PROBLEMATIZING LANGUAGE STUDIES

निष्ठा धृतिः सत्यम्

PROBLEMATIZING LANGUAGE STUDIES

Cultural, Theoretical and Applied Perspectives

Essays in Honour of Rama Kant Agnihotri

Edited by

S. IMTIAZ HASNAIN

SHREESH CHAUDHARY

AAKAR

PROBLEMATIZING LANGUAGE STUDIES
Edited by S. Imtiaz Hasnain & Shreesh Chaudhary

First Published, 2010

ISBN 978-93-5002-084-5

Published by
AAKAR BOOKS
28 E Pocket IV, Mayur Vihar Phase I, Delhi 110 091
Phone : 011-2279 5505 Telefax : 011-2279 5641
aakarbooks@gmail.com; www.aakarbooks.com

Printed at
Mudrak, Delhi 110 091

Foreword

"mozhi-t tiRattin muTTaRuttoor viiDupeeRu eytuvar"

'Those who cut the knot of language will reach (the truthful state of) the heaven'.

A quote from the famous Tamil saint Kumarakuruparar (1625-88) who spent thirty years in Kashi, when it was under the rule of Aurangazeb. He was exposed to Tamil, Sanskrit and Persian. (Courtesy Dr. E. Annamalai)

Here the great 17th century Tamil seer sage indicates the path to salvation; a realization of the Indian soul's culturally driven eternal quest for "*moksha*" - to attain that blissful divine state which is really one's due on having been born human- and this *self realization,* it is suggested, will come to those who shall severe their ties with language to enter the unconditioned state of meditative speechlessness... the Oneness of being ....

The present collection of most commendable essays, written by scholars of distinction with diverse backgrounds in honour of Professor Rama Kant Agnihotri, thoughtfully brought together by S. Imtiaz Hasnain and Shreesh Chaudhary, inform us that the goal of achieving that speechless state is problematic, to say the least, for our entire experiential world is tangled within the knots of language, and its tentacles reach out in all directions- biological, cognitive, social, cultural, political- and, therefore, what can be done at best is to examine the nature of those inextricable ties. Rama himself has been engaged tirelessly in understanding the nature of language from diverse or alternative perspectives and many of the authors have chosen the complex themes that have engaged his attention over the last four decades. The compilers are aware that their attempt to broadly categorize the same under three headings-cultural, theoretical and applied- may be insufficient, for the essays move beyond the beaten path traversing into unpredictable territories, striking the readers imagination in exciting ways, defying any categorization........

The *Indian pluralistic ethos-* starting with the seminal essay on *syncretic* or *sanskritic-* is a recurrent theme in variant forms. In the background are those high brow traditionalists who have a deeply ingrained sense for purity of codes and expect all branches of ancient linguistic science *–Shiksha, Nirukta, Vyaakaran and Chhandas-* to be directed at safeguarding the ancient oral cultural texts, predominantly Sạnskrit. And then on the foreground at various points of time, under changing historical and social conditions, as the authors of essays illustrate, surface texts and writers that herald the coming into being of new speech forms and belief systems that may have their origins in roots of diverse coexisting sources; these purposive communicative acts of identity-some as an expression of defiance- often a matter of choice for those who have refused to be divided by diversity and valued it instead, creating in their integrating performance the deeper connection of values with overt connections of form. India emerges through these multifaceted discourses as a country with a human face which has not been always scarred by history though traces of conflict abound and creative tension prevails.......

The dynamicity of societal multilingualism is another key theme. While code-production and code-differentiation are shaped by the inner workings of the mind, the cognitive processes-including code-switching- are socially assisted and constrained by the outer workings of society. The study of Hindi, Urdu and Hindustani bring to the fore the complexity of historical and political forces at work; the partitioning of the mind and diversification of linguistic resources-the oral with its gamut of inter-graded variations and the literary in various genres as embodied in *Devnagari* or *Perso-Arabic* scripts - accompany identity formation and assertion. A language being associated with religious identity is not new, of course, for even in the past Sanskrit being associated with Hindus, Pali with Buddhism, Prakrit with Jainism are known examples and in the more recent past Punjabi embodied in *Gurumukhi* script has become the marker of Sikh identity. Surely the association of Urdu with the Muslim identity is a publicly stated perception which has influenced policy matters so much so that census of India (1991) chose to correlate the two and present a demographic profile on the matter in its atlas!

The forms of multilingualism in everyday life, with notions of the relatively stable societal *code –matrix* and the ever evolving individual *verbal repertoire,* are also enriched when the regional mother tongues like *Braj Bhasha* are brought in to the arena of the HUP (Hindi-Urdu-Punjabi) region and the dynamics of exchange and code production acquire new forms and signification. The way litterateurs proceed to articulate-traversing the sacred, secular, profane and erotic- provides us an insight in to the society of yesteryears and helps in enlivening the past as located in the concerns of the present, even as it unravels the universal spirit to transcend and explore the intrinsic abilities and give form to language potential. The picture of India is brought out from many linguistic perspectives engaged in managing its show.......

Hindi as a *'speaking Banyan tree'* with over 49 mother tongues *as its roots and branches* is portrayed by the census as monolingual, which must annoy Rama -who feels to be human is to be multilingual- and he would retaliate that the actual reality is deliberately being distorted by those who shortsightedly proceed to smother diversity. But Hindi, some would say, is privileged to enhance its size because it is the official *Raj Bhasha*, though its proponents would claim their aspirations to have been pruned for Hindi was meant to be the language of the entire Hind - an expression of *'Swaraj' rather than 'Raj'*- and deserved its promotion as the national language. The *de facto* position, especially outside the Hindi states, in the nation at large is that it is English which rules the roost. Hindi gains flesh only from its conscious attempts to delve in to the Sanskritic world where it finds other Modern India Languages as partners, which strengthens its role as a link language even as it proceeds towards common strategies of standardization and modernization with translation of knowledge-based texts from English.

The stability of Indian multilingualism is also brought to question in this volume. The often repeated position of Prabodh Pandit (Rama's revered teacher at Delhi University) that in India maintenance of the language even outside its own territory is the norm and loss of language is an exception has been given a reality check. The issue of endangered languages, amidst UNESCO reports of India being the home for the largest number of such languages, surfaces as of vital concern for theorists as well as those engaged with applied aspects of language planning. It is as if a hierarchical order has emerged with the policy driven dominant official languages (16 in number when the state languages are included besides Hindi and English) posing a threat not only to mother tongues and dialects but to hundreds of languages including minor and tribal. Some make even a more exaggerated claim that all Indian languages are under threat from the dominance of English! It is as if English is cast in the role of adversary though Rama may not be easily convinced with this picture.

Ramakant would want to further the multilingual competence that Indians have through institutional support to all languages regardless of their size and status, with more informed pedagogic practices which will allow for teaching of English at appropriate points in keeping with the context and social aspirations. The quest for empowerment is linked to the learning of English and the nation with its many states has arrived at a consensus of sorts that English has come to stay and so an attempt must be made to enrich the expression systems of all Indian languages by using its presence. The policy initiatives from many states to introduce English from Class one may have its share of supporters but to translate this as a mission as the National Knowledge Commission envisions has also invited its critics. The role of English is a matter of constant debate......

India is in the grip of rapid social change and emerging as a dominant player which also portends an era of maximization of conflict for the focus is less on cultural diversity and more on social disparity. No Indian can disown connections with diverse others, who speak dress or act differently, but with whom one may share a sense of common identity with a shared past as a given. But for a shared destiny as a mature nation we will have to work out what is it that we want to give to each other for the destiny of man is inextricably linked to language........

Imtiaz and Shreesh have gifted us this book for which a sense of gratitude must be conveyed by all Indian linguists. To sit back and read under the gaze of Ramakant is to ignite our understanding.......

The Tamil saint heard the divine prophecy that he will meet his master in whose presence he would become speechless.......

Rama, however, would want us to speak...... for he is a master of another kind.

Professor Rajesh Sachdeva
Director i/c
Central Institute of Indian Languages,
Manasagangotri,
Mysore - 570 006.

Contents

Section B: Theoretical Perspective

About the Contributors

Aadil Amin Kak, Ph.D. (University of Delhi) is Assistant Professor in the Department of Linguistics, University of Kashmir. He has co-authored three books and published a number of research papers on syntax, language technology and online language resources for Kashmiri. He was awarded the FLOSS fellowship for localization. His interests include Sociolinguistics, Syntax, and Computational Linguistics. *aadilaminkak@yahoo.com*

Achla M. Raina, Ph.D. (Indian Institute of Technology Kanpur) is a Professor of Linguistics in the Department of Humanities and Social Sciences at Indian Institute of Technology Kanpur. She works in the areas of Cognitive Linguistics and Natural Language Semantics. Her current interests include grammar and conceptualisation, semantics of events, non-literal language, and sign language semantics. *achla@iitk.ac.in*

A.L. Khanna, Ph.D. (University of Delhi) teaches English in Delhi University. He is interested in Applied Linguistics & English Language Teaching. He has written extensively and has taught in this field for several years. He co-edits, with Rama Kant Agnihotri, the Sage series on Applied Linguistics. *amrit.l.khanna@gmail.com*

Anju Sahgal Gupta, Ph.D. (University of Delhi) is a Professor of English in Indira Gandhi National Open University. Her interests are ELT, Applied and Sociolinguistics, and material production. She has published extensively on grammar and speaking and listening skills. She has several articles in both national and international journals. *anjusgupta7@gmail.com*

Annie Montaut, Ph.D. in Hindi Verbal System, D. Lit. in Indian Linguistics and Hindi Stylistics, is Professor of Hindi and General Linguistics at Institut National des Langues Orientales, Paris. She is the author of *A Grammar of Hindi* (Lincom-Europa, 2003) and has published several papers on syntax of Hindi, and has translated in French a large number of Hindi novels. *annie.montaut@free.fr*

Arthur Dudney, is a Ph.D. candidate in the Department of Middle Eastern, South Asian and African Studies, Columbia University. His main interest is Persian and Urdu literary theory in the late pre- and early colonial periods. *add2115@columbia.edu*

Ayesha Kidwai, Ph.D. (Jawaharlal Nehru University) is Associate Professor at the Centre of Linguistics, JNU where she teaches generative syntax. Currently on a fellowship from the New India Foundation, she is working on the translation of Begum Anis Kidwai's *Azaadi ki Chaon Mein*. *ayesha.kidwai@gmail.com*

B.N. Patnaik, Ph.D. (English and Foreign Languages University, Hyderabad) was Professor at the Indian Institute of Technology Kanpur and a Senior Fellow at CIIL, Mysore. He has published extensively on computational linguistics and in the syntax and sociolinguistics of Indian languages. His current interests include discourse linguistics, linguistic communication, protest literature, and Oriya folk literature. *patnaik@iitk.ac.in, bn.patnaik@gmail.com*

Caroline Fèry, is Professor for "Theory of Grammar/Phonology" at the Department of Linguistics at the University of Potsdam, Germany. Her interests lie in the prosodic and tonal structure of languages, and in the theory of grammar. She has edited several books. *caroline.fery@googlemail.com*

Gisbert Fanselow, Ph.D. (Passau University) is Professor of syntax in the Department of Linguistics of the University of Potsdam, Germany. He researches in generative syntax, word formation, empirical methods for grammar, and syntax processing. *fanselowster@googlemail.com, fanselow@rz.uni-potsdam.de*

Haobam Basantarani, Ph.D. (Osmania University) has published several papers on issues of identity, multilingualism and code switching. *basantarani@gmail.com*

Kay McCormick, is Emeritus Professor in the Department of English at the University of Cape Town. Her research fields are sociolinguistics, particularly language contact, and narrative studies, in particular the analysis of oral life histories. Her current sociolinguistic work is on changing forms and uses of bilingual and multilingual vernaculars. *kaymc@iafrica.com*

Madhu Gurtu (late), Ph.D. (English and Foreign Languages University, Hyderabad) was a Reader in Delhi University. Her interests were ELT, syntax, language testing and translation. She was actively engaged in acquisition of vocabulary towards the end of her life.

Mahendra K. Varma, is an Honorary Fellow of the University of York, UK, where he taught Linguistics and Hindi for thirty three years. His publications include edited books: *Working With Bilingual Children; Adult ESOL Learners in Britain; Sociolinguistics, Language and Society; Bolchal kii Hindi*, etc. His current interests include impact of globalization and English on Hindi in India; and, Language Policies and Minority South Asian Languages in the UK. *mkv1@york.ac.uk*

Michael J. Franklin, Ph.D. (University of Wales, Cardiff) is a Senior Lecturer in the Department of English, University of Wales, Swansea. He has published books on *Sir William Jones* and edited a volume on *Eighteenth-Century British Orientalist Discourse*. Currently he is working on a biography of William Jones, to be published by Oxford University Press. *mjf@swansea.ac.uk, mjranklin@swansea.ac.uk*

Mi Yang Cha, Ph.D. (Jawaharlal Nehru University) is currently teaching English in Namseoul University, Korea. She is interested in language teaching, Second and Foreign language learning and Second Language Acquisition.

Mohammad Aslam, Ph.D. (University of Kashmir) is Professor of English, University of Kashmir. Some of his books include *Trends in English Language Teaching in India, Developing a Learner-Centred ELT Curriculum in India, Teaching of English for B Ed, A Practical Course in English Phonetics and Phonology,* and he edits *English Studies in India*. *miraslam@rediffmail.com*

Omkar N. Koul, is the Chairman of Indian Institute of Language Studies and is currently the Editor of *South Asian Language Review*. He retired as the Director of Central Institute of Indian Languages, Mysore. He has published extensively on different aspects of the Kashmiri language. *onkoul@yahoo.com*

Panchanan Mohanty, Ph.D. (University of Hyderabad) is a Professor at the University of Hyderabad. He has edited *Indian Linguistics* and *Translation Studies* He has published extensively on language in culture and society. *panchanan_mohanty@yahoo.com*

Paroo Nihalani, Ph.D. (University of Edinburgh) is Chair Professor of English Language and Applied Linguistics at Universiti Brunei Darussalam. His research interests include speech production processes; Acoustic Phonetics and Phonology of English; World Englishes; Corpus Linguistics, etc upon all of which he has books and journal articles. *nihalani@fass.ubd.edu.bn, nihalani@hotmail.com*

Pramod Pandey, Ph.D. (University of Pune, Pune) is currently a Professor at the Centre for Linguistics, Jawaharlal Nehru University, New Delhi. He has books and journal articles on Hindi and English phonology and phonological theory. His special interests are linguistic theory, speech sounds and writing systems. *pkspandey@yahoo.com*

Priya Hosali, Ph.D. (English and Foreign Languages University, Hyderabad) is a former Professor of EFL University. She has books and articles in Sociolinguistics, Phonetics and Lexicography. Her work on *Butler English* has earned her a position of authority on pidgins and creoles. *phosali@rediffmail.com*

Probal Dasgupta, Ph.D. (New York University) is a Professor at the Linguistic Research Unit, Indian Statistical Institute, Kolkata. He (co-)edits *Language Problems and Language Planning* and has co/authored a number of research articles and monographs on the linguistics of English and Indian languages. His *The Otherness of English: India's Auntie Tongue Syndrome* has been widely noticed. *probal53@yahoo.com, probal53@gmail.com*

Raj Nath Bhat, Ph.D. (Kurukshetra University) teaches linguistics at Banaras Hindu University, Varanasi. He has published books and articles in *Psycholinguistics,* on phonetics and phonology of Kashmiri and he edits *Bhasha Cintana- A Research Journal of Linguistics'. rnbhat2k2@gmail.com*

Rajendra Singh, Ph.D. (Brown) is Professor Titulaire of Linguistics at UniversitÈ de Montreal, Montreal. He is interested in Linguistic Theory, Phonology, Morphology, and Sociolinguistics. His books include *Trubetzkoy's Orphan* and *Lectures Against Sociolinguistics.* He edits *The Annual Review of South Asian Languages and Linguistics. rajendra.singh@umontreal.ca*

Rajesh Kumar, Ph.D. (University of Illinois at Urbana-Champaign) is an Assistant Professor of Linguistics and English at the Indian Institute of Technology Patna. He has also taught at the University of Illinois, University of Texas at Austin, and IIT Kanpur. He is interested in Natural Language Syntax, Sociolinguistics, and Language in Education. *kumar@uts.cc.utexas.edu*

Rajneesh Arora, Ph.D. (Panjab University, Chandigarh) is Associate Professor and Head, Department of Linguistics and Contemporary English in the English and Foreign Languages University, Lucknow Campus. His research interests include critical discourse analysis, pragmatics, language of advertising, and history of English language teaching in India. *rajneesharora13@yahoo.co.in*

Rakesh M. Bhatt, Ph.D. (University of Illinois) is Professor of Linguistics at the University of Illinois, Urbana-Champaign. He is also the Director of the Program in Second Language Acquisition and Teacher Education (SLATE) at the university. His research is concerned with different aspects of acquisition and use of multilingualism. *bhattrm@gmail.com; rbhatt@illinois.edu; rbhatt@uiuc.ed*

Rama Mathew, Ph.D. (MS University of Baroda) is Professor, Department of Education, University of Delhi. She has published in the areas of English language education, language teacher education and assessment. Her current interests include language teacher education, online teaching and testing and qualitative approaches to curriculum inquiry. *ramamathew@yahoo.co.in*

Ranjit Singh Rangila, a product of Punjabi University, Patiala, and University of Delhi, has been on the faculty of the Central Institute of Indian Languages, Mysore since 1976. He has published several books and articles in the areas of theoretical linguistics, philosophy of language, semiotics, Indian grammatical tradition and sociolinguistics. *ranjitsrangila@gmail.com*

Rizwan Ahmad, Ph.D. (University of Michigan, Ann Arbor) is Assistant Professor of English at the American University of Kuwait. His main research interests are language ideology, multilingualism, sociolinguistics of orthography, and Urdu in India. *rizzahmad@gmail.com, rahmad@umich.edu, rahmad@auk.edu.kw*

S. Imtiaz Hasnain, Ph.D. (Jawaharlal Nehru University) is Professor of Sociolinguistics, Department of Linguistics, Aligarh Muslim University. He has published articles and books in the areas of sociolinguistics, critical discourse, language planning and minority language rights. He was a Fellow of East West Center, Hawaii, and a Senior Fellow at CIIL, Mysore. *imtiaz.hasnain@gmail.com*

S.R. Prahlad, Ph.D. (English and Foreign Languages University, Hyderabad) is Professor in the Department of Materials Development at the EFL University, Hyderabad, where he teaches curriculum design, materials and teacher development. He also translates from Kannada into English. *sr.prahlad@gmail.com*

Shailendra Kumar Singh, Ph.D. (University of Hyderabad) is presently Chair of the Department of Linguistics, North Eastern Hill University, Shillong. He is the author of *Multilingualism* (2001) and has co-edited other books on language and culture. *tosksingh@rediffmail.com*

Shreesh Chaudhary, Ph.D. (English and Foreign Languages University, Hyderabad) is Professor, Humanities and Social Sciences, Indian Institute of Technology Madras. He has published articles and books in the areas of phonology, applied linguistics and in the history of foreign languages in India. *shreesh@hotmail.com*

Tanmoy Bhattacharya, Ph.D. (University College, London) is Associate Professor of Linguistics, University of Delhi. He has published books and articles on syntax. He co-authored an article on Wh-superiority in Bangla which has appeared in *Linguistic Inquiry*. He is also interested in Psycholinguistics, Pragmatics, and Sign Language. *tanmoy@gmail.com, tanmoy@linguistics.du.ac.in*

Tariq Rahman, Ph.D. (Sheffield) is Distinguished National Professor and Director, National Institute of Pakistan Studies, Quaid-i-Azam University, Islamabad. He has published journal articles and books on language and education in Pakistan. His *Language and Politics in Pakistan* (OUP, 1996) and *Language, Ideology and Power: Language learning among the Muslims of Pakistan and North India* (OUP 2002) have been re-issued in India by Orient Blackswan. *trahman@nips.qau.edu.pk, director.nips@yahoo.com*

Udaya Narayana Singh, Ph.D. (Delhi University) currently holds the Tagore Chair at Rabindra Bhavan, Visva-Bharati. He has been the general editor of the 'Language and Development' series from Sage, Chief Editor of *Indian Linguistics*, and general editor of the Longman–CIIL series of bilingual dictionaries from Pearson. Singh is interested in poetry, literary criticism, linguistics and language studies. *unsciil@yahoo.com ; uns@vis-bharati.ac.in*

Vaishna Narang, Professor of Linguistics at Jawaharlal Nehru University, started her career over three decades ago in General and Applied

Linguistics and Speech Science with special focus on application of linguistics in pedagogy, speech and language pathology. She has published several books and journal articles on these subjects.
vaishna_narang@yahoo.com

Introduction

The academic career of Rama Kant Agnihotri has been clearly synchronous with the growth of Linguistic Studies in modern India.

India, of course, has had a long and continuing tradition of linguistic studies. There was Linguistics in India in the Pre-Christian Era as well as in the 19th century, and the work of linguists from Panini (C. 6th Century BC) to Ram Gopal Bhandarkar (19th-20th century AD), by any standards, is no mean achievement. However, linguistic studies in India until mid-20th century, generally meant, interpretation and re-interpretation of Panini's *sutras*, i.e. aphorisms, or attention to Philology, or to the meaning of language as a mirror of cognition, practiced mostly as epistemology, ontology, philology and other related branches of philosophy barely reaching beyond the circle of its practitioners. Even in the late 1960s, when Rama Kant joined the post graduate diploma class in Linguistics at the University of Delhi, Linguistics was narrowly confined. Ramakant says[1],

> ... I was in for certain surprises... I realized that linguistics had nothing to do with the English language and literature... more seriously... I was told that a linguist does not have to know many languages...

Since then linguistics has enlarged its vision and observations like the following seem valid now,

> ... We need to examine the implications of some of our most powerful theories of language coming from predominantly monolingual contexts and from monolingual linguists It is now widely recognized that multilinguality is a natural human condition; it is monolingualism, which may be treated as an exception. Effortless multilingual first language(s) acquisition remains a mystery for the science of language... The ways in which languages are kept separate from each other and the ways in which they simultaneously flow into each other are not sufficiently well understood.... Any theory of language which does not keep multilinguality at the centre of its investigations is bound to be inadequate[2].

During the last four decades, studies in the Indian linguistics, both in India and abroad, have rapidly grown. It is no longer an esoteric science practiced by few; it is a welcome resource in Humanities, Sciences, and Social Sciences. A variety of monographs, papers, books, journals, conferences and workshops on Indian languages and linguistics happen every year.

Rama Kant may not have been the sole leader of this growth, but he has surely been among its most ardent workers. There is hardly a field of Linguistics where Rama Kant has made no significant contribution. With his numerous talks, notes, papers, book chapters and books, both original and translations, he has memorably contributed to Phonetics and Phonology, Morphology, Syntax, Sociolinguistics, Applied Linguistics, English and Hindi Language Teaching, Material Production, Literacy and Primary Education, and Human and Linguistic Rights.

And in all of this Rama Kant has asked, and often tried to answer, questions that can be asked only in a multilingual speech community such as India. Linguistics today is expected to describe and explain not just the design of the lexicon and the constraints on the rules of the grammar of a language; today it is also being asked to describe and explain links and layout that enable a multilingual person to not only learn all of the many languages he knows, but also to access and draw from them at will, as and when required. What grammar is that which regulates a speech that draws from a variety of grammars and produces all and only grammatically acceptable output? Though a grammar of this kind is yet to be written, we are past the time when as linguists we felt happy describing the syntax and word formation rules of a language in isolation of the context of its use. Rama Kant is easily the most visible presence of this school of thought in the Indian linguistics today.

We bring this Festschrift to honor Rama Kant for his interests and work, for the questions and concerns he has raised, and for the subtle and not so subtle ways in which he has influenced and even altered our agenda. We bring together in this volume a selection of articles reporting nearly all that is currently happening in Indian linguistics and language studies worldwide. We have, accordingly, decided to call this volume ***Problematizing Language Studies***.

Nearly all contributions here look at some aspect of the problem of language studies. We have, therefore, grouped the articles according to the major class of problems they address. The book, accordingly, has three sections, one each on cultural, theoretical, and applied issues. Articles in the cultural section dwell upon issues that influence the form and use of language. Issues pertaining to the theory of grammar in general, and of syntax, morphology or phonetics and phonology have been grouped together in the theoretical section. Articles in the section on applied linguistics discuss the problems of language pedagogy, language planning, data bases, etc.

The cultural perspective section has articles which problematize Hindi-Urdu, mourn the loss of Hindustani – the idiom of the street, and dwell upon the politics of multiculturality in India. Some articles reflect upon the phenomenon of code switching in terms of politics of nostalgia, and situate the discourse of identity in post-partition India. The account of the people of the Jenu Koruba tribe here demonstrates that though the majoritarian discourse has dominated the aesthetic expressions of the people with an exclusive existence, the minoritarian discourse is still capable of arts and expressions.

During the better part of the last century, communal question has dominated not just politics in India, but practically everything. **Michael**'s article on communal disharmony in contemporary India notes the instances of attacks upon heritage sites. Moving on to the 18th century India, he shows what Orientalists, like William Jones, Francis Gladwyn and others in the service of the East India Company, did to discover the works of prophets of syncretic culture and communal harmony. Michael particularly mentions Amir Khusro, Akbar the Great, Dara Shikoh, and other scholar-patrons of Islamic-Hindu tradition of art and literature. He, thus, refutes the charge that the Orientalists were determined to discover only the Hindu past of India.

Colonial India also saw much activity in the field of what was generally called vernacular language studies. Linguists in the late 18th and early 19th century were faced with the formidable task of studying India's vernacular languages. Vernacular was seen as a continuum which defined non-literary languages from the high-prestige languages of the time, namely Persian and Sanskrit. The British wanted to describe these non-literary languages for the purpose of learning them for more profitable business. In the process of looking into some colonial approaches to Hindi dialects, **Arthur** re-invents *Braj Bhasha* and observes how the British understanding of this literary dialect can show the divergence between indigenous and the British perceptions of language use. The paper sheds light also on the colonial language policy.

Colonial linguists have considerably influenced modern Indian linguistics. A different insight into the motives and works of the colonial linguists is provided by **Annie**'s paper on the consequences of the so-called "Orientalists vs Anglicists" quarrel in the first three decades of the 19th century. Today English is an official language of India, yet it is spoken only as a second language and only by a minority of (eight to eleven percent) all Indians. Is English then a chance for India to converse with the world cultures, and even lead a globalized liberal world, in compensation for centuries of domination, or, conversely, is it an inherited burden still preventing this conversation from taking place on equal terms? The paper explores the present dialectics of power among languages and cultures, with special attention to the "vernacular" like Hindi/Urdu.

By about the end of the 18th and the beginning of the 19th century, Hindi/Urdu was emerging as the popular language of South Asia - used and understood by many, but the mother tongue of none. Today Urdu is identified with Islam, with Muslim nationalist discourse in pre-partition India, with nationalist political discourse in Pakistan now and with Muslim identity politics in post-partition India. But during the 19th century, it was associated with the masses, both Hindu and Muslim, and with many subjects, both spiritual and amorous. The political and ideological associations of Urdu have been strengthened by the imperatives of the last century. **Tariq** presents evidence to argue that strands of various associations existed in the very being of Urdu, but they need to be understood with reference to the world view of the Muslim elite of the time. Understanding this may serve as a corrective to the sanitized versions of linguistic history. It can also help appreciate the non-Islamic associations of Urdu better.

Two other articles make the two sides of the debate in India about the identity and status of Hindi/Urdu. Describing the sociolinguistic factors that led to the evolution of Hindi-Urdu, **Shreesh** re-presents the view which treats Hindi and Urdu as 'one language with two scripts'[3]. Between Hindi-Urdu, there is the variety called "Hindustani" that the masses speak and understand. In an appropriate script, Hindustani can become the national language of India, argues Shreesh. But **Ayesha** questions this construct of the Hindi-Hindustani-Urdu continuum. She feels that this hypothesis cannot capture the linguistic and sociolinguistic identities of Hindi and Urdu. Rather than as a continuum, Hindi and Urdu may be conceived, according to this view, as two distinct languages that share some linguistic contexts.

Actually, a text can be treated as a "language" in a context. The concept of inter-textuality, therefore, can show how different contexts influence and are influenced by texts and social practices in the creation of meaning. **Imtiaz's** paper, based on advice literature (called *Bihishti Zewar*), has been used for demonstrating the usefulness of Giddens' '*structuration theory*' and for showing how this theory and the concept of '*inter-contextuality*' can supplement analysis based on context. Even taboo words can cease to mean or sound offensive in contexts. Analysis of "Puri Boli" by **Patnaik** shows just how and why taboo words heard in the course of annual Chariot Procession, "Rath Yatra", in Jagannath Puri causes no offence. Context can significantly influence the definition of standard forms of language to be learnt and taught. Is the 'Received Pronunciation' of English a valid pedagogical standard for students in India any longer to strive for? This question can be answered satisfactorily only with reference to the context of its use. **Nihalani** examines the issues of 'comprehensibility', 'intelligibility' and 'interpretability' from the perspective of spoken communication in the global context, and presents a pragmatic model of English for the World.

The Himachali languages, such as Pahari, Mandiali and Garhwali, have received relatively little attention from linguists or the government. In the official records, these languages are seen as the dialects of Hindi. They receive nearly no governmental support by way of education, publication or documentation. Official communication here uses Sanskritized Hindi, and commercial mass communication happens in English and/or Hindi. Speakers of these languages migrating to urban centres encourage their children to learn English and/or Hindi, seen as "linguistic capital". A situation of this kind, **Mahendra** fears, can lead to the death of these languages.

The future of languages spoken in the North-Eastern regions of India does not seem to be any rosier. Demographic changes in Tripura have rendered the tribals there, in majority a century ago, a minority community today, and except Kok Borok, their languages have no official support or place in the school curriculum. But the "tribals" of Tripura are not one monolithic ethnic group; the Census of India reports 14 groups there, each with its own mother tongue and inter-group dynamics and politics. **Tanmoy and Haobam Basantarani** plead for situating language and minority rights within a liberal and plural democratic framework. Languages in the hills and forests of India do not lack in resources. **Ranjit**'s paper offers a view of the sophistication and efficiency in the discourse of the Jenu Kuruba tribe which inhabits the jungles of Karnataka-Tamil Nadu border. Once a verb is realized as an act, then all the extensions of the verb in this language start showing up as extensions of the act. Jenu Koruba people can match act for act with sophisticated dramatic performances like *Yaksha Gana*.

Newly independent and developing nations everywhere are demanding re-arrangement of tradition, including tradition of language use. But language eventually remains a "tribal" affair, where "tribe" means an ethnic community identifying itself with certain overt practices, or ways and means. **McCormick** reports how popular television in South Africa balances the pulls of tribal loyalty with the pushes of the national loyalty, how TV allocates broadcast time to the major languages of the country, and, how it serves the cause of its "imagined nation" by broadcasting, at least in major cities, in a speech that mixes Afrikaaner, Zulu, Xoso, etc. with English, just as the national anthem of South Africa does. In India, however, television seems to have promoted use of Hindi even in the English newspapers. With data from two newspapers, **Rakesh** observes that increased use of Hindi words in English discourse has been synchronous with the rise of the forces of *Hindutwa,* or Hinduism.

Articles in **Section II** of this volume look into the **theoretical and empirical problems** in the study of Indic and some other languages. Two papers in this volume, one by **Pramod** and the other by **Udaya,** express theoretical worries. Linguistics in the past fifty years has been approached by two contending theories, namely, the knowledge of linguistic structure, or the Chomskyan view; and, the use of that knowledge, the view held by Halliday and others. This standoff has not helped us understand the puzzle of the human faculty called language. Pandey sees the need for a synthesis of the two approaches. Singh is anguished that much more needs to be done to bring the opportunities of a democratic and free world to all, in countries such as India. He argues for inspiring, rather than only knowledge imparting, education to turn the country into a genuine "knowledge society".

Some other contributions in this section address specific problems in syntax, morphology, or phonetics-phonology. **Carolene** observes that a new category of intonational systems is needed for 'phrase languages' like Hindi, Bengali, Tamil and Malayalam which are similar in their prosodic and tonal structure. Lexical stresses and pitch accents, if present at all, are less important in these languages than they are, for instance, in English. Rajendra **Singh** argues that the concept of "Morphological complexity" is redundant for the linguistic theory, since there is nothing that cannot be accounted for with the notion of 'length' (or 'weight'). The concept of "weight" finds favor also with **Probal** who suggests that the Hindi long vowel in morphological alternation can be better accounted for by expanding the data base so that the rule can cover verbs and lead to a phonological alternative.

Some papers argue for the reformulation of the existing theory so that it can adequately account for the facts of even the European languages. Formation of nominal compounds in German, for instance, is a productive process, but there are restrictions. These restriction can be better accounted for, says **Gisbert**, by invoking the constraints on words as part of the syntax rather than as part of the morphology or the lexicon. Syntax of Indian languages can be more baffling for existing theories. Infinitive phrase in Hindi for instance, can behave like both

VP and NP. A syntactic study of Hindi, **Rajesh** says, can proceed best if infinitives are treated as noun phrase externally, but as verb phrase in their internal structure. Similarly, the current theoretical approach to the description of complex predicates does not offer an elegant description of certain kinds of verbs in complex predicates. **Achla** proposes a predicate-predicate composition procedure involving argument and event structure unification to account for the compositional aspects of semantic restructuring in Complex Predicates (CPs). **Rajneesh** suggests that the building-block model is inadequate and that only a holistic view can explain the compositionality of meaning in all discourse.

Based on his field experience in Delhi, **Rizwan** argues that the notion of 'insider'and 'outsider' in Sociolinguistic researches is quite complex. Social identities and boundaries are often flexible, and can be perceived differently in different social contexts. Indian linguistics can actually be an economic asset, says **Shailendra** in the final paper in this section.

The Applied Perspective section has articles dealing with Second and Foreign Language Acquisition/Learning in the backdrop of linguistic diversity and multicultural identity, Spread of English and its current position as the sole global language is a social and economic opportunity for India. **Raj Nath** cites the idea of Basic English and suggests that ways and means should be found to bring English within easy reach of all.

Khanna reviews the position of second and foreign language theorists and practitioners regarding the influence of the learner's mother tongue upon the learning of a second / foreign language. The mother tongue may raise the learner's meta-cognitive awareness and may raise the learner's potential for learning the target language. Of late, however, English has found place as a subject even in the Class One curriculum of the mother tongue medium government primary schools. Yet this is not helping the learners as desired. **Rama** observes that something more than mere provision in the curriculum needs to be done. **Panchanan** has found that the accepted principles for producing materials for teaching vocabulary are not being followed by the textbook writers causing frustration among learners. Many materials producers know little about the learners' wants and needs, their learning styles and preferences, etc. **Prahlad** discusses some principles for designing a sourcebook which does not intimidate the learners with the texts or the tasks included in it.

An important aspect of learning English as a Second/Foreign language is its pronunciation where many non-native learners experience difficulties. **Aadil** identifies some phonological features of

English that cause difficulties for its Kashmiri speakers. **Vaishna Narang and Mi Yang** look at the 'errors' of Koreans learning English as a Foreign and Second language, and suggest that the nature of processing involved in an SL situation may be different from an FL situation, leading to 'acquisition' in the former and to 'learning' in the latter. **Aslam** recalls the basic principles of Communicative Language Teaching (CLT) and suggests ways to make language classrooms learner-centred and successful.

Like other pidgins and creoles, Indian Butler English (IBE) draws lexical items from native and other sources, such as Portuguese. Priya **Hosali** believes that IBE may tell us much about the nature of human interaction – from the first halting attempts at communication to the ultimate recognition of a shared identity. Now Indian languages and literatures are taught in many universities and institutions abroad. They are also taught as heritage languages to the Indian immigrant children. **Koul** suggests some principles for teaching Hindi and Urdu, the two Indian languages that attract largest number of students.

Anju and **Madhu** observe that an important part of language acquisition is the ability to comprehend and produce "lexical phrases". Many words in any language seem to go together as lexically generated single units. If true, this hypotheses can have interesting and far reaching consequences for the theory of grammar.

The volume, thus, touches a wide variety of issues and topics currently engaging linguists interested in the languages of developing communities. We make no claim to originality, but on the basis of the foregoing survey it will be accepted by all that this volume is a representative slice of linguistics in our time, which is also the time of Rama Kant Agnihotri.

There were many friends of Rama Kant who had wanted to offer their intellectual gratitude to him. We are sorry that we could not approach all who might have liked to contribute. Some did commit to send their papers but later sent regret for not being able to meet the deadline.

Our special thanks are due to Shagufta and Preeti for the editorial assistance rendered by them. We are also thankful to Asad for harmonizing the formatting of the papers included in this volume.

We would also like to thank Ms Saumya Sharma for the meticulous copy editing of all the papers; our publisher, Mr Saxena, who ungrudgingly accepted to publish it. We were as much unfamiliar to Mr Saxena as his publishing world was to a discipline located outside History. Thanks to Jaya, Supriya and Ishrat for breaking that barrier and introducing us to him.

NOTES

1. Agnihotri, Ramakant 2001. *Half the battle and a quarter*, Foundation Day Lecture, Central Institute of Indian Languages, Mysore, July 17-18, 2001
2. Agnihotri, *op cit*
3. King, Christopher R 1994. *One language two scripts: The Hindi movement in nineteenth century Northern India*, Delhi: Oxford University Press.

Section A

CULTURAL PERSPECTIVE

1

Sanskritic vs Syncretic: Sir William Jones and Indian Pluralism and Plurality[1]

Michael J. Franklin

On the 9 February 2005, *The Hindu*, 'India's National Newspaper' headlined a story by Mandira Nayar, entitled 'Lost in minutes: 800 years of history':

> NEW DELHI, FEB. 8. The tomb of Delhi's foremost poet, Amir Khusro, at the Nizamuddin dargah in South Delhi was vandalized early morning today, allegedly by a man from West Bengal. Wreaking havoc at the tomb, he single-handedly broke the intricately carved marble 'jaalis' adorning the poet's grave and vandalized more than three finials. While the police suspect he is mentally unstable, over 800 years of history have been lost forever. The accused, identified by police as Mohammad Bukhal Khan, has been arrested.

Almost exactly three years earlier, on 27 February 2002, a mob of angry Muslims set fire to the packed Sabarmati Express at Godhra in the western state of Gujarat, killing at least 58 people. The train had been carrying Hindu activists or 'Ram sevaks' returning from the northern town of Ayodhya, where they had been campaigning for the building of a temple on the ruins of the Babri Masjid, a mosque, the destruction of which ten years earlier by Hindu zealots provoked the worst rioting in India since partition, killing more than three thousand. This horror provoked an enormous wave of communal violence in which over two thousand people, mainly Muslims, were killed. The 'collateral' cultural damage was also appalling; in Ahmedabad, as Luke Harding reported for *The Guardian* on the 29 June 2002:

> Two hundred and thirty unique Islamic monuments, including an exquisite 400-year-old mosque, were destroyed or vandalized [...] Experts say the damage is so extensive that it rivals the better publicised destruction of

> the Bamiyan Buddhas in Afghanistan or the wrecking of Tibet's monasteries by the Red Guards. [...] Hindu gangs have smashed delicate mosque screens, thrown bricks at Persian inscriptions, and set fire to old Korans. [...] One of the monuments razed was the tomb of Vali Gujarati, the grandfather of Urdu poetry and inspiration of many later poets and singers, who died in Ahmedabad, the state's main city, in 1707. [...] On the night of March 1 Hindu gangs with pickaxes smashed it and replaced it with a small brick temple dedicated to the Hindu monkey-god Hanuman. [...] Several of Vali's fans have pointed out his own verse almost anticipates his ending:
>
> The city of whose songs I have always sung
> Why can I not bear to live in that city now?

Thus Godhra, and what became known as the 'post-Godhra riots', imperilled a long and valued tradition of Gujarati religious tolerance. As Harding points out:

> [L]ike many of India's Muslim rulers, Ahmedabad's 15th-century sultan and founder, Ahmad Shah I, married a rajput (Hindu) princess. His mosques and civic buildings incorporated Islamic and rajput elements and he employed Hindus in the highest offices of state.

These disturbing twenty-first-century developments cast a long and deep shadow over both the past and future of the peaceful, plural, and often syncretic co-existence of the two great religions of India. But one of the ironies that unites both the New Delhi and the Ahmedabad desecrations is that the lives and writings of the two poets whose tombs were targeted, Amīr Khusrau of Delhi (1253-1325), and Vali Mohammed Vali (1667-1707), aka Vali Aurangabadi, Wali Daccani, or Vali Gujarati, exemplify a sympathetic and productive mingling of Muslim and Hindu traditions. This essay is an attempt to illustrate the fascination with such Indian pluralism and multi-culturalism among some of the foremost Orientalists of the Hastings circle. It also seeks to demolish the persistent idea that Sir William Jones and other Asiatic Society members were exclusively concerned with the glories of a Hindu past, whether it be classical Sanskrit Gupta culture as exemplified by Kālidāsa's *Śakuntalā*, or twelfth-century *bhakti* devotional literature such as Jayadeva's *Gītagovinda.*[2]

To facilitate the transition from saddening postmodern times to the revolutionary 'Modern Times' of northern India in the last quarter of the eighteenth century we can do no better than to enlist the aid of Ghulam Husain Khan Tabatabai (1727-1806) whose fascinating history of India from the time of Aurangzeb down to 1781, the *Sëir Mutaqharin* [*View of Modern Times*] was published in Calcutta in 1789.[3] This fascinating history was written in Persian and translated into English (with a little help from Jones) by a remarkable exemplar of hybridity, M. Raymond, a French Creole born in Constantinople, who assumed the Muslim name Hājī Mustafā along with his conversion to Islam.[4] The *Sëir Mutaqharin* contextualizes the *inqilab* (reversal of fortune, revolution) effected by the East India Company as these 'alien' capitalists consolidated colonial hegemony in Northern India. The Mughal empire was in terminal decline; in 1788 heated wires were to be drawn across the eyes of Emperor Shāh 'Ālam in Delhi.[5] Ghulam Husain attempts in his history to come to terms with a world changed utterly, a world where Mughal nobility, customary authority and good nawabi government had been displaced. As the prestigious Mughal poet of Urdu, Mīr Taqī 'Mīr' (1722-1810) observed:

> This age is not like that which went before it.
> The times have changed, the earth and the sky have changed.[6]

Ghulam Husain was a friend of Sir William Jones who had praised this respected Muslim historian in his presidential 'Tenth Anniversary Discourse, On Asiatick History, Civil and Natural', addressed to the Asiatic Society of Bengal on the 28 February 1793.[7] What underscored Jones's praise of Ghulam Husain's 'impartiality' was the Orientalist's appreciation that the best traditions of Mughal government had indeed encouraged peaceful prosperity and cultural synthesis. Jones had read the historian's celebration of Indian Emperors who had 'cherish[ed] (their subjects) in the palm of the hand of benevolence' until mutual strangeness grew into familiar coalescence:

> And although the Gentoos seem to be a generation apart and distinct from the rest of mankind, and they are swayed by such differences in religion, tenets, and rites, as will necessarily render all Musulmen aliens and profane in their eyes; and although they keep up a strangeness of ideas and practices, which beget a wide difference in customs and actions; yet in process of time, they drew nearer and nearer; and as soon as fear and aversion had worn away, we see that this dissimilarity and alienation have terminated in friendship and union, and that the two nations have come to coalesce together into one whole, like milk and sugar that have received a simmering (*Sëir*, 2: 584).

This trope of the mingling of milk and sugar resents an image of reconciliation that was close to the heart of the regime instituted by Warren Hastings, Governor and Governor-General of Bengal from 1772 to 1785. His introduction of rigorously Orientalist government policies ensured that British sovereignty was exercised in Indian ways, and his models were the very same as those esteemed by the Mughal historian. In his admiration for the *Bhagavadgitā*, which he viewed as 'almost unequalled in its sublimity of conception, reasoning, and diction; a work of wonderful fancy',[8] Hastings not only proved his appreciation of the splendours of Hindu culture, but also mirrored the cultural sensitivities of the Mughal Emperor Akbar, whose court had been famed for religious tolerance, bolstered by philosophical investigation and artistic collaboration between the Muslim and the Hindu. Hastings's Judicial Plan to 'found the authority of the British Government in Bengal on its ancient laws' involved establishing authoritative texts of both Hindu and Muslim law. In this fashion, the practical politics of governance coincided with his own Orientalist intellectual avocations as (in best Mughal tradition) he patronized texts reflecting Hindu tradition and Mughal culture to foster reconciliation and mutual respect. The Governor-General's attempts to underpin notions of legitimacy and continuity thus necessarily involved the patronage of works such as Francis Gladwin's translation of the *Ā'īn-i Akbarī* ('Institutes of Akbar'), providing valuable insights into Mughal statecraft and political theory.[9]

Hastings's skill in gaining the confidence of native intellectuals, and his encouragement of the founding of Sir William Jones's Asiatic Society of Bengal in 1784 facilitated the substantial intercultural cooperation of the Calcutta Orientalists. Furthermore Jones's attempts to problematize and reconfigure the binaries of imperialism were also characterized by a similar emphasis upon cultural synthesis and syncretism. Jones's admiration for the eldest son of Shah Jahān, the scholar prince Dāra Shikūh, who had inherited the syncretic mantle of his great-grandfather, Akbar, was doubtless influenced by his reading of the sympathetic portrait within the pages of Ghulam Husain's *Sëir Mutaqharin*. Dāra Shikūh had translated some of the *Upaniṣads*, and composed a Persian text entitled *Majma 'al-bahrayn* or 'The Mingling of the Two Oceans' which maintained that the fundamental tenets of Hinduism were essentially monotheistic and identical with those of Islam.[10] According to Ghulam Husain, Dāra Shikūh 'seemed to inculcate the precepts of Quietisme and Mysticisme, and openly to give his approbation, and even preference, to some tenets of the Gentoo law' (*Sëir*, 3: 348). In describing his execution at the hands of his strictly orthodox Sunni brother, Aurangzeb, Husain refers to Dāra Shikūh as 'the unfortunate prince [...] made an example of, to terrify the pretenders to the crown' (*Sëir*, 3: 349).

When Jones introduces Dāra Shikūh into his essay 'On the Mystical Poetry of the Persians and Hindus' (1792) he echoes Ghulam Husain's epithet, referring his readers for 'detail of their [Sūfi] metaphysicks and theology to the *Dabistan* of MOHSANI FANI, and to the pleasing essay, called the *Junction of two Seas*, by that amiable and unfortunate Prince,

DÁRÁ SHECÚH'.[11] It is, however, important to contextualize this foregrounding and juxtaposition of Mohsanī Fani's *Dabistan* and Dāra Shikūh's *Majma 'al-bahrayn*.

Since arriving in Bengal late in September 1783, where so many had found disturbing otherness, Jones had been discovering similitude and inter-relationship everywhere. The groundbreaking essay, 'On the Gods of Greece, Italy, and India' (1784), had exploited cultural relativism and a syncretic approach to familiarize Europe with the 'alien' beliefs of the subcontinent. His subsequent learning of Sanskrit, undertaken primarily for practical legal reasons, led to world-changing ideas concerning both Indo-European linguistics and the common identity of Platonic and Vedantic metaphysical thought, which he published in his 'Third Anniversary Discourse: On the Hindus' (1786). It might seem that in travelling further east to South Asia, he had moved on from the Middle East; whereas he had written from London in 1768 in Latin to the Polish Orientalist-Count Charles Reviczky:

> From my earliest years, I was charmed with the poetry of the Greeks; nothing, I then thought, could be more sublime than the Odes of Pindar, nothing sweeter than Anacreon, nothing more polished or elegant than the golden remains of Sappho, Archolochus, AlcÊus, and Simonides: but when I had tasted the poetry of the Arabs and Persians ... [12]

By 1784 in Calcutta he was enthusing to his friend Richard Johnson about Sanskrit literature with all the *bhakti* (loving devotion) of a devout Hindu:

> I am in love with the *Gopia*, charmed with *Crishen*, an enthusiastick admirer of *Rām*, and a devout adorer of *Brimha-bishen-mehais*: not to mention that *Jūdishteir*, *Arjen*, *Corno*, and the other warriours of the M'hab'harat appear greater in my eyes than Agamemnon, Ajax, and Achilles appeared, when I first read the Iliad. (*Letters*, 2.652)

But although this appeared an even greater revelation than his earlier discovery of Arabic and Persian poetry, it by no means displaced his first Oriental love; he was, after all 'Persian' Jones, and India was affording still more Persian delights. In delivering his 'Sixth Anniversary Discourse: On the Persians' to the Asiatic Society on the evening of the 19 February 1789, he acknowledge both his excitement and a debt of gratitude at being introduced to the *Dabistan*: 'A fortunate discovery, for which I was first indebted to *Mìr* MUHAMMED HUSAIN, one of the most intelligent *Muselmàns* in *India*, has at once dissipated the cloud, and cast a gleam of light on the primeval history of *Iràn* and of the human race, of which I had long despaired, and which could hardly have dawned from any other quarter'.[13] This excitement was shared in

Calcutta, and almost immediately the enterprising Francis Gladwin set about translating the *Dabistan*, selections from which he speedily published in his periodical, *The New Asiatic Miscellany*.[14]

Thus we can appreciate that his essay 'On the Mystical Poetry of the Persians and Hindus' reflects further attempts at detecting similitude and syncretism in a synthesis which includes his beloved Sa'dī and Hāfiz, whose poetry had filled the pages of his 'poet's' *Grammar of the Persian Language* (1771). The synthesis now embraced two other Oriental religions: Christianity and Islamic Sūfism, and having cited a passage from the mathematician and theologian Isaac Barrow (1630-1677), Jones comments that it 'differs only from the mystical theology of the *Súfis* and *Yôgis*, as the flowers and fruits of *Europe* differ in scent and flavour from those of *Asia*, or as *European* differs from *Asiatick* eloquence; the same strain, in poetical measure would rise up to the odes of SPENSER on *Divine Love* and Beauty, and, in a higher key with richer embellishments, to the songs of HAFIZ and JAYADÉVA, the raptures of the *Masnavì*, and the mysteries of the *Bhágavat*'.[15]

Jones reveals his fascination with the mystical allegories of Sūfism and with how to the zealous admirers of the poet of Shiraz (Hāfiz), a glass of Shiraz might signify a toast to sublime devotion; to illustrate this he cites in full a literal translation of 'a most extraordinary ode' by the celebrated Ismat of Bokhara [Ismat-e Bukhârâ'î (d. 1436)]:

> Yesterday, half inebriated, I passed by the quarter, where the vintners dwell, to seek the daughter of an infidel who sells wine.
>
> At the end of the street, there advanced before me a damsel with a fairy's cheeks, who, in the manner of a pagan, wore her tresses dishevelled over her shoulder like the sacerdotal thread. I said: *O thou, to the arch of whose eye-brow the new moon is a slave, what quarter is this and where is thy mansion?*
>
> She answered: *Cast thy rosary on the ground; bind on thy shoulder the thread of paganism; throw stones at the glass of piety; and quaff wine from a full goblet;*
>
> *After that come before me, that I may whisper a word in thine ear: thou wilt accomplish thy journey, if thou listen to my discourse.* [...]

Intoxicating stuff, and insofar as the damsel wears her tresses in the style of the Brahman's sacred thread which she advises the poet to bind on his shoulder, this Sūfi ode serves to some extent to prepare the metropolitan reader for the bold luxuriance and divine eroticism of that more explicit Hindu 'Song of Songs', Jayadeva's *Gītagovinda*, which explores the mutual attraction of the *gopi* (cowherdess/milkmaid) Rādhā and the divine Krishna, and which Jones's essay introduces.[16]

In this way Jones makes his own important contribution to the

'Mingling of the Two Oceans' of Islam and Hinduism. He also followed Dāra Shikūh's lead in being drawn to the late Vedas, the *Upaniṣads*. Dāra Shikūh had assembled a team of Benares pandits to translate the *Upaniṣads* into Persian, producing in 1657 the *Sirr-i Akbar* ('The Great Secret'). Jones was also about the business of revealing great secrets and, although Abraham Hyacinthe Anquetil-Duperron had translated four of the *Upaniṣads* from the *Sirr-i Akbar* into French in 1787, and later published the influential *Oupnek'hat* (1802) which included the entire fifty-one *Upaniṣads* of the *Sirr-i Akbar*, Jones's *Isa-Upaniṣad* was the first direct translation of an *Upaniṣad* from the Sanskrit into a Western-language.[17] In introducing the *Ísávásyam* or *Isa-Upaniṣad*, Jones refers to the *Sirr-i Akbar*, a copy of which he had obtained from his friend Colonel Antoine Polier, with some reservation:

> but though sublime, and majestick features of the original were discernible, in parts, through folds of the Persian drapery; yet the Sanscrit names were so barbarously written, and the additions of the translator has made the work so deformed, that I resolved to postpone a regular perusal of it till I could compare it with the Sanscrit original.

Such comments have been seen as reflecting a certain condescension towards Persian and Indo-Persian scholarship, but this is not the case. It simply reveals the enthusiastic necessity for the linguist, who must believe that any translation constitutes something of a betrayal, to study the original; doubtless he would have found a Sanskrit translation of Hāfiz equally irritating. In the same way when Jones pursues his path-breaking ethnomusicological research into Hindu music via a study of Sanskrit, rather than Persian texts, his remark: 'that a man, who knows the *Hindus* only from *Persian* books, does not know the *Hindus*; and that an *European*, who follows the muddy rivulets of *Muselman* writers on *India*, instead of drinking from the pure fountain of *Hindu* learning, will be in perpetual danger of misleading himself and others', underlines both his determination to study original sources, and a certain proud self-awareness of his priority in having mastered Sanskrit.[18]

Only a very few of the slender but considerable number of Company servants who devoted some of their leisure time to Orientalist researches had learned the refined 'language of the gods', but Persian, perceived as an eminently useful political tool of diplomacy, had been much more widely studied by the members of the Asiatic Society. Since 1780 Richard Johnson, a scholar of Arabic, Persian and Urdu, had enjoyed the lucrative post of Deputy to the Resident at the court of the wazir of Oudh, and his experience in Lucknow, effectively the foremost centre of artistic patronage since Mughal decline in Dehli, encouraged him to commission a lithographic edition of Hafiz.[19] In Calcutta, Johnson had helped Jones investigate Hindu mythology, but they also shared an immense respect for Persian literature and the friendship of poets and scholars such as Abú Tálib Khān Isfahānī, the editor of Hafiz, Mir Muhammed Husain, and Mir Qamar ud-Din Minnat, whose diwan, dedicated to Johnson, and containing elegant miniatures of both Johnson and Hastings, earned for Minnat the Governor-General's accolade of 'King of Poets'.

An interesting note to Colonel Allan Macpherson, which escaped Garland Cannon's masterly edition of the letters, reveals that even in snatched moments on the judicial bench Jones found time to seek patronage for a talented Persian poet fallen upon hard times:

> In Court, 6th Jan. 1786.
>
> Dear Sir,
>
> Mirza Zainuddin Ishky is a man of genius and probity. I presented the Governor General last year with his works, and an Ode which I translated. He has been so poor that he has been forced to sell his darling books: but his son- in-law, who is in the service of the Vizier's Minister, has now invited him to settle at Lucknow. It would be very honourable to him if the Governor would favour him with a recommendatory letter to the Nabob Vizier. His literary merit I can answer for.[20]

Jones had listed some of his favourite Sūfi poets in 'On the Mystical Poetry of the Persians and Hindus', including 'SÁIB, ORFÌ, MÍR KHOSRAU, JÁMI, HAZIN, and SÁBIK, who are next in beauty of composition to HAFIZ and SADI', mentioning also 'MESÍHI, the most elegant of their *Turkish* imitators; [...] a few Hindi poets of our own times, and [...] IBNUL FÁRED, who wrote mystical odes in *Arabick*'.[21] Such poets featured largely among the manuscripts and books which lined the shelves of the study in his Garden Reach bungalow on the banks of the Hughli;[22] they were also widely enjoyed and translated by many other Company and Crown employees in Calcutta and the other Presidencies.

Abundant evidence for this may be provided by a single number of Francis Gladwin's Calcutta periodical, *The New Asiatic Miscellany* (1789) mentioned above. Apart from Gladwin's own translations of sections of the *Dabistan*, the contents include Captain William Kirkpatrick's 'Introduction to the History of the Persian Poets'; translations of 'The Death of Mahomet' and 'The Death of Fatima' from one of the first Urdu prose works of North India, the *Deh Majlis* by Faz'li; a letter from Emperor Akbar to the Ruler of Turan, translated by John Stonehouse;[23] 'The Institutes of Ghāzān Khan, Emperor of the Moghuls', translated by Kirkpatrick;[24] substantial extracts from Sa'dī's *Bostan*; and a fascinating example of enlightened Calcutta relativism entitled 'Doctor Franklin's Celebrated Parable against Persecution, Compared with a Passage in the Bostan of Sādi'.[25]

This comparativist article describes Sa'dī's *Bostan* as 'a work abounding in the purest morality, and in some of the highest strains of piety', and perfectly exemplifies the same open-minded syncretic acceptance of both Oriental poetry and Oriental piety to be found in the writings of Jones. Furthermore, the whole periodical, the pronounced scholarly bias of which is attested by the fact that many of the translations are accompanied by the originals set in Persian *nasta'līq* types, reflects a virtually exclusive focus upon Persian and Arabic literature (much of which is concerned with ethics and good Mughal government). The only specifically 'Hindu' contents are the opening item which was the first publication of Jones's own 'Hymn to Lacshmi', a Pindaric ode to the beauteous Hindu goddess of prosperity, and 'The Stanzas called the Five Gems ('Pánca Retnáni'), composed by five Poets, who attended the Court of ADÍSŚRA, King of Bengal'.[26]

One other significant item in *The New Asiatic Miscellany* is a poem entitled 'Raikhtah, or Ode from Wulli', which is printed in *devanāgrī* characters with an interlineal transliteration and following translation. This 'Wulli' is Vali Gujarati, the first poet to compose *ghazals* in an Indian language, Urdu, rather than in Persian and whose tomb in Ahmedabad, a site of pilgrimage for Indian poets and writers of all languages, was desecrated in 2002.[27] Vali, though not a Sūfi poet, was greatly inspired by Sūfi themes, and Urdu poetry has continued to reflect the profound influence of Sūfism. Vali was a revolutionary integrator and his celebrated visit to Delhi in 1700 encouraged poets to combine the dynamic vigour of Persian diction and imagery with the sensuous Indianized beauty of Urdu vocabulary.

'Rekhtah' was the old name for Hindi/Hindvi/Urdu,[28] and Vali's example not only encouraged a new wave of Indo-Muslim poets to use Rekhtah but, as Shamsur Rahman Faruqi has pointed out: 'By the mid-eighteenth century the Hindus, too, who had also been concentrating on Persian, began to adopt Rekhtah'.[29] The fact that this *ghazal* by Vali is printed by Gladwin in *devanāgrī* (Skr. 'language [or 'town-script'] of the gods) rather than Perso-Arabic characters may be seen as evidence of important literary-cultural mingling. According to Gilchrist's *Dictionary English and Hindoostanee* (1787-90), 'rekhtu' can mean a mixture as in plaster or mortar and, in the building of the new poetics of Urdu, Muslim and Hindu elements combined.[30] Significantly, under the entry for '*ghúzul*' in Captain William Kirkpatrick's Vocabulary (1785), he has the following: 'the Hindvi ode is called *RaikhtÈh* (a Persian participle signifying *poured, scattered, diffused, shed*)', and it might seem that the connotations of this term possessed a more than merely linguistic significance.[31] Certainly, it is possible to trace a new and syncretic poetic idiom which excited young writers in Delhi at the beginning of the eighteenth century and which reflected the cultural and national mingling of milk and sugar to which Ghulam Husain referred.[32] Gopi Chand Nārang has maintained that the 'indigenous base and syncretic qualities' of Urdu enables it to perform a 'syncretizing role in a pluralistic, secular and democratic India', and it would seem that Vali Gujarati, whose poetry the Calcutta Orientalists were reading and translating in the late 1780s, played a key role in this process of reconciliation.[33]

What is remarkable about the selection of materials in Gladwin's *New Asiatick Miscellany* is the marked emphasis upon the poetry – and indeed the prose – of politics, a politics of reconciliation that had been central to Hastings's Orientalist government, although Hastings himself in 1789 was being harangued by Sheridan for his 'monstrous behaviour' towards the Begums. In Bengal Hastings had appreciated that Mughal policies concerning the exchange of cultural and doctrinal information and of artistic and intellectual collaboration were valuable means of creating a measure of integration in the vast heterogeneity that was northern India.[34] He had set the tone and it was generally followed by Company servants. As we have seen, there was certainly no anti-Muslim bias among these periodical contributors, quite the reverse, in fact, and they appeared to appreciate that in the building of empire the mortar of Rekhtah might prove useful.

The origins Rekhtah and of *sabk-i Hindī* (Indian-style diction)[35] are the subjects of heated dispute among linguistic and literary scholars of precolonial northern India, and I have neither the expertise nor the space to make any useful interventions here.[36] Whether the eleventh-century beginnings of Hindi/Urdu should be traced to Hindu or Muslim authors, there seems to be a general acceptance of the key role of Amīr Khusrau (1253–1325), the greatest of the pre-Mughal poets and the second victim of twenty-first-century tomb desecration, in the development of both *sabk-i Hindī* and Rekhtah.[37] From the perspective of late eighteenth-century 'British' India and the studies of the Calcutta Orientalists, there appears to be significant interest in this Indo-Persian Sūfi poet, whose writings seem to exemplify a profoundly multi-cultural or pluralistic position.

Amīr Khusrau was born in Patiali in Uttar Pradesh, of an Indian mother and a Turkish father, his life and his Arabic, Persian, and Hindi/ Urdu writings anticipate the cultural synthesis between Hindu and Muslim civilization that was later to flourish at the court of Akbar. This alone might have rendered him a fascinating figure to the Orientalists of the Hastings circle; Jones, in particular, would have been attracted to the polymathic versatility of this 'Indian parrot' and Turco-Indic 'Renaissance man'.[38] This historian, poet, literary critic, courtier, musician, and mystic was alive to the sensuality of India its beautiful Hindu women, its flora, fauna, and language; he not only thought that India was the Earthly Paradise but conclusively 'proved' it by means of seven arguments.[39]

Aziz Ahmad has observed unreconciled tensions in Khusrau's *'Āshiqa*, which celebrates the love of the Muslim Prince Khizar Khān for the Hindu princess Dewal Rānī. Whereas Wahīd Mirza described the poem as 'fragrant with the smell of *kewrā*, the *karnā*, the *champak*, and hundreds of sweet Indian flowers and spices, and is luminous with the bright Indian sun, and the pale cool moonlight', Ahmad points out that the poem reveals 'that the India he loves is the land of the splendour of Islam, where the *sharī'a* is honoured and secure, and Hinduism has been conquered and subdued'.[40] Whether such orthodoxy was demanded or expected by his Sultan patron remains unclear, but Ahmed cites many authentic contrasting examples of Khusrau's polemical defence of Hinduism, and his emphasis upon its essential similarities with Islam. What is important is that the lionizing of Amīr Khusrau is part of a long and revered tradition in India especially amongst those who have wished to stress the realities, or encourage the possibilities, of cultural harmony within the subcontinent. Carlo Coppola stresses this political motive in reviewing a 1975 tribute volume:

> Several of the essays [...] do little more lionize the poet—stressing his religious tolerance towards Hindus and other religious groups and his rapturous pronouncements about all things Indian. It is not by chance that the publisher of this volume is the Government of India.[41]

It would seem that the poetry of politics was operating along remarkably similar lines for the world's largest democracy in the 1970s as it had within the 'enlightened' despotism of British India two centuries earlier. Much of the Hindi/Urdu poetry attributed to Khusrau, it is now clear, was never written by him and, although there is conclusive evidence of his interest in combining Persian and Hindu traditions of music, the tradition that he invented the sitar, developing it from the indigenous *vina* which Jones and Francis Fowke had studied, is similarly apocryphal.[42] Amīr Khusrau, in his freedom from ethnic, religious or social prejudice, represents the kind of figure, that had he not existed, it might have proved expedient to invent such a symbol of India's plural heritage. But invention is not necessary, and even the attributions to this inventive genius remain inherently interesting.

Imre Bangha cites and translates 'a popular poem attributed to Amīr

Khusrau' in which 'the first half of each line is in Persian and the second in Brajbhasha a dialect of Hindi:

> ze hāl-e miskīn makun tagāful, durāe nainām banāe batiyām;
> ki tāb-e hijrān na dāram ai jān, na lehu kāhe lagāe chatiyām.
>
> Do not be indifferent towards the condition of the poor one. You hide your eyes and invent excuses.
> I do not have the strength for separation, oh my love, why don't you embrace me?[43]

It might be said that this mixing of languages can seen as symbolizing a cultural embrace, such as was not to be seen again until the time of Akbar.[44] Furthermore, it might not be factitious to compare this with the *viraha bhakti* ('love-in-separation') theme of Sanskrit poetry, for what was to develop in Rekhtah or Urdu was the fascinating 'gender-mingling' of the genre of *rēkhtī*, in which the female point of view is assumed by a male poet. This might well have much to do with the fact that the grammar of Urdu, unlike that of Persian, allows gender differentiation, which allows a poet such as Vali Gujerati to hymn the female beauties of Surat.[45] Beyond this, however, in an important article, Carla Petievich has shown that the assumption of a female voice in *rēkhtī* owes much to Sanskrit poetic conventions:

> The presence of this *'āšiq* (lover) is almost certainly inspired by the *virahinī* [a woman who dwells in separation from her beloved, in a state of *viraha*] of Indic poetry, and the significance of this inspiration should neither be overlooked nor underestimated. It indicates a recognition on the part of Dakani poets that the *virahinī*—who provides the voice of both *bhakti* poetry, [mystical/devotional poetry (which) celebrates a passionate even erotic devotion to Hindu deities, and represents the dominant voice of artistic expression over most of the Indian subcontinent for approximately the millennium between 800 and 1800 CE.] and secular Indic love literature—represents an expression fundamentally similar to that of the Perso-Arabic tradition's *'āšiq* who suffers the throes of *firāq-e yār* (separation from the beloved).[46]

These *rēkhtī* poets, as C. M. Naim has pointed out, were, almost without exception, male, but, interestingly for our purposes, one exception that Naim footnotes is Naubahār 'Zalīl', a maidservant of Prince Sulaimān Shikūh.[47] Scholars of British Romanticism will have encountered this brave and handsome son of Dāra Shikūh, within a largely female-authored genre, the sentimental novel. Sydney Owenson introduces Sulaimān Shikūh into *The Missionary: An Indian Tale* (1811) to complete both an erotic love-triangle (of Hindu priestess, Islamic prince, and Franciscan monk) and a triad of three great Oriental religions, whose major tenets are seen in terms of a Jonesian syncretism.[48] In this way a

Romantic novel, which has been described 'as a perfectly extraordinary fictionalization of the psyche of William Jones', popularizes a cultural synthesis in which *bhakti*, *śakti* (female divine energy) Vedantic philosophy, Sūfism, and deism commingle like the waters of sacred Hindu *tirthas* (confluences/river shrines) within a paradisal Kashmiri setting.[49]

To return to Jones and Amīr Khusrau via Owenson and Dāra Shikūh's son will by now, I trust, have a certain syncretic inevitability. Certainly, Jones, like Khusrau, celebrated India in all its bewildering multifariousness. Jones was discovering similitude and inter-relationship everywhere and it is likely that the work of Persian intellectuals played a far from ancillary role in the development of Jones's ideas. Jones knew the philological works of the eighteenth-century Mughal writer, Sirāj al-Din 'Alī Khān Ārzū (d. 1756), and would have read in his *Sirāj al-Lughat* of the correspondence (*tavāfuq*) between Persian and Sanskrit.[50] But Ārzū's findings had been anticipated by more than four centuries by none other than Amīr Khusrau. In his *Nuh sipihr* (The Nine Heavens/Spheres), a *masnavī* completed in the year 1318, Khusrau described Sanskrit in the following terms

> But there is another language more select than the others, which all the Brahmans use. Its name from of old is Sahaskrit, and the common people know nothing of it. A Brahman knows it, but Brahmanì women do not understand a word of it. It bears a resemblance to Arabic in some respects, in its permutations of letters, its grammar, its conjugations, and polish.[51]

While Jones the linguist would have been attracted to such comparative philology, Jones the poet would have admired Khusrau's linguistic experimentation, and the intriguing humour of his word-play. Aziz Ahmed informs us of Khusrau that: 'For the amusement of his friends he wrote mixed Persian and Hindi (pre-Urdu) verses. These *dhu'l-lisanāyn* (bilingual) quatrains tail off in *jeux d'esprit* which could be read with *double entendre* as Persian or as Hindi'.[52] Jones had also exercised his facility for virtually extempore composition by writing *jeux d'esprit* himself the society of the 'Druids of Cardigan' on the banks of the Teifi.[53] On the banks of the Hughli, devotion to his legal duties and tireless researches militated against the composition of humorous occasional verse, but there is evidence that he delighted in that of Khusrau.[54]

Included within a British Library collection of documents reflecting Jones's Persian studies in India is a contemporary Indian blind-stamped leather-bound book containing transcriptions and translations of poems by Amīr Khusrau. One of my (and presumably his) favourites is the following translation of a Khusrau quatrain, which perfectly exemplifies the bilingual quatrains described above by Ahmed:

> I went to recreate myself on the bank of a rivulet
> I saw on the brink of the stream a *Hindú* woman.
> I said: "My idol, what is the price of your locks?"
> She cried out: "Dur dur múy": that is, in *Hindy*,
> "Keep your distance, sirrah!"
> In *Persian*, "a pearl for each hair."[55]

Many aspects of intercultural relationship may be appreciated in this riverside meeting at the ghat or *tirtha*: the importance in both religions of water for recreation and for ritual purification (or indeed both, if we think of Krishna sporting with the *gopis* in the Yamuna river. It highlights potentially divisive but ultimately resolvable issues of idolatry/*fin' amour* (itself originally an Oriental discourse), for in this interracial relationship certain productive tensions play around upon the fact that the Hindu is both his worshipped 'idol' and an idol-worshipper.[56] The humour involved in the woman's rejection of what on one level is an impertinent and insolent question, perfectly caught in Jones's translation of the Hindi by the words "Keep your distance, sirrah!", which combines a mixture of contempt, reassertion of authority, reprimand, with a hint of playful rejection. The Persian meaning of the words adds a superbly haughty self-compliment simultaneously encapsulating the treasure of her own beauty and, by association, the beauty of the subcontinent.[57]

In his addition of a bilingual dimension to the rhetorical device of *īhām* (playing on multiple meanings of a word), Amīr Khusrau produces a highly sophisticated poetic which goes far beyond *double entendre*, or punning into the semiotics of the syncretic.[58] Its crucial importance in terms of cultural interaction lies in its power to disconcert, to recreate imaginative spaces (mirrored by Jones's choice of the Augustan-sounding term 'recreate myself') in the recreation of reading/translating, and to create new interrelationships between words, seemingly identical but etymologically discrete, within the diverse linguistic family which – as a result of Jones's researches – would be grouped as Indo-European.

In March 2003, I discovered a letter from Sir William Jones to Harford Jones, the East India Company Joint Factor at Basra, expressing his passionate desire to see '*Persia*, the most delightful, the most compact, the most desirable country of them all', to view its cultural treasures and ancient monuments, and to talk to its respected poets.[59] While I read his words: 'I burn with a desire of seeing Shiraz', Baghdad was in flames. Jones's enduring fascination with Indo-Persian linguistic and ethnological affinities, his intellectual investment in pluralism, and his enlightened commitment to a syncretic East-West synthesis remain something of a beacon in a world where 'intelligence' is squandered upon missiles.

NOTES

1. This paper was delivered to the Asiatic Society on Wednesday, 8 February 2006.
2. An otherwise valuable article by Kumkum Chatterjee repeats this misconception: 'Even British orientalist scholars who are known for their admiration of Indian culture and traditions confined their interests to ancient India and specifically to the achievements of the Aryans', 'History as Self-Representation: The Recasting of a Political Tradition in Late Eighteenth-Century Eastern India', *Modern Asian Studies*, 32:4, 1998, 913-48.
3. Ghulam Husain Khan Tabatabai, *A Translation of the Sëir Mutaqharin; or, View of Modern Times, being an History of India, from the Year 1118 to the Year 1195 (this year answers to the Christian year 1781-82)*, 3 vols (Calcutta: James White, 1789 [1790]). For important biographical material on Ghulam Husain, see Gulfishan Khan, *Indian Perceptions of the West During the Eighteenth Century* (Karachi: Oxford University Press, 1998), 84-92.
4. See 'The Palanquins of State; or, Broken Leaves in a Mughal Garden', in *Romantic Representations of British India*, ed. Michael J. Franklin (Routledge: 2006).
5. The benighted darkness, which seemed to encompass all of Northern India, was lamented in a 'Persian Ode, written by the still nominal Emperor of Hindustán, Shah Allum, during his confinement, after his eyes had been put out by the traitor Golaam Khader, translated by Captain M. Symes, Esq. Captain in the 76th. Regiment of Foot': 'Has BRITISH JUSTICE, BRITONS' boast, / With HASTINGS left Hindostën's Coast?', *The Asiatic Annual Register* (1798-9), 203-5; 204. Interestingly, Michael Symes, in comparing and contrasting 'the gloomy Islamite and tranquil Hindoo', is the first author I have encountered to use the term 'Hindooism'; see his *An account of an embassy to the Kingdom of Ava, sent by the Governor-general of India, in the year 1795* (London: Bulmer, 1800), 99.
6. Cited by Rajat Kanta Ray, 'Indian Society and the Establishment of British Supremacy, 1765-1818', in *The Oxford History of the British Empire*, vol. II *The Eighteenth Century*, ed. P. J. Marshall (Oxford: Oxford University Press, 1998) 508-29; 508, from Khurshidul Islam and Ralph Russell, *Three Mughal Poets: Mir, Sauda, and Mir Hasan*, (Delhi: Oxford University Press, 1991), 22.
7. 'GHULÁM HUSAIN, many of us personally know, and whose impartiality deserves the highest applause, though his unrewarded merit will give no encouragement to other contemporary historians, who, to use his own phrase in a letter to myself, may, like him, *consider plain truth as the beauty of historical composition*. From all these materials, and from these alone, a perfect history of *India* (if a mere compilation, however elegant, could deserve such a title) might be collected by any studious man, who had a competent knowledge of *Sanscrit*, *Persian*, and *Arabick*; but, even in the work of a writer so qualified, we could only give absolute

credence to the general outline; for, while the abstract *sciences* are all truth, and the *fine arts* all fiction, we cannot but own, that in the *details of history*, truth and fiction are so blended as to be scarce distinguishable', *The Works of Sir William Jones*, ed. Anna Maria Jones, 13 vols, London: Stockdale, and Walker, 1807, 3: 214; henceforth *Works*. In an attempt to secure financial security for this 'venerable old man', Jones had sent home a copy of the *Sëir Mutaqharin*, with warm recommendations, to C.W. Boughton Rouse, Secretary to the Board of Control for India. Jones described it as 'an excellent impartial modern History of India [...] containing very just Remarks on the Administration of Government and Justice by our Nation, but *sine irā aut odio*' (without anger or hatred), see *The Letters of Sir William Jones*, ed. Garland Cannon, 2 vols (Oxford: Clarendon, 1970), 2: 723-4; 805-6; henceforth *Letters*.

8. As he wrote to his Persian Translator, Jonathan Scott, on 9 December 1784: 'My letter to Mr Smith introducing Mr. Wilkins's Translation of the Gheeta is also Business, though began in Play. It is the effect of part of a System which I long since laid down, and supported for reconciling the People of England to the Natives of Hindostan, Hastings to Jonathan Scott, 9 Dec. 1784, BL Add MS. 29129, f. 275.
9. It was not only Eurocentric stereotypes that were being radically adjusted by Orientalist publications. Din Muhammad cites Gladwin's translation of the *Ā'īn-i Akbarī*: 'The native Indians, or Hindoos, are men of strong natural genius, and are, by no means, unacquainted with literature and science, as the translation of the Ayeen Akberry into English, has fully evinced', *The Travels of Dean Mahomet: An Eighteenth-Century Journey Through India*, ed. Michael H. Fisher (Berkeley: University of California Press, 1997), 83. The *Ayeen Akberry* (1783-6) is reprinted in *Representing India: Indian Culture and Imperial Control in Eighteenth-Century British Orientalist Discourse*, ed. Michael J. Franklin, 9 vols (London: Routledge, 2000), vols. 5 and 6.
10. Dāra Shikūh's enlightened attitudes are also praised by Joseph White in his edition of the 'Institutes of Timur', which included a translation into English by Major William Davy, Hastings's Persian secretary, and was published at the expense of the East India Company. Also included was a Brahmanical prayer to Rudra, the Vedic storm-god, translated by C.W. Boughton Rouse 'from a Persic Version of Dara Shekoo'; see *Institutes Political and Military ... by the Great Timour* (Oxford: Clarendon, 1783), xiv; xlv-xlviii.
11. 'On the Mystical Poetry of the Persians and Hindus', *Works*, 4: 211-68; 232. Elsewhere he describes Dāra Shikūh as 'That amiable, but impolitic prince, who sacrificed his throne, and his life, to a premature declaration of his religious opinions', *Works*, 13: 365.
12. *Works*, 1: 78; Teignmouth's translation.
13. *Works*, 3: 110. Jones had quoted an elegy of Mir Muhammad Hussain in his 'On the Orthography of Asiatic Words', *ibid.*, 301-305.
14. *The New Asiatic Miscellany. Consisting of original essays, translations, and fugitive pieces* (1789), 86-136.

15. *Works*, 4: 216. On the remarkable parallels between Sūfism and Hindu mysticism; see Aziz Ahmed, *Studies in Islamic Culture in the Indian Environment* (Oxford: Clarendon, 1964), 119-39.
16. 'After having translated the *Gìtagóvinda* word for word, I reduced my translation to the form, in which it is now exhibited; omitting only those passages, which are too luxuriant and too bold for an European taste', *ibid.*, 235. Stuart McGregor demonstrates that such *bhakta* poetry was certainly to the taste of many Muslims: 'The popularity of Krsna songs right across north India's culturally mixed society is suggested in the *Haqāiq i Hindī* (Realities of India) of Mīr Vāhid of Bilgram (Hardoi district,1556). This work provides Islamic interpretations of personas and places in the Krsna story, 'The progress of Hindi, Part 1: The Development of a Transregional Idiom', in *Literary Cultures in History: Reconstructions from South Asia*, ed. Sheldon Pollock (Berkeley, University of California Press, 2003), 912- 57; 921-2.
17. This was first published posthumously in the quarto edition of *The Works of Sir William Jones*, ed. Anna Maria Jones, 6 vols (London: G. G. and J. Robinson, 1799), 6: 423ff. Nathaniel Brassey Halhed, a protÈgÈ of Hastings, friend of Jones, and author *A Code of Gentoo Laws* (1776) and *A Grammar of the Bengal Language* (1778) also translated the *Sirr-i Akbar* in 1787; the manuscript was never published, but its introduction was recently edited by Rosane Rocher, 'Nathaniel Brassey Halhed on the Upaniṣads (1787)', *Annals of the Bhandarkar Oriental Research Institute* (1977-78), 279-89. For a comparative study of the two friends' representations of Islam and Hinduism, see my 'Cultural Possession, Imperial Control, and Comparative Religion: The Calcutta Perspectives of Sir William Jones and Nathaniel Brassey Halhed', *Yearbook of English Studies*, 32, (2002), 1-18.
19. Jones wrote to compliment him on this commission, which appeared as *Divānī Khvajāh Hāfiz Shirāzi ā dibāchāh va qaṣaid. The Works of Hafez; with an account of his life and writings* (Calcutta: Upjohn, 1791), planning to take a copy to take the volume to Shiraz on his projected return to Europe via Persia: 'An impression of your Hafiz will, indeed, be a valuable acquisition to the publick; and I hope some years hence to offer up a copy of it on the tomb of the divine poet near the crystal stream of Rucnabad', *Letters*, 2: 702.
20. *Soldiering in India 1764-1787*, ed. W.C. Macpherson (Edinburgh: Blackwood, 1928), 345. Jones had presented Zainudeen's works, together with 'a hasty translation [...] of the best couplets', to Sir John Macpherson on Sunday, 22 May 1785, and arranged for the poet to receive an interview with the Acting Governor-General on the following Wednesday; see *Letters*, 2: 673-5.
21. *Works*, 4: 232.
22. Mere enumeration of items is obviously a crude indicator, especially considering the greater relative scarcity of Sanskrit manuscripts, but, according to Charles Wilkins's catalogue of Jones's Oriental Manuscripts, at his death he possessed 59 Sanskrit as compared with 77 Persian and 36

Arabic MSS. Some of the annotation which Wilkins records provides a better insight into his passion for Persian poetry. On the cover of item 81a, a copy of that thirteenth-century classic text of Islamic mysticism, from which he quoted in 'On the Mystical Poetry of the Persians and Hindus', Rumi's *Masnavi*, Jones wrote: 'So extraordinary a book as the Mesnavi was never, perhaps, composed by man. It abounds with beauties, and blemishes, equally great; with gross obscenity, and pure ethicks; with exquisite strains of poetry, and flat puerilities of wit; with ridicule on established religions, and a vein of sublime piety: it is like a wild country in a fine climate overspread with rich flowers and with the odour of beasts. I know of no writer, to whom the Maulavi can justly be compared, except *Chaucer* or *Shakespeare*', *Works*, 13: 401-26; 417.

23. Akbar stresses how throughout 'the vast country of Hindustan [...] many and various descriptions of people, though differing widely in manners and in customs, now maintain the most friendly intercourse with each other', *New Asiatic Miscellany* (1789), 75.
24. In his introduction Kirkpatrick writes: 'Out of a great variety of similar passages, with which Oriental writings abound, I have selected a distich on the kingly duty; which as it is contained in a work popular beyond all others, may be almost said to be in the mouth of every Asiatic possessing the smallest tincture of learning: (he cites Sa'dī in the original) Wrong not any of the people in the value of a mustard-grain: since the prince is a shepherd and the people are his flock', *ibid.*, 165.
25. The parallel is a fairly close one; in Franklin's version, the stranger announces 'I do not worship the God thou speakest of; neither do I call upon his Name; for I have made to myself a God, which abideth alway in mine House, and provideth me with all Things', in Sa'dī's he is actually a 'Gueber', or Zoroastrian, who declares: 'I practise no rite, which I have not heard from my priest, who worshippeth fire'. In both parables the devout man drives away the 'pagan' and is reprimanded (in the Franklin) by God: 'Have I born with him these hundred ninety and eight Years, and nourished him, and cloathed him, notwithstanding his Rebellion against me, and couldst not thou, that art thyself a Sinner, bear with him one Night?' or (in the Sa'dī) by Gabriel who reprehends: 'O friend, I have supported him through a life of an hundred years; and thou hast conceived an abhorrence for him all at once', *ibid.*, 235, 238. Jones was in fact a close friend of Franklin, both in London and Paris.
26. Gladwin prints the original of 'Pánca Retnáni' in *devānagrī* characters, *ibid.*, 61.
27. The nineteenth-century Delhi critic, Muhammad Husain Azad, uses an organicist trope for for the flourishing of Urdu: 'Although the tree of Urdu grew in the soil of Sanskrit and [Braj] Bhasha, it flourished in the breezes of Persian', cited and translated by Frances Pritchett, *Nets of Awareness: Urdu Poetry and its Critics* (Berkeley: University of California Press, 1994), 140.
28. Hindi-Urdu, the Indo-Aryan *lingua franca* of the Indo-Pakistani people, is one language with two names: Hindi when written in *devānāgrī* script

by Hindus and Urdu when Arabo-Persic *nasta'līq* script is used by Muslims. Sharing the same grammatical, syntactical, and phonological systems, Hindi vocabulary is largely derived from Sanskrit whereas that of Urdu is borrowed from Persian and Arabic. In the written language there are lexical differences, but as a means of oral communication in many ways there is an effective mingling and merging.

29. 'A Long History of Urdu Literary Culture, Part 1: Naming and Placing a Literary Culture', in *Literary Cultures in History*, ed. Pollock, 805-63; 849, n. 100.
30. *A Dictionary, English and Hindoostanee, in which the words are marked with their distinguishing initials; as Hinduwee, Arabic, and Persian. Whence the Hindoostanee ... is evidently formed*, 2 vols (Calcutta: Stuart and Cooper, 1787-90), 561, 648. Cf. 'Thus *rekhtah* became the name for a poem in which either Hindi/Hindvi was added to a Persian template or Persian was added to a Hindi/Hindvi template', Faruqi, 'A Long History of Urdu Literary Culture', 839
31. *A Vocabulary, Persian, Arabic, and English; containing such words as have been adopted from the two former of those languages, and incorporated into the Hindvi* (Calcutta: Joseph Cooper, 1785), 103.
32. According to Muhammad Husain Azad, the literary mingling wasn't always perfect; the addition of Persian to Urdu was 'as if someone had put sugar in the milk, but it had not yet been well dissolved: one sip is particularly sweet, one absolutely flavourless; then in another, the teeth crunched a sugar crystal', cited and translated by Pritchett, *Nets of Awareness: Urdu Poetry and its Critics*, 140.
33. Gopi Chand Nārang, *Urdu Language and Literature* (New Delhi: Sterling, 1991), vii. Two of Faruqi's section headings are entitled 'Vali's Literary Revolution' and 'The New Literary Culture', 'A Long History of Urdu Literary Culture', 843, 849.
34. 'Persian literary culture had a certain logical connection with the Mughal political ideology. It helped generate and legitimate the Mughal policy of creating out of heterogeneous social and religious groups a class of allies. Like the emperor and his nobility in general, this class also cherished universalist human values and visions, Muzaffar Alam, 'Persian in Precolonial Hindustan', in *Literary Cultures in History*, ed. Pollock, 131-98; 171.
35. According to Muzaffar Alam, 'The shaping of *sabk-i Hindī* signified a dialogue between the Persian language and the Indian cultural ethos', *ibid.*, 179.
36. Conflicting accounts may be found in Amrit Rai, *A House Divided: The Origin and Development of Hindi-Urdu* (New Dehli: Oxford University Press, 1991) and Shamsur Rahman Faruqi's *Early Urdu Literary Culture and History* (New Dehli: Oxford University Press, 2001), [a subsequently updated version appears in *Literary Cultures in History: Reconstructions from South Asia* (2003), see n. 22 above]. Imre Bangha has summarized their dissension as follows: 'Amrit Rai, reiterating the general (and official) Hindi stand, emphasises the composite aspect of Hindi encompassing

Avadhi, Bhojpuri, Braj, Rajasthani, Khar?ī Bolī and Urdu with examples taken from both Hindu and Muslim authors. This Hindi expansionist tendency is refuted by Faruqi, who examined the origins of Urdu as independent of the Hindi and indeed Hindu tradition and labelled Rai as 'full of tendentious speculation', 'Early Rekhta Poetry in the Nāgarī script' (forthcoming).

37. According to Imre Bangha, 'While Rai traces the development of early Hindi from Apabhramsha and considers Gorakhnāth (11th c.) and the Nāthpanthīs followed by Amīr Khusrau (1253–1325) to be the first Hindi authors, Faruqi starts Urdu literature with Mas'ūd Sa'd Salmān (1046–1121) of Lahore followed by Amīr Khusrau', *ibid.*
38. 'Since I am an Indian parrot, to tell you the truth, / Ask in Hindvi, that I may respond to you with elegance', cited in Muzaffar Alam, 'Persian in Precolonial Hindustan', 144. Cf. 'Amir Khusrau was the sort of multifaceted, multi-talented person to whom the term "Renaissance man" genuinely applies', Carlo Coppola, review of *Amir Khusrau Memorial Volume* (1975), *Journal of Asian Studies*, 37:4 (1978), 767.
39. Ahmed, *Studies in Islamic Culture in the Indian Environment*, 115-16
40. *ibid.*, 115.
41. Coppola, review, 767.
42. See 'On the Musical Modes of the Hindus', *Works*, 4: 166-210; Francis Fowke, 'An Extract of a Letter *on the Vina*', *Asiatick Researches*, 1 (1788), 295-99.
43. Imre Bangha also provides an even more remarkable of the macaronic in a poem attributed to Abd ur-Rahīm Khānkhānā, this quatrain is written in no fewer than ten languages: Sanskrit, Braj, Gujarati, Marathi, Marwari, Rajasthani, Khaṛī Bolī, Punjabi, Persian/Arabic and Telugu, 'Early Rekhta Poetry in the Nāgarī script', 2.
44. 'After Khusrau there followed centuries of mutual cultural distaste and indifference', Ahmed, *Studies in Islamic Culture in the Indian Environment*, 118.
45. '"Purity reaches its perfection in the beardless boys (here), / But Vali, the beauty of the women is (even) greater! He goes on to boast that all Krishna's legendary *gopis* are actually mere imitations of the beauties that exist here! Since both Urdu grammar and Vali's Dakhani poetic background, unlike Persian, permit gender differentiation, he includes women in his catalogue of beauties', Sunil Sharma, 'The City of Beauties in Indo-Persian Poetic Landscape', *Comparative Studies of South Asia, Africa and the Middle East*, 24:2 (2004), 73-81; 79. In translating the celebrated 'Persian Song of Hafiz', Jones had discreetly changed the sex of the beloved to a 'Sweet maid'; see my *Sir William Jones: Selected Poetical and Prose Works* (Cardiff: University of Wales Press, 1995), 186.
46. 'The Feminine and Cultural Syncretism in early Dakani Poetry', *Annual of Urdu Studies*, 8 (Winter 1993), 110-21; 112. I have reproduced her footnotes in square brackets.
47. 'Transvestic Words?: The Rekhti in Urdu', *Annual of Urdu Studies*, 16: 1 (2001), 3?26; 3.

48. See my 'Representing India in Drawing-Room and Classroom; or, Miss Owenson and "those gay gentlemen, Brahma, Vishnu, and Co."', in *Interrogating Orientalisms: Theories and Practices*, ed. Diane Long Hoeveler, and Jeffrey Cass (Columbus: Ohio State University Press, 2006).
49. John Drew, *India and the Romantic Imagination* (Delhi: Oxford University Press, 1987), 253.
50. On Jones's study of 'Sirajaid'din arzu'; see 'A Catalogue of Oriental Manuscripts', item 102n., *Works*, 13: 419.
51. Khusrau, *The Third Sphere* http://erga.packhum.org/persian/ We might compare Khusrau's references to the 'select' and polished character of Sanskrit with Jones's emphasis upon its 'perfect', 'copious', and 'refined' nature in the groundbreaking 'philologer' passage of his 'Third Anniversary Discourse: On the Hindus' (1786); see *Works*, 3: 34. Significantly, Khusrau, like Jones, stresses key similarities in grammatical forms.
52. Ahmed, *Studies in Islamic Culture*, 116-17
53. A most relevant one in the present context is 'Kneel to the Goddess whom all Men Adore' (1780), a mock-heroic address to Muslims, Christians, Hindus, Parsees, pagan Greeks and Romans to acknowledge that they all worship the same goddess be she called Diana, Mary, or Astarte, which, written as it was in the wake of the anti-Catholic Gordon riots, reveals Jones's Enlightened deism as it propounds a syncretic manifesto. See *Selected Poetical and Prose Works*, 58-61.
54. His first year in India did, however, produce the mock-epic, 'The Enchanted Fruit; or; The Hindu Wife' (1784), and the humorous ballad, addressed to his wife, Anna Maria, entitled 'Plassey-Plain' (1784), *Works* 2: 503-5, a holograph manuscript of which I recently discovered among Hastings's papers in BL Add. MS. 29, 235, ff. 158-9.
55. BL MSS Eur C 274. The Persian original, transliteration, and translation of this quatrain are available on the 'Amir Khusrau Website', posted by Yousuf Saeed at http://www.angelfire.com/sd/urdumedia/ : 'I went to enjoy the beauty of the river-side and saw an Indian lady at the ghat. "Oh, idol of mine," said I, "what is the price of your tresses?" and she replied, *dur dur muye- 'go away you wretch'* (so in Hindi) or *'every single hair of mine has pearls in it'* (so in Persian). (*dur dur muye* is a popular abusive word still found in much of north India)'. It has been pointed out to me by several experts that Jones's translation is much more precise.
56. Cf. the praise of a much later Urdu poet, Asadullah Khan Ghalib (d. 1869), for the beauties of the Benares ghats: 'Its land is the capital of idol-worshippers, / From one end to the other, it is a pilgrimage site of the intoxicated. / In essence, the beauties are ablaze like Mt. Sinai. / From head to toe, divine luminescence, "May the evil eye be far." / (They have) narrow waists and strong hearts, / They are innocently skilled in their work', cited in Sharma, 'The City of Beauties in Indo-Persian Poetic Landscape', 79.
57. Harish Trivedi, describing these 'light and even risquÈ verses in contemporary Khari Boli', links our two victims of tomb desecration, by

pointing out that 'the next major figure [after Khusrau] to write verse in a comparable idiom of Khari Boli occurs in Urdu not until Valī (f. c. 1700)', 'The Progress of Hindi, Part 2: Hindi and the Nation', in *Literary Cultures in History*, ed. Pollock, 958-1022; 969.

58. Mufazzar Alam interestingly connects the multiplicity of meaning characterizing *īhām* with Sūfi endeavours to find Islamic meanings for the narrative of Krishna and the *gopīs*, suggesting that Indo-Persian poetry may be read 'in the light of the extended connotative power of *īhām*, which creates space for possible meanings far removed from the explicit', 'Persian in Precolonial Hindustan', in *Literary Cultures in History*, ed. Pollock, 181.

59. 'The Sixth Anniversary Discourse; On the Persians', *Asiatick Researches*, II (1790), reprinted in *Representing India: Indian Culture and Imperial Control in Eighteenth-Century British Orientalist Discourse*, ed. Michael J. Franklin, 9 vols (London: Routledge, 2000), 8; 48. See my 'I burn with a desire of seeing Shiraz': A New Letter from Sir William Jones to Harford Jones', *Review of English Studies*, N.S. 56: 227 (2005), 748-756.

2

Braj Reinvented: Some Colonial Approaches to Hindi Dialects

Arthur Dudney

सूरदास प्रभु कहत प्रेम सौं, ये मेरे ब्रज लोग
"Surdas' lord says with affection, these are my Braj people."

"Why do you despise the culture of the language you speak every day of your lives?" was the question posed by a very frustrated Dr. J.R. Ballantyne to his Indian students at Benares College in the late 1840s (Rai 65-6). We can infer that the students responded with bemusement because in their opinion the "Hindi" that Ballantyne was attempting to teach them as their own language bore little resemblance to what they spoke at home. The students recognized that they all spoke rather differently from one another and that Englishmen like Ballantyne liked to compress all this linguistic diversity into an illusory thing called "Hindi."

This event dramatizes the fact that language is not just a code system for communication but also exercises a strong conceptual influence over a society. Language has a role in establishing a speaker's identity and the identities of others. Sociolinguistics teaches us that a descriptive analysis of a language (which is what linguistics attempts to construct) and the perceptions of it by its users can have little to do with one another.[1] The situation is even more complex when outsiders, who by definition have imperfect information about a society, try to define its languages. For Ballantyne, the students' dialects merged into one language because he was not concerned with the differences, but for the students one of the defining features of their speech was difference. Such paradoxes of usage and perception informed the ambitious British attempts to understand and catalogue vernacular languages in the north of India in the late eighteenth and early nineteenth centuries.

One of the languages to fall into the British classification scheme was Braj Bhāṣā, which is a fascinating test case for us because of its ambiguous status. It was a cosmopolitan literary language but it also had strong conceptual ties to its traditional base in the Braj country around Mathura and Vrindavan. For rhetorical purposes, it could be thought of as the everyday language of some cowherds in Mathura — whether it actually was or not is an entirely separate question — or as a mark of high refinement in the courtly literary tradition and in devotional poetry.[2] It existed in Sanskritized and Persianized idioms, and appeared in both Hindu and Islamicate contexts.

This essay will reconstruct some concepts of Braj that emerged in the early nineteenth century. I will consider writing by British scholars of the time, specifically John Borthwick Gilchrist (1759-1841), Thomas Duer Broughton (1778-1835) and William Price (1780-1830), and summarize their views on Braj and its relationship with other Hindi dialects. The primary texts I will consider are Gilchrist's *Oriental Fabulist* (1803), Broughton's *Selections from the Popular Poetry of the Hindoos* (1814) and Price's *Hindee and Hindoostanee Selections* (1827).[3] I will give special attention to the stated sources of their information so that the complexity of the interaction between British researchers and Indian intellectuals/ intellectual systems can be better understood in the context of Braj.

Because this essay is not a literary history, I will not attempt to sketch the development of the complex Braj literary culture across northern India as we understand it today.[4] My concern here will be to present British colonial approaches to Indian vernacular languages and to draw connections between research methodology and the conclusions colonial scholars drew about Braj. They made three significant assumptions about Braj: it was archaic, bucolic and strictly for Hindus. It was believed to be the precursor language to Hindustani (that is, what we would think of as Urdu) and other north Indian dialects. There was a trend of identifying a supposedly Hindu idiom against an Islamicate one without focusing on the divisions within the Hindu idiom. Thus, understanding the early nineteenth century attitudes towards Indian languages is made difficult by the fact that the terms "Braj," "Hindi" and "Hinduwee" are often used interchangeably in British sources. Furthermore, indigenous sources are not careful to distinguish between bhākhā (an alternate form of bhāṣā) as meaning vernacular language in general or the particular Braj Bhāṣā dialect (e.g. Ziauddin 34-5).

The British interest in Indian languages had a decidedly instrumental character.[5] They focused their attention on Urdu, which was the lingua franca of the army and used for administrative functions not conducted in Persian. Gilchrist writes that "the Hindoostanee is the most general colloquial tongue in India and one of constant use and occurrence with our servants, teachers and dependents of every description" (xiii; cf Das 62). Broughton claims that studies of Hindi had been neglected in favor of Urdu because Urdu was universally understood in administration (Bangha 36). However, he goes on to make the fascinating observation that

> with this language [Urdu], few of our Hindoo Sipahees are conversant when they quit their native villages. In the course of a long service they doubtless acquire more of it, but throughout their lives, they generally retain so much of their original dialect, that it not infrequently requires a third person to interpret between a veteran soldier and even his experienced officer.

Despite the fact that Urdu is seen as the common language of India, it is recognized that it is not everyone's language, being foreign in particular to village Hindus. Gilchrist implies much the same situation when he regrets not including Khaṛī Bolī (Hindi) translations for any but two of the fables in the *Fabulist*, "since this particular idiom or style of the Hindoostanee would have proved highly useful to students of that language" (v). There is a clear indication that access to a non-Persianized vernacular is a desideratum.

Despite the claims about the general availability of Urdu, Urdu is explicitly associated with Muslims. Gilchrist's *Anti-Jargonist, or a Short Introduction to the Hindoostanee Language* summarizes the differences in material culture between Hindus and Muslims, and argues that language is a critical feature by which Europeans can tell whether an Indian is a Hindu or a Muslim.[6] Price asserts that Urdu "continues to be the language of the Moosulmans, and especially of those of any rank or learning, or who affect precision in the words they employ" (viii). In the texts I have used, Gilchrist, Broughton and Price are all silent on the Islamicate influence on Braj, which is either a deliberate omission or a matter of not having had access to the right sources.[7] However, Broughton, who intends his collection to be a record of the "poetry of the Hindoos," writes of the poems he has gathered that, "I might have considerably enlarged the collection by admitting into it poems which contained a mixture of Persian and Arabic words, with the pure Hindee; but this would have been to deviate from the original plan and not do justice to the cause I have ventured to advocate" (49-50). In this case, Broughton was exercising a deliberate editorial choice, and Persian words were grounds for a poem's being excluded from this collection of "poetry of the Hindoos." However, he apologizes to the reader for having included two poems which contained the Persianate words "taksīr," "faryād," "kāġhaz" and "qalam" (Bangha 50). The excuse is telling: He argues that the words were in such common use that he had not noticed their origin. Clearly, the fact that his informants offered him poems with Persian words in them indicates that the "poetry of the Hindoos" was not conceived of by "the Hindoos" in quite the same way as by Broughton.

Broadly speaking, there were two kinds of informants used by the British to learn about vernacular language. Most of the informants about whom we have any record were members of the Indian secretarial class known as munshīs. They were formally hired as teachers and secretaries in colonial centers like Calcutta. However, there were also Indians who engaged with the British on a more ad hoc basis. The best evidence I have found for this latter category relates to Broughton's *Selections from the Popular Poetry of the Hindoos,* for which he gathered the raw material from among soldiers. He writes that "there is perhaps no set of men in India better qualified to afford the kind of information I sought for than the Sipahees of our own army" (38). He writes that many of the soldiers "belong to the higher orders of Brahmuns and Rajpoots... and not seldom have attained the degree of Pundit." Hindu munshis tended to be from high castes because of their responsibility for writing, but interestingly Broughton's soldier informants were also high caste. The literature of non-elite castes, inevitably marked as 'folklore,' would only interest the British later in the nineteenth century.

Fort William College in Calcutta was the nucleus for a great deal of British scholarship on Indian languages in collaboration with munshis. In 1805 there were 24 "established moonshees" working on a permanent basis and 26 "extra and certified moonshees" (Kidwai 25). Of these, only one was specifically employed as a Braj munshi, namely Śrī Lāl Kab, more commonly known to us as Lallūlāl, who was paid at the special rate of Rs. 50. It is not clear why he earned more than the pay of typical "established munshis," which was Rs. 40, but perhaps it reflects greater involvement in the College's publications.[8] Perhaps not surprisingly given that modern Hindi is kharī bolī, Lallūlāl is remembered today as the "father of [kharī bolī] Hindi prose" rather than for his services to Braj literature. The College printed several books written in or concerning Braj, including *General Principles of Inflection and Conjugation in Braj Bhasha* (1811), which is unfortunately not extant in any library today (Das 70). Despite an impressive record of publication (some 132 books were issued between 1802 and 1830, of which 65 were prepared by or under the guidance of Gilchrist himself), the influence of the College on later developments in Hindi and Urdu is a subject of debate (Das 68, Siddiqui 42, Kidwai 31). It took no Indian students and was threatened with closure and budget cuts from its inception (Sinha 16-7). The East India Company College (later known as Haileybury College), which was opened in Hertfordshire in 1805, superseded Fort William College as an educational institution because it took on the basic instruction of East India Company writers, the primary purpose for which Fort William College had been founded.

The relationships between Orientalists and their informants varied greatly. Rosane Rocher and Brian Hatcher paint a rich picture of Indian Sanskrit scholars adapting their traditional roles to avail themselves of the opportunities, financial and otherwise, offered by collaborating with British researchers. The details are not important here, but both Rocher and Hatcher argue that the milieu in which the Sanskritic knowledge of the colonial period was produced is important, and I have attempted to sketch very briefly what is known about the equivalent processes of knowledge production for vernacular languages. Gilchrist and Broughton, for example, have very different attitudes towards information gathered in India. Gilchrist has a deep-seated suspicion of his informants and accuses Indians of intentionally misleading Europeans as a matter of "low cunning or national policy." He specifically disavows the possibility of mere cultural misunderstanding, although he admits that some Englishmen are difficult to understand when speaking Indian languages, in favor of a more sinister explanation.[9] Broughton on the other hand finds his Hindu interlocutors "more intelligent and communicative, more abounding in interesting matter, and withal much less opinionated and arrogant than their fellow subjects of the Moohumedan faith"(38). He writes that his upper-caste informants "are always willing to repay any information on such subjects [as the customs of Britain], by communicating in return all they know of their own" (ibid.). It is fascinating that Europeans appear never to have described their working relationships with their native informants except in such strong terms; it is the bold manner in which these statements are expressed that is constant rather than what is said about the relationships themselves. Despite Gilchrist's condemnation of his informants, as mentioned above, elsewhere he lavishes praise on them, including in the preface to the *Fabulist*, in which he singles out the Second Munshi of the College, Tārnī Charan Mitr. (Second Munshi was the position below Chief Munshi, which was the highest position available to Indians at the College.) He warmly thanks Tārnī Charan Mitr for his contribution to the book, writing that to his "patient labour and considerable proficiency in the English tongue, am I greatly indebted for the accuracy and dispatch, with which this collection has been completed."[10] In comparison, we should consider the relationship of Sir William Jones with his close collaborator Rādhākānta, a Brahmin Sanskritist. As Rocher has documented, Jones alternates between high praise and outright condemnation (69). The pandit is called "learned" throughout Jones's letters and is especially praised when he discovers the similarity between English drama and Kālidāsa's plays, but when he refuses to provide good information on Buddhism, he is accused of being "blinded by the mercenary zeal of an intolerant priesthood."[11] As Rocher notes, "Jones took pains to show, wherever he could, that the pundits he consulted were unanimous in supporting the views he propounded" (65). Gilchrist, as we shall see below, was more confrontational towards his Indian subordinates.

The writing process for the *Oriental Fabulist* offers further conclusions as to how research was conducted at Fort William College. Although the book was compiled under the "direction and superintendence" of Gilchrist, the munshis appear to have had a surprising amount of editorial control. For one thing, Gilchrist's praise of Tārnī Charan Mitr implies that the Second Munshi had a significant, if undefined, organizational role in the project. More importantly, Gilchrist suggests that the munshis disobeyed his instructions to use a particular word in a passage in the *Fabulist.* To illustrate a point about how Hindustani is not yet a logical language, he writes:

> This I can avow, that in the present instance, I desired my people to use moontuzur instead of oommedwar, but they either forgot to do so or preferred the other, for they still defend it, as the synonymous word for moontuzur, while they also grant, that the last would after all be the most appropriate for the sentence under discussion. (32)
> [In modern transcription: muntazir (expecting; someone who watches expectantly) and ummīdvār (expecting; a suppliant; but in modern Urdu generally only used to mean "candidate").]

From this instance we can observe that the process of writing the passages had devolved to the munshis to such a degree that Gilchrist did not have or did not avail himself of the opportunity to overrule their choices before the Fabulist went to print. We also learn that Gilchrist debated word choices with his munshis. Although he appears to have been dictatorial in his lexicography, the munshis were not always convinced and indeed apparently disobeyed orders.

Despite having some sense of how the raw materials of language study — texts themselves — were produced, the sources for the sweeping philological assertions made by Gilchrist, Broughton and Price are not clear. The conclusion reached unambiguously by Gilchrist and Broughton is that Braj is a living fossil, the old language of northern India coexisting with more recent and consciously developed languages like Hindustani.[12] When Gilchrist was compiling his *Hindustani Dictionary,* which he intended to be a compilation of contemporary Hindustani, he clearly misunderstood the relationship of Hindustani to Hindi dialects with literary traditions like Braj and Avadhi and so rejected these out of hand as being archaic. During the process, his poor Persian prevented him from having direct access to indigenous linguistic works, notably those of Sirāj al-Dīn' Alī Khān "Ārzū," who wrote in the mid-eighteenth century (Kidwai 41). Ārzū himself refers to Braj (or, as he called it, "Zubān-i-Gvālyār"—"Language of Gwalior," which had been a major center of literary patronage for Braj) as an elite language.[13] There is no reflection of that opinion in Gilchrist or in Broughton. It is best to avoid discussing Gilchrist's stranger conclusions on language (for example, at one point he argues that Sanskrit was a recently perpetrated Brahmin hoax and was actually derived from the vernaculars) but he did recognize that what he called "Hinduwee" had many dialects (Kidwai 91). Indeed, "Hinduwee" apparently refers to all the Indo-European vernaculars of northern India because its variants, according to Gilchrist, include Bengali, Gujarati and Oriya.[14] Gilchrist does not set out his reasons for concluding unambiguously that Braj is "Old Hinduwee" but Islamicate sources, including the Tuḥfat al-Hind, a Persian courtly text dated 1675 CE which contains an account of Braj grammar, make an identical claim.[15] Even if Gilchrist himself was not conversant with Persian scholarship, it seems likely he could have picked up this idea from his Indian interlocutors who would have known the Persian linguistic tradition.

Broughton, for his part, uses what we would consider anthropological data to support his view of Braj as an archaic language. He finds the bucolic imagery of the poetry so compelling that he invokes a "Doric muse that would not have disgraced the pastoral reeds of Greece or Scotland" to explain its origin (Bangha 39). Since the poetry reminds him of the European classical tradition (he even refers to "the Hindoo nymph" as an archetype), he thought that it must similarly refer to an ancient Indian past carried forward. He refers to the "beautiful specimens of the ancient Hindoo poets" to be found in Braj Bhāṣā (qtd in Bangha 10). To him Braj is a "Doric tongue" and "a dialect that is perfectly rustic" (Bangha 45-46). Broughton has a belief in his ability to partake of this culture and describes overhearing everyday conversations in which poetic metaphors were used. Braj country is described in a note as "the Arcadia of India" and Broughton observes that "the Brij Bhakha, or language of Brij, is the dialect still spoken in this classic region" (Bangha 181). Ironically, as has been discussed above, Broughton praises his soldier informants for their learning but fails to acknowledge that the poetry he has collected from them is actually that of a highly refined literary tradition. He takes the simulated rusticity of the tradition at face value.

None of the authors is concerned with drawing distinctions among dialects they perceive as belonging to Hindus; the only important distinction for them is Islamicate Hindustani versus non-Hindustani. The greatest obstacle for our understanding of attitudes towards Braj in this period is the ambiguous conflation of the terms Braj and Hindi. All three authors argue that Hindi (or in Gilchrist's case "Hinduwee") is the spoken language of Hindus in northern India. Price refers to "Hindee or Bhakha" in the preface to his grammar and so considers the terms synonymous, in contrast to Hindustani (vii). Broughton refers to "Bhakha" just once in his preface and instead uses the term "Hindee" (Bangha 49). In his earlier book, *Letters Written in a Mahratta Camp* (1813), he refers to "Bhākhā or the language of Brij" (qtd in Bangha 10). He is conscious of Braj as a dialect tied to a place but for him what is important is that he is collecting "poetry of the Hindoos" and not allowing Muslim-influenced Hindustani to creep into his text. Having erased the distinction between Hindi and Braj, he adds in a note that the dialect spoken around Mathura is called Braj but does not attempt to clearly link the poetry he has collected with Braj country, except through the bucolic metaphor of Ancient Greece (Bangha 181). Gilchrist understands "Hinduwee" to be the modern non-Islamicate language of North India and Braj to be an archaic form of it. He therefore draws a temporal distinction between the two. He suggests in the preface of the Fabulist that in order to derive a Khaṛī Bolī passage from the text, one simply has to get one's favorite munshi to modernize one of the Braj selections.[16] (All of the fables have a Braj text but only two have an accompanying Khaṛi Bolī version.) None of these authors points out that Braj has had extensive influence from Khaṛī Bolī, which Bangha argues is the case for Broughton's poems and I will argue is also true of the Braj selections in the *Fabulist* (Bangha 24).

Colonial research into vernacular languages turned Braj Bhāṣā into a synecdoche for all non-Islamicate vernaculars in northern India. It was never properly understood in its literary context and was aggrandized as an old language which happened to coexist with newer languages. It served a symbolic role as a Hindu language contrasted with Hindustani, which was almost universally understood by the Indians with whom the British interacted (and was sometimes denigrated as a jargon), and yet was always associated by the British with Muslims. The role of Braj in British colonial research declined as Khaṛī Bolī prose was amplified by projects like Lallulāl's *Prem-sāgar*, and Kharī Bolī became seen as more useful than Braj because it was the "modern" non-Islamicate dialect. Thus, an 1838 grammar by J.R. Ballantyne was entirely Braj Bhāṣā, but in the 1868 edition it was called *Elements of Hindi and Braj Bhakha Grammar*, and the Braj elements had been relegated to footnotes (Dalmia 138).

Appendix – Āzād on Braj

Although this is a slight digression from what I have considered in this essay, we should explore briefly the possibility of whether a later theorist on language was influenced by the conflation of Braj and Hindi. At the beginning of his magisterial though problematic history of Urdu literature, *Āb-e ḥayāt*, Muḥammad Ḥusain "Āzād" (1830-1910) makes the highly political claim that "Everybody knows this much — that our Urdu language has emerged from Braj Bhasha. And Braj Bhasha is a purely Indian language."[17] As Frances Pritchett observes in the preface to her translation (with Shamsur Rahman Faruqi) of *Āb-e ḥayāt*, Āzād is inconsistent in his use of the term "bhāśā", which can refer to Braj or to vernacular language in general. Indeed, both the claim that Urdu descended from Braj and the ambiguity of the term "Bhāśā" (or Bhākhā) are present throughout the Islamicate linguistic tradition since at least the late seventeenth century (Ziauddin 34-5). Āzād clearly starts with that premise but goes further. To explain the provenance of Urdu, he is really claiming an aesthetic, which he believes that Urdu's precursor must have had, rather than making a linguistic argument about a particular dialect of Hindi. Specifically, he recognizes the poetic richness of the Hindi tradition (and I deliberately say "Hindi" rather "Braj" because Āzād appears to be referring to the whole of northern India) and then claims — entirely falsely — that Braj literature makes no use of metaphors. Whatever the Braj poet experiences, Āzād claims, "he very clearly describes in his sweet language, spontaneously, without exaggeration" (56). Anyone who knows about Āzād's aesthetic program immediately recognizes that this stripping away of pretense is exactly his prescription for improving contemporary Urdu by abandoning the decadence of the classical tradition. Since real Braj Bhāṣā cannot provide examples to support Āzād's thesis, Pritchett writes, he "simply makes up his own examples; he doesn't bother even pretending to attribute them to anyone else." If Āzād had approached the question as a linguist, he would have observed that Urdu has the same grammar as Kharī Bolī and that they obviously have a close relationship. Incredibly, Āzād does not address this in spite of the fact that he points out that Urdu was developed in Delhi — the geographic center of Kharī Bolī — and contrasts its cosmopolitan origins with that fact that Braj was only "the bazaar language of a district" (51). In Āzād's telling, the language of some cowherds near Mathura was the mother of Urdu while Khaṛī Bolī Hindi, which happens to share the same geographical origins and the same grammar, is irrelevant. Pritchett notes that Āzād never once uses the term "khaṛī bolī" in *Āb-e ḥayāt*.

REFERENCES

Primary Sources

Bangha, Imre 2000. *Thomas Duer Broughton's Selections from the Popular Poetry of the Hindoos*, 1814. Delhi: Rainbow.

Gilchrist, John Borthwick et al. 1803. *The Oriental Fabulist, or Polyglot Translations of Esop's and other Ancient Fables from the English Language into Hindoostanee, Persian, Arabic, Brij Bhakha, Bongla and Sunskrit in the Roman Character by Various Hands under the Direction and Superintendence of John Gilchrist for the use of the College of Fort William*, Calcutta.

Letters = Cannon, Garland (ed.) 1970. *The Letters of Sir William Jones*. Oxford: Oxford University Press.

Price, William 1827. *Hindee and Hindoostanee Selections to which are prefixed the Rudiments of Hindoostanee and Bruj Bhakha Grammar*. Calcutta: Hindoostanee Press.

Secondary Sources

Bailey, T. Graeme 1936. Does Khaṛī Bolī Mean Nothing More than Rustic Speech? In *Bulletin of the School of Oriental Studies*, University of London, Vol. 8, No. 2/3, Indian and Iranian Studies. 363-371.

Dalmia, Vasudha 1997. *The nationalization of Hindu traditions: Bhāratendu Hariúchandra and nineteenth-century Banaras*. Delhi: Oxford University Press.

Das, Sisir Kumar 1978. *Sahibs and munshis: An account of the college of Fort William*. New Delhi: Orion.

Hatcher, Brain 2005. What's Become of the Pandit? Rethinking the History of Sanskrit Scholars in Colonial Bengal, in *Modern Asian Studies* 39 (3), 683–723.

Kidwai, Sidiq-ur-Rahman 1972. *Gilchrist and the 'Language of Hindoostan'*. New Delhi: Rachna Prakashan.

Majeed, Javed 1995. The Jargon of Indostan: An Exploration of Jargon in Urdu and East India Company English. In Peter Burke and Roy Porter (eds.) Languages and Jargons: *Contributions to a social history of language*. 182-205. Cambridge (UK): Polity.

McGregor, Ronald Stuart 2003. The Progress of Hindi, part I: The Development of a Transregional Idiom, In Sheldon Pollock (ed.) *Literary cultures in history: Reconstructions from South Asia*. 910-957. Berkeley: University of California.

McGregor, Stuart 1984. *Hindi literature from its beginnings to the nineteenth century*.

Wiesbaden : Harrassowitz.

Pritchett, Frances W. Everybody Knows This Much. Preface to translation of *Āb-e ḥayāt* by Frances Pritchett in association with Shamsur Rahman Faruqi. <http://dsal.uchicago.edu/books/PK2155.H8413/0001fwp.html>

Rai, Alok 2001. *Hindi nationalism. Tracts for the times* 13. New Delhi: Orient Longman.

Rocher, Rosane 1995. Weaving Knowledge: Sir William Jones and Indian Pundits In Garland Cannon and Kevin R. Brine (eds.) *Objects of enquiry: The life, contribution, and influences of Sir William Jones (1746-1794)*. 51-79. New York University Press.

Romaine, Suzanne Socio-historical linguistics: Its status and methodology. *Cambridge studies in linguistics 34*. Cambridge: Cambridge University Press.

Siddiqi, M Atique 1963. *Origins of modern Hindustani literature* (Source Material: Gilchrist Letters). Aligarh: Naya Kitab Ghar.

Sinha, D.P. 1964. *The educational policy of the East India Company in Bengal to 1854*. Calcutta: Punthi Pustak.

Ziauddin, M. 1935. *Mirza Khan's grammar of the Braj Bhakha*. Calcutta: P. Knight.

McGregor, R.S. 1968. *The language of Indrajit of Orcha: A study of early Braj Bhāṣā prose*. Cambridge: Cambridge University Press.

Snell, Rupert 1991. The Hindi Classical Tradition: A Braj Bhāṣā Reader. SOAS *South asian Texts*, 2. London: Routledge.

NOTES

1. Cf. Romaine 7. I find Romaine's work useful because its style makes sociolinguistics — a very important technique for understanding how language operates in society — accessible to non-linguists.

   Referring to what non-linguists call a "language" as a "variety" is a sociolinguistic convention because this term avoids the often irrelevant question of whether what laymen call a language is, in fact, a dialect or a language under the rather strict definition of language used by linguists. In this essay, any reference to "a language" or "a dialect" should be read as "a variety."
2. For example, what are we to make of the fact that a scholar named F.S. Grouse lived in Braj country in 1872 and considered himself to be studying Braj Bhāṣā, which was, according to him, "the typical form of modern Hindi, which I hear spoken about me" (qtd in Pritchett)?
3. The term "Hindustani" presents a problem because it was the most common name in the nineteenth century for what we now call Urdu. Hindustani took on a different meaning in the early twentieth century, namely as a simplified Hindu-Urdu meant to unify the inchoate Indian nation-state, and I do not use it in that sense.
4. McGregor 2003 is a good overview of the Braj literary field (especially 940-1) but McGregor 1984 is more comprehensive.
5. Gilchrist distinguishes between those "who wish to learn the languages of the East, rather as acquisitions subservient to the due execution of

their duty, than as classic accomplishments for the improvement of their minds, as men or scholars" (ix). He bemoans the fact that not enough Englishmen study Indian languages for purely scholarly reasons.

6. Majeed 197. Majeed addresses the question of whether Urdu is a jargon or not — it is not a subject for this essay to attempt to discuss.
7. A good summary of Islamicate influence on Braj appears in McGregor 2003: 942-4.
8. Siddiqi 123. Later a munshi named Gangaprasad Sukla was employed for Braj (the date is not known). Indreswar Pandit (1815) and Khelaram (January 1827) were also hired (Das 124-5). We have no further information on these scholars.
9. "Independent of the natural stupidity and apathy, which too often disgrace the Hindoostanees on such occasions, there is a species of low cunning or national policy, about many of them, which is no less vexatious in its consequences to a young scholar. He probably asks a very plain, disinterested question, which the native perfectly comprehends and could answer immediately. His suspicious temper or guilty conscience takes the alarm, he fears there is something insidious in the interrogation, and to prepare his mind for an evasive or defensive reply, he very adroitly pretends not to have understood the speech, which was addressed to him. I appeal to the careful observer of Asiatic manners... for the truth of these remarks" (xxii).
10. xxiv. The other scholars who participated in the project are listed on xxiv. "Sree Lal Kub" (or Lallūlāl) is listed as the munshi responsible for Braj.
11. E.g. *Letters* 459, 465; the preface to Jones's *Śakuntalā* translation; qtd in Rocher 69.
12. "Before the irruptions and subsequent settlement of Moosulmans the Hindooee or Hindi was to India, what the Hindoostanee is now to Hindoostan, varying more or less in its territorial excursions from the pure speech called by way of pre-eminence Brij Bhasha or the language of India. This ancient tongue, under various modifications is to Hindoostan, exactly what Saxon was to England, before the Norman conquest" (*Oriental Linguist* iv qtd in Kidwai 90).
13. ibid 89. Also, the *Tuḥfat al-Hind*, a Persian courtly text, states that "Ornate poetry and the praise of the lover and the beloved is usually written in this language [i.e. Braj]" (Ziauddin 34).
14. The full list is "Bungalee, Rajpootee, Poorbee, Dukhunee, Ooreea, Mulwaree, Gujratee, Tilungee, Kishmeere, etc" (xxii-iii in the appendix to the *Oriental Linguist* qtd in Kidwai 91).
15. Gilchrist ii. However, it does make some sense in light of the indigenous linguistic tradition, because in the *Tuḥfat al-Hind* the author notes that the "application [of the term Bhākhā] is generally inclusive of all other languages" (Ziauddin 34). However, despite this claim and the claim that Bhākhā is "the language of the world in which we live," it is localized as being "particularly the language of the Brij people. Brij is the name of a country in India..." (ibid.). This is precisely the same problem as the British faced in trying to identify Braj as a local or a translocal language.

16. "The real *Khuree bolee* is distinguished by the general observance of Hindoostanee Grammar, and a nearly total exclusion of Arabic and Persian words; the scholar therefore has frequently little more to do than, with the aid of an expert Moonshee, to modify the present Brij Bhasha version, by the modern rules of the language..." (v).
17. The translation is Pritchett's but page numbers refer to the Urdu text. The original reads: "itnī bāt har śakhs jāntā hai kih hamārī urdū zabān braj bhāṣā se niklī hai aur braj bhāṣā khās hindustānī zabān hai..." (6).

3

The Language of Love: A Study of the Amorous and Erotic Associations of Urdu

Tariq Rahman

Abbreviations

OIOC Oriental and India Office Collections, British Library, London.
RRL Rampur Raza Library, U.P, India.

Haris Chandra Bharatendu (1849-1882), the father of modern Hindi literature (Dalmia 1997), said in his statement before the Hunter communion (1882).

> There is a secret motive which induces the worshippers of Urdu to devote themselves to its cause. It is the language of dancing-girls and prostitutes. The depraved sons of wealthy Hindus and youths of substance and loose character, when in society of harlots, concubines, and pimps, speak Urdu, as it is the language of their mistresses and beloved ones. The correct pronunciation of Urdu, with its *shin*, *ghain*, and guttural *kaf*, is indispensable, and one unable to twist his tongue into unnatural and unpleasant distortions is not a welcome or an agreeable companion (Edn. Com.NWP 1884: 201).

Another respondent, Siva Prashad, said that 'some of the women take up also amorous and vicious books, such as Mir Hasan ki Masnavi, Indarsabha, etc. etc' (ibid., 327). Even books in Urdu translation, such as the *Alif Laila* and *Qissa Tota Maina*, were blamed for creating mistrust for women and obsession with sex. Thus in Opandar Nath Ashq's short story *'Chetan ki Maan'*, Pandit Shadi Ram locks his wife in the house when he goes out because of his reading of these works. Both the respondents were supporters of Hindi against Urdu and the Hindi-

Urdu controversy was going on during this period. Could it be that the association of Urdu with love and eroticism which they had brought up was merely an allegation? A stratagem to defeat the pro-Urdu lobby? An anti-Urdu (and possibly anti-Muslim?) prejudice? Or, could it be that Urdu really did have such associations in the minds of many members of the intelligentsia? And, if so, why is there so much silence about them nowadays? Does this silence itself indicate the presence of certain ideological and political imperatives which can be understood once the erotic and amorous themes are documented?

These are the questions which this article will attempt to answer.

The Amorous and the Erotic Associations of Urdu

The major aim of this article is to document the presence of the amorous and erotic themes in Urdu writings of the nineteenth century. While scholars of Urdu are well aware of the erotic in the literature of the language, other scholars of South Asia would find it useful to have such a theme placed in a historical context. This is all the more necessary because the erotic associations of Urdu are suppressed by the Urdu-using community in both Pakistan and India in order to protect itself against charges of obscenity, decadence and backwardness. The construction of the modern, sanitized Urdu needs re-examination and the restitution and acceptance of the erotic, rather than its suppression. Frances Pritchett, who has described this process through the works of Mohammad Hussain Azad (1830-1910) and Altaf Hussain Hali (1837-1914), two of the greatest critics of Urdu literature in the nineteenth century, argues that modernity, spearheaded by these two great trend setters, discredited the themes, values and ideas of the classical Urdu literature (Pritchett 1994) and one major area under attack, as it were, was the treatment of beauty, love and sex. However, despite the incisive analysis of scholars like Pritchett, the 'South Asian Victorians remain' and they not only 'view the ghazal through the special distorting lenses provided by Azad and Hali' as Pritchett says (ibid xvii), but also suppress the more overtly erotic associations of genres other than the *ghazal*. Indeed, while the ghazal 'continues to be vigorously alive' (ibid., 189), partly because it is more amorous than erotic and also because it is possible to take advantage of its ambiguity to claim that the amorous symbolism is, in fact, mystical in nature, it is the other genres – *hazal, rekhti, vasokht, sarapa sukhan, masnavi, nazm* and the *dastan*—which are in danger of being lost sight of by all except a few specialists of Urdu literature.

This article, then, brings out the erotic and amorous associations of Urdu writings in the late eighteenth and nineteenth centuries so as to question and deconstruct the puritanical, modern, identity which the 'South Asian Victorians' – to use Pritchetts' apt phrase—construct. Such themes have been mentioned in several contexts by several scholars who will be mentioned below but there is no attempt to explore the reasons why Urdu was associated with the amorous and the erotic during the period of our study. Moreover, the vast archive which is known to specialists of Urdu is scattered in many works and one advantage if this article may be that it is brought together here.

It should be mentioned at the outset, however, that the nineteenth century was a period of several themes in conflict the major ones being identity and religion but, because these non-erotic associations are very well documented, they will not be referred to in detail. To put the rest of the discussion in context they should be mentioned here, however. Very briefly then, Urdu became the symbol of the Muslim political identity in India during the Pakistan movement and helped 'imagine' or 'construct'—in Benedict Anderson's sense (1983)—both Muslim and Hindu 'nations' (Brass 1974: 45-46; King 1994). After partition Pakistan's ruling elite used the symbol of Urdu to construct a Pakistani identity which would dominate and suppress the ethnic identities of the country, an attempt which the Bengali, Sindhi, Pashto-speaking and Balochi ethnic elites contested (Rahman 1996). Since these ethnic elites often espoused non-establishment, left-leaning views, Urdu came to be associated with official Pakistani nationalism and Islam. It is also associated with non-elitist schooling in Pakistan (the elitist one being in English) as has been brought out in several publications (Rahman 2004). However, the association with Islam was gaining in strength and salience since the nineteenth century when Urdu started replacing Persian and Arabic as the major language of South Asian Islam (Rahman 2006). In post-partition India too Urdu remains a symbol of Muslim identity and is very much in evidence in Muslim minority politics (Farouqui 2006).

In view of the salience of these political and ideological identities of Urdu, it is ignored that from the late eighteenth century onwards till almost the end of the beginning of the twentieth century the language was associated with the amorous and the erotic as well as some other variables of Muslim identity - Islam, Muslim political aspirations in South Asia and education - which have been mentioned already.This particular association, with the amorous and the erotic, was primarily with Urdu poetry but, since the language was taught through literature, it extended to the language itself. The reformers of Muslim society, aware of this nexus, tried to break it and, instead, strengthened the association with Islam which, too, was formed during the same period.

As the educated gentry (*ashraf*) studied Persian texts till the middle of the nineteenth century, the British officials and the Muslim reformers made deliberate attempts to purge the curricula of them. The erotic and the amorous was associated with moral degeneration, decadence and blamed for backwardness and political defeat of the Muslim ruling elite. For the *ulema* (clergy) it was not only associated with all these but was also a great sin. Thus, in order to regenerate a powerful Muslim 'nation' (*qaum)* a new literature, chaste and moral, had to be created. This moral and political imperative and the steps taken to bring the amorous and erotic themes in Urdu literature in disrepute and create a culture shame and silence about them have been described in some detail in Rahman (2002: 499-515). Indeed, they continue to this date with the textbook committees excluding love poetry, even from the masters of the *ghazal*, out of the curricula and the Pakistan Television being squeamish about a married couple holding hands on the screen.

The erotic is excluded to such an extent from the officially constructed identities of Pakistani Muslims that the classics of Persian and Arabic, which are proudly owned as being Muslim heritage languages, are not taught in unexpurgated editions in Pakistani universities. Hardly any scholars touch the erotic as a subject of serious research though any writings on the subject become popular among that group of the intelligentsia of Urdu letters which can only be described as the equivalent of 'the Other Victorians'. For instance, Zamir Uddin Ahmad's study of the sexuality of the beloved (Ahmad 1990) created a sensation and has had several reprints. Works of scholarship on such themes have been published by South Asians living, or at least publishing, in the West (notably Vanita and Kidwai 2000) but those published in Pakistan and India – a study of sexuality in the Urdu short story (Khan 2002) and boy-love in Urdu poetry (Azhar 1995) for example – are superficial and lack analysis. This is hardly surprising considering that in Pakistan the construction of the Muslim identity suppresses the erotic, associating it with the decadent 'West' or the sensational nudity of Bollywood. And in India it is a theme which does not bear placing in a serious context either in Muslim politics or in the Hindutva one for in both it is a stigma to be shunned. In short, the reformist discourse excludes the erotic and amorous for ideological and political reasons.

Such exclusion began in the nineteenth century and some of the reformist themes of the literature produced in Urdu during this period bears closer re-examination because it tells us what kind of associations existed in the minds of the educated public about much of Urdu poetry.

Reformist Urdu Literature on the Erotic Theme

Nazeer Ahmed's novel *Fasana-e-Muttila* (1887) begins with the following reflections regarding Urdu poetry:

> What is there in our poetry except love affairs (*ishq bazi*) and lack of manners (*be taehzeebi*). Boys of respectable (*sharif*) families learn habits leading to corruption from this very school.... (Ahmed 1887: 64).

The protagonist, Muttila, was taught Persian because it was assumed that one could not learn Urdu without knowing it but he was harmed by it i.e. got conscious of his beauty (Ahmed 1887: 78). Boys oggled the good-looking Muttila making him narcissistic (ibid., 83). Women—albeit after his family had rejected the match for their daughter— called him *'hijra, zankha'* (effeminate, eunuch, hermaphrodite) (Ahmed 1887: 92). He was always staring at the mirror at himself and was not interested in his plain wife (ibid., 92). The author describes Muttila's getting facial hair in a full page. He tells us how the youth's male admirers abandoned him and how he became lonely and sad (ibid., 98). But now Muttila turns to women and, of course, his taste for Urdu poetry becomes stronger. Among others, he praises Rind Lakhnavi's *Sarapa* called *'Muraqqa-e-khubi'* which describes and praises all parts of a woman's body as, indeed, do most poems of this genre (Mohsin 1861?)

In *Taubat un Nusuh* (1874), another novel by Nazeer Ahmed, Nusuh, the protagonist who turns reformer after nearly dying in cholera, tells his wife that poetry is considered bad because the poets express the unclean (*napak*) ideas of love and sensual gratification (*ishq o ayyashi*) (Ahmed 1874: 260). He finds his eldest son Kaleem's books obscene (*fahesh*), removed from modesty (*haya se dur*), immoral and so on. So he burns them. This act is described by Frances W. Pritchett as 'a powerful, drastic act of cultural destruction' (Pritchett 1994: 187). The books which are burnt include the classics of Urdu poetry and were read by almost all educated people of the day though they are confined to specialists today [1].The Persian ones are *Bahar Danish* and even Insha Ullah Khan's *Darya-e-Latafat*. A 'good' boy—Bi Sahib's grandson—tells Saleem, Nusuh's younger son, that the *Vasokht* is a dirty (*gandi*) book (Ahmed 1874: 256). Later, Kaleem meets the Sadr-e-Azam, a *maulvi* in Daulatabad state, who tells him in Arabicized Urdu that poetry is a corrupting influence and he considers it worthless (Ahmed 1874: 323).

To take another example from literature, Abid Hussain, the protagonist of the novel *Shareef Zada* by Mirza Hadi Ruswa (1857-1931), was not like other youths of Lucknow who were notorious for debauchery. While most young men acquired the habit of falling in love and took to versification which enabled them to express lust in beautiful words, Abid Hussain worked hard (Ruswa n.d: 534). Such works, products of modernist, reforming Muslims as they were, reinforced the association of the erotic with Urdu poetry in the public imagination.

Both the exemplars of modern Urdu literature, Azad and Hali, discredited the medieval world view which included the description of female and boyish beauty as a perennial theme. Hali argues against the description of boyish beauty because, in his view, it is unnatural. As for female beauty it is condemnable because if she is a beloved, one is revealing one's vices and if a wife, it is shamelessness (Hali 1893: 112-113). Besides these great names, other reformers too associated Urdu literature with eroticism. Mumtaz Ali (1860-1935), a pioneer of Urdu journalism for women, wondered whether Meer Amman's *Bagh-o-Bahar*, that classic of Urdu prose for a century, was 'appropriate for either boys or girls' (Minault 1998: 83). Syed Husain Bilgrami, an influential man from Hyderabad, considered Urdu literature as 'coarse, pernicious, and unclean' being a product of decadent, aristocratic (*nawabi*) culture (Bilgrami 1900). In short, there was an association of Urdu with the erotic and it was a source of anxiety for the reformers of the Indian Muslim society. The reformers dealt with it in various ways: modernizing literary norms in Urdu with reference to English literature (Azad and Hali); creating new reformist texts (Nazeer Ahmed); purging the canon of classical Urdu literature to create a sanitized, highly puritanical, pedagogical model for the mass consumption of the Urdu-reading public, especially students; and abandoning Urdu for English literature or language-teaching without the literary component (educational decision-makers; school and college teachers and even academics in universities).

But why did this association, disquieting as it was to people who wanted to break the British stereotype of Muslim sensuality and aristocratic (*nawabi*) decadence, come into existence? Did it have any basis in reality? These are questions which the following sections will attempt to answer.

The Place of the Erotic in Muslim Literature

Medieval literature in Muslim cultural languages – Arabic, Persian and Turkish – had an erotic content. This was natural, one part of life among many others, and was not the exclusive focus of the narrative. It was formulaic in the sense that beauty, both female and boyish, was described in certain fixed, conventional terms. Sexual desire was also described as the normal response to beauty. The sexual organs and intercourse itself were described in metaphorical, stylized, language though at places body parts were also referred to in words normally tabooed in society. This, however, was not in an erotic context as it is in pornography. The point is that, unlike the pornographer, the authors of classical literature in Muslim cultural languages were representing life—the whole of life that is—through certain conventional narrative devices.

Abdelwahab Bouhdiba, writing on the role of sexuality in Islamic cultures, suggests that eroticism 'is integrated in the Islamic view of the world and is situated at the heart, not at the periphery, of ethics' (Bouhdiba 1975: 127). Elaborating upon this theme he introduces the concept of *mujun* which he explains as follows:

> Observe the ambiguous and equivocal richness of the root *ma ja na*, which signifies, according to the *lisān al 'Arab*, the density, the depth, the lack of shame, the frivolity, the gratuity, the art of mixing the serious and the lighthearted, pretended austerity, true banter. *Mujūn* is the art of referring to the most indecent things, speaking about them in such a lighthearted way that one approaches them with a sort of loose humour. In principle *mujūn* ought not to go beyond words. It is oneirism, collective experience and liberation through speech (Bouhdiba 1975: 127).

The *One Thousand Nights and One Night* (*Alf Laila wal Lail*) is considered an example of a narrative with erotic passages of the *mujūn* genre. But the famous *Alf Laila*, paradigmatic though it is, is not the only example of literature with a healthy, accepting, attitude towards the erotic. Almost all the classics of Arabic, Persian and Turkish literature have the same attitude.

The *Masnawi* of Mawlana Jalal-ad-Din Muhammad Rumi (1207-1273), considered one of the most influential works in the Muslim world, and one which educated South Asian Muslims were acquainted with and held in high esteem, is said to embody the esoteric meaning of the Qur' an (*hast Qur' an dar zaban-e-Farsi* is the Qur' an in the Persian language). It is a six-volume work about the concept of the oneness of God (*tawhid*), redemption of the soul through mystical processes, the desire to seek union with the deity and other moral and spiritual themes. It is full of anecdotes, fables and aphorisms somehow related to the above deeply religious themes. And yet, in common with medieval norms of writing in the Muslim world, there are fables which would now be considered erotic and even obscene. The Mawlana also uses both the accepted, respectable words for the human anatomy and also ones which have earthy connotations and are tabooed in respectable writings today (collected in an appendix and defended against the charge of indecency by Iqbal 1956: 284-314). Modern Pakistanis would find them shockingly indelicate and teaching them to students of any age would be out of the question.

Boy Love in Muslim Literature and Society

The pervasiveness of boy-love in Persian and Turkish Muslim cultures is brought out, respectively, by Najmabadi (2005) and Andrews and Kalpakli (2005). Najmabadi makes the astute observation mentioned above, that the pre-modern beloved was a boy (*amrad*) who, like women (*zan*), belonged to the category of those who could be penetrated. Modernity changed this and Iranians became ashamed of this fact of their cultural past. The public space became hetero-socialized and male homosociality was heterosexualized during this era. Women's education too was seen in the light of this new female identity as it was in India (Najmabadi 2005: 196). The *amrad* disappeared from cultural imagination. Even the feminist reading of sexuality and gender identity has 'contributed to this historical amnesia by doing gender analysis without regard for the historical transformations of sexuality' (ibid., 235). Such an analysis is required for the Urdu-using culture of North India where gender was perceived in the same way as in Iran. The role of the *amrad* in this culture, as expressed in the Urdu language, has not been fully analyzed.

The lines along which the culture of 18th century Indian Muslim elite can be analyzed is provided by *The Age of Beloveds* (Andrews and Kalpakli 2005). The authors contend that in the long sixteenth century — a period running from the late fifteenth century through the early seventeenth century (Andrews and Kalpakli 2005: 10) — the ideal beloved was an adolescent youth (an *amrad*) who also symbolized the absolute ruler as well as the immanent deity in mystic love. During this period 'power relations of all kind, from the most personal (adult-child, husband-wife, lover-beloved) to the most public (courtier-monarch, patron-client, even empire-empire), were eroticized on a consistent pattern. That is, they were imagined in the forms, the language, and the metaphors of love' (ibid., 28).

The authors contend that the *seherengiz* was written as a catalogue celebrating the beauty of boys, generally artisan lads (ibid., 40). This is common to Urdu poetry (*shahr ashob*) also. Then the gender of Ottoman literature is masculine and 'reflects and scripts the (adult) masculinity of public space' (ibid., 54). This is true of Urdu culture again. The authors describe how, during this age, it was fashionable to be enamoured of boys, use the *ghazal* (in Turkish *gazel*) as a medium of communicating about the beloved and the use of certain literary practices and conventions for the above (ibid., 90). This, again, is true for the Urdu culture. It needs to be investigated (for initial steps in this direction see Naim 1979: 120-142; Rahman 1990: 1-20).

It seems to be a fact that 'the traditional scripting of the erotic in the Persian tradition emphasized love between males and that it was important for literate Ottomans to see themselves as custodians and perpetuators of that tradition' (ibid., 130). This is true of Indian Muslims who saw themselves as perpetuators of the Persian tradition. The two authors connect Ottoman sexuality with politics. They write:

> From our perspective, because the absolutist monarchy, and the society that it rules, is also phallocentric, its pedophilia (placing the object of desire in the role of child, either actually or structurally) is also fundamentally homoerotic (the hierarchy of domination is male on top of male) (Andrews and Kalpakli 2005: 269).

Decadence and Loss of Political Power

One popular theory in modern Indian Muslim writings is that the decadence of society was a consequence of the loss of political power. However, one can explain the presence of the erotic in Urdu literature with reference to history and convention without appealing to such theories.

A reading of texts from the medieval Indian period clearly shows that power was manifested in the possession of coercive ability which gave a person the ability to gratify himself (women were generally excluded from power) by possessing tangible and intangible goods (such as prestige). Among the tangible goods were sex objects — women and beautiful boys. Thus the Mughal rulers had large harems (Lal 1988) and a very active sex life. It was when political power was lost that people, especially reformers and apologists of this ruthless power, started propagating the theory that sexual excesses or promiscuity brought about the ruin of the Mughal (or other) empires.

Although Muslim political power was challenged by the eighteenth century in India, their cultural dominance was very much in place. Indeed, the British rulers themselves adopted the dress, etiquette, cuisine and the values — and sometimes even the religion — of the aristocratic Muslims becoming what William Darlymple calls the 'white Mughals' (Darlymple 2003). Thus, it was not a new breakdown of sexual norms but a continuation of older established patterns — established during the age of political power — which oft-quoted works like the *Muraqqa-e-Dilli* represent. The *Muraqqa's* author, Dargah Quli Khan (1710-1766) was a nobleman from Aurangabad who lived in Delhi from 1738 to 1741. He describes the capital of the declining Mughal empire as a place devoted to pleasures of all kinds. The public places were full of beautiful women and boys and the powerful indulged themselves with both (Khan n.d.). The descriptions of boy dancers and women who painted their bare legs as if they were wearing tight trousers may give one the feeling that Delhi was the most decadent of cities in the eighteenth century. But Paris and London, at the height of their colonial power, had all the pleasures which Delhi possessed (Bloch 1958: 217-252). Similarly the Lucknow of the Nawabs which Abdul Halim Sharar describes was not more profligate than, say, London, though, of course, the practice of having many women in the harem was reminiscent of medieval Muslim capitals at the height of their power. The social and literary norms for describing the sexual practices of European cities were, of course, different. But they were not any more virtuous even in Victorian England than Indian cities. Thus, the real reason why the erotic element in Urdu literature is condemned so unequivocally these days is not because such pleasures were found in certain urban centres or the rich indulged in them but because it is the product of a militarily defeated culture. And when one is defeated everything one does or possesses can be, and generally *is*, condemned. The defeat is not easy to explain and the tendency of everyone, most of all the reformers of the defeated party, is to blame pleasure, especially sexual pleasure, for the defeat.

The Erotic Theme in Early Urdu Writings

The earliest specimens of the erotic in Urdu poetry go back to the time of Muslim power not to its decline. A certain poet called Qureshi wrote a *masnavi* called 'Bhog Bal' in 1613 in Dakkani Urdu. It has twelve chapters describing sexual matters. Chapter 11, for instance, gives 84 positions for coitus (Shareef 2004: 170).

However, since Urdu came into its own at the time of the decline of Muslim political power, probably the most obscene of the Urdu poets is also one of the earliest, at least in north India. This is Meer Mohammad Jafar Zatalli (d. 1713). He was a satirist in both Persian and Urdu and the obscene words he uses are not a part of the Urdu erotic tradition. Nor are they meant for evoking sexual pleasure. Instead, they are obviously meant to shock, outrage, express contempt and belittle others. Zatalli lived at a time of political instability after Aurangzeb's death. He responded to it by making fun of it. He was murdered, probably at the instigation of King Farrukh Siyar (r. 1713-1719), in 1713 (see his works edited by Khan 2003). Zatalli created no tradition. His effect on Urdu literature is minimal. So it is not because of his use of obscenities that Urdu literature came to be associated with love and sex.

Another 18th century work is Sayyid Sirajuddin Aurangabad's (1715-1763) *Bustan-i-khayal* (written before 1783 when he stopped writing poetry). This is actually a *sufi* narrative — major theme of both Persian and Urdu poetry — about finding the source of permanent bliss. The narrator loves a boy who is indifferent to him. Although another boy, the son of a chief (*Sardar*), gives him attention, the narrator remains disconsolate. The beloved alternates between warmth and cold disdain till the narrator turns to God in whom he finds real love (Sarwari 1998: 149-246).

Najmuddin Shah Mubarak Abru (1683-1733), a poet of Urdu, wrote a poem called 'Advice for the adornment of a Beloved'. In this the narrator meets a beautiful boy who was, however, unsophisticated in the art of charming men. The narrator starts advising him how to behave like a 'beloved'. Above all, the boy must know when to stop behaving like a 'beloved'(*mashuq*) and become a lover (*ashiq*)in his turn. So, when the hair on his face coarsens, he must 'then give up the desire to be adored/don't overdress or act coy any more'. That is when he must transit to the role of the lover and 'enjoy the company of beauteous ones' (Abru c. 18c: 298-308). Available in English translation in Vanita and Kidwai 2000: 161-168).

But Abru's focus is not pornography; nor even erotica. He is discussing the norms of role-playing in a conventional society. Moreover, he is upholding decency because, like the behavioral norms enjoined upon the Greek boy (*eromenos* or *ephebe*) (Dover 1978: 16), there were certain forms of good behaviour expected from the *amrad* also. Abdul Haleem Sharar also tells us that adolescent boys combed their hair in such a way on their foreheads that 'attraction like women was created in them also' (Sharar 1927: 261).

Modernity has changed the categorization upon which boy-love was based. The word homosexuality has now been imported in Urdu as '*ham jins parasti*' (the worship of the same sex). In short, as Afsaneh Najmabadi puts it, 'the heteronormalizing dynamic of Iranian modernity' (Najmabadi 2005: 231), tends to bring in modern, Western categories of sexual identities in Pakistan as well. Though older attitudes persist residually in less Westernized parts of Pakistani society, there is considerable anxiety to wish away the presence of *hijras* (transvestites or eunuchs) in Pakistani cities and many people deny the presence of the boy-beloved in Urdu literature and, indeed, of anything but heterosexuals (most notably the President of Iran declared there are no homosexuals in his country in his visit to the USA in the end of September, 2007).

The Pornographic Minority

There were, to be sure, pornographers (*fahash go*) also. They wrote poetry called the *hazal* or, more loosely, *kalam-e-fahash* (obscene verse). One of them, Saiyid Imam Ali Khan of Bilgram, writing under the pseudonym of Sahib-e-Qiran, has left behind a collection of verse (*divan*) written in black in the *nastaliq* script (Qiran n.d). He flourished during the rule of Asif ud Daulah as he has been mentioned in several couplets. At one place the *Nawab* has been praised as a promoter of concupiscence (*shahwat*). Most of the verses are obscene and some mention the poet's exploits in the brothel. In some cases the names of prostitutes are also mentioned but mostly, like all pornographers, the poet is concerned with types of fornication. He even goes to the extent of creating an indecent parody of Amir Khusrau's famous poem with the refrain (*nami danam che manzil bud/shab jae ke man budam*= I did not know which place it was; the place I was last night...). According to Sharar, Mian Mashir, another *hazal go*, perfected Sahib Qiran's style of using language idiomatically in this sub-genre (Sharar 1927: 122).

Another notable pornographic poet (*fahesh go*) is Kallan Khan who wrote under the poetic name of Bechaen (1907-08; No. 1401 RRL). Bechaen was from Rampur. He was a student of Jan Sahib of Lucknow who is well known for his *rekhti* poetry. Bechaen was in the court of the Nawab of Rampur as well as the Maharaja Ranbhir Singh. His verses were collected together by Qudrat Ali Qudrat in 1907-08. Out of all the *hazal go* poets of the period, Bechaen's work is among the most pornographic. He writes mostly in Urdu but there are poems in Persian too.

> *Angia pe hath dala ye dilka futoor tha*
> *Mera qusoor tha na tumhara qusoor tha*
>
> (that the hand went on your brassiere was the fault of the heart it was neither my mistake nor yours). (N. pag)

Other verses refer to all sorts of sexual activities: anal sex, cunnilingus etc.

But perhaps the only pornographer with any influence was Sa'adat Yar Khan Rangin who wrote vis *Diwan-e-Amekhta* as well as *Divan-e-Angekhta* an erotic themes. Like the work of Sahib Qiran, Rangin's work is also full of obscenities and boastful exploits of copulation with prostitutes. It begins with praise for the Satan which is not the usual pattern of Urdu pornographers who do not begin with the usual *bismillah* (in the Name of Allah) but sometimes have merely *'ya Shaitan ul rajeem'* is Oh! The Accursed Satan!) and most often no prefatory formula at all.

> *Lanat men koi sharik nahin tera dusra jitney hain randi baz tu ūnka hai raehnuma*
> (No one shares with you in the distinction of being the accursed one. Thou art the guide of all the world's womanizers).

Here too some prostitutes are mentioned by name but most remain anonymous. The *divan* ends with the praise of Satan as the provider of carnal pleasures.

The *Divan-e-Angekhta* is about women's language which, according to the author, he heard during his womanizing days. Apart from the prostitutes themselves, he claims to have had access to married women (*khangi*) from respectable families who formed occasional liaisons with men for fun or, possibly, some personal income. This language is called '*Rekhti*' and Rangin is said to be the author of this genre of poetry which will be mentioned in more detail later (see Rangin n.d, Insha 1802: 86).

Elements of the *hazal*—couplets and even complete poems—are found interspersed in the works of some of the classical poets. Only a few, however, are mentioned as '*hazal go*': Mir Zahik, father of Mir Hasan, for instance, was one of them (Qureshi 1966: 9). These days they are either not printed or printed with blank spaces in their poetic collections.

The Rampur Raza Library has a large collection of *Hazliat*. Out of these seven handwritten manuscripts, though all entitled *Maj' mua Hazliat*, are all written by different people. One (No 1411) carries the names of two authors: Miss Flora and Sharir or Mir Hasan Ali. Others are by Mir Ashiq Hussain Bazm (Bazm 1908; Nos 1403 and 1404); Agha Wasi Ali Khan Lakhnawi Mazhar (d. 1912) (Mazhar n.d; No. 1407); Hayat Baksh Mustafa Abidi Rasa (d. 1913) (Rasa n.d; No 1409); Syed Jawad Husain Amrohi Shamim (d. 1915) (No. 1410); Syed Ali Husain (Husain n.d; No. 1412).

An oddity among these kind of poets is Chirkeen whose *Divan* (No. 100 RRL) falls in the sub-genre of the *hazal* but is distinctive in that he refers more to excretion than to sex. He is also one of the few, even among the *hazal gos*, to write on menstruation. Excretion is an obsession with him and even when he is mentioning sexual acts he brings in some allusion to excretion.

The other collections of the *hazal* use sex in order to continue the war of words between poets—or a hapless victim of a poet's satirical wit — through invective. Sex is used as a weapon; a device for insulting people; a means of embarrassing them. And this usage is based on the assumptions and values of a feudal society in which the crude use of power is a reality of life. This society was rigidly hierarchical and the male gender role was placed higher than the female one. Sexual acts outside the institution of marriage—in which case they were not discussed—were seen as conquests. For the male they brought honour; for the female, dishonour. And if a male (boy, eunuch or man) took the female role (of being penetrated) there was dishonour for him. It is in the context of these power relations and perceptions of reality that the world view of these anthologies of the *hazal* must be understood.

It is necessary to state, then, that the *hazal* — taking these collections as a whole — is neither part of erotica nor even of pornography. It is really part of satire (*hajw*) but it uses sexual invectives, tabooed words and acts in order to insult a person and continues to attack and humiliate its victims through sexual allusions and imagery. It yields no sexual pleasure, not even of the kind which pornography can and, of course, it is not erotic in any artistic sense of the word.

To give a few examples: Bazm narrates the story of a woman who has five lovers from the working classes – the lowest of the low in society, association with whom brings dishonour even if it is not of a sexual nature. Her husband, who cannot satisfy her, sees his insatiable wife's goings-on with all of them and is happy to yield to them himself as it is only a non-male, a passive homosexual, who can tolerate such disgrace. The purpose of the poem is to insult the man and his wife and not to excite lust. The poet sometimes names the butt of his insults—a certain Mazhar—who is said to be a passive homosexual and whose wife and daughter are sexually exploited by the poet (Bazm 1908).

Rasa insults a man called Sameem boasting about taking his mother, wife and daughter. He even mentions bestiality but, again, to insult Sameem whose sister is sexually abused by a bull dog. It is worth mentioning that the poetic collection does not begin with the usual '*bismillah*'; it begins with '*Ya Shaitan ul Rajeem*'. Rasa also mentions a European woman (*Mem*) called Flora by name (Rasa 1909). In short, the overall impression one gets from the *hazal* is that most of it is an extension of the *hajw* tradition rather than the erotic tradition in literature. It is also distinct, despite using sexual themes and obscene words, from the writings of pornographers such as Sahib Qiran, Bechain and Sa'adat Yar Khan Rangin whose works are confused with the satirical *hazal*.

While the works of Rangin and maybe some other pornographers may have reinforced Urdu's association with the erotic, it was not the major factor in creating this association. Obscenity, after all, is a part of all languages and remains on the margins of all literatures. Much more was contributed to the creation of this association by the erotic sub-genres in Urdu which were not, however, pornographic.

The Erotic Genres of Poetry

One of these, the *Sarapa Sukhan*, description of the female body, is beautiful. The other, the *Rekhti*, degenerates into the ridiculous, the frivolous and the misogynist. The *Sarapa*, as mentioned above, is a collection of couplets on every part of the beloved's body starting from her hair to her heels. The breasts, buttocks, legs and vagina are all described through metaphors and poetic similes. The beauty is always described in formulaic terms without any attempt at individuation. Obscene words are never used but the poet does use the more sophisticated Persian words for body parts: breasts (*pistan*); buttocks (*suraen*) and so on.

Examples are as follows:

Feet: *Aur jo hathon men utha lun to ajab lutf uthaun*
Phir jo vo lutf uthana tujhe bitha ke dikhlaun (Jurrat).
(And if I lift the feet I would find a strange pleasure/
And then to make you sit and watch that pleasure-taking)

Breasts: *Gol ubhre hue kya us ke hain pistan dono*
Must karne ko hain ma' jun ki dibyan dono (Himmat)
(How rounded and raised are breasts both.
To intoxicate, these are containers of intoxicants both)

Buttocks: *Koh-e-suraen dekho to sur phoro tum*
& thighs *Ranen makhmal si hain khuab-o-khurash choro tum* (Mahar)
(And if you see the mountains of the derriere you would knock out your head/ and the thighs are like satin-enough to make you leave all dreaming and thinking)

Vagina: *Aur kya is ke siva kejiye mudhat us ki*
Do hilal ik jagah dekhe hain qudrat us ki (Aesh)
(What other praise can I lavish upon it/Two crescent moons were seen at one place — God be praised!)

The *sarapa* is interspersed in the versified tales of the *masnavi* and the *vasokht*, especially the latter. The *vosokht* is a formulaic story of the narrator wooing a beautiful beloved who is described in detail. The beloved alternates between indifference and passion. The narrator takes revenge of her indifference by pretending to love somebody else who, in turn, is described much in the same conventional terms as the first beloved. The drama succeeds in bringing the lovers together again. Sometimes, however, the ending is tragic (see the work of Fida Ali whose poetic name is Aesh. Ali 1829).

Among the books read by the Muslim gentlemen of India was the notorious Persian work, *Bahar-i-Danish*, which was condemned by many Victorian British officers in various reports. These tales not only have erotic scenes but also feature a kind of defiant, and wayward, female sexuality which expresses itself by cheating the husband in a dare devil way. For instance, some of the women fornicate with a youth in the presence of their husbands. This book was eventually thrown out of the curricula but it was translated into Urdu, notably by Mirza Jan Tapish. He translated the Persian work during his stay in Fort William College Calcutta in 1802 (the history is in *Bagh-o-Bahar* which adds up to 1802 or 1217 Hijri). Modern translations purge out some couplets which are considered obscene but, in 1802, the work was acceptable to the authorities of Fort William College who are praised in it.

Another widely circulated tale (*dastaan*) was *Talism-e-Hosh Ruba* or *Dastan-e-Ameer Hamza*. This was translated from Persian to Urdu by Munshi Syed Mohammad Husain Jah (1908-1915). The stories of the great primal battle between good and evil—good personified by Amir Hamza and evil by the magician Afrasyab—have all elements of public entertainment: magic, war, deceit, trickery, sex and merry-making. These tales were read out by professional story tellers (*dastangos*) who acted out the dramatic scenes and mimicked the actors' voices to create a riveting rendition which reached audiences which could not themselves read the seven thousand plus pages (in the present Sang-e-Meel edition). The tales describe scenes of drinking and female beauty every now and then. As in other works, the descriptions of women (*sarapa*) are in the same formulaic terms as in Persian and Arabic literature: long black tresses, large dow-like eyes, full sensual lips, full breasts, narrow waist, curvaceous hips, rounded buttocks and sensual thighs. Sexual organs are described in metaphors, as is common in the *sarapas*, and if body parts are named sophisticated Persian words are used for them. In the ambience the tales create, the erotic, as in other Muslim literature, is very much a part of life and it is life which the tales reflect. The *Talism*, with its wide popular appeal, took the erotic expressed in the Urdu language to the literate public.

The *Rekhti* is written in a 'feminine' voice but this voice is satirical and mocking. It makes fun of the feminine, trivializing and vulgarizing it. It has already been mentioned that Rangin is credited with having pioneered it though, in fact, there are occasional poems in a pseudo-feminine voice from earlier poets. However, Insha's claim that Rangin invented it to induce women to such lewdness that he could seduce them (Insha 1802: 86), is an exaggeration. In any case, this claim has been made by a comic character in *Darya-e-Latafat* called Mir Gafar Ghaeni and it is not possible to determine what truth value the author wishes to ascribe to it.

Rekhti is course, facetious and licentious though hardly seductive. It provokes either disgust or risibility though hardly lust as erotica should (for study of Rekhti in Urdu with many examples see Mushir 1974; also see Kazmi 1930).

The *rekhti* presents a lustful, aggressive, rather high spirited woman.

She is not idealized like the beloved of the *ghazal*. Instead, she is constantly being held to ridicule and has to hold her own against seducing men and scheming women. Very often she has a not-so-secret liaison with another woman: either a girl friend (*dogana, ilaichi*) or the nurse (the ubiquitous *anna*); and sometimes an older woman (*baji*). However, because of the earthiness of these goings-on, the voice of the *rekhti* is a full-blooded one; a real life one. In real life, however, there is much more than sex; the *rekhti* has disproportionately large amounts of it. However, to be fair to the *rekhti* poets, they do include much more of the daily lives of women than a mere erotica writer would (see Jan Sahib n.d). Unfortunately, this glimpse into the lives of women has a slant towards the ludicrous. Its purpose is not to represent women but to ridicule them.

While the Urdu sources — Kazimi (1930) and Mushir (1974) — merely give samples of Rekhti couplets along with literary appreciation modified by the presently mandatory condemnation of indecency — recent criticism in English engages with more complex dimensions of this unusual sub-genre of Urdu literature. Ruth Vanita and Saleem Kidwai (2000: 193) defend it on the grounds that it 'represents women stating that they prefer women to men when they have access to both' (ibid 193). Petievich argues that the new criticism, that of the Hindu right in India and the Islamists in Pakistan, have created a culture shame for the *rekhti* because it was women's language and expresses lesbianism (Petievich 2001: 248). Moreover, according to Ruth Vanita the *rekhti* was purged from the Urdu canon because it draws upon 'literary conventions and social actions drawn from non-Persianate and Hindu sources' (Vanita 2004). In short, being in ordinary Urdu (Hindustani), it was linguistically subversive during a period of hardening Muslim/ Hindu identities. C.M. Naim, however, defends the more orthodox view that it is trivial, misogynist and meant only for male titillation (Naim 2001).

While interpretations of the *rekhti* in terms of identity, realism and the expression of lesbian feelings is new and interesting, it does not seem to be convincing at least for this writer. A full reading of the original sources reinforces the earlier view that the *rekhti* was written by men and it was used to entertain men. Indeed, it is recited even now in all-male gatherings in Pakistan and India to make men laugh. It was a joke and, like all jokes, it created stereotypes and figures of fun. It was obviously a bawdy relief from the high minded, idealized, romantic love of the *ghazal*. But it was not even subversive of the universe of the *ghazal*. It merely confirmed its existence by pointing out that real people, in moods of banter, could exist on much lower planes where women were not the androgynous ethereal beings of the *ghazal*.

The *rekhti* poets — Insha (1756-1817); Mir Yar Ali Jan Sahib (1810-1881); Nisar Husain Khan Shaida (b. 1868); Saiyed Sajid Sajni (1922-1993) — have not been ranked high among Urdu poets for their *rekhti* works at least. In Mirza Hadi Ruswa's novel *Umrao jan Ada* (1905), the *rekhti* poets are ranked as non-serious (Ruswa 1905: 84). Some of the poets themselves have written of their work in terms of macho self-confidence expressed in terms of ridicule for the feminine. As Jan Sahib has it:

> *Qadr kya nā mard janen, mardue jo mard hain*
> *Jan Sahib shad hote hain vohi sun kar mujhē*
>
> (The unmanly would never appreciate me; only men would who are real men/And they, Jan Sahib, are entertained when they hear me).

The 'real men' heard about women talking about their under garments, especially the brassiere (*angia* or *mahram*) to the confidante: the nurse (*anna*) or a friend. The *angia* is a subject of great fascination. There are complaints about its being too light; too heavy; too gaudy and that the male lover (*mardua*) has torn it to pieces or thrown it away. Sometimes she demands it as a present while at others she hides it from prying eyes of intrusive men. Sometimes the female friends—the words used by Rangin are *dogana, ilaichi* and *zannakhi*—are also sexual partners. In such cases they ridicule the men and indulge in tabooed pleasures. However, it is only rarely that this is expressed without ridicule and when it is, as in the *chaptinamas* of Jurrat, it is to provide sexual pleasure to men. Qalandar Baksh Jurrat (1748-1810), noted for salaciousness even in his *ghazal*, has written about two women, Sakkho and Mukkho, who complain against their husbands and invite all women who 'are given to clinging' (Vanita and Kidwai 2000: 222). They make love passionately as described below:

> When you join your lips to my lips,
> It feels as if new life pours into my being,
> When breast meets breast, the pleasure is such.
> That from sheer joy the words rise to my lips.
> The way you rub me, oh?...
> (English translation by Vanita and Kidwai 2000: 223).

In such samples the passion dominates the ridicule. In most others, however, the dominating tone is satirical, marginalizing, ridiculing. One couplet is as follows:

Rangin qasam hai teri hi hun maile sir se main
Mat khol kar ke minnat o zari izar band(Rangin)
(Rangin I swear to you I am having my periods
Do not keep pestering me to open the band of my trousers)

It seems to me that it was not because of the use of easy Urdu — the *doha* remains respectable though of minor interest despite its use of 'Hindi' words even in Pakistan (see the works of Jamiluddin A'ali, Partau Rohila etc) and Nazeer Akbarabadi's poems on the poor remain popular even today and are included in the curricula — that the *rekhti* was purged. It was simply too unrestrained, non-serious, sexist and rumbunctious. In an age of increasing puritanism when even the Persian classics were purged, it could not be countenanced by reformers wishing to assert the respectability of their literary legacy. However, it would not really be accurate to say that it was purged; it was never actually included in the canon of Urdu literature to begin with. It was a joke to begin with and remained one throughout its career. However, because it was quoted for fun in male gatherings as a joke, it may have contributed to the impression that Urdu was the natural language of erotica.

The *masnavi*, which is a love story in the medieval fairy tale tradition, has more erotic descriptions of feminine beauty and scenes of love-making than any other genre of canonical Urdu literature except the *vasokht* which, in a sense, is a formulaic *masnavi* in miniature.

There are, however, two traditions in the *masnavi*, like the *ghazal* but unlike the *vosokht*, that of 'earthly' and 'celestial' love (Suvorova 2000). The earliest *masnavi* were written in the southern centres of the Urdu language, the Deccan and Gujrat. The earliest one, called 'Kadam Rao, Padam Rao' is ascribed to Fakhruddin Nizami (1397-1462). It was written between 1421 and 1435 and it describes how the antagonist's soul takes over the hero's body and how he regains his true form (Jalibi: 1973). The early *masnavis*, both in the Deccan as well as Gujrat, had many elements from the indigenous culture and very often one of the lovers was a Hindu (Suvorova 2000: 1-44).

When the centre of Urdu literature shifted to the north, the masters of the *ghazal*, like Mir Taqi Mir (1724-1810), continued to write *masvavis* too. Mir, for instance, wrote eight *masnavis* of a romantic nature. Like his *ghazals*, they are more concerned with deep, romantic love than ephemeral lust. The erotic *masnavi*, still masquerading as a love story, came into its own in Awadh. Mir Hasan (b. 1727), born in Delhi but settled in Faizabad, is famous for his *masnavis* such as '*Sehrul Bayan*'.

The story is about Prince Benazir, and Princes Badr-i-Munir. They fall in love and Najmunnisa, the Vizier's daughter, advises her to yield to passion. Badr-i-Munir allows Benazir to make love to her. The scene of copulation is described in a formulaic manner (an early example being from Manjhan for the translation of which in English see Behl and Weightman 2000: 190).

This is true of most *masnavis* of Urdu — especially those written in Lucknow or under the influence of Lucknow's eroticism. According to Suvorova, 'we come across similar more or less uninhibited descriptions of amorous intimacy in most of the Urdu *dastans* or '*dastan*-like' *masnavis*' (Suvorova 2000: 146).

The *masnavis* of Diya Shankar Nasim ('*Gulzar-i-Nasim*') and of Tasadduq Husain Khan (Nawab Mirza Shauq) (1773-1871) ('*Zahr-i-Ishq*') are famous for their stylistic beauty. However, Shauq is an innovator in that he introduces realism in the *masnavi*. While the previous *masnavis* mostly described fairy-tale characters, this one describes the passions of the boys and girls of contemporary Lucknow.

In '*Fareb-e-Ishq*' Shauq describes a rendezvous with beautiful, veiled young ladies who are initially tricked by the lover into meeting them. The girl usually has a cunning maid servant who is bribed into making her palanquin-bearers leave her in a vacant house or garden. There the lover approaches her with seductive words and professions of ardour. She rejects him initially but eventually yields. When discovered the girl suffers and dies. However, in '*Bahar-e-Ishq*' the lovers get married and in '*Zahr-e-Ishq*' they both try to commit suicide though only the girl dies (Shauq n.d).

Abdul Halim Sharar blames Wajid Ali Sha's debauchery, or rather his advertisement of it, on his reading of Shauq's *masnavis* (Sharar 1927: 96). As Suvorova points out, this is unproven and unprovable (2000: 218), but Shauq, as well as the Nawab, contributed to the association of eroticism with Urdu poetry, and indirectly with the language itself, at least with reference to Lucknow and its Urdu poetry.

Nazeer Akbarabadi (1735-1830), often called a people's poet or a 'realist', has erotic appeal in many of his poems. Aditya Bhel, in his insightful analysis of the poet, claims that 'Nazir's poems about sexual experience need to be viewed as expressive of an engagement with pleasure, a sensual sensibility' (Bhel 2005: 194). Thus the poet, writing *nazm* instead of the more restrictive *ghazal*, found it possible to situate sexual desire in stories of daily life in north India. Whether on a festive occasion—Eid, Shab-i-Barat, Holi, Divali or a fair (*mela*)—he mentions beautiful women and boys. Incidents like a storm are occasions for kissing or fondling a beauty and dreams, of course, are an excuse for describing them. In Nazeer, because of the quality of realism, we get a sense of how forbidden pleasures made people yearn for them and act, even if in imagination, as thieves and robbers of delights (see *Kulliyat-e-Nazeer*). Nazeer uses words in common use, including obscene ones, which have been expurged in modern editions so that there are blanks in many poems, especially those describing festive occasions. For instance, he uses the excuse of showing exotic pet animals to boys in order to take sexual advantage of them (*'Biya'*, *'Gilehri ka bachcha'* etc).

The Seductive Charm of the Urdu *Ghazal*

The *ghazal* contributed most to the image of Urdu as an amorous and erotic language. While the risquè Lucknow school of poetry with descriptions of women or seduction (*mu'amala bandi*) may be called erotic, even such descriptions do not use explicitly sexual words nor are they the major theme of the poetry which remains love. Indeed, most of the *ghazal* poetry is amorous rather than explicitly erotic but it is the *ghazal* which is associated with the amorous as well as the erotic in the pubic mind. One reason for this is the popularity and wide availability of the genre while the others are neither so easily available nor so often quoted as cultural icons. However, while the references are to the *ghazal*, there is an understanding —based upon allusions to other, less available genres — that there is a concealed, subversive literature in Urdu which is highly erotic and of which the *ghazal* is merely that tip of the iceberg which is visible.

Let us now look a the world of the *ghazal* through some examples. The beloved of the *Ghazal* — whether the elusive deity, courtesan, veiled lady or adolescent boy — is beautiful but indifferent. The poet-lover's passion is, therefore, unrequited. Thus, the poet accuses the beloved of being cruel and faithless (*bewafa*).

> *Chara gari bimari-e-dil ki rasm-e-shaher-e husn nahin*
> *Varna dilbar nadan bhi is dard ka chara jane hai* (Mir)
> (It is not the custom of the dwellers of the city of beauty to give solace to anybody. Otherwise even an innocent beauty knows how to provide a cure for the disease of love)

The beloved appears to favour the rival (*dushman, ghaer, raqib*). And Ghalib invests the situation with inimitable humour.

> *Main ne kaha bazm-e-naz men chahiye ghaer se tahi*
> *Sun ke sitam zarif ne mujh ko utha diya key yun*
> (I asked the beloved that this gathering of charm should exclude the rival/ upon hearing this she made me get up saying 'like this' (present author's translation)

The lover is condemned to separation (*hijr*) from the object of his love.

He cries, sighs and grows pale and ill with the pain of separation.

> *Chupke chupke rat din ansu bahana yad hai*
> *Ham ko ab tak ashiqi ka vo zamana yad hai* (Hasrat Mohani)
> (Shedding tears night and day quietly I remember/ the days of that love affair I remember)

These themes — romantic love, separation, fidelity on the part of the lover, indifference and fickleness on the part of the beloved — were reiterated throughout the three-hundred year tradition dating at least from Vali Dakkani (1667-1707) (even if the earlier one is not part of the common people's consciousness) of the Urdu *ghazal*.

The *ghazal* had a special place in the lives of educated people — both Hindus and Muslims —in North India. Even in other parts of India — Hyderabad, Murshidabad, Mysore, Lahore etc. — the educated elite enjoyed the *ghazal* as a distinctive cultural artifact. It was customary for educated, urbane men to learn several hundred couplets of the masters of the Urdu *ghazal*. These would be recited to make the conversation interesting. *Mushairas* (poetry recitations) were common and are held even now among the diaspora settled in the United States and Europe where Urdu poets are welcomed and people come to listen to them and enjoy the *ghazal* as well as the more recent genres of poetry. People played *bait bazi* in which one person recited a couplet The other player had to recite a couplet in response beginning with the last sound (denoted by the letter of the Urdu alphabet) of the last line. This went on till one of the parties ran out of couplets. The other one was the winner. This has changed into *antakshari* in Hindi where film songs, instead of the classical works of the Urdu poets, are used. However, if the official language of the songs in India is said to be Hindi it is that version of the shared language of North India and urban Pakistan which was called Hindustani and which is closer to the Urdu end of the linguistic spectrum. In any case the Hindi movie is strongly influenced by the amorous orientation of Nawabi Lucknow and, therefore, reminiscent of the link between Urdu and the life of love (Kesavan 1994: 255-256) Very often couplet after couplet by the great masters were recited only for the pleasure of it. Such an evening and the special romantic atmosphere it created is described by E.M. Forster in his novel *A Passage to India* (1924) as follows:

> They listened delighted, for they took the public view of poetry, not the private which obtains in England. It never bored them to hear words, words; they breathed them with the cool night air never stopping to analyze; the name of the poet, Hafiz, Hali, Iqbal, was sufficient guarantee (Forster 1924: 38).

This kind of enthusiasm for poetry was common. Every student of Aligarh Muslim University who has written memoirs has attested to it. Since the *ghazal* mentioned love and beauty repeatedly, Urdu itself came to be associated with romance and eroticism in the public mind. This image proved to be harmful for Urdu during the Urdu-Hindi controversy when some Hindu spokesmen said that they did not want their children to learn Urdu as, being taught through its literature, it would spoil them. This criticism is still repeated by the partisans of the indigenous languages of Pakistan who claim that Urdu, being nurtured in the decadent and effete culture of the *nawabs* of India, is a decadent language.

The Defeat of Eros

The reformers crusaded against the eroticism of Urdu in ways which have been described earlier (Rahman 2002: 508-515). They won and slowly Urdu started becoming associated with Islam and Pakistani nationalism in Pakistan. In India it remains associated with the Muslim identity. But this identity can be politically-oriented or a nostalgic throwback to the Mughlai past like Nur, the failed poet in Anita Desai's novel *In Custody* (1984). In the latter case there are some fading associations with romance and beauty but hardly the erotic. However, as the *madrassas* teach Urdu more often than secular schools in India, even the association with romance is fading away though the *ghazal* is still responded to among middle-aged, educated, urban people with much nostalgic enthusiasm. In India, particularly in the north, Urdu is a matter of demands, protests and political mobilization, and remains a symbol of identity of the Muslim community. (Farouqui 2006) In Pakistan it is a contested terrain — opposed by the supporters of ethnic identities as well as those of English (Rahman 1996) — and more often viewed as part of the Islamic-Pakistani identity than the language of love and longing.

Conclusion

In short, the nineteenth century witnessed battles, so to speak, for the soul of Urdu. It was a period of transition and the formation of new identities for groups of human beings (Muslims, Hindus etc). Language was part of the construction of these identities. The Indian reformers' desire to purge the language of its erotic associations was motivated by their political agenda for the construction of a 'nation' which was respectable, serious and modern. They felt compelled to defend their culture and literature, and by extension the whole Muslim community, against the British and Hindu charge of concupiscence, decadence and lethargy of which the literature of Urdu, as known up to the reformist movement, seemed to be an obvious and painful reminder. This went hand in hand with the ideological imperative of emphasizing the Muslim identity which tended to push Urdu towards an Islamic orientation. As Muslim separatism needed it as a symbol of the Muslim political identity mobilized against a Hindu version of a similar but opposing identity, it took on new features of a strident nationalism which is perennial in Urdu textbooks in Pakistan. During the same century the new language — the older one being Persian — continued to express the medieval themes of redemption and spirituality of which the erotic was always a part.

During the same period Urdu produced all of its canonical literature in poetry which is predominantly associated with love and sometimes with the erotic. Thus the different, and often paradoxical, associations of Urdu kept in conflict with each other with the public mind responding alternately to different ones according to the demands of the situation and whether the occasion was public (when Iqbal's nationalistc and Islamic poetry was quoted) or private (when Ghalib's love odes were more appropriate). However, the public mode gained ascendancy and the amorous and erotic associations were suppressed in the wake of the political urgency and identity politics of the Pakistan movement and then the perpetual struggle the Pakistani ruling elite waged against the ethnic elites of Pakistan on the one hand and the Western and Indian 'Other' on the other. We now live in a highly politicized age where the amorous and the erotic are tolerated far less than ever before though, ironically, it is also the age of mass production and of and easy access to commercial pornography through the internet. So, although the beautiful aspects of the *ghazal* are moribund and still draw the ire of hardline Islamists as well as the Westernized professionals for their purported eroticism or romantic frivolities, a new generation of young people are being exposed to the commodification of the body in ways never imagined by even the most erotic poets of Urdu.

NOTES

1. The following books were found by Nusuh in his son Kaleem's room and burnt. They are mostly books of Urdu poetry, either the *ghazal* or erotic stories in verse. However, books other than poetry are also included.
   Kulliyat-e-Atish (ghazal)
   Divan-e-Sharar (ghazal)
   Vasokht-e-Amanat (amorous story in verse with erotic description of female beauty)
   Fasana-e-Ajaib (Prose story in very Persianized Urdu)

Qissa Gul Bukaoli (amorous story in verse)
Araish-e-Mehfil (1801) by Sayyid Haider Baksh Haider. A tale (*dastan*) originally said to be in Persian and rendered into ornate Urdu prose in Fort William College. Like other tales it belongs to the fantasy world of magic, adventure, romance and necromancy.
Masnavi Meer Hasan (amorous story)
Waqa'e-e- Nemat Khan Ali. The author's full name is Nuruddin Muhammad Shirazi (d. 1710-1711). The book is in Persian and it describes the victory of Bahadur Shah, son of Aurangzeb, over Golcunda (Hyderabad) in 1687.
Ghazliat-e-Chirkeen (scabrous poetry)
Hazliat-e-Ja'far Zatalli (satirical and indecent verse)
Qasaid-e-Hajwia Mirza Rafi Sauda (satirical and highly polemical verse)
Divan-e-Jan-Sahib (Rekhti poetry)
Indar Sabha (amorous drama with descriptions of female beauty)
Divan Nazeer Akbar Abadi (with couplets of Mian Hud Hud) (some poems are erotic)
Vasokht (the author is not specified but the *vasokht* is amorous and erotic at places)
Kulliyat-e-Rind (mostly ghazal). (Ahmed 1874: 253-255).

2. European translators of the *Masnavi* were so embarrassed by the erotic content of some of the fables that Nicholson who translated it in English between 1925 to 1940 rendered them (133 out of 25, 700 couplets) in Latin so that only a few scholars could have access to them. He considered them 'too outspoken for our taste' but now that they are perhaps no longer unsuitable for Europe, they are not acceptable in Pakistan. Even in 1956, when the Pakistani scholar Afzal Iqbal sarted writing his book on Rumi he was anxious to defend Rumi on the possible charge of sensuality (see Iqbal 1956: 284-314).

REFERENCES

Abru, Sirajuddin Shah Mubarak.c.18C. 1990. *Divan –i Abru* (ed.) Mohammad Hasan. New Delhi: Taraqqi Urdu Bureau.

Ahmad, Zameeruddin 1990. *Khatir-e-Masoom.* Karachi: Ahsan Matbuat.

Ahmed, Nazeer 1874. *Taubat-un-Nusuh.* Edition used. Lahore: majlis Taraqqi-e-Adab, 1964.

Ahmed, Nazeer 1887. *Fasana-e-Muttila.* Edition used. Lahore: Majlis Taraqqi-e-Adab, 1962.

Ali, Fida 1829. *Shola Jawwala: Maj mua' Vosokht.* (Aesh takhullus) Lucknow: Nol Kishor.

Andrews, Walter G. and Mehmet Kalpakli 2005. *The age of beloveds: Love and the beloved in early-modern Ottoman and European culture and society.* Durban and London: Duke University Press.

Azhar, Shahdad 1995. *Urdu ghazal mein shahid bazi.* Srinagar: Gulshan Publishers.

Bazm, Mir Ashiq Hussain 1908. *Maj'mua Hazliat.* 120. Mss No. 1403, Rampur Raza Library (RRL).

Bazm, Mir Ashiq Hussain 1909. *Maj'mua Hazliat*. 123. Mss No. 1404, RRL.

Bechaen, Kallan Khan n. d. *Divan-e-Bechaen*. Mss No. 1401 RRL.

Behl, Aditya and Simon Weightman and Shyam Manohar Pandey 2000. *Mir Sayyid Manjhan Shattari Rajgiri, Madhumalati: An Indian Sufi Romance*. Behl *et. al.* (trans. with introduction) New York: Oxford University Press.

Behl, Aditya 2005. Poet of the Bazaars: Nazir Akbarabadi, 1735-1830. In Kathryn Hansen and David Lelyveld (eds.) *A wilderness of possibilities: Urdu studies in transnational perspective*. New Delhi: Oxford University Press. 192-222.

Bilgrami, S. Husain 1900. *Presidential Address at the Fourteenth Meeting of the Mohammedan Education Conference held at Rampur, December 1900*. Quoted from Minault 1998: 207.

Bloch, Ivan 1958. *Sexual life in England*. London: Corgi Edition, 1965.

Bouhdiba, Abdelwahab 1975. *Sexuality in Islam*. Trans. from French by Alan Sheridan. London: Routledge and Kegan Paul, English edn. 1985.

Brass, Paul 1974. *Language, religion and politics in North India*. London: Cambridge University Press.

Chirkeen n.d. *Divan-e-Chirkeen*. Mss. No. 1400 RRL.

Dalmia, Vasudha 1997. *The nationalization of Hindu traditions: Bhāratendu Harischandra and nineteenth-century Banaras*. Oxford University Press, New York.

Darlymple, William 2003. *White Mughals: Love and betrayal in eighteenth-century India*. London: Harper-Collins Publishers Ltd. Sharar 1929

Desai, Anita 1984. *In Custody*. Harmondsworth: Penguin Books.

Dover, K.J. 1978. *Greek homosexuality*. New York: Vintage Books Edition, 1980.

Edn. Com. NWP 1884. *Report by the North-Western Provinces and Oudh Provincial Committee with Evidence Taken Before the Committee and Memorials Addressed to the Education Commission*. Calcutta: Supt'd. of Govt. Printing.

Farouqui, Ather 2006. *Redefining Urdu politics in India*. New Delhi: Oxford University Press.

Flora and Sharir or Mir Hasan Ali. n. d. *Maj'mua Hazliat*. 24. Mss No. 1411, RRL.

Forster, E.M. 1924. *A passage to India*. Oliver Stalybran (ed) Harmandsworth: Penguin Book, 1978.

Foucault, Michel 1984. *The Foucault reader: An introduction to Foucault's thought*. Paul Rabinow (ed.) Harmondsworth: Penguin Books, 1991 reprint.

Foucault, Michel 1976-1984. *The History of Sexuality*. 3 volumes New York: Pantheon

Hali, Altaf Husain 1893. *Muqaddamah-e-Sher-o-Shairi* [Urdu: Introduction to poetry and poetics]. Lahore: Kashmir Kitab Ghar, 1971.

Hussain, Syed Ali n.d. *Maj'mua Hazliat* 33. Mss. No. 1412.

Insha, Insha Allah Khan 1802. *Darya-e-Latafat*. Maulvi Abdul Haq. (comp.) Pandit Brajmohan Dataria Kaifi (trans.) Lahore: Anjuman Taraqqi-e-Urdu, 1988.

Iqbal, Afzal 1956. *The life and work of Jalaluddin Rumi*. Islamabad: Pakistan National Council of the Arts, 1991 edition.

Jah, Muhammad Hussain 1908-1915. *Talism-e-Hosh Ruba* . Lahore: Sang-e-Meel.

Jalibi, Jamil (ed and comp) 1973. *Masanvi Kadam Rao Padam Rao.* Delhi: Educational Publishing House. This ed. 1979.

Jan Sahib, Mir Yar Ali n.d. *Divan-e-Jan Sahib.* Lucknow: Sadiq Press.

Kazmi, Tamkin 1930. *Tazkirah-I Rekhti.* Hyderabad: n.p.

Kesavan, Mukul 1994. Urdu, Awadh and the Tawaif: the Islamicate Roots of Hindi Cinema. In Zoya Hasan (ed.) *Forging identities: Gender, communities and the state in India.* Colorado: Westview Press.edition used, New Delhi: Kali for Women. 244-257.

Khan, Abdul Rasheed 2002. *Urdu Afsane Mein Jinsi Jazbat* Srinagar: Gulshan Publishers.

Khan, Dargah Quli c.18C. *Muraqqa-i Delhi.* Persian with Urdu translation. Khaliq Anjum (ed.) and (trans.) New Delhi: Anjuman Taraqqi Urdu, 1993.

Khan, Rashid Hasan (ed. and comp) 2003. *Zatal Nama: Kulliyat-e-Ja'afar Zatalli.* New Delhi: Published by the Compiler.

King, Christopher R. 1994. *One language, two scripts: The Hindi movement in nineteenth century North India.* Bombay: Oxford University Press.

Lal, K.S. 1988. *The Mughal Harem.* New Delhi: Aditya Prakashan.

Mazhar, Agha Wasi Ali Khan Lakhnawi n.d. *Maj'mua Hazliat.* 94. Mss No. 1407, RRL.

McIntosh, Mary 1968. The Homosexual Role. *Social Problems,* 16 (2), 182-192.

Mohsin, Mohsin Ali 1861?. *Tazkara-e-Sarapa Sukhan.*(no Publication details).

Mushir, Khalil Ullah Ahmad Siddiqui 1974. *Rekthi ka Tanqeedi Mutaela.* Lucknow: Naseem Book Depot.

Naim, C.M. 1979. The Theme of Homosexual (Pederastic) Love in pre-Modern Urdu Poetry. In M. Umar Memon (ed.), *Studies in the Urdu ghazal and prose fiction.* Madison: University of Wisconsin; 120-142.

Naim, C.M. 2001. Transvestic Words?: The *Rekhti* in Urdu. *The Annual of Urdu Studies*: 16 (2001), 3-26.

Najmabadi, Afsaneh 2005. *Women with maustaches and men without beards: Gender and sexual anxieties of Iranian modernity.* Berkeley: University of California Press.

Petievich, Carla 2001. Gender Politics and the Urdu *ghazal:* Exploratory observations on *Rekhta* versus *Rekhta. The Indian Economic and Social History Review,* 38 (3), 223-248.

Plummer, Kenneth (ed.) 1981. *The making of the modern homosexual.* London: Huchinson

Pritchett, Frances W. 1994. *Nets of awareness: Urdu poetry and its critics.* Third edition. Karachi: Oxford University Press, 1995.

Qureshi, Waheed 1966. Introduction. *Mansaviat-e-Husan,* Vol 1 (ed. and comp) Waheed Qureshi. Lahore: Majlis-e-Taraqqi-e-Adab.

Rahman, Tariq 1988. Ephebophilia: The Case for the Use of a New Word. *Forum for Modern Language Studies* 24 (2), 126-141.

Rahman, Tariq 1990. 'Boy-love in the Urdu Ghazal', *Annual of Urdu Studies* 7, 1-20.

Rahman, Tariq 1996. *Language and politics in Pakistan.* Karachi: Oxford University Press.

Rahman, Tariq 2002. *Language, ideology and power: Language-learning among the muslims of Pakistan and North India.* Karachi: Oxford University Press

Rahman, Tariq 2004. *Denizens of alien worlds: A study of education, inequality and polarization in Pakistan.* Karachi: Oxford University Press.

Rahman, Tariq 2006. Urdu as an Islamic Language. *The Annual of Urdu Studies* 101-119.

Rangin, Sa'adat Yar Khan n.d. *Masnavi Ma'a Hazliut Tasnif Sa'adat Yar Khan Rangin Dehlavi.* Oriental MSS Or. 385, 010 C.

Rasa, Hayat Baksh Mustafa Abedi n.d. *Maj'mua Hazliat,* 53. Mss No. 1409, RRL.

Rumi, Jalaluddin c. 13 C. *Masnavi Maulvi Ma'navi.* 6 Vols Original Persian with Urdu Tqazi Sajjad Hussain (trans.) Lahore: Al-Faisal Nashran, 2006.

Ruswa, Mirza Hadi 1899. *Umrao Jan Ada.* Islamabad: Alhamra Publishing, 2000.

Ruswa, Mirza Hadi n.d. *Shareef Zada.* Lahore: Kitab Ghar.

Sahib Qiran, Syed Imam Ali c. 1811. *Muntakhab Divan Sahib Qir 'an.* Ms. No. 771 Delhi, Persian, OIOC, British Library, London.

Sahib-e-Qiran, Saiyid Iman Ali Khan n.d. *Divan-e-Sahib-e-Qiran.* Oriental MSS. Egerton 1040, Folio 49, 010C.

Sarwari, Abdul Qadir 1998. *Kulliyat-i Siraj.* Delhi: Qaumi Council Barai Farosh-i Urdu Zaban.

Shamim, Syed Jawad Husain Amrohi 1915. *Maj'mua Hazliat.* 154. Mss Np 1410, RRL.

Sharar, Abdul Haleem 1927. *Guzishta Lucknow: Hindustan mein mashriqi tamaddun ka akhri namunu* (ed. and comp). M. Ikram Chughtai (Lahore: Sang-i-Meel Publications, 2006). This is available in English as *Lucknow: The Last Phase of an Oriental Culture.*

Shareef, Mohammad Jamil 2004. *Dakan Mein Urdu Sha'vri Vali Se Paehle.* Hyderabad, India. Idara Adabeat Urdu.

Shouq, Nawab Mirza n.d. *Masnaviat-e-Shauq* (ed.) Tabassum, Israr Ahmed Lahore: Tahliq Markaz, n. d.

Suvorova, Anna A. 2000. *Masnavi: A study of Urdu romance.* Karachi: Oxford University Press.

Vanita, Ruth and Kidwai, Saleem 2000. *Same-sex love in India: Reading from literature and history.* New York: St. Martins' Press.

Vanita, Ruth 2004. Married Among Their Companions: Female Homo erotic Relations in Nineteenth-Century Urdu *Rekhti* poetry in India. *Journal of Women's History* 16 (1), 12-52.

4

Himalayan Languages, Hindi and English: Contentment or Containment?

Mahendra K. Varma

It is axiomatic to say that multilingualism and multiculturalism are parts of the fabric and ecology of the Indian society irrespective of its hierarchical social structure and its diversity of landscape. It is a country in which the diversity of languages and cultural traditions have been matched by its bio-diversity. The aim of the paper is to describe the nature of multilingualism in the Himalayan region, with particular reference to Uttarakhand and Himachal. In an ideal society and in a progressive and secular socio-political system linguistic choices could be viewed as indices of negotiated exercises of linguistic rights and obligations. There are several sociolinguistic questions to be addressed in this context. Is the support for multilingualism in the Indian constitution just politically-driven linguistic correctness and idealism, or a genuine belief in the various smaller languages as inherited assets, and the will to secure their preservation. In the Himalayan regions of Uttarakhand and Himachal, as in other Hindi states, Hindi and English are the languages of education, government and administration. English is also the language of intra-national and international diplomacy, business, science & technology. In varying degrees both Hindi and English are perceived by both parents and young children as symbols of status, entertainment and success, whereas the smaller local languages are symbols of local cultures. Has the society begun to believe that English is ' an open sesame' by means of which one can attain unlimited vertical socio-economic mobility? Could the interpretation and embrace of the mother tongue local languages as simply the inherited ' social capital' and of Hindi and English as 'linguistic capital' in varying degrees lead to language shift? Are the local languages, like Gaelic in East

Sutherland and Hungarian in Oberwart, beginning to be identified with 'rural' and 'peasant' predicaments? Does Hindi in the curriculum create a protected environment for the so-called local dialects? Are the 'enclosed speech communities', which have propered for centuries in the relative isolation of the hills being affected by the growing presence of Hindi in the media and cable and satellite TVs by urbanization and education? Have globalization and English - the dominant language of the superhighway, caused *E-Vibhajan* (BBC, 2001) in the country? Would the fear of linguistic and economic exclusion lead to language shift?

In the Himalayan region and among its languages, both majority and minority in terms of their power, pride and progeny, I have chosen to look at Himachal and Uttarakhand. According to the 1991 census the four 'numerically biggest mother tongues in descending order of strength in these states were:

State	*Number of persons who returned the Mother Tongue as their mother tongue.*						
	Mother Tongue	*Persons*	*% state pop.*	*Rural*	*Urban*	*% Rural*	*% Urban*
	1	2	3	4	5	6	7
Himachal	1. PahaaRii	2,165,562	41.88	2,090,490	75,072	96.53	3.47
	2. Hindi	1,032,369	19.97	808,373	223,996	78.30	21.70
	3. Kaangrii	485,137	9.38	461,276	23,861	95.08	4.92
	4. Mandealii	440,164	8.51	404,653	35,511	91,93	8.07
Uttarakhand	1. Hindi	114,240,698	82.12	94,601,785	19,638,913	82.81	17.19
(UP)	2. GaRhwaalii	1,829,530	1.32	1,691,496	138,034	92.46	7.54

According to the 1991 Census the 'rate of national average of bilingualism was significantly higher (99.44%) than that recorded in the earlier three censuses, and the national average rate of trilingualism was 7.26%. However, the Census does not give us a true picture of bilingualism in the rural areas in the Hindi belt. The Census subsumes a large number of languages under the **superordinate language label Hindi**. The absence of opportunity to register smaller languages as mother tongues in the Hindi belt in general and in the Himalyan part of the Hindi belt in particular, gives a misleading picture of linguistic diversity in these regions. The emergence of KhaRii Bolii Hindi as one of the national official languages, as the regional state language in the Hindi belt, and as the language of literacy, has led to the reaffirmation of its staus and 'capital'. Bourdieu claims that a language granted official status 'can be considered as linguistic capital which affords its holders symbolic power.' (Bourdieu.1992: 46-48)

Although the Indo-Aryan languages within the Hindi provinces as well as the languages across the provinces are in continuum, the big question is: why do the Hindi states have a high degree of illiteracy, in particular in the rural areas? Despite the family relationship between languages like PahaaRii and Hindi and a degree of mutual intelligibility, these languages have indivdual grammatical characteristics. Let us just look at a passage from GaRhwaalii and its translation in Hindi to illustrate the point.

GaRhwaalii

Kai aadmii kaa dvii nyonyaal chayaa, uunmaan choTaa naunyaal na apNaa baabaajii maa bole: "he baabaa jii, birsat maan mero jo hissaa cha mai saNii de devaa". Tab uuN apNii birsat baaT diye.

Hindi

Kisii aadmii ke do laRke the. Unme se choTe laRke ne apne pitaa jii se kahaa, " pitaa jii, jaayadaad me se jo meraa hissaa hai, mujhe de do." Tab umhone apnii jaayadaad baaT dii. (Shailesh, 1976)

Smaller languages and rural locations with populations of less than 100,000 people do not have the facilities for media publications. In her research of the press in India, Nair concluded:

> The masses in India do not read newspapers either because they are illiterate, or because among the few who can read, the majority cannot afford to purchase them... An important clue to the negligible influence of newspapers on the masses lies in the fact that English dailies together still have a larger circulation than dailies in any vernacular including Hindi...whereas 41% of the *urban* population is literate, only 7.18 per cent of them subscribe to a daily. (Nair, 1978: 57-58)

Confirming this Southworth, says, "Reports from rural parts of the Hindi area indicate that there is, on the whole, very little reading of newspapers." (Southworth, 1978: 41)

Southworth points to the increasing distance between the smaller languages and the developing Sanskritized Hindi. The spread of standard Hindi through language planning in education and administration in these areas and its acquisition by children has made it the symbol of being educated and literate and urban. Since the linguistic ecology of towns and cities has been increasingly becoming predominantly Hindi and for the select few English, the younger generation is likely to be turning away from their rural heritage, in particular their language. They could also be the agents of change in their families.

In most recent times the shift from an industrialized to a knowledge-based economy has highlighted the need for workers with higher levels of literacy and numeracy than was previously the case. Within this context, there is considerable consensus among the educated and the educational stakeholders that **English alone** can equip the young generation to meet the challenges of the 'information age'. The **internet** and the associated language often called 'technospeak' or 'netspeak' has, with great rapidity, been revolutionizing people's lives and work across the globe. It has invariably and unquestionably once again brought to the fore the sociolinguistic issues of inequality and inequity, to which English in the colonial and post-colonial times has contributed to.

The launching of INSAT (Indian National Satellite) I and II series marked a new era in the history of electronic media and gave Indian TV a tremendous boost in its ability to reach rural India. In 1997-98 Doordarshan had 80% of urban and 95% of rural viewership. The arrival of the Satellite and Cable TV: STAR, ZEE, JAIN, SONY and others have revolutionized TV viewer's market and choice of programmes in English, Hindi and other major regional languages. There has been a growing influence of globalization and of the multinationals with media buying power on the economic landscape and job opportunities of India. Bhatia said:

> Make no mistake, electronic media, particularly TV, is becoming more modern, western, and even bold. The satellite channels are constantly beaming with western movies, fashion shows, and shows glamorizing the lifestyles of the west. (Bhatia, 2000: 36)

One of the most potent media of selling your goods and the associated western/urban cultures is visual and print media advertising. Despite their dislike of and resistance to the association of 'desirable goods' with 'desirable bodies' the rural communities are not, and can not afford to be, averse to the benefits of the new 'information and knowledge'. But the urban elite are familiar with the 'super highway' which is progressively being used by the mughals of globalization to superimpose their own culture, commodities and language. Bhatia, quoting Lee and Lee (1985: 8), said:

> ...multinational corporations cater highly profitable commodities to the interests of urban elites who in turn act as agents of the promotion of their products in rural areas. (Bhatia, 2000: 39)

The advertisements are not surprisingly not in their rural languages, but in English and Hindi, both of which have been promoted as 'capital' possessions, which have associations with power, prestige and progress. In the Hindi belt, in particular in the Himalayan belt, languages like PahaaRii, Kumauni, MaNDialii, Raajii or GaRHwaalii are at the bottom of the language hierarchy. Bourdieu (1992) further says that the more linguistic capital an individual or a group possesses the more they are able to assert symbolic power in the market. In the case of the Hindi belt, it is not their amount of linguistic capital that is important, it is the possession of Hindi and English as linguistic capital which matters.

There is a strong link between language and heritage, and this is what has encouraged a large number of the speech communities of rural India, and the isolated communities living in the hills and valleys to transmit their heritage languages (often called dialects), across generations. Like other natural languages they have undergone change but have been resisting shift. However, in the fast growing Information-driven urban Hindi belt, only Hindi and English languages are likely to be perceived as the **capital**. The smaller languages, with no literacy tradition and no state support, are beginning to appear more as symbols of past heritage encapsulated in folk-lore. The younger generation which does not receive any support for the heritage mother tongue in the school curriculum, nor does it find it as the language of jobs and opportunities, nor of media and of the glamour of advertising, nor of the superhighway, aspires to follow the road to the city to have the share in the economic boom.

Saville-Troike (1982: 193), Gal (1979), and Dorian (1981) found that the non-maintenance of the mother tongue resulted from the communities' perception that their heritage languages were not economically and culturally attractive. Dorian saw this as the progressive erosion of interest in the traditional lifestyles as peasants or fishermen. Giles et al describe the situation:

> For some linguistic groups, the past offers mobilizing symbols, while for others, the past may offer only demobilizing symbols leading individuals to forget or hide their linguistic identity thereby diluting the vitality of the group as a collective entity. (Giles et al. 1977: 311).

The migrants to the urban centres of Dehradoon, Lucknow and Delhi are beginning to be attracted by new enterprise, opportunities and modern facilities. The dominant languages of the urban ecology, being Hindi and English, could begin to induce the process of language change and choice among the younger generation. If first generation migrants to these cities decide not to pass on their heritage language Kumaoni or PahaaRii to their language children, and the schools do not respond positively to their rural languages then the children's choice of language will be curtailed. This leads to the reduction in the ethnolinguistic vitality of these rural languages. According to Giles et al (1977), status, demographic strength and institutional and educational support are the main variables which influence ethnolinguistic vitality. Appel and Muysken (1987: 41) say that the new languages seem to ' conquer domain after domain via the intermediate stage of bilingual language use.' Thus the language(s) the minorities begin to internalize and use are determined and decided by the urban job providers and the Internet and the media custodians whose horizons are urban and international. They are invading the village community centres and the 'baiThaks' of individuals' homes too. Talking of the smaller languages of South Africa, August D.de V.Cluver says:

> Minority languages or languages of lesser diffusion tend to be associated with negative concepts such as 'inferior', 'powerless', 'uneducated', and 'lack of expressive power.' (de V. Cluver, 2000: 77)

Very little work has been done on the smaller languages in the Himalayan region from a macro-sociolinguistic point of view in studying any possible stigmatisation in progress. In the context of the growing pervasiveness, power and prestige of Hindi and English, we do not have empirical data on the patterns of language use, in particular the use of the rural mother tongues in the Himalayan regions, in different domains. We don't have detailed authentic data on the attitudes of the speakers of MaNDealii, PahaaRii or Kumauni towards the encroachment of both Hindi and English in the domains which have traditionally been reserved for their heritage languages. Pattanayak points to the likely change in the linguistic culture of India:

> During the last thousands of years large and small languages have coexisted in India without the threat of being assimilated. Colonial languages which emphasise the notion of superiority and inferiority and threaten to assimilate **smaller, weaker and unequal languages** create a situation where balance is lost in the relationship among languages. From a situation where language maintenance was the rule, they move over to a position where language loss becomes the rule. Selective language standardization and modernization give rise to indigenous dominant languages which begin to oppress smaller languages. (Pattanayak, 1996: 104)

The question I asked in the title of the paper was: Is the linguistic situation of change and shift an indication of the contentment of the smaller speech communities in the persuit of a pragmatic approach of acceptance of Hindi and English, or is it a case of the smaller language groups being 'contained' by the supremacy of Hindi and English over which they have no control. The answer to my question and the testing of the validity of Pattanayak's prognosis would need ethnographic research. I have tried to illustrate and highlight the sociolinguistic situations in which the future of the smaller languages might well be determined by the speed of urbanization and migration. On the other hand, the hills and the isolation, and close-knit community might help them retain their language vitality to survive for a long time to come. Language contact with Standard Hindi in the curriculum and government institutions, with English through TV, Satellite, Cable and the Internet may still take some time before the symptoms of *shift* and *deestabilisation*, so characteristic of urban environment, begin to appear in rural Himalayan regions. Romaine comes to similar conclusion:

> ...not all cases of language contact need to result in language loss. Individual variability and cultural attitudes about assimilation and integration on the part of the minority group are just as important to take into account as those of the majority. (Romaine, 1983: 127).

The transition from 'moTii bolii' to 'saaf bolii' (Gumperz. 1964) and 'safed bolii', resulting in a change from one diglossia to another diglossia, if it does happen, will not be a case of contentment but of containment.

REFERENCES

Apte, M.L. (ed.) 1978. *Mass, culture, language and arts in India*. Bombay: Popular Prakashan.

Appel, Rene and Pieter Muysken 1987. *Language contact and bilingualism*. London: Edward Arnold.

Bhatia, T. K. 2000. *Advertising in rural India*. Tokyo: Tokyo University of Foreign Studies.

Bourdieu, P. 1992. *Language and symbolic power*. Cambridge: Polity Press.

Crystal D. *Language death*. 2000. Cambridge: Cambridge University Press.

deV.Cluver, August D. 2000. Changing Language Attitudes: The stigmatisation of Khoekhoegowap in Namibia. *Language Problems and Language Planning* 24, 1.

Dorian, N. 1981. *Language death: The life cycle of Scottish Gaelic dialect*. Philadelphia: University of Pennsylvania Press.

Gal, S. 1979. *Language shift: Social determinants of linguistic change in bilingual Austria*. New York: Academic Press.

Giles, Howard, Richard Y. Bourhis, and Donald M. Taylor 1977. Toward a theory of language in ethnic group relations. In Howard Giles (ed.) *Language, ethnicity and intergroup relations*. London: Academic Press.

Gumperz, J.J. 1964. Linguistic and Social Interaction in Two Communities. In John J. Gumperz and Dell Hymes (eds.) *The ethnography of communication*.

Nair, K. 1978. Forms and Functions of Mass Media-The Press. In Apte (ed.).

Pattanayak, D.P. 1996. In S.K.Verma and D. Singh. (eds.) *Perspectives on language and society*. Delhi: Kalinga Publications.

Romaine, S. 1983. Problems in the sociolinguistic description of communicative repertoires among linguistic minorities. In S. Mancho (ed.) *Status of migrants mother tongue*. Strasbourg, ESF.

Shailesh, Hari Datta Bhatt 1976. *GaRhwaali bhaasha aur uska saahitya*. Lucknow: UP Govt.

Southworth, F.C. 1978. Language and Mass Communication in India. In Apte (ed.)

5

English in India and the Role of the Elite in the National Project

Annie Montaut

"In India, English is the language spoken by the ruling class. It is spoken by the higher class of natives at the seats of Government. It is likely to become the language of commerce throughout the seas of the East". Thus ended Macaulay's most famous minute, in 1835, a report aimed at instructing the Indian elite in the English language, in order to produce "a class of persons Indian in blood and colour, but English in taste, in opinions, in morals and in intellect". This most famous sentence, to be later quoted everywhere, summarized the explicit intention "to form a class who may be interpreters between us and the millions whom we govern"[1]. Hundred and seventy years later, most of the reports devoted to the use of English establish similar conclusions regarding the sociology of English[2]: the small proportion of people using English corresponds to the social class which is tightly integrated to world economy and techno-structures. This is particularly true for the millions of expatriates of the Indian subcontinent who are at least as close to the foreign techno economic trusts as to their own country and people, an elite whose belonging to the world, linked to the English language, is sharpened by the new technologies (Bhattacharya 1998: 45)[3].

Introduced in India by the British colonizers, English today is the associate official language of the State, along with Hindi, a status first suggested for fifteen years in 1950, then renewed *sine die*, largely because of the protest of Dravidian speakers against Hindi. Although it was not mentioned in the original list of the 14 constitutional languages ("major regional languages)" listed in the Eighth schedule, nor in its successive amendments, English is the official language of 4 North Eastern States and of 8 Union Territories[4].

Is English a chance for India, to voice her mind, in compensation for centuries of domination, to enter on equal footing in the dialogue of today world cultures, or, on the contrary, is a paradoxical denial of this opportunity stolen by language otherness? Such a question will be addressed in section 3, after a try for evaluating the role of English in the plural culture of contemporary India (section 1) and a look at the weight, today, of the introduction of English in the Indian colonial system (section 2).

1. The Indian pluralism and the English language

It can be said about many former colonies that the idea of nation in its homogeneity dissimulates an heterogeneous reality which accommodates ethnical, religious, linguistic contradictions. But it is probably nowhere as striking as it is in the case of India: not infrequently its very existence as such a single concrete entity has been questioned.[5] I leave it to Shashi Tharoor (2000: 7-8) to express the degree of that authentic pluralism rather than to Nehru, first because his are contemporary writings, second because he belongs to this class of writers who could make English a language for intellectual essay as well as for novel.

> How can one approach this land of snow peaks and tropical jungles, with seventeen major languages and twenty-two thousand distinct dialects (including some spoken by more people than those who speak Danish or Norwegian), inhabited in the last decade of the twentieth century by nearly 940 million individuals of every ethnic extraction known to humanity? How does one come to terms with a country whose population is 51 percent illiterate, but which has educated the world's second largest pool of trained scientists and engineers, whose teeming cities overflow while four out of five Indians scratch a living from the soil? What is the clue to understanding a country rife with despair and disrepair, which nonetheless moved a Mughal emperor to declaim, "If on earth there be paradise of bliss, it is this, it is this, it is this . . .?" How does one gauge a culture that elevated non-violence to an effective moral principle, but whose freedom was born in blood and whose independence still soaks in it? How does one explain a land where peasant organizations and suspicious officials attempt to close down Kentucky Fried Chicken as a threat to the nation, where a former prime minister bitterly criticizes the sale of Pepsi-Cola "in a country where villagers don't have clean drinking water," and which yet invents a greater quantity of sophisticated software for U.S. computer manufacturers than any other country in the world? How can one portray the present, let alone the future, of an ageless civilization that was the birthplace of four major religions, a dozen different traditions of classical dance, eighty-five political parties, and three hundred ways of cooking the potato?

The extreme linguistic diversity is then one among other extremes in a

Sub Continent which is prominently multicultural, a qualification now quite usual to define India. Its twenty major languages (see note 5) and its hundreds of dialects mapped into four genetically distinct families, overlap in the complex picture of a generalized multilingualism. Not only none of the States is monolingual, but more than half of the districts are multilingual (Srivastava 1994), let alone the regional local varieties and the important diglossia between written and spoken registers[6]. There is no speaking community which does not handle at least three distinct language codes, and there is no language whose speakers don't have at least two other contact languages. Similarly, there is no regional language whose speakers are not also present in a sizable amount in another State where the given language is not dominant: for instance, in Andhra Pradesh, a telugu-speaking State which was separated from Tamil-speaking Tamil Nadu after a language movement for the recognition of a Telugu territory[7], Urdu is also spoken by two and a half million speakers, as well as Rajasthani, Tamil, Marathi, Oriya, Malayalam, Panjabi, Kond, Jatapu, Savara, Koya, Yerakula, Gondi, etc. Reversely, important Telugu-speaking communities live in Tamil Nadu, Karnataka, Maharashtra, Orissa (Srivastava 1994: 102), and Delhi[8].

It is well known that the verbal tradition in India is an organic multilingual one, a grassroot plurilingualism where the various language identities of the plurilingual user behave as a global communicational unit (Le Page 1992, Le Page & Tabouret Keller 1985). This grassroot multilingualism is both societal and spontaneous: since it activates in a fluid way an heterogeneous repertoire mainly in its low nonstandardized varieties, in conformity with an organic stratified model. It relies on the integration of differences and on serendipity, within a shared communicational ethos which is widely spread across India. Khubchandani (1991: 16-17, 1997) defines it as a functional heterogeneity, with each segment of the repertoire having a specific function and a well defined sphere of use in social, cultural and economic activity. The dynamics of such a common ethos is thus non competitive. Each of the speeches involved in the various exchanges is, as nicely coined by R.N. Srivastava (1994), "a part of the whole" and none of them is "apart from the whole"[9].

Or maybe we should say 'was' rather than 'is', since this non competitive dynamics got recently changed under the competing forces towards official recognition, the market pressures, and competition for hegemony at a local or regional level (see section 2).

One of the features nurturing the vitality of the traditional spontaneous plurilingualism and the extraordinary resilience of language diversity in India (Pattanayak 1991, Pandit 1977) may well be, apart from the fluidity of language identities and grammatical tolerance operating in serendipity, the structural convergence of the various Indian languages which, in more than forty centuries of co-habitation on the same spatial area, has deeply transformed all the local speeches. It is today more legitimate from a scientific viewpoint to hypothesize an Indian family than four distinct families such as Indo-Aryan, Dravidian, Austric and Tibeto-Burman, to the extent that each of the Indian members of such families have now more structural affinities with other Indian members of other families than with non-Indian members of their own family (Emeneau 1980)[10]: neighborghood links are stronger than brotherhood links structurally speaking.

Clearly English is a newcomer in the picture and several reasons suggest that it got added more than integrated within the family-linguistically speaking at least: word order remains SVO, main syntax retains prepositions, etc.[11]. A language acquired more often at school than through spontaneous interaction, it plays a major role in the repertoire of a minority, the intellectual elite, without belonging to the list of "minor languages".

The number of speakers who return English as a mother tongue (MT) is estimated to be about 0,03%, with little variation between the various Census since in 1981 the number of English MT speakers was about 202 000 and in 1991 about 179 000 (that is, hardly more that the number of Ao speakers, a Tibeto-Burman language spoken in the North East of the country and practically ignored in instruction as well as in the job market).[12] The number of bilingual speakers with English as L2 is however far more difficult to estimate. According to the *Census of India*, they represented approximately 65 millions (slightly more than the Marathi speakers, which amounts to 8% of the population. But the appreciation on bilingualism can highly vary, since, according to the 1981 Census of India, there were 13,3% bilinguals with Indian languages and 1% with English, whereas in the same year the Anthropological Survey of India estimated that bilingual speakers were 66% of the population, and in 1993 almost half of them with Hindi as L2 - Hindi being equally spoken as L1 by approximately 40% of the Indian population. The use of the language as a language medium in schools may also be an indication of the literacy rate in English, and similarly the choice of the language as a subject (the topic for L2 or 3 for instance): the quasi totality of universities and prestigious schools or institutes use English as the teaching medium. If English was in 1992 the teaching medium of 13% of the high schools, 4% of the middle schools, 3.4% of the upper middle Schools, and 1.3% of the primary schools, the proportion is quickly increasing[13] - but how do we estimate the ratio between alphabetisation and real ability to communicate at both oral and written levels? The diffusion of newspapers in English may be the most reliable criteria, and the evolution of English publications in this respect is interesting: the 49 145 newspapers and periodicals published in 2002, 7125 were in English (19 685 in Hindi), whereas, according to Kachru (1986 : 12sq.), the number of newspapers in English twenty years before was 3582: the proportion was slightly less than 19% at the beginning of the eighties, and about 17% in the first years of the twenty-first century. In the same period, the proportion of newspapers in Hindi increased considerably, since it has nowadays reached 40%. As for the number of copies diffused, they probably represent a readership which we can multiply more for vernacular newspapers than English ones, and the official statistics give the following (*India 2002* : 19): 1 687 099 copies for the *Times of India*, the most widely read English daily (1 243 573 copies in 2004), 847 346 for the *Hindustan Times*, figures comparable to the Bengali newspaper which sells the best (*Ananda Bazar Patrika*), the Hindi daily which sells the best is close to the Times of India with its 1 138 035 copies (*Dainik Jagaran*), as well as Malayali with its 1 208 001 copies (*Malayala Manorama*). Readership was estimated in 2006 (National Readership Survey) to be the highest for *Dainik Jagran* (with 21.2 million readers) and *Rajasthan Patrika* (with 21.0 million readers), both published in Hindi. *The Times of India* is the most widely read English language newspaper (7.9 million), followed by *The Hindu* (4.05 million), *Hindustan Times* (3.85 million). The *New Indian Express* is also most widely read [English] (4.0 millions).

Taking all these various indicators into account, it can be admitted that a proportion of 3 to 11% master enough English to be able to benefit from it in the job market, both national and international, but having a BA in English is not always a passport for the proliferating call centers in big cities where one can earn quick money – they may welcome people without any diploma but with a language capacity acquired independently from the academic system.

2. The historical antecedents of today contradictions

It is well known that English as an Indian language is one of numerous legacies of the British colonization which already started with the growing impact of the East India Company. But it may not be so well known that the introduction of English in the relations of dominants and dominates has not been immediate. It was the formation in the "vernacular" languages (at the time Hindostanee in its two forms, Hindee or Urdoo) that was the first large scale language schooling,[14] when Lord Wellesley decided in the very first years of the 19th century to open a language school in Fort William College in Calcutta, whose direction was entrusted to Sir John Gilchrist. From this College, devoted to the teaching of what was then called "vernacular" (a term I will be using for that reason), emerged, between 1800 and 1810, the first educational texts, grammars, dictionaries, literary or narrative texts, in modern Hindi, later on compiled in an anthology called the *Gutkā*, which were used as textbooks in schools until the end of the 19th century. James Mill, from the India Office, indicates in 1833 that a position such as member of the Board of Revenue could satisfactorily be entrusted to persons without knowledge of English. And Hobson, author of the first glossary of the Indian words in the English language, the famous *Hobson-Johnson*, was in favour of the vernacular languages in the quarrel opposing the Orientalists (favouring Indian languages, that is, mainly Sanskrit or Persian, in education) and the pro-English modernists (favouring English as an instruction medium and topic). What inspired Macaulay, nominated in 1834 by Lord Bentinck as Director of the General Committee for Public Education, is in conformity with a general political as well as cultural trend. This trend was in its turn in conformity with the shift from a purely economic relation between Great Britain and India (resource extraction, payment of tribute) towards a modern industrial mode of exchange, with the colony serving as a market for the goods manufactured in Britain, as well as a source of raw produces, the wish for cultural, and eventually religious, domination being an additional change in conformity with the colonial ideology (Bhattacharya 1998)[15].

The famous "minute" issued by Macaulay in 1835 is located in the main stream of a liberal ideology, associated to the utilitarian trend of J.S. Mill and Lord Bentham, which can be clearly decoded in the Charter Act of 1834: it states, notwithstanding the interests of the Company, that "no native of India nor any natural born subject of His Majesty should be disabled from holding any place, or employment, by reason of his religious, place of birth, descent or colour". The same Charter Act decides for an amount of money allocated for supporting education in India which is ten times higher than the previous subsidy allocated in 1813. Such conceptions (right to education for the people, including girls, the trust in the equal value of all human beings, the faith in progress) had reached the Indian elite through the contact of the English language and the philosophical and ideological trends it conveyed in its then literature. And this is one of the reasons why the "reformist" Indians of the time[16], who considered themselves as enlightened and modern, were often in favour of the pro-English modernists in the above mentioned controversy. Ram Mohan Roy, the famous reformist, for instance, of the Bengali Renaissance, advocates as soon as 1823 the introduction of English in the academic curriculum. While giving to the British the credit of progressive and philanthropic motivations, he strongly criticizes the traditional Indian educational system as obscurantist and backward: "The Sanskrit system of education would be the best calculated to keep this country in darkness, if such had been the policy of the British legislature"[17].

Besides, the abolition of the "Sanskrit system" (or the Persian system, in *madrasas*) did not altogether mean that vernacular modern languages should be ignored, and the British themselves were far from agreeing together on the role they should play in the educational system. We can hardly have any doubt that Macaulay himself – who confessed a total ignorance of either ancient or modern Indian languages – did not hold them in a high esteem[18]. But the reform of the system of public education which was to be voted a few years later, known as the Vernacular Dispatch or Charles Wood's Education Dispatch of 1854, clearly states that, even if the knowledge of English will always be an essential requirement for those Natives of India who want to achieve higher education (article 11), even if English cannot be dispensed with in urban surroundings, the knowledge of English remains essentially a means for acquiring a good education and should in no way be an aim in itself (article 12). Consequently, the knowledge of English should never replace a good knowledge of the vernaculars, *because the languages understood by the masses are more important*, and they are the ones which have replaced Persian in administration and in the Court[19] (article 13); it is then desirable to teach English only where there is a demand for it, and to always teach it in combination with the vernacular languages *of the district* and the general culture conveyed by these languages. The 14th article of the Dispatch concludes that vernaculars should be used to instruct the *larger classes* of the population who ignore English or have no sufficient knowledge of it. As for the instructors, they should know both languages, because this double knowledge only will enable them to enrich the vernacular languages and cultures by means of ideas and words to express them[20].

These two historical documents (Macaulay's Minute and the Vernacular Dispatch) clearly show the double tension which is at work, right from the beginning, in the language policy of the British domination: the diffusion of English aims at fabricating this class of intermediaries between dominants and dominates which Macaulay was dreaming of (a tool for collaboration), but it is also the vehicle for the progressive ideology which favours mass education and is praised for that by the reformists. English is the language of the elite, but it is also the vehicle for such notions as social progress and mass education. On the other hand, the education of the masses, which Macaulay does seem to care of, can only be achieved through the vernacular languages, and even, as is very clear from the 1854 Dispatch, in their local variety – not in the learned speech such as high Hindi or Urdu which already differ from oral speech by their sanksritized or persianized lexicon respectively. The same is true for all other regional languages, which have a high learned speech far enough from the spoken language not to be understood by children from underprivileged backgrounds or living in villages where the local dialect is quite distinct from the regional language.

The end of the colonial period is then dominated, as far as language is concerned, by this schism between masses and elite (Di Bona, 1998: 370), a schism which still prevails in today's independent India although in a different way since it got reframed into the modern dialectics nation/local.

The desirable balance could indeed never be achieved, and the "combination" advocated by the 1854 Dispatch between English (the means for accessing power) and vernacular languages in their local "district" form could never be implemented. In reality, the introduction of English in the academic curricula was accompanied by a growing neglect of the vernacular languages, and similarly, the emphasis on the so-called vernaculars was translated into an elimination of the languages of the people: the real evolution was "a process of disprivileging folk languages (*lokbhasha*) or dialects vis-a-vis sanskritized chaste Hindi or *shisht bhasha* (cultivated language)" according to S.C. Shukla (1998: 45 sq.). Shukla then tries to find the reason for this perverse side-effect of the introduction of English in the education system, and identifies it in the total apathy of the elite regarding the education of masses, and notes that the middle classes had gone so far as to oppose the attempt for taxation on land which aimed at opening schools for poor children at the end of the twenties. A similar conclusion is reached by Jha (1998: 224-6) who shows that the vernaculars as school medium have constantly decreased in the period because of the promotion of English– and to a lesser degree of Sanskrit. The dominant classes founded schools, mainly in towns, with the single purpose of promoting their own members by educating them in English so that they may get a job in the administrative services[21]. Bhokta (1998: 217) similarly attributes the "marginalisation of folk languages" to the search for well paid jobs, an Indian teaching English earning far more than an Indian teaching a vernacular language – and far less than a British. In the hierarchy thus emerging in the second half of the 19th century and prevailing during the next century, the local speeches of the Chotanagpur and Santhali Parganas for instance are downtrodden by Hindi, Hindi by English – a language which gets, just before Independence, associated with the "service-seeking mania" (Bhokta: 1998).

So, when the Congress Party and Gandhi started debating about a pan-Indian language during the first decades of the 20th century, the situation was burdened by the colonial contradictions in the field of language policy. The contradiction however shifts: in the 20th century, English, which remains the language of the elite, is no longer perceived as the vehicle of modernity and of the social project but rather as the only real pan-Indian language. Besides it conveys the trans-local notion of an abstract nation: a nation abstracted from its concrete components, whether religious, regional or linguistic, which could not be fitted into a common project, as convincingly argued by Khilnani for the Nehruvian idea of India (1997).

Gandhi made the nationalist movement a mass movement by directly reaching the masses, on the first hand by the symbols he manipulated, both moral and concrete (like the charkha), more infused with religiosity than marked with a specific religion, and on the second hand by the use of popular language[22]. The nationalist ideology and the nationalist discourse were born in the Anglophone intelligentsia, but with Gandhi the movement goes down to the street and to the fields with the use of vernacular languages, particularly Hindustani, which was the most widely spoken and understood all over Northern India. This is the reason why Gandhi views "Hindi or Hindustani" (*"Hindi yani Hindustani", "Hindi athwaa Hindustani", Hindi yaa Hindustani"*, according to his phrasing in the 1936 Nagpur Session of the Bharatiya Sahitya Parishad) as the future national language of independent India (*swaraj*), and why he advocates its diffusion in all the Dravidian speaking provinces[23]. Even more than the English, he insists, those who enslaved India are our Anglophones. And indeed, "if we spend only half the efforts we do in learning English in the learning of Indian languages, there will be born a new atmosphere in the country and a good measure of progress will be achieved". Since 1925 it was agreed that the regional meetings of the Congress should be held "in Hindustani as much as possible", and if not, in the regional languages (Amendment of article 33 of the Constitution of the Congress), yet a common language was needed for the national meetings, and this common language should represent a *swaraj* which is not the *swaraj* of the Anglophone elite but the *swaraj* of the millions of hungry illiterate people, of the women and the untouchables, of all the dominated people" (*Young India* 1931). Until the end, Gandhi tried to make this language the cement of national feeling in the Dravidian provinces: "I want a pledge from you here and now that you will all learn Hindustani. I say it is your *dharma* to learn Hindustani which will link South with the North" (*Jubilee Celebration* 1946).

Gandhi has of course another reason to stand in favour of Hindustani "or" Hindi as he also calls it[24]. This composite language, "Hirdu" in the terminology of some contemporary linguists, is the common legacy of both Hindus and Muslims in Northern India[25], and the major danger at the time is the communal division ending in the partition of the country.[26] Hence Gandhi's emphasis on the spoken language, which is common to both communities and may then help neutralizing the tensions: the language he supports is "a resultant of Hindi and Urdu, neither highly sanskritised nor highly persianised or arbianised" (*Young India* (27 August 1925), "a harmonious blend of the two will be as beautiful as the confluence of Ganga and Yamuna". Hence, also, Gandhi's tolerance regarding the graphic problem (*Young India* 26 December 1924), a crucial choice in this context since Hindi has started identifying with nagari, the Sanskrit alphabet, whereas Urdu is written with modified Arabic characters. Gandhi's adamant promotion of Hindustani/Hindi amounts to asserting that freedom is not obtained in and with the language of the colonizer, and that the integration of the poor in the new nation will not be obtained in the language of the elite, but it also amounts to indefatigably emphasizing the cultural and linguistic unity of the Muslim and Hindu communities.[27]

Once Partition has been decided, once the creation of Pakistan has been announced according to the wish of the Muslim League, with Urdu as its national language, the Congress Party stops insisting on Hindustani and the debate is then restricted to the nature of the Hindi language consensually chosen for the new Indian nation: for the "Hindiwallahs" like Seth Govind Das and P.N. Tandon, the official Hindi can be only a sanskritized Hindi, explicitly attached to its cultural "origin", that is, aryanized and hinduized[28]; for the liberals and moderates, among whom Nehru and Patel, such a choice would serve as an incentive for religious sectarianism and support the obscurantism, bigotry and reactionary forces that British reforms tried to fight. But there were also certain liberals who, before the consensus in favour of Hindi in July 1947, had stood for English. It is the case of Dr Ambedkar, the leader of the Untouchables, who converted to Buddhism, for whom the choice of Hindi represented a symbol of identification to the Brahmanic orthodoxy, Hinduism and the cast system. Hindi written in nagari was however chosen as the official (not national) language, after a very hot debate which almost degenerated into an ideological war, leading to a violence never attained during the three years of the elaboration of the Constitution[29]. But the Hindiwallah did not win, since the official language is explicitly described in the Constitution as reflecting the composite culture of India and its ability to integrate vocabulary and idioms from various origins (article 351). The provisions regarding the "development" and "modernization" of the language suggest borrowings from Hindustani, other major regional languages, and their dialects as well as from Sanskrit.[30]

The way these directions were implemented during the fifty years of independence has largely betrayed the hopes of the moderates and confirmed the fears of the supporters of English. Over burdened by a proliferation of sanskritized neologisms and obscure technicalities unintelligible for the villager even educated, the official language has become strictly similar to that stigmatized by Macaulay's minute as well as the Vernacular Dispatch one and a half century ago. It is as cryptic and esoteric for the uneducated citizen as was Persian in 1836, and already in 1950 Nehru, presented with a Hindi translation of the Constitution of India, complained that he could not understand it – no more did he understand the Urdu translation. Official Hindi today has become the new symbol of oppression and of the power of the State (Rai 2000), so that in the early sixties, close to the end of the period when English should remain the associate official language, the leader of the supporters of English, Frank Anthony, clearly voiced what many non Hindiphones as well as non Anglophones thought: "The new Hindi is a negation of secular democracy": it has become a symbol of religious sectarianism, it is the ruin of minor regional and local languages[31]. Besides, it is English and not Hindi or other languages which secures good jobs, partly because official Hindi, due to its artificiality, could not impose itself even in central administration. We are consequently left, in the beginning of the 21st century, with a situation burdened by as much tension and inner contradiction as Macaulay might have contemplated one and a half century before.

English remains the language of the elite and can hardly serve as the integral expression of an authentic project for social democracy – from the central government to the actors most crucially concerned, the underprivileged masses who remain largely marginalized from the conception, the expression and the implementation of developmental devices. It is however the only trans-regional trans-religious language, supposedly able to transcend local chauvinisms and group interests. As a matter of fact, group interests have taken a more and more visible shape during the period, in the form of identity claims sometimes leading to extreme violence: their politization ended in polarizing religious identities up to the point of secessionist claims in Punjab during the early eighties of in Kashmir just after, and in polarizing linguistic and regional identities up to the point of creating new States: a Telugu speaking Andhra was created in 1953 out of the Tamil speaking State, then a Kannada speaking Karnataka and a Gujarati speaking Gujarat, separated from Maharashtra in 1966, before a further "bifurcation" into Konkani speaking Goa-Diu and a Marathi speaking Maharashtra in 1994, Hindi speaking Aryana was separated from Punjabi speaking Punjab in 1966, Nagaland was separated from Assam in 1971, and the year after Mizoram (Mizo speaking), Meghalaya (Khasi speaking), Tripura, etc. This process seems a never ending one since in 2000 again, the Santhali speaking Jharkhand was carved out from the Urdu/Hindi speaking Bihar[32]. English in such a context may appear as an integrative force barring any chauvinism, because of the secular ideology it conveys as well as the lack of link with any local culture. It thus remain for quite a few, as it was for Nehru, the language most fit to express the idea of India as a nation, beyond group identities, whether minor or major, beyond the local roots necessarily articulated in the mother tongue. A novelist like Salman Rushdie shows it in a gorgeous way in *Midnight Children* or *The Maure's Last Sigh*, and Shashi Tharoor argues for it in a more sober way: "There are many of us, but, among India's multitudes, we are few. We have grown up in the cities of India, secure in a national identity rather than in a local one, which we express in English better than in any Indian language. We rejoice in the complexity and diversity of our India, of which we feel a conscious part; we have friends of every caste and religious community, and we marry across such sectarian lines. We see the poverty, suffering and conflict in which a majority of our fellow citizens are mired, and we clamor for new solutions to these old problems, solutions we believe can come from the skills and efficiency of the modern world. We are secular (...) and, in Indian politics, we are pretty much irrelevant (...). We tell ourselves we are able, but not electable" (2000: 42-43).

But yet, even for this minor Anglophone elite — with the exception of the 0,03% speakers with English as their mother tongue and of the minority of intellectuals sharing Tharoor's legacy – English remains a foreign language. A language learned soon in life, but always more or less associated to what many consider as the "fatality of the colonial fate", with the alienation resulting from a mandatory bilingualism.[33]

In the contemporary education system, the "three language formula" adopted by the Constitution and later revised by the Kothari Commission in 1966, requires that school children learn their mother tongue first, then the regional language and the official language.

Although implemented everywhere except in Tamil Nadu, it reflects the contradictory tensions between the wish for national integration and the respect of minority rights, an awkward compromise which rarely allows children to be taught in their mother tongue if it is a non schedule language. Even schedule languages like Urdu are strikingly disfavoured compared with Hindi or English. Hasnain, (2006 a) mentions the perverse effect of the lists among which the student has to chose his topics, referring to cases where "at a point of time Urdu was bracketed with science and Urdu and Urdu speaking students could only opt for Urdu at the cost of science in secondary schools. Besides, the poor facilities for Urdu teachers training often leads to position in Urdu being left vacant, "to be abolished subsequently or diverted to some other subject",[34] and the unavailability of Urdu textbooks has resulted in the "total disuse of Urdu in the State of Uttar Pradesh, except for the backyard of the traditional madrasa-maktab system."[35]

3. No salvation without English?

3.1. The market realities

Between center and periphery, between mass and elite, is the compromise difficult to find or is it simply impossible to find? How indeed could an equal weight be given to the official language, the regional language and the mother tongue, to English and to Hindi, when universities have systematically imposed English as a teaching medium and as a medium for evaluation during exams for all scientific subjects including human sciences?[36] The very notion of university in India is linked with the success of the pro-English modernists in the early 19th century, and the foundation in 1857 of the first universities, in Bombay, Calcutta, Madras, with their deemed colleges, corresponds right from the beginning to the exclusive valorisation of English – to such an extent that the vernacular languages were totally suppressed, even as a subject, from the curricula in Bombay university in 1862. The Indian university tradition was born from the conviction that it was impossible to teach modern knowledge and do scientific research in local languages, although as soon as 1843 Delhi College (the very College stigmatized by Macaulay) had produced numerous reference books in the various fields of mathematics, from trigonometry to algebra, as well as in astronomy, blood circulation, or various technologies such as water mills, steam boats, etc., thanks to the efforts of Ramchandra et Munshi Zakaullah (Habib 1998: 348-352). Given the reluctance against Hindi in Dravidian surroundings and against regional languages in Hindi speaking surroundings, English finally remains the only language creating unanimity all over India in secondary schools. If, as noted by

Pandit in 1977, "mandatory bilingualism" fails whereas grassroot bilingualism is a traditional speciality of India, it is because the choice of English, in conformity with its exclusive use in higher education, does not need to be imposed.

Whatever the strength of 'linguistic loyalties', the passion for English has today stronger reasons, whether institutional or economic, than in colonial India. It is no longer conceivable to acquire a thoroughly vast culture without English, whereas it was still conceivable until Independence.

It is English and not Hindi which is the language of government and administration, a choice largely due to the artificial character of Hindi's syntactical and lexical modernization (Koul 1994). Consequently it is English and not Hindi (nor other regional languages) which leads to attractive careers, Hindi being an advantage only at the lower grades of the civil service. In the federal government for instance, mail is systematically written in English (almost 95% of it), and this even when answering letters, written in Hindi. Debates in Parliament are held in English, and the language in the Supreme and High Courts is English – in conformity with the provisions in the Constitution, providing there is no objection from Parliament (article 348). In prestigious examinations leading to top careers in administration such as the Indian Administrative Service (IAS), excellence in English is more and more a pre-requisite. Already in 1965, 18% of the candidates admitted where from Tamil Nadu only, a State which had only 8% of the national population but more English medium schools than many others. Reversely, there was not a single candidate admitted from Gujarat, a State which at that time had not developed English medium education. During the eighties, a notable decrease in the proportion of successful Tamil candidates appeared to be related with a decrease in the English level in the schools of the State. As expected, the ratio between the population and the candidates admitted in IAS is particularly high in the Northern States where English medium schools are a tradition. Regarding the very prestigious scientific examination of the Indian Institutes of Technology (IIT), it is theoretically acceptable for a candidate to present without an excellent level in English, but such cases are very rare, an indication that scientific excellence is formed only in English medium schools. Among those rare cases of students who have chosen Hindi and not English, the example of Shyam Rudra Pathak is interesting: he submitted in 1885 a 96 pages memoir on bio-gas written in Hindi. The memoir was not evaluated, a series of contestations and even trial went as far as to reach Parliament, and the affair was disclosed in the medias. A translation was asked, which the Institute did not provide quickly, so that the affair dragged on for years, giving time to the unhappy candidate for losing his job at Tata Electronic & Co....[37]

Whatever the field of specialization (except for regional literatures), there is no doubt that being educated in English is a great advantage for practical purposes. And indeed, education in English medium school has increased at a very quick pace during the last years: national enrolment in the upper primary sections (grads I to VIII) of English medium schools rose by 74% between 2003 and 2006, according to the National University for Education Planning and Administration (NUEPA). The highest jump is recorded in Tamil Nadu and Maharashtra.[38]

If at the end of the 19th century the wish for mastering English echoed the "service seeking mania", not without servility, according to its detractors, then today the lucrative job mania even more requires English. The blooming proliferation of the call centers in big cities during the last decade is a particularly striking example. For a few hundred rupees you can buy the directions for use, the first of such pamphlets has been published in a book form in 2004 by Arjun Raina, under the significant title: *Speak Right for a Call Center Job: A Complete Guide for International Interface.*

Among the some thirty call centers based in Delhi, the ten biggest employ between 1000 and 5000 employees, the smallest have between 40 and 50 employees. These delocalized call centers, which control the sales by phone for American and British companies have as their customers distant buyers who may be residents in London, Toronto, Manchester or any western English speaking city. The operator who answers them on the phone must not only speak in a non regional English[39], which he/she learns during the formation, an intensive training of four to six week, but also know the commercial rivals in the given sector, the name of all the relevant shopping centers and their location there, the legal systems prevailing in the country if for instance he sells life insurance contracts, and he must have a minimal knowledge in law in order to minimize the possible contestations or grievance regarding insufficient or wrong information. The center Infovision in Delhi provides various formations in the form of intensive trainings (8-10 hours a day) according to the degree of qualification aimed at (that is to say the kind of sell and the variety of customers dealt with by the operator once properly qualified) and according to the level of the candidate. The center selects only thirty among the some 300 persons who apply for the job as "Anglophone" candidates; the criteria for qualification are speed, perfectibility and linguistic competence rather than diplomas. Salaries vary from a minimum of 7000 rupee without extra (3 to 4 thousands) for a beginner with no previous experience to 25 to 35 000 Rs after two years experience. The staff is provided transportation in private car and food during working hours[40]. Progression is thus far quicker than in any other job, in the short term, but such well-paid jobs have their drawbacks: jobs in call centre are highly unstable (they are often chosen by brilliant students in order to self finance their studies), they always result in tension, fatigue, lack of long term perspective as well as boredom too, so that very few people stay more than two years in call centres. The risk of jeopardizing one's studies as well as health risk (high blood pressure particularly) has caused in the recent years many colleges to ban call center recruiters from campus, like Venkateshwara College in Delhi. Yet the boom is powerful enough to have been staged in May 2008 at a Belgian theatre (Inabox de Hang) in *Call...Cutta* by the Berlin collective Kaegi and Wetzel with the Rimini Protokoll, which shows a girl operating for Descon in Bangalore.

Although English may enable people to earn quick money and is still the language of power as well as of the national and international markets, the lower working exchanges at work are almost entirely in Indian languages and dialects. It is true in the agricultural universe which still largely dominates India (4/5), but it is also true in industrial surroundings: various lingua franca are reported to develop there among workers from various origins, which differ from the standard official Hindi almost as much as from English. According to Jason Baldrige's enquiry [(1996) 2002] on the verbal interaction among workers between themselves and with their immediate superiors in the TISCO Company of Jamshedpur[41], the lingua franca developed by the workers is a simplified Hindi which integrates various dialectal and regional words in a language mixture closer to a pidgin than to any specific mother tongue spoken by a given community there. Such pidgins, which are determined by the necessities of communication and not by official directives, exist all over India. Some are quite well known, such as the speeches used in big cosmopolitan megalopolis (Bombay Hindi or Calcutta Hindi), or in big slums such as Dharavi in Bombay where Marathis, Biharis, Tamils and Kannadigas mix and interact daily together. But there are also non urban lingua franca such as the Sadari in the tribal Bihar and Orissa developed by tribes with non inter-intelligible Austric mother tongues which have chosen an Indo-Aryan non standard speech for the basis of their common language rather than any of their own languages or any regional standardized language in order to be able to trade with all other tribal communities in Orissa or Bengal as well. Some of these speeches have been described as

Languages of Wider Communication, between pidgins and creoles, by Acharya and al. (1987). Other, such as Nagamese (a mixture of Indo-Aryan Assamese and various Tibeto-Burman Naga languages) have already become full fledged creoles, and have their own channels in the medias (radio or TV) with a wide and diverse sphere of use (Shridhar 1975, 1985).

It is not English which is used as an inter-language at the grassroot level neither for economic transactions nor for daily exchange. The major regional languages are no more used for these purposes, at least not in their standardized form which is the one taught in school. This standardized formal level of the languages (Hindi particularly but other major regional languages too), far from really allowing communication between the various dialectal speeches at a grassroot level, has usually resulted in the same perverse side effects as had previously Persian before 1836 or later English for low educated classes. Hindi is probably the most striking case, since it subsumes extremely different regional varieties (331 according to Srivastava 1994) and it is the official language in some of the less literate States in Northern India (Rajasthan, Bihar, Uttar Pradesh). The imposition of standard Hindi, in the first years of primary school, to children whose mother tongue is a so-called "dialect" of Hindi non recognized as a teaching medium, amounted to creating what some scholars labelled semi-lingualism or even a-lingualism.[42]. Such is for instance the case of Bundelkhandi speakers, a "dialect" of Hindi spoken in Madya Pradesh[43] and of Chattisgarhi speakers, another "dialect" of Hindi influenced by Dravidian tribal languages[44]. Practically, the use of standard Hindi as a medium in schools, far from reducing the distance between official Hindi and regional Hindis ("local speeches"), dramatized the consequences of this distance, by lowering the status of such speeches[45]. A similar conclusion was reached by Tiwari (1995), in a report published in the *International Journal of Dravidian Linguistics* after it spent ten years unnoticed by the very commission which had asked for it. The title itself is very much telling: "Linguistic deprivation among the socially disadvantaged in Bihar". The author shows that the children from lower-middle and lower classes, who master only to their 'dialectal' speeches (Bhojpuri, Magahi, Maithili), cannot manage to master standard Hindi, and remain limited to the 'restricted code' (in Bernstein's terms); this language restriction increases their economical distress, preventing them to ever become "empowered" actors in a region known for its feudal ways. Nambissan (2000) convincingly argues that dalit and tribal children are not given equality of chance at school due, largely, to the negative attitude towards their native language, an attitude fostered by the competitive dynamic in favour of 'powerful' languages as well as by the implicit power of the market. The role played by market forces in this attrition process of minor languages (Romaine 2002), particularly the role of the Structural Adjustment Program (SAP) imposed by the New Economy Policy has been rightly emphasized by Hasnain (2006a), making the provisions for protecting "endangered" languages more and more irrelevant: "if the dominant group is not going to get benefits from [it], the policy will not be implemented at all (...) No language can escape the wrath of linguistic market". On the whole, "developmentalism and the power of development in the context of restructured globalized world have far reaching implications, much more than the colonial mission of "civilizing the barbaric natives'" (Hasnain 2006b).

3.2. *Attitudes in front of such realities: what about language as something else than a market?*

With the above mentioned consequences of teaching in the language(s) of power only, we are back to the initial schism between the ruling elite and the mass of the dominated people: the persistence in India of English as the lingua franca of politics, education and commerce, notes Di Bona (1998: 370), echoes or results from a persisting schism between the world of success and achievement and the larger world of those left alongside the road to success. To know English means to belong to the elite, not to know English means being relegated in the provincial margins of intellectual life, the road for success today is English, as it was in 1850, and government school teaching in regional languages are left to those who cannot afford English medium private schools. Education in the major languages only, and particularly in English, has resulted in increasing this schism and marginalizing more and more the disadvantaged, which constitute the bulk of the 19% dropping-out schoolboys in primary schools today. That is why Di Bona (1998) concluded in condemning English education as "deeply anti-democratic", as well as did Gandhi in his own terms (see infra).

It is fairly clear how the new competitive dynamics of languages, supported by the institutionalization and politization of the language hierarchies, echoes the change in the social tissue, more and more distant from the old pattern which was the soil for the traditional grass root multilingualism. The reasons for the proliferation of enquiries and critical analysis of the school system, aiming at improving literacy rates (still around 50%, with huge disparities between urban and rural populations, haves and have-nots, boys and girls), are also obvious: what is at stake is the fate of the lower classes, hence the possibility of a truly social democracy in India.

Given the depth and width of the question, it may be vain to summarize the sociolinguistic studies quantifying and comparing the subjective attitudes of speakers vis-a-vis English and major regional languages in the various areas of verbal interaction (family, friends, school, university, entertainment, work, etc.), because they are only concerned, by necessity, with a very limited sampling of the population and cannot represent the mass.[46] It may equally be irrelevant, in this context, to collect the various contexts for code-switching with English: whether one enjoys or hates the new "Hinglish", the language of the English speaking urban bourgeois classes in the Hindi belt, propagated by Z TV for instance, it has hardly any relation with the "Hirdu" claimed by some scholars to re-unite the common origin and history of the two languages separated by politics. It may finally be vain also, in this context, to analyse the degree and forms of the native "appropriation" of the Indian "brown" English.[47] The point is that the Indian masses, crucial as they are for the national project of the Founding Fathers who made the Constitution of India, do not master English, and do not master the regional standard when their mother tongue is a minor language or a local variety of the regional language, and are, finally, illiterate up to about 50%.[48] Has the national project of the fifties been successfully implemented, we may wonder.

This project aimed at protecting minority rights by a politic of positive discrimination, while at the same time promoting the notion of a secular democratic nation, a difficult contradiction between the wish to erase group specificities (the section of the Fundamental Rights constructs a notion of citizenship devoid of any reference to cast, religion, language, etc.) and the wish to protect disadvantaged groups (the section of the Minority Rights emphasizes these specific references). The very idea of protecting disadvantaged groups implies of course that they are constructed into identified categories – whether thinking of languages (non scheduled or minor languages as opposed to scheduled languages) or of social groups (SC, ST, OBC).[49] As a matter of fact, the construction of distinctive categories has been shown to increase, leading to the making of "inner boundaries", from colonial India throughout Independent India, both in the field of religion (Hasan 2005) and of languages (Montaut 2005). Linguistically, what increased too was the deficit of the disadvantaged in favour of the Anglophone elite.

If we now try to answer the question of language attitudes in light of this question, we could start listening to the more personal reflections of some of the main actors of Indian culture now. For lack of space here, I will only consider the two extremes.

The first position is Shashi Tharoor's, already mentioned above.

Tharoor views English as the ideal and in fact the only vehicle for expressing the nation, an idea of the nation in disjunction from any community belonging which ordinarily stems for a particular local language and culture. The English language is thus paradoxically associated with the expression of secular democracy, in a context where communalism is more and more perceived as a disintegrative force threatening democracy. Tharoor's vision, unaware of his own cast until other schoolboys question him about it, is not radically different from Nehru's, and does not fully embrace the position of the optimistic neo-liberal or of the businessmen who only care for immediate profit, even at the cost of their own people, sold to the interests of a globalization which directly serves a tiny fringe of the population, and indirectly a more considerable minority (the middle class), but never the lower classes. The way Tharoor relays Nehru's ideology is eloquent in its soberness (2000: 15): commenting Nehru's address on the Independence night, right after the Partition blood bath, he emphasizes its last sentence – "it is fitting that at this solemn moment we take the pledge of dedication to the service of India and her people and to the still larger cause of humanity" – as characteristic of an elevated thought. Such a "dedication" finds no room in group identities, since they define us by what divides, and make us believe that it is more important to be a Muslim, a Bodo or a Yadav than an Indian. When our politicians, he goes on, have created a discourse loudly claiming for Assam for Assamese, Jharkhand for Jharkhandis, Maharashtra for Marathis, who still believes in an India for Indians? (2000: 58). In such a view, the nation, its English voice, non-alighment, are consonant with democracy. But the inherent contradictions in its very foundation of the Constitution pave in a certain manner the way for those politicians who are today blamed for threatening the principle of secularism.

This viewpoint is radically confronted by many intellectuals who, since Gandhi, have experienced English as alienation: "The pillory began with the fourth year", says Gandhi. "I know now that what I took four years to learn of Arithmetic, Algebra, Chemistry and Astronomy, I should have learnt easily in one year, if I had not to learn them through English but Gujarati. My grasp of the subjects would have been easier and clearer. My Gujarati vocabulary would have been richer. I would have made use of such knowledge in my own home. This English medium created an impassable barrier between me and the members of my family, who had not gone through English schools. (...) I was fast becoming a stranger in my own home".[50] Ray too, a well-known chemist, tried to oppose in 1932 education in a foreign language, foreign therefore bound to extinguish all creativity and originality: "Imagine for a moment what would happen if the English lads were compelled, first of all, to learn Persian or Chinese, and then had to read through the medium of such a tongue".

The depth of the ensuing alienation, has been described by the Anglophone writer Keki Daruwala: "Colonial history shows that language can be as domineering as any occupational army. It supplants myths, whole iconographies, world-view, ideology. It ushers in its own symbols and its own values. An armada of new texts sails in. Old dogmas and bigotries are swept away and exchanged for new ones."[51] What is at stake is a deep modification of cognitive schemes, which may also permeate Indian languages and produce novels simply translating into the bhashas Western mentalities and forms of knowledge (Rao 1995)[52]. The educational and institutional system of the country now carries on the Western modern frames favoured by the colonial then national "great narrative" in such a way that it is even possible to ignore English and still be 'translated' by English and western values.

At the bottom of this alienation, variously described by its victims and similarly analysed, is a conflict between cognitive and perceptual patterns: the Western rational consciousness, which has been inherited from the colonial past by the Indian national ideology, relies on the externalization and objectification of the very notion of "culture", whereas such an externality is totally alien to the indigenous perception. The "Indian" feeling of belonging as an empathic relation with the moving intertwined layers of shared knowledge, beliefs and symbol, nature and culture, experienced from within and not seen as an historical legacy, experienced from the outside, has been described by many writers from as different intellectual and social stocks as A. Coomaraswamy, Nirmal Verma (2000: *India and Europe*), Ashis Nandy (1980: *The intimate Enemy*), Anantha Murthy (2008), Gandhi, as well as by foreigners such as Richard Lannoy (*The Speaking Tree*) or Eric Erikson (on Gandhi). In the absence of clear-cut demarcation between the outside and the inside, the I and the objects, man is not to be conceived as the central dominating figure in the universe but as a place for interrelation with the whole of the living (and non living) beings in the creation. As a part of the whole which gives him his identity as much as a man contributes to giving its identity to the other components of the whole, mankind participates in a global ecosystem where social equity and respect for nature cannot be separated from the local beliefs and their expression in myths or folk tales. The "Indian environmentalist credo" (Agarwal 1994), by offering strong alternatives to the western developmental conceptions, without any statu-quo-ist nostalgias towards past models, and by digging innovative solutions from the wealth of tales and folk wisdom, confirms that the regional and local languages convey specific creative categories and mental frames. The whole work of Anupam Mishra (2007), in Hindi, is a witness for such creativity, particularly in the Rajasthani culture and idioms, giving ample evidence that we don't think the same in a regional language, taking into its folds the whole of the folk and literate culture, and in English. But a dialogue can start, as proved by the social forum in Bombay, between both modes of thinking, if the English culture/ language is not given absolute prevalence – indeed is treated as one of the many non central traditions that India has incorporated for centuries.[53]

Conclusion: the real predicament

If English becomes the only medium for 'real' serious education[54], such a chance for dialogue vanishes and the above commented schism has more and more dramatic consequences. Twenty years ago in a remarkable paper, the Hindi writer Krishna Baldev Vaid, who was then a professor of American literature in the US, developed the consequences of that growing schism associated with the growth of secondary English medium schools. He starts wondering why English failed allowing India its legitimate place within the cultural, particularly literary dialogue between cultures in the world: why is the dialogue not in equal terms? Why (and even today when English Indian literature seemingly achieved that goal) are the regional literatures still ignored by their legitimate partners in the West, which is not the case for Chinese or Japanese literatures, with practically no evolution since 1950, although English should have helped transcending the de-colonization misunderstandings and bitterness. He then notices that English has created an "enchanted circle" and imposed among Indians a mode of communication which bans the majority of Indians out of its "enchanted circle". Leaving aside the unprivileged, most writers themselves largely ignore the creation going on in regional cultures other than theirs. Among our own literatures, he says, we know only the literature written in our mother tongue, or poor (English) translations of other literatures; *because we have relied on English,* we have failed creating a culture of literary translation and consequently failed establishing an internal dialogue among Indian cultures. Symmetrically, our cultural relations with the West have impoverished by getting limited to this "enchanted world", and have perverted the way we perceive each other.[55] Without acknowledging (and first knowing) what is going on intellectually and culturally outside the enchanted circle, there will be no scope for a true dialogue (in equal terms) with the West. The prerequisite for the international dialogue is of course the inner dialogue, which means, in the matter, gapping the schism created by English.

The state of affairs in translation is certainly far better today than twenty years ago, although there are still not enough direct translations between regional languages, but what has on the contrary fast worsened is the state of cultural awareness and knowledge, as stated by Pollock (2003: 3) regarding the state of scholarly knowledge on literary culture:

> With different historical and textual critical methods added to the traditional repertory, vernacular intellectuals well into the 20th century produced works of enormous learning evincing mastery of the entire history of their traditions. Over the past fifty years, however, the ranks of this category of scholar have gradually diminished – so much so that the study of South Asian literary archives in their historical depths has lost two generations of scholars. There is now good reason to wonder whether the next generation will even be able to read Pingal texts in old Gujarati or *riti kavya* in Brajbhasha or ghazals in Indo-Persian. After a century and a half of Anglicization and a certain kind of modernization, it is hardly surprising that the long histories of South Asia literatures no longer find a central place in contemporary knowledge in the subcontinent itself, however much a nostalgia for the old literary cultures and their traditions may continue to influence popular culture.

Such an anxiety is not only valid for the scholarly sphere of production: the state of the educational machinery also affects the roots of creation. By no means does it result in endangering the constitutional languages, at least those having a regional status of major language: the market for Hindi and Malayali books is flourishing, to take only extreme cases in the scale of literacy in major languages, but most of Malyali printing consists in translations of the cheapest American literature or Japanese mangas, whereas we could recently find in the Hindu as an example of the revival in Hindi writing a full column of Ramdas' 50th novel, a very poor accumulation of clichés and artificial imagination with equally poor and artificial language.[56] So, if "heavy" regional languages are not endangered as tools for communication, they are quickly ceasing (they already have ceased?) to voice Indian civilisation, if Indian civilisation relies on the complex and rich links between *mārg* and *deshi* culture, respectively the "frontyard" of the "high" culture and the "backyard" of the "little" traditions, in Ananthamurthy's words (2008: 198-9).

> The tradition of lively dialectical contention between the royal highway and the indigenous in India will be marginalized if globalization encroaches over everything: if everything looses out to the corporate world. This is the danger in India today. Even Yadavs, who are supposedly born into the lowly but noble cast of Krishna in India, have begun to rule in the manner

> of barbarians. Even the so-called sons of the soil, such as the Shiv Sena in Mumbay, seem only to eager to sign a memorandum of understanding with polluting and exploitative industries which threaten to deplete the fertile backyard. There is still a fertile backyard. But if this continues, there will be no place for either a leisurely frontyard or for a dark and fertile backyard, in the industrial and corporate no-man's land which we increasingly inhabit in India today.

Along with Anglicization and within the "certain kind of modernization" mentioned by Pollock, we can range language modernization, specially for Hindi, which evolved into such a lexically Sanskritized and syntactically or discursively Anglicized cryptic construct that it totally lost touch with the lived-in culture of people: "the new Hindi is a dead language", said U.N. Tiwari as soon as the mid sixties, becoming alien to the writers who started living in a Hindi lived-in culture such as Kamleshwar, Krishna Sobati, Krishna Baldev Vaid opened to the Urdu and Panjabi culture and language (Bhalla 2006). A dire statement echoed by Agnihotri (2002: 33) more than ten years ago, commenting the politization of the mutual alienation of Hindi and Urdu: "by the 1990s, the linguistic consequences of these primarily political moves were becoming increasingly transparent. A new generation had grown up: unfamiliar not only with Ghalib and Faiz but also with Kabir and Premchand; nor could they understand Prasad or Nirala (...); the staple diet was Bombay film Hindi. The damage that inevitably accompanies the loss of literary sensitivity in a community is there for everyone to see".

REFERENCES

Agarwal, Anil 1994. An Indian Environmentalist Credo. In Guha (ed.) *Social ecology*, Oxford University Press: 346-386.

Agnihotri, Ramakant 2002. On a pre-partition partition: the question of Hindi-Urdu. In *Pangs of partition: The human dimension*, Vol. 2, S. Settar and L.B. Gupta (eds.) New-Delhi: Council of Historical Research and Manohar, 29-46.

Ananthamurthy, U.R. 2008. M. Manu Chakrawarthy (ed.) *Omnibus*. Delhi : Arvind Kumar Publishers.

Bhalla, Alok 2006. *Partition dialogues*. Delhi: Oxford University Press.

Bhattacharya, Sabyasachi (ed.) 1998. *The contested terrain. Perspectives in education in India*, Delhi: Orient Longman.

Bhokta, Naresh Prasad 1998. Marginalisation of Popular Languages and Growth of Sectarian Education in Colonial India. In Bhattacharya (ed.) 201-216.

Daruwala, Keki N. 1995. The Decolonized Muse. In Shantinaath K. Desai (ed.) *Creative aspects of Indian English*, Delhi: Sahitya Akademi: 30-34.

Di Bona, Joseph 1998. Going Back to the Educational Future Using Indigenous ideas to meet the Challenge of the 21st Century. In Bhattacharya (ed.) 357-379.

Dua, Hans Raj 1986. *Language use, attitudes and identity among linguistic minorities: A case study of Dakkhini Urdu speaker in Mysore*. Mysore: Central Institute of Indian Languages.

Dvivedi, S. 1981. *Hindi in trial*. Delhi: Vikas.

Emeneau, M.B. 1980. *Language and linguistic area*. Delhi: Motilal Banarsidass.

Ferguson, Charles A. 1959. Diglossia. *Word* 15, 325-340.

Fishman, Joshua 1967. Bilingualism with and without diglossia; diglossia with and without bilingualism. *Journal of Social Issues* 23, 29-38

Garg, B.R. 2001. *Policy documents on Indian education*, Delhi: The Associated Publishers.

Ghosh, Suresh Chandra 2000. (rev. ed.) *History of education in modern India; 1757-1998*. Delhi: Orient Longman.

Gupta, R.S., A. Abbi and K.S. Aggarwal (eds.) 1995. *Language and the State: Perspectives on the Eighth Schedule*. Delhi: Creative Books.

Habib, Irfan 1998. Teaching Sciences through the Local Language. In Bhattacharya (ed.) 342-353.

Hasan, M. 2000. *Inventing boundaries*. Delhi: Oxford University Press.

Hasan, M. and A. Roy 2005. *Living together separately: Cultural India in history and politics*. Delhi: Oxford University Press.

Hasnain, S. Imtiaz and K.S. Rajyashree 2004. Hindustani as an anxiety between Hindi-Urdu commitment: Linguistic engineering of language patterns. *The Year Book of South Asian Language and Linguistics* (Mouton de Gruyter): 247-265.

Hasnain, S. Imtiaz 2006a. Minority Rights and Education: Question of Survival of Minority Languages. In Joseph Benjamin (ed.) *Minorities in Indian social system*, Vol. I-II. New Delhi: Gyan Publishing House. Also at *Language in India* http://www.languageinindia.com.

Hasnain, S. Imtiaz 2006b. Globalization- Language, Culture and Media: Some Reflections. In B.N. Patnaik and S. Imtiaz Hasnain (eds.) *Globalization: Language, culture and media*. Shimla: Indian Institute of Advanced Study.

India. 2002. Delhi, Ministry of Information and Broadcasting in India.

Jain, M.P. 2003. (rev. ed.) *Indian Constitutional Law*. Delhi, Wadhwa.

Jha, Hetukar 1998. Decline of Vernacular Education in Bihar in the 19th Century. In Bhattacharya (ed.) 218-228.

Kachru, Braj 1986. *The Indianization of English. The English language in India*. Delhi: Oxford University Press.

Kachru, Braj 1997. World Englishes and English-using Communities, *Annual Review of Applied Linguistics* 17: 66-87.

Khilnani, Sunil 1997. *The idea of India*. Delhi: Oxford University Press.

Koul, Omkar N. (ed) 1994. *Language development and administration*. Delhi: Creative.

Khubchandani, L.M. 1997. *Revisualizing boundaries. A plurilingual ethos*. Delhi: Sage Publications.

Khubchandani, L.M. 1991. *Language, culture and nation building: Challenges of modernization*. Shimla: Indian Institute of Advanced Study.

Krishna, Sumi 1991. *India's living languages: The critical issues.* Delhi: Allied Publishers.

Le Page, Robert & A. Tabouret Keller 1985. *Acts of identity: Creole-based approaches to language and ethnicity.* Cambridge : Cambridge University Press.

Le Page, Robert 1992. You can never tell where a word comes from: language contact in a diffuse setting, in Hgkon Yahr Ernst (ed.) *Language contact: Theoretical and empirical studies.* Berlin/New York: Mouton de Gruyter, 71-102.

Mallikarjun, B. 1995. The 8th Schedule : A critical Appraisal. In Gupta et al (eds.): 59-83.

Mishra, Anupam 2007. Bhaashaa aur paryaavaran. In *Saaf maathe kaa samaaj,* Delhi: Penguin India (Hindi), 1-5.

Montaut, Annie 2005. Colonial Language Classification, Postcolonial Language Conflicts and the Grassroot Multingualism. In Hasan and Roy (eds.).

Mukherjee, Aditi 1996. *Language maintenance and language shift: Punjabis and Bengalis in Delhi,* New Delhi: Bahri Publications.

Nambissan, Geetha B. 1995. Language and Schooling of Tribal Children : Issues Relating to Medium of Instruction. In Gupta et.al (eds.) 178-200.

Nambissan, Geetha B. 2000. Language and Schooling of Tribal Children: Issues Relating to the Medium of Instruction, *Economic and Political Weekly* XXIX (42).

Pandit, P.B. 1977. *Language in a plural society.* Delhi: Dev Raj Chanana Memorial Committee.

Pattanayak D.P. 1991. *Multilingualism in India.* Avon, Multilingual Matters, 61.

Rai, Alok 2000. *Hindi nationalism.* Delhi : Orient Longman.

Rai, Amrit 1987. *A house divided.; the origin and development of Hindi/Hindavi.* Delhi : Oxford Universisty Press.

Raina, Arjun 2004. *Speak right for a call center job: A Complete Guide for International Interface.* Delhi, Penguin India.

Rajyashree, K.S. *An ethnolinguistic study of Dharavi: A slum in Bombay.* Mysore: Central Institute of Indian Languages. n.d.

Ramanujan, A.K. 1999. *The collected essays.* V. Darwadker (ed.) Delhi: OUP.

Rani, Asha 2004. Languages as a Marker of Religious Difference. In Imtiaz Ahmad and Helmut Reifeld (eds.) *Lived Islam in South Asia: Adaptation, accommodation and conflict.* Delhi; Social Science Press.

Rao, Ragavendra K. 1995. Translation, the Fate of Colonial Bilingualism. In Desai (ed.) *Creative aspects of Indian English.* Dehli, Sahitya Akademi: 26-91.

Romaine, Suzanne 1995. *Bilingualism.* Blackwell.

Romaine, Suzanne 2002. The Impact of Language Policy on Endangered Languages, *International Journal of Multilingual Societies* 4 (2), 194-212.

Saxena, S. and K. Mahendru 1995. Politics of Language. In Gupta et. al (eds.): 144-151.

Sharma, R.N. 2000-2001. *Indian education into millenium.* Delhi: Subhi Publications.

Shreedhar, M.V. 1975. *Naga Pidgin: A Socio-linguistic study of interlingual commicational pattern in Nagaland.* Mysore, Central Institute of Indian Languages.

Shreedhar, M.V. 1985. *Standardized grammar of Naga Pidgin*. Mysore: Central Institute of Indian Languages.

Shukla, Suresh Chandra 1998. Nationalist Educational Thought: Continuity and Change. In Bhattacharya (ed.) 29-53.

Srivastava, R.N. 1994. *Literacy and bilingualism*. Delhi: Kalinga Publications.

Thakur, R.N. 1999. *Plight of the minorities: Problems and grievances in their education*. New-Delhi: Gyan Publishing House.

Tharoor, Shashi 2000 [1997]. *India*. Delhi: Penguin India.

Thirumalai, M.S. and B. Mallikarjun (eds.) 2002. *Language in India*. vol. 2, online (3 May), site consultÈ le 14 sept 2004.

Thirumalai, M.S. et al (eds.) 2003. *Language in India* vol. 3, online (5 May), site consultÈ le 14 sept 2004.

Tiwari, K.M. 1995. Linguistic Deprivation among the socially Disadvantaged in Bihar. *International Journal of Dravidian Linguistics*, juillet : 8-81.

Tiwari, U.N. 1961 (1995). *Hindii bhaashaa kaa udgam aur vikaas*. Delhi: Lokbharati Prakashan.

Vaid, Krishna Baldev 1988. The Burden of Ambivalence, *Bahuvachan* 1. Vaid, Swaminathan and Vajpeyee (eds.) : 87-94.

Verma, Nirmal 2000. *India and Europe*. Shimla: IIAS.

NOTES

1. The complete text of the minute is available on-line: the original reason prompting this momentous report was the concern about the use of the British financial support in educational institutions, particularly the "misuse" of it in Delhi College and Banares Hindu College for Persian and Sanskrit respectively, both curricula leading to the unemployment of the graduates and an intellectual bend towards obscurantism and non-modernism, thus considered as useless studies.
2. The available data is not as important as expected, and lacks reliability: "there is little information on the extent of knowledge of English in India. Books abound on the place of English in the Indian educational system, job competition, and culture; and on its socio-linguistic aspects, pronunciation and grammar, its effect on Indian languages, and Indian literature in English. Little information is available, however, on the number of people who "know" English and the extent of their knowledge, or even how many people study English at school" (website of the US Library of Congress).
3. The category of NRI (Non Resident Indians), is commonly re-spelled in parody by the resident Indians as "Not Really Indian" or "Never Relinquished India".
4. Of the twenty languages officially recognized (Manipuri, Nepali, Assamese, Bengali, Oriya, Urdou, Marathi, Konkani, Gujarati, Sindhi, Panjabi, Kashmiri, Sanskrit, Telugu, Kannada, Tamil, Malayalam, Santhali, Chattisgarhi, plus Hindi outside the list of the VIIIth Schedule) and used in administration, all were Indo-Aryan or Dravidian until 1994, when Manipuri was the first Tibeto-Burmese language to be officially

recognized as a "constitutional language", before Santhali for the new State of Jharkhand (100th amendment of the Constitution), from the Auso-Asiatic family, in 2003 (100th amendment of the Constitution), Chattisgarhi being expected to be the official language in the new State of Chattisgarh. The four States whose official language is English are Meghalaya, Nagaland Sikkim and Tripura.

5. Khilnani (1997), in *The Idea of India,* has convincingly argued for the impossibility of defining the Indian nation on anything else than an abstract idea of the nation (that of Nehru), neither history, nor geography, nor local culture, nor religion, nor uses and lore, nor languages, allowing for a single homogeneous definition.
6. Whether the term "diglossia" is taken in its restricted meaning which was originally implied in Ferguson 1959 (two related languages, as for instance Singhalese in South Asia) or in its extended meaning as in Fishman 1967 (two possibly non related languages) or Romaine (1995).
7. Andhra Pradesh was officially created in 1953, after the death of Potti Sriramulu, the leader of Vishal Andhra, thus opening the not-yet-ended silsila of "bifurcations" (separation from a State on language basis), opposed by the Congress up to that time and since 1928 (JVP committee in 1948, Monford Commission, etc.) : after the State Reorganization in 1956, numerous "bifurcations" were still to come, and the creation of Jharkhand in 2002. See Montaut 2005.
8. Where they nurture their ancestral language better than Punjabis and less than Bengalis according to Mukherjee 1996.
9. An oft quoted example in the ample literature on the question since Pandit (1977) is that of the Gujarati merchant, who speaks the local variety of Gujarati at home, Kacchi and Konkani in his professional activities, as well as Marathi, who communicates in Hindi with the milkman and the railway employees, in English in more formal occasions, and uses sant bhasha in his religious practice when singing bhajans, along with old Hindi, Urdu, Persian and eventually Arabic if he is Muslim, Sanskrit and Braj if Hindu, who reads Gujarati newspapers and sometimes English, who hears Hindustani at the cinema hall.
10. Hindi or Bengali (IE) is then closer to Tamil (Dr) than to French or English (IE), Santhali, an Austric languaage, is closer to Bengali than to Austronesian languages. In the whole Indian family, retrofexes or cerebral consonants are phonologically opposed to dentals, word order is the same (final verb, postpositions and not preposition, anteposition of the genitive complement, anteposition of the adjective, postposition of verbal auxiliaries after the verbal base, causative derivation from intransitives, compound or serial verbs for expressing aspect and mental attitudes, reduplication with grammatical and expressive functions, "dative subjects", etc. A 30 pages bibliography is available in Montaut 1997 on these questions.
11. It is a different matter if we view things in a cultural or stylistic way of course (Kachru 1986).
12. Results of the 2001 Census not yet published.

13. Fifth All India Education Survey, 1992. For the proliferation of English medium schools (an average 75% increase between 2001 and 2006), see note 38. We must also take into account the considerable disparity between rural and urban zones (English is the first language in only 0,6% or rural schools, even if the proportions are almost equal for English as a second or third language in high schools).
14. Hindostanee or Hindustanee. The terms 'Hindi' ('Hinduī', 'Hindavī') and 'Urdu', often substitutes for 'Bakha' (lit. "language", were not yet (end of the 18th c. and early 19th c.) associated to the respectively Sanskritized or Persianized styles which marked the emergence of the written literature created out of the common speech of the Gangetic plain. On the contrary, one of the very first texts produced in these years, *Raanii Ketkii kii kahaanii*, The story of the Queen Ketki, by Inshallah Khan 'Insha', explicitly states in the prologue that the new language (hindi, hindavi) should avoid all words alien to Hindi, such as Sanskrit, Persian, Braj and regional dialectical words. On the complex question of the origin of the distinction of Hindi, Urdu, see Rai 1984, also Hasnain and Rajyashree, (2004).
15. This is what the Indo-Anglian writer Keki Daruwala humorously registers in his own way more than one and a half century later: "We are all trapped in History. The Europeans came to trade, hung on to fight, intrigue and conquer, and stayed on to instruct. Their colonies became markets for their textiles and their language. Conversions followed, to another way of life and on occasions to Christianity. When they went back, they left their language behind, and half-castes. In an alien land, language itself turns brown and half-caste... Colonial history shows that language can be as domineering as any occupational army. It supplants myths, whole iconographies, world-view, ideology. It ushers in its own symbols and its own values. An armada of new texts sails in. Old dogmas and bigotries are swept away and exchanged for new ones" (in Desai 1995: 30).
16. Most reformists societies (like the Brahmo Samaj of Ram Mohan Roy in Bengal and the Arya Samaj of Dayanand Saraswati in Panjab) reject bigotry, ritualization and superstitions (including local beliefs and popular devotion) and promote a coming back to the "purified" religion of ancient times (essentially vedic and vedantic), while in the social sphere they condemn castes, child marriage, sati, and seek to promote instruction for women, all features in consonance with the Western liberal philosophy.
17. Letter quoted in Garg (2001: 67). However, a (pre)reformist such as Bhartendu, a Hindi speaker from Benares, thinks on the contrary that the progress in the Hindi language and education in Hindi alone (in the region) can lead to progress and modernity, although by many sides his positions echo the reformists ones (faith in rationality and technological progress, in modernity, enthusiastic admiration of the 19th century British society for these achievements, etc.).
18. Macaulay goes so far as to compare the whole bulk of Sanskrit and Persian scientific, moral and philosophic literature to an obscure imbroglio, in order to oppose wasting public money in publishing "eastern" books,

and to blame Delhi College (Persian) and Sanskrit College for creating a population of jobless graduates useless to their country and to their own family.

19. Persian was given up as a court language in 1836 after numerous protests, since neither the accused nor the complaining person was usually able to understand the language used in trials, and in a more general way, the average man was unable to understand the language of administration. Italics by me.
20. Document quoted in its integrality by Garg (2001: 164-68).
21. For instance, the Bhumihar Brahma Sabha and All India Kayastha Sabha associations, respectively founded in 1889 and 1887, have the declared objective of developing education and social progress, but their practical intention is to promote cast interests.
22. All the movements directed against official power, that is, in India, Brahmanic orthodoxy, have succeeded in using the strength of the spoken folk language in order to express heterodoxical ideologies: it is particularly true for the various medieval *bhakti* movements which renewed the literary idioms by using the language spoken by the people including low cast people, but it had already been the case for Buddha using Pali and not Sanskrit to convey new ideas.
23. In 1918, he creates the *Dakshina Bharat Hindi Prachar Sabha*, to diffuse Hindi in South India. The oscillation in the denomination of the language, from Hindi to Hindustani, is linked with the complex politics of Hindi and Urdu and the positions Gandhi took in these (see Asha Rani 2004: "The category of Hindustani remained ambiguous and fuzzy in content while, at the same time, it was used as a category of political mobilization and collectivization of the two communities between 1920-40", 150)
24. An alternative (*yani, ya, athwa*) misunderstood or misused by both supporters of Hindi (who understood the equivalence Hindustani/Hindi as a way of accommodating Urdu in Hindi) and of Urdu (who understood Hindustani as a synonym for Hindi).
25. On the community of language uses in the zone, see the concept of fluid zone forged by que Khubchandani (1997) under the sign HUP (Hindi-Urdu-Punjabi); on the cultural community developed in the North West (Pakistani and Indian Panjab in particular), see the contributions of historians (Hasan 2000) and writers such as Krishna Sobati, Krishna Baldev Vaid, Kamleshwar interviewed in Bhalla 2006.
26. The situation is so explosive that Census at the time suppressed to mention Hindi and Urdu.
27. Followed on this ground by Nehru: "Hindi or Hindustani or whatever it is called. It is the content of the language that counts and not the name so much", notwithstanding that "no language is closer to Sanskrit than Persian" (National Herald, 13 February 1949).
28. Seth Govind Das and P.N. Tandon, who favour Sanskritized Hindi, do not hesitate to blame those who refuse nagari as a national script for betraying the nation. P.D. Tandon for instance writes on the 8th of April 1949 : "those who oppose acceptance of Hindi as a national language

and nagari as the single national script are still following a policy of anti-national appeasement". Similar accusations are still commonly heard in the form of suspicions against Muslims: "foreign script, alien culture, semitic language", etc. The presence of *Mein Kampf* in popular bazars (noted in the recent years and still 2007) may have indirect links with this conception of the Hindi language as an Aryan symbol opposed to Urdu as a semitic foreign symbol.

29. It is the language question (besides differed till the last year of the debates of the Constituent Assembly) which compelled Nehru to rely on votes and not to the consensus he privileged. And it is the question of the script, ultimately of the script for numerals, which was the more difficult of these votes, won by one voice only: "The question of numerals was the most controversial of all the issues debated in the Assembly" (Dvivedi, 1981 : 19).
30. Here is the text of Article 351, in view of developing Hindi "so that it may serve as a medium of expression of all the elements of the composite culture of India and to secure its enrichment by assimilating, without interfering with its genius, forms, style and expressions used in Hindustani and the other languages of India specified in the Eighth Schedule, and by drawing, whenever necessary or desirable, for its vocabulary, primarily from Sanskrit and secondarily from other languages".
31. Report of the Committee of Parliament on Official Language, quoted in Dvivedi (1980 : 210).
32. On this complex question of the role played by clear cut categories in the "Linguistic States" following the States Reorganisation Act of 1956 and its colonial antecedents, see Montaut 2005.
33. Pour reprendre une expression de Ragavendra Rao (1985).
34. Sources in *Muslim India* 9, 1983 (quoted in Hasnain 2006 a) : out of 211 posts in government schools for Urdu medium teachers, 53 are lying vacant, while, out of the remaining 158, 63 are occupied by non trained teachers who simply know Urdu.
35. Ansari, I.A., 1997, "Inadequacies of constitutional protection of minority languages in India", *in* S. Singh (ed.), *Language problem in India*, New-Delhi, Institute of Objective Studies. Quoted in Hasnain 2006 a.
36. A university can impose the use of a language other than English for exams only if it can prove that the level will not be downgraded because of this choice – which is generally the case for literature in Indian or other languages only – and the Supreme Court alone can take a final decision in case of contestation (Jain 2003 : 616).
37. Krishna 1991. Mallikarjun (1985 : 59-83) quotes numerous other cases, including in the field literacy. The National Literacy Mission conducts literacy campaigns in the regional languages, including Tulu in South Karnataka where it was a considerable success, but the national competition for essay in literacy and adult education is limited to Hindi and English. As for the admission exams for Management schools, they are all in English.

38. There are still more than half of the Indian school children who enrol in Hindi upper medium primary school (783,74, 227, or 52% in 2006, more than in 2003 where they were 50%). But the general tendency in the whole country is to shift from the regional language to English as shown by the decrease in the (nation wise) proportion of enrolled children from 2003 to 2006 (for Marathi, 9% to 8%, for Telugu, no change, 6%, for Tamil, 6% to 5%, for Gujarati, 5% to 4%, for Kannada, 4% to 2%, for Assamese 2%, no change, for Urdu, 2%, no change, for Malayalam, 3% to 2%). As expected, English medium primary school are massively dominating in the Northern States (90% of the schools).
39. If he answers from Delhi or Madras a British customer, the customer from Bedford or Soho is not aware of that, since he is simply calling a London electronic or paramedical company.
40. A waged tailor earned from 2 to 3000 rs, the minimal salary amounting to 30 rupees a day in agriculture et 50 in industry in 2003. Other call centres may pay less for beginners and slightly more for experienced workers (from about 180 to 500 dollars in Purple). During the last year an important crisis is reported to strike call centres because, on one hand, other job availabilities have recently opened (engineering), making student unemployment less dramatic and, on the other hand, the working conditions in call centres are more and more criticized, particularly on internet, people complaining of being pressurized and even verbally assaulted (racist insults).
41. Tata Iron and Steel Company, one of the most ancient industrial group which employs workers from several States of India.
42. Such cases have been commented by Geeta B. Nambissan ("Language and schooling of tribal children : issues relating to medium of instruction" in *Language and the state* (1985 : 178-200). See also Shailendra Kumar Singh "Suicide of language identity" (ibid. : 220-225). Theoretically, as part of the Minorities Rights in the Constitution of India (articles 29, 30), a given linguistic community has the right to register the children in a school using their language as teaching medium providing this language is recognized for such purposes and there are at least fourty children in the school and ten in the class. Practically, such directives are seldom implemented. None of the 100 tribal mother tongues spoken in Orissa is used in primary schools, although 81 were recognized as 'school medium' in 1981, 58 in 1990: Ho, Kurukh, Mundari, Kharia (Austro-Asiatic) as well as Maithili had, among others, been suppressed. Note that the same is true for some major languages when they happen to be in a the situation of minor languages in a district: this is particularly frequent for Urdu in Hindi-speaking States.
43. The Hoshangabad Science Teaching Program, which reaches 50 000 primary schools in the early nineties, records the following results: After five years in a Hindi school, the children are unable to understand and to communicate in the language, because the local variety of their 'Hindi' is linguistically very distant from the regional standard variety. Commenting these results, Sumi Krishna (1991: 92) concludes: "Hindi

had made these children inarticulate students". The distress of these children taught in Hindi when the standard variety is not their mother tongue can only compare with the distress recorded by Gandhi taught in English (see *infra*). Useless to say that in tribal zones the general result is a "linguistic de-tribalization". (1991: 72). The situation far from having improved, has rather further deteriorated, according to Udayan Narayan studies on the state of tribal languages (Communication in Jaipur festival, January 2008).

44. According to Saxena and Mahendru (1995), who supervised in the nineties a literacy program in Raipur district, the instructions given in the text books were not understood by the children, and even the simplified Hindi used by the field workers did not allow for communication. Although a specific text book in Chattisgarhi was available, thanks to the efforts of a group of young dynamic teachers, it was severely criticized as a potential trigger of disintegrative forces, and not used in the classroom. At the same time, most teachers felt that only the teaching in the standard language will free the pupils from their 'backwardness'. Even worse: the authors relate that two workers of a literacy campaign lost their jobs because they contested local elections in favour of the Kisan Mazdoor Sangathan against the powerful Malguzar family: when they were sanctioned out of their job, they were served a conference in purely *shoudh* Hindi mainly aimed at humiliating them. The situation is of course going to drastically change with the official recognition of the new State of Chattisgarh.
45. "Why does the police prepare charge sheets in unreadable language and always give a bad copy to the victims, specially if he or she is poor ? Why are land records maintained in such esoteric language that it requires a Patwari to interpret them, seldom without a bribe ? How could there be any communication in Hindi with people of Jhabua who are going to be affected by Sardar Sarovar ? How could a migrant worker of Chattisgarh explain her pain and suffering to a labour officer who does not understand Chhattisgarhi ? Standard languages divide society" (in Gupta & et. al, *Language and the state* (1995: 144-151). Jhabua belongs to the area where the Narmada dam has severely endangered the traditional patterns of life and society.
46. The results are quite divergent according to the populations and regions studied, Bengalis being probably the most attached to their mother tongue, and Panjabis at the other extreme (Mukhherjee 1996). According to Anniko Henthal ([1998] in Thirumalai 2003), conversations within the family among educated urban people occur mostly in the mother tongue, but Tamils alternate L1 and English whereas Bengalis do not. As for friendly conversations, they occur in English (41%), or in alternance L1/ English (65%), Hindi is exceptionally used among Tamils and Bengalis (for commenting Hindi programs seen on TV).
47. See on these points the pioneering work of Braj Kachru (1986) and his followers.
48. In spite of the many studies and statistics, it is difficult to exactly evaluate

the ratio of literacy in India, and there is considerable divergence in the figures (depending on what is meant by literate, loss of literacy following school dropping , etc.: 64% according to the more optimistic, National Readership Survey). According to Sharma (2000-2001) who compares various results, "about half of the population enters the millenium unable to sign their name, and the two thirds of this half are women. And Indian illiterate people are half of the world illiterate population. Just remember that only 53.04% villages have at least primary schools somewhere near by."

49. Scheduled Casts, Tribal Casts, Other Backward Casts and Tribes. What is a minority language is more ambiguous and no has ever been sought for according to Thakur ((1999: 28-9) quoted in Hasnain 2006a).
50. *Harijan* 1938.
51. Cf. note 15.
52. See also Ananthamurthy (2008) : "In reaction against the Orientalists and the westernisers, some of our very intelligent and sophisticated writers have created a new kind of work of art which, apparently, looks Indian and original. Yet, in a very subtle manner, these works are also Indian equivalents of western models. The conceptual framework into which the material is organized is western. The material is Indian – the details of life, the myths, the folklore, the legends are all there, but you feel, "Why should I read this after reading Kafka or Camus? You cannot borrow the style of form of these writers without their philosophy, their concept of man", reprinted from 1976, "The search for an Identity" (paper delivered at a seminar on "Identity and Adulthood", in IIT Delhi in 1976).
53. On this location of English culture as one of the many "subcultures" of India, see Nandy's *Intimate Ennemy* (1980: 60sq, 107). Ramanujan's vision of Indian culture as essentially 'reflexive" (1999: "Where mirrors are windows"), that is, proceeding by commentaries and critical re-readings as well as uncritical enrichments of the works of the past, commentaries which may be quite subversive, in an interactive and multilayered model, goes well with the vision of Indian culture as a mosaic of subcultures with no hierarchic center.
54. Which it is fast becoming : poor state of Government schools, explicit selection of English medium private school as the only access to success and "good life", etc.
55. My italics. Cf. also: "Intellectual inertia and educational errors that have landed us in this morass..."
56. Devoid of all the (bollywood-like) qualities which made the success of popular writers like Gulshan Nanda during the 70-80's.

6

Has Globalization Given a New Legitimacy to Diversity?

Paroo Nihalani

Introduction

One of the buzzwords of the 21st century is 'global connectivity'. Thanks to the revolution in communication technology, the entire universe today has become a tiny 'Global Village'. As markets and geographic barriers become increasingly blurred and even irrelevant, globalization is no longer an objective but imperative. The last five centuries or so have seen a radical transformation of the existing world order and the subsequent creation of the modern Global era that has inescapable interrelationships in virtually all spheres of activity such as economics, trade and commerce, industry, international diplomacy, communications, transport and travel, defense matters, education (science and technology), entertainment, etc. These global infrastructures in English have become the bases for the emergence of an *inextricably interconnected world* – a world we describe by the clichÈ: the 'global village'. The key word here is '*interdependence*'.

With the dawn of the Internet age and the trend towards globalization, proficiency in English is perceived as a crucial skill for survival. It is like a driver's license or computer skills. It is no longer sufficient to be literate in one's own local language. A monolingual society is en route to extinction and total isolationism in the modern world. Proficiency in English is necessary to be globally literate. Discerning parents therefore would admittedly like to give a bilingual edge to their children. Zhou Min, who hosts several English programs at the Beijing Broadcasting Station, says some pregnant women speak English to their foetuses in order to give their children a 'head-start'. Along with computers and mass migration, The English language has proved to be the turbine engine of globalization.

Global Spread: Multiple International Identities

In recorded history there has never been a language to match the present global spread and use of English (Strevens 1982, Quirk and Widdowson 1985, Kachru 1986, Smith 1983, 1986). The second half of the twentieth century has witnessed an emergence of institutionalized varieties such as 'English as an African language' and 'English as an Asian language'. New Englishes are mushrooming all over the world, ranging from Englong (Tagalog-infused English spoken in the Philippines) to Hinglish (the mixture of Hindi and English in India), Singlish (spoken in Singapore), Japlish in Japan and Spanglish (spoken in Spain). Who is to say what is 'real' English in a world where native speakers of British and American English are in a minority? There has never before been a language that has been spoken by more people as a second language than a first, observes David Crystal (1997). The new-English speakers are not just passively absorbing the language; they are *shaping* it. India, Nigeria, Singapore, South Africa, the Caribbean, and long ago America, have taken the language of their overlord and made it uniquely and distinctively their own. And by doing so, they are changing the world's definition of what it means to speak English. Veteran actor John Kani recently told the BBC: "We speak English with a Xhosa accent and a Xhosa attitude." In the words of Kachru (1986), "English has thus acquired, and is in the process of acquiring, multiple ownerships and multiple international identities." The English language has become a global product (an abstract entity like a phoneme) that has its various manifestations (allophones) available in different local flavors.

With the global spread of English, three most important related questions come to our mind:

(a) Variation and multi-cultural identity
(b) Intelligibility, and
(c) The pedagogical issue of an 'education target'.

With the demographic distribution of its speakers all over the world, *diversity* seems inevitable. It is at the phonological level that the New Varieties of English differ most from each other. The learner of English therefore is dealing with a language that offers a bewildering variety in its main transmission phase– its pronunciation. Language learners, on the other hand, have pleaded for some kind of 'international uniformity', which has undoubtedly existed, to some extent, in grammar, lexis and its written form. Diverse as it may appear to be, there still has to be some kind of 'unity' in the so-called apparent 'diversity' that should enable it to function as an effective tool of international communication.

This paper focuses on intercultural communication in the global context and examines the three much-debated notions of 'comprehensibility', 'intelligibility' and 'interpretability' from the perspectives of linguistics and social psychology. A pragmatic model informed by the multi-dimensional view of intelligibility and multicultural interpretability will be discussed in great detail as a solution that is guided by the philosophy that underpins the rhetoric "unity in diversity".

Comprehensensibility & Intelligibility

Smith (1992) defines comprehensibility as 'word recognition', intelligibility as 'utterance comprehension' and interpretability as 'understanding the pragmatic meaning of the utterance'. The consonant system of English, as we all know, is relatively uniform throughout the English-speaking countries. Accents of English are mainly known to differ in terms of their vowel systems as well as in the phonetic realizations of vowel phonemes. Descriptions of vowel quality based on auditory perceptions are impressionistic and rather subjective. The use of the sound spectrograph in describing the vowels enables reliable and objective measurements of the vowels based on formant frequencies. The vowel chart given below is reconstructed on the basis of the mean frequencies of F1 and F2' (the distance between F2 and F1) computed for 6 tokens of all vowels for Japanese subjects (Nihalani, 2001).

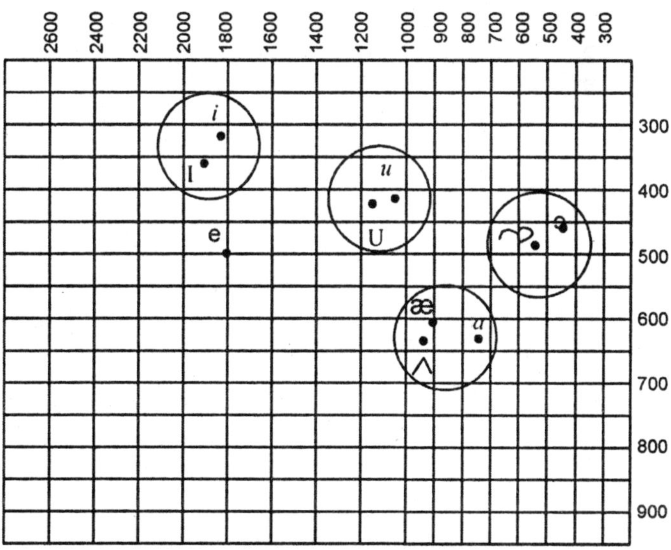

Formant Chart for Vowels in JE

This acoustic study provides sufficient evidence that a Japanese English (JE) speaker fails to maintain sufficient perceptual distance between two vowels in each pair. A similar acoustic study undertaken on Standard Singapore English points to a similar phenomenon of conflation of the same pairs of vowels (Nihalani, 1995). Given below is a Formant chart for the vowels in Standard Singapore English (SSE):

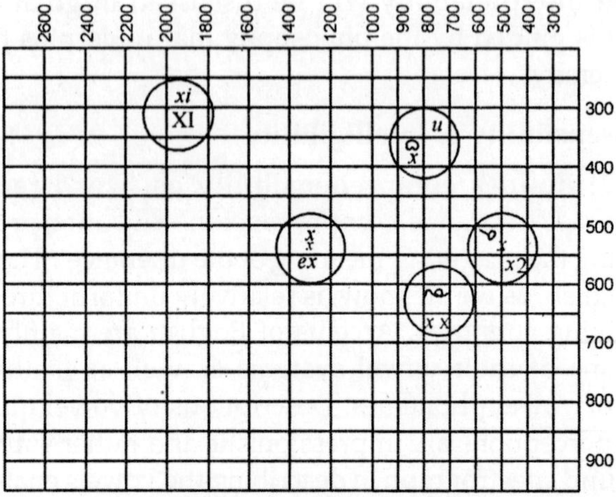

Formant Chart for Vowels in SSE

Tay (1982), Brown (1988) and Ong (1994) have also referred to a similar phenomenon in Educated Singapore English. Bansal (1966) refers to the loss of a distinction between such pairs of vowels in Educated Indian English (EIE). Given below is the comparison of the vowel phonology of five different varieties of English from Kachru's three concentric circles:

Vowel Systems of Standard Englishes

	SSE	EIE	JE	SCOTTISH	RP
bead	i	i	i	i	i
bid				I	I
bed			e	e	e
bad					æ
bard		a			
bud					
pot					
port	ɔ	ɔ	ɔ	ɔ	ɔ
pull	u	u	u	u	U
pool					u

Conflation of Pairs of Vowels

A cursory look at the data above, based on acoustic investigation, clearly brings out the fact about the conflation of pairs of vowels such as /i/ and /ɪ/, /v/ and /ʊ/, /ɒ/ and /ɔ/, and finally /ɛ/ and /æ/ in the varieties of English spoken in the 'Outer Circle' (including Nigeria, Pakistan, Brunei and Malaysia) and Japan, which belongs to the 'Expanding Circle'. The opposition of 'tense' versus 'lax' is systematically seen between these pairs in British Received Pronunciation (RP) where each of these pairs is reported to have a high functional load. Textbooks on English pronunciation, therefore, have repeatedly pointed out that if a speaker of non-inner circle English fails to maintain this distinction, it could cause a lack of comfortable mutual intelligibility when (s)he interacts with speakers of other varieties of English. Their view, I am afraid, sounds rather ethnocentric and displays intolerance of diversity that has been unfortunately perceived as a threat to the Western cannon. Such a view also presupposes a kind of superiority of experts' linguistic norms.

American speakers and Standard Scottish English speakers do not distinguish the vowels of '*cot*' and '*caught*', and American speakers fail to distinguish between '*bomb*' and '*balm*'. Both Indian and American speakers of English distinguish between '*caught*' and '*court*', but this distinction is lost in British English in the sense that these are homophones in RP. The two words '*psalm*' and '*Sam*' are homophones in Standard Scottish English. To illustrate my point further, here is an anecdote.

A British visitor to New Zealand decided while he was in Auckland he would look up an old friend from his war days. He found the address, walked up the path and knocked on the door.

> *'Gidday', said the young man who opened the door. 'What can I do for you?'*
> *'I've called to see me old mate Don Stone', said the visitor.*
> *'Oh he's* **dead** *now mate,' said the young man.*
> *The visitor was about to express condolences when he was thumped on the back by Don Stone himself.*

You will have rightly noted that the two words '*dead*' and '*dad*' are homophones in the New Zealand variety of English. If keeping the segmental distinction were the primary purpose of teaching spoken English, we would have to teach speakers of General American and RP speakers to keep the distinction they do not maintain in their varieties of English. Bansal (1969), Tiffen (1974) and Tay (1982) point out that the diphthongs /eI/ and /əu/ are realized as monophthongs in Educated Indian English, Nigerian English and Standard Singapore English respectively. The same is true of Japanese English. But is this not true for most North American varieties and Scottish English as well? I wonder why no segmental interference of any kind has ever been reported in respect of native varieties.

We do not speak isolated sound segments. We use words in a social context, which serves to help with comprehensibility. Speakers of non-native varieties of English have been using their vowel phonological systems for ages and they have been able to communicate with a fair amount of success across the national boundaries. In the context of the global spread of English and multilingualism, what one comes across, more often, is the 'conflation of pairs of vowels' rather than the 'tense/lax opposition'. One should therefore be raising a fundamental question as to why most of these non-native varieties share the phenomenon of the conflation of pairs of vowels. Further research perhaps needs to be done in this area in order to explore a common substratum that cuts across all these non-native varieties even though this phenomenon seems to be absent in the two varieties of General American and British RP. I cannot help but reflect here whether this linguistic feature of conflation, which is shared by most of the non-native varieties, will eventually constitute an integral part or the core of the emergent Global English for international communication.

Allophonic Features

Jennifer Jenkins' study (2000) has admittedly been the most extensive and comprehensive investigation of the notion 'intelligibility' available in the literature so far. Jenkins (2000: 159) demonstrates, in general, a profound sympathetic understanding of the socio-psychological issues. In her discussion of the LFC segmental features, she refers to 'aspiration', 'allophonic vowel length' and the fortis/lenis consonantal distinction as an essential part of the core. Our experience in the Commonwealth will bear me out that speakers of L2 varieties have been communicating fairly successfully without such allophonic features in their speech. This seems to me a rather over-rated/over-exaggerated claim on the part of Jenkins.

It has been asserted in the literature that the recognition takes place not always because of the phonemic distinctions but rather more significantly because of allophonic features [see O'Connor 1973]. For example, the distinction between the two words *pin* and *bin* is maintained not because of the presence or absence of [voice] feature. Perceptual studies have been cited to show that it is the [+aspiration] feature that distinguishes /p/ from /b/ at the beginning of a stressed syllable. Let us consider another example of a pair of words *seat* and *seed*. Once again, the distinction between [t] and [d] is maintained mainly because of the vowel length which gets comparatively reduced when followed by a voiceless consonant in word-final position. Thus 'there are many clues (allophonic features) to a particular distinction that are located right outside the segment with which the distinction is usually associated' (O'Connor 1973: 133).

In this connection, Gleason (1961: 265) points out that 'the use of allophones is more important socially than it is linguistically'. Hayes (1968: 51) remarks: 'It is the mismanagement of allophonic differences that accounts for much of what we call a foreign accent. He who wants to avoid a foreign accent must use allophones in a way which is ***normal in the language concerned***' (emphasis is mine). The foreignness in foreign accents is obviously ascribable to allophonic deviations. These allophonic features such as 'aspiration', 'allophonic vowel length' etc. are normal in RP accent, and the L2 learners do not aspire to it any more. Attitudinal studies undertaken in India, Malaysia, Nigeria and Singapore at the undergraduate level have clearly revealed resentment against the native-like use of allophonic variants such as syllabicity, aspiration and dark [ɫ]. Non-native speakers have invariably expressed their fear of alienation from their peers, and the society in general.

Let me now present linguistic arguments here. Sounds of one language are known to differ from those of another because of the phonetic value of the segments along the same continuum. To take an example, the linguistic specification that distinguishes between [p] and [b] in English is that they are [-voice] and [+voice] respectively. The articulatory instruction that accompanies the feature [+voice] is "vibrate the vocal cords". In order to implement this instruction, a number of articulatory gestures have to be performed, such as keeping the vocal folds sufficiently lax, reducing the distance between the vocal folds, keeping the airflow through the glottis powerful enough to cause vibration, and maintaining the difference between the sub-glottal and supra-glottal air pressure by lowering the larynx, allowing air to escape through a small velic opening, and/or expanding the walls of the pharynx. "Vibrating the vocal folds", however, is the primary instruction that is associated with the linguistic feature [+voice], and the rest of the articulatory gestures are ways of implementing this instruction. Speakers of different language backgrounds choose different combinations of parameters for the implementation of voicing in stops. The phonetic implementation of these differences is as much important as those in the sound patterns. As phonologists, we tend to get involved in the description of the sound patterns so much so that we forget to point out that many of the sounds of English, for example, are not the same as the similarly specified sounds of, say, Hindi, Sindhi, French or Telugu. Let us consider sounds like [b] voiced stops in Sindhi and English, as an illustration. It is common practice to represent these two sounds with the same symbol [b] and they have the same set of feature specifications at the phonemic level. However, when one listens very carefully to the sounds produced by an Englishman and a Sindhi speaker, one would unhesitatingly say that they sound far from being alike; the phonological instruction to vibrate the vocal folds fails to apply prepausally and postpausally during the closure period of voiced stops in languages like English, voiced stops in English are partially devoiced pre-pausally and post-pausally whereas these are fully voiced in Sindhi during the entire period of closure and are characterized by a slight nasalization (Nihalani, 1972, 1975). When a Sindhi speaker uses his own voiced sounds in English, he perhaps will not need to acquire the allophonic features of vowel length or fortis/lenis consonantal distinction, and the inner-circle speaker should not have any problems with his English speech. Further cross-linguistic research perhaps needs to be done in this area so as to explore how the sounds of one language differ from those of another because of the phonetic value of the segments along the same continuum.

Since in our proposed model, it is claimed that the national identity is characterized by the phonemic vowel system of the local variety, there is not much motivation for the learners to change their phonemic/phonetic segmental system; in fact, that helps them acquire their national flavor. Ironically, Jenkins' LFC segmental core features are heavily grounded in RP and, in many ways, provide further evidence of what Kachru (1992: 362) describes as 'the continuing grip ... on the profession of the traditional paradigm. What makes matters more complex is the fact that active interest groups want to maintain the status quo'.

Educational Target: Standards and Models

Communication is one of the keywords that most often go with globalisation. The term ordinarily conjures up the image of "oral communication" or "spoken interaction", even though the other two kinds of communication (the information related communication technology [ICT], and mass media communication technology (such as journalism, advertising, Radio, TV, etc.), have significantly contributed to the process of globalisation in the modern capitalist economy. Recently, the Strategic Management Unit (SMU) at the UBD conducted an in-depth two-pronged research project to identify the extent of employer/stakeholder satisfaction with the skills of UBD graduates who had entered the local labour market. The second objective was to identify the students' viewpoints regarding the range of skills and competencies that they feel are necessary for their future employment. Preliminary results from the two-pronged study conclusively reveal a perceived skills and competencies gap between the calibre of the graduates that is expected to fulfil the labour requirement in the work force and the actual output from the university.

(*i*) UBD graduates are considered less 'employable' by employers as they tend to have significantly lower skills, competencies and attributes that are prerequisites for effective employment.
(*ii*) Employers appear to rate oral communication as the most important skills but it is here that UBD graduates tend to exhibit the greatest deficiencies.
(*iii*) Students are aware of the skills that are valued by employers. They identified various skill deficiencies in the following areas: oral communication skills, interpersonal skills, critical thinking, adaptability, independence and self- confidence.
(*iv*) Students perceived that their academically oriented programmes should be more practical based and that opportunity for student skills and competency development in the university should be made more readily available.

The implication of the findings has highlighted the need for radical changes in the academic curriculum toward a more practical based and market oriented one from the current pedagogical approach to learning. Such findings remind us of a similar phenomenon in the eighties and nineties in Britain when the Thatcher government underwent a change in the perception of knowledge to be viewed operationally, in terms of competencies, and seeing education as 'training in skills'. With globalisation, this emphasis on skills has been increasingly marked. The new capitalism is dominated by forms of work in which the use of oral communication (mobile technology) and interpersonal communication (being pleasant, and attentive to customers and clients in face-to-face talk or on the telephone) is an integral part of almost every worker's function. Employers who are asked to specify their needs consistently stress that what matters to them is not the specialist subject knowledge new recruits bring with them from education, but rather the transferable or 'key' skills - among which oral communication skills are ranked as particularly important. As a result, the practice of instructing people in 'speaking' and 'listening' is gaining ground in educational institutions. The present preoccupation with communication skills is solely a reflex of recent and ongoing changes in the economic sphere, or that instruction in oral communication is a purely vocational enterprise aimed at increasing the employability of entrants to the workforce. Communication is emerging as the supreme value of language teaching for first language users as well as second language learners.

It is interesting to see how the whole notion of new work order has impacted the educational patterns and established a new set of priorities in the modern service-oriented capitalist economy. In the fast-shrinking world of today where the spoken word reigns supreme, the 'speaking' skill will have to assume a prominent role in English language education, and there will be once again renewed energetic interest in the systematic teaching of phonetics in our English curriculum.

Once we are agreed upon the importance of speech in the new scenario of global economy, we are immediately involved in the pedagogical issues of 'standards' and 'models', and our concerns for international intelligibility are highly justified. The obvious question at this stage arises: What should be the 'educational target'? Is it convergence or divergence from the mainstream or a hybrid?

In principle, the pedagogical models for English are primarily what linguists have termed RP and General American. In practice though, it is always the teacher's model whatever be the model laid down on paper. In the Outer Circle countries where English is a second language, RP is the model described in textbooks and in theory is therefore the model for teaching. Textbooks aside, the reality is that the majority of those who speak English in Brunei, India, Malaysia, Nigeria, Pakistan, Singapore and some other countries in the Commonwealth have never been taught by native speakers, and those who have been taught by native speakers have not had necessarily RP speakers; there are just not enough to go round, not even in England. Any language model to be followed in instruction and learning has to be a living model. This does mean in effect that the teaching of English is significantly different from what the theory would lead one to believe. Abercrombie (1967) observes that RP is an anachronism in the present-day democratic society. In this connection, Gimson (1970) remarks: "There are indeed clear signs that in the less rigid structure of present-day British society, the younger generations feel little of the veneration for the so-called 'received pronunciation' (RP) which used to characterize the attitudes of their elders". The so-called "Received Pronunciation" (RP) was indeed adopted fifty years ago by the BBC for use by its newsreaders and remains still valid as the foundation of a model for imitation abroad. R.P., to my mind, is a dead horse in the 21st century, and I hate to beat the dead horse.

As an educational model, no purely imported standard can ever be practicable in countries where there is an extensive intra-national use of English. In our increasingly networked world, I believe there will be increasingly greater realization that native-speaker like attainment is certainly NOT a basic criterion. The aim should be for foreign learners to acquire a form of pronunciation that is 'universally intelligible' and 'socially acceptable'. Let me quote here Larry Smith: "Non-native speakers must develop a fluency in **educated** English but they do not have to have native-speaker pronunciation as their target. In contrast, they should be trained to be examples of educated speakers of Standard English, *identifiably from their own country...* A good pronunciation is one that a variety of educated listeners find intelligible." (Smith 1985)

With the internet-oriented world, English is beginning to assume a new role as a global language for international communication. Globalization, however, has by no means, eclipsed various countries' efforts to defend their national identities. National flavor is seen, nowadays, as a distinct advantage in speech, provided the 'national distinctiveness' doesn't interfere with 'international intelligibility'. These two tendencies are to be perceived as complementary rather than contradictory. It should not represent a kind of tension between 'nativists' and the 'purists', or a dilemma between 'national identity' and 'international intelligibility'. What I am recommending here is the emergence of home grown varieties of English (called World Englishes) that are globally intelligible without sacrificing their own local (national) identity. This I prefer to call 'Borderless English' or "GLOCAL ENGLISH" (to use Ann Pakir's term), which retains its own segmental features, particularly the vowel system, to characterize its national identity, and incorporates the larger units such as stress and pitch to render it internationally intelligible. Such endocentric models will be the major codes of communication in the context of globalization.

In the multiculural, multilingual and multiethnic world order, people are now getting more and more inclined to view 'diversity' in positive terms. Globalization has given a new legitimacy to diversity that seems to have been validated and revitalized in the 21st century. In the conceptualization of World Englishes, there is a sobering message in what Hughes says:

> "In society, as in farming, monoculture works poorly. It exhausts the soil. The social richness of America, so striking to the foreigner, comes from the diversity of its tribes. Its capacity for cohesion, for some spirit of common agreement on what is to be done, comes from the willingness of those tribes *not to elevate their cultural difference into impassable barriers and ramparts*". [Cited in H. Gates Jr. New Yorker, April 19, 1993 p. 115)

This vision must now be taken beyond the confines of the USA and applied to the English language education in the global context, observes Kachru (2002: 10)

Speech: A Collaborative Enterprise

I consider RP or American Standard English as 'normative models' that limit themselves to the consideration of communicative intentions attributed to the speaker only. I would like to argue here in favor of a communicative model, which goes by the measure of success with which a transaction between the two participants, (either individuals and/or groups), is negotiated. These two models have a set of rules prescribed for the speaker, whereas the two-way interactional model considers the listener as an active participant because it is after all up to the listener either to accept the speech act as a successful speech act or reject it as more or less inappropriate. But only the observation of the hearer's answer can tell whether the speaker has succeeded in performing his/her speech act. Within the framework of Speech Act theory, an utterance is treated as an act performed by a speaker in a context with reference to an addressee. This pragmatic model focuses on strips of activity and speech acts as 'occurring in interaction'. Central to the understanding of communication as information transaction is the construct known as 'negotiation for meaning'. According to the Vygotskian perspective, meaning is inherently relational and is socially constituted through interaction and discourse. Speech, by definition, is a collaborative activity, where the listener is an equal partner. 'Intelligibility' has, unfortunately, emerged as the point of encounter between conventional meanings that are given by dictionaries. However, the individuals and groups elaborate on these conventional meanings through negotiation and discourse. The listener empathizes with the speaker (which I call 'mutuality of cognition' or 'reciprocity'). In passing, I would like to comment that spending time on teaching sound segments seems rather counter-productive in my opinion. We do not speak individual segments. These differences do not take us very far. We always speak in a social context, which helps the listener understand the meanings of even the homophones that are common in any variety of English. So learning to distinguish the individual sounds in isolation is not such a fruitful activity from the point of view of human interaction, and should be played down in our curriculum.

Speech is a mirror of the soul. As a man speaks, so is he. According to Ms Jessica Seet, a voice coach with the Art of Voice in Singapore, "The human voice is an exquisite and expressive instrument which reveals your individuality and thoughts, and sometimes even your soul." [The Straits Times Forum, 28 June 2006]. We can generalise, with a reasonable amount of accuracy, whether a person is pleasant, affectionate, polite and friendly, or aggressive, assertive and rude. A whole gamut of emotions and feelings is reflected in one's own speech.

Psychological markers of personality and mood are often taken to reside in a speaker's tone of voice. The voice is the very emblem of the speaker, indelibly woven into the fabric of speech. Your voice is you. Your voice defines you in the ears of others just as much as your dress sense or hairstyle defines you in their eyes. Millions of dollars are spent on cosmetics, clothes, courses for body and mind, books to shape up the image. Personnel directors cannot help but be influenced by the voice applying for a job. Entirely aside from appearance and manner, the voice can be a liability, or an asset. The tone of voice not only tells us a great deal about a person, it also arouses differing attitudes, varying from great respect to instant dislike. *The voice sets the key.*

A sequence of consonants and vowels is a good guide to the general dictionary meaning of the word but it is the intonation that gives it precision and a point. Perhaps, it may not be so important for a foreign student to master all the individual sounds, but it is crucial that he masters the intonation that is known to encode inter-subjectivity between the speaker and the hearer. A beautifully articulated 'Good Morning' said with the wrong intonation 'characteristic of anger' may have more disastrous results than saying nothing at all. Intonation is one of the chief means by which a speaker gives exactness and subtlety of meaning. Intonation and tonal units serve to relate the segmental and syllabic material to the higher-order grammatical level and, most importantly, to the pragmatic level of interaction between the speaker and the hearer. Intonation is crucial to the art of communication.

Conclusion

The key to international intelligibility, in fact, lies more in knowing how to move the voice according to accepted patterns of stress and melody than in making or recognizing correctly the component sounds. If we want to be understood and accepted internationally, we should learn to pay attention to the larger units of pronunciation (intonation and word stress). These units, called supra-segmentals, are relatively much more important than the smaller units of pronunciation (vowels and consonants) because they help us convey the meaning of an utterance, and also develop richer relationships. I therefore recommend the 'top-down' approach in which the emphasis is shifted from the teaching of segments to the teaching of supra-segmental features. Instead of taking the learner systematically through each English vowel and consonant, perhaps one could concentrate on the *'gross' regional features*, and then quickly move on to features such as word accentuation and intonation. Admittedly, intonation IS a notoriously difficult area of phonetic investigation and the differences in intonation are harder to learn and teach. Since the implications are so serious, it is indeed a real challenge for the teaching community. Such an understanding will shift the focus from 'what is *convenient* for teachers to teach' to 'what is *effective* for learners to learn'. What is asserted here is that it is still realistically conceivable that a speech style could be constructed which includes the essential elements of stress and pitch that are most significant in the communication process, and it also retains its national segmental variations that help the speaker maintain a sense of national identity. This use of English in the expression of national identity is well stated in the words of Professor Tommy Koh, Singapore's Ambassador-at-large:

> "...when one is abroad, in a bus or train or aeroplane and when one overhears someone speaking, one can immediately say this is someone from Malaysia or Singapore. And I should hope that when I'm speaking abroad my countrymen will have no problem recognizing that I am a Singaporean." [quoted in Tongue 1974]

Dr Lee Siew Peng, a Singaporean living in Harrow (Britain), observes:

> "...despite my clearly Singaporean accent, I can address international audiences in English and still be comprehensible. That is what our younger Singaporeans should achieve." [The Straits Times Forum of 26 June 2006]

I personally envisage that the preferred pronunciation model for global communication will be that of the fluent bilingual, perhaps a multi-lingual, 'non-native' speaker. Such a model:

(*i*) will be well within the reach of learners under normal school and college conditions,

(*ii*) will not encounter any psychological barriers arising out of social inhibitions. Furthermore,

(*iii*) the task of training teachers in the use of this model will be much easier. It will be a realistic situation for students and teachers both.

A shift towards this new paradigm is socio-linguistically realistic and pragmatically sound in the planning of courses in the transferable 'soft' skills of oral communication.

The implications of this pragmatic approach to 'oral communication' in the global context can now be summarized as follows:

(*a*) It may be rewarding for the learner to be exposed to many varieties of pronunciation, including native and, more importantly, non-native as well, in order to enrich his repertoire. Undoubtedly, one meets many varieties as one listens to radio, television, and films. But exposure of this kind should also be *systematically incorporated in the learning programs.*

Listening, unfortunately, is one skill that has received the least attention in our language teaching programs. Many people have great difficulty with listening because they have never been instructed in the 'active listening' skills. It has been pointed out that most people listen at a 25 per cent level of efficiency. This is of a particular concern in the context of advanced mobile technology- based communication when the absence of visual cues makes it more important to demonstrate listening. Structured listening comprehension tasks may therefore form a part of the language teaching program.

(*b*) We must abandon the teaching of Phonetics of English *per se.* At the moment, both trainers and trainees are grid-locked within the narrow borders of RP or GA, and anything deviating from the two systems is perceived as an error. Training in General Phonetics will raise awareness and a kind of sensitivity, among learners, towards the total repertoire of human articulatory possibilities. That is when the world opens up, getting them out of that rigid box to one that's much bigger; no longer will they be constricted by the boundaries erected around them. A sound grounding in General Phonetics will create more space and help learners with broadening their perceptual skills, which I may call 'multi-dimensional view of intelligibility'. A sound grounding in General Phonetics will better equip learners to appreciate a whole range of L2 sounds that they might encounter, anyway, in the speech of the international community of interlocutors. Courses in General Phonetics thus will help learners of English acquire greater flexibility, empathy and tolerance. Most importantly, it will be the trained phonetician who will be the expert; a native speaker shall hold no canon or be a gatekeeper anymore.

(*c*) Students also should be given training in some of the supra-segmental features (such as nuclear stress, word groups and pitch movement) that constitute a core as outlined in my presentation. Such a core will hopefully contribute to developing richer human relationships, making our language learning more relevant and socially more meaningful. By no means is this core drawn from one specific culture; it will be multicultural in its character, and yet universal. There are universal norms for relating yourself to other people through talk. For example, speaking positively is better than criticizing; negotiating is better than arguing; sharing your feelings is better than remaining silent and withdrawn, etc. Intonation convincingly helps to characterize human diplomacy through these universal norms.

To conclude, the pragmatic model outlined here will be a *hybrid;* it will be characterized by 'divergence' at the segmental level and 'convergence', in some ways, at the supra-segmental level, and shall serve to harmonize the two seemingly opposing tendencies of 'national identity' on the one hand, and 'international intelligibility' on the other. Such a hybrid form of global pronunciation will create a ***synergy*** that will bind all the three concentric circles (so-called diverse periphery and central communities) together, and will certainly prove to be highly vibrant and truly international. Above all, the endocentric model, as proposed here, will promote respect for one's own social identity, one's own national identity, without sacrificing international intelligibility and multicultural interpretability, and truly epitomizes the rhetoric "unity in diversity".

REFERENCES

Abercrombie, David 1965. *Studies in phonetics and linguistics*. London: Longman.

Bansal, R.K. 1966. *The intelligibility of Indian English*. Unpublished Ph.D. dissertation. University of London.

Bansal, R.K. 1969. *The intelligibility of Indian English*. Hyderabad: Central Institute of English and Foreign Languages.

Block, D. and Deborah Cameron. 2002. *Globalization and language teaching*, London: Routledge.

Brown, Adam 1988. Vowel differences between Received Pronunciation and the English of Malaysia and Singapore: which ones really matter. In *New Englishes: The case of Singapore*, Joseph Foley (ed.) 129-147, Singapore: Singapore University Press.

Crystal, David 1997. *English as a global language*, Cambridge: Cambridge University Press.

Gimson, A.C. 1970. *An introduction to the pronunciation of English*. London: Edward Arnold.

Jenkins, Jennifer 2003. *Phonology of English as an international language*. Oxford: Oxford University Press.

Kachru, Braj B. 1985. Standards, codification and sociolinguistic realism: the English language in the Outer Circle. In Quirk and Widdowson (eds.)

Kachru, Braj B. 1986. The power and politics of English. *World Englishes* 5 (2), 121-40

Kachru, Braj B. 1990. World Englishes and applied Linguistics. *World Englishes* 9, 3-20.

Kachru, Braj B. 1992. (ed.) *The other tongue: English across Cultures*, Urbana and Chicago: University of Illinois Press.

Lee Siew, Peng 2006. *The Straits Times*, Forum, 26 June 2006, Singapore: Singapore Press Holdings.

Nihalani, Paroo 1972. *The articulation of stops in Sindhi: An aerodynamic and physiological study*, Unpublished MLitt dissertation. Edinburgh University.

Nihalani, Paroo 1975. Velopharyngeal opening in the formation of voiced stops in Sindhi, *Phonetica* 32, 98-102, 1975.

Nihalani, Paroo 1995. Phonology of non-native accents of English: Evidence from Singapore English In *Proceedings of Thirteenth International Congress of Phonetic Sciences*, Stockholm, Sweden, 3, 504-507.

Nihalani, Paroo 1999. Vowel Phonology of Asian Englishes: Towards a characterization of International English. In *Proceedings of Fourteenth International Congress of Phonetic Sciences*, San Francisco, USA, 1, 97-100.

Nihalani, Paroo 2001. Phonology of non-native accents: Evidence from Three Concentric Circles. In Thumboo (ed.) *The three circles of English*, 67-76, Singapore: Unipress.

Ong Hwee, Ping 1994. *An acoustic analysis of vowels in Singapore English*. Unpublished Honors thesis. Department of English. National University of Singapore.

Quirk, R and Henry Widdowson (eds.) 1985. *English in the world*. Cambridge: Cambridge University Press.

Seet, Jessica 2006. *The Straits Times*, Forum, 28 June 2006, Singapore: Singapore Press Holdings.

Smith, Larry E. (ed.) 1983. *Readings in English as an international language*. London: Pergamon.

Smith, Larry E. 1992. The Spread of English and Issues of Intelligibility, In Braj B. Kachru (ed.) *The other tongue: English across cultures*. 2nd ed. Urbana: University of Illinois Press

Strevens, Peter 1983. What is Standard English. In Larry E Smith (ed.) *Readings in English as an international language*.

Strevens, Peter 1992. English as an International Language: Directions in the 1990s. In Kachru (ed) *The other tongue*, Urbana and Chicago: University of Illinois Press.

Tay, Mary 1982. The phonology of educated Singaporean English. In *English World-Wide*. 3(2), 135-145.

Thumboo, Edwin. (ed.) 2001. *The three circles of English*, Singapore: Unipress.

Tiffen, B. 1974. *The intelligibility of Nigerian English*. Unpublished Ph.D. dissertation. University of London.

Tongue, R.K. 1974. *The English of Singapore and Malaysia*. Singapore: Eastern Universities Press.

Wong Soon, Fen. 1987. *The formant structure of vowels in Singaporean English*. Unpublished Honors thesis. Department of English Language and Literature, National University of Singapore.

7

Hindi, Urdu, Hindustani : Evolution of the Language of a People

Shreesh Chaudhary

Section I : Socio-Linguistic Context

"Hindi, Hindustani and Urdu are different names for the same speech form, just as the dialects of Cornwall, Lancashire, and Middlesex are different names of the same speech", says Gandhi[1]. Its birth and growth is a result of some socio-linguistic phenomena, seen as follows:

(1) a. contact between culturally different communities,
b. link language for multilingual commercial centres, and
c. link language for multilingual courts and gentry.

Pre-Islamic Aryans followed the policy of exclusion of the natives of India, as untouchables, *mlechchhas*, or *yavanas* - other names for Greeks and Bactrians, and others that generally came from the West and spoke "strange" languages[2]. The Portuguese in India insisted upon compulsory use of their language and upon the exclusion of the native languages in territories occupied by them[3]. The British, for a relatively long time, followed the policy of isolation - keeping themselves to themselves, as far as and as long as possible, away from the local people, making their own "civil lines" and "cantonments"[4]. Islamic invaders expanded their community and included all who accepted, or could be forced into accepting, Islam. The lower caste Hindus, who had mostly been kept outside the main Hindu villages, towns, cities and forts, after conversion to Islam, were admitted inside, and were allowed to pray and inter-marry with the followers of Islam[5].

The lower caste Hindus included attendants, barbers, boatmen, butchers, cobblers, carpenters, confectioners, elephant-drivers, gardeners, horse-minders and grooms, palanquin carriers, smiths, soldiers, tinkers, water carriers, weavers, etc. Muslim conquerors and their armies and civil bureaucracy came from different linguistic backgrounds. Muhammad Ghori spoke Arabic, Babar spoke Turkish, Nadir Shah, a native speaker of Arabic, preferred to speak Persian in the public domain, and Ahmadshah Abdali spoke Pushtu and hardly any Arabic or Persian. In India their allies and collaborators spoke several different languages. Even those who aided Babar against Ibrahim Lodhi, hoping that the former would go away after the plunder, handing the throne of Delhi over to them, came from different religious, ethnic and linguistic backgrounds. This caused intense interaction between speakers of Arabic, Persian, Pushtu, Turkish, etc on one hand, and those of the many Indian languages on the other, triggering the process of pidginization, creolization and nativization (PCN) of the mixed speech forms[6]. These speech forms, rarely written and more rarely used in formal and public domains until mid-19th century, came to be variously known, in various times and places, as Hindawi, Hindustani, Moors, Hindi, and Urdu[7].

Even languages spoken only by the primitive tribes[8] could not escape contact with these new languages. And through sheer frequency of use, these words became integral parts of the many Indian languages. Describing language use during the time of Slave and Khilji kings of Delhi, Law (1916: 65) says, "...both the Hindus and the Muslims were gradually learning languages – the former of the ruling race, and the latter, of the subject people". A random list of some common Perso-Arabic words found in many modern Indian languages is given below.

(2)	**Persian**	**Gloss**	**Arabic**	**Gloss**	**Turkish**	**Gloss**
	aazaad	free	akhbaar	newspaper	baabaa	father
	aabaadii	population	aksar	often	darogha	policeofficer
	aamad	income	aadat	habit	chogaa	mantle
	aamdani	income	aadmii	man	bahl	cart
	afsos	regret	amiir	rich	bahalwaan	cart driver
	aakhir	finally	aakhirii	last		
	aaraam	rest	ijaazat	permission		
	aasaan	easy	aam	common		
	aawaaz	voice	asal	real/genuine		
	aasmaan	sky	ijzat	prestige		

The list in (2) above, hardly a fraction of the total, shows the variety of lexical sources for this language, and, the extent of its reach. This language is clearly a product of intense and significantly long contact between two populous and powerful multilingual groups.

Another factor in the birth and growth of this language has been the emergence of rather new and multilingual cities in the wake of relatively long period of Muslim rule in India. This also enhanced sea-borne and over-land domestic and foreign trade. And more trade brought more visitors to and from these major cities. By the beginning of the 17th century, that is when Akbar the Great died and his son Jahangir sat upon the Mughal throne, several cities in India had merchants and missionaries from different nations of Europe. Principal among these cities were Agra, Ajmer, Allahabad, Benares, Balasore, Chittagong, Cochin, Delhi, Dhaka, Goa, Hugli, Masulipatnam, Murshidabad, Patna, and Surat. Describing Surat during 16th–17th centuries, the Portuguese traveler Manuel Godinho[9] writes,

> ... In Surat we find Spaniards, Frenchmen, Germans, English, Dutch, Flemish, Dunkirkians, Italians, Hungarians, Poles, Swedes, Turks, Arabs, Persians, Tartars, Georgians, Scythians, Chinese, Malabaris, Bengalis, Sinhalese, Armenians and an endless variety of other strange barbarian people... Surat is the biggest trading centre of India, and I may say the richest in the whole world, because the best merchandise from all over flocks there, both by land and by sea...

Surat[10] at this time was a Tower of Babel. It had speakers of all principal Indian languages and of many foreign ones. Says Anderson[11],

> Perhaps no city in the world contained a more varied and mixed assemblage of people. In its thoroughfares were to be seen not only the natives of the Gujarathi and Marathi provinces; but also Sindians, Persians, Arabs, Armenians, Parsis and Jews, together with English, Dutch and Portuguese. Mussalmans and intelligent Bohras, all thronged there for sale or purchase of indigo, spices, pepper, lead, quick silver, tin, copper, porcelain, jewels and many other profitable commodities...

"From a perusal of the inscriptions on the Christian graves"[12] in Agra, we find that

> ...from 1600 to 1800 persons of all European nationalities, the English, the Dutch, the French, the Portuguese, the Italian, the German, the Flemish, and even the Swiss were from time to time buried at Agra. The Jesuits, of course, account for a considerable number of inscriptions. Indian converts to Christianity who assumed European names and the off-spring of mixed marriages account for others...

In a similar way, Delhi attracted ablest men and women from all over the world, because these people knew their abilities would be recognized and rewarded here. According to Percival Spear, Delhi by the middle of the 17th century,

> was a great and imperial city... with anything between one and two million inhabitants. It was the largest, and most renowned city, not only of India, but of all the East, from Constantinople to Canton. Its court was brilliant, its mosques and colleges numerous, and its literary and artistic fame as high as its political renown.[13]

About the language of its bazaars, an early 19th century account[14] says,

> Oordoo or camp language is a mixture of Arabic, Persian and Hindooee. It is a written language only as concerns the Europeans; it was first established as a conventional means of communication at Delhi, by the people of the various nations who resorted to its markets to dispose of their commodities. It is, as observed, a colloquial language, and is understood from the plains of Tartary to Cape Comorin...

Benares, another metropolis of the 19th century India, was a similar polyglot. There is scarcely a province in the country, an account says, "that is not more or less represented in this peculiar city." About the general language here, this account observes,

> But the general basis of the population of the city is, of course, the same as that of the surrounding country; both Muhammedans and Hindus being ordinary Hindustanees. The Muhammedans generally speak the Urdu language, while the Hinduis is most used by the rest of the people. A good many of the Hindoos, however, speak Urdu, and, unless among the Brahmans, the Hinduis is usually spoken, with a considerable admixture of Urdu words. The Hindui, however, which derives most of the words from Sanscrit, though *in general not very purely spoken*, may still be said to be the language of the city, as it is used by the great mass of the Hindoos, who constitute the great majority of the people; while Urdu, which derives most of its words from the Arabic and Persian language, is not much used, *in any considerable degree of purity*, except among the Muhammadans, who do not likely form above a sixth, or seventh, of the entire population. Urdu, however, is used by a small body of Hindoos, mostly of the writer caste, many of whom are employed in the government, and other public offices[15] (Italics added).

This was, as the italicized words indicate, not a "pure" but a popular language. This language was without much written literature for a long time, and its first codified grammar appeared in the 19th century, as Heber (1828: 225-6) says,

> ... by the labours of that Leviathan of Oriental literature, Dr Gilchrist, Europeans have had for some time the benefit of its being put to paper; and hence the means are offered of obtaining grammatical accuracy in the acquirement of it.

Even today the popular varieties of Hindi-Urdu, or what we would, following Gandhiji, call Hindustani, take words from anywhere they can, so that they are spoken and understood by lot more people than only those who claim to be the native speakers of Hindi/Urdu. A popular television show or a popular Bombay film abundantly shows this. To use a clichÈ, it seems to be there in the idiom of this language to use words that may convey best, regardless of where they come from. So it has words from Portuguese, like *girja* "church", *boiyaam* "glass jar", or *paraat* "an over sized dining plate", as well as words from Pushtu, such as *aasaan* "easy", *ajubaah* "wonder", *talaaw* "pond/ tank", etc

Yet another factor that helped the emergence of Hindi-Urdu on the national scene was the multi-lingual composition of most ruling courts in India during 13th–19th centuries. Here is a glimpse of the mightiest of them.

(3) Racial & Religious Composition of Aurangzeb's Nobility, 1679–1707 : Mansabdars of 5,000 and Above[16]

Iranian	*Turanian*	*Afghan*	*Indian Muslim*	*Other Muslim*	*Total Muslim*	*Rajput*	*Maratha*	*Other Hindus*	*Total Hindus*
14	6	10	10	13	53	5	16	5	26

And this was the situation not just with the Mughal courts or with the Muslims, Hindu royal courts were not very different. Even Marathas had Muslim and Portuguese generals and soldiers, Tipu Sultan had a Brahmin for his prime minister. It was a status symbol for many petty Hindu land lords to have Pathan body guards, just as it was a mark of prestige for several Muslim nobles and rulers to patronize Sanskrit and Persian poets. The greatest Sanskrit poet of the 17th century, Kaviraj Jagannath, was on the personal pay roll of Shah Jehan's father-in-law. A great deal of public domain and quite a bit of formal domain even in private situations cut across ethnicity, necessitating the use of a language with greater reach and comprehensibility.

Until a long time Sanskrit, and later Persian, served as the common language of royal courts in India, but because of too much rigidity, and often because the number of people proficient in these prestige languages was too few, in their lighter, informal and intimate moments, Urdu/Hindi had started appearing even in these courts. By the middle of the 18th century, the Mughal court accepted Urdu even for formal use, though not yet so enthusiastically as the use of Persian. This connection with the royal courts, however, gave Hindi-Urdu the "prestige", or to use a Mughal symbol, the *masnad,* "pillow", and the *qaaliin,* "carpet". Though not yet quite at ease here, it could now compete with, and, later, snatch domains from, Persian.

The royal army camps had a similar ethnic diversity. The word "Urdu", of Turkish origin, means "Horde", crowd, or an army, or a camp. "Ever since the 11th century", Kripalani (1975: 307) observes,

> when the Muslims invaded India from the North-West, the rulers, whether Afghans, Turks, or Mughals, used Persian as the language of the Imperial court. Their army, belonging to different races, also spoke the same language, although the soldiers in course of time picked up the rudiments of local dialects so as to communicate with the common people, mainly Hindus or Muslim converts. This crude speech form, thus. born of the confluence of Persian and a Western Hindi dialect came to be known as Urdu....

It was a language of contact, a link in a polyglot market place, or army camp, or a king's court.

It is commonly believed that Urdu had its birth in the bazaars of Delhi and growth in the camps of Mughal army. The word "Urdu"was first used in Shah Jehan's time to refer to a mixture of Hindi and Persian[17], but it must be recognized that by then the essential part of this language had been in existence in India for at least four centuries and had been the popular medium of speech as well as a popular link language between Deccan and Delhi, and between Chawl and Chittagong. The Mughals and the Iranians, who learnt and used Persian for literature and culture, called it Hindi to indicate its Indian origins. At this time it was also called *Rekhta*, i.e. scattered, to indicate its non-settled nature. This also indicated the mixed, i.e. pidgin like, structure of this language.

Because it was the language of bazaar, without a written grammar or canon, it suited the temper of the time, and no body minded if there were any "errors", because there was no "grammar". People spoke, understood and ignored its plebian connections and "form:", thus making it the language of widest reach even by about the early 17th century. That this language was of a reach much greater than any during its time is borne out by many accounts. Reverend Terry, a member of Thomas Roe's Embassy in the early 17th century, observes[18],

> The language of the Empire, I mean the vulgar, bears the name of it, and is called Indostan; it hath much affinitie with the Persian and Arabic tongue... a language which is very significant and speaks much in a few words....

Section II : Linguistic Context

Theoretically, Hindi/Urdu is a product of free interaction among speakers of a large number of diverse languages through nearly 600 years of contact: "... after the formation of Delhi Sultanate, Punjabi and

Persian words got interwoven with the language which was spoken there and which was a mixture of Khari Boli[19], Brij, Rajasthani and Hariani..."[20]. The birth of this new language can be traced to the early years of the 11th century. Words from Perso-Arabic languages began getting mixed in the speech of the North –Western parts of India even before the consolidation of Muslim rule here. In *Prithvi Raj Raso* of Chand Bardai, we can find Arabic and Persian words. These words acquired currency in parts of Northern India before Muslims occupied Delhi.

Amir Khusro (1253-1325)[21] counts Khwaja Masood Saad Salman (1048-1122) among the first poets of this language. A little later, Khwaja Moinuddin Chishti (1146-1236) became another early but powerful and popular voice in this new language. Chishti's compositions mark the beginnings of *Sufi* poetry. In course of time, other poets further added to this genre. The likes of Kabir (1425-1505) just did not care where their words came from – they had to reach the lowest of the low, and used the language that came naturally to them. See the following, for instance:

(4) *Kabir*: yah to ghar hai prem kaa *khaalaa* kaa ghar naanhi
siis kaaTi bhuinyaan dharo tab paiTho ghar maanhi

Khaalaa, i.e. aunt or mother's sister, is a Persian word, and *siis*, i.e. head, is the Apabhramsha form of Sanskrit word, *shiirsha*. These words were in currency across many languages of North India in the days of Kabir. In spite of their different lineages, they are both used in the same couplet, and fit so well that for a lay person they are both parts of the lexicon of the same "language". The power and popularity of Kabir endures in no small measure due to his language, as due to his message. Though Kabir presumably was a native speaker of Bhojpuri, as spoken in Banaras, Gorakhpur and Mirzapur[22], the language of his *Bijak* is believed to be of a wider area. The about a thousand couplets collected in the *Bijak* have more than 235 words of Persian, Arabic and Turkish origin. Undoubtedly, this is how the people's language was heard then[23]. Kabir used to say that Sanskrit was like a well, but the popular language he was using in his couplets was like the flowing water of a river. And just like Kabir, other Sufi poets and writers used popular language in their compositions.

Actually, the first works of literature in this kind of mixed language appeared in the Sindh – Rajasthan – Doab region[24]. Two important land marks in this literary tradition are Chand Bardai's *Prithviraj Raso* and Jagnayak's *Alhakhand*, both composed before the end of the 13th century. Then in the 16th and 17th centuries there were poets like Sarangdhar and Lal who, respectively, wrote the heroic tales of Hammeer and the history of Mewar. Then came the line of religious poets like Kabir, Vidyapati, Meera, Jayasi, Tulsi, Suur, Raskhan, who wrote between the 14th and 17th centuries in a language which reflected the popular, and not the elite, idiom of their times, mixing, as we have said above, words from Persian, Arabic, Turkish, Pushto, Sanskrit and modern Indo-Aryan (MIA) languages, as their fancy took flight.

Many historians of Hindi/Urdu recognize Khusro as the first truly original poet of this language. Chatterji (1960: 203) goes to the extent of saying that a writer like Khusro "essaying in the Indian vernacular in literature was an exception" for his time. He combined words from Sanskrit and Arabic, Persian and Turkish with those from the vernaculars around Delhi with such felicity that his lines became popular soon. Some examples follow:

(5) *Khusro*[25] *je hale miskan makun tagaaaful,* duraay nainaa banaay batiyaan
kitaabe hizraan na daaram e jaa, na lehu kaahe lagaay chhatiyaan
shabaane hizraan daraaj chun julf, wa roje waslat chu umra kotaah
sakhii piyaa ko jo main na dekhuun, to kaise kaaTuun andherii ratiyaan

Paraphrase : Mine is the fate of a destitute beggar, she talks even while she looks away! The book of separation is not dear to me, O Dear!, why do you not embrace me! The night of separation is long like your hair, and the day of union is short like my life! How am I going to pass the dark night without the sight of my beloved!

All italicized words in the extract above have been taken from Persian. Other words are either from Sanskrit or its derivatives current then. Khusro, beside his Persian tomes, also wrote romance, riddles, and spiritual verses in a popular idiom using words from all the different languages he knew, And, as Chauhan (1970: 51) says, Khusro knew Sanskrit, Persian, Arabic, Turkish, Hindi and eight other Indian languages. Yet he was a people's poet, using the speech of the street, used by both the Hindus and the Muslims, the rich and the poor, the learned and the lay, and, thus, watered the plant whose seeds had already been sown.

The son of a Brahmin mother, Khusro held the Sanskrit language, the *Vedas* and the *Smritis* in great esteem. The Persian word *Rekhta,* which Khusro used for this language, is derived from the Sanskrit root *ris,* meaning to flow ceaselessly. Khusro composed a grammar for *Rekhta.* Because of extreme flexibility in the lexicon and grammar, this new language soon spread to principal cities, towns and fair grounds, and became most widely used language of contact in India. It began just as pidgins do - driven by need, and taking from available languages as required. In this manner, in less than 300 years, during 12th-15th centuries, Hindi-Urdu established itself in the principal courts and markets of India, as the link language, though not yet the language of and for the elite.

A survey of literature in India during the Mughal rule shows that many Hindu poets wrote in Persian. Important among them were poets like Gang, Manohar, Kishan Das, Pushkar, Chintamani, Bihari, Matiram, Bhushan, Padmakar, Ghananand and Thakur. All of these poets even in their non-Persian compositions freely used "more Arabic-Persian words than their Muslim counterparts", such as Rahim, did.

There also were those that did not belong to the royal court, but wrote in a language that freely used Perso-Arabic and Sanskrit words side by side with words from the local languages. Important among such poets of the period are Kabir, Sur Das, Malik Muhammad Jayasi, Tulsi Das, Mati Ram, Sundar Das and Raskhan.

There was hardly any difference between the pragmatic and linguistic features of the works composed by Hindu and Muslim poets during this period in this language. They were both writing for the same audience, in the same idiom, the same style, the same prosody, a similar beginning and a similar end. Scripts occasionally differed – Jayasi write in Arabc script, and Tulsidas is believed to have written in Devnagari. But lots of Hindu writers until about the beginning of the 20th century wrote in Arabic script.

One of the best works of this new language of people during this period is known as *Padmaawat.* Malik Muhammad Jayasi composed it in about 1540. According to Grierson (1989:xviii), "it gives us a representation of the speech and pronunciation of those days...". Commenting on the significance of the contribution of Jayasi, Grierson further says,

> Hindu writers, tied by the fetters of custom, were constrained to spell their words not as they were pronounced, but as they were written in the old Sanskrit of their forefathers. But Malik Muhammad cared not for Hindu customs, and wrote his work in the Persian character, thus giving necessarily a phonographic representation of every word he wrote...".

See the following, for example:

(6) prem piriit purukh ek kiyaa, naaw Muhammad duhu jag diyaa
andhkuup bhayaa ahaa niraashaa, onke priiti joti parkaashaa

(Jayasi, *Chitralekha*)

sershaah dehli *sultaanuu* , chaariu khand tape jas bhaanuu

....

Diinh asiis Muhammad, karahu jugahi jug raj

Badshah tum jagat ke, jag tumhaar *muhtaaz*.[26]

(Jayasi, *Padmaawat*)

Paraphrase: God created a man in love and affection, and in both the worlds gave him the good name of Muhammad. The world had been like a dark and narrow well without hope or light but the light of His love illuminated it.
Shershah, who is the king of Delhi, shines all around like he very sun.
Muhammad blessed him, and said may you rule for eternity.
You are the emperor of the world, and the world is beholden to you.

Words like *sultaan*, *baadshaah*, i.e. King, and *muhtaaz*, i.e. beholden, had by the time of Sher Shah, i.e. mid-16th century, got into common use in the popular language of the Northern India. There are many instances of pidgin pronunciation even in this short extract. *Sultaan*, for instance, has been rendered as *sultaanu*. Similarly, the Sanskrit word *ashiish* has been given as *asiis*, and *paadshash* has been renderd as *baadshaah*. Of interest in this extract is the rhyming of Arabic *Sultanu* with the Sanskrit *bhaanu*. Thus, a language with free use of frequently occurring words from different language families was emerging. in India in great and unrestricted use. "With Malik Muhammad", Grierson (1889:xviii) says:, "the period of apprenticeship of vernacular literature in Hindustan may be said to have come to a close. The young giant had bestirred himself, and found that he was young, and strong and lusty as an eagle, he went forth rejoicing to run his course...".

This idiom did not change significantly between communities of Hindus and Muslims. Tulsidas uses the same prosodic structure, as does Jayasi, and a similar idiom to tell similar tales. In his prologue to the *Ramacharitmanas* , invoking gods, Tulsidas says:

(7) *Tulsidas*: bandaun guru pad param paraagaa
suruchi subaas saras anuraagaa

....

bandaun sant samaan chit
hit anhit nahi koi
anjali gat subh suman jimi
sam sugandh kar doi

....

bahuri bandi khal gan satibhaaen
je binu kaaj daahinehu baaen
par hit haani laabh jin kere
ujaren harash bishaad basere

Paraphrase: (I) bow to the feet of the guru that are like the buds of lotus that are pretty, fragrant, lustrous and loving.

Like a recluse, (I) bow to all with a like mind
without deeming anyone a friend or a foe.
Like a handful of holy flowers
It can only perfume both.

With many a prayer I bow to the vile
Who without purpose can dwell to my left and to my right
Harm to others is the gain to whom
Who relish causing destruction and doom

We can note some similarities in the two invocations – they both begin with invocation of God and then go to other – benign or malignant – powers, as was the accepted idiom in India for telling any great tale those days. In *Ramcharitmanas* and other works written for people at the behest of his guru Ramanand, Tulsidas freely used words, inflexions and derivations from all the speech forms current in a metropolis like Varanasi, and in his experience from further west then. He uses words like *sahib*, "master"; *gariib nawaaj*, "protector of the poor". *majuurii*, "wages"; etc from Arabic/Persian. Inflexions like "hoihain", i.e. will happen, come from Bhojpuri, and "soi", i.e. that, from Awadhi, as in the following.

(8) *Tulsidas* : hoihain soi jo raam rachi raakhaa
ko kari tarak badhawahin saakhaa

Paraphrase : That will happen what God has designed
Why debate what is already assigned

In his zeal to use the popular idiom, Tulsidas went so far as to render even Sanskrit words in popular pronunciation. Thus, we find, for instance, "saakhaa", i.e. branch, rendered with the dental /s/, as popular then, rather than the palatal /sh/, as standard Sanskrit would have it. Tulsidas followed the popular idiom closely.

We find similar examples of composition by other contemporaries. They composed in the local languages with many words from Arabic and Persian. Among relatively unknown but important works of Rahim in Sanskrit literature must also be counted his *Kheta-kautukam*, i.e. Wonders of Sky. This is an astrological work making generalized predictions about people born under different zodiac signs. It uses Sanskrit mixed with Persian and Arabic. Rahim says that many of his predecessors have also used this kind of language[27]. Some examples are given below[28]. Persian words are given in italics.

(9) *Sanskrit* : yadi bhawati *jalaadulkalkako moutkhaane*
"Mars" "eighth house"
satam ahitbhaasii guhyaruk striisukhonah
*mutfaki*r badaame *johari* soath *jakhmii*

"worried" "expert" "wounded"
kamfahamanah syaallaagaroasrigwikaaraih.
"Dull-witted"

Paraphrase If mars is in the eighth house, the person in question talks rudely, suffers from venereal diseases, and is wretched in conjugal love. Worrying, suffering from sores, lacking in intelligence becomes physically weak due to Anaemia, itching, or sores.

(10) *Sanskrit*: *tarwagaras* jachaatmajasoukhyayuk
"rich"
syaaddaanaagraniirbhuupapriyas *sipaahii*
"soldier"
sardaarakah paakdilo dawiirulkalko
"leader" "golden-hearted" "Mercury"
yadaa *yaapti makaan-gah* syaat
"eleventh house"
yadaa *maadaraagaar agahsamsh*akhetah
"Mother's/4th House" "Sun"
sukhiino samsah *pareshaanakah* syaat
"worried"

Paraphrase: If Mercury stays in the 11th house, the person in question becomes wealthy, famous for fighting, a leader, and a human being endowed with a golden heart.

If one has sun in the Mother's/4th House, one is constantly worried.

Sometimes Rahim opts for hybrid compounding, making one phrase out of words from different languages. A good example here is *maadaraagaar*, i.e. "mother's house", where the first word, *maadar*, is Persian, and the second, *aagaar*, is Sanskrit. If Rahim had followed the rule of compounding from Persian he would have rendered this phrase as *maadar-e-makaan*, or at least *maadar – e – aagaar*, granting that as user of the language he can choose words from either of the two languages. But after choosing words from two different languages, Rahim chooses to apply the rule of compounding from Sanskrit and goes for *Sandhi*, i.e. phonological assimilation, of compatible vowels, rather than for the infix from Persian. It is difficult to explain the choice of one over the other, unless we presume that habit of derivation formed by frequency of use of Indian languages nearly naturally suggests this as the first choice. It is interesting to see how the process of pidgnisation cuts across boundaries of language and forms new expressions.

There were others, including Hindus, who composed in this kind of language. Possibly, it was non-standard, but was in fashion then. Some extracts from Lakshmipati's *Nripati – niti – garbhita – vritta* or

Farruk-siyar Charita, for instance, is given below[29]. Lakshmipati was a court poet of King Jagachchandra of Kumaon. It is most likely that he composed this work at the behest of his king in the first quarter of the 18th century[30].

The book, presumably, teaches political truths with reference to contemporary politics. He has chosen a "mixed language", mixing Arabic and Persian words in Sanskrit text. The author says that this was in keeping with the times and could make his work more popular than other wise possible. The subject, according to Lakshmipati, demanded this language which was "simple Sanskrit with an admixture of those words that were in common use in the Muslim dominated parts" of India[31].

The book describes the events following the death of Aurangzeb leading to the battle of succession among his children amidst which comes the life and coronation of Farrukhshiyar. It describes the politics and treachery of Syed Brothers, who became famous as the "King makers". The Brothers finally got rid of Farrukhshiyar, by first blinding him and then imprisoning him and poisoning him to death in the prison itself. In the meanwhile, the new king had been found and coronated. Lakshmipati describes this story in very simple unexaggerated verse using Arabic-Persian words wherever apt within the Sanskrit lexicon and syntax. Some examples follow[32].

(11) *Lakshmipati* : maduktam manyate mithyaa twaya chet sarwa bhaawatah
tarhim swa-*maadaram* prichchh saadaram priitipuurwakam
"mother"
prasanna chetsaa yudhham kartu gachchhati yo narah
dast niilofare tasya samaayati jayo drutam
"hands" "lotus"

Paraphrase : If you do not trust what I have told you, you can go and respectfully ask your mother.
To the King that goes to the battle field cheerfully, the Goddess of Victory herself gives in his hands the Lotus of success.

Lakshmipati also subjects Arabic and Persian words to the inflexional rules of Sanskrit. Persian, for instance, may render "Own Mother" as *maadar-e-khaas,* genitive infix and the possessive word coming after the head word. But following the Sanskrit lexicon, the Relative marker "Swa" is brought at the head of the word followed by "Maadaram" in the appropriate case. Another interesting example of adherence to Sanskrit syntax while using a hybrid code is the way phrase "*dast niilofare* tasya" has been rendered. Had it followed the Persian lexicon, the genitive particle "-e" would occur between the two words, and not at the end of the second word, and would, thus, read "*dast – e-*

niilofar" and not "*dast niilofare*".

Once again what is interesting here is not just the mixed code, but the ease with which these poets and writers put them together in a context. We get to see this process not just in poetry, though more profusely and clearly there than elsewhere, but in other genres too, and not just in high literature written by the court poets, but also in ordinary everyday use. That is how Pidgins are born.

This language grew in popularity and attracted more poets and writers with time. Prose compositions began appearing in this language in the early 19th century when College of Fort William, ran by the East India Company for the training of its civil servants, encouraged production of anthologies in this language. The Company wanted its servants to be proficient in the modern Indian languages, and, so, it helped in the production of books in this language. Raja Shiva Prasad, Sitar-e-Hind, Lallooji Lal and Sadal Mishra created a new genre in this language, and added to its popularity. The Book Society of Calcutta produced close to eight thousand copies of Hindi/Urdu books in 1834. This number today does not appear to be big, but it is several times larger than just about 50 books sold in Arabic and only a few more in Sanskrit and twice as many as bilingual English-Persian books[33].

Soon plays, novels and short stories followed. *Inder Sabha*, the Court of Indra, the King of gods, written by Agha Hasan Amanat (1816-59) broke all records of literary popularity then. It was played throughout the sub-continent and translated into other languages in India and beyond. Amanat was a court poet of Wazid Ali Shah of Lucknow. He wrote in both Brajbhasha and Persian. Here in this dance-drama he has used the traditional metrical structure of *ghazal, thumri, hori,* etc in a language that mixes Awadhi, Brajbhasha, Bhojpuri and Khariboli with Perso-Arabic words[34]. An extract from Amanat follows:

(12)[35] raajaa huun main *kaum* kaa aur indar meraa naam
Gloss "nation"
bin pariyon kii *diid* ke nahiin mujhe aaraam
"sight"

Paraphrase King I am of this land, and Indar is my name
Without the sight of the fairies, I am disconsolate.

Many Hindus before and since wrote in Urdu, the last and perhaps the greatest being Dhanpat Rai (1880–1936), who in the middle of his career switched to writing in Devanagari and acquired fame as Premchand. His works became so popular and went into so many editions that they supported an entire printing press, Saraswati Press, by themselves. At about the same time, Devaki Nandan Khatri's *Chandrakaanta* and *Chandrakaanta Santati* (1870 C) came to the popular notice and helped create the much needed literature of the people, and a mass base for the same.

Section III : Social Context

Mixed language gained in popularity between 13th century, when Amir Khusro wrote in this language, and 1839, when Persian was replaced with English and Urdu/Hindi, this new language, as the languages of administration in the British India. By about 18th century, Hindi/Urdu became the language of common man in a great part of the Indian sub-continent. And by the end of the 19th century, it became the most widely understood language in India. It is true that the Urdu/Hindi in Hyderabad or Cochin differs from that of Lucknow and Delhi, but these differences should be seen as dialectal, just as English differs between Bristol, Brighton and Birmingham, or between Sydney and Chicago. As Kim says in Rudyard Kipling's deservedly popular novel after his own name *Kim*, Hindustani was understood from Kabul to Calcutta even before the end of the 19th century. The Khan who takes Kim under his wings speaks with Kim in this language, not in his native Pushtu.

East India Company realized that "though the Persian language is useful on application to the great men, yet the Moor's language has its advantage too"[36]. Like many among the early British, Gilchrist foresaw that his residence in India may not be much useful without the knowledge of "Hindustani". My residence in India, he wrote, "in any capacity, would prove as unpleasant to myself, as unprofitable to my employers, until I acquired an adequate knowledge of the current language of the country, in which I was now to sojourn. I therefore sat resolutely down to acquire what was then termed as the *Moors*...".[37]

Urdu had already gained the support of the College of Fort William. Hindi was not taught seriously until 1815, and did not receive formal recognition as an important vernacular until 1825, when a judge of the Patna City civil court came up with a clinching argument[38]. Morris, that judge from Patna, argued that in case of any choice between Urdu in the Persian script and Hindi in the Nagari or Kaithi script, the government should adopt Hindi "upon the principle of the convenience of the larger body of people"[39]

The British had, thus, been favourably disposed towards the use of Hindustani. But there were no dictionaries or grammars or no other materials for learning it. Actually many among the British suspected that the powerful sections of the Indians were against the British learning the Indian languages, lest they should establish direct and "immediate communication" with the Indian masses and render the Indian middlemen powerless. Gilchrist, the author of the first modern dictionary and grammar of Hindustani, suspected,

> That it is not at all improbable, that the cormorant crew of Dewans, Mootsuddies, Sirkars, Nazirs, Pundits, Munshis and a tremendous roll call of harpies who encompass power here see with jealous solicitude every attempt in their masters to acquire the means of immediate communication with the great mass of the people who those locusts of the land conceive their lawful prey[40].

In the meanwhile, opposition to the use of Persian had also been growing. The main thrust of the anti-Persian argument was that this language was no longer comprehensible to a very large majority of the ruled and the ruler, and, therefore, it was time that this language was replaced with something more easily comprehensible and in popular use. The following, written in the early 1830s, is typical:

> The continued use of the (Persian language) is an unaccountable absurdity, and the parent of exceeding injustice to the huge mass of the population. The Moslems, in the true spirit of conquerors, introduced the Persian, which was almost their own language, (as it was certainly the great conventional one of the East,) into the Courts of Law, and established it as that of the Court, and the medium of communication in all political relations, even with the Hindoo princes. It was, of course, a great evil to the Hindoos, who not only were subjected to foreign law, but were obliged to seek it through the medium of the (foreign) language, and the interpretation of their conquerors.
>
> It is strange that the English have never thought of abrogating so vicious a form, and bestowing upon their subjects, in its stead, the great boon of having the law administered in the language of the country... Why the Persian has not been discarded, and either the English or Hindoostani, which is the colloquial language of all India, substituted, and which is understood by Hindoo and Moslem, is a matter known best to the Court of Directors. The Hindoostani would have this advantage over the English, that the people speak it, and a competent knowledge of it is very easily acquired by Europeans with whom it is rendered familiar by being the universal means of communication between them and their servants, as well as *the natives of all castes and descriptions*[41].

But by this time several of the Company's servants were learning Hindustani and they found it very useful. Reginald Heber, a missionary campaigner of this kind, for instance, was able to distribute copies of the Hindustani prayer book and gospel at Buxar, in Bihar, in course of his journey through "the Upper provinces of India" in the 1820s[42]. In 1839, accordingly, Persian was removed and replaced, in Bengal Presidency, with Urdu and Bengali at the lower echelons of administration and English at the higher which the EIC, and, after 1857, the Imperial Government, continued until India's independence from the British Rule[43].

But the question was still far from settled – the problem of over-Sanskritization / over-Persianization persisted, and the government of the Company had difficulty deciding on the identity and the form of the official language. After another enquiry into the subject, J.C. Nesfield, then Director of Public Instruction in North Western Province, i.e. much of the Western U.P. and Haryana of today, with Agra as its capital, announced that he was about to change the curriculum of the government schools of "Oude" to include Kaithi writing and Kaithi arithmetic along with Nagari in the lower classes. Nesfield deplored the tendency of Hindi school books to use "obsolete" words of Sanskrit origin, and called Hindi "a language which no one speaks, and which no one, unless he has been specially educated, can interpret"[44].

The division of the same language on the basis of scripts started in the last quarter of the 19th century itself when extreme positions were adopted by contending parties such that Urdu got identified with Arabic script and Muslims, Hindi was identified with Devanagari script and Hindus. This division is well documented in at least two studies, namely by Rai (1984) and King (1994), and I need not repeat that story here. The British government in its final move went along with the opinion of Judge Morris of Patna and declared Hindi in Devanagari script to be its language of administration at the lower echelons of government in much of Bengal, Bihar, U.P., etc[45]. English replaced Persian at the higher echelons.

Section IV: Ethnic Context

Institutionalization of the popular language also introduced stratification. The choice of Gilchrist, the first grammarian of this popular language, was deliberate. He recognized that there were at least three social varieties of Hindustani current in his time. The first was the Court variety saturated with Persian words, as found in the poems of Sauda, Vali, Mir, Dard, etc. This is the "pompous and pedantic language of literature and politics", Gilchrist observed, and it drew heavily on Arabic and Persian. Another variety was in use "in Mr Foster's translation of the Regulations of the Government... in the greatest part of Hindostanee compositions written in Nagaree character, in the dialect of the lower order of servants and Hindoos, as well as among the peasantry of Hindostan". The variety of Hindustani that Gilchrist selected for codification was something between these two[46].

By the end of the 19th century three kinds of Hindi-Urdu had emerged – one, that was highly Persianized; a second, that was highly Sanskritized; and a third, the neutral form spoken and understood by the masses. By this time their stratification seems to have become complete and total, and claims were being laid for representative status. So which variety, it was being asked, has the rightful claim to be called the language of the people of Hindustan. Following is the answer from Gandhi (1918)[47],

> It is necessary to give some thought to the definition of the Hindi language. I have often said that Hindi is that language which is spoken in the North by both Hindus and Muslims and which is written either in the Nagari or the Persian script. This Hindi is neither too Sanskritized, nor too Persianized. The sweetness that I find in the village Hindi is found neither in the speech of the Muslims of Lucknow, nor in that of the Hindu *Pandits* of Prayag. The language which is easily understood by the masses is the best...

Gandhi's conclusion, that Hindustani is understood by most people not only in the North, even in the South of India is widely shared. Hindustani is understood by more people than is English. So is it in Pakistan, Bangladesh, Nepal, Sikkim, Bhutan, Burma, Srilanka and Maldives. As is Spanish in South America, Chinese in South East Asia, Arabic in North Africa & West Asia, Swahili in East Central Africa, etc, so is Hindi-Urdu the language most widely understood in South Asia.

It must also be recorded here that Urdu is not the language of all Muslims nor only of Muslims in India. I know many Muslims in Tamil Nadu and Bihar who think I speak Urdu, but they do not. There are Muslims in Assam, Kashmir, Punjab, Mithila or Northern Bihar, Bengal, Orissa, Tamil Nadu, Kerala, Karnataka, etc. A Muslim in Bengal speaks Bengali just as another Muslim in Kerala speaks Malayalam. One of the most popular novelists of Malayalam, and also one of its most translated, is a Muslim, Vaikkom Mohammed Basheer. Hindustani, however, can claim to be the best understood second language in India.

The reach of Hindustani has tremendous increased with 24-hour satellite television and Hindi films. They both enjoy audiences rivaling those of English, French, Spanish and Chinese. Telecast and film exhibitions in all other languages in India are region and group specific, but, like English, Hindi films and television are shown and seen everywhere. But then a serious constraint on this popular language of the people of and from the Indian sub-continent restricts it to the spoken form – Hindustani is best understood in the spoken form, in print it is group specific.

Section V : A Script for Hindustani

A serious and related question, therefore, has to do with its script – which script can take it to the largest numbers in its written form. Currently, there are at least three claimants for this role – Arabic, Devanagari and Roman. In this section, we will discuss the merits of each of them and then will reach some conclusions on this question.

Arabic's claim is backed by chronology, this script has been used for longest to write this language. Arabic is as efficient a script as, if not more than, any other script. In North-Western parts of the Indian subcontinent, Arabic has been used for writing Sindhi, Pushtu, Sanskrit, etc. Of late, at least in modern India, it has been identified with the Muslims here. Most Muslims learn this script any way, the *Holy Quran* is written only in this script. But it has now become almost exclusive to the Muslims, few other than Muslims learn to write in this script. For this reason alone the constitution of India recognizes Urdu as another language, different from Hindi, which is written in Devanagari.

The claim of Devanagari is backed by numbers. This is the most well known script in India and from India. Most speakers of Hindustani any way know Devanagari. Even in the South Devanagari is learnt by may people as the script essential for reading Sanskrit texts. Bhojpuri, Chhattisgarhi, Dogari, Haryanawi, Marathi, Maithili, Nepali, Tibetan, etc are written in this script. As to the correlation between sound and symbol, Devangari seems better than both Arabic and Roman.

But if today there is one script that most educated Indians surely learn then that distinction goes to the Roman script. That is why most Hindi films and televisions shows write titles and other graphics in the Roman script rather than in any other. Thus they reach very large numbers of users of this language all over India and abroad. Roman is used extensively by the Indian Armed Forces and is well understood by its men from all over India. Roman script does not have half or quarter letters and numerous diacritics, unlike Arabic or Devanagari. Consensus can be built in favour of using only lower or upper case letters and the Roman writing system can be further simplified and adapted for writing Indian languages. Even since this script arrived in India in the 16th century, it has been used for producing translations of the Holy Bible and other books in this script. Early Christian books in the languages of India, prepared by the Portuguese and other Chrisitian missionaries in India were prepared in this script. Some mismatches between the Roman symbols and Hindustani sounds can be easily fixed and standardized.

Gandhiji suggested that this "sweet Hindi" could be written in Devanagari script so that the language can come within the easy reach of every one. On an experimental basis, Gandhi says, an edition of *Gitanjali* of Tagore had been brought out in Devanagari. This edition had also been well-received. This will also "bring Hindus and Mussalmans together", Gandhi thought. He also suggested that Hindus ought to learn Urdu, and Muslims ought to learn Hindi, to come "nearer to their brethren"[48]. Gandhi rejected Roman script as a compromise calling that script "imperfect" for Hindustani. He also hoped that "Hindustani speech will be a mixture of words indifferently borrowed from many languages according to the tastes and equipment of its multitude of writers and speakers"[49]. Only this language, according to Gandhi, can be the "National language of India". "If we want every one to be able to follow what we say", says Gandhi, "we should use in our conversations and speeches a mixture of Hindi and Urdu"[50].

Besides, it is said, adopting Roman script to write Hindustani can render all that has been written in Devanagri beyond the reach of generations to come, and India does not have the resource to transcribe all the existing Hindi works into Roman script. Therefore, the practical choice can be between Arabic and Devanagari.

Interestingly many Urdu writers and their publishers even from Pakistan now tend to bring out an extra edition of their works in Devanagari script, and this brings them good revenue[51] without causing them I any manner a loss of identity. Turkish is written in the Roman script now, but that does not make Turkey a Christian country, it still remains an Islamic country. Use of Devanagari does not make Tibetan a Hindu language, neither does the use of Arabic script for writing Sanskrit, as happens to be the case with Hindus in Sindh and Western Punjab, etc, make Sanskrit a Semitic language. Script has little to do with identity, it seems.

Many languages in the world have changed script and have prospered. The classic case is that of English. It used to be written in its native Runic script until about thirteenth century. But after the rise in French influence in the royal court of London, the Roman script replaced the Runic. This replacement made old English literature opaque to the successive generations of English people, but it gave this otherwise until then relatively underdeveloped language a good chance to become first the language of Europe and then of the world.

Even in India there are many languages that have changed their script and have preferred to survive rather than hold on to their script and perish. A good example here is Maithili which gave up its Tirhuta script in the early 20th century and decided to adopt Devanagari to write its literature. As a result even today all its children who can read and write Hindi, that means nearly all of their literate population, can also read and write this language. This can not be said to be the case with all non-native speakers of Hindi. There are many Bengali, Gujarati, Malayalam, Marathi, Oriya, Punjabi, Tamil, Telugu and Urdu speaking children that can not read their languages in print.

Konkani is written in many different scripts today none of which is "native" to it. Tulu, spoken in coastal Karnataka, is no longer written in its "native" script; in about 15th century or so its speakers adopted Kannada script for its graphic version. So the change of script does not mean the end of that language. Until about the 15th century, Marathi was also written in Modi script. But it switched completely to Devanangari with the advent of printed books in this language.

That script is not integral to the language finds some support also from the view from the converse – that knowing a script does not necessarily give one proficiency in language. Persian printed in Devanagari, such as in the following verse, may still be incomprehensible to those without the knowledge of Persian, even if they know Devanagari script.

(13) बनामे आँकि ऊ नामे नदारद
बहर नामे कि ख्वानी सर बर आरद[52]

कुफ्रो इस्लाम दर रहश पोयाँ
वहदहू लाशरीक लहू गोयाँ[53]

हमसाय: व हमनशीं व हमरह हम: ऊस्त
दर दलके गदा व अत्लसे शह हम: ऊस्त[54]

Similar experiments have been made for rendering Tagore in Devanagari. But they are of little help to the readers of these works because Hindi and Bengal, and Hindi and Persian, more than the Hindi and Bengali, are two totally different languages, and the knowledge of the script alone may not lead one to the meaning of these timeless verses.

Conclusion

The case of Hindi-Hindustani-Urdu, however, is different. Here it is one and the same language made two by the choice of scripts. Different scripts are keeping this language from occupying its rightful place, with one script it may become the mass language of unprecedented reach and can truly be called "the language of India". It may truly became the most preferred second language for most Indians if it adopts a script of wider and greater reach. That will obviously make Roman script the first choice, followed by Devanagari and Arabic in that order. But for some historical reasons, this does not appear to be possible.

Then they can both continue to be used. Efforts must, however, continue to be made to publish literature and other kinds of writings by Muslims also in Devanagari. All that is published in India in Arabic script can also be transcribed and published without much change of language in Devanagari. That will render all publications in this language within the reach of all users of this language, Hindus and Muslims. Writers of Urdu will get nine times more readers and will stand to make as many times more money publishing in this way. That will also give India something like a national language that India has never had. It will, most importantly, re-open the channel of communication between Hindus and Muslims, so badly needed, but so unavailable today. It requires use of pragmatic common sense. And soon Hindustani can be among the languages spoken by most people in the world.

REFERENCE

Ali, M. Athar 1966. *The Mughal nobility under Aurangzeb*. Bombay: Asia Publishing House.

Anderson, Philip A.M. 1854. *The English in Western India*. London.

Archer, Major 1833. *Tours in Upper India, and in parts of the Himalaya Mountains; with accounts of the courts of the native princes, & C.* 2 Vols. London: Richard Bentley.

Ayyar, Chandrika 1987. *Educational and intellectual pursuits*. Kanpur: Prajna Prakashan.

Basham, A.L. (ed.) 1975. *A cultural history of India*. New Delhi: Oxford University Press. pp. 303-09.

Buyers, Rev William 1848. Recollections of Northern India with observations on the origin, Customs, and moral sentiments of the Hindoos, and remarks on the Country, and principal places on the Ganges, & C. London: John Snow.

Chatterji, Suniti Kumar 1960. *Indo-Aryan Hindi*. Calcutta: Firma K.L. Mukhopadhyay.

Chaudhary, Shreesh 2009. *Foreigners and foreign languages in India: A sociolinguistic history*. New Delhi: Cambridge University Press.

Chaudhuri, Jatindra Bimal (ed.) 1954. *Khan Khanan Abdur Rahim and contemporary Sanskrit literature*. Contributions of Muslims to Sanskrit Learning Series, Vol. 2. Calcutta: Prachyavani.

Chaudhuri, Jatindra Bimal (ed.) 1959. *The Nripati – niti – garbhita vritta* or *Farruksiyar carita*. Calcutta: Prachyavani.

Chauhan, D.V. 1970. "Sanskrit inflence on Amiir Khusrau" in *Annals of the Bhandarkar Oriental Research Institute*. Vol. LI, Parts I-IV. pp. 51-58.

Correia-Afonso, John (ed.) 1990. *Intrepid itenerant : Manuel Godinho and his journey from India to Portugal in 1663.* Bombay: Oxford University Press.

Grierson, George A. 1889. *The modern vernacular literature of Hindustan.* Calcutta: The Asiatic Society.

Hasnain, S. Imtiaz and K.S. Rajyashree 2004. "Hindustni as an anxiety between Hindi-Urdu commitment" in *The Yearbook of South Asian Languages & Linguistics.* pp. 247-265.

Heber, Reginald 1828/1833. *Narrative of a journey through the upper provinces of India from Calcutta to Bombay, 1824-25 with notes upon Ceylon, etc.* 3 Vols. London: John Murray. pp. 225-6.

Hedayetullah, Muhammad 1977. *Kabir: The apostle of Hindu – Muslim unity.* Delhi: Motilal Banarsidass.

Hingorani, Anand T. (ed.) 1965. *Our language problem* by M.K. Gandhi. Bombay: Bharatiya Vidya Bhavan.

Hussain, Yusuf 1971. *Indo Muslim polity: Turko-Afghan period,* Simla: Indian Institute of Advanced Study.

Kelkar, Ashok 1978. *Studies in Hirdu Phonology.* Poona: Deccan College.

King, Christopher 1994. *One language, two scripts: The Hindi movement in nineteenth century north India.* Bombay: Oxford University Press.

Offredi, Mariola (ed.) 2000. *The banyan tree: Essays on early literature in new Indo-Aryan languages.* Vol. 1. New Delhi: Manohar. pp. 97-112.

Parasher-Sen, Aloka 1991. *Mlechchhas in Early India.* New Delhi: Munshiram Manoharlal.

Pathak, Jagannath (ed.) 2005. *Dara Shikoh Wirachit Mazm ul Bahrain (Samudra Sangamah)* with Sanskrit-Persian-Hindi text and annotation. Shimla: Indian Institute of Advanced Study & Allahabad: Raka Prakashan.

Qadir, Sir Shaikh Abdul 1942. *Urdu language & literature,* Maharajadhiraj Sir Rameshwara Singh Bahadur of Darbhanga Lectures Series No. 2, University of Allahabad.

Rai, Amrit 1984. *A house divided : The origin and development of Hindi/Hindawi.* Delhi: Oxford University Press.

Russell, Ralph and Khursidul Islam 1994. *Ghalib: Life and letters.* Delhi: Oxford University Press. p. 21.

Shadap-Sen, Namita Catherine 1981. *The origin and early history of the Khasi-synteng people.* Calcutta: Firma K L M Private Limited.

Singh, Rajendra 1997. *Grammar, language & society.* New Delhi: Sage Publications.

Singh, Rajendra 1998. *Linguistic theory, language contact, and modern Hindustani: The three sides of a linguistic theory.* New Delhi: Munshiram Manoharlal Publishers Pvt Ltd.

Singh, Samar Bahadur 1961. *Abdur Rahim Khan-e-Khana: A critical study of his life and works,* in Hindi. Chirgaanw, Jhansi: Sahitya Sadan.

Sinha, Surendra Prasad 1978. *English in India: A historical study with particular reference to English education in India.* Patna: Janaki Prakashan.

Talugdar, J.C. 1931. "Sidelights on the settlements and history of the Christians in Agra in the seventeenth century as revealed from a study of their Tombs" in *Bengal: Past & Present*, Vol. XLII, Part II No. 84, Oct-Dec 1931, pp. 109-16.

Wilson, C.R. 1900/1983. *The early annals of the English in Bengal*, Vol II, Part I. Calcutta: W. Thacker & Co/New Delhi: Bimla Publishing House.

NOTES

1. *Harijan*, May 16, 1936, cited in Hingorani (1965: 49).
2. See Parasher -Sen, Aloka (1991) and Chaudhary (2009: Chapter 2).
3. See Chaudhary (2009: Chapter 4).
4. See Chaudhary (2009: Chapters 5 & 6).
5. See Chaudhary (2009: Chaper 3).
6. For a brief discussion of this process, and for references to the more detailed ones, see Chaudhary (2009: Chapter 1).
7. There are many other local and caste specific names for the numerous varieties of this speech form in India. An interesting new name, showing its bi-culturality, comes from Kelkar (1978) who calls it "Hirdu".
8. See Shadap-Sen (1981).
9. See Correia-Afonso (1990: 47-49).
10. See Anderson (1854) cited in Sinha (1978: 5).
11. See Anderson (1854).
12. Talugdar (1931: 109).
13. Russell & Islam (1994: 21).
14. Hebber (1828: 225-6).
15. Buyers, Rev William (1848: 386).
16. Ali (1966: Table 2(b)).
17. See Qadir (1942: 1) .
18. Cited in Cohn (1997: 34).
19. His first serious piece of literature in Khari Boli appeard only in the late 18th century in the translation of *Bhaagwat Puraan* into *Kharii Bolii* by Munshi Sadasukh who wrote his translation of Bhaagwat in prose and published it as *Sukh Saagar*. See Chatterji (1960: 211).
20. Also see Husain (1971: 68).
21. Cited in Ali (2000: 12).
22. See Kripalani (1975: 306) in Basham.
23. See Hedayatullah (1977: 133-4).
24. Grierson (1889: xvi-xvii).
25. See Singh (1961: 265).
26. Ali (2000: 39-40).
27. Rahim says: "phaarsiiyapadamilitagranthah khalu panditaih kritaah puurvaih/sapraapya tatpadpathamkarawaani khetakautukam padyam".

Gloss: Persian mixed works many pundits have composed even before. For *Khetakautukam* I am merely following that path. See Chaudhuri (1954: 28).

28. All extracts of discourse mixing Persian and Sanskrit have been taken from Chaudhuri (1954: 28-31).
29. See Chaudhuri (1959).
30. See Chaudhuri (1959: 11 and 85).
31. Chaudhuri (1959: 11).
32. Taken from Chaudhuri (1959: 12, 26, 31 and 60-65, and the main text, 1-5)
33. See Ayyar (1987: 26).
34. See Hansen (2000) in Offredi.
35. See Hansen (2000-102-09) in Offredi.
36. Wilson (1900/1983: lxvi-lxvii).
37. Cited in Cohn (1997: 34).
38. King (1994: 27).
39. This principle was endorsed also by the University Education Commission (1940) and the Official Language Commission (1956) which felt that "the language of the large advanced groups with a current literature, practice and tradition" were the only fit media of inatruction (Official language Commission, 27 cited in Singh (1997: 299-301).
40. Cited in Cohn (1997: 35).
41. Archer (1833, Vol. I, Pp. 321-22). Italics added
42. Heber (1828: 333).
43. In Bombay Presidency, Persian was replaced with Urdu, Gujarati and Marathi; in Madras Presidency with Tamil and Telugu.
44. King (1994: 73). Nesfield also wrote a pedagogical grammar of English which became very popular and is used in many regions of Northern India even to day.
45. See King (1994: 54-78).
46. See Cohn (1997: 36).
47. From Gandhiji's Presidential Speech at the 8th Session of the Hindi Sahitya Sammelan, Indore, 1918, cited in Hingorani (1965:13-14).
48. Hingorani (1965: 28).
49. *Harijan*, Feb 8, 1942, cited in Hingorani (1965: 65).
50. *Harijan*, August 9, 1942, cited in Hingorani (1965: 75).
51. Rajkamal & Sons, a noted Hindi publisher from Delhi, have brought out a Devangari edition of the collected short stories of the well-known Urdu writer, Ismat Chugtai, and has had good business on this account. The most well-known instance of increased business due to change of script in Hindi is that of Premchand. Some books of Rabindranath Tagore have been issued by the Sahitya Akademi, Government of India's Academy of Letters, in New Delhi, in the Devanagari script.

52. By the name of the One who has no name
    Call Him by any name, He raises his head.
53. Infidelity and Faith they are both galloping to Him
    They are one, there is no division in His kingdom.
54. He is the neighbour, the friend, the fellow traveler
    In the rags of the beggar, in the attire of the King is he.
    All Persian verses have been cited from Pathak (2005: 33).

8

The Case for Hindustani Revisited

Ayesha Kidwai

In a contribution to a Festschrift for someone so dear to so many linguists, educationists, and social scientists for his commitment to learning and knowledge infused with social responsibility, it would be singularly inappropriate to confine oneself to a topic that is not infused with a similar passion, and does not strive to take us beyond the formulations with which we have been satisfied thus far. Accordingly, this paper re-examines the issue of the 'Hindi/Urdu/Hindustani continuum' - a subject on which Rama Kant Agnihotri himself has written much - and argues that characterisation of the linguistic space defined by these three language labels as a 'continuum' serves to obfuscate the true nature of the linguistic and communicative competence of individuals who command these three varieties. In making this argument, I will be informed by a work of translation into English of Anis Kidwai's Urdu memoir of the first eighteen months of Independent India, *Aazaadi ki Chaon Mein* (*In Freedom's Shade*) that I am currently engaged in, as this experience has led me to rethink some of my own (Abbi, Hasnain, and Kidwai 2004) characterisations of the distance between these varieties.

Hindustani and the promise of release

To encapsulate in a few pages, a long and contentious debate such as the Hindi-Urdu-Hindustani one is virtually impossible. As my intention in this paper is not to examine the causes of, and events in, a historical progression to the current state of affairs in which Urdu is, by and large, considered to be a Muslim language, Hindi is the language of the Indian nation-state's nationalism, and Hindustani has been murdered (see Rai (2000), Rangila, Thirumalai, and Mallikarjun (2001), Hasnain and Rajyashree (2003)) but a more specific examination of the continuum hypothesis as a solution, I will take the liberty of a more impressionistic account of the divide and the solution that is offered. A series of quotation below bring out both the social and cultural costs of the divide, as well as the solutions that have been offered.

The first is a quote from Rama Kant Agnihotri's biographical note about his encounter with the loss of Urdu through his recovery of it in adulthood, and his awareness that the loss is inextricably linked to the Partition of India and the communalisation of Indian polity:

> In the small sleepy town of Nahan in the Sirmaur district of Himachal Pradesh, my parents, very liberal otherwise, forbade me to associate any longer with two of my very dear schoolmates, Shaheed and Anwar; that is the time when I think **I lost touch with the idiom of the street** and could never return to flying kites and making fire-crackers; ... and later when I came to Delhi, **I noticed that the language in which contemporary Hindi poetry was being written was a part of linguistic engineering in which the language spoken inside the walled city was being kept out.**
>
> Very often, some friends would get together in the evening in the lawns of India Gate, recite poems and critically evaluate them and in the end **almost always return to the increasing separation between the language of the people and the new 'pure Hindi' of All India Radio, nascent Doordarshan, Hindi newspapers and magazines and most of all of Hindi literature.**
>
> ...In 1970, I found a copy of the poems of Faiz (1969) in the *naagarii* script. I was simply overwhelmed by the simplicity and power of some of his poems and asked myself and my friends whether he was simply not still the greatest Hindi/Urdu poet. I think it is in Faiz, Kaifi Azmi, Dhumil, and other similar poets, both in India and Pakistan, that we may trace the natural descendants of Kabir or Tulsi . . . **Are poems like *ham jo taariik raaho me maare gaye, yah fasl umiido kii hamdam, shaam, kab Thahregaa dard, paas raho*, etc., Hindi poems or Urdu poems?** Decide it for yourself:... Agnihotri , 2002 (*emphasis mine*)

This sense of mourning for a lost 'idiom of the street', this sense of distance between pure Hindi and 'the language of the people' is also to be found in the text that I am currently translating Begum Anis Kidwai's (1906–1982) memoir, *Aazaadi ki Chaaon Mein* (written in 1949, published 1970), where she suggests that this distance was borne at the very first moment of the birth of India itself. Consider the following extract from her despairing account of the celebrations of the first 15 August:

> On that day, India took its first steps back to the past. Foreheads were being anointed with tilaks. Why were Brahmins from Benaras being summoned? Why the frenetic search for karis to enunciate the Quran? Why was chandan being prepared? Why are those long beards being carefully groomed? What could Buddhist monks possibly have to do in the Government House? Were we to grow accustomed to the sight and

sound of wooden kharauns slapping on its smooth floors?

Fretting and fuming, I made my way to the Government House. At the threshold, my head lifted with pride – this imposing entrance to this magnificent building, on which the tricolour proudly waves, was now to be the thoroughfare for all citizens — everything here is now ours, and everyone who lives here, our comrades.

As quickly, however, the light in my heart was extinguished. The language being spoken around me was even more alien than English – in the words of Josh:

That which can be comprehended by no one but aliens
Is the tongue, my saki, that is in currency these days.

Seated all around on chowkis were Buddhist monks, Brahmin priests, Muslims clerics, and God knows who else. Many languages were spoken that day – English, Sanskrit, Arabic, difficult Hindi, but not the tongue that belongs to us all, every expression of which a hundred flowers scent the air. (Chapter 1)

Over the years, these laments have been consolidated into an appeal for the cultural retrieval of the middle of 'Hindustani', as in the promise of the existence of that language lies the possibility of relief from the phantom pains borne by the social and cultural amputation brought about by Partition. Hindustani decreases the distance between Hindi and Urdu, and can facilitate even the closing seditious question of Agnihotri's note – is the distance between the two languages quantifiable in the first place?

This theme of Hindustani as the release from the divide between Hindi and Urdu is itself gives birth to what I am terming the Continuum Hypothesis. Consider one statement of this hypothesis:

> **...The language of every day life [is] synonymously referred to as Hindi, Urdu, Hindustani – not as three language categories defining the existence of three distinct linguistic entities, but constituting a single structure, verging on mutual intelligibility and sharing the social and inner space.** ...The common language of the common man, which shows a remarkable resilience to rise above the manoeuvring of communal constructionists of both Hindi and Urdu. Yes, indeed, a defence of a social mind that enjoys Hindi-Urdu speech and literature in spite of a "pre-partition partition", and a narrative of intimate destabilization and dispossession. (Hasnain and Rajyashree 2004)

Claims of linguistic identity are made at various points of the continuum according to different formulations. In Hasnain and Rajyashree's conception of the continuum:

> Hindi-Urdu-Hindustani forms a continuum of speech repertoire where identities are crystallized. **Both Hindi-Urdu form one end of the continuum where they survive by acquiring the language of aggression and identifying with the ideology of ... communal constructionists.** The

> writers of Hindustani, on the other hand, are situated on the other end of the continuum, who merely wish to reflect reality. ...Their use of Hindustani is a reflection of 'voluntary inner exile,' consciously chosen to obtain the freedom to separate reality from the language of ideology....

I find this contention that to claim either Hindi or Urdu as one's language to be a collaboration with, or at least a co-option by, communal ideologies very intriguing. An extreme view, no doubt, but nevertheless one that can be argued to be an entailment of the continuum hypothesis *per se*. If what lies at the base, in the words of Abbi, Hasnain, and Kidwai (2004), is "a distinct composite linguistic identity forming the substratum upon which the claims of Hindi and/or Urdu speakerhood [are] overlayed", then to depart from making this common core the locus of linguistic identity ascription must be occasioned by something "extra". In this case, the only other historically relevant factor is religion.

Notice that in all these comments, it is the language of the everyday that invokes "the ghostly persistence of Hindustani" (Rai 2005). Importantly, Hindustani is seen as a locus in which linguistic identities are freed from the shackles that communalism has imposed on them, and becomes "the natural vehicle of popular democracy as well as of secularism (Rai 2005)." What of the language of literary production? If Hindustani is indeed pregnant with the possibility of popular democracy and secularism, why have so few amongst the ranks of secularists and democrats claimed the language as the one they compose or write in? Notwithstanding, however many seditious questions linguists and students of literature may ask, Faiz or Kaifi Azmi would not hesitate to identify themselves as Urdu speakers and writers, as would Dhumil and Nirala call themselves speakers and writers of Hindi.

The Impossibility of Hindustani

At a more general level, as is well known by now, the political appropriation of Hindustani by Gandhi as an antidote to the Hindi-Hindu-Hindustan slogans of the intolerant Hindu Right was a miserable failure, and Partition killed Hindustani altogether. As Rai (2005) points out, between 1931 and 1951, the numbers of people claiming Hindustani as their mother tongue in U.P. declined by 86.4 percent, and by 98.5 percent in the period 1951–1961. ... The 1971 census still recognized Hindustani, albeit grouping it under Hindi, but subsequent censuses have eliminated Hindustani altogether." In the main, claims of language identity have pooled around *either* Hindi *or* Urdu, and not for Hindustani (Rai 2001, 2005). To deny these ascriptions as owing to claims of privilege or religious identity is to elide the subjectivity inherent to all self-identifications. If no one claims Hindustani anymore, an insistence that it is the solution is an exercise in irrelevance, and it cannot even initiate, let alone accomplish, the task of cultural recovery that we have entrusted it with.

At least part of the reason why Hindustani only evades the problem of division between Hindu and Muslim, and Hindi and Urdu, and does not solve it, is because much of the so-called Hindustani canon is a construction of not the 'producers' of the code, but of its receivers, who make intelligibility as the site of language identity. Linguistic identities are for the wholes of languages, and not just their literary or quotidian or religious, etc parts, so to be a producer of a Hindi or Urdu text is merely a matter of choosing one of these registers and still be speaking the same language, *without reference to the notion of Hindustani.* So Kaifi Azmi may write in simple or high-flown Urdu, but the Urdu-ness of his language is not at issue.

Moreover, it is also true that this common core of the quotidian is conceived of differently by Hindi and Urdu speakers. Russell (2004) shows, quite factually, that the distance between Hindi and Urdu is always demonstrable, and indeed infinitely extendable:

> Lelyveld is right to describe the *One Language, Two Scripts* of King's [(1994)] title as an "unfortunate over-simplification." King's description is valid only for one level of the language, the language of everyday conversation on mundane themes, and even there the correspondence is not quite a hundred percent. The vocabulary used in Snell and Weightman's *Teach Yourself Hindi* (1989) illustrates this very well. Pages 252 and 253 — the first two pages of their Hindi-English vocabulary — have a total of 73 entries .... Of these, 54 can equally well be called Urdu... Another 18 are Hindi, and not Urdu, but one finds elsewhere in the vocabulary synonyms for some of them, which are as current in Urdu as they are in Hindi. For example, *adhik* on p. 252 is matched by *zyaadaa* on p. 270 and *aakaash* on p. 253 by *aasman* on p. 255. ... Substantial random sampling of other pages suggests that a complete analysis of the whole vocabulary would yield similar results.
>
> But to equate Hindi with just this range of Hindi would be absurd, and to do the same sort of thing with the comparable range of Urdu would be equally absurd. It is true that the Hindi equivalent of "How far is the station from here?" is identical with the Urdu equivalent. And it is equally true that the Urdu for "The eighteenth century was a period of social, economic and political decline" is "athaarviiN sadii saamaajii, iqtisaadii aur siyasii zavaal ka daur thii," while the Hindi equivalent is "atharaviiN sadii samaajik, aarthik, aur raajniitik giraav kii sadii thii" (and in the Hindi version, Rupert Snell tells me, one could say "...*shataabdii*" instead of "sadii" and "tathaa" instead of "*aur*").

Russell's conclusion that "for all practical purposes, therefore, Urdu and Hindi are two separate languages and should be described as such, despite their almost completely common structure and less completely common stock of everyday words" keeps alive the space for mutual intelligibility, but casts it only in terms of an act of *comprehension*. If one speaks and writes *either* Hindi or Urdu, then the shared space belongs to no one, and cannot be wilfully accessed as a site of production by a speaker of Hindi or Urdu. Only passive receivers constitute Hindustani, and a speech act in Hindustani is in essence doomed to failure.

Even at the level of reception, it must be said, that the notion of Hindustani falls short of defining a common core that underlies both languages. I will assume that the similarity in the basic syntactic structure of the two languages, by virtue of the fact that they are built on a Khari Boli base, is not seen as speakers as definitional of the common core, as many languages share a basic syntactic skeleton (the classic case being Flemish and Dutch), but nevertheless serve as sites for identity formation. Furthermore, no reference can be made to some sort of 'standard Hindustani' – if that indeed existed, then this discussion would be irrelevant – or to stock-based notions like 'if Perso-Arabic, then Urdu, if Sanskrit then Hindi' – if this were true, then neither the Hindi or the Urdu language could be constituted, given the degree to which expressions from each stock is in forming the syntax and semantics of Khari Boli. In effect, then, mining for Hindustani is a lonely act of an individual receiver, and therefore an intensely dynamic one. Just for fun, consider the process of Hindustani mining to be algorithmically expressed as follows:

Hindustani Mixing

For any utterance EXP, EXP is a Hindustani utterance if and only if:

(*i*) EXP falls into the class of utterances/lexical items that is understood by a speaker who claims to be a Hindi speaker, and

(*ii*) EXP falls into the class of utterances/lexical items that is understood by a speaker who claims to be a Urdu speaker

Example: *xariid* 'buy' is an expression that is understood by both Hindi and Urdu claimants, but *faroxt* 'sell' will only be understood by an Urdu claimant and thus will not be considered Hindustani.

This algorithm necessarily requires the existence of both Hindi and Urdu in the same linguistic space, as without such contemporaneous existence, no perception of commonality and sharing can arise. In such a situation, dynamic contact is inevitable, and speakers constantly encounter the other language, and learn it; and the Hindustani extraction algorithm that we have just formulated, everything that is called Hindi or Urdu has the potential to be subsumed into the linguistic code of Hindustani. To see this, consider someone who has claimed to be a Hindi speaker. Say, that she encounters the Urdu word *faroxt*, and learns it; furthermore, this knowledge does not have any fundamentally disastrous consequences for her ascription to a Hindi identity. Consider her next encounter with the word – now that she knows it, the algorithm will class it as an EXP that falls within Hindustani, although she 'knows' it is from Urdu. This procedure can iterate in this fashion infinitely, preserving both the knowledge of a 'non-Hindi-ness' or 'non-Urdu-ness' of an utterance, as well as its inclusion into one's verbal repertoire, *without making reference to notions like a common core, or a composite identity.*

A good example of this point is a footnote in Anis Kidwai's text, where the inclusion of a Hindi word in her verbal repertoire does no elide or political identities and tensions are elided or resolved:

> *A special gift of the times was the word used for refugees from Pakistan – sharanaarthi, 'he who had gained refuge'. For many days we could not even pronounce it properly – such a fat, unwieldy word that it would simply fill up one's mouth – but just as we were getting used to it, Punjabi newspapers protested its use for Punjabi migrants on the grounds that they were not charity-seekers, living off those who gave them refuge. They took up the cause for the use of the word purushaarthi – 'he who labours' – in recognition of the fact that the refugee's own labour rebuilt his life. Later, some also argued for the use of the word muhajir – 'emigrant'. I do not know which to use: the word panaahguziin and muhaajir are Arabic and Farsi words, and the word purushaarthi smells of manual labour, so sharanaarthi will have to do.* (Chapter 2)

This is no pristine untouched common ground, immune from religious distinction and strife. Just as in Hindi/Urdu, even in this terrain, an Arabic or Farsi word should not be used to signify a Hindu.

The Possibility of Multilingualism

If, as I have argued, this conception of Hindustani is in the ultimate analysis, unable to bear the weight of either speakers' ascriptions of identity or yield a definable linguistic object, the question that we must ask what can we erect to stand in its stead.

It seems to me that even as there can be no doubt of the validity and the necessity of the task of cultural recovery, to place its entire burden on the reconstruction of a quasi-mythical common core is mistaken. In my current thinking, it is far more appropriate to characterize the shared space between Hindi and Urdu as not a "core" but as a *register*, a mode of speech employed as appropriate for a particular context, most commonly the quotidian, but also extendable to encompass the literary and other formal discourses. This register is what each language owns individually, but is also shared by the other; as a result, this shared space may be continually enriched by both languages.

So central is this intersected space for both Hindi and Urdu individually, that attempts to liberate it into an autonomous language are viewed with suspicion by Hindi and Urdu-*waalas*, with "each side seeing it as merely a Trojan horse of the other; or, occasionally, in moments of cultural confidence, greedy to annex it by infecting the middle domain with their kind of extremism" (Rai 2005). As a consequence, too, identity claims to only *either* Hindi *or* Urdu by "ordinary people", as the "middle" of a language does not offer a peg to hang an identity on, and particularly when this middle is included in more than one language.

To be a Hindi or Urdu speaker and writer before the pre-Partition partition of the two languages was to exploit the latitude afforded by this shared cross-fertilised register. Creativity in language use lay in the ability to, as Rai (2005) observes, "play with polymorphous perversity ... over the entire range, from fairly *tatsama* Sanskrit all the way to fluent Persian and guttural Arabic, providing cross-border frissons to a genuinely multilingual community." For some, the movement is genuinely pole to pole, for others it signals a liberty to cavort between the end one has pitched one's tent in and the vast middle beyond. What has been lost by 2008, most evidently in literary production, is the right of both Hindi and Urdu to enrich and access this middle, as well as the right to 'listen in' to what the other is saying.

REFERENCES

Agnihotri, R.K. 2002. On a pre-partition partition: The question of Hindi-Urdu. In S. Settar and I.B. Gupta (eds.) *Pangs of partition: The human dimension.* Vol. 2. New Delhi: Indian Council of Historical Research and Manohar. 29-46.

Abbi, Anvita, S. Imtiaz Hasnain, and Ayesha Kidwai 2004. Whose Language is Urdu? *Heidelberg papers in South Asian and comparative politics,* No. 24. Available online at <http://www.hpsacp.uni-hd.de/>

Hasnain, S. Imtiaz and K.S. Rajyashree 2004. Hindustani as an Anxiety between Hindi-Urdu Commitment. In Rajendra Singh (ed.) *The yearbook of South Asian languages and linguistics.* Berlin: Mouton de Gruyter. Also in *Language in India* 3. Available online at http://www.languageinindia.com.

Rai, Alok 2001. *Hindi nationalism.* In *Tracts for the Times.* New Delhi: Orient Longman.

Rai, Alok 2005. The Persistence of Hindustani. *The Annual of Urdu Studies*, 20. Available online at <http://www.urdustudies.com>

Rangila, R.S., M. Thirumalai, and B. Mallikarjun 2001. Bringing Order to Linguistic Diversity: Language Planning in the British Raj. *Language in India* 1. Available online at <http://www.languageinindia.com>

Russell, Ralph 2004. Some Notes on Hindi and Urdu. *The Annual of Urdu Studies* 19. Available online at <http://www.urdustudies.com>

9

The Politics of Multiculturalism

Tanmoy Bhattacharya and Haobam Basantarani

Introduction

In spite of its engagement with application, and in spite of its concern for social justice, sociolinguistics, according to some, has had negligible impact beyond academic circles (Bargiela-Chaippini, 2004). The theoretical agnosticism of sociolinguistics and the relatively unengaged attitude of current sociolinguistics towards social theory (Coupland, 2001), no doubt, contributed to this impasse. The present paper, as a tribute to the responsible teachings of Rama Kant Agnihotri, redresses this allegation to some extent by situating language rights movements and minority rights in general within the broader spectrum of a liberal, plural democracy framework.

In the aftermath of recent events that urged political scientists to promptly designate a *pre-* and a *post-* period of these events, the spirit of liberal democracy has been under threat in the form of exclusionary gestures towards integrating multicultural policies concerning immigration and ethnicity in general. The notion of an undifferentiated citizenry in the public sphere has been compromised by western societies and governments. This is further compounded by the philosophical retreat from such policies as amounting to a denial of individual freedom and equality. This, in short, is the politics of multiculturalism; however, it is also becoming clearer that there cannot be a political car of multiculturalism without its philosophical engine. Throughout the following discussion, it becomes evident though, that the thread that runs through – or the oil that runs the car – the politics and philosophy of multiculturalism is the liberalist dilemma of coping with the opposing demands of liberty and equality.

The Philosophy of Multiculturalism

Multiculturalism attains a philosophical underpinning by virtue of the discord it brings about with the notion of individual freedom enshrined within the western liberal tradition of political philosophy. However, this was not always the case; the *individualistic* turn in philosophical thought in the 18th century gives rise to this modern discordance. Let us unravel this in some detail.

In one famous mapping of the notion of identity (Taylor, 1994) – that which engenders recognition – individualistic identity figures prominently. That is, the concerns of a community, a group or a nation, are the concerns of individuals that comprise it. Identity, in this regard, provides the social form that shapes individuality. However, such a particularized identity (the *one that I find in myself*), comes along with an ideal of being true to myself and my way of being. Thus, a sense of the moral is acutely attached to identity, making *ethical individualism* one of the central heritages of liberalism.

The pre-18th century view of morality was concerned with divine punishment and reward. This gave way to the sense or feeling of what is right or wrong – the "voice" within. Taylor (1994) identifies Trilling's (1969) use of the term "authenticity" to identify the displacement of this voice as an ideal that humans strive to attain. This shift in focus can be read as the passage from the moral to the ethical, the former being only a part of the broader tradition of the latter. The distinction comes out clearly in Dworkin's (2000) formulation where ethics "includes convictions about which kinds of lives are good or bad for a person to lead, and morality includes principles about how a person should treat other people."

Over the centuries and decades the notion of an ethical life has undergone various transformations. One of the modern views of a well-lived life recognizes it as the principle of *expressive liberty* which ensures "individuals and groups leading their lives as they see fit, within a broad range of legitimate variation, in accordance with their own understanding of what gives life meaning and value. This principle implies a corresponding presumption against external interference with individual and group endeavours" (Galston 2004). The ethical turn, in the shape of how to lead a well-lived life, finds identity (among others) as an important tool to attain this ideal.

However, "authenticity" makes its appearance most directly in the form of the principle of originality – each of us with a unique way of being human.[1] Thus, for the first time, the difference between human beings attained a moral significance: in articulating my true self, I am also defining myself, my authenticity. Determination of one's identity through social positioning now had to be discarded in favour of authenticity where you are called upon to determine your own original way of being. However, being a true communitarian, Taylor (1994) warns against an inward generation of the self, rather, it depends crucially on the dialogical relations with others.

In the public sphere, however, this gives rise to the politics of difference in our times, which seems like a negation of the main tenet of liberalism, namely, equalisation of rights, itself derivable from the notion of equal dignity. Thus the demand for equality through recognition of identity of individuals and groups unsettles the universal foundations of liberalism as it plays out in the public sphere.

Constitutional Democracy

Thus multiculturalism compromises individual freedom by privileging groups over individuals and equality by treating people differently on the basis of group traits such as race, gender or ethnicity. However, a far more alarming prospect is the attempt to associate multiculturalism with the rise of a concern for national security in some western societies. The disquieting belief is that multicultural policies of a state provide the basis for installing institutional structures within minority communities that promote sectarian ideas.

A different concern in circulation coterminous with this is the sociological worry that multiculturalism weakens the welfare state, it gradually erodes trust, solidarity and coalition essential to sustain the good health of a welfare state (Banting and Kymlicka, 2006). It may not be difficult to assess which came first, the threat to national security or the threat to welfare state. From the early days of liberalism, many liberals including Mill (1956) had agreed that liberalism is only viable in countries that share a deep sense of common nationhood. The recent events alluded to above have only thus accentuated the nationalistic fear to national security.

Above all however, the claims for multiculturalism have been firmly set within the basic principles of justice, especially in its relation to human rights norms. Rights in this sphere increasingly have acquired a relational character which expresses the mutual recognition of the citizens articulating them, though for Kant, for example, the law in general was regulated by reason and situated in the realm of morality. The legal positivists rejected this moral legitimacy of law and instead identified political status as the source of legitimacy for the law. That is, a law is legitimate only when socially and politically recognized authorities posit it. However, in the past decades, a Neo-Kantian notion of law has prevailed which emphasises subjects constructing intersubjective worlds through their own faculties and actions, termed as "Kantian Constructivism" by Rawls (1980). This is also the tenor of a Habermasian legal theory with its focus on human practices of world construction, on citizens' creation of legal norms through discourse. Habermas (1996) calls his core argument (for the derivation of a system of rights), "the logical genesis of rights". In this, democracy and law come together in organising peoples' lives to enable them to see one another as equal citizens - as "free and equal consociates under law."

Thus we see that the beginning of multiculturalism can be philosophically traced to the liberal notion of individuality with its political ending with the liberal notion of the system of rights. Multiculturalism is thus codified into specific enactments in the form of constitutional democracy.

Reconstruction of Rights and the Politics of Segregation in Tripura

Habermas' "reconstructions" of human practices is a process of interpretation in which a practice's full meaning, in terms of its internal structure and sets of presuppositions, must be understood. Thus rights are reconstructed through discourse by the consociates. Given his emphasis on reconstructing the implicit presupposition of a practice, by analogy to language, Habermas's work can be considered as a reconstruction of norms and rules that define the actual practice of the democratic rule of law. For example, the right to privacy in the U.S. constitution is not there in the text of the Bill of Rights but is considered to be an implicit right.

Similarly, Article 29 of the Indian Constitution, falling under cultural and educational right, although named as *Protection of interests of minorities* never actually uses the word 'minorities' in the text, yet is assumed to relate to minorities:

Article 29: *Protection of interests of minorities*

(1) Any section of the citizens residing in the territory of India or any part thereof having a distinct language, script or culture of its own shall have the right to conserve them.
(2) No citizen shall be denied admission into any educational institution maintained by the State or receiving aid out of State funds on grounds only of religion, race, caste, language or any of them.

Thus in its scope, Article 29 is not confined to minorities, since it is available to "any section of citizens resident in the territory of India." This may well include the majority, as pointed out by Chief Justice Ray in the case 'Ahmedabad St. Xavier's College Society v. State of Gujarat',

AIR 1974 SC 1389. (Bakshi, 2009)

In fact, the word 'minority' has not been defined in the Indian Constitution. The U.N. Commission on Prevention of Discrimination and Protection of Minorities has defined minorities as follows:

> (i) The term 'minority' includes only those non-document groups in a population which possess and wish to preserve stable ethnic, religious or linguistic traditions or conditions or characteristics markedly different from those of the rest of the population; (ii) such minorities should properly include a number of persons sufficient by themselves to preserve such traditions or characteristics; and (iii) such minorities must be loyal to the State of which they are nationals.

Article 27 of the International Covenant on Civil and Political Rights does not define the expression but renders the following right to them:

> In those States in which ethnic, religious or linguistics minorities exist, persons belonging to such minorities shall not be denied the right, in community with the other members of the group, to enjoy their own culture, to profess and practice their own religion or to use their own language.

If a government or state fails to administer Article 29 within the ambit of minorities, it can be deemed to have failed in "reconstructing" the implicit rules of a democratic legal practice. It thus exposes the failure of the political system to follow through its commitments (hypocrisy) or its inconsistency in embracing a new principle but not its implicit preconditions.

However, a clear grasp of the reconstruction of the rights is clearly not enough since the enactment of the laws themselves are sites for discontent and strife, precisely because they have been, to a large extent, non-discursive. Within the context of the case study that we later report, namely the tribal in-group out-group behaviour in Tripura, this gives rise to a politics of segregation and/ or self-rule in the form of a creation of an autonomous council. Note in this connection the contentious clause (iii) above of the U.N. Commission definition of 'minority'. This restrictive clause is also a reflection of Galston's (2004) liberal strand of value pluralism which calls for certain restrictions a liberal public institution may observe for several reasons, preventing and, when necessary, punishing transgressions individuals may commit against one another to guard the boundary separating legitimate from illegitimate variations among ways of life. A few among them ensure that adherence to State laws however non-discursively they are enacted – for the parties under conflict – must be observed at all times.

This conflict in the case of the tribals in Tripura becomes apparent when we consider certain assertions that the politics of multiculturalism makes. It is asserted in Banting and Kymlicka (2006) that western democracies have never retreated from granting rights to the indigenous and substrate population, neither have there been any instances of backlash towards these groups or rolling back of rights granted to them in the past; it is only the immigrant groups that have faced such treatments recently. This is exactly the opposite of what we find in the case of a state within a nation, such as Tripura, where the rights and the demands of the majority indigenous historic population of the Tripuris have been compromised or suppressed by the minority ruling Bengali population, whereas no major backlash against recent migrants from other states have been reported.

Thus, it becomes clear that the non-recognition of Constitutional demands made by an ethnic group, within this Habermasian model, in addition to indicating a lack of discursivity at the level of enactment of the law governing the conduct of individuals that make such a group, is a direct reflection of a failure of reciprocal, mutual granting of autonomy between "consociates" under law. The misrecognition of a group is then the deliberate act of denial of presuppositions implicit within a democratic legal practice.

Plural Democracy

The situation in Tripura thus presents a critique of the constitutional democracy in such an analysis by exposing its hypocrisy and inconsistency in reference to the particular legal practice. In other words, reconstruction is able to provide a critique but not a direction. We need to now shift our gaze from the codification of a democratic practice to the politics of it in terms of how it is contested by affected groups.

For this, the reworking of the Gramscian notion of hegemony as 'articulation' in Laclau and Mouffe's (1985) seminal work *Hegemony* is found useful:

> ... (W)e will call articulation any practice establishing a relation among elements such that their identity is modified as a result of the articulatory practice. The structured totality resulting from the articulatory practice, we will call discourse. The differential positions, insofar as they appear articulated within a discourse, we will call moments. By contrast, we will call element any difference that is not discursively articulated.

As it will become clear from the exposition of the situation in Tripura (next section), borrowing from Haobam (2003), the linguistic demand of a tribal population in general is an articulation, with its discursive background being greater political autonomy. On the other hand, extending the analysis presented in Bhattacharya and Haobam (2003) and Haobam (2007), an 'element' in this framework is shown as the language right movement of a minority tribal group.

This reinvestigation reveals to us that if a direction, referred as above, is to be sought, it is most likely to be found in the plural, radical democracy model enunciated in *Hegemony* and specially, in Mouffe (1993, 1996, 2000). Although on surface it may seem to be another recalcitrant thread from Gramsci, especially his proposal of a formation of a 'historical bloc', it is a more complex notion arising out of the typical liberalist tension between liberty and equality. In addition, the treatment the model is subjected to in our analysis can make sense only in this extended, a more tempered notion of plural democracy found in Mouffe's later works[1]. Before we proceed further, let us now examine the ground realities of the political and linguistic situation in Tripura.

Tripura: Where the majorities are a minority

Tripura is one of the North-Eastern states of India, sharing its national border with Assam and Mizoram in the east and the international border of 839 km constituting nearly 84% of its total land frontier in the north, south and west with the neighbouring country of Bangladesh. Comprising of four districts, namely, North Tripura, South Tripura, West Tripura and Dhalai, the total geographical area of Tripura is 10,491 sq. km, the total population being 27,57,205. (Census of India, 1991)

The remarkable growth in the population of Tripura in terms of percentage variation is as shown in the Tables below:

Table 1: Growth of the Population in Tripura

Year	*% Variation*
1911	+32.48
1921	+32.59
1931	+25.63
1941	+34.14
1951	+24.56
1961	+78.71
1971	+36.20
1981	+31.90
1991	+34.30

Table 2: Change in the total population of Bengali and Tripuri speakers over time

Year	*Bengali %*	*Tripuri %*
1911	42.71	40.93
1921	42.18	41.32
1931	44.65	38.78
1951	60.51	23.49
1961	65.22	24.86
1991	68.88	23.50

The major cause of the rise of population is found to be the large number of immigrants from outside the state and country, particularly, from adjoining Sylhet and Bangladesh. Being bounded on its three sides by Bangladesh, the geographical position of Tripura also makes it vulnerable to such a movement of population. As can be seen from Table 1, the total population of Tripura increased by 78% between 1951 and 1961 alone. This heavy influx of population into Tripura from the adjoining territories mainly comprises of the Bengali speaking immigrants. Such influx has been an ongoing process and by 1961, the Bengalis had emerged clearly as a dominant group and the Tripuris were effectively reduced to a meagre 25% of the total population.

These factors had a significant impact on the population, economy, culture and language of the region. The Bengalis being the economically, educationally and numerically more stronger group became the dominant group. They came to be the people in power, administration, business, educational institutions etc. Based on the numerical strength of the Bengali speaking population and their economically and politically advantageous position, Bengali is today the official language of Tripura and also the medium of instruction. *Kok Borok*, the native language of the Tripuris and spoken by 84% of tribal population of Tripuris is taught in schools but only at the primary level where the children have to shift to Bengali from standard six onwards. The script used is also Bengali. However, as will be discussed shortly, this is beginning to change. One major outcome of such a scenario is a situation where the indigenous people and their languages emerge as minority groups and the immigrants as the dominant group.

There are two prominent trends that can be witnessed among the tribal population of Tripura (Haobam, 2003; Haobam, 2002). On the one hand, a trend of assimilation, culturally and linguistically, towards the dominant group can be seen among sections of tribals in urban areas, particularly in Agartala and surrounding areas in West Tripura. For example, there already is a language shift in the direction of Bengali. This is evident from the fact that as many as 5,354 (0.7%) Tripuris returned Bengali as their mother tongue according to the 1991 Census of India. On the other hand, there is also a strong resistance building up against the dominant group.

Tribal unrest in Tripura

Tribal political mobilization against Bengali inflows was first articulated in 1947 by *Seng Krak*, an organization (mostly drawn from Tripuri and Reang group of tribals) which was banned shortly afterward. The history of the tribal insurrection in Tripura is closely linked to the history of the Communist movement in the state which started as early as 1946 when *Tripura Rajya Praja Mandal* and later in 1948 *Gana Mukti Parishad* were formed by progressive young tribals, where the Congress party, the major national level party, was dominated by the Bengalis. However, the Communists who were largely responsible for spreading awareness among the tribals and later, articulation of their demands, fell from favour and were largely seen as not representative of the tribal struggles.

A new organization, the *Tripura Upajati Juba Samiti* (TUJS), was thus born in June 1967 and began a political campaign to create an autonomous tribal district council which had a four-point agenda, two out of which had to do with language:

(*i*) Recognition of the *Kok Borok* language

(*ii*) Adoption of Roman script instead of the Bengali one

Anti-Bengali activities surfaced with the reformation of *Seng Krak* in 1967 and the Government in 1968 declared Bengali as the official language. TUJS formed *Kok Borok Sahitya Sabha* as a cultural and literary front at the same time.[2]

However, the left front, led by the Communist Party of India (Marxist) received a massive mandate in the 1977 elections winning 56 of the 60 seats, TUJS forming the main opposition with 4 seats and 7.9% share of the total votes cast. Due to internal division, Congress drew a blank. The government recognised *Kok Borok* as the tribal representative language and the Tripura Tribal Areas Autonomous District Council (TTAADC) Bill was adopted as the entry 5, list 2, Schedule VII of the Constitution of India on 20th July 1979; the district council realised in 1982.

Demands for language and script

Kok Borok falls within the Boro group of Tibeto-Burman branch of Tibeto Chinese family of languages and as such, recognised as a language in Grierson as early as 1904. The Tripuris can study up to standard Xth in *Kok Borok*. As a language subject, it is taught up to standard XIIth. Since the last few years, Tripura University has started a one year Diploma course in *Kok Borok*. This was a result of first Education Commission since 2005 to implement the study of the language at primary, secondary and higher secondary levels.

A look at the proposals of the government of Tripura with regards to Education in the form of a 25 Point Tribal Development Package (1999 to 2002) is instructive; it is clear that none of the points in this package mention anything about mother tongue education or a language policy. In fact, by looking at this proposal, it appears that there is no language issue involved in education in this area, which is a major blunder.

The emergence of *Kok Borok* as the most important language of the tribals of Tripura is accompanied by controversies regarding the issue of script and the renaming of the state. The script issue emerged as a major bone of contention after the Congress-TUJS coalition government came to power in 1988. While regional parties favour the Roman script, the Left parties go for the Bengali script. As a result, the primary and secondary schools of the council areas, which teach *Kok Borok*, are thrown into turmoil because the script, the textbooks and pedagogic strategies change with bewildering regularity.

Both the controversies regarding the language and script are statements of assertion of the linguistic rights of a minority. However, at the same time as this demonstration of assertion is taking place, a different, hegemonic dominance begins to play out its tune (Haobam, 2002).

Kok Borok as the articulation

Though the tribals of Tripura have been successful in carving out a new identity for themselves through *Kok Borok*, other several tribal languages of Tripura have been inadvertently put to a greater disadvantage. The state today comprises of nineteen different types of tribal communities. They are Tripuri[3], Reang, Jamatia, Chakma, Halam, Noatia, Mogh, Kuki, Garo, Munda, Lushai, Orang, Santhal, Uchai, Khasi, Bhil, Chaimal, Bhutia and Lepcha. Among these, the Tripuris and the Reangs are the biggest and the earliest inhabitants (Das, 1982).

We have seen so far that *Kok Borok* has achieved the status of the representative language as a symbol of success of the struggles of the indigenous tribal population of the region. In terms of Laclau and Mouffe, thus, *Kok Borok* is the articulation of the movement for language rights of the minorities. As a result, all the other tribal languages which are significantly different from each other and from *Kok Borok* have been conveniently grouped as dialects of Tripuri and their differences are identified by Tripuris as minor differences emphasising only the language-dialect difference. However, in the model of plural democracy, the representative articulation is also to be widely acceptable as a new collective identity, but is it really the case?

The Census of India, 1961 and 1951, list Tripuri, Jamatia, *Kok Borok*, Murasing, Noatia and Reang as dialects of Tripura (and Tripuri, respectively). However, the Tripuri of 1991 census subsumes at least three other languages, namely, *Kok Borok*, Tripuri and Reang. Comparing the mother tongue tables of the relevant years, the number of *Kok Borok* speakers show an increase from 3 to 5,16,749 in 30 years. Note in this connection that the number of so-called Tripuri (as a dialect) speakers has reduced from 2,11,883 in 1961 to 73,147 in 1991. Since Tripuri is standardly considered to be the language of the Debbarmas, it is assumed that the reduction is due to identification with *Kok Borok* as the representative language of the Debbarmas. The corresponding figures of the number of Reang speakers also reveal the fact that many of the Reang speakers identified with *Kok Borok* as their mother tongue in the 1991 census. Thus the inflated figure of *Kok Borok* speakers is not only due to identification with *Kok Borok* by the Tripuri tribe but also because of some Reangs, Jamatia and Noatias identifying with *Kok Borok* as a reaction to dominance of Bengali as the major language. However, this state of affairs also points to the hegemonic role that the major tribal language, in this case *Kok Borok,* ends up playing.

The trend of switching over to the dominant minority language was already visible in the mother tongue and bilingualism data of the 1961 census. The following table shows the figures for minor tribes (Reang, Jamatia and Noatia) identifying Tripuri as the mother tongue:

Table 1: Minor tribes identifying with Tripuri as MT

Tribe	MT in the tribe's name	MT as Tripuri
Reang	52,926	3,645
Jamatia	14,137	10,203
Noatia	4,433	11,535

The arrows indicate increase in numbers. Thus we can deduce that the Noatia are the most willing to give up their linguistic identity whereas Reangs are the most resistant to sacrificing their linguistic identity. The table is thus instructive in not only showing us how switching over to another linguistic identity is already set as a trend in 1961, but also that Reangs as a group are resistant to this switch-over.

Thus, *Kok Borok* does not really satisfy the criterion that 'demands of each group are articulated equivalently', however problematic the term equivalent may mean in this model. The articulatory stance of *Kok Borok* as the representative language of the minority tribal groups is thus flawed. This is might as well since in the model of plural democracy the end of each hegemonic practice is an impossible one, each hegemonic formation necessarily encounters 'frontier effects' (Laclau and Mouffe, 1985) with other articulatory practices. We shall see that Reangs and their language constitute one such frontier effect.

Rise of the Reangs: A minority within the minorities

The Reangs as a tribal group constitute about 14% of the tribal and 4% of the total population of the state. By no means, the presence of the Reangs is a recent phenomenon in Tripura. The 1875 census reports

2435 of them, which even then constituted 3% of the total population. By 1901, their numbers had increased to 15,115 which was then a healthy 8.72% of the total population; the increase itself was comparable to that of the Tripuris.

In 1990, the Reang Democratic Convention Party was formed with the aim to protect and promote Reang culture. This brought about opposition to the domination of Christian Mizos. The Reangs won in seven village council elections and a seat to the Lai Autonomous District Council in 1992. In 1997, another organisation — the Bru National Union — demanded an Autonomous District Council. It was also during this period that the Bru National Liberation Front — a militant body — was born. The BNLF, floated in 1997, had demanded a separate autonomous district council for the Brus carved out from the north-western parts of the state. The opposition to the Reang demands was led by the Mizo Zirlai Pawl (Mizo Students Federation). Mizos accused National Liberation Front of Tripura, a banned group dominated by Reangs, of providing arms and training to BNLF cadres. Due to infighting among these groups, an exodus to Tripura and Cachar in Assam began. Other Brus joined them later in 1998, swelling their numbers, and they were treated as refugees by Tripura and the Government of India and lodged in six different camps. Repatriation of the refugees has not yet taken place and the conditions of the camps continue to be inhuman, with lack of drinking water, health care, education. 'Education for All' (*Sarva Siksha Aviyan*) of the Government of India which has been successfully launched in many districts of Tripura, has not been started in these camps and as a result, a whole generation of Reang children (about 5,000) remains illiterate. The refugees get Rs. 87 a month compared to Rs. 800 that displaced Kashimiri pandits get.

With respect to linguistic minority rights, although Reangs constitute 14% of the population, their language has not been adopted by any institution as a medium of instruction even in the areas dominated by the Reangs. Subsuming *Kai Bru*, the language of the Reangs, under *Kok Borok* as one of its varieties deprives *Kai Bru* of its status as a different language in its own right. Though, we have taken up the case of Reang and *Kai Bru* for the purpose of our paper, this observation holds true of the case of other minority languages of Tripura which face the threat of being reduced to varieties of *Kok Borok*.

It must also be realised that since Grierson's *Linguistic Survey of India* (1904), Reang has been recognised as a separate language. Grierson's survey was based on the 1891 census data. It is thus all the more surprising that even now the language of the Reang is considered to be simply a variety of the language of the dominant group, that is, Triupris. Furthermore, the census of 1961 clearly identifies Reang as one of the three strongest languages of the state.

Predictably, by June 2003, the Reangs pressed for demands for a formal recognition of *Kai Bru* as separate language from *Kok Borok*. Several seminars and meetings have been held in the Reang-dominated areas of Kanchanpur in North Tripura and Shantir Bazar in South Tripura to press for the demand. A Reang-dominated group, Bru National Renaissance Organisation (BNRO), is spearheading the struggle for recognition of *Kai Bru*.[4] However, it is in subjecting a demand like this to the model of plural democracy that true chances of it succeeding are revealed.

Agonistic Pluralism as 'Civil Association'

In *Hegemony*, radical democratic pluralism is a struggle that superimposes a 'new common sense' that alters the identity of the different groups in such a way that the demands of each group are articulated equivalently with those of the other groups. In light of the case-study discussed in earlier, *Kok Borok*, at the first glance, seems to attain the hegemonic articulation or the new common sense. The suspicion that was consequently attributed to such an articulation was discussed in previous section with respect to the language rights movement of the Reangs. It now becomes clear that such a suspicion emanates from the correct interpretation of the term 'equivalence' above, the model is unclear about how equivalence is to be construed. In fact, Wenman's (2003) employment of a broadly Saussurian semiotic theory in this regard successfully accentuates the political difference between *Hegemony* and the tempered notion of plural democracy of Mouffe. Thus the absence of a synecdochic replacement (a part standing in for the whole) in Mouffe's pluralism highlights the formation of a condensation of a new common sense that is at the same time indifferent to each particular demand.

Returning somewhat to the liberal themes, an agonistic form of pluralism, unlike other strands of liberalist political philosophy, is not relegated to the private sphere so that a rational political consensus can emerge in the public sphere but rather creates a situation where identification with different positions in the public sphere becomes possible. It is only a real struggle against different positions advocated by agonistic pluralism that creates a vibrant democratic life as opposed to a deliberative model of democracy.[5] In the localised context of our discussion, such a form of political engagement is able to construct the possibility where Reangs can see themselves also as Reangs and not just as tribal Tripuris.

The challenge for this new notion of radical democracy is 'to envisage a form of commonality strong enough to institute a "*demos*" but nevertheless compatible with certain forms of pluralism: religious, moral and cultural pluralism, as well as a pluralism of political parties' (Mouffe, 1999). That is, to identify a common political identity among persons engaged in different enterprises. In this view, a radical democratic community is devoid of any aspiration of any single group so that the principle of pluralism is not violated. Viewed from a semiotic lens, synecdoche fails to provide us any 'direction' we may be seeking, but rather a metaphoric condensation does.

The well-known challenge to liberalism's preference for the individual at the cost of the community is also partly met by Mouffe in her notion of the 'demos'. Her commitment to liberalism is clear in what she takes to be its most important contribution to democracy, the idea of pluralism. Her idea of a community in the form of a "demos" is a combination of the best of the liberal and communitarian world views. The tempered notion of pluralism thus ensures that in addition to what we have in common, the particularities are also taken into account.

Furthermore, her notion of the *societas* or 'civil association' emphasise the bond between radical democratic citizens that is defined not by an engagement to pursue a common purpose or to promote a common interest, but by the notion of loyalty to one another. It is in this light of political action that the language rights demands of the Reangs must be seen. Although a politics of multiculturalism when translated in terms of a constitutional binding comes with certain restrictive preconditions, it is only a tempered notion of pluralism that lends its acquiescence to a "co-articulation" of a demand. Thus, on surface, such a co-articulation may seem contradictory to the strategy outlined in *Hegemony*, capable of inviting an allegation of dissent, civil association, especially at the time of 'revolution', leaves enough space for it in the true spirit of the liberal democratic tradition.

REFERENCES

Bakshi, P.M. 2009. *The Constitution of India*. 9th Edition, New Delhi: Universal Law Publishing Co. Pvt. Ltd.

Banting, Keith and Will Kymlicka (eds.) 2006. *Multiculturalism and the welfare state: Recognition and redistribution in contemporary democracies*. Oxford, New York: Oxford University Press.

Bargiela-Chaippini, Francesca 2004. Introductions: reflections on a new research paradigm. *International Journal of Sociology of Language* 166, 1-18.

Bhattacharya, Tanmoy and Haobam Basantarani 2003. 839 Kms: Language Hegemony and Social Identity in Tripura. Paper presented in 9th Himalayan Language Symposium, CIIL, Mysore.

Census of India 1961, 1971, 1981 and 1991. New Delhi: Registrar General of India and Census Commissioner.

Coupland, Nikolas 2001. Introduction: Sociolinguistics theory and social theory. In N. Coupland et al (eds.) *Sociolinguistics and social theory*. 1-26, Harlow: Pearson Education.

Das, A.K. 1982. *Assam's agony: A Socioeconomic and political analysis*. Delhi: Lancers Publishers.

Dworkin, Ronald 2000. *Sovereign virtue: The theory and practice of equality*. Cambridge: Harvard University Press.

Galston, William A. 2004. *Liberal pluralism: The implications of value pluralism for political theory and practice*. Cambridge: Cambridge University Press.

Grierson, G.A. 1904. *Linguistic survey of India* (Vol.III, part 2). Calcutta: Government of India; (reprinted by Delhi: Motilal Banarasidas 1967).

Habermas, Jürgen 1996. *Between facts and norms: Contributions to a discourse theory of law and democracy*. William Rehg (trans.) Cambridge, Mass.: MIT Press.

Haobam, Basantarani 2002. Tribal-non-tribal contact situation, the case of Kok Borok in Tripura, Paper presented at the Non- Scheduled Languages conference, Gandhi Hindustani Sahitya Sabha, Delhi.

Haobam, Basantarani 2003. *Tribal bilingualism: Borrowing and assimilation in Kok Borok*. MS. University of Delhi.

Haobam, Basantarani 2007. Multilingualism endangered. In R. Elangaiyan et al (eds.) *Vital voices: Endangered languages and multilingualism*. Mysore: CIIL.

Laclau, Ernesto and Chantal Mouffe, 1985. *Hegemony and social strategy*. London: Verso.

Mill, John Stuart 1956. *On liberty*. Currin V. Shields. (ed.) Indianapolis: Bobbs-Merrill.

Mouffe, Chantal 1993. *The return of the political*. London: Verso.

Mouffe, Chantal 1996. Radical Democracy or Liberal Democracy? In D. Trend (ed.) *Radical democracy: Identity, citizenship, and the State*. New York: Routledge.

Mouffe, Chantal 1999. *The challenge of Carl Schmitt*. London: Verso.

Mouffe, Chantal 2000. *The democratic paradox*. London: Verso.

Rawls, John 1980. Kantian Constructivism in Moral Theory. *Journal of Philosophy* 77, 515– 572.

Taylor, Charles 1994. *Multiculturalism: Examining the politics of recognition*. Amy Gutmann, ed. Princeton, NJ: Princeton University Press.

Trilling, Lionel 1969. *Sincerity and authenticity*. New York: Norton.

Wenman, Mark Anthony 2003. Laclau or Mouffe? Splitting the difference. *Philosophy and Social Criticism* 29 (5), 581-606.

NOTES

1. See section on agnostic pluralism later.
2. Herder, J.G. 1877-1913. Ideen Chapter 7, Section 1. In Herders Sämliche Werke, ed. Bernard Suphen. Berlin: Weidmann.
3. Another non-political cultural society was formed in 1993 called Kokborok tei Hukumu Mission or KOHM to promote and to preserve the Kok Borok literature, culture, tradition and its heritage.
4. Also called Tipura/ Tripura or Tippera
5. Muzrati Bru, a Reang intellectual, who is a prominent figure in leading the movement for recognition of Kai Bru as a separate language, has emphasised the fundamental differences between the two languages. He believes the tribals were being forced to record their identity as Boroks and their language as Kok Borok in the census. Blaming the mainstream tribal parties and a section of militant outfits for trying to impose Kok Borok on Reangs, he has pledged to fight to elicit their demand on national and linguistic identity (*The Telegraph*, Kolkata, June 7, 2003).
6. As in the nature of the discursive in Habermas (1996) being the instrument of participatory democracy.

10

Contextuality, Critical Discourse Analysis and Structuration Theory: Sociological Basis for Analyzing 'Heavenly Ornaments' (*Bihishti Zewar*)

S. Imtiaz Hasnain

> *If we describe the context of situation in terms of ad hoc observations about the settings in which language is used, this could be said to be a 'social' account of language but hardly a 'sociological' one, since the concepts on which we are drawing are not referred to any kind of general social theory.*
>
> (Halliday, 1978: 34-5)

1. Introduction

An observation of the distinction drawn by Halliday marks the trajectory adopted in this paper since context is inextricably woven into texture and the expectancies, on which the text leans to be made sense of, are derived not merely from the textual environment but more pertinently from within the framework of a context. Context functions as the retrieval source to clear up indeterminacies of meaning. In Systemic Functional Linguistics (SFL) and Critical Discourse Analysis (CDA) context holds a prominent place in the analysis of language use and language change. Both examine interconnections between texts and contexts where they occur. Though CDA and SFL both provide contextualization of analysis, how far the context has a sociological basis in the analysis yet remains to be seen. The objective of this paper is to problematize the concept of social context by exploring the notion of intertextuality used in CDA and outlining Structuration Theory (ST) of Anthony Giddens, a sociological thinker, as a broad sociological foundation to account for context in analysis of texts. Inasmuch as context is reflected in the analysis of CDA and SFL, the paper provides a more explicit link between CDA and SFL, on the one hand, and ST, on the other, by highlighting the methodological commensurability between the two. In ST, we have taken the dimensions concerning role prescriptions, social practices, and social structures as rules/resources in the analysis of text. It has been suggested that should these dimensions be incorporated in SFL and CDA, both will be benefitting immensely from these theoretical principles developed by structuration theory. Structuration theory also assumes significance because, unlike CDA, it gives autonomy to individual action and helps in resolving tension between individual action and social structure. Further, taking cue from Muerer's notion of "intercontextuality", the paper also explores intercontextuality-based shared features of different contexts and looks at how rules and resources that cut across specific contexts intermesh to influence texts, discourse and other social practices. It needs to be emphasized here that my intention is not to provide SFL and CDA analysis through the exploration of tenor, field, mode and their corresponding metafunctions of language realized by the lexico-grammatical systems of transitivity, mood at the clausal level. Instead, what I intend to do here is to show how structuration theory helps in providing additional information in the construction of meaning through its dialectical nature of relationship with the text. The link between SFL/CDA and ST is made amply explicit through the analysis of *Bihishti Zewar* (Heavenly Ornaments), an advice literature concerned with the normative language and social behavior of women.

2. Systemic Functional Linguistics and Critical Discourse Analysis

There is an inherent methodological commensurability between Critical Discourse Analysis and Systemic Functional Linguistics since both are concerned with construction of meaning in the context. The SFL framework was developed by Halliday in the 1980s for describing what he termed the *context of situation*- the social context which allows exchange in meanings. It uses both the context of situation and its subfield called field, tenor and mode, and the context of culture to discuss "ramifications of language and context as they relate to register, genre and ... contextual configuration." (Muerer, 2004: 85) The principles and technique of the SFL approaches to language is to analyze and explain how meanings are made in everyday life or linguistic interactions, and how the social context of a text allows for meaning to be analyzed. SFL views language as a strategic, meaning-making resource. It not only shows how simultaneous strands of meanings (the ideational, interpersonal and textual metafunctions) are expressed in clause structures, but at a higher level of context it also gives sufficient attention to ideology. No text is free of ideology. It believes that our ideological positions and perspective influence our use of language. To quote Eggins, "whatever genre we are involved in, and whatever the register of the situation, our use of language will also be influenced by our ideological positions: the values we hold (consciously or unconsciously), the perspectives acquired through our particular path through the culture." (2004: 10)

Although in our use of language we encode particular positions and values, in practice, we tend to gloss over the ideological components embedded in the text. In fact, this gloss over is in itself ideological and most language users have not been educated to identify ideology in text. The language user believes that the text merely represents reality and, therefore, read texts as natural, inheritable representations of reality bereft of any ideological import. CDA analyzes the relationships between language and social. It views language as dialectically interconnected with other social elements and, thus, provides a framework for conceptualizing language use as an irreducible component of social life. (Fairclough, 2003) The demythologizing sociolinguistics enterprise associated with CDA challenges the naÔve and unquestioning borrowing of the concepts and social categories from social theory without making any critical reflection. CDA discusses the interconnections between texts and context where they occur, and handles the relationship between language and context by elaborating on socially-based topics and revealing underlying ideological bias and power relations. This is obvious from the following extracts:

(*i*) *Critical Discourse Analysis is essentially political in intent with its practitioners acting upon the world in order to transform it and thereby help create a world where people are not discriminated against because of sex, creed, age or social class.*

(Cardas-Coulthard and Coulthard, 1999: xi)

(*ii*) *Critical studies of language, critical linguistics, and critical discourse analysis have from the beginning had a political project; broadly speaking that of altering inequitable distributions of economic, cultural and political goods in contemporary societies. The intention has been to bring a system of excessive inequalities of power into crisis by uncovering its workings and its effects through analysis of potent cultural objects-text-and thereby to help in achieving a more equitable social order. The issue has thus been one of transformation; unsettling the existing order, and transforming its elements into an arrangement less harmful to some, and perhaps more beneficial to all the members of a society.* (Kress, 1996: 15) (*iii*) *This does not, I hope, mean that I am writing political propaganda. The scientific investigation of social matters is perfectly compatible with committed and 'opinionated' investigators (...) and being committed does not excuse you from arguing rationally or producing evidence for your statements.* (Fairclough, 1989: 5)

The connection between CDA and SFL becomes more apparent if we look at the constructive effects of discourse. According to Fairclough discourse has constructive effects in three domains, namely,

(*i*) as part of social activity,
(*ii*) in constructing identities and social relations, and
(*iii*) in representing the world.

These three constructive effects roughly correspond to three metafunctions of language outlined by Halliday, namely ideational, interpersonal and textual. Fairclough (2003) argues that SFL provides necessary linguistic tools, such as transitivity analysis, for examining the social embeddedness of discourse at the clausal level, and thus makes the theorizing more substantial. It is at the clausal level of a text where the metafunctions of language are manifested, while the conditions and consequences of discourse reach out towards social practices.

CDA is generally a cover term for different approaches to discourse. However, what remains common to all these approaches is its interest in the social conditions and consequences of language use. Discourse, in fact, is *language use as social practice*, and, as a social practice, it figures particularly in institutions, historical and political structures and processes. It is considered as an essential part of social phenomena, wherein also lies identity since it is constructed, i.e. construction of identity. As social aspects are foregrounded, the role and position of the individual get backgrounded or overshadowed.

Fairclough's social theory of discourse reflects the influence of Bakhtin's dialogical philosophy of language. Like Bakhtin he believed that language use is dialogical, which sets up relations between different voices. (Fairclough, 2003: 214) He uses the concept of *intertextuality* to describe this dialogicality of texts (Fairclough, 1992, 84,10).[1] Intertextuality suggests that language and social are dialectic in nature, i.e. they both have a mutually shaping relationship, which can best be appreciated from Bakhtin's conceptualization of language. (Choulliaraki and Fairclough, 1999: 49)

One source of the weakness of CDA is that it backgrounds the position of the individual. Individual as an agent of bringing social order is not only pushed to the background, but even his actions are said to be determined by the social structure. A central problem in any social theory is the relation between the autonomous actions of individuals and an overarching and stable social order, and the question of structure and agency. There is, therefore, a need to have a social theory that not only resolves the tension between individual action and social structure but also provide a broad sociological account for context in analysis of texts and their impact on social change. Giddens' (1984) theory of structuration is one such approach in social theory that can complement the framework provided by CDE.

3. Structuration Theory

Structuration theory is an attempt to develop a middle way in providing a relationship between the individual action and social structure, and the structure and agency. It views society as not existing independent of the individual as human agent. Rather it offers an explanation of the relationship between both individual human agency and the stable & patterned properties of society as a whole. It makes an investment in both the individual and the society since it believes that both must be given equal importance. The society provides stability and order on everyday events and activities on which individuals have no control, and thus provides constraint and control on the individuals for bringing and maintaining social order. The individuals, on the other hand, are capable of making sense of complex and often unique situation and maintaining the order, on the basis of their high level competency, vast stock of knowledge and range of skills.

In the process of going beyond the extremism, the ST has brought about the "duality" of agency and structure. With regard to the duality of pattern in social structure, Giddens points out that, as an organized and enduring character of social life, social structure provides a "duality of structure" in the sense that "it is at once external to the society's' members and internal (constituting the agent as a competent member of society)." The structural properties of social systems, as Giddens puts it, "are both medium and outcome of the practices they recursively organize." (Giddens, 1984: 25) The members of the society have the social structure existing in their *langue* or competence or mental knowledge. Embedded in this knowledge is the set of rules and resources, which the competent members of the society use for organizing their own social life. What is crucial to mention here is that agent, according to Giddens, is, however, not consciously aware of this set of rules and resources, and a great deal of this competence is non-discursive. This means that the individuals do know how to go about in a given situation, but are unable to provide a verbal account of this knowledge.

In the argument that language and the social have a mutually shaping relationship which is dialectical in nature; the notion of intertextuality is inevitably eluded in the study of CDA. However, in developing the notion of context, Meurer (2004) further takes the argument pertaining to dialectic relationship between the language and the social to its logical conclusion by suggesting the term "Intercontextuality" to refer to "the various contexts that intermesh the influence or determine and be determined by, texts, discourses and other social practices." (Meurer, 2004: 86) Notion of intercontextuality facilitates theorization of context and thus becomes a potential tool for broader contextualization in discourse analysis. Structuration theory enables the problematization of context in relation to discourse because it attempts to capture social life as "dynamically organized in a flux of interconnected practices". (Meurer, 2004: 87) These interconnected practices can, at one and the same time, either reproduce previous identities, relations and forms of conceptualizing the world or challenge and change them, thereby leading to new flows of social life.

4. Bihishti Zewar

Bihishti Zewar ("Heavenly Ornaments"), written in early 1900s by Maulana Ashraf 'Al-Thanawi, which was the major vehicle for bringing reform in the social milieu. Thanawi was a reformist who "sought to improve the quality of Islamic education, increase personal piety, and to spread the observance of Islamic law more widely among Muslims in India." (Minault, 1994, p. 109) Written at the beginning of the 20th century, it is considered as a model of informal, conversational prose style that took up many topics and issues for providing a standard guide to religious practice for Muslim brides, many of who "entered their husband's home with the Holy *Quran* in one hand and the *Bihishti Zewar* in the other." (Metcalf, 2002, p. 3) It is directed toward women and provides an excellent source for "a textured detailed presentation of the major themes of Islamic reform." (Metcalf, 2002: 2) As an advice literature, it has been, according to Metcalf, "one of the most influential texts of the scripturalist reform movements" (p. 1) aimed at creating "a properly ordered society in which people knew their place, fulfilled their responsibilities, and received their due." (2002: 2)

This text comprises eleven parts[2] dealing with various facets required in the conduct of social life as per religious practices of Islam envisaged by Thanawi.. Each part of the book begins with a verse from the Holy Quran followed by its translation in Urdu stating *nek biibiyaaN farmaabardaar haiN khayaal rakhne waalii haiN pith piiche Allaah kii hifazat hai* ("Righteous women are devoutly obedient and guard in their husbands' absence what Allah would have them guard."[3]) Further, after this translation what immediately follows is the translation of Urdu text *laRkiyoN aur aurtoN ko is aayet ke mazmoon par aml karne kaa tariiqaa batlaane ke liya yeh rasaala musamma bah* ("A pamphlet meant to instruct women and girls in the way to act on this Quranic verse")[4] mazmoon provided in the given verse. For the purpose of analysis, the sixth part of the book has largely been used, particularly the section "On women gathering for celebrations":

Text: (taqriiboN men aurtoN ke jaane aur jama' hone kaa byaan)
ON WOMEN GATHERING FOR CELEBRATIONS

The women of a family gather for many celebrations, including those described above as well as many others. All described here are illegitimate.

Celebrations aside, whenever women have a whim, they just think, "I have not seen so and so for ages!" Someone gets sick, and off they go to see her. They may hear of some occasion of celebration, and off they go to offer congratulations Some women are so free that they set out at night without even summoning a palanquin! Worse yet, as soon as night falls, they think of travel! To go out on a moonlit night is even more shameless. The point is that it is wrong for women to leave their homes and go about here and there.

At most, it is permissible for them to visit their parents or other close relatives, and then only once or twice a year. Beyond that, to go out imprudently, as is the custom, is simply illegitimate, whether it is to the home of relatives or someone else and whether the occasion be a wedding or a condolence, visiting the sick, offering congratulations, or joining the wedding procession from the bridegroom's house. It is not proper to go out for a wedding at all, even if it is at the home of close relatives. A husband who gives permission is guilty, and so is the wife. It is lamentable that in all Hindustan this rule is nowhere acted upon, and the custom is not even considered improper. Indeed, it is regarded as legitimate, although it is the source of so many sins. Now that you know the practice to be wrong, you must wholly repeat. This is the injunction of the shariat...[The text also provides a list of sins starting from sin one and reaching up till thirty second sin.]

...

[The following text is suggestive of women's language in Urdu]:

Now she has arrived at the house. She greets the women of the house. Fine, for many do not even take the trouble to speak but simply place their hand to their forehead in greeting. The hadiis says that this style of greeting is forbidden. Some say the word salaam, simply salaam. That too is against the sunna. One should say, as-salaamu alaikum. ("Peace be upon you"). Now just look at the responses:
"Keep cool!"
"May you live long!"
"Remain a beloved wife (suhaagan)!"
"Long life!"
"May you bathe in milk and enjoy grandsons!"
"May your brother live long!"

"May your husband live long!"
"May your children live long!"
It is easy to count off the names of the whole family but difficult to say as-salaamu 'alaikum, which in fact subsumes all the other prayers. ...

For providing meaningful discussion on intertextuality and intercontextuality sections from some other parts have also been taken.

5. Dimensions of the Structuration Theory: Tripartite Social Framework

How will the analysis carried out in SFL and CDA be enriched by incorporating the theoretical principles developed in structuration theory? Also, what is the justification of the notion of 'intercontextualization'?

Along the lines to answering these questions, in the following sections I will first discuss the tripartite social framework at length. The theoretical discussion will then be substantiated by illustrations from the selected text to show how additional information can be accrued, which will enrich the analysis carried out in SFL and CDA in the construction of meaning.

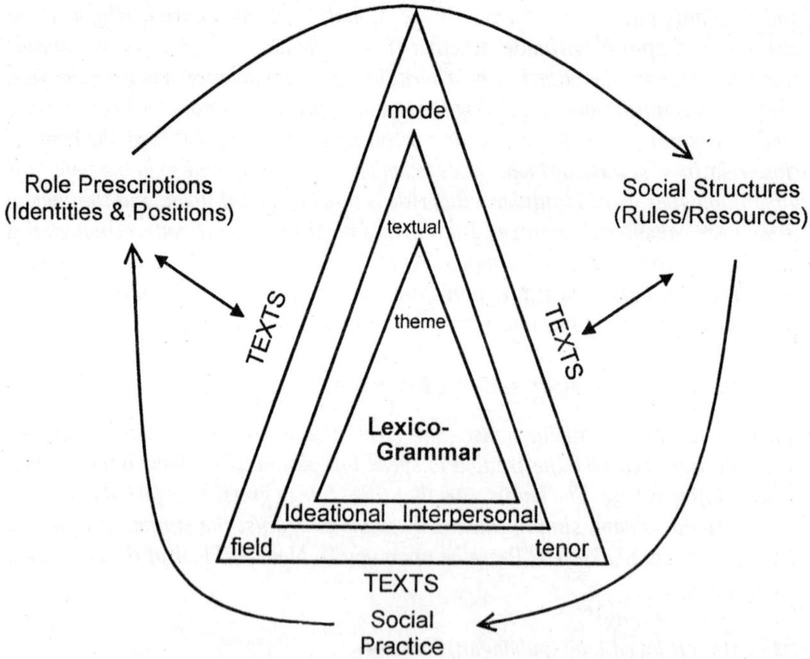

Figure 1: *Shows how each aspect of dimension from structuration theory is dependent on each other and also there is a dialectical relationship between texts and these dimensions. (Adaptation based on Giddens, 1979/1994)*

The three dimensions of the structuration theory which constitute the tripartite social framework for the analysis of text are:

(*i*) role prescriptions,
(*ii*) social practices, and
(*iii*) social structures as rules/resources

(*i*) Role Prescriptions

Role prescriptions enable us to conceptualize social positions and social identities. Social position, according to Giddens, is "a social identity that carries with it a certain range of prerogatives and obligations that an actor who is accorded that identity (or is an 'incumbent' of that position) may activate or carryout: these prerogatives and obligations constitute the role prescriptions associated with that position." (1979/1994: 117)

Role prescriptions are, therefore, the privileges or rights and duties or responsibilities that are associated with specific social identities. CDA borrows tools from SFL for analyzing the role prescription through the exploration of tenor and its corresponding interpersonal function realized by the lexicogrammatical systems of mood. Since there are various contexts that intermesh to influence or get influenced by texts, discourses and other social practices *(a la intercontextuality)*, CDA and SFL will definitely benefit if it analyzes the role prescriptions by incorporating theoretical principles, developed in structuration theory, related to role prescriptions, social practices and rules/resources embedded in social structures.

(*ii*) Social Practices

Social practices are the various activities on human actions that people actually engage in as they conduct social life in different domains of culture and everyday life. These activities, according to structuration, are dependent upon other dimensions from structuration theory. No social practice is independent of role prescriptions and larger social structures, which is evident from Figure1. This interdependency is best realized by the notion of intercontextuality. For, as different social practices are carried out, interdependent role prescriptions, social structures and contexts may also in the process get implicated.

(*iii*) Social Structure

Social structure indicates some regular and stable patterning of social action and social institutions. Structuration theory treats it as "primarily expressed in the things that people do in a regularized and institutionalized way." (Giddens and Pierson, 1998: 78) Giddens further conceptualizes social structures as constituting "rules and resources recursively implicated in social reproduction." (Giddens, 1984: 17) He treats these rules and resources as the "structural properties" in which neither rules nor resources can be conceptualized apart from each other. They exist across varying spans of time and space, like the way social practices do. The stability and institutionalized orderliness in the social structures are, therefore, produced by the involvement of agents' role prescriptions and social practices.[5]

In structuration theory, one may discern overlapping and loosely connected set of rules in a given social practice. Rules are always associated with practices. There can be two aspects associated with the rules, namely, normativity and codes of signification.

(a) Normativity: The normative or regulative elements of rules relate to the sanctioning of modes required in the conduct of social life.
(b) Codes of Signification: This relates to the constitution of meaning.

While the regulative elements of rules may invoke negative or positive sanctioning of the social activities, the signification aspect of rules enable the agent to ascribe meanings to his activities as well as to the activities of others, and also to the "socially constituted context generated as meaningful to agents when activities are established and maintained." (Cohen, 1989 cited in Meurer, 2004: 90)

In structuration theory, resources are medium as well as outcome of structuration processes in which individuals recursively produce and reproduce social life. There are two types of resources, namely allocative and authoritative.

(a) Allocative resources: These are governed by material resources i.e. they are controlled by "material products or aspects of the material world". (Giddens, 1984: 17)

(b) Authoritative resources: These are those transformative capacities that generate "command over persons or actors." (Giddens, 1984: 33)

Since both rules and resources are properties of social structure, rules can not be conceptualized apart from resources. As structural properties of social systems, they are implemented simultaneously in different social realms and at different levels of social life. Further, both rules and resources constitute the means and the outcome of social practices, i.e. both give rise to the *duality of structure*.

6. Modalities of Strucuration

According to Giddens (1984) there are three modalities of structuration, namely signification, legitimation and domination. The actor uses appropriate rules and resources to give to situations of action by "interlacing..... meaning, normative elements and power." (Giddens, 1984: 28-29) Rules governing signification enable meaningful communication and the rules governing legitimation allow moral sanctioning. As for power resources govern domination that allows command over people and over objects.

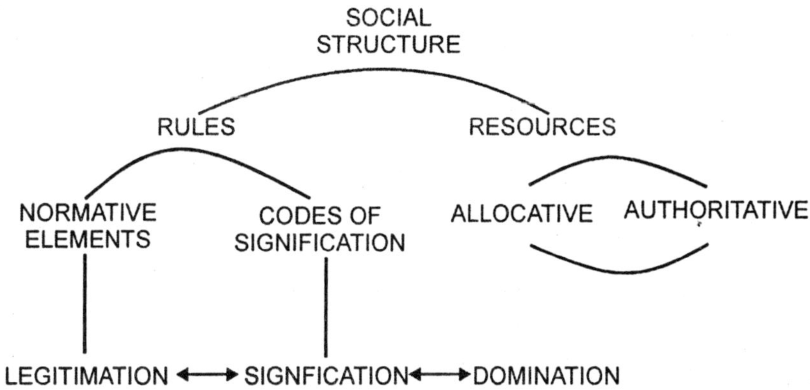

Figure 2: *Modalities of Structuration (Source: Meurer 2004)*

All the three modalities of structuration have an intimate interdependence. Bidirectional arrows clearly suggest that significations have to be grasped in connection with legitimation and domination. When the structures of domination are mobilized, structures of legitimation and signification may be reproduced in a constant interaction between rules and resources, implemented in specific social practices. When the structures of legitimation are mobilized then structures of signification affect structures of domination by either reproducing on challenging them, and, thus establishing the potential for social change.

Exemplication

In Thanawi's text, the most significant identities and positions associated with role prescriptions include those of Thanawi himself, the *'ulemaa'*, the state, reformist concern with women's and men's lives, *'shariat* norms for communicating correct teachings, correcting wrong attitudes about women that identify them with *juhhal* ("deemed innocent of knowledge"), etc. These role prescriptions are intermeshed with different social practices and rules and resources, which have interdependence relationship. No social practice is independent of role prescriptions and social structures.

Social practices constitute the activities that people actually engage in as they conduct social life. They may typically involve habitualized actions, including everyday life, in certain domains of economy, politics and culture or they may even include unexpected action. As an advice literature, Thanawi's text is engaged in instructing women and girls to conduct their social life in the way suggested by the Quranic verse. In order to make these activities become part of their habitualized action particularly in the specialized domain of culture. Thanawi resorts to using mixture of the genres. In this mixture there is:

(a) 'narration', which is simply recounting sequence of events in casual conversational style;

(b) 'description' of how women behave in a social gathering, what or how someone or something looks like through creation of imaginary landscape, strategically positioning a dominant impression for making comparison & contrast, and deliberately providing an objective description with the focus on the behavior.

(c) 'persuasion' where the force of persuasion is coming from the factual information contained in the text. Here the author or writer is anticipating the extent of familiarity that the reader has with the topic and he has chosen a style which shows his passionate involvement with the subject expressed through evangelical tone. Along with persuasion is the 'argumentation' in which the author or writer moves its readers to adopt a belief, position or follow a course of action by appealing to the emotions, ethics and reason. Hence a constant reference to commitment of sin whose number goes up to thirty second time.

A close analysis of the text reveals an occurrence of a chain of practices (in an analogy to Bakhtin's, notion of 'chains of texts'. In the text *taqriib* ('celebration') is a social practice in which women of a family gather to celebrate the occasion of happiness. But this practice is not just confined to *taqriib* alone. The text also talks about events that are besides the celebration marking joy and happiness- there is a clear statement of *taqriiboN ke alaava* ('celebration's aside') in the text. These events outside *taqriib*, which women engage in or actually do as they conduct social life, involve practices like social visit to the *falaani* ('someone') who has not been seen or met for ages, or visiting the sick person, or visiting for offering congratulations, or simply venturing out at night without any reason. These are suggestive of chains of practices. Every social practice interrelates with other social practices within a larger social structure. This interrelatedness is captured by the notion of intercontextualization. This interrelatedness of every practice with other practices is also evident in the said text in which several other contexts are implicated, such as *nafaqaa* and *mehr*. These are suggestive of an aspect of intercontextuality.

Yet another case where other contexts are implicated can be seen with reference to women's language (*begamaati zubaan*) in Urdu. (Second half of the text given above is illustrative of *begamaati zubaan*.) Thanawi considered women's language from religious point of view to be "incorrect", "uninstructed or un-Islamic" because "it goes against religion." (Minault, 1994: 109)

The negative and positive sanctions for carrying out social activities can be seen from the use of the following expressions: *na jaaez* ('illegitimate"), *agar chaandnii raat huii to aur bhii behayaayii* ('to go out in moonlit night is even more shameless'), *gharz ke aurton ko apne ghar se nikalnaa aur kahiiN aana jaana bawajah bahut sii kharaabiyoN ke kissi tarah durust nahii* ('the point is that it is wrong for women to leave their homes and go about here and there')[6], *gharaz ke ab ma'luum ho jaane ke baad bilkul choR denaa chaahiye aur tauba karnii chaahiye yeh to shariyat kaa hukm hai* ('Now that you know the practice to be wrong , you must wholly repent. This is the injunction of the shariyat.')[7]

Intercontextuality, whereby contexts are implicated in different social practices within larger social structures and interdependency of each dimension of structuration theory can also be seen with reference to letter writing. Thanawi suggests that letter writing is a planned activity operating through the interplay of normative elements of rules and codes of signification and resources. Depending on the hierarchy of relationship between the addressor and the addressee, letters are classified and salutations are used. "A letter from an elder is called waalaa *naama* ('an eminent letter'), *sarfaraaz naama* ('a letter conferring distinction: lit. 'a head raising letter'), *iftikaar naama* ('a letter of generosity'), *e'zaaz naama* ('an honoring letter'), *sahiifa-e 'alii* ('a lofty epistle'), *sahiifa-e garaaamii* ('a precious epistle')." Salutations must therefore be used in an appropriate manner. For instance, the text prohibits using of *aap* (the respectful second person plural form)[8] for a person who is extremely superior to the addressor. Instead it positively sanctions the use of *aanjanaab* ('Sir'), *janaabe aalii* ('exalted sir'), *janaa-e waalaa* (eminent sir'), hazrate *waalaa* ('the eminent person'), *hazrate 'aalii* ('your highness', 'lofty sir'). It further prescribes that "if you intend to write 'your letter came', write *janaabe waalaa kaa safaraaz naama aaya* ('the honour-bearing letter of your eminence came'). And instead of *aaya* ('came') write *saadir huaa* ('was issued') or *musharaf farmaayaa* (conferred honour, nobility'),"[9] These are the regulative aspect of rules playing the role of structuring properties because they are deeply embedded in the production and reproduction of human practices. If the regulative aspects of rules are not applied in a legitimate manner, the result is breach of codes of signification The following extract depicting the life history of Bibi Ashraf aptly captures the failure in the constitution of meaning related to the codes of signification:

> *I knew only one way to address someone [alqaab] and used that form all the time, regardless of the age and relationship of the addressee. One lady had me write letters to her husband. This was the way I addressed her husband on her behalf: " Dear young man, light of my eyes, comfort of my life, pupil of my eye, may your life be long!" I can fully understand your letters, for their language is just like your own speech. But tell me this, where did you find this strange scribe who knows only one way of addressing people.* (Naim, 1987: 110)

As mentioned earlier, Thanawi's discussion of letters required competence in the set of rules, which an individual is not consciously aware of. Since a great deal of this competence is non discursive, the agents do not know how to go about using it in a given situation. Bibi Ashraf did not possess this knowledge. As a young Muslim woman she taught herself to write in the mid nineteenth century against all odds, but she lacked the required knowledge of rules constituting structuring properties to carry out specific activity of scribe for the women of her family. She carried out the activity of letter writing in an inappropriate manner and was not able to ascribe tacit and discursive meanings to her own activities as well as the activities of others. This ensued negative sanctions and she, thus, miserably failed as a scribe.

Further, as a leader of the Deobandi reform movement and as *ulamaa*, who was always "sought out for his erudition , his passion for reform, his integrity, and his spirituality as a sufi elder" (Metcalf, 2002: 4), Thanawi wielded resources in the form of "transformative capacities" required for controlling and coordinating the activities of human agents which is revealed through the use of commands like *ab suno* ('now listen'), *tum dekho* ('you look'), *tum* ('2nd person singular form').

The text, therefore, clearly indicates that the CDA and SFL must not only incorporate the notion of chains of practices but should also explore the elements of intercontextuality for looking at the way every social practice interrelates with other social practices. Depending upon the complex interrelations between dimensions of signification, different identities are instantiated, relations are established and different representations of reality and significations are created. Also, all these aspects of social life mutually influence each other thereby socially creating an interconnected structures for legitimation and domination.

REFERENCES

Caldas-Coulthard, Carmen and Malcolm Coulthard (eds.) 1996. *Texts and practices: Readings in critical discourse analysis.* London: Routledge.

Fairclough, N. 1989. *Language and power.* London: Longman.

Giddens, A. 1984. *The constitution of society.* Cambridge: Polity Press.

Giddens, A. 1976/1994. *Central problems in sociological theory.* Berkeley, CA: University of California Press.

Giddens, A. and C. Pierson 1998. *Conversations with Anthony Giddens.* Cambridge: Polity Press.

Halliday, M.A.K. 1978. *Language as social semiotic.* London: Edward Arnold.

Kress, G. 1996. Representational resources and the production of subjectivity: Questions for the theoretical development of critical discourse analysis in multicultural society. In Caldas-Coulthard and Coulthard (eds.)

Metcalf, Barbara D. 2002. *Perfecting women: Maulana Ashraf 'Ali Thanawi's Bihishti Zew -A partial translation with commentary.* New Delhi: Oxford University Press.

Meurer, J.L. 2004. Role prescriptions, social practices, and social structures: A sociological basis for the contextualization of analysis in SFL and CDA. In Lynne Young and Claire Harrison (eds.) *Systemic functional linguistics and critical discourse analysis: Studies in social change.* London: Continuum.

Minault, Gail 1994. Other voices, other rooms: the view from the zenan. In Nita Kumar (ed.) *Woman as subjects: South asian histories.* Charlottesville and London: University Press of Virginia.

Naim, C.M. 1987. How Bibi Ashraf learned to read and write? *Annual of Urdu Studies* 6.

Parker, J. 2002. *Structuration.* New Delhi: Viva Books Pvt. Ltd.

NOTES

1. This term owes much particularly to Julia Kristeva's reading of Bakhtin.
2. Thanawi uses the term *hissa* starting from one to eleven, which has, however, been translated by Metcalf as 'Book'. The appropriate translation, according to Steingass, or Platts, should be either 'part', 'division', 'segment'. Even 'chapter' or 'section' could have been used.
3. Metcalf has used a generic term 'women' in the specific sense for connoting 'wife'. In fact, *bibi* as a vocative particle subsumes both 'lady' and a wife, and, therefore, the attributes of being 'righteous', 'devoted' and 'caring' go to the generic *bibiyaN* ("ladies and wives"). This translation fails to capture the tacit and discursive meaning that the verse intended to communicate.
4. Here *mazmuun* means "sense, meaning, subject matter, subject, contents of a letter). Suggestion to simply act on the said Quranic verse will fail to appreciate the aspect of discursive meaning embedded in the text.
5. Although one may find certain stability and orderliness in the social structures, there can also be disruption and chaos in structures. This,

perhaps, is evident from 9/11 event or even all other aberrations that one may witness in society.

6. The emphatic aspect associated with the prohibition of leaving the house is lost in translation. Emphasis in the Urdu text has been underlined through the use of *gharazke* ('to sum up', 'on the whole') in the beginning and *kisii tarah durust nahii* ('not justified at any cost') towards the end of the sentences.

   Further, the phrase *bawajah bahut sii kharaabiyoN ke* has been completely omitted in the translated text. If one carefully follows the discursive tenor of the text one understands that this has clearly been used as a cohesive device to bind the narration of events concerning commitment of various sins that appears later in the text- *ab iskii buraaiyaaN aur kharaabiyaaN suno.* Interestingly, the entire line is omitted in the translated version.
7. Omission of the entire line - *ab iskii buraaiyaaN aur kharaabiyaaN suno.*
8. Contrary to Metcalf's observation, *aap* is the respectful second person singular form in Urdu -Hindi. *aap log, aap sab* are the respectful second person plural forms.
9. What is missed out here is the following: *aur aayaa kii jagah likhte haiN sarfaraaz naama saadir huaa – sarfaraaaz naama ne musharaf farmaaya.* Linguistically, *ne* is an ergative marker indicating subject position. Discursively, it has been used with *safaraaz naama* occupying subject position to suggest that the letter has arrived from an eminent source and as an honor bearing letter it has bestowed honor and nobility. Embedded in this expression is the role responsibility and rules/ resources.

11

On "Puri Boli"

B.N. Patnaik

This short essay aims to introduce a very interesting and only inadequately studied variety of Oriya known as "Puri boli", i.e., "the language / tongue of Puri", a variety that is spoken by the traditional local people of the temple town of Puri in coastal Orissa. There is an inner Puri, partly geographical, partly cultural, and an extended, outer Puri, likewise partly spatial, partly cultural. The population of the inner town comprises almost exhaustively those who are associated in some way or the other with "Bada Deula" ("the Big temple"): the temple of Lord Jagannath. Those who inhabit the outer Puri are mostly the ones who have moved into this temple town from the nearby villages and towns, and some other parts of Orissa, and even Bengal. This process of movement seems to have gone on for at least two hundred years. Then there is another category of people who live in outer Puri – most of them are associated with modern institutions of education, public health, and governance, and the rest have other modern occupations connected with transport, trade, and commerce, etc. Even now, some inhabitants of the inner town consider those who live in the extended parts as kind of outsiders, and the so-called "outsiders" look upon the inhabitants of the inner town as different. In this sense the linguist Bijoya Mohapatra characterizes Puri as a dual town. The "divide" is cultural, and being soft, does not give rise to tension among the inhabitants. As Mohapatra rightly observes, there is much more interaction between the people of the two parts of the town now than, say, half a century ago. But all this may not be unique to Puri; in its essentials this situation invites comparison with any ancient temple town in India. The outsider-locals of Puri sometimes refer to the speech of the locals in a rather dismissive manner as *pandaa padhiaari bhaasaa* ["language of the *pandas* and *padhiaris* (the servitors at the temple)"], which is commonly known as "Puri boli".

Incidentally, Puri boli is not the same as what is often called *deula bhaasaa* ("language of the temple (of Jagannath)"), which comprises expressions associated with the rituals (and related matters) in the temple of Jagannath. For example, consider the word *murti*. In standard Oriya, it means the idol of a god or a goddess made of clay, stone, metals, wood, etc. In *deula bhaasaa* it roughly means "a piece". Thus in this variety, three separate pieces of *jhili*, a kind of pancake, offered to the Lord, is *tini murti jhili*, whereas in coastal Oriya spoken in the Puri and Cuttack districts, which is also the standard Oriya, the same is referred to as *tinigoti / tinoti jhili* ("three pieces of *jhili*"). The item made of crushed pieces of various kinds of sweet, deep-fried pancake mixed with ghee is called *cadeinadaa*, for which there is no lexical equivalent in any variety of Oriya. *Deula* or in more informal terminology, *deuliaa bhaasaa*, as distinct from Puri boli, is yet another term of the outsider, and his attitude towards this variety is no less dismissive. It is best characterized as a register of Puri boli. Although the term Puri boli is used to describe the language of the inhabitants of inner Puri, it may not be really exclusive to this group. One would find the inhabitants, especially brahmins, of the nearby *saasanas* ("brahmin settlements") using such language, which may not be surprising, because of their past (and in some cases, continuing) association with the temple. Now for some decades the traditional locals have been increasingly interacting with the outsider-locals, and participating in the economic activities unconnected with the temple. On account of this, they are using Puri boli for in-group communication, and a mixed variety – Puri boli mixed with standard Oriya - with outsiders. There are quite a few among them who have acquired university degrees, and have shifted to the so-called "secular" professions, and they generally use standard Oriya outside of the domains of home and the temple.

Because of the various (and well known) pressures of modernization, which include those of modern education in the form of dissemination of scientific ideas in particular, and of modern technology entering traditional households, and the even more powerful pressures of secular economic activities leading to the kind of prosperity and life style considered by the local population to be virtually impossible for those living within the traditional temple-based economy, Puri boli now is certainly under some threat. It is aggravated by the negative attitude towards it by the non-local people in general, a fact that the traditional locals can no more ignore. Some years ago the charioteer's extremely colloquial, verse-like exhortations containing explicit sexual references, calling upon people to pull the chariots during *ratha jaatraa* ("The Chariot Festival", often referred to as "The Car Festival"), were discontinued on the ground of obscenity. The *daahuka boli* ("the charioteer's ritualistic sayings") was part of the tradition of *ratha yaatraa*, but had come to be viewed by the intelligentsia as something that was in dissonance with the modern ethos (they, incidentally, most likely, do not have had any such problems with regard to the writings of Kundera or Marquez, and Amitav Ghosh – see his *Sea of Poppies*), and its discontinuance had popular support. There was hardly any protest when it was discontinued or afterwards. Those so-called obscene expressions were not directed towards any individual, and were not uttered out of any desire to cause offence, and one might say with confidence that they were not uttered for the pleasure of saying "dirty" things in public. *Daahuka boli* was just part of the ritual of the pulling of the chariots. It was a *tantric* element in the composite ritual structure (into which are woven the brahminical and the vaishnavic and the tribal elements too) in the worship of Jagannath. This practice would bring to mind the human figures engaged in various sexual postures carved out on the outer side of ancient Orissan temples (in temples elsewhere as well, Khajuraho temple being a famous example), including the temple of Jagannath. When the belief system on which the charioteer's call was founded disappeared from the consciousness of the people, the significance of the *daahuka boli* was lost. What remained were expressions divested of their deeper meaning, and they sounded obscene, and the intelligentsia wanted the entire discourse to be sanitized. A part of the culture was consigned to oblivion when *daahuka boli* was abolished. It was like hammering down those figures in sexual postures on the temple walls, and substituting them by the ones in, say, the mood of meditation or prayer, as part of some reformation process. De-legitimizing the traditional *daahuka boli* was like slicing off a bit of Puri boli. Quite a few sex-related expressions and some of the others that are taboo in standard Oriya occur in this variety, and the speakers use these without embarrassment. These are not excluded from any domain, including the family, and these are not always used in order to insult or abuse.[1] Consider the following which are generally considered indecent. For us, however, this labeling is just an instance of the power of the standard variety.

(1) *gaanditaaku tikie thoi dabaara hau aagyaan* [Kindly place your buttocks (on it), Sir.]

(2) *bele bele rajaa pua gaangitaa pache miliba, khandi taae miliba naain* (Sometimes the buttocks of a prince would be available, but not a piece of clay pot.)

(3) *kouthire sahasra dipa jaliba? gaandire sahasra dipa jaliba* [On what

will the thousand lighted lamps burn (i.e., be placed)? On the buttocks will the thousand lamps be placed.]

More than forty years ago I was the recipient of (1) and (2), and (3) was said in an interaction in my presence. With increasing care in dealing with the outsiders, I am not sure whether these or similar utterances would still be part of an outsider's experience today. The word *gaandi* is considered indecent now, as it was four decades ago.[2] It would have been quite the expected thing to consider the above as indecent language, but from only the outsider's perspective. For the insider there was nothing indecent about the utterances. Consider the use of the highly polite verb form in (1), reserved only for the most revered in highly formal situations, the polite address form, *aagyaan*, and the polite particle, *tikie*, indicating deference towards the addressee. Consider the context. The servitor who said it to me was feeling uncomfortable that I kept standing and waiting for service, and he was not able to attend to me. He pushed a seat to me and said (1). Both the expression and the accompanying gesture were polite. Technically, he of course had the choice of an alternative that avoided the "indecent" word: *aagyaan basantu* (Sir, please sit) - the norm in standard Oriya. But in terms of form, it is the less polite expression. If he did have these expressions to choose from, I had no doubt in my mind that he had chosen the more polite one.

Turning to (2), a servitor said this to me in some desperation when he was unable to find at hand a piece of broken clay pot on which to give me some *mahaaprasaad*, (very roughly, "sacred cooked food").[3] After a while he, an elderly man, rather heavy, had to get up with some effort to look for one, and that was when he said (2), which has a proverbial ring about it: there are times when one can get the near impossible, but not the simplest of things. The speaker meant no disrespect at all towards the addressee in saying (2), and saying the way he did. If one is not already negatively predisposed towards this variety, one would note the economy of expression, the alliteration, and the novelty of contrast in the expression.

As for (3), it is part of an exchange involving a lower level temple official and a servitor who were arguing on some matter concerning a ritual, when the former asked the question. The latter gave that answer which was an expression of his annoyance, probably because he thought that the official was asking too silly a question, and he thought he should be silenced. In any case, the answer was not to be understood literally, and was indeed not, by the addressee. The official understood that the addressee was not going to be helpful. He simply changed the topic and asked him to attend to his work.

Since they look upon Puri boli as impolite, sometimes indecent, and at times rude, outsiders tend to avoid situations where they might receive it. Many pilgrims take offence at the language they receive from the servitors of the temple and their employees. The need for change in the behaviour on the part of the latter has been stressed for quite sometime even by a section of the traditional locals themselves. More recently some influential servitors of the temple supported the temple administration in its effort to encourage the servitors and others associated with the traditional pilgrimage structure to use polite language, i.e., not use the "offending expressions" of Puri boli, while speaking to the pilgrims. In all probability, in two or three generations, the speakers of Puri boli would themselves feel embarrassed to use this variety at all. One might however argue that in spite of all the pressures, it would survive because of its association with the temple rituals. But such hope may turn out to be unfounded; what will indeed survive is just the temple register, which is just part of the variety under discussion.

An appropriate response to such a possibility would be to document this variety of Oriya carefully and exhaustively. Some creative writers have used bits of Puri boli in their writing, but none as copiously and creatively as has the novelist Surendra Mohanty in his classic *Neela Saila* ("The Blue Mountain"). This qualifies as some documentation at the discourse level. Like all varieties, Puri boli has the so-called low and high layers used in their appropriate situations. The general attitude to it is so negative that the high layer has hardly ever been noticed, let alone studied. All existing studies of Puri boli deal with the low layer, and the present attempt is no different.[4] Sidheswara Mahapatra's *Puri Boli* is a creditable piece of work in the field. It is essentially a dictionary of the terms used in this variety (including *deula bhaasa*) with their meanings given in standard Oriya with a useful introduction to the subject. Much of the existing scholarship on this variety deals with its lexicon. Here a small attempt is made to invite attention to some stylistic aspects of Puri boli at the discourse level. Extracts from Mohapatra's *Puri Boli* and Mohanty's *Neela Saila*, and spoken data from personal experience have been used for the purpose. The written material has been evaluated for its authenticity. Some who are familiar with Puri boli have attested that the extracts sound natural, and not contrived for aesthetic or some practical purposes. Because of the introductory nature of the discussion, only a few examples are dealt with here.

Consider the following exchange:

(4) **A**: *kichi kam kara* (Please reduce (the price of the pot of rice) a little at least); **B**: *kanute kam karibi – paisaa taa na annutaa* (What shall I reduce – the price (of rice) or the amount (of rice)?

A, the educated outsider, asked B, a servitor who was selling *mahaaaprasaad* (which is sold in the temple premises), the price of a *kuduaa* (clay pot) of *anna* ("cooked rice already offered to the deities"). A found the price quoted by B rather high and somewhat unreasonable. What followed is (4). B's response was sharp, witty and spontaneous, and the utterance was balanced in structure and rhythm. He played on the unspecified object (of the verb *kam kara*: "reduce") in A's utterance. Although the object is unambiguously interpretable in the specific context, he pretended that he was unclear about its antecedent: he suggested that since it referred ambiguously to the price (as intended by the speaker) and the quantity of *anna* (as unintended, but quite logical, if not natural in the context), A must make it clear for him what he wanted B to reduce. B imaginatively transformed a simple request to a verbal duel, and registered a victory over A.

Consider (5):

(5) *e emti maada cadheibi je maaka gotie bi tale padibani* (Hey, I'll give (you) such a thrashing - not even one hit will fall on the floor.)

I have heard speakers spontaneously saying (5) or some version of it, all of which contain the adjunct *gotie bi tale padibani*. Sometimes it is said seriously and sometimes, in jest. When said seriously, on account of the adjunct, the threat acquires intensity, and when said in jest, the utterance is humorous, on the same account. The adjunct is redundant from the point of view of information content, which is what makes it unexpected and therefore interesting – one doesn't expect blows to miss the target during a severe thrashing, and one surely doesn't have to spell out the same in advance in such specific terms, almost in the manner of a guarantee to the potential target. And consider the visual metaphor: a hit missing the target's body is one falling on the floor, which invokes the cultural meaning that whatever falls on the floor is wasted.

Still on thrashing, consider (6):

(6) **A**: *...debi jodie bajeibi je* (I'll give you two. I'll drum on your back = I'll give you a beating.) **B**: *...ete bajaanaa ma. haadinka daanapaani maaribuki* (Don't beat so much drum. Are you going to render the professional drum beaters jobless?) *Puri Boli* (p.18).

A threatens to beat up B, and uses the metaphorical *bajeibi* ((I) will beat a drum) in preference to the literal *pitibi* ((I) will beat), evoking the beating of a drum. Puri boli typically uses the former verb in this context. B derisively dismisses the threat (notice the dismissive particle *ma*, and of course the slighting (understood) pronoun *tu*, and the associated verb forms) and in doing so, plays on the drum idea by interpreting the verb literally, rather than metaphorically. His repartee is sarcastic, as he mockingly advises A not to do the job of the drummers and make them jobless. The simplicity, directness, and economy of expression make the response (6) so effective and artistic.

Puri boli is colourful. Simile, metaphor, sarcasm, onomatopoeia, indirectness of expression, etc. make the utterances both effective and interesting. Consider some more examples:

(7) **A**: *kana bhitaraku jiba* (Will you go in (to the temple)? **B**: *mun para niti jaauci* (I have been going there everyday.) A: *hah niiti jaauthibu. deula jie tiaari kalaa taara ta maaka niti dekha darsan naahin ie kahilaa kana na niiti jaauci*...(Going everyday, huh! The one who built the temple isn't to be seen in the temple everyday, and this one says he goes there everyday!) (*Puri boli*, 18)

(8) *kiere sethi khuntataa pari thiaa hoici* (Who is there standing like a post?) (*Neela Saila*, 8)

(9) *aare ethi kaudi pakaa, jagiaa hanumaana paakhare kaudi napakaai, dian darsanaku sidhaa tang tang baahari jaaucu je* (Hey, put some coins here. Without putting money here at Hanuman temple, you are heading inside for *darsan* (of Jagannath))! (*Neela Saila*, 9).

In (7), A belongs to the servitor community, and works as a guide for the pilgrims. Many of these guides wait outside the entrance gates of the temple for a willing pilgrim. B is more likely to be an outsider-local who is a regular visitor to the temple. A's first utterance is polite, as the verbal agreement shows. When B indirectly rejects his offer to be his guide, he immediately uses impolite verb form: *jaauthibu*, *jaauci*. He uses the dismissive particle *hah*, suggesting that B was lying. Then juxtaposing B's claim of coming everyday with the king's not coming there regularly, he makes a connection that is bizarre. In abstraction it might not look illogical, but in the specific conversational context it does. If it doesn't look illogical, it is because in a decontextualized situation one would ordinarily tend to associate "the one who built the temple" with the existing king of Puri. By convention the king of Puri does not come to the temple everyday, but only on some special occasions, something that everyone in the town knows. Thus A's utterance is completely without content in this regard, and only expresses his disappointment. The indirectness of expression, the juxtaposition of two entirely unconnected things, giving rise to a bizarre contrast, the sarcasm, and the dismissive expression make his utterance so colourful.

The context of (8) is the following: there is some unfamiliar, crazy looking person standing motionless near the temple gate for sometime without showing any intention to either go into the temple or leave. This makes the guards suspicious, and they shout at him (8). The simile in it is authentic, connecting a person standing unmoving, to a post— one comes across this simile in the day-to-day use of language among the locals. It is typically used in an utterance intended to reproach the addressee, and the slighting particles *re* and *taa* heighten the tone of reproach. It is well known that day-to-day use of language is not merely informative, it is imaginative too; however, each such instance of language use arrests attention and sensitizes one to the flavour of ordinary speech.

(9) is interesting on account of the elegant use of the secondary onomatopoeia *tang tang*. The speaker, a servitor, deprived of a little income, mildly reproaches the addressee for directly heading for the main temple without having first put some coins at the Hanuman temple (of which he is the priest). The addressee surely knew that if he lingered, the man would pressure him to leave some money at the temple; so he was hurrying into the main temple with quick steps. It is this manner of walking that the secondary onomatopoeia captures here. *Tang tang* and *daga daga* are secondary onomatopoeic expressions for hurried walk in other varieties of Oriya too, but these appear to be used a great deal more frequently in colloquial Puri boli. Besides, although (9) is uttered to show displeasure, *tang tang* is not necessarily uncomplimentary in this variety. In contrast it would be considered rude in other varieties.

In *Neela Saila* there are examples of servitor talk with villagers living in distant villages, and the language sounds entirely authentic. There is the familiar ring about it, and the style is unmistakable. While talking on some religious matter, a not-very-educated servitor would cite a proverbial expression or a memorable line or a couplet from some religious text to support his point. Whether this strategy has the desired effect on his audience or not is a different matter, but the strategy makes the discourse persuasive, interesting and weighty. Incidentally, the servitor in all probability would not have first-hand acquaintance with the relevant text, but would have just picked a line or a couplet from the environment in and around the temple, and would put it to good use when there is the occasion. In the following example, the speaker is a servitor who is persuading a rich elder of a farmer's family of a village to go to Puri for Rath Yatra that year. He addresses him pleasantly, using the kinship term *ajaa* ("maternal grandfather"). He assures him that he would take care of his family there. He would in the process have a good income. But as a strategy he would conceal this selfish objective, and express it in an other-oriented perspective. But there is no cynicism; neither is there any lack of understanding of the speaker's intentions on the addressee's part. Deep thoughts about the transitoriness of human life are expressed in a very simple, and colloquial idiom. In the unsophisticated language of the servitor, *shastra* becomes *sahastra*, and *mokshya* becomes *mocha*.

(10) *e sana ratha jaatraaku aasiba naa ajaa? sahasra boilaa, "kali kaalare deha bahi, jale jesane candra chaai!" aaji achi, kaali naahin. basi thiba talipadiba. Taa aagaru cakaadolaaku thare dekhi aasile ekaathare jibana mocha*...(Are you coming to Rath Jatra this year, grandfather? The text says," The body in this (uncertain) age of Kali is like the shadow of the moon." Today it's there, tomorrow it is not. You'd be sitting, then suddenly collapse. Before that you must see The Round Eyed One (Jagannath) once. Then you'll directly get *mokshya*.) (227-228).

Consider the following discourse of hospitality in Puri boli:

(11) *aare haneicu kana de baabunka patarare...kana aagyaan etikire hadeigale. ie kana kaama? aau punje anna hau? di oli khiraa? gaandi kachchi kari khaantu*. (What are you staring at? Put some more on the Babu's leaf...What, Sir! You're backing out with only this much! Is this fair? Please have a little more of rice. A couple of *olis* (earthen cups) of *khiraa* (a sweet preparation of thickened milk)? Please do hit your buttocks and eat (eat your bellyful) (*Puri Boli*, 8)

The speaker is an inhabitant of the inner Puri, and speaks of Puri boli, and the one receiving his hospitality at a community feast is most likely an outsider local – he is referred to as "Babu", a respectful term used for an educated outsider, who might also be holding a position of some power and authority in some secular set-up. Polite address form *aagyan* and polite verb form *le* (in *hadeigale*), and *ntu* (in *khaantu*) and the more polite indirect request with the subjunctive verb form *hau* instead of direct request verb form *khaantu*, are used for him. The first sentence in (11) is addressed to the one who is serving rice and other items of *mahaaprasaad* (sacred food), and the rest, to the guest. Contrast the polite forms in the sentences addressed to the guest with the informal and impolite address form *aare*, and the verb forms *cu* (in *haneicu*), and *de* used for the addressee in the first sentence. The speaker pays special attention to his local outsider guest. He sees to it that his leaf is filled.[5] He entreats him to have more. And then he most naturally and most politely and quite appropriately says the last sentence, which an outsider would consider indecent. He would feel embarrassed when it is uttered in his presence, let alone when it is directed to him. For the outsider, this last sentence might even be sufficient to neutralize the warmth of the foregoing sentences. It is the case of a word marked as taboo in the variety of the language spoken by those who are privileged in many ways, and unmarked in a variety that is spoken by people most of whom are poor and marginalized, and who are also the victims of an attitude that regards all those associated with religious practices and institutions as obscurantist, backward, and even corrupt.[6] The expression *gaandi kachchi khaaibaa* is an idiom now; it's a dead metaphor. It is a creative extension of the familiar practice of hitting the bottom part of a sack as one fills it with grain so that all inside space can be fully used.

Puri boli awaits a great deal more scholarly attention than what it has received, and perhaps no variety of Oriya has been generally more negatively viewed than this one. Its speakers are also among the more misunderstood, more unsympathetically thought of, and the more marginalized speakers of Oriya. As they would increasingly shift to the standard variety that surrounds it, Puri boli would shrink, and in all likelihood not many would feel concerned – like not many were with the discontinuance of *daahuka boli*. It is time serious effort is made to document Puri boli at all linguistic levels, describe it, and also discuss it as a carrier of a rich history and culture. It is time too for the attitude of others towards it to change, and scholarly work of the kind mentioned above can certainly play an important role in this regard.

Colophon

I am thankful to Achla M. Raina, discussions with whom on certain conceptual aspects of this paper have been helpful.

REFERENCES

Mahapatra, Sidheswara 1996. *Puri Boli*. Bhubaneswar: Orissa Sahitya Academy.

Mohanty, Surendra 1979. *Neela Saila*. Cuttack: Cuttack Students' Store. (4th Edition).

Patnaik, B.N. 1979 The Jagannath Temple Register of Oriya, *Language Forum* 6, 3-4.

NOTES

1. This may be an over-statement. There may indeed be constraints; such as many of such expressions may not be used by the male in the company of women and girl children, and even among the males, some of these may be excluded in certain relationships, such as father-son. More work is needed to arrive at the precise constraints on the use of these expressions.
2. The linguist D.P. Pattanayak told me (on 16.10.05) that there is no general agreement with regard to the taboo status of this word. He told me of Pandit Neelakantha Das, the great Oriya intellectual, linguist and freedom fighter, who once ruled as the Speaker of the Orissa Assembly, that the word is parliamentary, and in support of his view had cited a couplet that contains this word in the poetry of the eighteenth century poet Krushna Singh. The couplet under reference is: *sabhaare basanti jete karpura*

maaliaa / samastanka gaandi maana jesana oliaa. I have heard some local (outsider-local) people of Puri using this word, but I am aware that the same people feel considerably uncomfortable if someone of the inner Puri uses it while talking to them. It is as though the status of the speaker decides whether a word is taboo or acceptable – the familiar instance of the power factor in language use.

3. Since metal utensils are not used for the purpose in the temple compound, using broken pieces of clay pots for the purpose is quite the norm when one buys small quantities of *mahaaprasaad* – rice, dal, etc.
4. It appears that the high layer Puri boli is, for the most part, Sanskritized Oriya.
5. Traditionally *mahaaprasaad* is partaken of on banana leaf, and one is supposed to sit on the floor (i.e., not on any *aasana* (seat)) for the purpose. But these days even many local outsiders are using metal, porcelain, etc. at home for the purpose, and many sit on newspapers, sheets, carpets, etc. Other constraints associated with the partaking of *mahaaprasaad*, and the relaxations in urban households these days can constitute the subject matter of a separate study.
6. I personally know quite a few of them who are liberal and modern in their outlook in the best sense of these terms.

12

On Unearthing a Civilization*

Ranjit Singh Rangila

To Celebrative

This writing is offered as a celebrative token in the honour of a shared childhood with Rama, the Pandit.

As an opening approximate the writing takes 'civilization' as a conceptual continuum that lies between earth and truth (see Rangila 2004b-06 also Rangila and Sholapurkar 2010). One unearthens it every bile-second to realise that there is more to it. The engagement keeps confirming the truth that civilization is a baseline to walk on; it is a resource potential to live on; and it a completion to leave behind. That also makes civilization a 'speak' of collctage that continues as a shared presence.

The writing almost follows an affirmative tangent as it probes a simple question: could civilization be unearthened through conscious means? The materials explored come from the lives of Jenu Kurubas and the toolkit is sourced through C-semiology.

The Range of Criticality

It is quite likely that established disciplines may not own the language of a place as their data. Such attitude stems from self-righteous sense of rationality. To theorise the unfolding reality of the life of Jenu Kurubas as a case, therefore, in this writing, is to invite 'civilization' as the richest and widest nod of reference.

A C-semiological inquiry takes place on multiple axes, where linear ('syntagmatic') and hierarchical ('paradigmatic') readings are just points of preliminary reference. As a matter of fact such a characterisartion does account for some facets of reality (see Saussure 1964), but it does not match the observational requirements when it comes to observing n-dimensional reality.

One is faced with the n-dimensional reality, because discovering a civilization is to land in a multi-dimensional reality. The problem of discovering Jenu Kurubas civilization should follow the rule in principle. It should show, therefore, that C-semiology neither in general, nor in this writing in particular, is addressed to 'language' within the intuitions developed within some version of linguistic theory or the other.

Once the traditional axes, called *syntagmatic* and *paradigmatic,* are received as two dimensions, it is logical then to look for methodologies which may be rich enough in their descriptive potential to handle n-dimensional reality. Within the craft of C-semiology now we have a fairly efficient facility called *floral architecture* (see Rangila 2004-06) that serves n-dimensional reality rather resourcefully. The architecture below presents an abstract version of it:

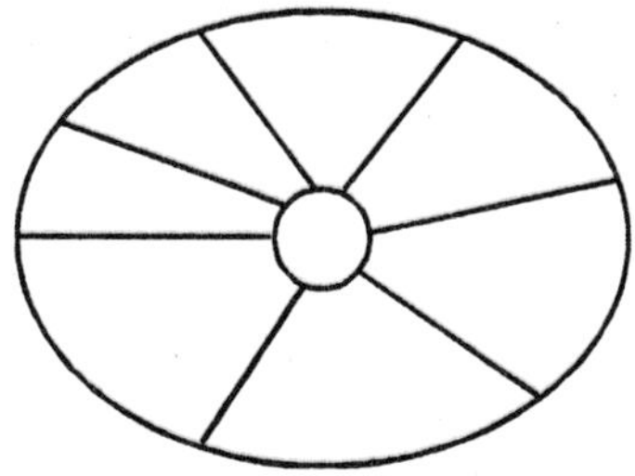

Formal means of its operations are also developed in a previous writing called *Power to Act Civilized* (Rangila 2004-06). Lot much subtle facilities are developed to provide ways of making descriptive statements even on linear entities (Rangila 2001b, 2002).

Dramatology is one of the most sophisticated spheres of a culture. Proof of the skill in the sphere is presented with power of the artistry. Since culture is the immediate point of reference in the C-semiological vision (Rangila, 2002), in this sense the proof is right there.

A Moot Question

The patches of the information gathered so far build up a case for there being a resounding success of Jenu Kurubas in the performance of the play. A moot question surfaces at this stage: Should it have happened with a fluke? Is it as simple as that? Is it a simple case where Narayan goes to Heggada Devana Kote jungle on an official assignment from the Central Institute, collects *linguistic data* for the purpose, writes his report, and then, one fine morning just casually goes back, meets some Jenu Kuruba individuals, tells them to participate in the performance of the drama that he writes? They leave their daily earning chores and join him for the fun. Is this that mundane a happening?

For the sake of argument, even if every thing happens according to the script in the paragraph above, one must face an even more basic question: How could Jenu Kuruba friends rise to the performing standards that Sathyu Sahab could set with Balraj Sahani in *Garam Hava*?

Research on Jenu Kurubas has helped Narayan to peep through the layers of the oral society. He has been able to fathom the depth of excellence that the people exhibit. Like most oral societies, Jenu Kurubas are great story tellers. The tales and texts that Narayan has collected are not only the products of the Jenu Kuruba textual consciousness; they are also the source materials on which any narrative text can be built.

As has been shown, for example, in Rangila (2001a), the codification happens when people create knowledge and in the process also invest it. These codifications are investments of wisdom to enrich the existing pool. At a mega level codifications are part of wealth creation. Civilization is consequential upon this strategic wisdom.

Further, in all these thirty odd years, Narayan must have put in a considerable amount of time and effort to train his literary intuitions in the conceptual resources of the people. At every stage his eye should have been centered on the aesthetic sensibility of the people. He must have been discovering literary shades of the gathered data and just not the linguistic stock. I am witness to the struggle that Narayan had to put up in creating songs for the play. All along, it must have been a struggle to imbibe the Jenu Kuruba cosmology (see also Narayan 2001). The mystic, the cryptic, the enduring, the sublimate and the forerunner of the felt realization – all meet in this sphere of the luminous.

Play At the Higher Echelon of Glitter

It is a scene from Bangalore, the capital of Karnataka state and an important city of India. Nth production of the Jenu Kuruba play is in order. The occasion in itself is unfolding into a phenomenon. The surging crowd is a normal expectation.

The fact that the Jenu Kuruba play has run into as many performances is in itself significant. But we have something even more significant to note. The professional significance of the event is measurable from the fact that the Kannada matinee legend, Dr. Raj Kumar attends it and sits through the show. The excellence is revealed. The Jenu friends have crossed another level of success.

Raj Kumar is on the stage now. The Jenu Kurubas climb upon the stage and touch him. There is applause, there is celebrity and celebration, but the scene on the stage is that of admiration. No power play, or creation of a visual field of strength, it is an artist meeting the artists.

The civilized honours the civilized.

Ordinary people from the woods may not have lived with electric lights, but the evening has produced an absolute bloom. The power of the evening is better expressed with the following architecture:

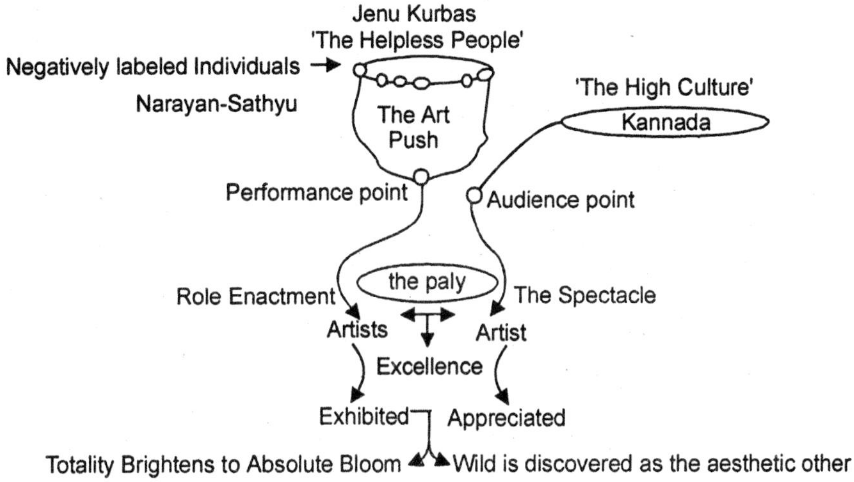

Even though there is nothing professional about the performance that the Jenu Kurubas have put up to-day, yet this is the ultimate that one may dream of in dramatic arts....

The show still goes on. Wherever art lovers come to know, they invite Jenu Kurubas for performance. Even Doordarshan – the state media in India puts up a show once a month. With inherent power to create charming spectacles that *the civilized* can afford the Narayan-Sathyu duo has placed Jenu Kurubas on a measure of excellence.

In his CNN interview Narayan supports the happening as a *celebration of the voice of the marginalized*. Sathyu has expressed his appreciation of the performative skills of the discovered artists.

On the Banks of River Tungabhadra

Bapat (Guru Rao) arranged a show of the Jenu Kuruba play on the banks of river Tungabhadra near Sagar. Experience has it that the one who can do it in woods may do it even on moon. It does not suffer a daunting break of the so-called civilized. To use Levi-Strauss like idiom, ***it is a continuity of the savage*** all along. Jenu Kurubas were more at ease on the river bed. Sagar being unique with its cultural repository and strong tradition of learning and valor, it had a good share of the Art Jenu Kuruba.

As the show came to close, someone got up out of the audience and came forward. He proposed that anyone out of the Jenu artists should compete with him in dance. This person's name was Karanth. Remember the other Karanth, Shivarama, the Yakshagaana maestro. The modality of dance was that the Karanth would dance Yakshagaana steps and the Jenu Kuruba person could dance his/her own parallel.

A lean and thin looking Jenu Kuruba youth accepted the challenge. With some dress adjustment and minimum of the other paraphernalia, the dance started. A Yakshagaana beat was received with a Jenu Kuruba parallel, a taal had its taal parallel; and the abhinaya as such was as skillful as it was thrilling.

The audience that came to watch the play got additional entertainment. It continued till the Yakshagaana dancer realized that he was no comparison to the man from the woods. He stopped dancing, walked up to the Kuruba youth and touched his feet. One should not forget to mention that the Kuruba youth had already been through the performance, and the body could have been tired a bit. No problem with the Karanths. Here is the architecture:

Civilizational Roots		
The I	::	The Other
The Lived Experience	::	The Discovery
Will to do	::	The Jenu Kuruba Body
Challenge	::	Physical Agility Aesthetic Sophistry
Reassurance	::	Power to act civilized
		Civilization

The individuation that the civilization of the people sustains Jenu Kurubas in their real life activity is unfolded to its best possible. Even though it is just a slice; given the narrative, it brings in the aesthetic power and body agility to a level of bloom.

Cosmology Has It

To discover a people on the strength of their creative genius as they engage themselves with the people 'out there' is a fairly respected strategy. For instance, in terms of the ancient Tamil wisdom, it is recognized as an area of 'Puram', which has its essential and parallel half in 'Aham'. Both *Aham* and *Puram* are two consonating spheres of soul. The architecture has it:

The facility that the Puram strategy provides is that it helps to tap the doings of *the soul* of a people from the point of view of the perspective that may be chracterised as 'out there'. In the case of the present writing, the Puram perspective offers insight to observe Jenu Kurubas doing their performance for others. This should project Puram as the externity side of the soul, whereas Aham performs as the internity of it. The discovery of Jenu Kuruba civilization, therefore, could be gainfully progressing not just on the basis of the Puram-externity perspective as has been done in this writing so far. To have conceptual, as well as, informatic balance the writing should open to the Aham-internity perspective also.

Needless to add that scope for the balance surfaces only when the problematics of the inquiry is placed in cosmology. Most of the other levels of observation prove too narrow and limited for the surfacing. The cosmology requirement demands an extension of the above architecture as follows:

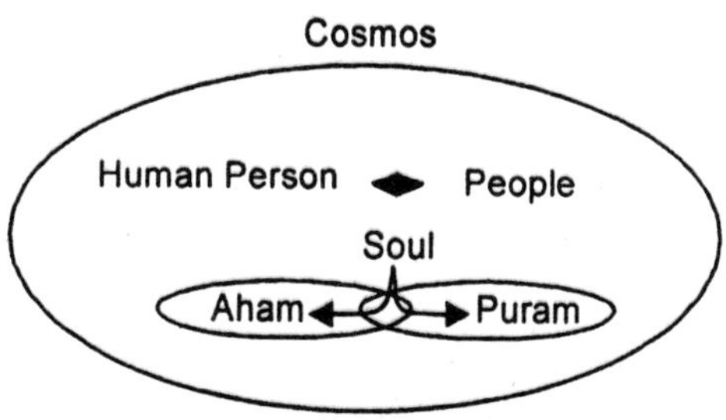

Cosmos is meant here in a conceptual sense of the term such that has its physical correlates, yet to make sense of it, people workout their typologies which give primacy to conceptual dimension of things they live with. C-semiology, in this sense, is addressed to a cosmos that includes multiple dimensions of it. The conceptual and physical are two important ends between them.

Incidentally, compare Chomsky's well known choice for i-language perspective that does not bother about the balance. Neither human consciousness, nor human societies function without balanced participation of both of the sides (i.e. Aham and Puram), unless one is theorizing of rare and extreme cases of emergency, where some force of imbalance takes over to drive certain irregularities out. Surely, neither Chomsky, nor I, in fact, none of us, can theorize some definable emergency situation. Cosmology, in the present inquiry in particular, and in C-semiology in general, provides a conceptual source pool for balance, on the one hand, and it also acts as the relevant level of abstraction where the scope and wisdom for consonating functioning of both externity and internity axes surfaces in recognizable force and clarity.

To appreciate the perspective and to use it productively in the C-semiological vision in general, and in the Jenu Kuruba series in particular, it makes sense to discover soul to some detail in the first place. This is specifically so because soul is placed in the cosmology so far.. In operation the statements get applied in the stipulated sequence. Each statement stands in the set for a specific role. On completion of its specified job it gives way to the next. The set of the definationals stands for the function that has traditionally been played by definition. None of the definationals in the set is a preposition.

May be it makes the effort at the discovery even more interesting as one adds that while elaborating Panini's characterization of soul, together with its role and function 'soul' is accorded the following architectural shape that is created in a recent piece of writing (see Rangila 2008):

The architecture there carries an elaborative statement, which more or less confirms the over all spirit of the elaboration of the Tamil wisdom.

Such a conception of soul should explain in the first place Panini's motivation in giving an all-pervasive role to it in his conceptualisation.

The Spheres of the Discovery

The opening into the slice of cosmology above is helpful to the effect that it marks out the spheres in which the present inquiry may hopefully be conducted. It also brings in the wisdom that should be helpful in setting up explanatory basis and criterion of justification.

In the absence of the two facilities, as is known, any piece of observation stands risk of being *intentional*. From my personal point of view, this is the best caution that one can sound. If there is any lesson to be learnt from the failure of *logical inquiry* in India after Panini, it is this: To base ones inquiry on 'intention' is fine, as our logicians are fond of doing, but the same intention may lead to fallacy of intention as well!

The caution is relevant to the present inquiry also, because without proper balancing, check and probe most of the statements in the forgoing sections can be termed as intentional to say the least. Therefore, in this sense a step into cosmology has its role both in theory and methodology of C-semiology at least.

Framework Has It

The forgone considerations should suggest that one should strive to look for possibility of discovering Aham-internity perspective in the life of Jenu Kurubas. Two problems are quite evident for such a venture.

The first problem is that of identification of the relevant universe of data, and some reasonable data fields therein. The second problem is toolkit that should be appropriately suited to reach at least some preliminary statement of an Aham-internity perspective. Viewed together, both of the problems put forth need for some kind of framework of doing such things on a single platform.

Approached intuitively, it makes sense to suggest that language is the best universe of data, locale, as well as, the tool of reaching the Aham-internity perspective of a people. In that language does provide the required balancing weight and insight into the discovery of civilization, as well as, building the same.

The statement above makes better sense when it is realized that the search for an Aham-internity perspective is invited to participate in an inquiry engaged in discovering a civilization, and that the perspective has to play a balancing act also. If such a help comes from the study of Jenu Kuruba language, the move is welcome.

In Search of Framework

Seen from the framework end, it is important to realize that civilization as a construct in C-semiology refers to past, present and right now, the three points relevant to the occurrence of any act, and to the realization of any fact. None of the three is exclusive in this case. They not only work in consonance, but they also present civilization as a living force within a cosmos in the life of people.

The main point of time in the life of Jenu Kurubas is 'Right Now'. As an act comes up, including an act of speaking, all other points in time are pushed into background in an individual's consciousness. These points start acting as the resource materials for the effective Right Now. The architecture clarifies:

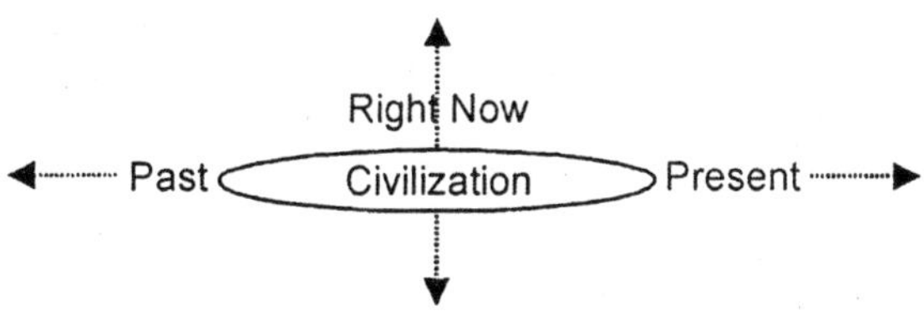

There is every reason to believe that the point identified as Right Now effective in terms of Time, and all the references to tense formations coming from language and similar sources are relegated to secondary processings.

It may, therefore, be clear that to the vision of C-semiology any resources are normally in the care of one's consciousness. As and when it happens, unconsciousness speaks tonally and offers insights. Therefore, it is fair to say that the ultimate seat of civilization is unconsciousness, though it speaks only at times.

If civilization were to be some fact situated in some distant past or in some present out there, then it should not have mattered to people in general. Few human beings, who could have afforded leisure and patience, might have shown some interest in it and, again, up to a limited degree. Civilization, then, would be a time pass hobby for a few.

That, however, is not the case. Civilization matters in life for its instant role and relevance. This explains why 'future' as a point in time is optional in the architecture above. No act and articulation is possible without its being sourced through value attribution. It is this attribution that has led to formation of civil societies, even though it has been put to pretentious usage world over to denigrate 'the other', yet the fact remains that civil society as a project of civilization is a game in value. Therefore, the architecture suggested above can play the role of a seed in creating a framework.

Incidentally, when formal ways of developing descriptions are tried, which is not being done here to save space for developing other basic requirements of the writing, the simultaneity of the three time points may be captured by denoting it with 'T'. The minimum that may be committed at this stage is to add that it is possible to develop formalisms of many types within the C-semiological framework, depending, of course, on the analytical needs of a given problem.

One can foresee the possibility where the facilities that are created with the formalisms that are visualized may be helpful to explain the wisdom of Tholkappiar, the ancient Tamil thinker, where he separates Time from tense and places Time at a higher plane. The simultaneity of time points in 'right now' presented above has another dimension. It behaves as a wider phenomenon, where the above architecture works as an *anchoring base*. The actual processing schedules that take place in cognition use, the base for working out conceptual maps of the moves, as well as, that of the priorities that may be thought better, but the base as such does not surface in the whole process, as it works as the base for any other actential move.

The subtlety of the issue at hand must be underscored. To say that Jenu Kurubas, like any other people, are able to perform the play reported above as they use their knowledge base is to say the least.

More important from the point of view of the present writing is to discover as to how do they muster that unique wisdom that bears them marvelously well when it comes to performing an act?

The main query, therefore, is not the issue of wherefrom their knowledge comes. Rather, it is to know from where do the Jenu Kurubas get the unique wisdom of life making. And, how are they able to use the same to make it a very successful and lived experience? There is, surely a double-ended game at hand: The Jenu Kurubas have the required wisdom to conduct a job at hand quite efficiently, and their bodies have the required energy to make it happen in a razor cut sharp fashion. The issue to be inquired into is: where does the wise energy come from?

The architecture above indicates a possibility. Put more bluntly, it should be said that the civilization of Jenu Kuruba people offers all the relevant resources for its individuals to acquire and develop an ***act orientation*** as more of a natural endowment. Here is a case for a rule like situation:

> To have a 'naturally' engrained orientation is not only to be unique, it also signifies there being a civilization to source it.

Given the orientation, the individuals among these people have developed wisdom to merge their individualities. It ends up in creating a pool of power that bears them out in a collective or individual job situation. At such sites of act and role enactment, they are more people than individuals. That is, every act, fact, concept, percept and driving move of Jenu Kurubas stems from an anchoring base that works on a principle of simultaneity, where under conditions of role enactment individual distinctions have wisdom to merge together to create greater power. This determines their aptitude, as well as, their chances to survive. The distinctions surface as they return to their individual selves for short durations of privacy.

Said differently, though the actual thinking among Jenu Kurubas seems to happen right there and in the immediate, termed as 'Right Now' in the architecture above, yet the whole round of processing in the active consciousness actually uses the information sources and data fields that are far more vast and wide spread in the experience of the Jenu Kuruba individuals. This is how they get deeply rooted in their civilization.

Seen from the end of consciousness as it helps the people to make their lives with whatever resources they do, they have a very accomplished and well mapped up anchoring base like any people from any other civilization. The 'anchoring base' acts as a bridge-house to build links among sites of processing and localities of wisdom (Rangila, 2001). The following architecture shows the vision in praxis:

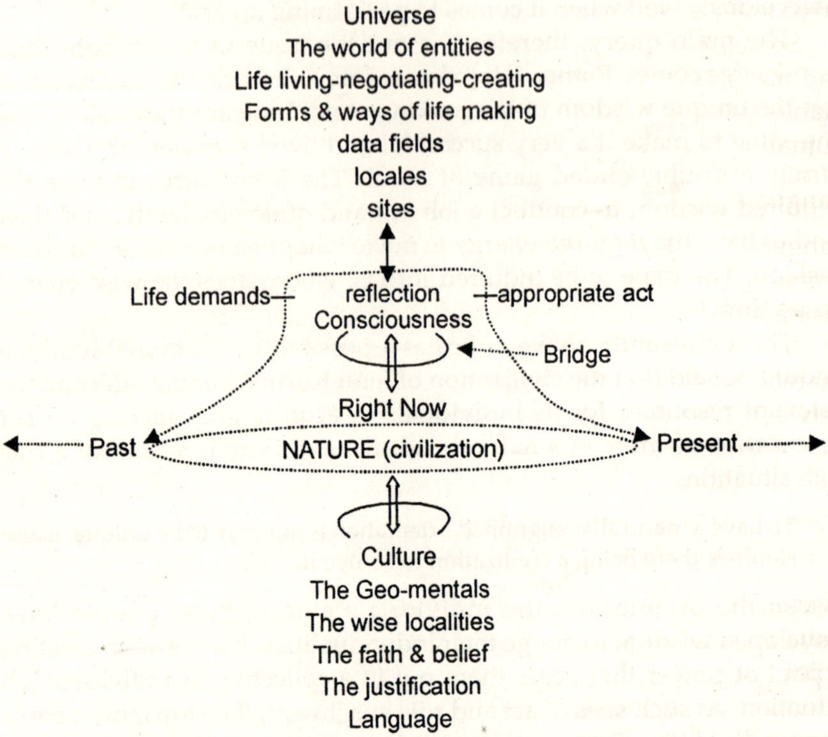

The architecture presents a part picture of what possibly happens as Jenu Kuruba individuals enact any life situation. It suggests that every incidence of reflection in their life is an act in the first place and then something else. An idea, for instance, enters much later in the processing hierarchy in their thinking. The secondary status for ideation flows from the observation of there being the ***act orientation***. The proposal of primacy of act among Jenu Kurubas must be understood from the end of the drive of life. That is where the 'act orientation' gains its place and relevance: Among Jenu Kurubas it seems to act is to ideate. Whether it is a trait of the people or a wide generalization should be left to further investigation.

The primacy to act and be guided by the tested wisdom seems to be at the core of Jenu Kuruba cosmology. That unfolds their civilization in a big way: The will to live with 'right now' in the life of Jenu Kurubas is both responsive to the immediate out there, as well as, sourced through their unconsciousness in the sense already discovered. Since the *act orientation* among the Jenu Kurubas does not lead to primacy of ideation among them, it ensures endurance to sustained act and fast reflexivity.

This also ensures speedy composition of an act, and explains, for instance, creation of the dance parallel to Yakshagaana dance. It is their drive to act and let that do the talking that makes Jenu Kurubas click.

Somewhere and in some sense a discovery is an act of understanding and realisation. The offered picture is termed 'part' because a lot more than what is counted seems to participate in an act performed by a human being (Narayan, 2001).

Language Has It

Language in such a framework does not play a central role as it primarily articulates universe with all its rich phenomenal diversity. This gets displayed in the architecture above with language and universe sitting at the two opposite ends. The links between the two may be characterized by a scale of all pervasiveness. There is more of a parallel between the two and that is captured in the architecture below:

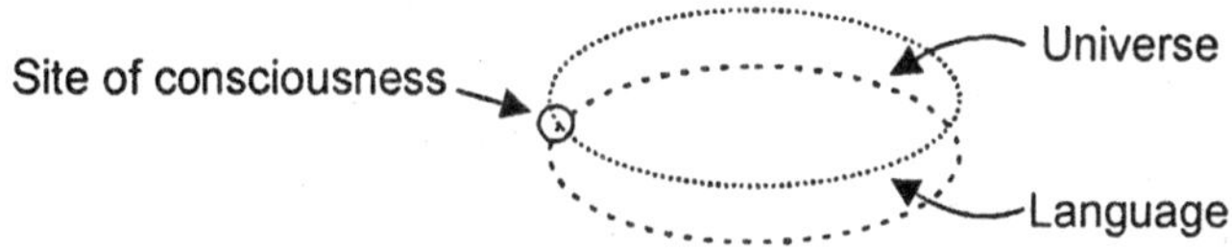

Ever since *Amar Kosh,* there has been a tradition of language studies in India that addresses the all pervasive side of language. But from the point of the present writing this is where the first sign of the Aham-internity perspective of Jenu Kurubas surfaces, because language of a people looks at the universe from the end of their psyche. Every thing, including conception of the Other, is articulated from that end. Out of the universe of possibilities, call it Amar plain of language, people workout their cosmos on the basis of their ability to make statements. The statements are made with reference to sites of experience and localities of life making practices. It may be said, therefore, that the cosmos of Jenu Kurubas is made up of that description of the universe that they can make in their lives at any point in time, termed above as Right Now.

The statements that build cosmos determine the possibilities of acts in actual life, where people live. The experience of doing acts and thereby playing doers is much different from their being a statement. In other words, the possibility of a statement and the act of making a statement are two different things. Acts of people create their world, as shown in the architecture below:

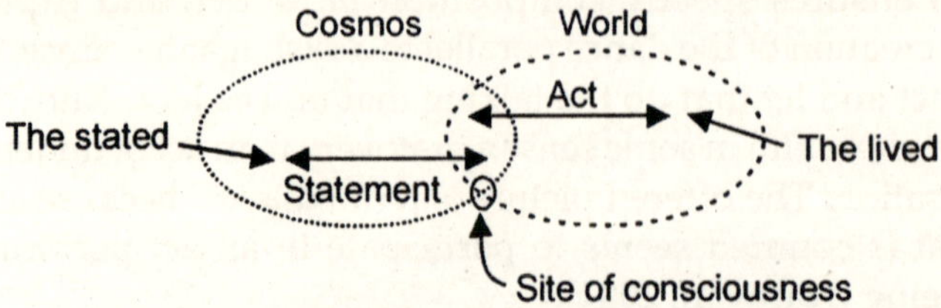

There is a very subtle distinction to be grasped at this point, and that concerns relationship between universe, cosmos and world. By using an insight developed long back (Rangila 1989a: 39-41), the distinction can be profitably drawn:

- Universe is a broad *potential* that language of a people draws from bit by bit.
- Cosmos is a grand realization of the universe that people make with their statements. It is a sphere of possibility of statement.
- World is the sphere of act that people live with guidance from their consciousness.

People are one end of the power to negotiate. The other end is polity with all its governing might that it has been made to accumulate over the ages. Though there is nothing natural about it, as it is a historical incidence, yet it is the case that it is polity that holds the bigger chunk of the balance of power. In the case of Jenu Kurubas there is no scope of negotiation even at the lowest ebb of polity.

NATURE facilitates Jenu Kurubas to build up their cosmos. They get guided by NATURE for making statements in language, and for doing acts in life. Within their world, they negotiate their practices. In fact there is a layer of actential life that does not move at all without some possibility of negotiation. This can be shown even in acts that may be called intransitive. So within the cosmos they do negotiate their life practices. That explains as to how Jenu Kurubas are able to co-inhabit the H D Kote forest with the other beings, 'animals' like tigers especially, also with the spirits of their ancestors. Methodologically, therefore, it could be a useless generalization to categorize their co-inhabitants into categories like nature and culture.

But the negotiative ability of Jenu Kurubas suffers a huge loss when it comes to living with the polity – the most powerful, big and by far the least known to these people. The only direct experience of the polity among these people is the administrative machinery of the forest. Unfortunately the administration believes that the Jenu Kurubas cannot live in their ancient *homes* as the forest officials treat these groups of trees as nothing more than a forest, and a forest is reserved for *the animals* only. Any attempt by Jenu Kurubas to live in their homes is met with vigorous physical assault.

In the world of Jenu Kurubas, it is not ***proper to act civilized*** (Rangila 2004-06). That the people may own the power through the depth of their civilization is altogether a different matter. Once you see the life with reference to the polity, it is ***power to rule*** that plays the civilization. This is where the Jenu Kurubas are no match to the state power, and are driven to live their lives in absolute powerlessness. At a more delicate level of observation, it is a case where those who are authorized to administer people in a polity do it by imposing their own categories of knowledge upon those whom they administer. It goes unrecognized that at least Jenu Kurubas categorise their universe, cosmos and their knowledge systems differently. For instance, the will to co-inhabit with a tiger and developing the knowledge required for the purpose has led the people to categorise tiger as just another living being in the forest. They have age old ways to protect themselves against all those eventualities they may come across due to co-inhabitance. The best that the so-called civilized society of the administrators, on the contrary, could do is to turn a forest into a reserve place restricted for the 'animals' without realizing that segregation may create a natural imbalance.

Language of Jenu Kurubas, like any other people's anywhere in the world at large, does multiple things. The considerations above should single out at least three things, as follows.

1. Language of a people draws the universe of them bit by bit and creates at least a working picture of the same for every individual.
2. Language describes cosmos with the possible statements that people make in their lives.
3. But when it comes to actual life making, then language is put to very complexly distributed functions, as for instance, given below.
    - Language serves to articulate acts by describing them.
    - People negotiate the cosmos with their life practices and use language as one of the means of negotiation.
    - People negotiate their acts also, where language either plays a parallel code, or means of negotiation, or tool of description, or even as a weapon of defence and protection.
    - Language may signify even an act, fact, concept, precept and all that may be lingualised.

The suggested functional inventory should help in observing the life of Jenu Kurubas, and in that they are like any other people – civilized in their own typical way. Yet the inventory fails to capture three most important facts:

1. Where from do Jenu Kurubas gather such a strong capacity to put up quality acts?
2. Why can the Jenu Kurubas not out-smart the forest administration?
3. How did the Jenu Kurubas come to be cheated and robbed of their land?

It is this 'act orientation' that helps their survival in situations like an animal attack. They cannot afford to sit, survey, write report, debate conclusions and then venture an act, which may be termed as 'idea orientation'. Since they have to act instantly to protect themselves, it seems their bodies are conditioned to retain some measure of optimum power against the forces of co-inhabitance in forest.

In the daily life of Jenu Kurubas, it seems idea has an equally strong tendency to merge with act and thereby allow an act to play the lead. In other words, somewhere in the depth of consciousness, call it unconsciousness; Jenu Kurubas are tuned to survive against adverse forces.

The act orientation has consequences for language. The age old wisdom has it that the so-called 'verb' does act articulation. It may, therefore, be a good hypothesis to believe that as they are driven by act orientation in their life in general, the verbal system of the Jenu Kuruba language should show at least some signs of the orientation. If the hypothesis gets support from the available data, then it should be a one of the major discoveries of the present writing. A life making orientation among Jenu Kurubas is found affecting the verbal base of the language of the people.

It is important to recall that Narayan (2008, also see Rangila 2008) in his presentation termed 'daatī/u' as a 'movement verb'. Seen from the perspective of C-semiology, a movement denotes act. That is how his discovery of a *movement verb* makes his data relevant for discovering what is termed as 'actential spread'. To workout the data for the purpose, each of the units is taken as a verbal composite, which includes the verb, an overt case marking and a nominal form. It is given a *pictorial graph* that makes the composite more than a Verb Phrase. The 'verbal composite' carries an element of specifier which signals the specifics of act and actential typologies (Rangila 2006a, 2006b). This is a new development in C-semiology.

As regards the construct 'typologies', it may help to know that in all those data fields where information about 'type' of a unit in question plays some role and the unit is expected to be identified as such, those cases are thought to be *typologies*. However, it makes a good piece of practical wisdom to take each and every unit of a cosmos as a typology, and then look for further and subtle distinctions within it. Other than presenting a concretized shape of a verbal composite, a *pictorial graph* prepares the 'linguistic description' for certain C-semiological readings, which come up shortly. The description has it:

1. 'manegu daatī':	'daatī' gu	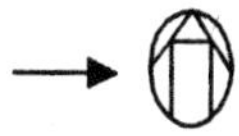
house to go	go to	house
2. 'maneyinna daatī':	'daatī' yinna	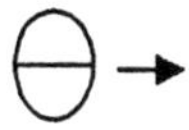
house from go	go from	house
3. 'mara daatī':	'daatī'	
tree climb	climb tree	
4. 'marayinna daatī':	'daatī'	
tree from climb down	climb down tree from	
5. 'alla daatī':	'daatī'	
river cross	go across river	
6. 'akki daatītade':	'daatī tade'	
bird flies	fly + s	bird
7. 'kasta daatīna':	'daatī na'	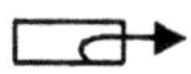
difficulty came out	came out	
8. 'kadu daatīna':	'daatī na'	
forest crossed he	crossed forest	
9. 'daatīne':		
get out, get lost.		

When data given above are considered together with their graphs, it makes a bigger piece of information. The interesting fact about the information package that each of the 1-9 cases comes from at least three channels of information:

1. Linguistic channel;
2. Physical channel – the one that linguistic channel creates by standing for a *state of affair* in the physical world; and

3. Visual channel that each of the 'pictorial graph' builds up.

It should suggest that if one wants to actually map up the linguistic spread of the verb 'daatī/u', then first channel is in the focus. While looking for 'case markers' and to discover the relations with the nominal, it leads to a discovery of syntax of the same. The wisdom of linguistic analysis, however, does not work if one were to look for a 'state of affair'.

Once a verb is realized as an act, all its extensions start showing up as extensions of the act. This gives rise to actential spread. So, instead of considering a verb in participation with doer and thereby looking for the syntactic caliber of the data, one may look for the actual spread that the verbal composites based on the verb show up together. The 1-9 digit description above, therefore, presents actential spread of the single verb 'daatī/u'.

An equally difficult problem is that of capturing the thus called *actential spread* in methodological terms. In this case how can one, for instance, decide if the 1-9 digit description of the data actually describes the actential spread that one is searching for?

One of the ways tried in the opening writing of the series is to create a 'verbal topograph' (Rangila 2008), which is reproduced so as to extend the idea. The picture has it:

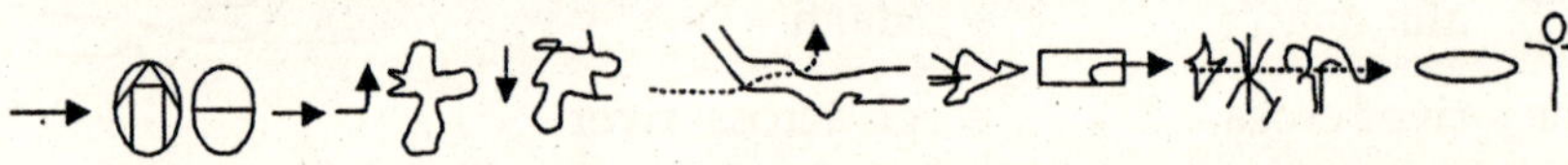

There are two levels at which the topograph may be seen. First, that topograph walks in to get integrated within the toolkit of C-semiology. Second, the verbal topograph opens door right in the centre of the Aham-internity of the Jenu Kurubas.

More important fact from the point of view of the present writing is that the topograph is exhaustive enough. It can afford to accommodate act as a general methodological tool and accommodate much larger or smaller sets of pictorial graphs. The topograph in these terms can be accepted as the relevant description of the actential spread of the Jenu Kuruba verb. Verb may be considered in its driving capacity. It is nice, and meaningful too, to extend the problematics of verb to act, as it brings to light many hitherto unknown facts to light, but in so doing one must not deny its due to the verb. To Jenu Kurubas it does not take any special effort to realize their act in actential chains. It happens involuntarily. At this moment, one does not know why the language should possess a long range of spread of a verb.

There is another methodological problem to be addressed. Since the data field concerns just one verb, it is possible to dismiss it as a non-representative sample. Once that happens, the offered reading does not have to survive.

No amount of linguistic analysis can explain why a single verb of Jenu Kuruba language projects a topographic spread. The analysis is rigorous as it picks up each case, establishes the type of 'case' and specifies the range of its function. Unfortunately, it stops at that and does not look for any way to take the observation further. Once the verbal universe is opened to a conceptual investigation, it rewrites the modalities of the analysis set by linguistics. One of the further openings could be to see how the Jenu Kurubas manage with the spread of the act. Within the framework of C-semiology, two separate answers are possible to the query. One is to realize each of the nine cases as separate entities such that have their own individual realities, and then suggest that human mind puts these realities into a ring, turn them into *the ringed realities* (Rangila 2002-06 for details) and live with them. The other way out for the human mind may be seen as the analytical facility termed as floral architecture (Rangila 2004-06), where human mind not only moves in linear progression, but the mind moves in all directions and even beyond them.

A floral architecture offers n-dimensional space to work with. The space has a base to set an operation on and then it may take to all the possible directions that a circle may allow. Approached the details of the verb above within this facility we may arrive at the following picture of the spread already captured in the verbal topograph:

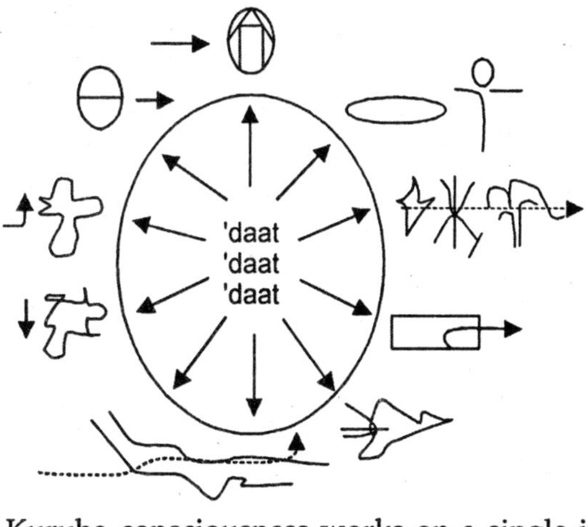

The Jenu Kuruba consciousness works on a single insight which may be called, following Panini 'Vridhi'-expansion. It may not be surprising to find that many Jenu Kuruba verbs may still be in the process of expansion.

You May Have It

How does one explain the fact that Jenu Kurubas excel others or call them so that they can compete with others when it come to performance, but they cannot defend themselves when it comes to withstanding the forest machinery?

It is not only Jenu Kurubas that are powerless against forest management machinery. On the global scale, I am looking for a new world. I hope you were careful when I drew the three distinctions like 'universe', 'cosmos' and 'world': A world, where people are respected as people along with the differences that they stand for.

If it turns out to be majority-minority configuration issue, as in present India, for instance, then you not only have it, like the poor Jenu Kurubas, but you are at the verge of getting wiped out also, because all the basic categories of the guiding wisdom of the polity are sourced in the so-called *educated elite*. Is it not absolute elitism that those who declare H D Kote forest as National Park, reserved only for 'animals', do not even qualify to understand that the forest has been an existential universe also for human beings since ages?

The so-called development thesis fails to realize that in Mysore city people refuse to take a house on rent if death has taken place in the house, whereas the Jenu Kurubas have an opposite cosmological value for death. If one is so adamant to suggest that let them die in some number, they will learn new value in the process, then of course, there is no argument with such developed souls acting a polity itself.

Using death as a teacher in the place of wisdom can act as a great leveling super power, because in that case both elite and poor Jenu Kurubas are to die. I am not interested in creating a brute force out of death. It is a great celebrative force that must be treated as a decent completion. My issue is what does one leave behind? Is it worth forcing people to die before their civilized death?

You yourself have spoken to me in great detail that this is what a civil society is doing in the name of saving animals and the human being together. And the result is destruction of both of the halves of the thus 'saved' ones. They are disappearing at faster speed. To me it is one single problem that has its multiple dimensions that deserve to be appreciated at one platform. The architecture has it:

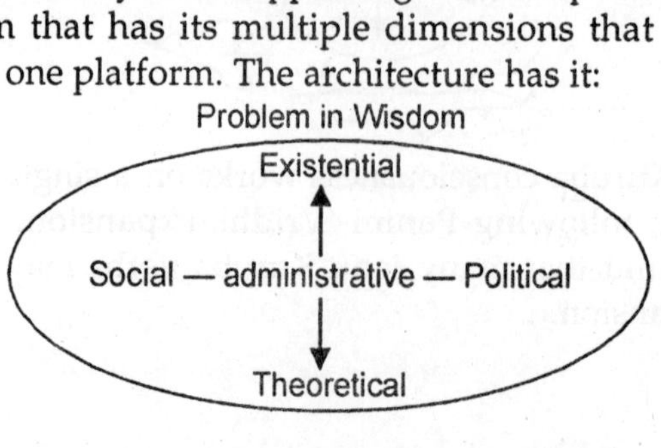

Yes, of course, if you want to play too innocent, you can talk of doing better discipline like many of those inspired by Chomsky would have it. You can go, collect data, do a minimalist analysis and come out with syntax of Jenu Kuruba language which could be better than the one you already did. Never mind the people, after all no critique can be built into the theory. If you try, it looses its scientific rigour and charm.

To support life I am trying to redefine 'science'. Please do not read it as something anti-science, anti-rigour and anti other known attributes of science. My principle of beauty of description does not depend on the elemental compositions and the compulsions that they may lead to. Quite opposite to it, I look for the mended compositions that may be conducive to life growth. Only then any description can be beautiful.

Importantly so I am not willing to concede any 'application' metaphor in my vision of *science*. It is a single continuum for me. This is the case in spite of very temptingly convincing local typologies.

The science that I am looking for strives to discover even elemental structures that support life in a big way. Had it been otherwise, life should not have grown on earth in the first place. To me there is a level of discovery at which NATURE supports life. Any other level of discovery is non-science.

For me there is no line between better analysis and better life, better theory and better society, as well as, better knowledge and better governing polity. If someone cannot theorise the society-theory combine, it is not my problem.

When someone moves from one form of act to another act, it is a movement from one theory to another theory. And in each case the movement is integrated with life directing societal wisdom. It works both ways. The Jenu Kurubas could do it, because human persons by nature are both knowledge (theory) making and knowledge implementing beings. I have shown that there is no rupture between the so-called two.

I do my version of science, because I am convinced that it must be done. It must be done because this is how people do it in their innocent or clever lives. You cannot show me just one and invite me to spend my life with a hope that others will some day do something that will bring it for my analysis in a discipline to be better and respectable. Why should not I myself do it?

The only test of one's theory and application that interests me is whether the pursuit can show it to modes and levels of governance that it is better for them to look for judicious distribution of power space among the knowledge systems that it governs. It is not a lofty idealism; rather it is an urgent need of polities the world over.

May I add, civilization never concludes, it continues as a discovery.

REFERENCES

Chandarshekhar, S. 1991. *Truth and beauty: Aesthetics and motivation in science.* New Delhi: Viking.

Gill, Harjeet Singh 1981. *Semiotics of conceptual structures.* Patiala, publisher not mentioned.

Gill, Harjeet Singh 1996. *Semiotics of conceptual structures.* New Delhi: Bahri Publications.

Narayan, K. 1997. Towards An Integrated Theory of Developing Writing system for Oral Language. In K.P. Acharya (ed.) *On writing.* 15-20. Mysore: Central Institute of Indian Languages.

Narayan, K. 2001. Space and Cosmology of Jenukurubas. In Udaya Narayana Singh (ed.) *Culturation – Essays In Honour of Jawarlal Handoo.* 156-173. Mysore: Central Institute of Indian Languages.

Narayan, K. 2008. Planning Modalities That Jenu Kurubas Deserve. *Workshop on language planning and language policies.* Jointly organised by Department of South and Central Asian Studies, Stockholm University, Sweden and Central Institute of Indian Languages, Mysore, India – in cooperation with the Nordic centre in India (NCI), 4-6 March 2008. Mysore: CIIL.

Rangila, Ranjit Singh 1989a. *Problematics of linguistics – Metatheoretical and analytical considerations.* New Delhi: Bahri Publications.

Rangila, Ranjit Singh 1989b. Relevant other and its implications in learning-Behaving. *Language Forum* 15 (1) 1989.

Rangila, Ranjit Singh 1995. Grammaticalisation and Narrative. Papers IV, 65-82. *XI Congress of the International Society for Folk-Narrative Research,* January 6-12, 1995. Mysore: Central Institute of Indian Languages.

Rangila, Ranjit Singh 2000. Sites in C-semology. A talk for the Discussion Club of the Central Institute of Indian Languages, Mysore.

Rangila, Ranjit Singh 2001a. The Wise Localities. In U. N. Singh (ed.) *Culturation.* 79-100. Mysore: Central Institute of Indian Languages.

Rangila, Ranjit Singh 2001b-05. The Invisible Trees. Paper presented in Seminar on *Language and Modes of Interpretation and the Concept of Tradition and Modernity,* Pune. Also available on http://www.languageinindia.com, Vol. 5, 12 December 2005.

Rangila, Ranjit Singh 2002-06. The ringed realities. Paper for *ZICR 21st century reality: Language, culture & technology.* October 29, 31, 2002, Joint: Central Institute of Indian Languages, Mysore and Mahatma Gandhi International Hindi University, New Delhi. Also available on http://www.languageinindia.com Vol. 6, 7 July 2006.

Rangila, Ranjit Singh 2004a-06. Power to act civilized. *The national seminar on language and power and communication,* February 4 – 6, 2004, jointly held by SNDT Women's University, Mumbai and Central Institute of Indian Languages, Mysore. Also available on http://www.languageinindia.com Vol. 6, 5 May 2006

Rangila, Ranjit Singh 2004b-06. The Geo-mentals. The writing prepared for *International Seminar on Construction of Knowledge,* April 16-18, 2004 at Vidya Bhawan Society, Udaipur, Rajasthan organized by Rama Kant Agnihotri. Also available on http://www.languageinindia.comVol. 6, 9 September 2006.

Rangila, Ranjit Singh 2005a. Of dream – SOVERIGNITY. . The paper is presented in *National seminar on semiotics of conceptual structures – Polity praxis and Mahatma's Swaraj,* February 1-4, 2005, Bhavnagar. Jointly organized by Central Institute of Indian Languages, Mysore and Samaldas Arts College, Gijubhai Badheka Marg, Bhavnagar.

Rangila, Ranjit Singh 2006a. The concretisers. The writing is presented in *National seminar "Theorizing 'Region': Configurations, alliances, contestations", 10-12 February 2006,* Centre for Comparative literature, University of Hyderabad.

Rangila, Ranjit Singh 2006b. Leap beyond eco. This paper is prepared for the First International Conference of Organisation for Studies in Literature and Environment-India on ECOLOGY AND CULTURE: Interdisciplinary Approaches, September 18-19, 2006, Loyola College, Chennai 600034, organised by Nirmal Selvamony.

Rangila, Ranjit Singh 2006c. Rural Punjab speaks English. The paper is presented in *International conference on improving spoken English in rural Punjab,* November 2006 at Mukandpur in Punjab.

Rangila, Ranjit Singh 2007. Sign measures life praxis in C-semiology. The paper is presented in *National seminar on the legacy of saussure and contemporary Indian experience,* February 9-11, 2007 at Mukandpur in Punjab.

Rangila, Ranjit Singh 2008. Language in the care of civilized societies – Jenu Kurba: A case. *Workshop on language planning and language policies titled* COMPETING LANGUAGE LOYALTIES IN SOUTH AND CENTRAL ASIA: THEORIES VERSUS CASE STUDIES. Jointly organised by Department of South and Central Asian Studies, Stockholm University, Sweden and Central Institute of Indian Languages, Mysore, India – in cooperation with the Nordic centre in India (NCI), 4-6 March 2008, CIIL, Mysore.

Rangila, Ranjit Singh and Sholapurkar, Sunetra 2010. Celebrative. A monograph. Mysore.

Saussure, Ferdinand de 1964. *Course in general linguistics.* Wade Baskin Tr. London, Peter Owen.

* The Jenu Kurubas materials in this writing come from Kikkeri Narayan's life long work. One is also thankful to many of those colleagues who made wise comments on an earlier writing titled 'C-semiology Discovers Jenu Kurba Civilization'.

13

From Margin to Mainstream: The Growing Domain of Language Switching and Mixing in Contemporary South African Television Drama

Kay McCormick[1]

I. Introduction

Writing about language and ethnic relations, Ross argues that '... where physical segregation is practiced, and where group relations are manifestly or latently competitive, linguistic differences are maintained as mechanisms of boundary maintenance '(1979: 7). As South Africans respond to the erosion of racial segregation which is occurring as a result of political change, and as they try to develop cooperative relationships with those with whom they seldom associated before, we see language losing some of its force as an intergroup boundary keeper. During the apartheid era part of the dominant ideology was that racial/ ethnic and language boundaries could be identified, and among those in power there was a belief that these boundaries should be institutionally consolidated. Of course social and linguistic mixing had always occurred and continued to occur in spite of these notional, protected boundaries[2]. But it occurred in the margins, out of the mainstream. Sometimes it constituted a conscious act of resistance, sometimes not. Now it is to be found in the mainstream.

Probably the most striking instance – and symbol – of this is the new national anthem which, in the conventional view, uses five of the eleven official languages, and switches between them both inter- and intrasententially. See Figure 1 below. It is important to note that, while the stanzas can be looked at through one lens and seen as being assignable to particular languages, other lenses would reveal commonalities accounting for the fact that lines 1-4 are easily understood by speakers of all the languages in the set to which Xhosa and Zulu belong; and that lines 5-9 are easily understood by speakers of other Sotho languages (Mantoa Smouse, personal communication). These two linguistic continua or sets were carved up and reified as distinct languages in the 19th and 20th centuries by various religious and secular institutions. (Going much further back in time, one would of course find that the two continua in turn come from one language family.)

(Xhosa) Nkosi sikelel' iAfrika Maluphakanyisw' uphondo lwayo, **(Zulu)**Yizwa imithandazo yethu, Nkosi sikelela, thina lusapho lwayo.	God bless Africa May her glory be lifted high Hear our petitions God bless us, Your children
(Southern Sotho) Morena boloka setjhaba sa heso, O fedise dintwa le matshwenyeho, O se boloke, O se boloke setjhaba sa heso, Setjhaba sa South Afrika - South Afrika	God we ask You to protect our nation Intervene and end all conflicts Protect us, protect our nation, our nation South Africa - South Africa
(Afrikaans) Uit die blou van onse hemel, Uit die diepte van ons see, Oor ons ewige gebergtes, Waar die kranse antwoord gee,	From the blue of our heaven, From the depths of our sea, Over our eternal mountain ranges, Where the cliffs give answer,
(English) Sounds the call to come together, And united we shall stand, Let us live and strive for freedom, In South Africa our land.	

Figure 1 South African National Anthem

Source: Wikipedia. http://en.wikipedia.org/w/index.php?title=National_anthem_of_South_Africa&oldid=243058909

Between the singing of the national anthem on the one hand and street corner talk on the other, there is a range of other public sites of language switching and mixing. This chapter explores one of them: the dialogue of locally made television drama. It shows how policy decisions and practical constraints interact in the shaping of linguistic choices in that field, and it considers whether the observable increase in code-switching might be an index of a new 'imagined community', to use Benedict Anderson's term for the concept of nation (Anderson 1991).

In the early 1990s protracted negotiations between the government and representatives of the liberation movements lead to a new political dispensation underpinned by the 1996 Constitution which lays the ground for a different 'imagined community'. It envisions a society very different from that of the apartheid era: one which is not segregated, where all people are regarded as equal, and in which there is respect for diversity. Government and the corporate world have, for different reasons, used the media in their attempts to establish attractive, feel-good images of a new national identity in which people of different backgrounds come together harmoniously. This is most evident in television advertisements for products, businesses, institutions, local tourism, and even for government and parastatal initiatives. Viewers are meant to follow the lead of these advertisers by - literally in some cases - buying into 'the new South Africa'.

A less rosy, more nuanced media picture of the difficult processes of constructing a new order of social and economic relations can be found in newspaper editorials, articles, reports and letters to the editor, in radio and television phone-in programmes and panel discussions and also in some radio and television dramas. As a genre of television drama, soap operas are not concerned with articulating the major political and economic forces that shape societies, but those which are in a 'realist' tradition as distinct from an 'escapist' tradition[3] do present individuals trying to find their way through a series of challenging personal, family and work situations that would be recognizable and interesting to their target audiences (Kilborn 1992, Wittebols 2004).

The switching and mixing of languages and dialects is becoming a conspicuous feature of South African prime-time soap operas and other local drama series. This is in stark contrast to what was allowed during the apartheid era, where strict policies of language separation and linguistic purism in broadcasting indexed the dominant ideological concern for ethnic purity and separateness. What has prompted the change in policy, and what shapes the linguistic practices in the production of prime-time drama? The rest of the chapter addresses these questions.

Part II sketches the historical and contemporary contexts of broadcasting policies and practices of the apartheid and post-apartheid eras. Part III comments on relevant aspects of recent research on South African television soap operas. In Part IV I give an account of my data on language switching and mixing in prime-time television drama and how I gathered it. Part V is an analysis of the data. In the concluding section of the chapter I return to the question with which I started out, namely whether the increase in multilingualism and in code-switching in these dramas can reasonably be seen as, among other things, an index of a socio-political shift towards a new 'imagined community'.

II. Contexts of television broadcasting policies and practices

Television came late to South Africa. The first programmes were aired in 1976. Prior to that there had been long debates in government circles about the threats that television might pose to apartheid ideology and practices. The higher echelons of the South African Broadcasting Corporation (SABC), which also controlled radio broadcasting, were packed with members of the Afrikaner Broederbond, a secret political organisation of white Afrikaans-speaking men[4]. They were ultra-nationalists who had worked tirelessly since 1918 to place Broederbonders in all spheres of influence, local, provincial and national. Once Broederbond members had secured high political office through the Nationalist Party victory in the 1948 elections, broadcasting was identified as a key propaganda tool and was relentlessly exploited as such. From 1960 to 1972 Dr Piet Meyer was simultaneously chairperson of the Broederbond and of the SABC. He also chaired the Bantu radio programmes control board[5]. It was during this period that the framework for television was established. A Broederbond document from that period show that the service was conceptualized as serving 'Afrikaans-, English-, and Bantu-speaking *national communities* in our country' (cited in Wilkins and Strydom 1978: 280, my italics.)

In 1976, after what is known as the Soweto Uprising, the Broederbond strengthened its commitment to apartheid, which it envisioned as resulting in 'a commonwealth of South African states' (Wilkins and Strydom 1978: 212). It produced a set of guidelines by which the Bantustans should establish political control and create favourable public opinion. Guideline 8.7 begins 'Power of the mass media. The radio services for the respective black nations must play a giant role here' (Op. cit. 213). Until 1982 there were no television channels dedicated to African languages, hence the emphasis on radio.

Note how in these instances of Broederbond discourse from 1969 and 1976, separate black nations are spoken of as if they already exist, 'naturally', so to speak. There is an underlying assumption that for every language there is a nation. (English and Afrikaans could not so easily be associated with separate nations, nor even with one race, ethnicity or culture. No official attention was drawn to this evident weakness in the language/nation equation.) When black people were forcibly assigned to particular 'homelands' (in which they might not previously have set foot), the assigning was done largely on the basis of language. Another assumption was that a family would have one home language, and in urban areas particularly this was (and is) simply not the case for the majority of families. Partitioning on the basis of language and assumed ethnicity, and the changes that came with it, were loathed by the people it affected. It caused enormous hardship, destroying social networks, disrupting and sometimes destroying employment and schooling.

In the 1987 Annual Report of the SABC we find slightly changed terms. No longer are black (and other) South African 'nations' mentioned. Instead we find terms such as 'language and cultural groups', 'communities' and 'population groups'. (South African Broadcasting Corporation 1987: 1). However, distinctiveness and separateness are still assumed to be important.

Separate institutions existed for the development of South African languages. The first of these had been founded in 1929, long before the advent of the apartheid era. It was for the development of Afrikaans. In the first decade of the apartheid era language boards were established by the government to promote the development of indigenous African languages[6]. This reflected the nationalist claim that under apartheid groups of people (more or less ethnically defined) would be treated as separate but equal. (Something of an anomaly is that there was no equivalent state language board for English, but nobody seemed particularly exercised by that.) The approach of those officially entrusted with the development of South African languages was linguistically conservative: if new words were needed in a language, they should be constructed from that language's existing lexical and morphological stock, rather than be obtained from other languages as borrowings. Needless to say, language mixing and switching were anathema to these language authorities who acted as watchdogs (some fiercer than others) over what was happening to languages in the public domain, including, of course, broadcasting.

As I hope will be clear from this sketch of the apartheid context for broadcasting, there was a policy of 'divide and rule'. Language differences were exploited wherever possible to promote separateness of groups of people. Post-apartheid language policy has to take into account people's memories of that strategy, and the effects of that exploitation. It has to tread a fine line between recognizing and celebrating diversity but promoting unity. It has to do this nationally and in particular domains, the most crucial of which in this regard are probably education and broadcasting.

I turn now to those aspects of the new SABC Language Policy which show the contrast between its concepts of 'nation' and 'diversity' and those which had informed the apartheid policy on language in broadcasting. The 2006 language policy document opens with a recognition of the SABC's 'constitutional duty to treat all the official languages equitably and with equal respect' (South African Broadcasting Corporation 2006: 26). Unlike the apartheid policy, the new policy's valuing of diversity is not linked with promotion of group separateness. Quite the contrary: almost every mention of languages and cultures in the plural is counterpoised, usually in the same sentence, with reference to national identity or national unity in the singular.[7] Examples include the broadcaster's acknowledgement of its responsibility to 'broadcast programmes that promote development of national identity while supporting development of our languages and cultures'(ibid.); and the following guideline: 'The obligation to reflect the linguistic and cultural diversity, and multilingual nature of South Africa while promoting national unity' (ibid.). Furthermore, the policy explicitly recognizes 'The unique potential of television to showcase cultures and languages creatively; to nurture people's knowledge and experience of one another, and to contribute to developing a national identity' (op cit 30).

In the implementation of language policy, the options are different for radio and television. It is financially viable to have radio stations dedicated to each of the official languages, but not television channels. Consequently, alternatives have to be devised. One of the principles is that the SABC 'creatively combines unilingual and multilingual programmes, and uses broadcasting technologies such as subtitling, to reach its language goals' (op cit 31).

Thus far - and indeed in the rest of the policy document - the driving force in the recognition of the value of multilingual programming might seem to be ideological. However, in the previous year's Chairperson's Statement, the Chairperson of the SABC Board had drawn attention to economic and financial factors that shape what happens. In my interaction with people working on SATV soaps, it became very clear that these factors influence soaps in a range of ways, from time of airing, to plot, to language choice. Reflecting on diversity, Sonwabo Eddie Funde said:

> A fundamental feature of SABC activities is reflection of the diversity of our nation. *At the top of the list of factors here is recognition that black consumers are playing an increasingly important part in the media marketplace, and that addressing the burgeoning black middle class is imperative for advertising and marketing. Language delivery is part of this,* as is local content[8]...' (South African Broadcasting Corporation 2005: 25, italics mine).

In a paragraph headed 'Reaching out', he goes on to say:

> We are committed to the SABC's role as a corporate citizen, and undertake to support the SABC in its efforts to *strengthen the bonds of unity* in South Africa and *to invest in South African society; to celebrate our cultural and linguistic diversity*; to project an image to the outside world that *attracts foreign investment* and promotes this country as one of the world's most desirable tourist destinations; and *to focus on the positive aspects of our country* (ibid., italics mine).

Although there is some difference of emphasis between the SABC

Language Policy and the Board Chairperson's report, the two documents clearly have in common the assumption that part of the work of the national broadcaster is nation building.

In 1998 a new channel, etv, was launched. Described in its website as a 'free-to-air commercial television station', it is now the second-largest channel, and the largest English channel. It claims viewership across all age, race, income groups. Although it is an independent commercial channel, like the public broadcasting channels it is subject to the control of the Independent Communications Authority of South Africa (ICASA) including its 'vernacular quota'. As I shall show in Section 5 of this chapter, etv handles the implementation of this policy in a different way from the way chosen by the public broadcaster.

III. South African television soaps and other drama series.

It is broadly agreed that there are two traditions of soaps: British and American. According to Wittebols (2004: 41), British soaps are produced in the tradition of public service, and thus story lines in British soaps are geared towards social realism and are set in working-class environments' while soaps produced in the United States 'focus on melodrama and romance in upper-middle-class settings'. South African soaps are in the British rather than the American tradition, but, as Lockyear suggests, the vertical class range is greater in local soaps than in those made in Britain (Lockyear 2004: 39).

South African audiences have been exposed to American soaps for more than two decades but not to British soaps. According to Neil McCarthy, who has worked in local television drama for more than 25 years, South African audiences do not distinguish between locally made soaps and other local prime time television drama series: 'the weird thing is that our viewers don't distinguish between the two. Soaps in this country are part of mainstream culture'. Perhaps this is because the local soaps are made in the British tradition in which a range of issues and intrigues (not only romantic) is explored. The viewership for these prime time programmes cuts across ages, races and income groups and they are popular with both men and women.

Almost all of the TV dramas – I use this term when it is appropriate to cover both soaps and other drama series[9] – are set in or around Johannesburg, a cosmopolitan city which is the centre of an enormous urban area. (The city is usually referred to as 'Joburg', and is affectionately known as 'Jozi'.) It is ideal as the site for tv dramas for various reasons. Johannesburg is the centre of the television industry, which means that the relevant physical and human resources are concentrated there. Thus, for logistical reasons it is easier to set the dramas there. The second reason is that all the issues which would make good story material can be authentically set in Johannesburg, with (apparent) excursions to other settings where necessary, for example to rural areas if the story deals with rural/urban or traditional/modern contrasts. Thirdly, with regard to soaps in particular, Neil McCarthy explained that 'Jo'burg is our great metropolis and since soapies[10] are all about aspiration, and since the sad fact is that the youth seem to share an aspiration to be part of the metropolitan life, they need to be set in the metropolis' (http://www.gautengfilm.co.za/live/content.php?Item_ID=488). For all these reasons 'Jozi is a soap dish', as the Gauteng Film Commission put it (http://www.gautengfilm.co.za/live/content.php?Item_ID=488).

Johannesburg is also by far the most multilingual place in South Africa. All South African languages are to be found there, with substantial numbers of speakers of each. Because of the long and continuing history of migration to this mining, industrial and financial centre, a wide range of foreign languages and also of regional and class dialects of local languages is also heard there. In addition, mixed language urban vernaculars have been in use for more than a century in predominantly black areas. They are a very important index of being urbanized. Local tv drama taps all aspects of this fluid multilingualism, but the processes involved are interestingly complex, as the analysis of my data shows.

Before turning to my own data, I wish to note relevant points made in a few recent research papers on South African soaps. Miki Flockemann speaks of the ways in which soaps

> generally serve to naturalize hegemonic value systems, while simultaneously, under certain circumstances, also serving as a vehicle for opening up a useful – and 'safe' – space for articulating alternative identities both in the public and in the private spheres during times of intense political and social transition (2000: 144).

She goes on to note that in some local soaps which have used the opportunities thus created, 'alternative (new) South African realities purporting to be 'real' or 'local' (...) often represent an unproblematically and already achieved 'new' rainbow-nationhood' (ibid.). What she says here is borne out by the people whom I interviewed. In the introduction to a paper on educational soap opera, Loren Kruger (1999: 106) notes that 'soap opera may seem an unlikely site for nation-building' and goes on to say that 'soap opera would appear to draw viewers away from an engagement with the "imagined community" of the nation that Benedict Anderson (15) finds in the "mind of each citizen" in the era of mass communication'. However, her analysis of *Soul City* shows that that soap did engage viewers with issues preoccupying citizens in the years of transition from apartheid. This article also gives an insightful analysis of the tensions besetting the national broadcaster at the time, including tensions that arise when the mission of a public broadcaster is to be 'relevant, accessible, diverse, and responsive to the communication needs of the country' but its 'primary source of revenue is advertising' (SABC Green Paper cited in Kruger 1999: 110).

Slabbert, Van der Berg and Finlayson (2007) give an economically and historically contextualized overview of multilingualism in South African soaps on the three SABC channels, examining it in the light of the language policy requirements for each channel laid down by ICASA. They discuss the extent to which the SABC shares key features of public broadcasters identified by Mendel. Two of these features are relevant here, namely 'concern with national identity and culture', and 'independence from both the state and commercial interest' (Mendel 2000 cited in Slabbert et al 2007: 333). The authors recognize that the SABC is not independent of state interest (in that its language policy is shaped by a state institution) or of commercial interest (since a very large proportion of its income comes from advertising). Their research indicates that although English has high aspirational value in this sector of the population, African languages are still highly valued.[11] They claim that the multilingual soaps are very successful commercially, and also that they are raising the status of marginalized languages. Their analysis of the dialogue in soaps from each of the SABC channels showed that there was not strict adherence to the guidelines as to which languages should predominate on each channels but '[r] ather, there is a mix of languages according to the scene, context and profile of the actors' (Slabbert et al 2007: 354).

So far, there is relatively little research on lexical and grammatical detail or on types of code-switching in the language of local tv drama programmes. However, the dialogue of an Afrikaans soap *7de Laan* has come under scrutiny in recent studies. In one of these, Klein draws on Bell's theory of audience design to account for the influence that the television audience can exert on the language usage in soaps. Speakers in dramas have two sets of interlocutors: the characters to whom they are speaking, and the audience which is not physically present. The latter group constitute what Bell refers to as 'referees' (1984: 186, cited in Klein 2007: 1) and they exercise an influence on the dialogue because the TV channel needs to please them in order to retain financial support from satisfied advertisers. This kind of influence was discussed by the script writers whom I interviewed.

IV. Data and data-gathering for this chapter

Policy documents and official reports dealing with the language of multilingual television soaps provide context, principles, guidelines and some indication of constraints on the deployment of South Africa's languages, but in order to understand the complex set of factors that actually shapes the language that we hear in these programmes, it was necessary to draw on the experience of people involved in programme creation and production: script writing, translating, directing and acting. Aware of how pressured this field of work is, I did not feel like asking for interviews with people whom I did not know at all. I thus needed an entrèe to a network, and sought help from two of my former students, Neil McCarthy and Maralin Vanrenen, both of whom have long connections with television drama in South Africa. Without them and the people to whom Neil McCarthy introduced me, this chapter would have been impossible. All of them were extraordinarily generous with their time and insights. A brief summary follows of the kinds of material I was able to gather.

Interviews

Because I was fairly ignorant of the processes and constraints that shape the production of television dramas, I used a relatively unstructured interview format so that interviewees could run with topics I raised, and could also branch out into anything else they thought was relevant. They did so. As a result the interviews are very rich in information and reflection. The topics I raised concerned: policy changes responsible for the move from monolingual to multilingual scripts; effects of this move on creative and production possibilities and practicalities, and also on audiences; the degree of freedom accorded to writers, translators, actors regarding the amount and nature of language switching and mixing; language switching and mixing as a possible index of values being promoted in the construction of a post-apartheid 'imagined community' in Anderson's sense.

I had an interview Maralin Vanrenen, who currently writes for *Muvhango*, a prime-time drama series and who has also worked in other capacities in tv drama. In my interview with Neil McCarthy who has worked in numerous television drama series and soaps as an actor and writer since 1980, he drew on this long history as well as on his current experience in creating and being head writer for a soap called *Rhythm City*. Through him I met and interviewed others involved in *Rhythm City*: the translator, Funeka Mpela, the language editor, Ferry Jele, and the music editor and storyliner, Percy Vilakazi. Neil McCarthy also arranged for me to meet and interview people working on *Isidingo*, a long-running soap which he had helped to create and for which he used to write. I had a long interview with *Isidingo*'s co-ordinating producer, Steven Raymond, in which the executive producer, Pumla Hopa and the head writer, Greig Coetzee, also participated for a while. All of my interviewees had previously worked on other South African soaps and drama series and commented on those experiences as well, during the interviews.

Observation

I sat in on a writers' meeting for *Rhythm City*, which was attended not only by the four writers, but also by two people whose task it is to advise on cultural and other aspects of the story. I sat in on the screening and discussion of some casting footage for *Rhythm City*, and I watched the rehearsal and filming of several scenes of *Rhythm City* and *Isidingo*.

Scripts

I was given translated scripts for one episode each of *Rhythm City*, *Isidingo*, and *Muvhango*.

V. Analysis and commentary

I turn now to what happens regarding language in the space between the proclaiming of language policy and the screening of the dramas. I explore a range of factors that in some way shape the language we hear in the episodes we watch, drawing primarily on interviews and supplementing that with what I learned from observation and from my reading of the multilingual scripts. My commentary is, of course, informed by my reading of the language policy documents and of other people's research. I start by describing some aspects of language policy requirements, and go on to show their ramifications in practical aspects of creating and producing tv drama series.

The Constitutional framework for how languages should be treated with regard to status, respect, rights and domains of use provides guidelines for ICASA's directives to each channel, and for the broadcasters' conceptualization of what they should and could do in order to comply with the directives. The Constitutional framework remains stable, the public broadcaster revises its policy every now and then[12] – there have been three policies in the last 14 years - but ICASA's directives concerning relative proportions of air-time for various languages on the different channels change more frequently, resulting in the channels' needing to adapt the implementation of their own policies. Usually this means speeding up the increase in use of languages other than English. (Among people working in tv drama these languages are collectively referred to as 'vernac' and I will follow this usage.) The heads of all channels are answerable to ICASA in respect of their channel's compliance with ICASA directives, and there is downward pressure from them to the programme producers and from them, in turn, to the head writers.

The first post-apartheid language policy for the public broadcaster allowed the use of English on all channels, but assigned languages from the Nguni group (which is the biggest) to Channel 1; the Sotho group, plus Venda, Tsonga and Afrikaans to Channel 2; and English to Channel 3. This neat division did not prove easy to implement and produced some anomalies. For example, on game shows and other programmes requiring studio audience participation, the polyglot hosts would take their linguistic cues from interlocutors in the audience. In TV drama, a channel's language profile was sometimes at odds with channel policy to show and endorse diversity. This happened in the early days of Chanel 3's *Isidingo:* a core group of characters in this drama series was (and still is) the Matabane family, bilingual in Sotho and English. The characters' background would have determined that in family conversation at home they would have spoken Sotho to one another. How to signal that on the English channel? According to one of the original writers, strategies included having family members greet one another in Sotho, using Sotho terms of kinship address, and sprinkling a few Sotho borrowings in the otherwise English dialogue. These devices were meant to remind the audience that the characters should be regarded as speaking Sotho. In my experience as a viewer, this did not work. With the endorsement of multilingualism on all channels in the SABC's 2006 policy, came changes in the Matabane family's use of language. They and characters who are speakers of other languages now code-switch between English and those languages, thus retaining some continuity of experience for English-speaking viewers. Any text that is not in English is subtitled in English. Steven Raymond says that the shift in *Isidingo's* language profile has coincided with an 'astronomical growth' in black viewership, and some decline in white viewer numbers. He speculates that having to rely on reading subtitles may be a problem for those (mostly white) viewers who do not know Sotho and Zulu, and especially for those whose household activities during the viewing time would necessitate their taking their eyes off the screen and its subtitles, for example while cooking or eating.

It is important to note that ICASA and SABC language policies do not just facilitate multilingualism, they demand it, and that raises challenges for producers. ICASA sets the vernac target percentage for each channel but, according to Steven Raymond the broadcasters' planning on how to met the targets has not led to their commissioning enough new work which could from the outset be high in vernac usage. The result is that there is pressure on existing programmes, particularly local dramas, to change their language profiles in order to raise the channel's vernac percentage. According to Hopa, 'as per contract we [*Isidingo*] are supposed to deliver 5% of vernac, but we've been requested by the channel to give between 10 and 15, and we are doing it.' All locally produced tv dramas now have to use more than one language. This can be achieved by developing the story line in such a way as to require more vernac domains and vernac-speaking characters. Where that is too difficult to achieve in the short term, strategic casting decisions can help. For example, the most recent casting decision in *Isidingo* saw the appointment of an Afrikaans-speaking male actor, also fluent in English, to play the part of the new barman at a popular gathering place. His presence in bar scenes provides opportunities for Afrikaans dialogue which had not existed before. There are other actors who can speak Afrikaans, but the plot hadn't brought their characters together before in situations where it would have seemed authentic if they spoke Afrikaans.

Muvhango, a TV 2 drama series, underwent a change of language profile. It was conceived originally as a mainly Venda drama, with two important Zulu characters. It was set in a rural area. From the outset it was extremely popular among Venda speakers. This was at least in part because, being the home language of little over 2% of the South African population, Venda had previously had little airtime. Maralin Vanrenen, who has been writing for it since its seventh year (2006), classes it as a drama series rather than a soap because it is based primarily on character rather than being plot-driven, as many soaps are. Its producer is clear about the need for it to give insights into cultural beliefs and systems. In response to my question about why *Muvhango* had extended its linguistic profile, Maralin Vanrenen said this was partly due to the 2006 SABC language policy, and partly to the need to be able to broaden the story possibilites. This broadening stayed within the focal theme of *Muvhango* – the title means 'conflict' – and was achieved by having the leading Venda-speaking family set up a business partnership with a Sotho-speaking family. This provided scope for the exploration of cultural differences and rivalries, as well as for the inclusion of urban scenes. The change in language profile came at a time when there was a strong push for sub-titling in local dramas (into English). This combination of factors has widened the range of viewers, which in turn pleases advertisers.

When the SABC launched its 2006 policy it made a presentation on it to all producers, but according to my interviewees neither the presentation nor the policy in its present form has resolved practical implementation issues. One interviewee put this down to language being just one of a number of matters on which new policy had to be developed (others include race and gender issues), and indicated that it seemed as if some of the new policy specifications were reactions to the fear of being found wanting in the area of transformation, rather than the product of extensive, careful deliberation. According to Steven Raymond, for the *Isidingo* team the language policy and vernac quota are not experienced as onerous 'I can quite honestly say that for a large part, we pretty much just do what we want to do. We just do what organically seems to be right, and I think that's because the intention of the policy meets the intention of what we're trying to do.'

Elements of these policy guidelines seem to me to be in tension with one another, and with values among some sectors of the audience. They promise to ensure correctness while at the same time wanting to recognize and celebrate diversity and change. The practical implications of that tension for productions do not seem to have received sufficient attention from policy-makers. In the 2006 policy, the section headed 'Use of language in broadcasting' begins thus:

> In fulfilling its duty to protect and nurture South Africa's official languages, the SABC strives to ensure that they are all spoken correctly. In doing so the SABC commits itself to celebrating the rich diversity of dialects and accents in each language group.
>
> The SABC recognizes the languages are dynamic, continually developing and adapting to circumstances; language in broadcasting should therefore take account of the evolution of languages (South African Broadcasting Corporation 2006: 27).

The tension within these guidelines can be accounted for in terms of Bakhtin's concept of the everpresent tension between the centripetal and centrifugal forces at work in language. The centrifugal force allows for growth and change, while the centripetal force ensures sufficient core stability to prevent total dispersion of commonalities that are essential in a mode of communication (Bakhtin 1981). The SABC guideline on correctness explicitly links concern for correctness with respect for dialectal diversity. This strong linkage indicates a nuanced understanding of historical sociolinguistic realities surrounding the emergence/creation of standard dialects of indigenous languages. The opposites can thus be reconciled intellectually, but implementing both guidelines is not a simple matter and leads to some oddities in scripting for characters who need to use a mixed vernacular – in practice there are limits on ICASA's acceptance of language variety and contact-induced language change. I return to this point later.

In my view, the concern with languages being spoken correctly that is evident in the first guideline quoted above is unlikely simply to be the product of purist mindsets. There is a history here. During the colonial and apartheid eras it was only English and Afrikaans for which rules of correctness were enforced in the public domain. English and Afrikaans speakers felt entitled to complain about what they perceived as incorrect usage (or 'unattractive accents') in public use of those two languages. Even today, far less attention is paid to the promotion of high levels of competence and correctness in the public use of other South African languages. Among native-speakers of those languages there is considerable resentment about this, as it is regarded as a sign of lack of respect for the languages, and by implication for their speakers. Some of the negative audience reaction to language usage in soaps appears to be based on this perception. On the whole, though, linguistic fluidity of the dialogue in these dramas is accepted and enjoyed by their audiences.

Policy-makers' desire for maximum reach of multilingual programmes has had some rather bizarre consequences. One of the interviewees, Greig Coetzee, had worked as a writer for a bilingual comedy series in English and Zulu. He was told that no punning or word-play was to be allowed because that would reduce comprehensibility among sectors of the audience who did not have high proficiency in both languages.

Apart from policy, other loci of decision-making about language as it actually appears in the screened episodes are to be found in various stages of what practitioners refer to as the creative and the production phases. For the most part the two phases use different teams of people but over-all practical responsibility is taken by the head writer / co-ordinating producer, and over-all accountability upwards is taken by the executive producer of the series. These two have to work closely together. As will become apparent, there are some significant differences between processes generating SABC programmes on the one hand, and programmes for etv on the other.

Some of the high-level decisions taken at the outset when a new programme is being developed, such as decisions about setting and plot type, have consequences for language choices down the line. For example, stories set in deep rural areas will necessitate the use of what interviewees variously referred to as 'pure', 'clean', A-grade or 'hard-core' forms of the local language. Stories with corporate settings necessitate the inclusion of English, and those set in urban townships have to be multilingual. In long-running series new characters have to be created. When this happens, the writing team has to decide what the character's language background should be. That decision, in turn, has to be taken into account at the casting stage of the production phase. According to McCarthy, the teams have had to develop their sociolinguistic awareness considerably. He was one of the original *Isidingo* writers and spoke of what he called their 'naivete' in this regard when they started out. For example, when casting members of one of the central families in *Isidingo* they had simply looked for and cast good actors who were Sotho-speaking, unaware that dialect differences among actors playing this family, if not explicable in terms of the plot, would be picked up as inauthentic by the Sotho-speaking audience. Now, in most drama series there is far more consciousness of the role of subtle dialect and accent difference in constructing identity. Producers and writers are very aware of negative audience reaction to what they perceive as incorrect or inauthentic use of vernac. (I return to the casting processes later.)

The processes that generate episodes of *Rhythm City*, which were described to me and which I summarize below, are similar to those that used at the SABC, up to the point of getting scripts translated. That is where etv practices begin to differ significantly from those at the SABC.

Soaps usually weave together scenes from three story lines in each episode. These story lines are developed by a team of writers who meet weekly, together with cultural advisor(s) for the series. In these meetings possible long-term plot developments or shifts in balance between the various story lines are discussed as are writers' notes for the scenes that had been assigned to them for the next set of episodes. Where relevant, at the meeting writers can check out cultural or other contextual background with the cultural advisors who have insider knowledge of norms and practices in the communities represented in the fictional world. In the following week writers flesh out the stories for their scenes which go to and fro between them and the head writer until he or she is satisfied. The scenes are then woven into the episode structure by one of the writers. When the head writer regards the coherence of the episode's structure as sufficiently tight, the script is sent to a script editor who checks it for continuity. Only then do writers create the dialogue. These writers may be the same people who devised the stories, but often other people write the dialogue. This, too, is checked and edited by the head writer. Before it is sent on to those involved in the next phase, the script has to be approved by the executive producer as well.

Thus far in the process, everything is in English as this is the working language of both the SABC and etv.[13] There has to be an English version of every script for use by the production team. At present this is convenient for the writers, the majority of whom are English-speaking.[14] The completed English version of the script for each episode is handed over for translation. From this point on there are significant differences in process between etv and the SABC channels.

The provision of translation at etv is regarded by all interviewees as far better than that at the SABC. According to Neil McCarthy, this is because etv commissions production companies to 'deliver products' to them and it is the companies which decide how to go about that. 'So, in this case the details of language policy and the resources that are assigned to execute that policy are all decisions that are made by the production company, not the channel'. Clearly, the companies do what is most effective for them. The company that produces *Rhythm City* has the human and financial resources that allows it to appoint its own translator, and also a language advisor who sits in the box with the director throughout all the shoots. As I show later, series made for SABC do not have the same latitude

I interviewed Percy Vilakazi, now a music advisor, formerly a story-liner, who had done some translating for *Scandal*, an etv soap. He speaks five languages. I also had a long interview with the translator for *Rhythm City*, Funeka Mpela, who is proficient in seven languages and Tsotsitaal (which she did not include in the listing of her seven languages). She has spent a lot of her life in and around Johannesburg and is familiar with dialect differences in the languages heard in the area. From what they said, it is clear that both she and Percy Vilakazi work intuitively when translating. They spoke of allowing the flow of a character's speech to indicate where switches would occur. Neither of them mentioned the station's need to meet a vernac quota target as a factor to which they had to pay attention in translating dialogue. When I asked how she made decisions about where and when characters would use vernac or English, Funeka Mpela explained that:

> You have to understand your character first .... You have to understand their moods ... you have to bear in mind that this character would not necessarily say this, which is written in English, so when you do your translation you must make it so that it accommodates the personality of that character.

She also takes into account what a character might want to suggest about himself/herself in a particular situation, and used this example:

> You start thinking like Fats. That, no he would want to prove that he is intelligent here, and his English is very good, so he will mix it in such a way that it's going to end up in English. So I use these big words.

She spoke of needing to be aware of the affordances of each language in relation to various situations, for example 'There are certain ways of being romantic in Tswana, but it's not as lovey-dovey or as cheesy as you want it to be, you know. It's got a formality to it'.

Her work schedule allows time for watching the filming of scenes when, for example, she wants to get a feel for a new actor's range. Because she works at the studio, she can speak to the head writer and the producer whenever she needs to. Etv's language policy does not lay down any rules about the forms that multilingualism can take in the dialogue. The translated *Rhythm City* script which I was given shows a wide range of language alternation phenòmena: lexical borrowing, intersentential switching and intrasentential switching, and language mixing.

At the SABC there is no direct contact between translators and creative or production teams. SABC policy is to develop a pool of skilled translators who can be drawn on by any programme needing translated material. These translators do not work in the buildings that house the studios. Producers and head writers have no control over who does the translation of the sections that are to be in vernac. They do not know who the individuals are who do the translating or whether the same person / people are assigned to their series for the translation of all episodes. They do not even know whether the translators watch the series. Having been told about this impersonal outsourcing, I expected uniformity in the way translating was done for all the SABC drama series, but that is not the case.

The entire *Muvhango* script that I saw had been translated from English into Venda for some scenes and Sotho for others, depending on situation and characters. Thus there is no code-switching in the script. Nor is there any indication as to which bits of the dialogue would or should be performed in vernac and which in English. According to Maralin Vanrenen, the default setting is that characters speak in the vernac appropriate for the interaction, and tend to use lexical borrowings only for untranslatable phrases. The decisions about code-switching are made by the director. The translation of the *Isidingo* script that I was given had been differently handled. It would appear that the translators made the decisions about how much code-switching there should be and where it should occur, and translated the bits that they thought should be in vernac (with one exception, which will be discussed below). It is not clear whether the SABC's language monitors send clear guidelines to the translators as to what kinds of language alternation are allowed, but I noticed that in the translated script for *Isidingo* there is more situational code-switching (which is usually intersentential), than conversational code-switching (which is often intrasentential). I found no instances in the translated script of a 'mixed code[15]', although such a code is part of a key character's linguistic repertoire, and although such usage is common in and around Johannesburg, which is where *Isidingo* is set. The translators leave the lines of this character, wheeler-dealer Georgie Zamdela, in English and the actor decides how and where to vernacularise his speech. The idiolect which he developed for the character draws on Afrikaans, English, Sotho, Zulu and tsotsitaal.

Tsotsitaal (originally 'gangster language') or flaaitaal (etymology unclear) is a form of language mixing that originated in the Johannesburg area but is now also found in other cities. There is debate as to whether there are recognizable, stable sub-varieties of this practice. The *Rhythm City* translator believes that there are, and says that the varieties are regional, with subtle differences that can immediately place a speaker within a particular part of Soweto or a nearby township. In her recently completed doctoral dissertation, Ellen Hurst argues convincingly that it is more appropriate to regard tsotsitaal as what she calls a 'stylect' than as a language variety. She proposes the term 'to distinguish Tsotsitaal as a code which is style-related and linked to extra-linguistic markers: a style-lexicon' (Hurst 2008:2). Hurst's characterization of tsotsitaal could explain how it is that the speech of *Isidingo's* Georgie Zamdela (a shebeen owner involved in various dodgy practices) is so readily accepted and enjoyed by black male viewers of approximately the same age as the character[16], in spite of the fact that it is an idiolect developed by the actor for the role. Although this character's speech is accepted by the audience as local vernacular, and although it is more multilingual that that of any other tv drama character with which I am familiar, *Isidingo's* producer says that it does not count towards programme's target percentage for vernacular because ICASA doesn't recognize his speech as a language. This seems to be an instance of the tension I mentioned earlier between the guideline on 'correctness' and guideline on 'respect for variety and change' which I discussed earlier. It produces an anomaly. The existence of variation and change is recognized (and this should include the consequences of language contact, such as tsotsitaal) but only discrete languages can be identified and counted in the drive to increase the airtime of languages other than English.

Pumla Hopa feels that the current language policy strictures on language switching and mixing result in some falsity in the representation of urban speech. It seems that things could have been different in this regard, had an earlier policy suggestion been taken up. Slabbert et al quote from a 1994 SABC discussion document. One of its suggestions was that 'To facilitate comprehension, the use of urban languages could be considered. Perhaps a relaxation of the stringent puristic use of languages could be to the advantage of certain commercial services and programme types' (cited in Slabbert et al 2007: 338). Other SABC interviewees agreed with Hopa, saying that at times the translated lines are not an accurate reflection of the writer's intended meaning, and they reported that actors sometimes complain that the translated lines use vocabulary or a style would not come across as authentic for that character. When this happens the director allows the actors to make whatever amendments they deem necessary and their decisions are final. However, on the whole, in order to safeguard the intention of the scene, actors are not given a great deal of scope to change the language in the script. According to Maralin Vanrenen, some of the linguistic choices occur in a totally unplanned way as they are the result of actors not having learned their lines properly[17].

As I saw when I sat in on the shooting of scenes of etv's *Rhythm City*, some decisions about code-switching are made at that stage by the director's team. One scene involved a series of short job interviews. From where I was sitting I could read the translated script the director was using, and noted with interest that in her short piece an actress playing a minor role as a job-seeker switched from English at the point in the script where that was indicated, but she switched into Tswana not Zulu, which was the language in the script. No-one in the box commented on this. I presumed that the actor felt more confident in Tswana than Zulu, and since her preference didn't skew the scene in any way it was accepted. Later in the scene, the language advisor intervened, telling the director that it would be better if another job-seeker character didn't use so much English but rather 'put in more vernac'. She did not specify which other language should be used. The instruction was relayed to the actor who had no trouble at all in spontaneously code-switching between English and Zulu. The role of the language advisor, who needs to be someone with stage experience, is to see that the language used feels and sounds right at the shoot. SABC production teams do not have anyone with that final responsibility.

Thinking that an actor's linguistic repertoire could have an impact on the range of potential directions the story line involving the character could take, I asked interviewees at etv and SABC whether an actor's linguistic repertoire was taken into account at the casting stage. Answers varied. Maralin Vanrenen explained that for *Muvhango*, an actor's ability to speak Venda well was crucial. She reported having noticed over the years working on other productions, that audiences don't mind how characters speak English, but they are offended if an actor acting as an Afrikaans character, or as a character whose home language is a 'black language', doesn't get the accent right. It is acceptable to 'get it wrong' only if the character is not supposed to be a mother-tongue speaker of the language. I noticed in the casting tapes which I saw that one of the questions asked of each actor at the beginning of the audition was which languages he or she was comfortable speaking. Both Steven Raymond and Neil McCarthy said that they paid careful attention to actors' command of the dialects and accents of a language because these could be used in signaling a character's background.

According to McCarthy, while established actors are willing to act in vernacular languages, actors who are still trying to get a foot in the door are sometimes unwilling to use vernacular in their roles because they feel that

> real acting is in English and that you're making them look like they're kind of degraded and working-class if they're having to talk their own township language, and they want to speak English. And sometimes our language advisor has gone to them repeatedly and said 'No, please would you just do it in tsotsitaal or in local, township.' No! They will refuse and they'll do it in English because English is regarded as a posh language.

Such is the power of the image of English as an 'Open Sesame' code that an aspiring actor will take the risk of disobeying directorial instruction in order to make an opportunity to showcase his or her English abilities. (They sometimes get away with it because the production schedule is too tight to allow a search for a more compliant actor.) Here we see an example of how the 'real world currency' of two languages can negatively affect the dialogue in the fictional world.

V. Conclusion

The brief comparison of public broadcasting in two political eras shows that dominant political visions of the ideal nation feed directly into broadcasting policies, and that they do shape linguistic practices in programmes. However, translating broad policy into guidelines for implementation is no simple matter. Nor is policy implementation a straightforward process because there are competing interests and practical constraints.

In the current dispensation, which is meant to redress the ills of the past, we see two soundly based policy guidelines in tension with each other, and resulting in problems at the language planning, implementation and monitoring stages. Interviews revealed several practical constraints on what is possible in relation to what is desirable. Implementation is affected by the availability of human and financial resources, the most striking evidence of which in my data is the contrast in translating practices between the public broadcaster and the commercial channel. Essential financing from advertisers depends on the dramas' appeal to those sectors of the public (and their aspirations) which advertisers target. That in turn has implications for choice of languages, dialects and accents, and how they are be deployed. And then there are the less weighty factors which can affect particular story lines or episodes, such as individual actors' competences, preferences and sociolinguistic sensitivity. Clearly, there are all sorts of contingencies en route from policy to product.

If one recognises the effects of these sometimes unpredictable pragmatic factors, is it at all justifiable to think of multilingual practices in our tv drama as an index of a new imagined community? Towards the end of each interview, I asked interviewees whether they saw their programmes – and the linguistic diversity within them - as being part of the creation of a new 'imagined community'. In his reply, Neil McCarthy said 'I don't think it is a conscious agenda, but I do think it's an unconscious agenda'. He saw soaps as being able to engage audiences with ways of living or issues that might not be part of their own experience in such a way 'as to make it a part of your understood world', adding 'I think that's the best thing soaps could do'. However, he reiterated what he had said earlier 'Fundamentally we're there to entertain, not there to educate'.

Steven Raymond's reply is a reminder of constraints on putting good ideas into practice. Referring to *Isidingo,* he said that the initial idea of the show was that it would try 'to create "one nation viewing" – you create stories, characters, people that connect to one world'. He went on to say that from the outset the soap, set in a mining community, had attracted 'a fascinating audience, but one which made the show unprofitable because advertisers didn't know how to categorise it' because it cut across linguistic, race and economic groups. The SABC told the producer to 'up the glamour' in order to target the highest 'lifestyle measurement band'. They had to comply. Now, ten years down the line, the team is thinking of other ways of creating 'one nation viewing' for *Isidingo* by showing a range of characters responding to issues which – it is clear – currently affect all sectors of South African society.

In her response, translator Funeka Mpela linked the new 'imagined community' more explicitly with linguistic practices in the tv dramas (and beyond):

> I think the whole mixing thing is trying to bridge that, [to say] that I am not better than you in any way. Because we are here together, we have to

> live together, we have to find a compromise so let's start by breaking a language[18], you know? I think it takes you back to how sacred is your language to you because it takes you to where you started, to your great grandparents, how they preserved it to actually bring it to a point where you receive it. So, breaking a language says 'I am breaking everything that you are and including myself in it. If we take this and this and this away, and put them together, we actually are one thing.' What it's saying is 'You can remove a bit of Zulu, bit of Tswana, bit of Sotho to have just a human being.' We're healing, we're finding ways to get along with one another. We will formulate a language that we will all understand each other and I will not feel that Zulu is taking over, or Tswana is taking over. We've got a mixed language that we are speaking so we are equal in that sense. Whereas if we are going to separate ourselves and say 'You speak pure Zulu', 'you speak pure Tswana' then you've said, 'I'm not included in this, I'm not part of this', whereas breaking it says 'We're one'. We are actually coming together.

Taking together all that has emerged from documents, interviews and observations, I would say that, although it clearly occurs for a variety of reasons – some idealistic and some mundane - the flexible weaving of languages in South African tv drama is an index of a new 'imagined community'. It is a way of working with what we have to create the stories that engage us. As Lerner says 'The nation comes to life in texts other than those which are ostensibly nationalist' (1993: 1). Wittebols uses the metaphor of 'the electronic hearth' to talk about the place of prime-time television drama in contemporary life and says 'By looking at the kind of stories being told in prime time television, one can get a sense of what matters most – what our society celebrates, what it fears, what it aspires to' (1994: 151). The dialogue of South African television dramas recognizes a characteristic style of using our linguistic repertoire and endorses it in the public domain and, according to Anderson, 'Communities are to be distinguished, not by their falsity/genuineness. But by the style in which they are imagined' (1991: 6).

REFERENCES

Anderson, B. 1991. *Imagined communities: Reflections on the origin and spread of nationalism.* (2nd ed.) London and New York: Verso.

Bakhtin, M.M. 1981. *The dialogic imagination.* Michael Holquist (ed.) Caryl Emerson and Michael Holquist (trans.). Austin: University of Texas Press.

Dyers, C. 2008. Truncated multilingualism or language shift? An examination of language use in a new non-racial working-class township in South Africa. In *Journal of multilingual and multicultural development* 29 (2), 110-126. etv http://www.etv.co.za

Flockemann, M. 2000. Watching soap opera. In S. Nuttall and C.A. Michael (eds.) *Senses of culture: South African cultural studies.* Oxford: Oxford University Press, 141–154.

Kilborn, R. 1992. *Television Soaps.* London: B.T. Batsford Ltd.

Klein, Y. 2007. Comparative study of code-switching, code-mixing and borrowing in two South African television dramas: reflections of reality or appeasement of the audience. Unpublished Linguistics Honours Essay. University of Cape Town.

Kruger, L. 1999. Theatre for development and TV Nation: Notes on an Educational Soap Opera in South Africa. *Research in African Literatures* Vol. 30 (4), 106-126.

Lerner, A.J. 1993. Introduction. In M. Ringrose and A.J Lerner (eds.) *Reimagining the nation.* Buckingham, Philadelphia: Open University Press. 1-5.

Lockyear, H. 2004. Multiculturalism in South African soap operas. In *Communication: South African Journal of Communication Theory and Research* Vol. 30 (1), 26-43.

Makhudu, K.D.P. 1995. An introduction to Flaaitaal. In R. Mesthrie (ed.), *Language and social history : studies in South African sociolinguistics.* Cape Town : David Phillip, 298-305.

"National anthem of South Africa." *Wikipedia, The Free Encyclopedia.* 4 Oct 2008, 23:30 UTC. 18 Oct 2008 <http://en.wikipedia.org/w/index.php?title=National_anthem_of_South_Africa&oldid=243058909>.

Nuttall, S. and C.A. Michaels, (eds.) 2000. Introduction: imagining the present. *Senses of culture: South African culture studies.* Oxford: Oxford University Press. 1-23.

Ross, J.A. 1979. Language and the mobilization of ethnic identity. In H. Giles and B. Saint-Jacques (eds.) *Language and ethnic relations.* Oxford: Pergamon Press.

SABC http://www.sabc.co.za

South African Broadcasting Corporation 1987. *SABC Annual Report.* Johannesburg: SABC Corporate Publications.

South African Broadcasting Corporation 2005. *SABC Annual Report.* Johannesburg: SABC Corporate Publications.

South African Broadcasting Corporation 2006. *Language.* http://74.125.95.104/search?q=cache:61vs3vo9BJYJ:www.sabceducation.co.za/VCMStaticProdStage/CORPORATE/SABC%2520Corporate/Document/About%2520SABC/Legislative%2520%26%2520Regulatory%2520Organs/language.pdf+%22 accessed October 19, 2008.

Slabbert, S. et al. 2007. Jam or cheese? The challenges of a national broadcaster in a multilingual context. In *Language Matters* Vol 38 (2), 332–356.

Smith, A.D. 1995. *Nations and nationalism in a global era.* Cambridge: Polity Press.

Webb, V. 2002. *Language in South Africa: The role of language in national transformation, reconstruction and development.* Amsterdam/Phildelphia: John Benjamins Publishing Company.

Wilkins, I. and H. Strydom 1978. *The Super-Afrikaners: Inside the Afrikaner broederbond.* Johannesbug: Jonathan Ball.

Wittebols, J.H. 2004. *The soap opera paradigm.* Lanham, Boulder, New York, Toronto, Oxford: Rowman and Littlefield Publishers, Inc.
http://www.gautengfilm.co.za/live/content.php?Item_ID=488 accessed 2008/08/1

NOTES

1. I wish to thank the following people for their time and insights: Neil McCarthy, Funeka Mpela, Percy Vilakazi, Ferry Jele, Maralin Vanrenen, Steven Raymond, Pumla Hopa, and Greig Coetzee. Without them, this chapter could not have been written. I am also very grateful for Tracey Denis for her untiring and efficient work as research assistant for this paper.
2. See for example Shell 1994, Nuttal and Michaels 2000.
3. This distinction is discussed in Part III.
4. The information that follows on the Broederbond has been taken from Wilkins and Strydom 1978.
5. As Wilkins and Strydom put it, at that time 'the SABC, like South Africa, [was] divided on ethnic lines with different services for the various language and colour groups' (1978: 12).
6. The first attempts at standardization of indigenous languages had been made by missionaries. The language boards established by the apartheid government '... were perceived as instruments of Apartheid, especially in progressive circles, and became totally discredited, losing all their legitimacy' (Webb 2002: 285).
7. This is in line with Smith's claim that 'not all nationalisms have equally striven for cultural homogeneity. What all nationalists demand is a single *public* culture. There are cases where they are happy to concede some degree of private culture for ethnic and religious minorities, provided these do not impinge too much on the national identity created by the public culture of the national state' (1995: 151).
8. Wittebols (2004: 29-30) quotes Allen on commercial motivation: ' ...the soap opera is and always has been a narrative text in the service of an economic imperative.'
9. I do not deal with the following kinds of series: police/crime series, hospital dramas, sitcoms.
10. In South Africa 'soapies' is a very commonly used term for soap operas.
11. This is endorsed by Charlyn Dyers, writing about findings from her research based in the Western Cape (Dyers 2008: 110).
12. I have not been able to obtain detailed information about etv language policies past or present.
13. Steven Raymond for *Isidingo*, is trying to change that with respect to that programme. He believes that the multilingualism of the programme should be not just in what is aired, but also in the working talk among team members.
14. There is a project at etv to develop writers who are native-speakers of

languages other than English. The project, led by Julie Barker, reverses the usual process by getting writers to write in their strongest language, and that is then translated into English where appropriate.

15. By 'mixed code' I mean a community's established way of drawing on its bilingual or multilingual linguistic repertoire in such a way that there is evidence of much embedded lexical borrowing and even some influence from the grammar of one language on the grammar of the other language.
16. Audience response was tested in a survey.
17. It needs to be noted that South African production schedules are very demanding: only one day is allowed for the shooting of an episode, so five episodes are shot every week, which makes huge demands on actors and the rest of the production team.
18. From what she had said earlier, it was clear that 'breaking a language' meant not being purist, being prepared to borrow from other languages and to switch from one language to another.

14

Code Switching and the Politics of Nostalgia

Rakesh M. Bhatt

1.0 Introduction

In this paper, I will present evidence to claim that the use of Hindi in Indian English newspapers functions as a rhetorical authentication of indigenous practices, as a form of discursive representation of traditional practices and values in a global-modern medium—English. Hindi mixing with English provides, *in other words* , an opportunity to present indigenous voices, local attitudes and dispositions, and cultural narratives of the past to articulate an identity that is bivalent: global (English/colonial) AND local (Hindi/indigenous). This linguistic production of bivalency, however, is properly understood within the context of the political ideologies that inform the mixed texts that appear in Indian English newspapers. The discussion of the data will reveal how the use of Hindi is strategic in terms of recalling the historical narratives (=cultural memory) in the present English texts, inserting, as it were, the *there* and *then* into the *here* and *now,* all in a bid to activate, and animate, the politics of nostalgia. This politics—return to the past—is part of the larger ideological project of the Hindu-nationalist political party, the Bhartiya Janata Party, which came to power in India in the late 1990s on the promise to promote nationalist ('Hindutva') ideologies. In the next section, 2.0, I discuss the political context of the data that is used in this paper , followed by the analysis of data in section 3.0. Finally, in section 4.0, I offer some general conclusions. Before I turn to the next section, let me quickly note here that code-switching in the "sphere" — dedicated interactional zone (Habermas 1991) — of newspaper journalism offers one of the ways in which cultural texts participate in the construction of wider cultural values and ideologies, and are, therefore, legitimate sites of investigating competing ideologies, expressed in code-switching (cf. Bhatt 2008).

2.0 Contextualizing Data and the Politics of Nostalgia

As I mentioned above, this paper will attempt to relate the linguistic practice of code-switching to ongoing socio-political transformations in order to fully understand the contemporary politics of identity representations. The 90s decade in India is generally characterized in terms of two important transformations: the economic—a move to liberal, market-economy—and political. The political end of the transformation began with the emergence of Bhartiya Janta Party (BJP), elected to government on the promise, and later successful implementation, of promoting nationalist ideologies, commonly known as Hindutva. Hindutva is an ensemble of doctrines, social movements and political formations of Hindu-supremacism emphasizing a return to the past: Sanskritization and Brahminical values. This new political ideology, seeking traditional beliefs and allegiances, has taken the form of 'return,' a rediscovery of indigenous (Hindu) identity. This politically-driven nostalgia—aimed at perpetuating the hegemony of the Brahmanical order in Indian society—appeals to a homogenizing requirement in the face of ethnic and cultural diversity, using it to manipulate and rewrite its own history by reconstructing 'the' national tradition (Bhatt 2008). Accordingly, textbooks, classrooms, research organizations, and even cultural institutions such as museums were being used as instruments of ideological propaganda to 'saffronize'—Hindu-ize— education (*The Hindu* , July 22, 2001). The political form of this ideology ('Hindutva') thus appears closely intertwined with its cultural expression: Hindi-language/Hindu religion (cf. Chand 2002). The Hindu cultural nationalism agenda of the BJP reached its peak in the years 2001-2002, when governance appeared to be taking a back-seat to the promotion of Hindutva, as the headline of *The Times of India* in Extract 1 below indicates.

Extract 1.

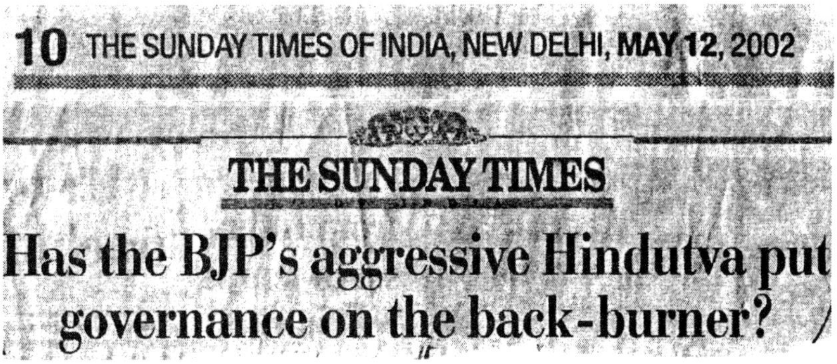
10 THE SUNDAY TIMES OF INDIA, NEW DELHI, MAY 12, 2002

THE SUNDAY TIMES

Has the BJP's aggressive Hindutva put governance on the back-burner?

In sum, the BJP government sought to ground its authority in traditional beliefs, and employed the tropes of 'return' to an imaginary earlier 'golden age' of tradition, offering the baldly religious political ideology of Hindutva in the face of the rapidly globalizing, secularizing society. The linguistic politics of these two trajectories have created conditions that simultaneously favor economic globalization, via English, and cultural nationalism, via Sanskritized Hindi, as a path for the country's progress and transformation into a modern nation. The data presented in this paper were collected from two Indian English newspapers, over a period of five years, 2001-2004 and 2006, of one-month long visits. The data collection coincided with the rise of Hindu cultural nationalism promoted by the BJP government. The two newspapers, *The Times of India* and *The Hindustan Times*, were chosen because (a) they are the two leading newspapers of India and have a combined largest circulation in North India where Hindi is the dominant first or second language, (b) they both cater to the English-knowing bilingual middle class, and (c) although both are known to take "pro-government" positions, there are slight perceived ideological differences: *The Times of India* is perceived as ideologically "conservative" whereas *The Hindustan Times* is generally considered "centrist," according to Worldpress.org. Out of a total of 1,627 tokens of code-switching that were collected, 856 switches (52.61%) came from *The Times of India* and 771 switches (47.38%) from *The Hindustan Times*. These switches were categorized in terms of five genre-types: domestic politics, sports, editorials-opinions, films, and advertising. The switches constituted single-word switches, phrases, and sentences. Care was taken to ensure that none of the data coded as a switch was a borrowed item. The breakdown for the total number of switches for the five years was: 2001 (N=356) , 2002 (N=228), 2003 (N=329), 2004 (N=291), 2006 (N=423) . The mean score for switches for this set of data is 325.4 (SD: 72.71). The frequency of these data was then compared with micro-filmed data obtained later from the Indian English newspaper *The Hindustan Times* for two months each of three (randomly chosen) years: 1990, 1995 and 1997. The comparisons were made to check if the trend of using Hindi in the register of English newspapers can be correlated with the rise of the Hindutva ideology that peaked during the government of BJP: 1998-2002 (cf. Excerpt 1). A total of 243 tokens of code- switching were observed, with roughly 67 percent of them (N=164) in 1997, 22 percent of them (N=53) in 1995, and only 11 percent (N=26) in 1990. The mean score for switches for this set of data was 81 (SD: 73.14). The t-test comparing the means of the two sets of data shows a statistically significant difference at $p < .01$. The tentative conclusion that can be drawn from these results is that there has been a significant increase in the use of Hindi in English newspapers since the Hindu-nationalist government came into power in India

3.0 Data and Analysis

The data I present in this section will show that language boundaries between Hindi and English, with their associated identities, are now beginning to unsettle in India as it enters what Chouliaraki and Fairclough (1999) call 'late modernity.' The inter-animation of global (English) and local (Hindi) in late-modernity produces, I argue, new forms of differentiation, a new collective agency and possibilities for creating new meanings. These new possibilities of meaning- making and representation become most visible in sociolinguistic performances, as in English-Hindi code-switching, that in turn produce a mutual and mutable representation, and recognition, of cultural difference and of cultural meaning. The excerpt in (2) below, the switch to 'Tandava', the celestial dance of destruction performed by Lord Shiva, makes reference to the destruction in the Hindu holy city of Varanasi after the terrorist attacks there. The switch shows how local meanings are strategically inserted in global texts producing discoursal hybridity, giving rise to a polyphony of voices, rendering texts, especially in post/late-modern context, as fundamentally heteroglossic. As such, the analysis of the code-switched texts thus follows the insights of Bakhtin (1981: 291), who correctly notes that: "[A]t any given moment of its historical existence, language is heteroglot from top to bottom: it represents the co-existence of socio-ideological contradictions between the present and the past, between differing epochs of the past and between different socio-ideological groups in the present." The discoursal hybridity in the context of Hindi-mixing in English newspapers in India allows the readers to (re-)position themselves with regard to new community-practices of speaking and writing, creating counter-discourses to the hegemony of the monoglossic standards of English and Hindi (cf. Bhatt 2008).

Excerpt 2:

THE TIMES OF INDIA

■ 16 Die As Serial Blasts Rock Holy City ■ Tuesday Devotees Of Hanuman Targeted ■ Attacks Bear Hallmarks Of LeT, Jaish ■ Nationwide Red Alert

TERROR TANDAVA IN VARANASI

EYEWITNESSES

'I owe my life to monkeys'

SANKAT MOCHAN TEMPLE

MAJOR ATTACKS

Similarly, in excerpt 3 below, taken from the *Times of India news-brief* www.timesofindia.com, (Oct 12, 2001), the switched items reflect local cultural embeddings in an otherwise global text. The mixing of Hindi words carry the load of cultural meanings that are available to the bilingual reader: the use of *saat pheraas* refers to the ritual in which the bride and the groom walk around the fire together, pledging commitment to each other for seven births; *agni* refers to the sacred fire in the wedding ritual believed to be the messenger (or priest) who operates on behalf of the people who perform the sacrificial ritual, takes the prayers of the people to gods in the heaven, and brings back their blessings to the people; *lakshmana rekha* refers to the line of protection drawn by Lakshmana (in the epic Ramayana) around Sita's hut to protect her from dangers of the external world. Maricha, the demon (in the form of the deer) disguised his voice as Rama's, and called for Lakshmana's help. This was a trick to lure Lakshmana away from Sita and give an opportunity to Ravana to approach Sita, who would be left unprotected. Lakshmana, however, draws a line around the hut and tells Sita not to cross it lest she will encounter a danger. Thus the term Lakshmana rekha has become a symbol of protection, and transgressing it has acquired the meaning of allowing undesirable results to occur.

Excerpt 3:

There have been several analyses of this phenomenon. First, there is the 'religious angle' which is to do with Indian society. In India a man feels guilty when fantasizing about another man's wife, unlike in the west. The *saat pheras* around the *agni* serves as a *lakshman rekha* (italics added).

The switch to Hindi in these English texts serves the bilingual readership well as it is observes both the (Gricean) maxims of Quantity (be as informative as required) and Manner (be perspicuous). The alternative, the monolingual English option, would have required elaborate rhetorical engineering without any guarantee of an articulation of the desired intentionality of the writer. To be sure, these switches are neither random nor a chance occurrence but appear rather regularly in Indian English newspapers as excerpts 4 and 5 below show. In excerpt 4, the news item is about the High Court's order to restrain (hence, 'lakshman rekha') the protesting airport workers from getting within a 500-metre radius of the airport terminal.

Excerpt 4.

HC draws 500m lakshman rekha

TIMES NEWS NETWORK

New Delhi: The Delhi High Court has come to the rescue of hurried air passengers trying to reach the Delhi airport, which has been under siege from striking Airports Authority of India employees protesting against the government's airport privatisation plan.

On Thursday, the court restrained the strikers from staging their protest within a 500-metre radius of the terminals. The AAI employees joint forum had begun an indefinite strike from Wednesday following the government's decision to hand over Delhi and Mumbai airports to private consortia.

Passing an interim order on an application moved by AAI, Justice Swatanter Kumar also asked the striking employees not to interfere in the functioning of the airports or cause inconvenience to the passengers.

The order came on a day when passengers faced tremendous harassment as the employees blocked all entry and exit points at the domestic terminals (I-A for Indian and Kingfisher, I-B for all private national carriers as well as arrivals) for several hours till about 4 pm. As a result, passengers — even pilots and cabin crew — had to walk long distances with their luggage to reach the terminals.

The strike led to massive traffic jams. People were seen leaving their vehicles and walking to the airport in an effort to catch their flights.

VVIPs bore the brunt of the strikers' anger. The tyres of BJP leader Venkaiah Naidu's car were deflated as he reached the terminal.

'Protests won't help them': P3

In excerpt 5 below, the switch to "kundali" (horoscope) makes clever reference to the traditional Hindu cultural practice of consulting Hindu Vedic Astrology for all important events, especially matrimony and health.

Excerpt 5.

Check your health kundali for happy union

Vivita Relan

Making preparations for an Indian wedding is an immense affair. Besides the razzmatazz of the wedding functions, the trouble that one has to go through to make sure that one is marrying the right person are manifold — checking the family background, caste, financial position and astrological compatibility. But often some of the most basic factors are overlooked such as a health *kundali*.

Recently started by health labs, such as Ranbaxy SRL, it's a simple genetic test which can detect any possible diseases, if any. A test like this allows a couple to make an informed difference between life and death of their child".

Dr Ashish Munjal, who has conducted the tests on over 200 couples so far, concurs, "According to recent statistics, for every one person that dies of AIDS in India, four people die of hepatitis. Only 10 percent know that they are hepatitis B carriers, a disease which can be transferred through sub-standard quality of life. A pre-natal test detects whether parents are both carriers – if one is just a carrier then there's little risk. If both are carriers, then there's 25 percent chance of the child being born with the disease.

Bajwa stresses that these tests are not done to break up a potential alliance, but rather to

Excerpts 2-5 above show, clearly, that code-switching to Hindi serves as a vehicle of **cultural memory** , insofar as the significations of the switched words are concerned. The Hindi items are rooted in the most important historical narratives (Vedas) and the great Hindu epic (the *Ramayana*) of India, and a full appreciation of the text, therefore, demands knowledge of the Sanskrit Vedic traditions and cultural-historical literacy of the indigenous peoples. Where the interpretive demands of text-in-context require bilingual AND bicultural competence — to be able to faithfully decipher the writer's (speaker' s) intention — the medium capably indexes (and serves as) the message.

The switches to Hindi in Indian English newspapers are not restricted in their distribution to main news-headlines, they appear in a range of other genres of this register. Strategic switches to Hindi appear in (i) opinion-editorial pieces as in excerpt 6 where the switch to a low-frequency, high formal-register Sanskritized Hindi word, SAMVAD, meaning discussion/debate, recalls local cultural history, denoting an older form of ritualized dialogue in political oratory; (ii) advertising, as in excerpt 7 where again the use of highly Sanskritized Hindi words (e.g., "Agnipareeksha") animates historical narratives in contexts of modern cultural products/performances such as the "Indian Idol" (a mimetic copy of the "American Idol") ; (iii) sports, as in excerpt 8 where the topic, "In Pathan land," and the comment, "Pesh hai war" (the creative use of the place Peshawar where the cricket match is to be played) brings into focus the two ideologies in action—the 'us' (local) and the 'them' (non-local): Hindi is used to galvanize local cultural nationalism, whereas English is used to present the Other with which the local must go to war.

Excerpt 6.

Remote Control Tax

Taxing emigrants will ensure reinvestment in the country that produced them

Mihir Desai
Asst Prof of Finance,
Harvard Business School

'Brain-drain' tax is the economic equivalent of a Berlin Wall for our emigrants

Jug Suraiya
Columnist and Associate
Editor, TOI

TIMES SAMVAD

(As told to Harsh Kabra)

Excerpt 7.

Excerpt 8.

In Pathan land, Pesh hai war

India Seek To Avenge Test Loss In ODIs

Two to tango

Indians miffed over Tri-colour goof-ups

Flag printed upside down on tickets

One of the strongest arguments for the politics of nostalgia, however, comes from the struggle in gender practices in contemporary India. This struggle is uniquely reflected in code-switching between English, indexing modernity, and Hindi, indexing traditional-indigenous identity. In excerpt 9 below, the news-report appears to be supporting the Italian-born wife of former Prime Minister of India, now the leader of the Congress Party, who was demonized by the then nationalist government of Bharatiya Janata Party. The semantics of *layak bahu* ('competent daughter-in-law') is socio-culturally grounded, its explication offered in the English relative clause that follows the Hindi noun *bahu*.

From timesofindia.com

Support for Sonia

I really don't like the way our ministers in Parliament treat Mrs Sonia Gandhi. What wrong has she done? Is she to blame for having fallen in love with an Indian and married him? Honestly, how can anyone be so unfair as to blame someone for having done that. We have all experienced love in one form or the other and we all know how beautiful it makes us feel. How enriching it is. I think we should respect her for the fact that she did not leave this country along with her children after her husband's assassination. What's more we should respect her for being a *layak* Indian *bahu* who stayed on to do her duty by her husband's family, she reared her children and instilled in them the best Indian values, she took care of her mother-in-law and husband's legacy — the Congress party. So let us not descend to targeting a poor defenceless woman.

Ambreen Zaidi, via e-mail

TOI, Lucknow, Mon. May 20 2002, p-10

Specifically, the switch presents a 'foreigner' as entrenched in indigenous discursive practices (men-women roles), authenticating her as (one of) 'us,' through the use of an indigenous language. The bilingual code-switched mode thus serves several interpretive functions: (i) it authentically expresses the socio-historical experiences of the English bilingual population, (ii) it captures the cultural-semantics of the utterance, and (iii) it reflects the hybrid, bicultural nature of identity. The practice of authenticating gendered practices in India appears in different possible variations. In Extract 10, for instance, the switch to Hindi in the fourth column (The young women—always overdressed—will typically say, *"Mummyjee, aap rahne deejeye, Chai mein bana ke laungi, mujhe apne kartavyon ka ehsas hai."*) presented in the "character voice", corresponds to the local cultural etiquette: it recalls a particular ritual-cultural practice that cannot be adequately translated into English without engendering cultural-semantic dispossession.

Extract 10.

GUEST COLUMN

KAVITA CHOUDHRY

The double standards in today's serials reflect real life

Does the adoption of traditional rituals free you from jealousy and selfishness? It's like going on and on about the cutlery in the absence of food. This is dangerous, especially when one considers the pious and self-congratulatory note with which these rituals are propagated.

(The writer is a serial maker)

TOI Sunday Times May 12, 02 Page 10

Lamenting the anachronistic representation of women in contemporary TV soaps, it becomes communicatively economical for the author to move from a 'modern' public voice (of English) to a distinctive 'ethnic voice,' embedded under quotation marks. The last part of the quote, 'I am aware of my (traditional) responsibilities,' recalls historical practices and gendered scripts and embeds them skillfully in contemporary discourses of social engagements by switching into Hindi. In other words, even contemporary gendered roles must reference traditional gender ideologies, made possible, of course, most authentically in the local language. Not surprisingly then, the international women's day is celebrated in local contexts by referencing traditional-local representations of women, "shakti", as shown in the excerpt below.

Extract 11.

Finally, the switch to Hindi in excerpt 12 below points to another historical-Hindu text, Mahabharata, to contextualize the text appropriately. The news-narrative that follows tells the tragic story of a woman who refused to be shared with her husband's brothers, reminiscent of the story of Draupadi married to the Pandava brothers in Mahabharata: The clever use of switch to Hindi clues the readers to the context of the narrative of Mahabharata.

Extract 12.

TOI, 3-7-2006, p.7

Salman withdraws petition after SC tells him to face trial, Page 15

KOLKATA LUCKNOW MANGALORE MUMBAI MYSORE NEW DELHI PATNA PUNE

Unwilling 'Draupadi' pays with her life

By Sonali Das/TNN

The politics of nostalgia—a return to the past—in gender -identity politics is not uncontested, however. Predictably, we find ample evidence of English-Hindi code- switching used as a form of discursive resistance, representing struggle for a space where the old/traditional is re-contextualized, as shown in the titles of a guest column, see excerpt 13 below.

Extract 13.

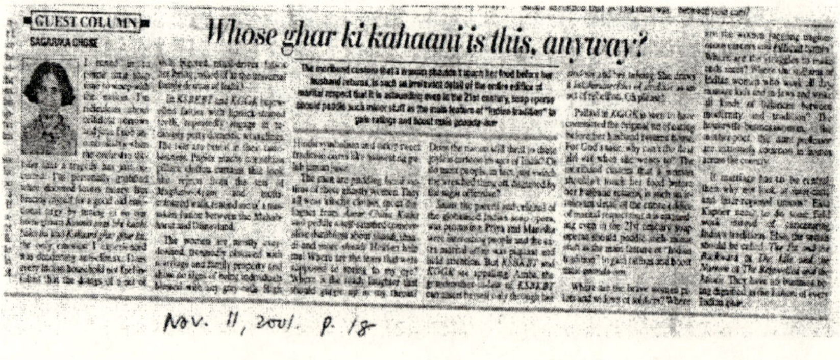
GUEST COLUMN

SAGARIKA GHOSE

Whose ghar ki kahaani is this, anyway?

Nov. 11, 2001. p. 18

The text in Extract 13, authored by Sagarika Ghose, a middle-class, middle-aged woman, 'voices' a modern feminist concern over (and a critique of) the production of gender ideologies in local (Hindi) soap operas that she finds, basically, anachronistic and outdated. The context of the text is the day-time soap operas producing images of women as homemakers following old traditional rituals and Hindu symbolism. The use of a Hindi noun phrase with a prepositional phrase complement [*ghar* [*ki* kahaani]] NP PP ('story of household') frames the established social (gendered) practices that are evaluated in the text, and transformed in recontextualization by embedding it in the matrix language frame, English.

The anachronistic representation of Indian women in soap operas is also noted by the local journalists who often write about it in local newspapers (see excerpt 14 below). For instance, writing for the Indian English newspaper, *The Times of India* , Dhawan (2006: 1) notes, "[A]lmost without realizing it, today's advertisers and soap script-writers have transformed the intrepid woman of the 1990s, and taken her back to where she was in the 50s—the kitchen."

Extract 14.

Spunky salesgirl gives in to family values

By Himanshi Dhawan/TNN

WHERE'S SHE GONE?

In sum, the tension between traditional and modern gender roles has become part of the local discourse. The overt form of ' resistance' in code-switching data, excerpts 13 and 14, does not oppose the 'compliance' use as discussed before. In fact, the apparent 'compliance' with traditional values of the modern middle-class women has a subversive meaning—of creative, non-overt resistance (cf. Mertz 1989; Reed-Danahay 1993), as discussed in Bhatt (2008). The willingness to accept dominant traditional values is arguably a bid to not lose solidarity/intimacy with the local as the modern woman assumes power/authority in their new contemporary roles (Bhatt 2008).

4.0 Conclusions

In this paper I have presented evidence to claim that the use of Hindi in English is arguably strategic: it activates historical-cultural memory in contemporary modern linguistic practices animating a politics of nostalgia, closely intertwined with Hindi- language/Hindu-religion as its cultural expression. Hindi mixing with English thus allows for an inter-animation of old-traditional and new-modern identities (cf. Hall 1997), creating in the negotiation between the old and the new a hybridity that enables a concatenation of the two. The hybrid code—mixed English-Hindi—offers multilingual experiences of cultural difference as well as a sense of the entanglement of different cultural traditions.

The code-mixed data presented in this paper—the juxtaposition of English, representing colonial traditions and associated with class ideologies, with Sanskritized Hindi, representing Brahmanic tradition and associated with caste ideologies—recalls Hall's comment: 'the notion of two histories, one over here, one over there, never having spoken to one another, never having had anything to do with one another, is simply not tenable any longer in an increasingly globalized world' (cited in King 2000: 155). The linguistic practice of mixing Hindi (embedding language) with English (matrix language) neutralizes the specific indexicalities of the participating languages—boundary erasure— and replaces them with a vernacular ideology; specifically, the disappearance of 'Englishness' with the entailed colonial inflections. The new English that emerges thus faithfully represents the various complexes of nuances of local cultural meanings, mobilizes new identity formations that are simultaneously local-traditional and global- modern, and successfully captures the generative capacity of bilinguals' creativity.

REFERENCES

Bakhtin, Mikhail 1981. *The dialogic imagination: Four essays.* Michael Holquist (ed.) Caryl Emerson and Michael Holquist (trans.) Austin, Texas: University of Texas Press.

Bhatt, Rakesh M. 2008. In other words: Language mixing, identity representation, and third space. *Journal of Sociolinguistics* 12 (2), 177-200.

Chand, Shyam 2002. *Saffron fascism.* Delhi: Hemkunt Publishers.

Chouliaraki, Lilie and Norman Fairclough (1999). *Discourse in late modernity: Rethinking critical discourse analysis.* Edinburgh: Edinburgh University Press.

Habermas, Jürgen 1991. The public sphere. In Chandra Mukherji and Michael Schudson (eds.) *Rethinking popular culture: Contemporary perspectives in cultural studies* . Berkeley, California: University of California Press.

Hall, Stuart 1997. Old and new identities: Old and new ethnicities. In Anthony D. King (ed.) *Culture, globalization and the world-system: Contemporary conditions for the representation of identity* Minneapolis, Minnesota: University of Minnesota Press. 19-40.

King, Anthony D. (ed.) 2000. *Culture, globalization and the world-system.* London: Macmillan.

Mertz, Elizabeth 1989. Sociolinguistic creativity: Cape Breton Gaelic's linguistic 'tip'. In Nancy Dorian (ed.) *Investigating obsolescence.* London: Cambridge University Press. 103-115.

Reed Danahay, Deborah 1993. Talk about resistance: ethnography and theory in rural France. *Anthropological Quarterly* 66, 221-22.

SECTION B

THEORETICAL PERSPECTIVE

15

Confessions of A Minor Morphologist: Some Remarks on 'Morphological Complexity'*

Rajendra Singh

In the remarks that follow, I shall attempt to sketch out my reasons for suspecting the notion 'morphological complexity'. It plays an important role in most contemporary theories of morphology, but it should really be expunged from morphology, because it does not have many correlates that cannot be accounted for with the help of the simple notion 'length' (or 'weight').

The earliest discussion of morphology and morphological complexity I know of is the one in which Patanjali (2BC) recounts, with obvious approval, Brahaspati's response of unknown antiquity, to his pupil, Lord Indra, that for learning a language, it was better to formulate generalizations and exceptions in terms of smaller units, as learning it one word at a time would take a thousand heaven years. His answer, though correct in emphasizing the size of lexicon, unfortunately, does not consider the possibility which could have taken the form of a question: "Given that you now have learnt several words of Sanskrit, what new words can you come up with yourself, dear pupil?" If he had asked the question, the ancient Indian grammarians may have evolved notions such as *qiyās* (analogy), *mitāl* or *binā'* (morphological pattern). The fact that he did not, led to Panini's *Astadhyayi*, the anti-syncategorematic, atomistic ontology of which inspired Thieme (1971: 617) to say that it wasn't a description of Sanskrit but an argument that tries to show that words are built up from simpler elements in a way that can be captured by rules and exceptions.

Even if we assume that morphemes and morphs can be flawlessly segmented, located, and identified – (for arguments opposing this , see Bazell 1949, Bybee 1985, Ford et al 1997, and Singh and Neuvel 1983) –

it is not clear if the notion of morphological complexity is of any use. Most contemporary formalist theories of morphology take it to be very crucial for morphology and insist on deriving the properties of what they call morphologically complex words from morphologically simplex words (cf. the very title of Baker 1988). According to these theories, all the words listed in (1) below are morphologically complex (because they all contain more than one 'morpheme', which contribute to their properties):

(1) a. boys (noun/plural)
b. chair (verb)
c. sang (verb/past)
d. goodness (noun)

In these theories, 'morphological complexity' is very important because they see the properties of words they regard as complex as derived from the properties of smaller pieces they say such words are made up of.

In Whole Word Morphology (WWM), the theory of morphology implicit in much of my work on morphology to date, the morphology of a language is a set of word formation strategies, a set of ongoing processes, that generatively accounts for all the possible words of that language, all of them, that is, that do not result from extragrammatical activities such as borrowing or the use of anagrams, initials, etc. (cf. Ford, Singh, and Martohardjono 1997). Under this mode of representation, words are members of classes and represented by the variables X and X' in word formation strategies of the general form (2):

(2) $[X]_\alpha \leftrightarrow [X']_\beta$

where : (*i*) X and X' are words;
(*ii*) α and β are major lexical categories;
(*iii*) ↔ symbolizes an equivalence relation, that is a bi-directional implication;
(*iv*) X and X' are semantically related;
(*v*) the prime ['] symbolises a formal difference between the two related elements, henceforth to be called the morphological operation;
(*vi*) the prime ['] may be null if $\alpha \neq \beta$.

Affixes and other formal markers of the morphological operation linking two classes of words α and β, all that is symbolised by the prime ['] in (2), are constants of the operation and do not need, for any linguistic reason I have been able to determine, to be grouped together in any way other than they are under this proposal. What is more important is that this relational theory of morphology does not allow one to talk about morphological complexity.

Whereas the words in (1) above are represented in morpheme based formalist theories as hierarchical arrangements of morph(eme)s, in WWM they are represented as phonemic envelopes without any 'syntax'. In (3) I provide popular morphemic and WWM representations for some words from (1) :

(3)	boy	[[boy]z]]	/bɔyz/
	chair (verb)	[[chair] 0]]	/tʃeər/
	sang	[[sing] 0]]	/sæng/
	goodness	[[good] ness]]	/gudnEs/

Both types of representations capture the fact that the words above are related to *boy, chair, sing,* and *good,* the morpheme-based representations by directly representing them as category-bearing constituents and the WWM representations indirectly by simply including the phonemic envelope needed to specify them when they are on their own.The difference is that whereas WWM assigns no pride of place to 'morphological complexity' and its representation gives no particular status to that envelope, the standard morphemic representation does. Morpheme-based formalist theories do finally get to the phonemic representations provided by WWM, but they do so with the help of a derivational history that uses mechanisms such as Bracket Erasure, Inheritance, and Percolation, all mechanisms to come to terms with what such theories consider to be the crux of the matter, i.e., 'morphological complexity'. *Goodness* is, thus, derived from *good.* Although the morphological relationship between *good* and *goodness* is acknowledged by both morpheme-based theories and WWM, the former sees it as derivationalist in nature. Under the WWM analysis, it is not necessarily derived from *good,* though it is necessarily related to it.Should one happen not to know the word *goodness,* one CAN, of course, derive it with the help of the WFS given in (4) below :

(4). /X/adj. ⟷ /XnEs/ noun

If WWM is correct, the only possible characterization of 'morphological complexity' would be :

(5) A word is morphologically complex IFF its representation is related, via some WFS, to a shorter/lighter representation standing for a word.

Under this sort of characterization, *goodness* is morphologically complex because its representation is related to the representation of *good* via (4) above and *boys* is morphologically complex because its representation is related to that of *boy* via the WFS in (6) below :

(6) /X/Nsg. ⟷ /Xz/Npl.

Since the other words in (3) above are neither heavier nor longer than the allegedly simplex words they are related to, they cannot be characterized as 'morphologically complex' under this view.

We must now ask (1) if there is any reason to believe that we need 'morphological complexity' in addition to simple length/weight and (2) if there is any theory independent criterion for saying that the words like *chair* (verb) and *sang* are morphologically complex. I believe the answer to both these questions is 'NO'.

One might point to some psycholinguistic studies that attempt to show or imply that 'morphological complexity' does have some correlates. It is reported in the literature, for example, that if one slices off the envelope for *boy* from the envelope for *boys* and presents it to hearers they hear something different from what they hear when presented with the envelope for *boy* — in fact, it is claimed that in the former case they sort of hear the plural. What is interesting about such studies is that they do not eliminate the length factor. In order to support the claim they make or imply, they must show that the /pɔy/ of /pɔyz/ is not heard as equally anticipating the missing /z/.

As for the 'morphological complexity' of English words like *sang* and Arabic words like *kitib* (or *katab*, for that matter), the complexity seems to reside not in these words, but in the derivationalist theories that insist on deriving them. There is, in other words, no reason to believe that they are 'morphologically complex', though their morpheme-based accounts certainly are.

Diachrony provides further evidence aginst the *Gesamtbedeutung* tradition of morphological analysis. Consider the case of Spanish *-azo*, whose history has been documented by Rainer (1992). In the Middle Ages, its appearance seems restricted to words like *azotazo* 'lash with a whip', words involving an instrument and some physical contact. During the Renaissance, however, one can also find it in words like *canonazo* 'cannon-shot' where the instrumentality is maintained, but physical contact is lost. Later, even the punitive aspect disappears, and one can get words like *trompetazo* 'blast of a trumpet' and *bombazo* 'explosion of a bomb'. Much later, one finds words like *obispazo* 'a politically spectacular letter from the bishop' and *telefonazo* 'a 100% increase in telephone rates'.The history of the uses of *-azo* in words from *azotazo* to *telefonazo* is a long history of heterogeniety, embedded in groups of words whose birthdays are known, thanks to Rainer's painstaking work. A *gesamtbedeutung* analysis that postulates an abstract "meaning" like 'physical impact' for *-azo* has to not only provide explicit rules for deriving what it sees as contextual variants but also to explain the existence of words like *obispazo* and *telefonazo* in addition to explaining what Rainer calls the implausibility of words like *boxeadorazo*.

It is, we believe, not an accident that the nodes in what I would like to call the FRP map of *-azo* largely reflects the history of *azo* words in Spanish. The early 90's creation of *telefonazo* is, thus, not to be explained in terms of a new meaning of *azo*, somehow related to the abstract meaning, but by saying that it is fashioned after the famous *catastrazo*. The only existence *azo* can be said to have is in these sets of words in which it has occurred in the past and in the sets of words it may occur in the future, for that is the only history it has or will have.

As for Inheritence and Percolation, it is perhaps useful to begin by pointing out that nothing even remotely resembling the ECP or the theta-criterion can be said to play a role in word-formation. It is, therefore, not surprising that there is tons of evidence against both these mechanisms, some of it provided by formalists themselves. Some of the facts that advocates of argument inheritance have to face are facts like the following: (1) *-er* agentives in German show argument inheritance but *-er* instrumentals do not, possibly because non-derived agentives, like *autor* and *pilot*, allow complementation but non-derived instrumentals,like *stift* 'pen' and *flugzeug* 'plane' do not, and (2) *-erei* in German regularly allows argument inheritance, quite possibly because the contribution it can be said to make is better handled in pragmatics than in semantics. Facts like these suggest that argument inheritance can be predicted from semantic considerations. Fanselow (1985), from whom I take these facts, demonstrates that quite convincingly.

Perhaps these principles and mechanisms do not work because 'complex words' do not get their properties from anywhere – they just have them, as their *nityatva* would require.

One might object to the position articulated above on the grounds that the multiple morpheme view of 'morphological complexity' allows one to capture the fact that whereas a word like *tables* is morphologically complex, a word like *abracadabra* is not, but WWM, on the other hand, would have to imply that when compared with *table, abracadabra* exhibits 'morphological complexity' . This is not a valid objection for two reasons: (1) although the WWM view jettisons 'morphological complexity', it does not license the view that length/weight in itself can be interpreted as 'morphological complexity' and (2) the import of capturing the fact that *tables* exhibits ' morphological complexity' and *abracadabra* does not remains far from clear – as *abracadabra* is not related to any shorter, lighter word, where would one need to state this 'catch' ? The knowledge that *tables* is 'morphologically complex' is based on the knowledge/ fact that *table* (and NOT *abracadabra*) is not. This is implicit even in the morpheme-based view of 'morphological complexity'. And to the best of my knowledge, morpheme-based theories of morphology have no place where they can store such 'catches', and rightly so.

The possible demise of 'morphological complexity' is another reason to be optimistic that the standard Paninian definition of morphology as a study of the internal structure of words will be replaced by the definition according to which morphology is that branch of the science of language which studies the patterns of co-variation of form and meaning which languages exploit or can exploit to form new words. When that happens, morphological complexity will be seen as what it is – an artefact of neo-Paninian theories of morphology. What is needed is NOT 'morphological complexity', inheritance, right-headedness, or percolation but an account of the interplay between variables and constants, which play their game of what Patanjali called *nityatva* ('lexical integrity'), in the playground of word formation-strategies in which they figure.

Despite the fact that I am inviting the reader to reconsider 2600 years of history, I remain optimistic because neither Bhartrhari's conclusive demonstration that only words can carry human intention nor Wittgenstein's underscoring of the integrity of words - a *broom-stick*, he said, is not a *stick* with a *broom* attached to it - can be ignored forever. Even those of us for whom these are names not of linguists but of philosophers and those for whom morphology began in 1976, should be encouraged by Fabb's (1992) demonstration that no language seems to allow more than a miniscule fraction of possible combinations of so called morphemes, quite possibly licenced directly by the patterns that do in fact exist in a language, the patterns captured by the sort of WFSs presented here. I am encouraged by the fact that most of the heavy gadgetry of the contemporary Paninian technology is, after all, designed to make the hierarchical brackets it sets up invisible to morphological and phonological operations.

NOTES

* The reflections on 'morphological complexity' contained in this contribution were originally embedded in a lecture I delivered as IMM Fellow at the National University of Singapore, February 11, 2009. I am delighted and honoured to offer this, possibly the last display of what JKL calls 'RMT' to Rama Kant Agnihotri, with whom I have had the pleasure of discussing morphology for more than a decade, on his 65th birthday. My apologies to MH for the title.

REFERENCES

Baker, M. 1990. How Complex Words get their Properties. *McGill Working Papers in Linguistics*.5.40-59.

Bazell, C.E. 1949. On the Problem of the Morpheme. *Archivum Linguisticum* 1.1-15. Reprinted in *Readings in Linguistics,* ed. by Eric Hamp, Fred Householder and Robert Austerlitz. Chicago: University of Chicago, 216-226.

Bybee, Joan L. 1985. *Morphology*. Amsterdam: Benjamins.

Fabb, N. 1988. English Sufixation is Constrained only by Selectional Restrictions. *Natural Language and Linguistic Theory*. 6: 527-539.

Fanselow, G. 1985. What is a Possible Complex Word? In Toman J (ed.) *Studies in German Grammar*. Dordrech: Foris. 289-318.

Ford, A., R. Singh and G. Martohardjono 1997. *Pace Panini: Towards a word-based theory of morphology*. New York: Peter Lang.

Patanjali 2BC. *Mahabhasya*.

Rainer, F. 2003. Semantic Fragmentation in Word-Formation: The Case of Spanish *azo*. In Rajendra Singh and Stanley Starosta, (eds.) *Explorations in seamless morphology,* New Delhi: Sage. 197-211.

Singh, R. and S. Neuvel 2003. When the Whole is Smaller than the Sum of its Parts. *Chicago Linguistics Society Papers* - 38.299-307.

Thieme, P. 1971. *Kleine Schriften*. Wiesbaden: Franz Steiner.

16

The Hindi Long Vowel Problem: A Substantivist Approach

Probal Dasgupta

1. Substantivism is a perspective in the study of language that methodologically distinguishes the social science considerations of macrolinguistics from the natural science considerations of microlinguistics. Descriptions of language phenomena that invoke this perspective occasionally blur the macro-micro boundary for expository convenience. Constant vigil is the only way to ensure that such shortcuts do not cost us the methodological care that continues to be necessary. Substantivism owes its name to its concern with the broad picture of how the written substance and the oral substance co-articulate with the form of language, universally and particularly.

2. The Hindi long vowel problem is discussed in detail by Singh and Agnihotri (1997: 62-4). They begin by presenting a phonologically slanted, formally "morphophonological" solution proposed by Elizarenkova (1988). They then explain why they reject it and offer instead a morphological analysis.

3. Their critique of Elizarenkova's analysis is a pedagogically useful exposition of the combination of Whole Word Morphology and Generative Phonotactics on which their description of Hindi is based. A representative passage from their discussion is cited below:

> "In her analysis of 'verbal word formation' (371-377), Elizarenkova tries hard to achieve a semblance of overall regularity in the formation of causatives in Hindi using processes such as 'quantitative alternation' and 'vowel alternations'. It is not only that different combinations of these processes are associated with different sets of words but also in each case there is a large number of exceptions, enough to motivate an additional strategy of word formation. After suggesting that vowel gradation is an

essential part of forming causatives in Hindi, she goes on to point out that words having the diphthongs *-ai-* and *-au-* do not undergo any vowel gradation in forming causatives. Similarly, in the case of diminutives of nouns, some involve vowel gradation, some vowel gradation with quantitative alternation, and some do not involve any morphophonemic change e.g.

ghoRii	ghuRiyaa	'mare'
aam	amiyaa	'mango'
boraa	boriyaa	'sack'

"There are thus multiple ways of achieving the same morphological change and each one of these ways may or may not have sound alternations associated with it. Any attempt to present these strategies in the garb of "phonological rules" will only lead to statements involving expressions such as 'generally', 'most of the time', 'except in the following words', 'but'. These formations are morphological formations par excellence" (Singh and Agnihotri 1997:63-4).

4. It is unlikely that any author who has faced the body of reasoning in Singh and Agnihotri's book and related work will find grounds for reviving Elizarenkova's proposal itself. However, other issues about the proper treatment of vowel length in a Hindi grammar do remain open; hence the need for further discussion.

5. Singh and Agnihotri incorporate their entirely morphological analysis in the Word Formation Strategies their book offers for Hindi. In particular, they propose the following strategies on p 119. Our reproduction of their proposals, here and in the passage cited above, employs transcription conventions distinct from those used in their book, a shift that is unlikely to impede comprehension:

95.

$(\text{Pii})_{\text{n, sing, fem}} \leftarrow\rightarrow (\text{PiyaaN})_{\text{n, fem, pl, nom}}$

96.

$(\text{Pii})_{\text{n, sing, fem}} \leftarrow\rightarrow (\text{PiyoN})_{\text{n, fem, pl, obl}}$

97.

$(\text{Pii})_{\text{n, sing, fem}} \leftarrow\rightarrow (\text{Piyo})_{\text{n, fem, pl, voc}}$

6. Word Formation Strategy 95 is intended, the authors explicitly state, to cover such examples as (1) below:

(1)

laRkii	'girl'	laRkiyaaN	'girls'
ghaRii	'clock'	ghaRiyaaN	'clocks'

Strategy 96 addresses the way /laRkii/ 'girl' is related to /laRkiyoN/ 'girls'. Strategy 97 expresses its relatedness with /laRkiyo/ 'girls!'.

7. Furthermore, Singh and Agnihotri design their Word Formation Strategies for verbs in such a way that vowel length does not become

an issue. On p 139, we find strategy 200:

$(X)_v \leftarrow\rightarrow (Xe)_{v, perf/pp, contin, masc, pl\ I/II/III}$

This is explicitly designed for cases like /khel/ 'play'←→/khele/ , or /bhaag/ 'run away'←→/bhaage/. The strategy does not mention any conditions on the form of the verb. Likewise, on p 140, we find strategy 205:

$(X)_v \leftarrow\rightarrow (XuuN)_{v, non\text{-}fut, opt, I, sing}$

This strategy, explicitly designed to cover the relatedness between /khel/ 'play', /khaa/ 'eat' and /kheluuN, khaauuN/, again refrains from mentioning any condition on the form of the verb. On p 142, strategy 212 states a condition on the form of the verb:

$(X)_v \leftarrow\rightarrow (Xyaa)_{v, perf/pp, masc, sing, I/IInh/III}$
condition: X ends in a vowel

The surrounding text clarifies that the authors' intention is to address pairs such as /ro/ 'weep'←→/royaa/ 'wept', /so/ 'sleep'←→ /soyaa/ 'slept'. However, vowel length, again, goes unmentioned in the formalism.

8. The difficulty with strategies 200, 205, and 212 as they stand is that they do not handle verbs in such examples as (2) below:

(2)

pii	'drink'	piyaa	'drank'
jii	'live'	jiyaa	'lived'
chuu	'touch'	chuaa	'touched'
cuu	'trickle'	cuaa	'trickled'

In these cases, the bare verb on the left ends in a long vowel, and the corresponding part of the verb on the right substitutes a short /u/ for a long /uu/ and a short /i/ plus glide sequence for a long /ii/. Verbs ending in a long high vowel in the bare form consistently exhibit a short high vowel in the past tense/ past participle form.

9. The difficulty with strategies 95-97 mentioned at point 5 is that, unsupplemented, they do not help us to make sense of such nouns as in examples (3):

(3)

bahuu	'daughter-in-law'	bahueN	'daughters-in-law'
aaNsuu	'tear'	aaNsueN	'tears'

10. Of course, these gaps can be filled, mechanically, by postulating further Word Formation Strategies that accommodate these paradigms along the lines of strategies 95-97 and 200, 205, 212. But that is not the

point. Surely any reader who has followed Singh and Agnihotri's reasoning with care will agree that the body of data presented here strongly suggests that in fact such an entirely morphological analysis would miss the phonotactic point.

11. The phonotactic point is that Hindi nouns and verbs with a final high vowel in the bare form do not let the vowel retain this length if a morphological process places it to the immediate left of another long vowel. Or, to move into real phonotactics by removing all reference to syntactic categories, the sequence */H:V:/ is starred by the Well-Formedness Constraints of Hindi, where /H:/ and /V:/ are a long high vowel and a long vowel, respectively. The Repair Strategies that come into play shorten the vowel and, given short /i/ followed by /V/, interpolate a /y/ glide. Notice that simply interpolating a /y/ is not the Repair Strategy of choice – in other words, the plural of /ghaRii/ 'clock' does not come out as /ghaRiiyaaN/ 'clocks'. Notice also that this phonological proposal involves recasting the Word Formation Strategies for Hindi nouns so that they simply add the necessary /eN/ or /oN/ or /o/ and leave the cleaning up to the phonotactics. Readers who have trouble with the technicalities of this may need to revisit Singh 1987 and Ford, Singh and Martohardjono 1997.

12. Is this a revival of Elizarenkova's proposal? Obviously not. She had argued for special dispensations for certain causatives and diminutives. At the heart of her story lay a "universal morphophonological rule" (1988: 269) that turned word-final long /ii/ into /iy/ if followed by a vowel – very different from our application of Singh and Agnihotri's strict distinction between phonotactic and morphological statements.

13. Does our proposal disregard the observations Singh and Agnihotri have adduced in their critique of Elizarenkova? Well, our proposals do appear to contradict their claim that "From the phonological point of view, there are many words in Hindi which allow the sequences of long and short vowels in any combination without any glide insertion. Words like *laaii* 'brought', *roaaii* 'weeping', *kaaii* 'moss' etc. are common enough to cast serious doubts on the phonologization of morphophonology proposed by Elizarenkova (1988)" (Singh and Agnihotri 1997: 63). But scrutiny of the data leads to the conclusion that they had gone a bit too far when they wrote that vowels in Hindi were indeed available "in any combination". In particular, Hindi seems not to permit H:V: – or even to permit i:yV: (in contrast to u:yV:, which appears in the name /ansu:ya:/).

14. If we make a fresh claim of this type, seeking to modify earlier ideas, obviously all the relevant data must be scrutinized with great care. Does

Hindi indeed prohibit i:yV: even in words from Sanskrit such as the words whose spelling would suggest the pronunciations /dvitiiyaa, tritiiyaa/ 'second, third unit of the lunar cycle'?

15. Speakers we have consulted assure us that everybody whose speech they have ever monitored consistently pronounces such words with a short /i/, as /dvitiyaa, tritiyaa/. If this is all that there is to describe, then the present paper ends right here, and substantivist principles as such do not come into play.

16. But we need to allow for purists in a language as contested as Hindi. Let us assume that there are purists who make a point of pronouncing these words in keeping with Sanskrit norms, as /dvitiiyaa, tritiiyaa/, perhaps even exaggerating the length of the /ii/. Does that take the wind out of our phonotactic sails and force all the phenomena back into the morphology as far as the lexicon of purist speakers of Hindi is concerned?

17. It is possible to take and even to defend such a position. However, we would like to propose, along substantivist lines, that even such speakers of Hindi essentially speak the same language as their non-purist brethren, and that their specially length-added renditions of / dvitiyaa, tritiyaa/ are to be treated as a special effect, an add-on, that counts as a derivative of written artifice rather than spoken spontaneity.

18. While we do not have the resources to test such a hypothesis, it is a straightforward matter to devise experiments that test it. Find speakers of the puristic and the non-puristic kinds in numbers sufficient to satisfy statisticians. Devise nonsense nouns and nonsense verbs that test the validity of the strategies we have proposed. Invite the speakers to form plurals for the nonsense nouns and pasts for the nonsense verbs. See if speakers of both types shorten the vowels that are at stake. If the relatively ordinary speakers do and their more Sanskritized neighbours do not shorten the vowels, we will have evidence that the special effects have entered our purists' bones.

19. On the way to such an experiment, there is a small practical difficulty to overcome. We have to first find the purists that all this fuss is about. My informants have absolutely never heard anybody say /dvitiiyaa, tritiiyaa/ with a long /ii/. However, the methodological position is clear, and our readers will surely know of situations elsewhere in the languages of the world where the principles are more amenable to direct testing without such a long wait.

Colophon

I thank Mamta Saini, Sanjukta Ghosh, Ravi Ranjan, Sarita Panda, Sanghamitra Khan, Rajat Ghosh and Shashi Mudiraj for empirical and theoretical discussion. Research for this paper was partially supported by the Indian Statistical Institute project on Generating a Differentiated Electronic Lexicon for Bangla. The usual disclaimers apply.

REFERENCES

Elizarenkova, T.Y. 1988. Morphophonology of Hindi. In M.S. Andronov and B.P. Mallik (eds.) *Linguistics: A Soviet approach*. Kolkata: Indian Journal of Linguistics 267-86.

Ford, A. et al. 1997. *Pace Panini*. New York: Peter Lang.

Singh, R. 1987. Well-formedness conditions and phonological theory. In W.U. Dressler et al (eds). *Phonologica 1984*. Cambridge: Cambridge University Press. 273-85.

Singh, R. and R. K. Agnihotri 1997. *Hindi morphology: A word-based description*. Delhi: Motilal Banarsidass.

17

Indian Languages as Intonational 'Phrase Languages'[1]

Caroline Féry

1. Intonation in grammar

Intonation has numerous facets. It reflects emotions and interests, it helps to identify speakers in society, and crucially for linguists, it plays an important role in grammar. This paper will not be concerned with what has been called 'the metalinguistic aspects of intonation,' as for instance, the increase in pitch range when we want to add emphasis to what we say. Also biological aspects, like the 'frequency code' (Ohala 1983) and the 'effort code' (Gussenhoven 2004), are not a primary concern of this paper. The biological codes express that some uses of fundamental frequency (F_0) are genetically and ontologically anchored. For instance, children have a higher pitch than both men and women, due to their shorter vocal folds. Tentative universal (cross-species) interpretations of this physiological fact have been provided in the literature as 'submissiveness' vs. 'dominance,' among other peculiarities like 'friendliness' vs. 'aggression.' However, biologists have taught us to be cautious with ready-made explanations in evolution, and research on pitch in birds shows us that higher pitch can have completely different motivations than social roles. In rain forests, birds living in the canopy sing with higher pitch than birds foraging on the ground because higher sounds travel better in higher altitudes (Morton 1975). Closer to the linguistic concerns of the present paper, it has been observed that tonal contours as social conventions are culturally and socially meaningful. Ladd (1996) gives striking examples of different interpretations of tonal contours in different varieties of English. For instance, a question with a rise-fall intonation is felt as neutral in British

English, but sounds condescending in American English. And, also for English, Gunlogson (2001) shows that a question with a declarative syntax like (1a) differs from its true declarative counterpart in (1b) only in terms of tonal contour. The question is rising and the statement is falling.

(1) a. It's raining?
    b. It's raining.

The syntactic fact that the verb occupies the second position in the sentence constitutes the declarative part. It expresses in both cases commitment to the propositional content of the sentence (in contrast to a syntactic question, which does not have this effect). The part played by intonation, that is, the rising contour in the question in (1a), is responsible for attribution of the commitment to the Addressee. In using (1a), the Speaker commits the Addressee to the fact that s/he knows whether it is raining and fails to commit him or herself to the content of the sentence. In this respect, rising declaratives are like interrogatives. A true declarative like (1b), by contrast, commits the Speaker to its content. Rising declaratives cannot be used 'out of the blue.' A question like (2a) is felicitous if the Speaker has no idea of the fruit being eaten by the Addressee, but (2b) is not well-formed in this context.

(2) a. Is that a persimmon?
    b. That's a persimmon?

Because of such (and other) constraints on the use of intonational patterns, it appears important to elaborate precise intonational grammars. Intonation is now classically studied with the help of autosegmental-metrical (AM) representations, a model with its origin in the work of Bruce (1977) and Pierrehumbert (1980). A sentence melody is analyzed as a sequence of tones and the association between tune and text proceeds according to certain rules. In this conception, tones are targets which the speaker's voice seeks to attain. The fundamental frequency defining the melody interpolates between the tonal targets, and produces tunes of smoothly decreasing or increasing frequency, or tonal plateaus between two tones. In Pierrehumbert's model for English, tonal targets are of three kinds. First, some tones seek to associate with prominent syllables. These tones are provided with a star and can be mono- or bitonal (H*, H*L, L*, etc.). The second kind of tones are boundary tones, which associate with edges of prosodic domains (H%, L% in some transcriptions). The third kind of tones are phrase tones, which define melodies between the last pitch accent and the final boundary tone (H^-, L^-). Pierrehumbert & Beckman (1988) have shown that these last tones are better understood as boundary tones of smaller prosodic domains. In the analysis of Indian languages proposed below, only pitch accents and boundary tones will be used. The phrase and boundary tones are subscripted for their domains, and are written H_I, H_P, L_I, etc.

2. Typology of intonation systems

In trying to locate Indian languages in existing typologies of intonation, it becomes conspicuous that these languages present properties which render them different from the usual classes. Traditionally, languages have been divided on the basis of their word melodies (Gussenhoven 2004, Hyman 2006, Jun 2005, Ladd 1996). Languages are then divided into classes according to whether they have a stress, a tone or a pitch accent on a designated syllable of each lexical item. This leads to a typology of the kind shown in (3). The first category (3a) consists of languages in which each word has a syllable specified for lexical stress, but the tonal realization of this stress is free. (3b) groups languages which have lexical stress, as in (3a), at least in part of their vocabulary, but additionally, this stress must be tonally realized in a certain way. Thus not only the position of the stress is specified but also the pitch accent coming with the stress. Tone languages in (3c) specify tonally all or nearly all syllables, not only the accented or stressed ones. There is no freedom as far as intonation is concerned, at least at the level of the word. And the last category (3d) contains languages in which words have no lexical stress and also no tonal specification. In the languages of the last category, it is of course the case that words have tones realized on them, but the claim here is that these tones do not occur at the level of the word, but only at the level of the prosodic phrase (called p-phrase in this paper).

(3) **Word-level accents and tones**

a. Main accent without tonal specification: English, Italian
b. Main accent with tone specification: Swedish, Japanese
c. Tone specification on (every) syllable: Yoruba, Cantonese
d. No lexical accent, no tone specification: Bengali, French, Malayalam

The typology on which this paper is based does not use word melodies as primary, but rather focuses on sentence melodies. It is assumed that word melodies as shown in (3) are only one of the components entering a classification of languages, the other being sentence melodies, coming from phrase tones. In other words, languages are classified not only according to the kind of tonal structure that the words have, but also according to the tonal pattern associated with the sentences. From this perspective, languages can be classified according to (4). The first class of languages, intonation languages in (4a), display a rich array of pragmatically triggered phrasal tones. Sentence melodies change according to the kind of pragmatic meaning they convey. English, Italian and German are languages of this type, but also French, which is a language without lexical stress. Swedish, a language which tonally specifies lexical accents, also has a free intonation at the level of the sentence. Second, tone languages in (4b) are pretty much constrained by the lexical tones and do not show a lot of intonational variation for the sake of pragmatic meaning. And third, the intonation of some languages comes exclusively from phrasal tones, that is, tones assigned at the level of intonational phrases. This is the group of phrase languages, to which Indian languages belong.

(4) Phrase-level tones
  a. Intonation languages: Rich array of pragmatically triggered phrasal tones on top of pitch accent
  b. Tone languages: Nearly no phrasal tones (correlating with rich lexicalspecification of tone)
  c. Phrase languages: Only phrasal tones (no pitch accent, no lexical tone)

3. Intonation of Indian languages

The similarity in intonational patterns of several Indian languages is striking, and in the remainder of this paper, I will sketch out the formal aspects of prosodic structure and tones which conspire to produce it. Two aspects of intonation will be particularly highlighted: first, the prosodic and tonal structure of declarative sentences, both in canonical and in marked word orders; second, the effect of focus, givenness and topic on the prosodic and tonal structure. As for the languages that are studied, we will look at two language families displaying the similarities. First, the intonation of Indo-Aryan Hindi is summed up and compared to Bengali, and in a second step the Dravidian languages Tamil and Malayalam are shown to have a similar intonation.[2]

3.1 Hindi

Good descriptions of Hindi intonation appear in Harnsberger (1994, 1999), Moore (1965) and Dyrud (2001), among others. The work of Nair (2001) and Dyrud (2001) suggests that Hindi has lexical stress, in the sense that every word has a designated syllable on which prominence is realized (but see Hayes 1995 and Moore 1965, who notice contradictions in the older literature). Both Nair (1999) and Dyrud (2001) find acoustic correlates of prominent syllables, like higher pitch and longer duration. The position of lexical stress is dependent on syllable weight, the heavier syllables attracting stress first (see Hussain 1997, who shows how the position of stress can be predicted by syllable weight). However, the assimilation of these correlates to the kind of pitch accents found in English is problematic. First, there is no necessity for a syllable to carry them. Second, speakers have no intuition about lexical stress, or the intuitions are inconsistent. The very fact that it is so difficult to pin down pitch accents speaks against their existence. Third, the tonal excursions are realized with a tonal pattern which does not resemble the kind of pitch accent found in intonation languages. The most striking difference is that the direction of the tonal excursion is always the same, but its exact position in the word is not. I argue here that the rising contour at the beginning of words is not triggered by pitch accent, but by phrasal tones.

All researchers of Hindi intonation agree that each content word except the final one is associated with a rising contour. The domain for this rise has a morpho-syntactic base, but is phonologically defined as a prosodic phrase, abbreviated as p-phrase. Harnsberger (1994) proposes that the low part of the rising contour is a low pitch accent, annotated as L* in the AM notation system. He presents an alternative analysis for the high part of the rising contour: it is either a trailing tone, thus the second part of a bitonal rising tone (L*H), or a boundary tone, in this case H_P. The subscript 'P' represents a boundary at the level of the p-phrase (see Hayes and Lahiri 1991 for this annotation convention). In the analysis proposed here, the low part of the rising tone is a low phrasal tone L_P and the high part of the rising tone is neither a trailing tone nor a boundary tone in the traditional sense, but also a phrasal tone, located after the L_P tone, but not obligatorily aligned with the end of the p-phrase. Between the initial L_P and the final H_P, interpolation is usually found, meaning that the voice of the speaker smoothly rises between the two tones in the course of the p-phrase.

Only two levels of prosodic phrasing are used in this paper, called prosodic phrases (p-phrases) and intonation phrases (i-phrases).[3] The i-phrase is the highest level of phrasing considered in this work. It includes a whole sentence, very often several p-phrases, and does not have the same tonal correlates as a p-phrase. The end of an i-phrase often has different tonal correlates from that of a p-phrase, because of finality. Another important difference between i-phrase and p-phrase is to be found at the beginning of an i-phrase. In this position, pitch is reset. These higher prosodic domains are primarily mapped to the syntactic structure, but in some languages, focus can have an influence on prosodic phrasing, as well, as has been shown by Kanerva (1990) for Chichewa. We will not show how the syntactic structure defines prosodic phrases, since this would lead us too far away from our subject, and the interested reader is referred to the relevant literature (Selkirk 1986, 1995, Nespor & Vogel 1986, as well as and many others). We assume that both p-phrases and i-phrases are recursive. The term p-phrase is used here for prosodic units roughly corresponding to maximal projections or lower domains, and i-phrases roughly correspond to whole sentences or higher domains. An example of the kind of phrasing used here appears in (5).

(5) [[Ms. Benwell]$_P$ [[[always]$_P$ [buys thyme]$_P$]$_P$ [at the market]$_P$]$_P$]$_I$

In many languages, information structural changes affect prosody, as has been shown for intonation languages (see for instance Féry & Kügler 2008 for a quantification of these effects in German), and it may be asked whether the same takes place in Hindi. Hindi is a head-final (SOV) language, with relatively free word order. Constituents may be scrambled to express different information structural configurations. Focused constituents typically occupy the immediately preverbal position. 'Focus' is understood, rather traditionally, as the part of the sentence which introduces alternatives (Rooth 1985, 1992). In the general case, an all-new sentence does not trigger a set of alternatives, although the possibility of focusing a whole sentence cannot be excluded in principle.

Focus has been claimed in the literature to have three prosodic effects in Hindi (see Harnsberger 1994, 1999, Moore 1965, Dyrud 2001, among others). First, the rising pitch pattern may be 'hyper-articulated' and show a higher excursion, a greater intensity and longer duration. Second, after the focused element, a phrase break may occur. According to Moore (1965), focus has a phrasing effect, as it inserts a prosodic boundary after the focused word, and separates it in this way from the remainder of the sentence. Third, postfocally, the pitch range may be compressed or even completely flat and deaccented (Harnsberger and Judge 1996), although rising pitch accents are still realized in the compressed pitch range.

In a production experiment bearing on the prosodic realization of focus in Hindi, Patil et al. (2008) have analyzed sentences spoken by 20 native speakers, in two word orders (SOV, the canonical word order, or OSV) and three focus contexts (subject focus, object focus or wide focus ('all-new' sentences)). Measurements of F_0 range, F_0 maximum and duration were performed on all sentences (1200 altogether).

Examples of the sentences included in the experiment are given in (6) and (7), with the prosodic phrasing and the tonal pattern (my analysis). A pitch track of this sentence in SOV order and in an all-new context appears in Fig.1. All pitch tracks are made with Praat (Boersma & Weenink 2005).

(6) SOV: L_P H_P L_P H_P H_P L_I
[[*adhyaapak ne*$_F$]$_P$ [moorti ko]$_P$ [banaayaa]$_P$]$_I$
teacher ERG sculpture ACC make-PAST
'The teacher made the sculpture.'

(7) OSV: L_P H_P L_P H_P H_P L_I
[[moorti ko]$_P$ [*adhyaapak ne*$_F$]$_P$ [banaayaa]$_P$]$_I$
sculpture ACC teacher ERG make-PAST

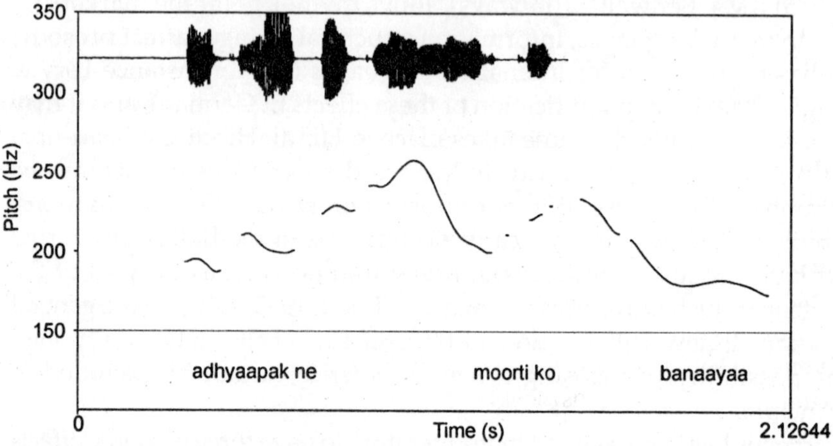

***Figure 1.** Illustration of a declarative Hindi sentence*

The averaged measurements of the F_0 pattern and of the duration, of all speakers and all sentences, delivered the following results:

- The tonal and prosodic representation in (6) and (7) and Fig.1 stands for all three focus structures and both word orders. Subject and object had a rising contour, and the final verb a falling one. A downstep pattern was realized in all conditions. The high tone on the first constituent (subject or object) was always higher than the high tone on the second constituent (object or subject), and the high tone on the verb was always the lowest. In all three focus structures and in both word orders, the prosodic and tonal structure remained unchanged.

- When focus was medial, as in (7), there was no change in the relationship of high tones as compared to the all-new pattern. There was no raising of the focused constituent, and no lowering of the given constituent. This result holds true for both word orders.

- When focus was initial, the focused constituent was raised relative to the all-new pattern, and the postfocal constituent was lowered. However the change in the melody was restricted to the quantity of downstep. There was no change in the overall tonal contour. The high tone on the focus was slightly higher than in the other two focus conditions, and, most importantly, all following postfocal tones were significantly lower, not only the high tones, but the low ones, as well. But there was no complete compression of the pitch range, as is observed in English or German in postnuclear regions. In other words, initial focus induces a postfocal reduction of the pitch range. However, the downstep relationship between the three high tones remains, as well as the basic prosodic and tonal structures. It must be added that not all speakers, and not in all instances, realized a higher initial focus followed by a compression of the postfocal domain. These strategies seem to be optional in Hindi.

- Duration of the initial focused constituent was also slightly longer.

- As for the effect of word order, SOV and OSV contours were very similar. The F_0 range on the initial constituent shows a small but significant effect of word order, though the F_0 maximum was not significantly higher in OSV than in SOV. Additionally, the duration of the preverbal constituent was significantly longer in OSV as compared to SOV. This is true for all focus conditions.

Summing up the results for Hindi declarative intonation, focus and givenness seem to only have a minimal effect on the prosodic and tonal structure. The only conspicuous result was raising of an initial focused constituent, as well as postfocal range reduction, and a small increase in the duration of initial focused constituents.

In phrase languages, the tonal structure of utterances is not changed much as an effect of information structure. This kind of pragmatic meaning is expressed by morpho-syntactic variation rather than by local prosody, as is common in intonation languages.[4]

3.2 Bengali

In this section, it is proposed that Bengali should be re-analyzed as a phrase language, rather than as an intonation language with pitch accent.

The intonation of Bengali has been described extensively by Hayes & Lahiri (1991). See also Fitzpatrick-Cole (1996), Fitzpatrick-Cole & Lahiri (1997), Lahiri & Fitzpatrick-Cole (1999), Selkirk (2006) and Truckenbrodt (2003) for further discussions of different aspects of Bengali intonation. Hayes & Lahiri's seminal paper fulfills two tasks: first, they present different 'tunes' relevant for the expression of pragmatic meanings and second, they introduce rules for the formation of p-phrases. It is conspicuous that, except for the focus tone, nearly only boundary tones can change for the sake of pragmatic meanings. Intonation patterns described by Hayes & Lahiri that we will not comment on any further comprise among others the yes/no questions

($L^*H_IL_I$) and the offering nucleus (L^*H_I), as well as patterns with continuation rise, like the declarative nucleus ($H^*L_PH_I$).

Like Hindi, Bengali is a head-final language (SOV), and the formation of p-phrases is primarily based on syntax. Every maximal constituent is a p-phrase, and the verb often forms its own p-phrase, obligatorily so when it is focused. Evidence for p-phrases comes not only from the tonal structure, but also from segmental processes like /r/ assimilation and voicing assimilation, which only take place inside of p-phrases. The absence of these processes correlates with p-phrase boundaries. Some variations in phrasing occur as a consequence of speed, style and givenness, but these variations are also subject to syntactic constraints. It is not the case that all kinds of restructuring are allowed. Hayes & Lahiri also show that the phrase construction rule is cyclic and recursive. A small constituent embedded into a larger one can form its own p-phrase, but can also be part of the larger one. The examples in (8) and (9), from Hayes & Lahiri (p.85), show some variation in the formation of p-phrases in sentences in the form of recursion. Prosodic constituents can be phrased together under the influence of rhythm and information structure, as in (8a-d), which show possible phrasings of this sentence; however the verb, which has the tonal structure of a focused phrase, and is thus the focused constituent of the sentence, must be phrased separately (8e).[5] In this case, restructuring is triggered by givenness, but it can also apply in rapid speech. According to Aditi Lahiri (p.c.), the original phrasing is not completely lost, so that the structure seen in (8a) is part of the other ones, though the internal p-phrases are no longer as clearly defined tonally.

(8) a. $(\text{ámor})_P$ $(\text{čador})_P$ $(\text{tara-ke})_P$ $(\text{diečʰe})_P$
b. $(\text{ámor čador})_P$ $(\text{tara-ke})_P$ $(\text{diečʰe})_P$
c. $(\text{ámor})_P$ $(\text{čador (tara-ke)}_P$ $(\text{diečʰe})_P$
d. $(\text{ámor čador (tara-ke)}_P$ $(\text{diečʰe})_P$
e. $^*(\text{ámor})_P$ $(\text{čador})_P$ $(\text{tara-ke (diečʰe})_P$
(Amor (scarf (Tara-OBJ (gave
'Amor gave the scarf to Tara.'

(9) shows that a complex predicate forms a single p-phrase, while with the same sequence of words used literally, as an object-verb sequence, the words are phrased separately. Again, phrasing is taken from Hayes & Lahiri (1991:90). In (9b) the verb is phrased separately.

(9) a. $((\text{aami})_P$ $(\text{bʰút dekʰlam})_P\ )_I$
I ghost-saw (I was startled)
b. $((\text{aami})_P$ $(\text{bʰút})_P$ $(\text{dekʰlam})_P\ )_I$
I ghost saw (I saw a ghost)

In an all-new declarative sentence, all non-final p-phrases, called 'heads' in Hayes & Lahiri's paper, have a rising pattern, analyzed here as the tone sequence L_p H_p, where the low phrasal tone is associated with the beginning of the p-phrase, and the high boundary tone with the end of the p-phrase. My analysis differs from the one proposed in Hayes & Lahiri, who assume that the initial low tone is a pitch accent L*. Against this analysis speaks the following fact. The association of the low tone shows some variation: it is sometimes linked with the first and sometimes with the second syllable of the p-phrase, as for example in their example (16) on p. 57. But this variation is expected if the early low tone is an initial phrase boundary tone rather than a true pitch accent. When the p-phrase is very long and is not initial in the sentence, the speaker may choose to realize the lower point of the phrase a bit later. By contrast, if this low tone is a pitch accent, no such variation in the alignment of the tone is expected, since a starred tone has to align with the stressed syllable. In many cases, the early low tone does not trigger any pitch movement at all.[6] When there are several small heads, Hayes & Lahiri assume that they also jointly form a head (maybe a super-head), which has a 'fall-rise' pattern, at least when it consists of two p-phrases. Not clear (because not addressed) is what happens when more than two p-phrases are grouped into a head. Logically this should then create a 'fall-rise-fall-rise' pattern.

In their analysis, the neutral sentence-final p-phrase is realized with a tone sequence H^*L_I, thus a high pitch accent followed by the low boundary tone of an i-phrase. In some cases, H* is downstepped relatively to the preceding H_p, a property that Hayes & Lahiri render by augmenting the high pitch accent with a preceding L tone, thus L+H*, since they assume that downstep is always triggered phonologically by a low tone. However, since the high boundary tone (H_p) of the preceding p-phrase is deleted when it finds itself before H* (because of the active OCP principle, which blocks the adjacency of two low tones, or of two high tones), it is not clear why downstep cannot be triggered by the unique tone remaining in the preceding p-phrase, namely L* (see Selkirk 2006:230 for a different analysis of H_p deletion).

In the analysis proposed here, in which Bengali does not have pitch accents, but in which all tonal excursions are phrasal tones, the H* tone of Hayes & Lahiri is reinterpreted as H_p.

A focused phrase causes dephrasing of the postfocal material. This is reminiscent of the effect of the nuclear stress in English, which destresses all postnuclear material. As a consequence, a focus always carries the last tonal excursion of the sentence. It has the same contour as a non-final declarative p-phrase L_pH_p, but additionally, it is followed by the final L_I, which delimits the focus domain. The focused p-phrase is rendered in Hayes & Lahiri by the tone sequence $L^{*}H_{P}L_{I}$. They claim that H_P is the focus tone, because the focus domain is delimited by a rise at its right edge (see Kahn 2007 for a different approach).

Compare the following pitch tracks from my own recordings. In (10), where the focus word is preverbal, the lower level is reached at the end of the focused constituent and the final L is aligned with this point. This lower point is retained until the end of the sentence.

In (11), the initial focused word *ami* 'I' also carries the entire focus tonal structure. The remainder of the sentence is low and flat. (10) and (11) differ in their word order, and this difference also brings along a difference in the F_0 contour. The object *Ram* has a secondary accent in (10), possibly because it is a topic, but in (11), it is just flat, as it would be in English and German in the postnuclear position.

(10) L_P H_P L_P $H_P L_I$
[[Ram-ke]$_P$ [*ami* $_F$]$_P$ [boke-che]$_P$]$_I$
Ram-ACC I scolded

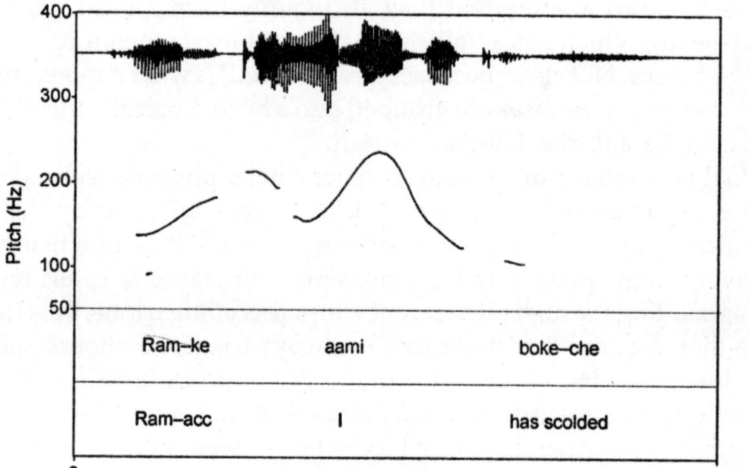

Figure 2

(11) $L_P H_P L_I$
[[*aami*$_F$]$_P$ [Ram-ke boke-che]$_P$]$_I$
I Ram-ACC scolded
'I scolded Ram.'

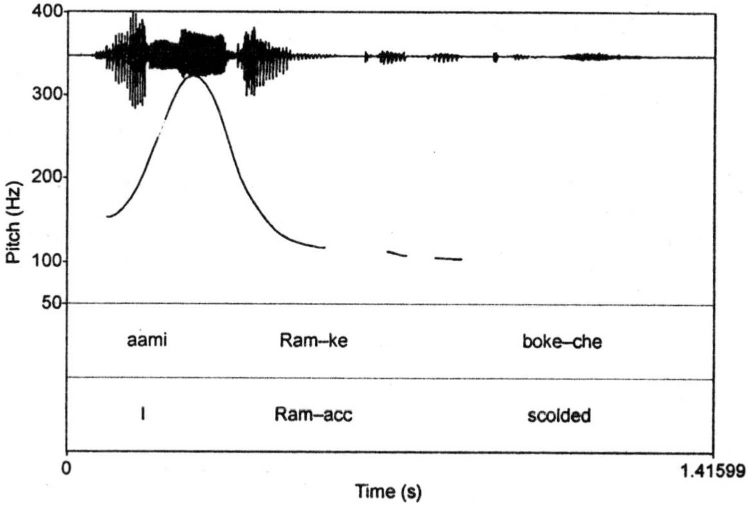

Figure 3

The choice of the one or the other word sequence is driven by the information structural context, or just by the preceding question (Gautam Sengupta, p.c.). The answer (10) is triggered by the question (12a) and (11) is a better answer to (12b). It must be noted that the pitch track of the question is identical to one of the answers. The word *ke* 'who' has the same role in (12) as the word *ami* in (10) and (11). Hayes & Lahiri postulate a complex boundary tone for the question intonation because they find that the high boundary tone of a question is higher than that of a focus. This suggestion needs to be confirmed with quantitative data.

(12) L_P H_P $L_PH_IL_I$

a. $[[$Ram-ke$]_P$ $[$*ke*$_F]_P$ $[$boke-che$]_P]_I$

Ram-ACC who scolded

b. $L_PH_IL_I$

$[[$*Ke*$]_P$ $[$Ram-ke boke-che$]_P]_I$

who Ram-ACC scolded

'Who scolded Ram?'

The next sentence in (13), which serves as an illustration of Bengali intonation in neutral utterances, has a complex syntactic structure and contains an embedded clause. Both the phrasal rising contour on all non-final p-phrases and the falling contour on the final p-phrase are clearly visible. Every p-phrase initial low tone L_P is linked to the beginning of the p-phrase which is projected from a full content word of the p-phrase. An example is *dekhā-korto* 'met', where the contour on the preceding word *sāthe* 'with', a function word, is just gently interpolated from the high tone of the preceding p-phrase to the low tone on the first syllable of *dekhā-korto*. I analyze this expression as consisting of two p-phrases, one embedded in the other. The L_p has to be aligned with the beginning of the embedded one in order to be relevant for both of them. The final H_p is always aligned as far to the right in its p-phrase as possible. In all non-final p-phrases, thus, the rising contour L_pH_p is clearly present. The final p-phrase is simplified to H_pL_I, rather than H_pL_p L_I, because there is no indication that two low tones are realized.

High pitch scaling across sequences of p-phrases reflects the syntactic structure. The first p-phrase *chele-belā-te* 'as a child' ends much higher than the second one *Pitr̃* 'Peter'. The third p-phrase *sku:l* 'school' returns to nearly the same height as the first one. The relationship between *tar bondhuder* 'his friends' and *sāthe dekhā-korto* 'is meeting with' is one of an inverted downstep relation which expresses the subordination of the argument relative to the verb. The same is true for the three final p-phrases. The high tone of the last p-phrase (the verb) is higher than the preceding ones. Remarkably, it is even higher than the first high tone in the sentence. As far as I know, pitch scaling relationships have not been studied in syntactically complex sentences in Bengali. This paper is not the place to go into detail on the correspondence between pitch height and syntactic structure, but since phrasing in Bengali plays the role of pitch accents in English, it is expected that some of the functions, if not all, fulfilled by scaling of pitch accents in intonation languages are to be found in other forms in phrase languages.

L_p H_p L_pH_p L_pH_p L_pH_p L_p H_p L_p H_p
(13) [[chele-belā-te]P [pitr̃]P [[sku:l]P sese]P]P [tar bondhuder]P [sāthe [dekhā-korto]P]P
child-as Peter school after his friends with meet-PAST-PROG3S

L_p H_p L_pH_p H_p L_I
[ebaN tāder]P [sāthe]P [anekhon khel-to]P]I
and them with many.hours play-PAST.PERF
'When Peter was a child, he used to meet his friends after school and play with them for hours.'

The verb can be integrated into the same p-phrase with the preceding argument (contra Hayes & Lahiri). This is illustrated in the following sentence in (14).

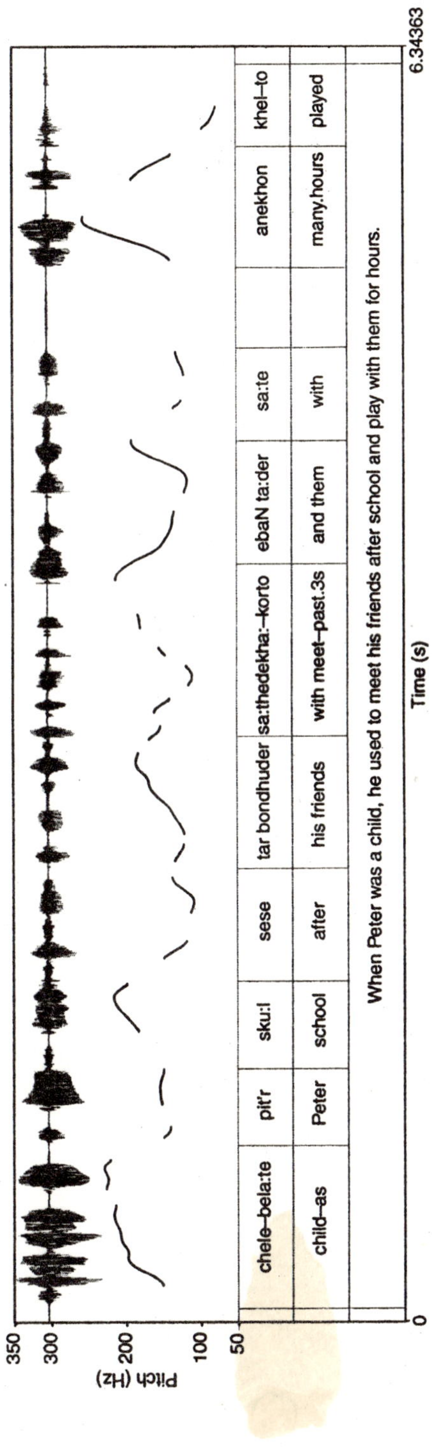

350
300
200
100
50
Pitch (Hz)
chele–bela:te
pit'r
sku:l
sese
tar bondhuder
sa:thedekha:–korto
ebaN ta:der
sa:te
anekhon
khel–to
child–as
Peter
school
after
his friends
with meet–past.3s
and them
with
many.hours
played
When Peter was a child, he used to meet his friends after school and play with them for hours.
0
Time (s)
6.34363

Figure 4

(14) L_PH_P $L_P H_P$ $L_P H_P$ $H_P L_I$
[[meri]P [onek]P [gulo]P [boi kine-che]P]I
Mary many-CLASS book buy-PR.PROG.3S
'Mary bought many books.'

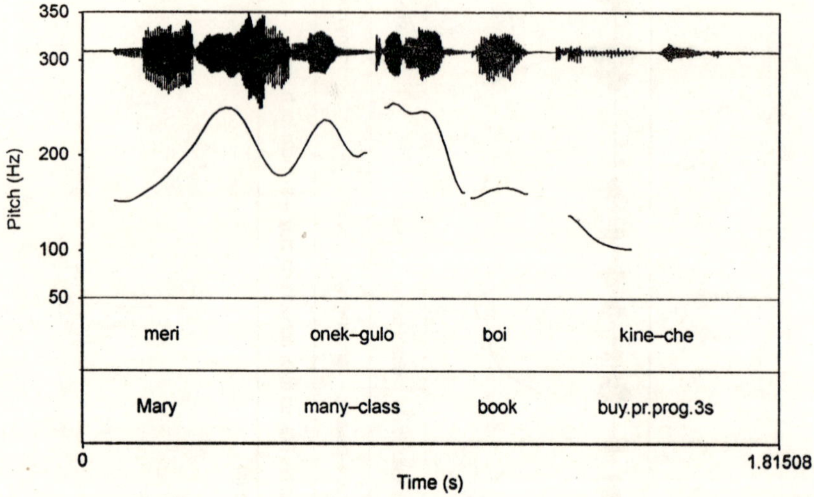

Figure 5

The following sentence (15), a reordering of the words in (14), shows a nominal phrase discontinuity: *boi* 'book' is topicalized, and the quantifier *ñ̃ek-gulo* 'many' occupies the same position as before. The quantifier is the focus of the sentence and has the effect that the verb is low and flat instead of gently descending, as before. The non-final p-phrases again have the typical rising contour and the last p-phrase is falling. In (15), the final rise for focus is on *ñ̃ek*. This high tone delimits the focus domain.

(15) L_PH_P $L_P H_P$ $L H_P$ L_I
[[boi]P [meri]P [ñ̃ek$_F$-gulo kine-che]P]I
book Mary many-CLASS buy-PR.PROG.3S

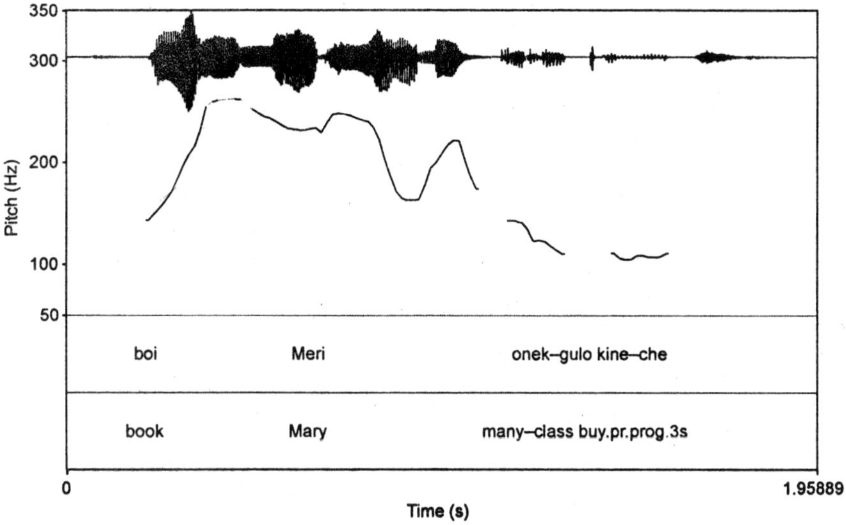

Figure 6

To sum up this section, Bengali has a phrasal intonation of the same type as observed for Hindi. In the default prosodic phrasing, every content word is phrased individually, but the phrasing can be an embedded recursive structure. All p-phrases, except for the final one, have the typical rising contour L_pH_p, whether focused or not. The very beginning, usually the first syllable of every p-phrase, is linked to a low tone L_p, and the last syllable of the p-phrase is associated with a boundary tone H_p. In the pre-final, prefocal position, the realization of the contour on all p-phrases is not guaranteed, since rhythm and speed can have the effect that some p-phrases are realized with a rather flat contour. Prominence or careful speech favor a rising pattern on every p-phrase. Focus also triggers a clear tonal pattern. A focus domain is delimited by a high tone H_p, immediately followed by the last L_I of the sentence. Pitch scaling between the high tones of a sequence of p-phrases probably plays an important role in the prosody of Bengali, but more research is needed here. The last p-phrase has a falling contour H_PL_I. It contains a high pitch accent, usually downstepped from the preceding H_p, and a low boundary, which is reached early in the final p-phrase. In the postfocal position, the tonal structure is eliminated, because the L_I is realized right after the H_P delimiting the focus domain.

As in Hindi, word order and pitch scaling are the correlates of information structure. But it is not the individual pitch accents which are in a downstep or in an upstep relation, as would be the case in an intonation language. Rather the range of an entire p-phrase can be larger or narrower, lowered or raised.

3.3 *Tamil*

The intonation of Tamil, a Dravidian language, has received some attention in the literature, recently from Keane (2006, 2007). In this language also, non-final p-phrases have a rising tonal contour and the final p-phrase is falling. Keane (2007) assumes that Tamil has pitch accents, and claims that the rise is L*H_p and the fall H*L_I. In her approach, the tonal structure of the non-final p-phrase consists of a fall-rise-fall. However, an examination of the contours in her papers confirms that the initial fall is the consequence of the interpolation between the preceding p-phrase final H and the initial L. In the same way, the final fall is the result of the interpolation between the final H_p and the L of the following p-phrase. For this reason, the intonation of Tamil's non-final p-phrases can be analyzed in the same way as that of Hindi and Bengali, namely as a rising contour. A further similarity with Bengali has to do with the status of the initial L tone, which is aligned with the first syllable of each content word. Keane analyzes this tone as a pitch accent, although she admits that Tamil does not have any lexical stress. The status of this tone is comparable to that of a postlexical pitch accent, which is not associated with a lexically stressed syllable, but rather with a position in a prosodic domain.

Exactly like Harnsberger for Hindi fifteen years before, Keane raises the question of the status of the high tone following L. The final high tone could be the trailing tone of a bitonal pitch accent or a boundary tone H_p. Keane seeks to find the answer in the alignment of this tone. Her argument goes as follows: either the high tone is aligned with the edge of the prosodic domain, and then it is a boundary tone, or it follows the L* at a fixed distance, and then it is a trailing tone. Keane (2006) finds that the location of the peak is variable. There are inter-speaker differences and also differences between lexical items, in which the peak can appear on the second or on the third syllable. Keane (2007) is an attempt to settle this issue experimentally. She measured the distance between L and H as a correlation of the duration of the word. But no stability of H relative to the end of the word could be found. Although the arguments do not all seem to point towards the same explanation, more evidence speaks for an analysis in terms of boundary. In short, her results are disappointing for an autosegmental theory of intonation which predicts that all tones have a role as either pitch accents or boundary tones.

In an analysis of Indian languages as phrase languages, the variable association of tones with syllables is a consequence of their status as phrasal tones. Tones have association domains rather than being necessarily associated with a prespecified syllable in the p-phrase.

Variation of the kind observed for Tamil, Bengali and Hindi is expected. The final H tone is associated with the phrase, and floats relative to the syllables it may anchor to.

The sentence (16), from my own recordings, illustrates the typical rising intonation of Tamil in non-final p-phrases, as well as the falling contour in the final p-phrase. It is conspicuous that in some of the non-final p-phrases, an additional but very reduced rising pattern is present, as on *oru* and on *amma* in the first and second p-phrases. I interpret these small rises as embedded p-phrases. The H tones at the end of the larger p-phrases are higher than those at the end of the smaller ones. No downstep is visible in this all-new sentence.

(16) $L_P H_P$ $L_P H_P$ L_P H_P L_P H_P L_P H_P H_P L_I

[[[Oru]$_P$ pe?]$_P$ [[ava? amma]$_P$ -vi?am]$_P$[pustakam]$_P$ [kodu-ta:?]$_P$]$_I$

one woman her mother-to book give-s

'A woman gives a book to her mother.'

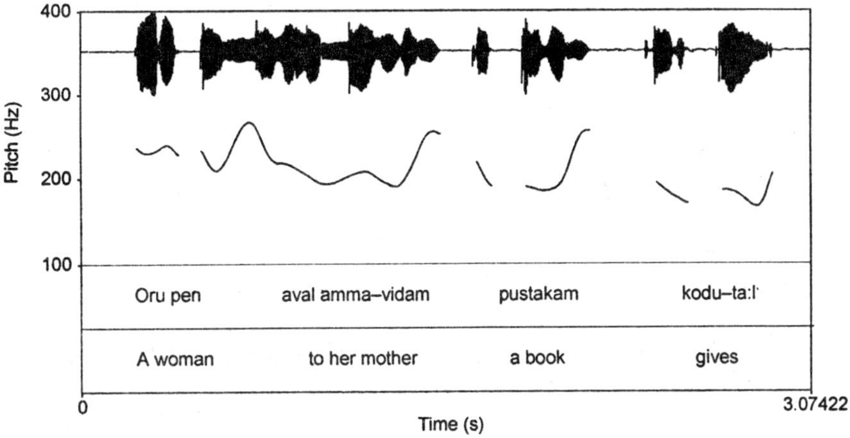

Figure 7

The next sentences illustrate that the phrasal intonation does not change much under different information structures. In (17), a sentence with canonical word order is shown.

(17) $L_P H_P$ $L_P H_P$ H_P L_I

[[meeri]$_P$ [niRaiya]$_P$ [ceer vaank-in-aaL]$_P$]$_I$

Mary many chairs buy-PST-PNG

'Mary has bought many chairs.'

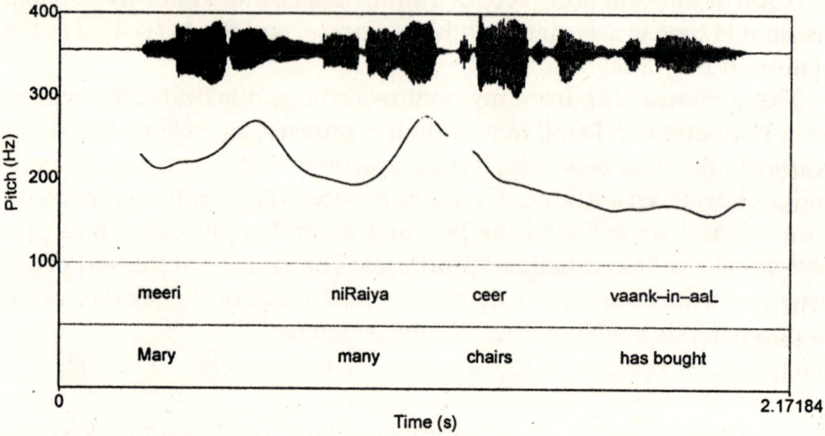

Figure 8

Sentence (18) keeps the wording of (17) but changes the word order. The direct object *many chairs* is topicalized and clearly separated from the remainder of the sentence. In none of the versions of this sentence are *many* and *chairs* included in a single p-phrase. In (17), *many* is a separate p-phrase and *chairs* forms another one together with the verb, and in (18), *many* and *chairs* each form their own p-phrase. I analyze the topicalized constituent as forming its own i-phrase.

(18) L_P H_P L_PH_P L_PH_P L_P H_I
[[[niRaiya]$_P$ [ceer]$_P$]$_I$ [meeri]$_P$ [vaank-in-aaL]$_P$]$_I$
many chairs Mary buy-PST-PNG
'Many chairs Mary bought.'

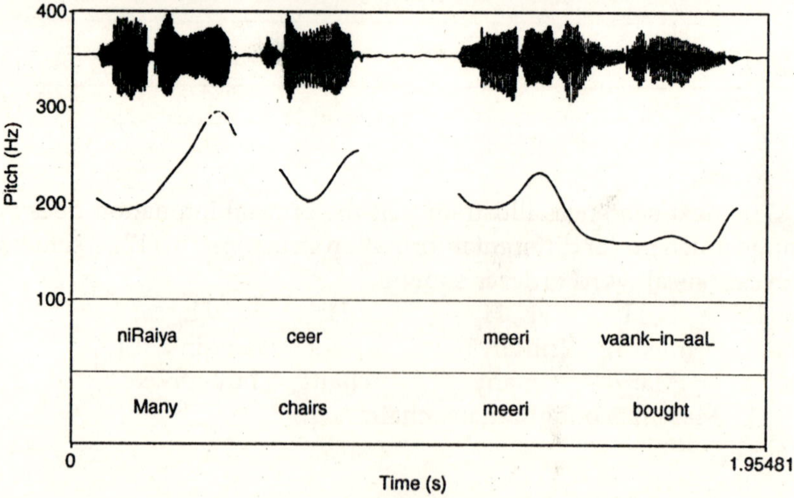

Figure 10

Sentences (16) and (17) do not show much downstep, but (18) clearly does. More data and controlled experiments of the kind conducted for Hindi by Patil et al. (2007) are needed before anything can be said about the significance of pitch scaling in Tamil.

To sum up this section on Tamil, a superficial review of some of the intonational properties of this language reveals that the prosodic and tonal patterns are similar to those found in the Indo-Aryan ones.

3.4 Malayalam

Turning now to Malayalam, another Dravidian language, we again find a language with a phrase intonation. There is no lexical stress, i.e., no lexical contrast on the basis of the stressed syllable.

The intonation of Malayalam declarative sentences is illustrated with a pair of sentences in a canonical and in a discontinuous version. Both show the typical rising intonation that we have already observed in Hindi, Bengali and Tamil. The subject in (19) has the highest boundary tone, and the following high tones are in a downstep relationship to each other. The lowest point in the second p-phrase *oru rasakaram-aya* 'one interesting' is on the first syllable of the adjective, rather than on the initial numeral, which speaks for an embedded p-phrase structure.

(19) L_PH_P L_P H_P $L_P H_P$ $H_P L_I$
[[Peter]$_P$ [oru [rasakaram-aya]$_P$]$_P$ [pustakam]$_P$ [vaichu]$_P$]$_I$
Peter one interesting book read
'Peter read an interesting book.'

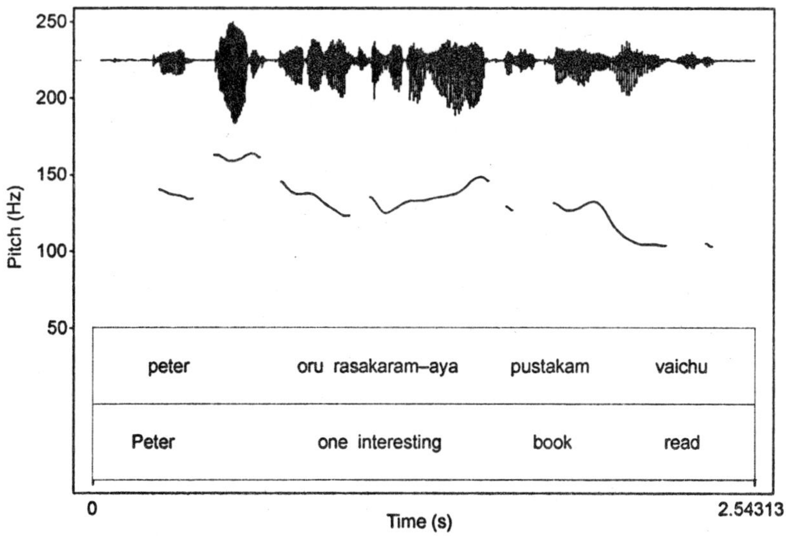

Figure 11

The same sentence with a changed word order in (20) shows that the individual p-phrases retain their phrasal intonation. But the relationship between the high tones is not the same as in (19). It is now the verb which has the highest tone, and the two preceding high tones are nearly as high but not quite. In both versions of this sentence, the verb is in a separate p-phrase. The topicalized constituent *pustakam* forms its own i-phrase.

(20) L_P H_P | L_PH_P | L_P H_P | H_P L_I
[pustakam]$_I$ | [[Peter]$_P$ | [vaicha-atu]$_P$ | [rasakaram]$_P$]$_I$
book | Peter | read-REL | interesting

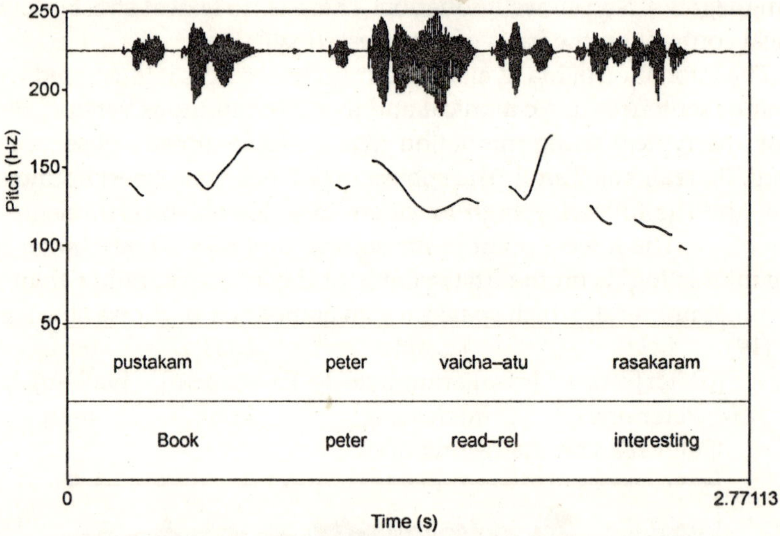

Figure 12

Obviously, more research is needed on the prosodic and tonal structure of Malayalam. However, judging from the two sentences and from the results obtained for the other languages, prosody will not play a very important role in the expression of information structure. For this part of the grammar, Malayalam has different strategies at its disposal, namely morpho-syntactic ones (see Jayaseelan 2001 for a syntactic analysis of focus movement). In (21), it is shown how a sentence changes its shape when put in different information structural contexts.[7] In the all-new sentence in (21a), a suffix *-anu* 'be' is attached to the verb, with the first vowel elided. This suffix is assumed to be a focus particle, which attaches to the focused constituent and which may be interpreted as the copula of a cleft construction (see Wiederhold 2008 for this interpretation). In the default case, when the sentence is all-new, the verb serves as the anchoring place for the particle. In (21b), the focus particle *-anu* is anchored to the narrowly focused subject *strii* 'lady'. This narrowly focused constituent is preverbal, which is the preferred, but not exclusive, focus position. The given object is moved into a postverbal position. In (21c), the verb is contrastively focused, and it takes the suffix again, but with a different verb form than in (21a). In both (21d) and (21e), the focused object is suffixed with *-anu*, but there is a difference in word order. The information focus in (21d) is located postverbally and the corrective focus in (21e) appears in the preverbal position. In (21f), with two foci, only the first focus takes the suffix and the other one is prosodically prominent. In short, Malayalam has at least two strategies for the expression of focus: suffixation of a focus particle and change of word order. It could be that prosodic means, like increase of register, are available as well, but again more investigation is necessary.

(21) a. {What is happening?}
strii veḷḷam kuḍikkun-nu
lady water drinking-ϕ-be
'The woman is drinking water.'

b. {Who is drinking water?}
strii-anu kuḍikkunnathu veḷḷam
strii-anu veḷḷam kuḍikkunnathu

c. {What is the woman doing?}
strii veḷḷam kuḍikuka-y-anu
(she drank the water, she did not spit it)

d. {What is the woman drinking?}
strii kuḍikkunnathu veḷḷam-anu

e. {Is the woman drinking wine?}
strii veḷḷam-anu kuḍikkunnathu

f. {Who is drinking what?}
strii-anu kuḍikkunnathu veḷḷam

To sum up, Malayalam has the same kind of prosodic pattern as observed for Tamil and the Indo-Aryan languages Hindi and Bengali. Like in the other languages, the prosodic pattern of both the pre-final and the final p-phrases does not change much under information structural influences. Malayalam illustrates that information structure is expressed by morpho-syntactic means rather than by prosodic ones.

4. Conclusions

It has been proposed in this paper that some of the main Indian languages, Hindi, Bengali, Tamil and Malayalam, show common intonational properties. They belong to a group of languages called *phrase languages*, which have no lexical stress and also no pitch accent.

Other languages in the same group are Korean and West Greenlandic. I propose phrase languages as a new intonational category, based on sentence intonation, besides the existing intonation languages, pitch accent languages and intonation languages. The four Indian languages examined in the paper organize the tonal pattern of their declarative sentences on the basis of phrase tones, which are anchored at the level of the prosodic phrase. Lexical items do not project any tones. Very few pragmatic meanings are conveyed by changes of tones, though manipulation of pitch range may be a more common device, requiring in-depth studies. The pattern exemplified by declarative sentences in Hindi, Bengali, Tamil and Malayalam consist in a rising contour, decomposed in a low tone associated with the beginning of the p-phrase, and a low tone associated with the end of the same p-phrase. Sentence-final p-phrases have a falling contour with an early high tone and a late low tone.

REFERENCES

Boersma, P. and D. Weenink 2005. *Praat: Doing phonetics by computer* (Version 4.5).

Bruce, G. 1977. *Swedish word accent in sentence perspective.* Travaux de l'Institut de Linguistique de Lund 12, Gleerup, Lund.

Dyrud, L.O. 2001. *Hindi-Urdu: Stress Accent or Non-Stress Accent?* Ph.D. dissertation. University of North Dakota.

Féry, C. and G. Kentner 2010. The prosody of grouping names in German and Hindi. Proceedings of Speech Prosody 2010 in Chicago.

Féry, C. and F. Kügler 2008. *Pitch accent scaling on given, new and focused constituents in German.* Journal of Phonetics 36, 4.

Fitzpatrick-Cole, J. 1996. Reduplication meets the Phonological Phrase in Bengali. *The Linguistic Review* 13, 305-356.

Fitzpatrick-Cole, J. and A. Lahiri 1997. Focus, intonation and phrasing in Bengali and English. In A.G. Botinis et al (eds.) *Intonation: Theory, models and applications. Proceedings of the ESCA Workshop*, Athens. 119-122.

Gunlogson, C. 2001. *True to form: Rising and falling declaratives as questions in English.* PhD Dissertation. UCSC.

Gussenhoven, C. 2004. *The phonology of tone and intonation.* Cambridge: Cambridge University Press.

Harnsberger, J.D. 1994. *Towards an intonational phonology of Hindi.* Unpublished manuscript.

Harnsberger, J.D. 1999. *The role of metrical structure in Hindi intonation.* South Asian Language Analysis Roundtable. Urbana-Champaign: University of Illinois.

Harnsberger, J.D. and J. Judge 1996. Pitch range and focus in Hindi. *The Journal of the Acoustical Society of America* 99, 2493.

Hayes, Bruce 1995. *Metrical stress theory: Principles and case studies*. Chicago: University of Chicago Press.

Hayes, B. and A. Lahiri 1991. Bengali intonational phonology. *Natural Language and Linguistic Theory* 9, 47-99.

Hussain, S. 1997. *Phonetic correlates of lexical stress in Urdu*. Northwestern University.

Hyman, Larry 2006. Word-prosodic typology. *Phonology* 23, 225-257.

Jayaseelan, K.A. 2001. IP-internal topic and focus phrases. *Studia Linguistica* 55 (1), 39–75.

Jun, S.A. 2005. Prosodic Typology. In S.A. Jun (ed.) *Prosodic typology. The phonology of intonation and phrasing*. 430–458. Oxford: Oxford University Press.

Kanerva, Jonni M. 1990. Focusing on Phonological Phrases in Chichewa. In Sharon Inkelas and Zec Draga (eds.) *Phonology-Syntax-Interface*. Chicago: University of Chicago Press. 145-161.

Keane, E. 2006. Prominence in Tamil. *Journal of the International Phonetic Association* 36, 1-20.

Keane, E. 2007. Distribution and Alignment of F0 Contours in Tamil. *Proceedings of the 16th International Congress of Phonetic Sciences*, Saarbruecken, Germany.

Khan, S. ud D. 2007. The Distribution and Realization of H tones in Bengali. *Working Papers in Phonetics* 106, 34-40. Los Angeles: University of California.

Ladd, D.R. 1996. *Intonational phonology*. Cambridge: Cambridge University Press.

Lahiri, A. and J. Fitzpatrick-Cole 1999. Emphatic Clitics and Focus Intonation in Bengali. In: R. Kager and Z. Wim (eds.) *Phrasal Phonology*. Nijmegen University Press 119-44.

Moore, R.R. 1965. *A study of Hindi intonation*. Ph.D. dissertation. University of Michigan.

Morton, E.S. 1975. Ecological sources of selection on avian sounds. *American Naturalist* 109. 17-34.

Nair, R. 1999. *Syllables and word edges*. Northwestern University. Unpublished Dissertation.

Nair, R. 2001. Acoustic correlates of lexical stress in Hindi. In A. Abbi, R. Gupta, and A. Kidwai (eds.) *Linguistic structure and language dynamics in South Asia - Papers from the proceedings of SALA XVIII roundtable*.

Nespor, Marina and Irene Vogel (1986) *Prosodic phonology*. Dordrecht: Foris.

Ohala, J.J. 1983. Cross-language use of pitch: An ethnological view. *Phonetica 40*, 1-18.

Patil, Umesh, Anja Gollard, Gerrit Kentner, Frank Kügler, Caroline Féry & Shravan Vasishth 2007. Focus, word order and intonation in Hindi. Journal of South Asian Linguistics 1. 53-70.

Pierrehumbert, J. 1980. *The phonology and phonetics of English intonation*. Ph.D. dissertation. MIT. Distributed by Indiana University Linguistics Club, Bloomington.

Pierrehumbert, J. and M. Beckman 1988. *Japanese tone structure.* MIT Press.

Rooth, M. 1985. *Association with focus.* Ph.D. dissertation. Amherst: University of Massachusetts.

Rooth, M. 1992. A theory of focus interpretation. *Natural Language Semantics* 1(1), 75–116.

Selkirk, Elisabeth O. 1986. On derived domains in sentence phonology. *Phonology Yearbook* 3, 371-405.

Selkirk, Elisabeth O. 1995. Sentence Prosody: Intonation, Stress and Phrasing. In Goldsmith, John (ed.) *Handbook of phonological theory.* Blackwell. 550-569.

Selkirk, Elisabeth O. 2006. Bengali intonation revisited: An optimality theoretic analysis in which FOCUS stress prominence drives FOCUS phrasing. In C. Lee, and D. Büring (eds.) *Topic and focus: Cross-linguistic perspectives on meaning and intonation.* Dordrecht: Springer, 215–244.

Truckenbrodt, H. 2003. Variation in p-phrasing in Bengali. *Linguistic Variation Yearbook* 2, 259-303.

Wiederhold, T. 2008. Discontinuous Noun Phrases in Indian Languages. Ms, Potsdam.

NOTES

1. I am indebted to my colleagues and informants for their help with the collection of the data which served as a basis for this paper, as well as for their patience in answering my questions. Thanks are due to Gautam Sengupta and Masum Ali for Bengali, Grace M. Temsen for Khasi, Kiran Kishore for Malayalam, Shravan Vasishth and Umesh Patil for Hindi, and Arathi Kannan for Tamil. This paper is dedicated to Ramakant, in sign of respect, admiration and friendship.
2. Other languages spoken in India have a completely different intonation pattern from the one introduced in this paper. Tone languages, like Tai (Khamti and Khamyang), Tibeto-Burman (Mishmi) or Mon-Khmer (Khasi), are to be treated differently. These languages are not part of the present study.
3. There is an ongoing debate in the literature as to the number of larger prosodic domains needed, and what they are called. Jun (2005) lists 'Accentual Phrase,' 'Intermediate Phrase' and 'Intonation Phrase' as prosodic units above the word. Other terminologies include 'Focus Domain,' 'Prosodic Phrase,' 'Phonological Phrase,' 'Minor Phrase,' 'Major Phrase' and many more.
4. Even more intriguing is a result by Féry & Kentner (in prep) which shows that prosody is not used in Hindi for the disambiguation of groupings of names, like (a and b) or c as opposed to a or (b and c).
5. According to Gautam Sengupta (p.c.), (8) has a scrambled word order. A more natural word order for this sentence places the direct object 'scarf' in the preverbal position.
6. See for instance examples (20) and (21) on pages 60 and 61 in Hayes & Lahiri's paper.
7. Thanks to Kiran Kishore for providing and discussing these data.

18

More Freedom on the Left

Gisbert Fanselow

This paper deals with a variety of aspects of German nominal compounds, and is concerned with a number of 'smaller' issues arising in the study of natural language. These smaller issues are possibly related to a bigger question: is there only one mechanism generating recursive structures in natural language, or are there more? More than two decades ago, I opted for the latter option (see Fanselow 1985a,b), but recent developments in the syntax and certain aspects of compounding in German now seem to favour the former alternative, but in a restricted way only. However, the process of extending the lexicon on the basis of word formation strategies (Agnihotri 1997, Singh & Agnihotri (1997) could constitute a second way of generating structures recursively.

The smaller (or, rather, descriptive) issues arise when one tries to implement the idea that compound formation is a process combining words – a very natural assumption that was spelt out in detail for Hindi morphology and compound formation by Singh & Agnihotri (1997) and Agnihotri (1997). The formation of nominal compounds is a very productive process in German, but there are restrictions on the form of the left part of a compound (e.g., a ban on regular *s*-plurals) showing that not all kinds of words may participate in compounding. At the same time, the choice of these left parts is quite unconstrained in other respects: very often, they are not even possible words of German. We argue that these problems find a solution in terms of the idea that some properties of and constraints on words are part of the syntax rather than part of the morphology (word formation) or the lexicon. Morphology and the lexicon are blind to these constraints imposed by syntax. In this sense, we can defend the basic idea underlying the model developed by Agnihotri and Singh, *viz.* that compound formation involves (morphological, but not necessarily syntactic) words.

The paper is organized as follows. In section 1, I give a brief summary of the idea that the formation rules for compounds and phrases are, essentially identical. Phrases and compounds are endocentric, but in compounds, certain classes of morphemes (e.g., prepositions) may show up in non-head positions only (section 2). We argue that this behaviour is due to a division of labour between syntax and morphology: morphemes combine freely in the formation of compounds, but syntax may filter out certain types of such combinations. In sections 3, 4, and 5, we use this insight to account for the fact that the left part of compounds may consist of combinations of nouns with prepositions, numerals, quantifiers, and particles that never show up as independent words, and that even *dvandva* compounds are licensed there in spite of the fact that they are generally banned in German. Section 6 considers combinations of adjectives and nouns, which illustrate the differences between constraints within the generation of compounds, and constraints that are syntactic in nature. In Section 7 we delevop the idea that AN compounds in German are not generated on the basis or merge, but by special word formation strategies as proposed by Agnihotri and Singh. We draw our conclusions in section 8.

1. Ever since Lees (1960), a seemingly natural assumption has dominated the generative analysis of word formation, *viz.* the idea that the nature of the rules of word formation and the nature of rules of syntax are, essentially, identical. On the side of word formation/ morphology, one major insight was that the rules of generating complex words should not be loaded with the burden of making the interpretation of the complex words explicit, so that the abstractness of the structures underlying complex words could be reduced substantially (see Chomsky 1970). Within an interpretive system for compounds such as the one proposed in Fanselow (1981), the combinatory rules can then be kept rather simple: they combine words of certain categories and have a word of a certain category as an output.

In a nutshell, when one considers German nominal compounds, the examples in (1) motivate the 'rules' given in (2), which can be generalized as in (3). In other words, German nominal compounds are (of course!) syntactically endocentric, with the head sitting on the right.

(1)	Garten.schlauch[1]	garden hose
	Rot.buche	red beech
	Geh.weg	walk way (sidewalk)

(2) $N \rightarrow N\ N$
$N \rightarrow A\ N$
$N \rightarrow V\ N$

(3) N → XN (X a lexical category)

Endocentricity and right-headedness characterize German compounds quite in general, as (4) and (5) illustrate for adjectival and verbal compounds, respectively. The most concise statement of German compounding thus appears to be (6).

4)	kirsch.rot	cherry-red	A → N A
	dunkel.blau	dark-blue	A → A A
	kopier.echt	copy-proof	A → V A
(5)	wasser.paddeln	water-paddle	V → N V
	heiss.laufen	hot-run (become heated)	V→ A V
	kennen.lernen	know-learn (get to know)	V → V V
(6)	X→ Y X	with X,Y ε {N,V,A}	

(6) guarantees that compounds are right-headed structures, see, e.g., Fanselow (1985b), Höhle (1985), Lieber (1980, 1983), Selkirk (1982), and much later work. (6) is reminiscent of the X-bar-theory (7) proposed for syntax by Chomsky (1970, 1981), so that the question arises whether the structure building mechanisms of compound formation and of syntax are identical.

A quarter of a century ago, one might have arrived at a negative answer on the basis of several formal differences between the mechanisms generating complex words and complex phrases (cf. also Fanselow 1985a), but syntax has changed substantially in the meantime so that the issue has now become much more subtle. E.g., the idea that syntactic structures involve an elaborate system of phrasal levels (maximal (X''), minimal (X), and 'intermediate' (X') projections) that are, arguably, non-existent in compounds, became doubtful after the important arguments elaborated in Speas (1990), so that phrasal levels were eliminated in the minimalist program (e.g, Chomsky 1993, 1995).

(7) $X^i \rightarrow \ldots X^j \ldots$, with $i > j$ or $i = j$

The assumption that syntactic structures show binary branching brings syntactic branching even closer to (6), so that (7) would be replaced by something like (8) for syntax.

(8) X → Y Z, with X = Y or X = Z

The far-reaching simplification of structure building in the syntax thus makes it possible to claim that both syntax and morphology apply the same merge operation combining two formal objects. Headedness may differ in the two domains[2], and it seems as if truly functional categories do not participate in word formation while they play a central role in syntax, but this does not affect the identity of the combinatory mechanism.

2. In the syntax, every category can be used both in head- and non head-positions[3]. This is different in compounding, in contrast to what

(6) states. It is easy to observe that rule (6) undergenerates. While the heads of compounds must belong to one of the lexical categories N, V, and A, some prepositions are allowed as left branches:

(9) Zwischen.bericht	Between-report (interim report)
Vor.zug	Before-train (train in front)
Nach.ernte	After-harvest (second harvest)
Neben.regierung	Beside-government (secondary/rival government)
Gegen.bericht	Against.report (counter report)
Mit-Autor	With.author (co.author)

Semantically, such compounds are endocentric[4] : a *Vor.zug* is a train going in front of some other train, not something going in front of some train. More interestingly, *both* semantic arguments of the preposition belong to the same class of objects: a *Nach.ernte* is a harvest following some other harvest (not a harvest after some contextually given event such as ploughing), a *Gegen.bericht* is a report against some other report. and a *Mit.autor* is an author writing together with some other author (not an author with a spouse). This constraint following from this general pattern[5] may explain the oddness of many P + N combinations in terms of the anomaly of the resulting semantics (**Auf.Zug* 'On-train', train on some other train, and not a non-derailed train), but some inacceptable words such as **In-Puppe* (doll in some other doll), **Ohne-Chef* (boss without some other boss) are ill-formed although their interpretation would make sense[6].

P+N compounds show that there are elements, viz. prepositions, that occur within compounds, but are confined to non-head positions there. In descriptive terms, (6) thus has to be replaced by (10).

(10) $X \rightarrow Y\ X$ with $X \in \{N,V,A\}$ and $Y \in \{N,V,A,P\}$

But why are there elements that participate in word formation, but not as heads? We could of course work with an unelegant generative rule such as (10), but that would imply that syntax and morphology differ with respect to structure building. As mentioned above, in syntax, there are (almost) no elements that are restricted to non-head positions.

We get a clearer picture of the nature of the special license for prepositions to act as non-heads in compounds when we consider further instances of morphemes confined to non-head positions such as those in (11). *Pseudo-* and *Euro-* 'euro' (in the sense of: (related to) the European Union, not in the sense of the name of the EU currency) do not occur as heads of compounds, and they fail to do so because they cannot appear as independent words either.

(11)Pseudo-Demokrat	pseudo-democrat
Euro-Parlamentarier	Euro-representative,

	'representative in the EU parliament'
*Sozialisten-Pseudo	socialist-pseudo
*Alt-Euro	Old-euro
Alt-EU	Old-EU

We can derive the latter property from the (inevitable) assumption that *Pseudo* and *Euro* lack a syntactic category specification, and the (equally natural) assumption that the generation of syntactic structures can only 'see' elements that have a category label. In recent models (Chomsky 2005), this follows from the assumption that the (external) merging operation must also be triggered by the checking of formal (categorical) features (coming close, thereby, to ideas entertained in Categorial Grammar).

Now, compounds are endocentric elements. Their syntactic category is determined by their right daughter. If the right daughter lacks a category specification, so will the compound. Both will be unusable as parts of sentences because they lack the category specification that is required for participating in syntactic structure building.

The ability of category-free elements to show up as left branches of compounds thus implies that elements can be merged without feature checking/categorical selection in the morphological component of grammar. Alternatively, we can have the merge operation apply freely, but assume that only those elements whose categorical features have been checked are transparent to further syntactic operations and operations at the interface. Compounds thus are structures that are built without feature checking. We are therefore replacing (10) by (12), and leave the nature of the parts of a compound entirely open within the morphological component: it is only the syntax that requires that a compound belong to one of the syntactic categories[7].

(12) a. Combine any two morphemes
b. The category value of a compound is identical with the value of its right daughter

We can now return to the absence of compounds with prepositional heads. The difficulty here is not that (12b) could not compute a syntactic category for the compound. Rather, an inappropriate label is derived. If the process of compounding is as such unrestricted, words such as **Tisch-unter* 'table.under' will be formed, but they will be blocked because of the endocentricity requirement of (12). Prepositions are (semi-) functional categories, and these come with syntactic selection features that cannot be and are not checked/saturated within word formation structures and a semantic argument place corresponding to the syntactic selection feature. In particular, prepositions select a D-feature of their complement, and the complex preposition **Tisch-unter* inherits this D-feature because of (12). However, the *semantic* argument place of the preposition corresponding to this D-features has already been closed in the complex preposition (it should get a meaning such as **λx (∃y (table (y) & below(x,y)))** by the semantic process of functional application), so that we end up with a mismatch between the semantic and the syntactic properties of $[_P$ N+P], making such words unusable from a syntactic point of view (Fanselow 1988). By the same reasoning, all categories are excluded from the head position of compounds that always come with a selectional feature, and this seems to hold for all functional categories. Consequently, compounds belong to the categories N, A, and V only.

Left daughters of a compound have been merged without feature checking. They are not affected by (12b). Consequently, the restrictions following from (12b) are not valid for non-head positions.

3. More complex compounds show that the picture is more complicated. 'Triple' compounds with the internal branching structure $[_C$ A $[_C$ B C]] do not bring any interesting new properties, and the same seems to hold for those with the structure $[_C$ [A B] C] as in (13)

(13) a. Nach.ernte..ergebnis After-harvest-result, results of the secondary harvest
b. Vor.prüfungs..termin Before.exam.date 'date of the preliminary exam'

However, in addition to (13), the patterns exemplified in (14a-d) are also well-formed. They differ from (10) and (13) in terms of interpretation. Recall that a *Nach.ernte* 'after-harvest' is a harvest following some other harvest. *Vor.weihnacht* in (14a) does not refer to some Christmas preceding some other Christmas, rather it refers to **λx (∃y (christmas (y) & before (x,y))**. The left branch thus has the semantics of an exocentric *bahuvrihi*-compound. Formulated differently, we observe that semantically, at least, the preposition is the 'head' of the left parts of the compounds in (14a-d).

(14)		
a.	Vorweihnachtszeit	Before.christmas-time (Pre-Christman period)
b.	Nach.festtags.übelheit	after.holiday.nausea (Post-holiday nausea)
c.	Zwischenkriegsdemokratie	between.war-democracy
d.	Überaugenstreif	above-eyes.stripe
e.	?*Gegen-Regen-Demonstration	against.rain-manifestation
	Anti-Regen-Demonstration	anti-rain-manifestation
f.	?*Mitkragenhemd	with.collar-shirt
	Kragenhemd	collar shirt

One should note that the pattern exemplified in (14a-d) is produced mostly with spatial and temporal prepositions. The prepositions *für* 'for' and *gegen* 'against' cannot be used in such compounds (14e). They appear to be blocked by *pro* and *anti* that fulfil the same semantic functions. However, many other prepositions like *in* fail to participate in such a compounding process, too. We have no definitive answers to the question as to why this is the case, but here is a speculation: Prepositions typically express thematic relations. The semantic vagueness of NN compounds such as *Kragenhemd* collar.shirt makes them compete with *Mitkragenhemd* for the expression of exactly the same content. (14e) may thus also be ruled out as an instance of some type of blocking triggered by NN compounds.

Returning to the productive cases in (14a-d), two questions arise. How are they formed, and why do they take the shape they have? Given the unrestricted nature of compound formation, nothing prevents the generation of words such as (14c) [[*Zwischen-Kriegs*]*demokratie*].

By (12), *Zwischenkriegs* would be a noun if inserted into a syntactic structure by a triggered merge operation, and at least semantically, this is incorrect, as we have just mentioned. We have also seem that the left part of a compound need not belong to any syntactic category at all, because it is merged with the compound's head without feature checking. This absence of a category specification implies a solution for the "headedness-problem" with *Zwischenkriegs*: we can have that element lack a category specification (so that the headedness problem is avoided), i.e., we can let (12b) apply only when the complex structure is in fact inserted into a syntactic slot. In other words, morphology 'avoids' the computation of a head (in a syntactic sense) unless this is required in the interest of identifying the category by which the morpheme complex can enter syntactic representations.

This still leaves it open why *[*Kriegszwischen*]*demokratie* "war-between democracy" is out, i.e., why prepositions have to *precede* their semantic arguments in the left branches of nominal compounds, too. It is tempting to derive this property from the word order we find in PPs, i.e. to assume that the combination P+N in the non-head part of the compounds in (14) is in fact due to the application of a *phrasal* rule. Such phrasal compounds built from PPs in fact exist in German alongside (14), as (15) shows:

(15) Seine "Ohne - Mich" Haltung
His without me attitude
"his attitude of keeping himself out of everything"
Ihre "Mit dem Kopf durch die Wand" Politik
Her with the head through the wall politics

"her politics of being hell-bent on getting her own way"

In a grammatical model in which there are explicit phrase structure rules and explicit rules for compound formation, the concept of a 'phrasal compound' is rather easy to identify, but a system in which the structure building components of grammar are kept as simple as possible, it is difficult to see whether 'phrasal compound' is more than merely a descriptive label. If a phrasal compound is a compound the left part of which is made up by a complete and potentially independent phrase (as in (15)), then the structures in (14) are of course not phrasal compounds. Likewise, if a phrasal compound is one in which the left part has been formed by the rules of syntax, then the words in (14) are not phrasal compounds either. Apart from linear order, *Zwischen.kriegs* has little in common with PPs: in the syntax (and in phrasal compounds), prepositions accept DPs as complements rather than nouns, but *Zwischenkriegs* does not follow that rule: P directly combines with N here. Given the selectional requirements of P, we must conclude that P and N have *not* been combined in the context of a feature checking operation. Their combination is not syntactic in nature.

Furthermore, the morphological shape of the noun *Kriegs* is typical for *Krieg* when it figures in compounds. The dative form *Kriegen* that would be governed by *zwischen* in a syntactic expression is NOT chosem. A PP-analysis for *Zwischenkriegs* would thus raise more questions than it answers, so that we will stick to analysing the word as a compound.

We are left, then, with the linear order problem. The idea that we will pursue here is that at least the merger of functional categories is a directional process. Prepositions, complementizers, determiners, etc., are always merged as left branches. This property holds of the merge process in general, both in the morphology and the syntax. With respect to merge, the absence of feature checking thus seems to be the *only* difference between syntax and morphology.

4. Our hypotheses and conclusions are confirmed when we consider further types of left branches of compounds. In binary compounds, numerals and quantifiers cannot show up (*All.Partei 'all party'), but they are fine as parts of left branches of more complex compounds:

(16)	a. 200-Seiten-Buch	200 pages book
	b. All.parteien-Regierung	all party government
	c. Kein.kind..familie	No-child-family

As in the case of prepositions, some quantifiers such as *jed-* 'every' cannot enter that pattern (*Jed.parteien.regierung "every-party-government"), in contrast to *all* 'all', *viel* 'many' (Viel.parteien.regierung), *mehr* 'several' (Mehr.parteien.regierung), and *kein* 'no' (16c). *Einige* and *welche* 'some' avoid showing up in complex left parts of compounds, too. This may be linked to the fact that the default interpretation of an NN compound AB is already "the set of B related to **some** A", so that there is no need for a triple compound "some.A..B". Finally, demonstratives and definite articles are also absent in left branches of compounds. Probably, nouns should not have truly deictic meaning parts, so that compounds using demonstratives and definite articles would be blocked.

An analysis of the forms in (16) in terms of a 'phrasal compound' would face the same difficulties that we have identified for P+N combinations above. The morphological shape of the noun is often not the one it would have in a syntactic phrase. E.g., *Ein.parteien.regierung* 'one-party-government' has the noun *partei* 'party' appear in a form that is a plural in phrasal syntax, even though *ein* 'one' requires a singular. It is just the other way round with *Drei.raum.wohnung* 'three-room-flat', with *Raum* being singular rather than the plural that *drei* 'three' should require.

Our treatment of quantifier/numeral + noun combinations raises the same issues that already came up in the previous section with P+N compounds. We assume that quantifiers and numerals strictly subcategorise a nominal projection, i.e., they possess an N-feature that must be checked. This N-feature of the quantifier will be inherited by a complex form such as *kinder.alle* 'children.all', while the semantic argument place of *alle* would already be saturated within this N+Q compound. Consequently, we are confronted with the same mismatch between syntax (X selects a feature) and semantics (the argument slot of X is already saturated) that we already found for N+P compounds, and that makes them unusuable in a syntactic context.

Furthermore, we assume that numerals and quantifiers, being functional elements, always take their arguments on the right, which blocks the generation of [[N Num/Q] N].

Functional application is the basic semantic operation combining the meanings of the parts of the compound, so that Q+N will be interpreted by the result of applying the meaning of a quantifier to the meaning of a noun, and we take this semantic object to not fit the meaning constraints for nouns (cf., e.g., Fanselow 1988)). The fact that left parts of compounds do not need a syntactic head while the complete compounds do thus implies that complete compounds need to fulfil constraints that their left parts do not have to.

5. We argued against an explanation of our critical examples in terms of 'phrasal compounding' on the basis of morphological evidence. A phrasal analysis of their left branches seems also unlikely for the compounds in (17): These left branches are *dvandva* (coordinative)

compounds, which cannot be formed productively as independent words in German.

(17) a.	CDU-FDP-Koalition	CDU-FDP-coalition
b.	Rhein-Main-Donau-Kanal	Rhine-Main-Danube-canal
c.	Eltern-Kind-Beziehung	parents-child-relation
d.	Kaiser-König-Herzog- Hierarchie	emperor-king-duke- hierarchy
e.	Mutter-Tochter-Oma- Konstellation	mother-daugher-grandma- constellation
f.	das Zwei Vorsitzende vier Stellvertreter System the two-chairpersons four-deputy system	

Coordinative (nominal) compounds are only used as names for (abstract) entities composed of formerly independent parts. Examples are state names such as *Baden-Wḷrttemberg* or company names such as *Daimler-Chrysler*. In the adjectival domain, coordinative compounds are more frequent (such as *rot-grün* 'red-green' or *süss-saue*r 'sweet.sour'). The examples in (17) show that the severe restrictions on nominal dvandva compounds disappear when they are used as left branches. The grammar of *Eltern-Kind* as in (17c) can be described easily: in a coordinative compound, the right branch is not a head. More precisely, there is no general rule that would determine the grammatical features of a coordinative compound. Lacking a category feature, coordinative compounds cannot be merged as part of syntactic structures. The merge operation in the morphological component is more liberal, however, and allows non-head left parts without a syntactic category. Thus, (17c) can be formed.

The examples (17b,d,e) suggest that dvanda compounds need not have a binary structure. Therefore, they cannot be generated by the standard (binary) merge operation of syntax. At first glance, this seems to imply that (17) could not possibly be analysed in terms of phrasal compounds, but we must not forget that syntax itself must be able to generate coordinative structures.

6. The examples discussed so far contrast nicely with other restrictions in compound formation. For P+N, Q+N, and Num+N compounds, we have argued that they can be formed in the morphological component of grammar. They are blocked as independent complex words because of a mismatch of their syntactic and semantic properties. However, in a context in which syntactic properties play no role, *viz.*, as left parts of compounds, they occur frequently.

With A+N compounds, the situation is different. The formation of A+N compounds is heavily restricted, but these constraints typically do not lose effect when AN is used as a left part of a compound. The non-head position of a compound thus serves as a testing ground for the syntactic or morphological nature of a restriction on compounding.

The formation of AN compounds is quite restricted in German. The presence of such restrictions constitutes a well-known fact about German, but they have rarely been analysed in rule-based approaches. Usually, AN compounds are, e.g., bad when N refers to a human being, as exemplified by *[*Klug*][*professor*] "smart professor" and *[*Munter*][*schüler*] 'alert pupil'. Note that the constraint does not affect (unproductive) *bahuvrihi* structures such as [*Schlau*][*kopf*] "clever head", [*Rot*][*haut*] "red skin" or [*Lang*][*nase*] "long nose". These compound structures are inacceptable when one tries to interpret then as standard *tatpurusha* compounds. In other words, it seems as if the adjective appearing in AN should not modify the referent of the compound. (18b) is good, while (18a) is not.

(18) a. λx (**clever (x)** & professor (x))
λx (**red (x)** & skin (x))
b. λy (∃y(**red (y)** & skin (y)) & HAS (y,x))

The absence of a morphological distinction between adjectives and adverbs in German obscures the ban on certain types of AN compounds to a certain extent. *Schnell.sprecher* 'fast speaker, a speaker who talks fast" (not a speaker fast in some other respects) violates the ban on AN compounds only superficially: it is a combination of an adverb and a noun. Surprisingly, secondary predicates also often do not count when the ban on AN formation is at stake, as *Nackt.tänzer* "naked dancer" (someone who dances naked) and *Nackt.modell* ("naked model", person who poses naked) show. Apparent adjectives are factually interpreted as adverbs outside the domain of human and animate nouns, too: a *Schnell.zug* ("fast train") is a train going fast). Likewise, a *Schwertransporter* "heavy transporter" is a transporter carrying heavy things, not a heavy transporter.

Interestingly, there are grammatical AN compounds which cannot be explained away in the way just sketched. This is, e.g., true of words such as those cited in (19). Very similar combinations of adjectives and nouns can be inacceptable, see (20).

(19) Jung.professor "young professor", Jung.unternehmer "young industrialist", Billig.flug "cheap flight", Edel.matraze "noble mattress", Gebraucht.buch "used book", Neu.ware "new goods", Frisch.fisch "fresh fish" , Leicht.waggon "light car, a light car", Leer.flasche "empty bottle"

(20) *Schwer.tisch "heavy table", *Beschädigt.buch "damaged book", *Teuerflug "expensive flight" *Vollflasche "filled bottle"[8]

As already mentioned above, ill-formed AN combinations do not improve when used in the non-head position of some compound: **Klug.professoren.auszeichung* 'smart-professor-award' and **Teuer flug.vermeidung* 'expensive flight avoidance' do not sound better than **Klugprofessor* and **Teuerflug*. Where there is a constraint on compounding in the narrow sense, it affects complex words in all contexts. When syntax filters out compound structures, it can do so only in domains within its rule.

7. The facts discussed so far support a model in which the structure building operations of syntax and morphology are nearly identical. The major difference lies in the fact that structure building in the syntax (merger) must be triggered, while it applies freely in morphology. The contrast between (19) and (20) presented in the preceding section has introduced a new type of problem, however: how can we account for constraints in compounding that are, apparently, item-specific? Do we have to generally allow AN compounds, and filter out illegal combinations? Or do we have to ban AN compounding, and rule in special combinations by some other mechanism?

I cannot offer a definite answer[9] to these questions for AN compounds, but the second option is, at least more easy to formulate. We can combine a very general constraint on, e.g., the merge operation forming AN compounds with human referents with the listing of a considerable number of items such as *Jungunternehmer* 'young industrial' in the lexicon, such that the list of these words can always be extended on the basis of analogy formation, e.g., along the lines suggested by Agnihotri (1997) and Singh & Agnihotri (1997) in their word-based account of word formation.

At least for interpretation, *no* account of compound formation can avoid reference to existing words and the extension of the lexicon based on analogy to these, so that the analogy induced generation of AN compounds does not really add a new component to grammar. The crucial observation is that new words may partially take over the idiomatic interpretation of existing words. A famous example of German is *Haus.mann* 'house man; man doing house work" formed in analogy to *Haus.frau* "house woman, housewife". *Kauf.frau* "buy woman, female merchant" (in analogy to *Kauf.mann* "buy man, merchant") and other words of this kind illustrate the same point: there is no (interpretive) rule for compound formation that could produce the idiomatic aspects in the meaning of *Hausmann* and *Kauffrau* by simply combining the words *Haus* and *Mann*, or *Kauf* and *Frau*. In order to account for newly formed but idiomatically interpreted compounds, the generative rule based model must take recourse to analogy, too.

It is a small step, then, to allow for analogy-based processes of extending the lexicon on the basis of already existing entries, as suggested by Agnihotri and Singh. Such a move, deriving from existing words a strategy as formulated in (21) along the lines proposed by Agnihotri and Singh, may be easy to accept for a domain such as human nouns in which compounding is heavily blocked, but its extension to AN compounds in general may seem a bolder move. Note, however, that (22), and the absence of a corresponding strategy for *TeuerN* (expensive) gives us a chance to describe why there are no words like *Teuer.flug* corresponding to *Billig.flug*.

(21) Ns ↔ *Jung*N (an N that is young and became an N only recently)

(22) Ns ↔ *Billig*Ns (an N produced or carried out in a cheap way)

For Hindi, it seems as if the whole compounding process, even nominal compounds is a result of such lexicon-based word formation strategies (Agnihotri 1997).

Two questions arise. First, we must describe and explain why the unrestricted merge operation we postulate for German compounding is inapplicable in certain domains, as we have just argued. I would suggest that we can make word formation strategies directly responsible for this in terms of blocking: the presence of more specific rules in a certain domain (word formation strategies) blocks the application of the more general process (merge). Second, one may wonder whether word formation strategies also yield recursive structures. Since *Edel.jung.unternehmer* 'noble-young-industrial' or *Billig.leicht.fahrrad* 'cheap-light-bike' are wellformed, the answer is positive.

8. The present paper has tried to capture a number of restrictions on compound formation in German. We have identified two types: P+N, Num+N, and Q+N combinations, and also dvandva compounds that are (generally) out as simple compounds but may figure as non-head left parts of larger compounds. Other constraints, such as those in the AN domain, are not ignored in non-head positions.

For the former type, we argued that the ill-formed structures are in fact generated by the morphological component, but they cannot enter syntactic structures because an incorrect category specification will be produced. In the model we propose, compound formation differs from the generation of syntactic (base) structures only in the status of merge: it applies optionally in the lexicon, but is always a triggered process in the syntax. To the extent that this difference can be ignored, this means that recursion in compounds and in phrases comes about by the same mechanism.

AN compounds suggest that this picture must be refined. The strong lexical restrictions we observe here do not disappear in non-head contexts. This suggests that these constraints are due to lexicon-internal regularities. We have speculated that AN compounds do not arise from the standard merge operation, but are rather due to word formation strategies in the sense of Agnihotri and Singh. If correct, this implies that recursive structures can indeed arise by two different mechanisms in natural language.

REFERENCES

Agnihotri, R.K. 1997. Is ghuRsavaar a compound? Hindi compounds revisited. Ms., Delhi.

Chomsky, N. 1970. Remarks on Nominalizations. In Jacobs, R. and P. Rosenbaum (eds.). *Readings in English transformational grammar.* Waltham: Ginn. 184-221.

Chomsky, N. 1981. *Lectures on government and binding.* Dordrecht: Foris.

Chomsky, N. 1993. A Minimalist Program for Linguistic Theory. In Ken Hale and Samuel Keyser (eds.) *The View from building 20.* Cambridge: MIT Press. 1-58.

Chomsky, N. 1995. *The minimalist program.* Cambridge, Mass.: MIT-Press.

Chomsky, N. 2005. On phases. Ms., MIT.

Fanselow. G. 1981. *Zur Syntax und Semantik der Nominalkomposition.* Tübingen: Niemeyer.

Fanselow, G. 1985a. Zur Stellung der Wortbildung im System kognitiver Module. *Linguistische Berichte* 96, 91-126.

Fanselow, G. 1985b. What is a possible complex word? In: J. Toman (ed.) *Studies in German Grammar.* Dordrecht: Foris: 289-318.

Fanselow, G. 1988. Word Syntax and Semantic Principles. *Yearbook of Morphology* 1988: 95-122.

Höhle, T. 1985. On Composition and Derivation: The Constituent Structure of Secondary Words in German. In J. Toman (ed.) *Studies in German grammar.* Dordrecht: Foris: 119-176.

Lees, R. 1960. *The grammar of English nominalizations.* The Hague: Mouton.

Lieber, R. 1980. *On the organization of the lexicon.* Bloomington, Ind.: IULC.

Lieber, R. 1983. Argument Linking and Compounds in English. *Linguistic Inquiry* 14, 251-286.

Selkirk, E. 1982. *The syntax of words.* Cambridge, Mass.: MIT-Press.

Singh, R. and R.K. Agnihotri 1997. *Hindi morphology – A word based description.* Delhi: Motilalal Banarsidass.

Speas, M. 1990. *Phrase structure in natural language.* Dordrecht : Kluwer.

NOTES

1. The internal structure of German compounds will be indicated by inserting a dot between the words the compound is composed of. Of course, this dot is not part of German orthography.

2. The differences in the location of heads between syntax and compounds is smaller than it appears, because movement may change linear order in the syntax but not in compounds.
3. Focus particles and coordinative conjunctions might be exceptions.
4. There are a few lexicalized exceptions, such as *Zwischen.eiszeit* 'between. ice age' (interglacial time), which refers to the warm ages between two ice ages rather than to an ice age sitting between two other ice ages.
5. Again, there are a few exceptions such as *Vor.garten* 'before.garden' referring to a garden in front of a house.
6. We have no answer to the question as to why compounds with e.g. *in* are blocked while *vor* and *hinter* participate in compounding easily.
7. Note that the lexicon itself is not governed by a principle requiring that each morpheme belongs to one of the parts of speech. Cf. our above discussion of *Pseudo* 'pseudo' and related items.
8. The word is acceptable and in use in its idiomatic reading "complete loser".
9. In fact, the item specific constraints on PN and QN compounds occur in a domain where the merge operation applies freely. This means that both options may be realized in natural language.

19

Morphosyntax of Hindi Infinitives

Rajesh Kumar

1. Introduction

Some elements in languages do not seem to have clearly distinct categorical status. Hindi infinitives seem to be one of them. In this paper, I suggest that infinitives in Hindi do not display the characteristics of a particular grammatical category or linguistic phrase. Further, I argue that they can be called mixed category. Mixed categories (MC hereafter) such as English gerund phrases, Koran Type III nominalization, and infinitive phrases in Spanish and Romance languages have been discussed in Pullum 1991, Yoon 1996a, b, Lapointe 1998 among others. Despite their divergent view on the analysis of the MC, there are some consistent and theory-neutral facts that every analysis must account for. First, internally MC shows verbal properties, while externally it has nominal distribution. Second, even though it may not be a universal property, as Yoon (1996a) points out, so-called nominalizer uniformity is cross-linguistically observed in languages such as English, Spanish, Korean, Quechua, etc. In other words, the same (de)verbal form is used in both lexical and phrasal nominalizations. Third, despite mixed properties of the MC, it is not clear whether the MCs are exocentric like genuine headless constructions. MCs have consistent endocentric phrasal properties which is hard to dispense with in any analyses. Hence most researchers try to analyze the MC in accordance with endocentricity. Fourth, as Malouf (1998) points out, so-called phrasal coherence is cross-linguistically observed in the MC. In other words, at some point in the structure of the MC nominal and verbal properties are categorically distinctive.

In this paper, we will examine Hindi infinitive constructions with regard to the above discussed four properties, in particular, and argue for the lexical and phrasal nominalizations on the basis of verbal infinitive form in Hindi. In section 2.1, we will briefly introduce the verbal morphology of infinitive forms in Hindi. In section 2.2 we will discuss the phrasal nominalizations on the basis of the verbal infinitive forms. In section 2.2.1 we will describe the internal nominal property of the infinitive phrase. In section 2.2.1 we will discuss the external nominal property of the infinitive phrase. In section 2.2.3 we will show that the infinitive phrase also has the verbal property internally. In 2.3 we will argue that the (de)verbal lexical noun is also derived on the basis of the infinitive form. Finally in section 2.4 we will summarize the discussion in section 2.

2. The morphology of the infinitive verb

The example in (1) shows the possible alternations of the verb 'play'. Traditionally the verb stem ending -naa has been analyzed as the infinitival form of the verb. Hence the example in (1a) corresponds to the infinitival form of the verb 'play'; (1b) corresponds to the third person masculine singular imperfective (present) form whereas (1c) is masculine singular perfective form. The examples in (1d) and (1e) are periphrastic expressions of the present continuous and the participle forms, respectively.

(1) a. khel-naa — to play (infinitive)
b. khel-taa — plays (present)
c. khel-aa — played (perfect)
d. khel rahaa hai — is playing (present progressive)
e. khel-te hue — while playing (participle)

There are certain auxiliary verbs which require infinitival verb forms, with no other forms allowed. For example, the auxiliary verb cahiye in (2), which corresponds to an English auxiliary verb 'should', can co-occur with the verb ending '-naa' only.

(2) aapko har din kriket khelnaa/*khel-taa/*khel-aa caahiye
you-DAT every day cricket play-INF/plays/played should.
'You should play cricket every day.'

The auxiliary verb hai 'is' always takes an infinitive complement in dative subject constructions as shown in (3).

(3) raakesh ko jaanaa/*jaataa/*gayaa hai
Rakesh DAT go-INF/goes/went is
'Rakesh has to go.'

The other auxiliaries such as paRnaa 'must' also take infinitival complements as shown in (4). The auxiliary paRnaa 'must' inflects for different tenses (present, past and future), aspects (perfect), numbers (singular and plural) and gender (masculine and feminine) and hence paR-taa in (4) corresponds to the habitual form and it should co-occur only with the infinitival form of the verb.

(4) mujhe har din skuul aanaa/*aataa/*aayaa paR-taa hai
I-DAT everyday school come-INF must (in HAB) is
'I have to come to School every day.'

Therefore agreeing with the traditional view, we also claim that the verb ending '-naa' corresponds to the infinitive form.

2. Phrasal nominalization (Internal syntax of an NP)

In this section, we will show that the infinitive phrase has some internal property of noun phrases. The subject argument (henceforth subjectoid) within the infinitive phrase is followed by a postposition which corresponds to the genitive case, while in the case of a pronoun it is inflected for the genitive form, just like regular noun phrases. That is, the subjectoids of infinitive phrases are exactly like the possessive determiners of ordinary NPs as shown in (5) and (6).

(5) a. mukesh kaa ghar
Mukesh GEN house
'Mukesh's house'

b. mukesh kii kitaab[1]
Mukesh GEN book
'Mukesh's book'

c. tumhaarii kaar
your (YOU-GEN) car
'your car'

(6) a. tumhaaraa naavel likha-naa mere liye ek sarpraaiz thaa
your novel write-INF me for one surprise was
'Your writing a novel was a surprise for me.'
(=/= 'Writing your novel was a surprise for me.')

b. tumhaaraa gaanaa gaanaa mujh-ko achaa nahiiN lagataa hai
your song sing-INF I-DAT good not seem-HAB is
'I don't like your singing a song.'
(=/= 'I don't like singing your song.')

c. mukesh kaa sigreT piinaa mujh ko achaa nahiiN lagtaa hai
Mukesh GEN cigarette drink-INF I- DAT like not seem is
'I don't like Mukesh's smoking a cigarette.'
(=/='I don't like smoking Mukesh's cigarette.')

d. raakesh kaa biif khaanaa uske dostoN ko pasand nahiiN thaa
rakesh GEN beef eat-ING he-DAT friend-OBL to like not was
'Rakesh's eating beef upset his friends.'
(=/= 'Eating Rakesh's beef upset his friends.')

As English translation shows in (6), the subjectoids are not associated with the following noun but with the whole infinitive phrase and function as a subject of the phrase. Hence the infinitive phrases in (6) suggest the following structure.

(7)

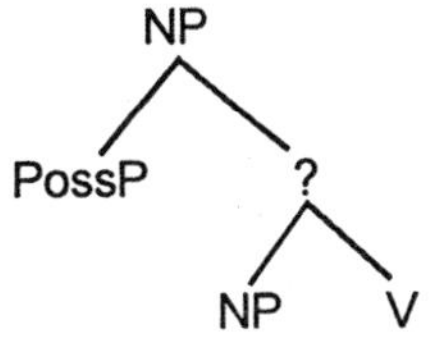

3. Phrasal Nominalization (External syntax of a NP)

This section shows that the infinitive phrases also have some external properties of noun phrases. First, no extraction is allowed from the subjectoid in an infinitive phrase just like a possessive in a normal NP cannot be extracted as it will result into violation of Ross's left branch condition. This is similar to the other languages such as English, Korean, etc. As (8a) shows, relativization of possessive noun phrases leads a sentence to ungrammaticality; similarly, (8b) shows, extraction of possessive phrase within the infinitive phrase also leads to ungrammaticality. The possessive phrase in (8b) is extra posed.

(8) a. *raakesh kaa$_i$ jo mohan ko t$_i$ ghar pasand nahiiN hai
rakesh GEN that Mohan to house like not is
'Rakesh's that Mohan does not like house'
(Intended: 'Rakesh's house that Mohan does not like')

b. */? sigreT piinaa mujh ko achaa nahiiN lagtaa hai mukesh kaa
cigarette drink-INF me to like not seem is Mukesh GEN
'Of Mukesh, I don't like (his) smoking a cigarette.'
(Intended: 'I don't like Mukesh's smoking a cigarette.')

Secondly, infinitive phrases can be the complements of postpositions. Postpositions can only take noun phrases as their complement as shown in (9). All the three examples in (9) have postpositions meN 'in', ke liye 'for', and par 'on'. They have kamraa 'room', raakesh 'Rakesh', and tebul 'table' as the compliments of the postpositions.

(9) a. kamrae meN koii nahiiN hai
room in anybody not is
'There is no one in the room.'

b. raakesh ke liye ek kursii laao
Rakesh for one chair bring-IMP
'Bring a chair for Rakesh'

c. tebul par kyaa hai

table on what is
'What is on the table?'

Exactly the same postpositions that are used in (9) can appear following the infinitive phrases, as shown in (10). In the presence of a, the verb forms other than infinitive are ungrammatical.

(10)a. raakesh ke biif khaane/*khaate meN uske dostoN ko koii
rakesh GEN beef eat-INF/while eating in he-DAT friend-OBL to any
aaptti nahiiN hai
objection not is
'Rakesh's friends do not have any objection in his eating beef.'

b. rakesh ke biif khaane/*khaata par uske dostoN ko koii
rakesh GEN beef eat-INF/eats on he-DAT friend-OBL to any
aaptti nahiiN hai
objection not is
'Rakesh's friends do not have any objection on his eating beef.'

c. rakesh ko biif khaane/*khayaa ke liye uske dostoN
rakesh DAT beef eat-INF/ate for he-DAT friend-OBL
ne majbuur kiyaa
ERG forced
'Rakesh's friends forced him to eat beef.'

Another piece of evidence for the nominal status of infinitive phrases comes from the variation on the ending -naa in infinitive verbs. In Hindi, nouns that end with -aa show systematic variation with -aa changing to oblique form -e when a postposition follows a noun. For example, as shown in (11), regular noun phrases ending with -aa become ungrammatical without replacing the ending by the oblique form when they are followed by postpositions.

(11)a. *laRkaa ko
laRke ko
boy to

b. *tangaa par
tange par
horse-cart on

Similarly we can find exactly the same variation in infinitive verbs when they are followed by postpositions as shown in (12).

(12)a. raakesh ne sariitaa se [paani laa-ne/*naa] ko kahaa
Rakesh ERG Sarita to water bring-INF for say-PST-mas
'Rakesh told Sarita to bring water.'

b. rakesh ne sariitaa se [caaye pii-ne/*naa] ko kahaa
Rakesh ERG Sarita to tea drink-INF for say-PST-mas
'Rakesh told Sarita to drink tea.'

In addition, in Hindi noun phrases, genitive markers usually appear between two nouns. It is evident in (13) when a genitive marker appears between the infinitive phrase and another noun phrase; also infinitive form changes to the oblique case due to the intervening genitive case marking postposition.

(13)ramesh kii dimaagii haalat ko dekhte hue maiN ne
Ramesh GEN mental situation DAT see PRSP I-ERG
dost ko apmaanit karne (kii baat) kii andekhi kar dii
friend DAT insult do-INF GEN matter GEN disregard do give-PST
'When considering Ramesh's mental situation, I disregarded insulting his friend.'

Finally we find another piece of evidence for the external nominal status of the infinitive phrases on the basis of the coordination. Noun phrases are coordinated by the conjunction aur 'and' as shown in (14).

(14)a. [raam aur shyaam] skuul jaa rahe haiN
Raam and Shyamm school go PROG are
'Ram and Shyam are going to School.'

b. maiN [seb aur kele] khaataa huuN
I apples and bananas eat-HAB am
'I eat apples and bananas.'

Note, that a regular noun phrases can also be coordinated with infinitive phrases as shown in (15).

(15)a. raakesh kaa kitaab paRnaa aur uskii imaandaarii ne mujhe
rakesh GEN book read-INF and his honesty ERG I-DAT
cakit kar diyaa
surprise do give-PERF
'Rakesh's reading the book and his honesty surprised me.'

b. raakesh kaa aalas aur uskaa der se ghar aanaa uskii maaN ko
rakesh GEN laziness and his late home come-INF his mother to
acchaa nahiiN lagtaa hai
good not feel is
'Rakesh's laziness and his coming home late bother his mother.'

Hence the discussion in this section strongly suggests that the infinitive phrase has the external distribution of noun phrases. Before proceeding to the next section, let us point out that with regard to the coordination fact, the following sentence in (16) also suggests that infinitive phrases have the internal structure of the VP. As far as the coordination is concerned, the bracketed phrase corresponds to the VP coordination.

(16)raakesh kaa [ghar becnaa aur kaar khariidnaa] uskii patnii ko
rakesh GEN house sell-INF and car buy-INF his wife to
pasand nahiiN thaa
like not was
'Rakesh's selling the house and buying the car upset his wife.'

The data examined so far lead us to the following conclusion about the syntactic structure of infinitive phrases in Hindi. Infinitive phrase externally have nominal qualities whereas, internally they have the features of a VP. Before we draw any final conclusion with regard to the syntactic structure of the infinitive phrase, we need to get more convincing evidence for the internal VP property of the infinitive phrase, which will be discussed in the next section.

4. Internal syntax of a VP

In this section we will show that part of the infinitive phrase following the possessive/genitive phrase have functions similar to that of a Verb Phrase. First, as we already saw in the preceding sections, the infinitive form of the verb takes a bare NP as its complement as far as it can take one. As the contrast in (17) shows, the genitive marker cannot intervene between the infinitive verb and its object complement, suggesting the verbal status of the infinitive itself.

(17)a. raakesh kaa kitaab paRnaa
Rakesh Gen book read-INF
'Rakesh's reading the book'

b. *raakesh kaa kitaab kaa paRnaa
Rakesh Gen book Gen read-INF
'Rakesh's reading of the book'

Second piece of evidence for the internal VP status of the infinitive phrase comes from the fact that it can be modified by adverbs but not by adjectives. As the examples in (18) suggest, adjectives modify noun phrases whereas adverbials are not allowed to modify nouns. The reverse will be true for the verb. That is to say, adjectives are not allowed to modify a verb phrase whereas the adverbs are permitted to modify verb phrases. Hence if the infinitive phrase has internal verbal property, the same adverbs disallowed in (18) should be permitted to modify a verb phrase while the adjectival modification allowed in (18) should not be permitted for VP modification. This prediction is borne out as shown in (19).

(18)a. *jor se aavaaz
loudly voice

a'. tej aavaaz

loud voice
'loud voice'
b. *dhiire kaar
'slowly car'
b'.dhimii kaar
'slow car'

(19)a. raakesh kaa jor se kitaab paRnaa
rakesh GEN loudly book read-INF
'Rakesh's reading the book loudly'
a'.*raakesh kaa tej kitaab paRnaa
rakesh GEN loud book read-INF
'Rakesh's reading the book loudly'
b. suniitaa kaa dhire kaar calaana
suniitaa GEN slowly car drive-INF
'Sunita's driving a car slowly.'
b'.*suniitaa kaa dhimii kaar calaana
Sunita GEN slow car drive-INF
'Sunita's driving a car slow'

On the same note, yet another piece of evidence comes from the placement of demonstratives. Usually, demonstratives are not permitted to modify the infinitive phrase. The examples in (20) clearly confirm the above mentioned point. Again, it suggests that the infinitive internally display verbal property.

(20)a. * yeh raakesh kaa US choRnaa
this Rakesh Gen US leave-INF
'*this Rakesh's leaving the U.S.'
b. *raakesh ka yeh US choRnaa
rakesh GEN this US leave-INNF
'*Rakesh's this leaving the U.S.'

Relativization provides another piece of evidence in support of internal verbal status of the infinitive phrase. Infinitive phrase do not seem to be modified by restrictive relative clauses, however, a regular noun phrases can be modified by a restrictive relative clause as shown in (21a). The same relative clause cannot modify the infinitive phrase though, as shown in (21b).

(21)a. kitaab jo raakesh ko pasand nahiiN hai
book that Rakesh DAT like not is
'the book that Rakesh did not like'
b. '*raakesh kaa sigreT piinaa jo raajesh ko pasand nahiiN hai
rakesh GEN cigarette drink that rajesh DAT like not is
'Rakesh's smoking a cigarette that Rajesh did not like'

Finally, infinitive phrases can undergo the VP-internal process such as scrambling while the noun phrase cannot. As shown in (22), the direct object and the dative object of the verb can be scrambled around.

(22)a. rakesh kaa sariitaa ko ek kitaab denaa
Rakesh GEN Sarita DAT one book give-INF
'Rakesh's giving a book to Sarita'
b. rakesh kaa ek kitaab sariitaa ko denaa
Rakesh GEN one book Sarita DAT give-INF

On the contrary, the scrambling inside the regular noun phrase is not allowed as the contrast in (23) shows.

(23)a. raakesh ka siiTii kaa vidhvans
rakesh Gen city Gen destruction
'Rakesh's destruction of the city'
b. *siiTii kaa raakesh kaa vidhvans
city Gen rakesh Gen destruction

Therefore the data examined in this section clearly suggest that the infinitive phrases have the internal VP structure. Putting the discussion so far together, we can propose the following syntactic structure for the infinitive phrase as in (24), which is not final and should be reconsidered with regard to endocentricity and phrasal coherence.

(24)

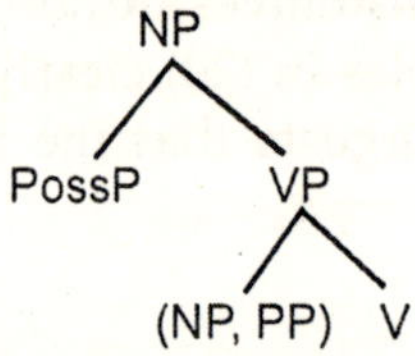

5. Lexical nominalizations

In this section we will show that the same infinitive form of the verb, which functions as the verbal head in the case of the phrasal nominalization, can also function as a lexical noun, i.e. deverbal noun.

First, the infinitive form of the verb itself can appear where regular noun phrases can occur, i.e., subject, object position of transitive verb, and in particular can be followed by postpositions. That is, they show nominal distribution to some degree, as shown in (25).

(25)a. likha-naa mere shOkh hai
Write-INF my hobby is
'Writing is my hobby.'
b. mujh-ko likh-naa pasand hai
I-DAT write-INF like is
'I like writing'
c. maiN likh-naa pasand kar-taa huuN
I write-INF like do-Hab am

'I like writing'

d. gaa-ne meN mazaa aataa hai
sing-INF in enjoyment come is
'Singing is fun'

In the above example the infinitive verb in (25a) functions as a subject of the sentence, in (25b-c) function as objects of conjunct verbs, and in (25d) is a complement of the postposition.

More direct evidence for the status of the lexical noun of the infinitive comes from the availability of the adjective modifiers, which contrast with the infinitive phrases as we saw in section 4 that the infinitive phrases cannot be modified by the adjectives. As the contrast in the English translation shows in (26), once the infinitive form of the verb is modified by an adjective as in (26a) and (26c), it does not function as a verb which is related to the event or process but it functions as a regular noun which is related to the result. On the contrary if it is modified by an adverb as in (26b) and (26d), it corresponds to the verb which is the head of the infinitive phrase as we discussed in section 4.

(26)a. raakesh ka tej gaanaa
rakesh GEN loud sing-INF
'Rakesh's loud song' (=/= 'Rakesh's singing loudly')

b. raakesh kaa jor se gaanaa
rakesh GEN loudly sing-INF
'Rakesh's singing loudly' (=/= Rakesh's loud song)

c. raakesh kaa mahNgaa khaanaa
rakesh GEN expensive eat-INF
'Rakesh's expensive food'

d. raakesh kaa dhire khaanaa
rakesh GEN slowly eat-INF
'Rakesh's eating slowly'

Another very strong piece of evidence in support of the claim that the infinitive form of the verb can be a (de)verbal lexical noun comes from the possibility of adding a plural marker –e to the (de)verbal counterpart of the infinitive, while the verbal head of the infinitive phrase cannot be attached with the plural marker as shown in (27).[2] As just pointed out, adjectival modification of the infinitives in (27a) and (27c) renders the infinitives (de)verbal lexical noun and hence they can be pluralized. On the contrary, true infinitive verbs in (27b) and (27d) cannot be pluralized.

(27)a. raakesh ke tej gaane
rakesh GEN loud sing-INF-Pl
'Rakesh's loud songs'

b. *raakesh ke jor se gaane

rakesh GEN loudly sing-INF-Pl
'*Rakesh's singings loudly'

c. raakesh ke mahNge khaane
rakesh GEN expensive eat-INF-Pl
'Rakesh's expensive food'

d. *raakesh ke dhire khaane
rakesh GEN slowly eat-INF-Pl
'*Rakesh's eatings slowly'

Furthermore we can find more evidence in support of the nominal status of the deverbal lexical noun. A (de)verbal lexical noun can be modified by demonstratives, whereas the modification of an infinitive phrase with demonstrative is not permitted. Hence as shown in (28), the (de)verbal lexical noun modified by the demonstratives in (28a) and (28b) are grammatical while the infinitive verb modified by the demonstratives in (28b) and (28d) are ungrammatical.

(28)a. voh tej gaanaa
that loud sing-INF
'that loud song'

b. *voh jor se gaanaa
that loudly sing-INF
'that singing loudly'

c. voh mahNgaa khaanaa
that expensive eat-INF
'that expensive food'

d. *voh dhire khaanaa
that slowly eat-INF
'that eating slowly'

Finally, it is possible to modify a (de)verbal noun by a restrictive relative clause. We pointed it out in section 4 that infinitive phrases cannot be modified by a restrictive relative clause. However, the (de)verbal nouns from an infinitive can be modified as shown in (29). The (de)verbal lexical noun modified by the relative clause in (29a) and (29c) are grammatical while the infinitive phrase modified by the relative clause in (27b) and (27d) are degraded in grammaticality.

(29)a. raakesh kaa tej gaanaa jo kisii ko pasand nahiiN hai
rakesh GEN loud sing-INF that anybody DAT like not is
'Rakesh's loud song that nobody liked'

b. *?raakesh kaa jor se gaanaa jo kisii ko pasand nahiiN hai
rakesh GEN loudly sing-INF that anybody DAT like not is
'Rakesh's singing loudly that nobody liked'

c. raakesh kaa mahNgaa khaanaa jo kisii ko pasand nahiiN hai
rakesh GEN expensive eat-INF that anybody DAT like not is

'Rakesh's expensive food that nobody liked'

d. *?raakesh kaa dhire khaanaa jo kisii ko pasand nahiiN hai
rakesh GEN slowly eat-INF that anybody DAT like not is
'Rakesh's eating slowly that nobody liked'

Therefore the discussion in this section strongly suggests that the same infinitive form of the verb that is used in the infinitive phrase can undergo lexical nominalization and hence can function just like a regular noun. This conclusion also suggests that the nominalizer uniformity, which was pointed out in Yoon (1996a), holds in Hindi as well. That is, the infinitive form of the verb can be the anchor of both lexical and phrasal nominalizations.

6. Vaalaa and infinitives

So far in this paper, we have observed that the infinitives do not seem to display characteristics of a particular phrasal category. On the contrary, they are exhibiting features of a verb phrase internally and the features of a noun phrase externally. The vaalaa suffix in Hindi further shows this tension. With the help of vaalaa we will show that infinites in Hindi really do not belong to a category; and it is a mixed-category.

Vaalaa attaches to may lexical and phrasal items belonging to many grammatical categories in Hindi. Two prominent of them are nouns and infinitives. It's not at all a problem when vaalaa attaches to a noun. The question is when vaalaa attaches to an infinitive, does it attach to a verbal infinitive or a nominal infinitive or a noun? The answer to this question substantiates the claim that the infinitives in Hindi are neither nouns nor verbs but, the mixed category. We will provide, in this section, an account of vaalaa constructions in Hindi. First of all, we present a brief distribution of vaalaa in Hindi.

It also functions like an agentive marker in Hindi as in (31) and (32).

(30) [N[N sabzi] + vaalaa] 'vegitable seller'
[N[N dudh] +vaalaa] 'milk man'
[N[N akhwaar] + vaalaa] 'Newspaper seller'

(31) sabzii-vaalaa aaj nahiiN aayegaa
vegetable seller today not come-FUT
'The vegetable seller will not come today.'

(32) akhbaar-vaalaa paise maaNg rahaa hai
newspaper seller money ask PROG is
'The newspaper seller is asking for money.'

Nouns with vaalaa suffixes can have distribution of an adjective.

(33) mujh ko duudhvaalii caay acchii lagtii hai

I DAT milk with tea good seem is
'I like tea with milk.'

(34) hindiivaale chhatra kal piknik par jaa rahe haiN
Hindi students tomorrow picnic on go PROG are
'Hindi students are going on a picnic tomorrow.'

To a great extent, vaalaa in Hindi behaves like a postposition. Unlike most of the postpositions in Hindi, vaalaa is not a morphological case marker. However, nouns that are followed by a vaalaa suffix are in the oblique form. Whether a morphological case marker or not, a postposition in Hindi converts a noun into oblique. This suggests that the vaalaa suffix can be classified as a postposition in Hindi. Let's consider examples in (35) and (36)

(35) a. *larkaa ko
boy DAT
'To the boy'

b. larke ko
boy (OBL) DAT
'To the boy'

(36) taangaa+ vaalaa = taangevaalaa 'horse carriage owner/driver'
rikshaa + vaalaa = rikshevaalaa 'rickshaw puller'
baajaa + vaalaa = baajevaalaa 'band man'

Let's now see what happens when vaalaa suffix is added to an infinitive. The outcome is definitely grammatical as this is a very productive pattern in Hindi. Once again, the question is whether we add the suffix to a nominal or a verb a verbal entity? Any of the answers to this question suggest that Hindi infinitives are really a mixed category. In other words, they are neither a pure noun nor a verb. Let's look at the following examples.

(37) *Karnaa + vaalaa
Do vaalaa
karnevaalaa
'doer'

(38) rakesh jaane vaalaa hai
Rakesh go-INF-OBL PP is
'Rakesh is about to go.'

(39) varsha hone vaalii hai
rain happen-INF-OBL-PP is
'It is about to rain.'

(40) yehaan kaar calaane vaaloN kii kamii nahiiN hai
here car drive-INF-OBL GEN-OBL GEN shortage not is
'There is no shortage of the people who can drive car.'

(41) mujhe jaane kii jaldii hai
I DAT go-INF-OBL GEN hurry is
'I am in a hurry to go.'

In the above sentences the infinitival forms of the verbs behave just like a regular nominal. We can add a vaalaa suffix to an infinitive just like can add the same to any other noun. This is yet another piece of evidence to argue that the infinitives in Hindi are sometimes like a regular noun. They occur in the subcategorized position of the verb just like any an NP. They are followed by a genitive case marker (40) where genitive case in Hindi connects the two nouns and specifies their relationship. Thus, Hindi infinitives are real type of mixed category. They have nominal as well as verbal properties.

7. Conclusion

In this paper we have examined the morphosyntax infinitive constructions in Hindi. We have shown that the Hindi infinitive phrase has the internal syntax of a verb phrase, the partial internal syntax of a noun phrase, and the external distribution of a noun phrase. We suggest that we should recognize both VP and NP structure inside the infinitive phrase. This conclusion, however, does not endorse the exocentric structure of the infinitive phrase. The infinitive phrase is too endocentric to analyze as the exocentric structure. As far as the proposed structure in this paper remains as it is, we come to admit the exocentric structure of the infinitive phrase, raising a lot of theoretical and empirical questions. Also we have shown that the same infinitive form that is used at the infinitive phrase can function as a lexical noun. We provided the empirical evidence showing that the lexical noun counterparts of the infinitives behave differently from the infinitive verbs, which suggests that they are genuine lexical nouns. We pointed it out that the nominalizer uniformity also holds in Hindi as far as the nominalization on the basis of the infinitive is concerned. At this point, the analysis that meets the theoretical challenge with regard to the endocentricity remains an issue of further examination. However, based on the empirical discussions, we suggest that the nominalizer uniformity and phrasal coherence hold in Hindi as well.

REFERENCES

Abney, Steven P. 1987. The English Noun Phrase in its sentential aspect, Ph.D. Dissertation. MIT.

Butt. M. 1994. The structure of complex predicates in Hindi-Urdu, Ph.D. Dissertation. Stanford University.

Grimshaw, Jane 1990. *Argument structure*. Cambridge, Mass.: MIT Press.

Lapointe, Steven 1993. Dual Lexical Categories and the Syntax of Mixed Category Phrases. In A. Kathol and M. Bernstein (eds.) *Proceedings of ESCOL*, 199-210.

Lapointe, Steven 1998. Dual Lexical Categories Vs. Phrasal Conversion in the Analysis of Gerund Phrases. Ms., University of California, Davis.

Malouf, Rob 2000. *Mixed categories in the hierarchical lexicon*. CSLI Publications: Stanford.

Pullum, Geoffrey 1991. English Nominal Gerund Phrases as Noun Phrases with Verb-Phrase Heads. *Linguistics* 29: 763-799.

Yoon, James 1996a. A syntactic account of category-changing phrasal morphology: nominalizations in English and Korean. In H.D. Ahn et al. (eds.) *Morphosyntax in generative grammar*. Seoul: Hanshin, 63-86.

Yoon, James 1996b. English Nominal Gerund Phrases as Phrasal Zero Derivations. *Linguistics* 34: 339-356.

NOTES

1. There are three different morphological variants of the GEN/POSS marker *ka* in Hindi: *ka* (masculine singular), *ke* (masculine plural) and *kii* (feminine singular and plural).
2. Similar to many other languages, plural formation of the (de)vebal noun is not a productive pattern in Hindi as well. In particular, for the lack of the plural formation of the phrasal nominalization, we can appeal to semantics. Given the observation in Grimshaw (1990) with regard to the 'complex event nominals' that plural marking is disallowed even in purely nominal constructions, we could invoke semantics to rule out plurality on the infinitive phrases as well as English gerund heads.

20

Compositionality in Complex Predicates

Achla M. Raina

Keywords: Complex Predicates, Grammaticalisation, Generative Lexicon, Argument and Event Unification

1. Introduction

Complex Predicates[1] (CP) consisting of an open-class host predicate and what is sometimes called a Light Verb (LV) are a common phenomenon in languages of the Indo-Aryan family, Japanese, Korean, etc. (Jesperson, 1940; Hook, 1991; Matsumoto, 1996). Complex predication has traditionally been associated with *grammaticalisation* of lexical elements such as verbs. The grammaticalised or semantically diluted light verb (LV) is assumed to restructure the semantics of a host predicate, imposing aspectual and other constraints on the event structure. However, the question of whether the semantics of CPs is non-compositional or composed from its constituents remains an open issue. In this paper, we consider the question of compositionality in CPs. We argue for a two-pronged approach that seeks to capture the semantic regularities (and irregularities) underlying complex predication at a finer grain taking into account argument and event structure, as well as aspectual and other temporal properties of complex predicates. We propose a compositional account in terms of a semantic type system along the lines of Generative Lexicons (Pustejovsky, 1995) that approaches the full semantic specification of complex predicates. Drawing on Indic languages such as Hindi, Urdu and Kashmiri, we propose a model involving event structure *unification* and *argument binding*. These compositional procedures are argued to be adequate for at least a class of CPs which exhibit a certain degree of transparency in semantic restructuring. Our investigation throws up instances of complex predicates that seem to resist a strict compositionality based treatment thus indicating that non-compositional, constructional mechanisms may be at work in these cases.

1.1 Predicate Composition

Syntactic aspects of complex predication have been analysed in terms of compositional syntactic rules (Jayaseelan, 1984; Matsumoto, 1996; Folli, et al. 2005; Yokota, 2005). Matsumoto offers a control analysis of complex predication, positing embedded sentential constituents with implicit arguments. Matsumoto's analysis of the Japanese complex predicates has been contested on the grounds that it does not address the semantic interrelationships between complex predicates composed from a given host predicate (Yokota, 2005). Yokota proposes argument transfer as the mechanism for restructuring the argument structure of the host in complex predicates. Yet another analysis addressing argument structure regularities can be seen in Butt's account of complex predication in Urdu (Butt, 1995; 2003), which relies on argument fusion in A-structure along the lines proposed in Jackendoff (1990). Butt posits a distinction between LVs and HVs in terms of event transparency, which is claimed to trigger complex predicate formation with LVs and an argument fusion at the A-structure level. Brugman (2001) in a cognitive grammar-based treatment of CPs, shifts the focus from argument structure to event structure, viewing HV-LV relationship as one of polysemy. Butt (2003), who opposes lexical compositionality for CPs, arguing that they be determined on a verb-by-verb basis, concedes that constraints on composition are semantic in nature: ". . .the CPs are not formed within the lexicon," but are "the result of the syntactic composition of two predicational elements." Yet, since CPs do form a composite unit, the compositional constraints must also reflect their semantics.

The LVs participating in complex predication have been traditionally considered to have undergone a process of *grammaticalisation* involving semantic dilution (also termed *bleaching*). The grammaticalisation process is viewed as a cline (Hook, 1991):

heavy (full) verb → light verb → auxiliary → clitic → affix

Here we show that LVs themselves are graded in the degree of semantic dilution; while a few retain some of their heavy verb (HV) semantics, and others undergo fuller grammaticalisation. We consider LVs as independent lexicalizations, although for some of the less diluted LVs it may be possible to obtain their semantics from the corresponding HVs through a semantic type shift.

The complex predication process affects both the argument and event semantics of the CP. The semantics of the composite are obtained by predicate-predicate composition, and we distinguish two compositional mechanisms:

(*a*) *Unification*: can apply to both argument and event structures of the two predicates. Typically the more specific constraint is retained in the complex predicate. The event structure of the CP results from event unification where aspectual and other fine-grained temporal constraints of the LV are imposed on the host.

(*b*) *Binding:* one of the CP constituents serves as an argument in a valence slot for the other. Argument binding between a superordinate type in the LV and a more specific type in the host tends to select the more specific type for the CP.

As pointed out earlier, LVs appear to exhibit a gradation from those retaining much of their HV semantics, mostly in AVs and NVs, to those performing a purely grammatical function, as in some VVs. In particular, VV composites exhibit a range of dilution behaviour, where some LVs seem to be completely divested of the full verb semantics, while others retain some semantic features, thus constituting a "semantic dilution cline".

1. 2 *Complex Predicate Exemplars*

As an example, consider the attributive/predicative adjective *pareshaan* 'upset' in Hindi/Urdu which is underspecified with respect to its argument structure and event structure properties. These properties are specified variously by the light verbs, *ho* 'be', *ho* 'happen/become' and *kar* 'do', as the following data show:

(1) a. raam apni asaphaltaa se pareshaan hai
Ram self-gen failure with upset be-pres
'Ram is upset over his failure.'

b. raam apnii asaphaltaa se pareshaan huaa
Ram self-gen failure with upset become-past
'Ram became upset over his failure.'

c. raam ne sitaa ko apnii asaphaltaa se pareshaan kiyaa
Ram erg Sita acc self-gen failure with upset do-past
'Ram upset Sita by his failure.'

The adjectival host *pareshaan* by itself takes an animate argument in an experiencer role, and has a stative event structure. This argument is retained in the CPs *pareshaan hai* in (1a) and *pareshaan huaa* in (1b) which take an experiencer as the sole argument. The CP *pareshaan kiyaa* in (1c) takes experiencer and agent as its arguments, where *kar* contributes the agent argument. In addition, these CPs may also take optional adjuncts such as cause which are contributed by the host *pareshaan*.

The event structure properties of the CPs composed with *hai, huaa* and *kiyaa* are as follows:

pareshaan hai: stative
pareshaan huaa: inchoative
pareshaan kiyaa: agentive

Accounting for such event structure distinctions is one of the main objectives of this work, and for this we propose a rich semantic lexicon for LVs such as *ho / kar*, which compose with adjective such as *pareshaan*.

Turning to VV composites, or the so called compound verbs, the host verb *nikal* 'leave' forms a complex predicate with LVs such as *jaa* 'go' and *paD* 'fall'. The host *nikal* is, by itself, underspecified with respect to the aspectual structure properties, which are determined by the LV it combines with.

(2) a. raam har din saat baje kaam par nikal jaataa hai
Ram daily seven o'clock work on leave go be-pres
'Ram leaves for work at seven o'clock everyday.'

b. raam har din saat baje kaam par nikal paDtaa hai
Ram daily seven o'clock work on leave fall be-pres
'Ram leaves for work at seven o'clock everyday.'

The VV predicates *nikal jaa* and *nikal paD* above represent event structure variations involving the completive and inceptive aspects. A similar aspectual contrast is at work in case of the LVs *jaa* 'go' and *uTh* 'stand':

(3) a. sabki ki baat sunkar raam bhi apnii baat keh gayaa
everyone-gen opinion hear-part ram emph self-gen opinion say go-past
'Having heard everyone else, Ram spoke his own mind.'

b. sabki ki baat sunkar raam bhi apnii baat keh uthaa
everyone's opinion hear-part ram emph self-gen opinion say stand-past
'Having heard everyone else, Ram spoke his mind.'

In (3a) *keh gayaa* expresses a completive aspectual structure, but *gayaa* is distinguished from other completive LVs such as *chukaa* in that *gayaa* also imposes a durative constraint on the event: the speaking must have been going on for some time. In terms of the traditionally held aspectual distinctions, *chukaa* imposes an achievement interpretation on the host predicate whereas *gayaa* appears to signal an accomplishment. In (3b), the CP *keh uThaa* exemplifies an inceptive aspect, with a degree of abruptness about it.

Clearly, the event semantic restructuring exemplified in (1-3) presents finely graded distinctions, which constitute a significant challenge for attribute-value models of semantic composition. We propose a semantic type shifting mechanism modelled along the lines of the Generative Lexicon (Pustejovsky, 1995), which employs a rich event and qualia structure, relevant in particular to the analysis of event structure modification in CPs. We show that such a semantic typing system together with compositional generative mechanisms can be used to lexically generate the complex semantic types under discussion here. To handle some of the finer distinctions of aspect, we also extend the event semantics to a schematic progression of the complex event in time.

In the next section we detail the semantic restructuring that adjectival and nominal predicates undergo in complex predicate composition, and discuss the type shifting mechanism that lexically generates such CPs. Section 3 looks at VV composites and models event structure modification by LVs. The semantics of LVs is analyzed and a semantic dilution cline is proposed to account for the varying degrees of LV grammaticalisation. Section 4 examines further constraints on composition involving inflectional variants and polarity effects.

2. NV and AV Complex Predicates

2.1 Event Structure Modification: AV Composites

The NV and AV composites resulting in complex predication in languages such as Hindi and Urdu are a practically unrestricted class. We have looked earlier at AV composites with *pareshaan*; the stative/inchoative feature of the event structure in *pareshaan hai* and *pareshaan huaa* can be elaborated further in the following contrastive examples:

(4) a. raam aajkal apnii asaphaltaa se pareshaan hai
ram nowadays self-gen failure with upset be-pres
'Nowadays, Ram is upset with his failure.'

b. *raam aajkal apnii asaphaltaa se pareshaan huaa
Ram nowadays self-gen failure with upset be-past
'Nowadays, Ram has become upset with his failure.'

c. *raam yeh khabar sunte hi pareshaan hai
Ram this news hear-emph upset be-pres
'Ram is upset on hearing this news.'

d. raam yeh khabar sunte hi pareshan huaa
Ram this news hear-emph upset become-past
'Ram became upset on hearing this news.'

In (4a), the stative *pareshaan hai* can take a durative adverbial, aajkal, which is ruled out with the inchoative *pareshaan huaa* in (4b). In terms of the compositional mechanism, the LV *ho* (become) imposes an inchoative event structure on the resulting CP which rejects the durative temporal structure of the modifier *aajkaal*. Similarly, in (4c), the stative *pareshaan hai* cannot take *sunte hi*, a temporal adjunct, which signals inception of the action denoted by the predicate *sun* 'hear' in the adjunct clause. The inchoative pareshaan huaa on the other hand does take *sunte hi* (4d).

Likewise, the stative/inchoative/agentive contrast between *pareshaan hai / pareshaan hua* on the one hand and *pareshan kiyaa* on the other, is brought out by the following data:

(5) a. *raam jaanbujh kar apnii asaphaltaa se pareshaan hai
ram deliberately self-gen failure with upset be-pres
'Ram is deliberately upset with his failure.'

b. *raam jaanbujh kar apnii asaphaltaa se pareshaan huaa
ram deliberately self-gen failure with upset become-past
'Ram deliberately became upset with his failure.'

c. raam ne jaanbujh kar sitaa ko apni asaphaltaa se pareshaan kiyaa
Ram erg deliberately Sita acc self-gen failure with upset do-past
'Ram deliberately upset Sita with his failure.'

The agentive predicate *pareshaan kar* in (5c) can take a volitional adverbial, *jaanbujh kar*, which is ruled out in both (5a) and (5b) containing stative *pareshaan hai* and inceptive *pareshaan huaa* respectively.

2.2 Event Structure Modification: NV Composites

As stated earlier, a large class of nominal and adjectival predicates forms composites with LVs such as *ho* 'be', *ho/aa* 'become' *kar* 'do'. To differing degrees, verbs such as *de* 'give' and *le* 'take' can also participate in NV complex predication. The data in (6) exemplify a nominal predicate *pasand* 'like' in a complex predicate structure:

(6) a. raam ko siitaa ka gaanaa pasand hai
Ram dat Sita poss sing-nom like be-pres
'Ram likes Sita's singing.'

b. raam ko siitaa ka gaanaa pasand aayaa
Ram dat Sita poss sing-nom like come-past
'Ram got to like Sita's singing.'

c. raam ne siitaa ka gaanaa pasand kiyaa
Ram erg Sita poss sing-nom like do-past
'Ram liked Sita's singing.'

The nominal predicate *pasand*, like the adjectival predicate *pareshaan* discussed earlier, is a stative predicate with an [experiencer, object] argument structure. In the data above, the arguments of *pasand* are retained in the composites with the LVs *ho, aa:* the argument structure for the CPs in (6a) and (6b) is [experiencer, object]. The agentive *kar* in (6c) imposes an [agent, object] structure, as is indicated by the presence of ergative *ne,* where the agent argument of the LV *kar* is unified with the experiencer in *pasand.*

In NV predicates, as is the case with AVs, the event semantics is inherited from the LV. The predicate *pasand* is a stative noun, with [experiencer, object] argument structure and stative event structure. This composes with *ho(*be*), aa,* and *kar* to generate a stative in (6a), an inchoative in (6b), and a processive in (6c). Note that the LV *aa* has lost the feature *motion* present in its HV semantics (*aa,* 'come'). In the compositional process, this semantic feature is imposed on the nominal host to generate the inchoative event type of the CP. These event semantic properties are attested in the following data:

(7) a. raam ko aajkal siitaa ka gaanaa pasand hai
Ram dat nowadays Sita poss sing-nom like be-pres
'Nowadays, Ram likes Sita's singing.'

b. *raam ko aajkal siitaa ka gaanaa pasand aayaa
Ram dat nowadays Sita poss sing-nom like come-pres
'Nowadays, Ram has begun to like Sita's singing.'

c. *raam ko siitaa kaa ganaa sunte hi pasand thaa
Ram dat Sita poss sing-nom hear-emph like be-past
'Ram liked Sita's singing on hearing it.'

d. raam ko siitaa kaa gaanaa sunte hi pasand aayaa
Ram dat Sita poss sing-nom hear-emph like come-past
'Ram got to like Sita's singing on hearing it.'

e. raam ne siitaa kaa gaanaa swayam pasand kiyaa
Ram dat Sita poss sing-nom himself like do-past
'Ram himself liked Sita's singing.'

f. *raam ko siitaa ka gaanaa swayam pasand thaa/aayaa
Ram dat Sita poss sing-nom himself like be/come-past
'Ram himself liked Sita's singing.'

The complex predicates encoding stative and transitional (inchoative) events yield well formed structures with the durative adjunct *aajkal* (7a) and the inceptive adjunct *sunte hi* (7d) respectively, whereas the process predicate *pasand kiyaa* takes the emphatic reflexive *swayam* as a modifier for the agent *raam* (7e). Semantic restrictions can be seen in the failure of the stative *thaa* to license an inceptive *sunte hi* (7c), or in the stative *tha* and the transitional *aayaa* rejecting the durative *aajkal* (7b) and the agentive *swayam* (7e).

2.3 Complex Predicate Generation

Turning to the mechanisms needed to generate the fully specified complex predicates from their underspecified constituent elements, we propose lexical structures for the host predicates and LVs with compositional devices based on unification. The lexical structures proposed for the predicates in question are modelled along the lines of one of the mainstream procedural models of lexical semantics, the Generative Lexicon theory (Pustejovsky, 1995; 1998). The Generative Lexicon (GL) model adopted here has many advantages over the competing models of lexical structure such as the Lexical Conceptual Structure (LCS) (Jackendoff, 1990). We mention two which are relevant to our present concerns. In the first place the model provides for fine-grained lexical decomposition which would be needed to account for the subtle semantic type shifts at work in complex predicate formation. Secondly, GL is a procedural model rather that a declarative one: lexical semantic shifts in this model are accounted for through generative mechanisms based on the principle of semantic type coercion operating on lexical representations.

The compositional mechanism proposed here constitutes a departure from the generative mechanisms proposed in the GL.[2] The predicate-predicate compositional mechanism proposed here is based on "term unification" and directly unifies parallel arguments or event structures of the constitutent predicates. It is argued that lexical structure for LVs is based on semantic type hierarchies. These along with an *argument unification* and *event unification* mechanism can account for the range of semantic properties triggered in complex predicate formation.

Adjectival predicates such as *pareshaan* in (1-3), are represented in the lexicon along with a specification of their argument, event and qualia structures. The CP construct emerges through unification of these structures with those in the LVs. Let us consider the non-CP usage of the predicates *pareshaan, ho(be), ho(happen)* and *kar* as in the following:

(8) a. mujhe aaj ek pareshaan laDkaa milaa
I-dat today a troubled boy meet-past
'I met a troubled boy today'

b. raam ek shikSak hai
Ram a teacher be-pres
'Ram is a teacher'

c. julaai me baarish hoti hai
July in rain happen-pres
'In July it rains'

d. raam ne kaam kiyaa
Ram erg work do-past
'Ram worked.'

The lexical semantic structure for *pareshaan* is represented in (9). The representation consists of ARGSTR (argument structure), EVSTR (event structure) and QUALIA (qualia structure) along the lines of GL. The argument structure of the adjectival predicate, for example, is represented as ARGSTR= [ARG1=x: animate], which captures the fact that this predicate takes one argument which is animate. The event structure representation denotes the stative attribute of the predicate. The QUALIA representation depicts a fine grained semantic information: FORMAL QUALE as the argument x in state of trouble and the AGENTIVE QUALE as the coming about of this state in x:

$$(9)\quad \begin{bmatrix} \text{pareshaan} \\ \text{ARGSTR} = \left[\text{ARG1} = \text{x} : \text{animate}\right] \\ \text{EVSTR} = \left[\text{E1} = \text{e1} : \text{state}\right] \\ \text{QUALIA} = \begin{bmatrix} \text{FORMAL} = \mathit{troubled}(x) \\ \text{AGENTIVE} = \text{exp\_}\mathit{act}(e1, x) \end{bmatrix} \end{bmatrix}$$

The LV *ho(be)* appears to be relatively undifferentiated from its heavy form, and refers to a state in its event structure, as captured in the lexical representation in (10). However, the properties of the arguments are modified by the host predicate in the compositional process in both AV usage (4-5) and NV usage (6-7) of this predicate.

$$(10)\quad \begin{bmatrix} \text{ho(be)} \\ \text{ARGSTR} = \begin{bmatrix} \text{ARG1} = x : \ \mathit{entity} \\ \text{ARG2} = y : \mathit{state} \end{bmatrix} \\ \text{EVSTR} = \left[\text{E1} = e1 : \mathit{state}\right] \\ \text{QUALIA} = \left[\text{FORMAL} = \mathit{is\text{-}a}(e1, x, y)\right] \end{bmatrix}$$

In its HV usage, *ho(happen/become)* usually denotes a process event, a sense closer to the English 'happen'. The LV, however, denotes a causal transition from event e1 to e2, resulting in the complex predicate *pareshaan hua* in (1b) with the semantics "became upset". The semantics of the HV *ho(happen)* appears to have been shifted into the transition sense of "become" resulting in an inchoative event structure for the stative host. This alternation, termed *bleaching* in Hook (1991), does not always reflect a semantic dilution but may reflect a shift to a new sense as in (11):

$$(11)\quad \begin{bmatrix} \text{ho}_{\text{LV}}\text{(become)} \\ \text{ARGSTR} = \left[\text{ARG1} = x:\ \text{state}\right] \\ \text{EVSTR} = \begin{bmatrix} \text{E1} = e1: \text{transition} \\ \text{M2} = e2: \text{state} \\ \text{RESTR} = e1 <_{\alpha} e2 \\ \text{HEAD} = e1 \end{bmatrix} \\ \text{QUALIA} = \left[\text{TELIC} = \text{act}(e1, x)\right] \end{bmatrix}$$

The semantic structure for *kar*, the agentive do, retains most of its HV properties:

$$(12)\quad \begin{bmatrix} \text{kar} \\ \text{ARGSTR} = \begin{bmatrix} \text{ARG1} = x: \text{animate} \\ \text{ARG2} = y: \text{action} \end{bmatrix} \\ \text{EVSTR} = \left[\text{E1} = e1: \text{process}\right] \\ \text{QUALIA} = \begin{bmatrix} \text{FORMAL} = \text{act}_{[y]}(e1, x) \\ \text{AGENTIVE} = \text{do}(e1, x, y) \end{bmatrix} \end{bmatrix}$$

Stative hosts such as *pareshaan* or *pasand* are type-shifted by the LV *kar* to agentive events in the CP. Thus, while *ho(be)* and *kar* are more or less undiluted in their LV semantics, *ho(become)* undergoes a higher degree of shift. However, as we will see in section 3, LVs participating in VV composites exhibit semantic shifts of even higher magnitude.

2.4 Predicate-predicate Co-composition

Next we elaborate the two generative mechanisms proposed for predicate-predicate co-composition: Argument Unification and Event Unification.

a. Argument Unification:

Argument unification refers to the semantic binding occurring between an argument of an LV and an argument in the host. In addition to filling an argument slot in the LV, the host argument may subsume the more general argument type in the LV. The type-narrowing effected in the CP through this operation distinguishes it from the arity based accounts such as *argument fusion*[3] as employed in Butt (2003). In CP generation, the semantic binding is more specific: the argument type of the host predicate is unified with an ontologically superordinate argument in the LV, and the resulting composite reflects the more specific argument structure of the host.

In the CP *pareshaan hai* in example (1a), ARG1 of *pareshaan* (type:

animate), as represented in (9) above, is unified with ARG1 of *ho(be)* (type: *entity*), as represented in (10). The resulting type for the ARG1 of *pareshaan hai* is ontologically the narrower type, i.e. *animate*. In (1a) and (1b) *pareshaan* satisfies the argument slot of the LV *ho(be)* and *ho(become)*, and hence, there is no argument binding. In (1c), *pareshaan* undergoes a state-process type-shift with *kar* and satisfies the ARG2 slot for *kar*, whereas the experiencer argument from *pareshaan* is retained in the final composite along with the agent argument of *kar*. The semantics of the resulting composites may be captured as follows:

(13) a.
$$\begin{bmatrix} \text{pareshaan hai} \\ \text{ARGSTR} = \begin{bmatrix} \text{ARG1} = x : \text{animate} \end{bmatrix} \\ \text{EVSTR} = \begin{bmatrix} \text{E1} = e1 : \text{state} \end{bmatrix} \\ \text{QUALIA} = \begin{bmatrix} \text{FORMAL} = \mathit{troubled}(x) \\ \text{AGENTIVE} = \text{exp\_act}(e1, x) \end{bmatrix} \end{bmatrix}$$

b.
$$\begin{bmatrix} \text{pareshaan huaa} \\ \text{ARGSTR} = \begin{bmatrix} \text{ARG1} = x : \text{animate} \end{bmatrix} \\ \text{EVSTR} = \begin{bmatrix} \text{E1} = e1 : \text{process} \\ \text{M1} = e2 : \text{state} \\ \text{RESTR} = e1 <_{\alpha} e2 \\ \text{HEAD} = \text{M1} \end{bmatrix} \\ \text{QUALIA} = \begin{bmatrix} \text{FORMAL} = \mathit{troubled}(x) \\ \text{AGENTIVE} = \text{exp\_}\mathit{act}(e1, x) \end{bmatrix} \end{bmatrix}$$

c.
$$\begin{bmatrix} \text{pareshaan kiyaa} \\ \text{ARGSTR} = \begin{bmatrix} \text{ARG1} = x : \text{animate} \\ \text{ARG2} = y : \text{animate} \end{bmatrix} \\ \text{EVSTR} = \begin{bmatrix} \text{E1} = e1 : \text{process} \end{bmatrix} \\ \text{QUALIA} = \begin{bmatrix} \text{AGENTIVE} = \text{trouble\_act}(e1, x, y) \end{bmatrix} \end{bmatrix}$$

Thus, predicate-predicate unification differs in one respect from argument-predicate binding: in argument-predicate binding, unfilled slots in the host are combined to obtain the argument structure of the resulting composite, whereas unification may result in some of these unfilled slots being merged. Note that in argument unification, the LV does not appear to modify the type structure of the argument in the host predicate. However, this is not true of event structure, where the LV modifies the temporal structure and imposes its own aspectual constraint. As noted by Hook (1991) and others, this may be one of the main functions of CP structures in language.

b. Event Unification:

Here the event structure of LV and host are unified, resulting in restructured event semantics for the CP. Each LV appears to carry fine-grained temporal semantics, and serves as a marker for aktionsarts. This semantic function also imposes selectional constraints, e.g. only hosts where a transitional event structure is possible can take the transitional LV *ho(become)*. In the AV examples (1-3) above, *ho(be)* (STATE) and *ho(become)* (TRANSITION) event structures are imposed on *pareshaan*, the resulting CP taking STATE and TRANSITION aspects. For the LV *kar*, the event structure is that of a PROCESS, and this results in a PROCESS interpretation for the CP. The same reasoning applies to the selectional constraints exhibited in (4-7): the incipient aspect in stative *pareshaan huaa* (4b) rejects the durative adverbial, *aajkal*. Similarly the rejection of the inceptive temporal adjunct *sunte hi* constitutes a test for the stative predicate *pareshaan hai* in (4c). Again, in example 5, the stative/inchoative interpretation rejects volition whereas the agentive one does not.

Although we have focused on the AV predicates in the above analysis, a similar analysis can be extended to NV hosts as in (6). Thus *pasand* takes [experiencer, object] arguments which combine with the [entity, state] arguments of ho (be) resulting event structures of the compounds are as follows:

(14) a. *pasand hai*: [STATE]
b. *pasand aayaa*: [TRANSITION]
c. *pasand kiyaa*: [PROCESS]

The argument structures of *pasand* in (14a-b) involve the experiencer argument from the host. We note that these descriptions, while being more refined than others, are still limited by the range of symbolic devices available, and are somewhat incomplete, e.g. in (6b), there is a hint of non-volitionality about the event, which is difficult to capture in the present account.

Predicate-predicate unification appears to impart a detailed event semantics with respect to certain LVs in VV composites as we shall see in section 3.1.

2.5 Constraints on AV/NV Composites

As already observed, complex predicate formation with underspecified nominal and adjectival predicates is a productive process in the languages under consideration. However, the process does appear to operate under some constraints. Hindi and Urdu NV predicates for example, show regular alternation between N *ho*, N *ho/aa* and N *kar*. But there are some nominal predicates, exemplified in (15-16), which resist one or the other of these composite semantic types:

(15) a. raam ko is baat ki samajh hai
Ram dat this matter-poss understanding be-prs
'Ram understands this matter.'

b. raam ko yeh baat samajh aayi
Ram dat this matter understanding come-past
'Ram understands this matter.'

c. *raam ne yeh baat samajh ki
Ram erg this matter understanding do-past
'Ram understands this matter.'

(16) a. *raam kaa giitaa ka pathan hai
Ram poss Gita-poss reading be-pres
'*Ram has a reading of the Gita.'

b. raam kaa giitaa kaa pathan huaa
Ram poss Gita-poss reading happen-past
'Ram has had a reading of the Gita.'

c. raam ne gitaa kaa pathan kiyaa
Ram erg Gita-poss reading do-past
'Ram has done a reading of the Gita.'

It appears that a strongly stative nominal such as *samajh* 'understand' resists being type-shifted to a process. Thus *samajh* can select the stative *ho*, as well as the inceptive *aa*, but not the active *kar* (*samajh kiyaa). On the other hand other stative nominals such as *pasand* do license type-shifting to bind with *kar* as in (6c). Similarly, a strong action nominal like *pathan* 'read' does not admit of the stative possibility (**paThan hai*).

3. VV Composites

VV composites constitute a large semi-productive class. The LVs participating in these composites appear to undergo greater degree of dilution compared to LVs in AV/NV composites. The host predicate remains uninflected in true VV complexes. Although usage patterns with an inflected HV form can also appear in a VV configuration, but these constructs may be treated as clausal constituents of the regular verb rather than a CP, as we shall see in section 4.1.

Consider the verb *nikal* 'leave' which forms a complex predicate with light verbs such as *jaa* 'go' and *paD* 'fall'. The verb *nikal* is, by itself, underspecified with respect to the aspectual properties, which are determined by the light verb it combines with.

(17) a. raam har din saat baje kaam par nikal jaataa hai
Ram daily seven o'clock work on leave go be-pres
'Ram leaves for work at seven o'clock everyday.'
b. raam har din saat baje kaam par nikal paDtaa hai
Ram daily seven o'clock work on leave fall be-pres
'Ram leaves for work at seven o'clock everyday.'

The VV predicates *nikal jaa* and *nikal paD* above represent event structure variations that have to do with the aspectual classes of completive and inceptive.

Aspectual modifications are a regular feature of VV compounds, observed also for other LVs such as *jaa* 'go' and *uTh* 'stand':

(18) a. sabki ki baat sunkar raam bhi apnii baat keh gayaa
everyone's opinion hear-part Ram emph self-gen opinion say go-past
'Having heard everyone else, Ram spoke his mind.'
b. sabki ki baat sunkar raam bhi apni baat keh uThaa
everyone's opinion hear-part Ram emph self''s opinión say stand-past
'Having heard everyone else, Ram spoke his mind too.'

In (18a-b), *keh gayaa* and *keh uThaa* express completive and inceptive aspectual structures respectively.

3.1 Event Structure Modification by LVs

It does not appear that the LV forms of *jaa* and *uth* in (18a-b) can be derived by bleaching the heavy verbs. For example, the HV form of *jaa* has the following semantic structure:

$$(19)\quad \begin{bmatrix} \text{jaa}_{\text{HV}} \\ \text{ARGSTR} = [\text{ARG1} = x : \text{human}] \\ \text{EVSTR} = [\text{E1} = e1 : \text{process}] \\ \text{QUALIA} = [\text{FORMAL} = \text{move}(e1, x)] \end{bmatrix}$$

On the other hand, the LV form of *jaa* reflects a completive aspect for the main predicate as evinced in the data above. Within the Generative Lexicon approach, we may encode the completive aspect using the notion of a moment, which is an "instant" event, indivisible in the scale of discourse under consideration. With this instant set at the endpoint or "finish" of the event, we can consider the head of the action as this instant, as in (20):

$$(20)\quad \begin{bmatrix} \text{jaa}_{\text{LV}} & \\ \text{EVSTR} = & \begin{bmatrix} \text{E1} = e1 : \text{process} \\ \text{M1} = e1.\textit{finish} : \text{instant} \\ \text{HEAD} = \text{M1} \end{bmatrix} \\ \ldots & \end{bmatrix}$$

We note that jaa_{HV} does not encode aspect – it assumes aspectual connotations (like most HVs in Hindi) using LV collocations as with *chukaa*, say. On the other hand jaa_{LV} has none of the motion connotation that is the defining element in jaa_{HV}. If we are to model this as a semantic shift, almost the entire structure of the HV will be lost and replaced by a new structure, a process that is perhaps better mapped as a complete re-lexicalization.

However, complete loss of HV semantics does not appear to be the case with certain predicates such as *uThaa*, 'stand-up', which in its heavy verb form, has an incipient nature characterized by sudden-ness. We may model this as a default manner for the event structure of the HV predicate:

$$(21)\quad \begin{bmatrix} \text{uThaa}_{\text{HV}} & \\ \text{ARGSTR} = & [\text{ARG1} = x\text{:human}] \\ \text{EVSTR} = & \begin{bmatrix} \text{E1} = e1\text{:process} \\ \text{D-MANNER} = \text{abrupt} \end{bmatrix} \\ \text{QUALIA} = & [\text{TELIC} = \text{standUp}(e1, x)] \\ \ldots & \end{bmatrix}$$

In the LV version, which picks out the details of the temporal role, the telic role is completely lost, and the abruptness at the start becomes the head, thus giving it an inceptive aktionsart. Indeed, it captures a more fine-grained abruptness than can be captured by the aktionsart alone – here the abruptness parameter is retained in a pronounced form, and is a default. Thus, one can have *dhire se* $uThA_{HV}$ (stood up slowly), but not *dhiire se gA* $uThA_{LV}$ (slowly started singing). Thus, the MANNER parameter is now enforced:

$$(22)\quad \begin{bmatrix} \textit{uThaa}_{LV} & \\ \text{EVSTR} = & \begin{bmatrix} \text{E1} = e1\text{:process} \\ \text{M1} = e1.\textit{start} \\ \text{HEAD} = \text{M1} \\ \text{MANNER} = \text{abrupt} \end{bmatrix} \\ \ldots & \end{bmatrix}$$

This intensification in the abruptness is perhaps better captured in a constructional schema (Figure 1), rather than in a symbolic model. The schema maps the energy function over the process interval:

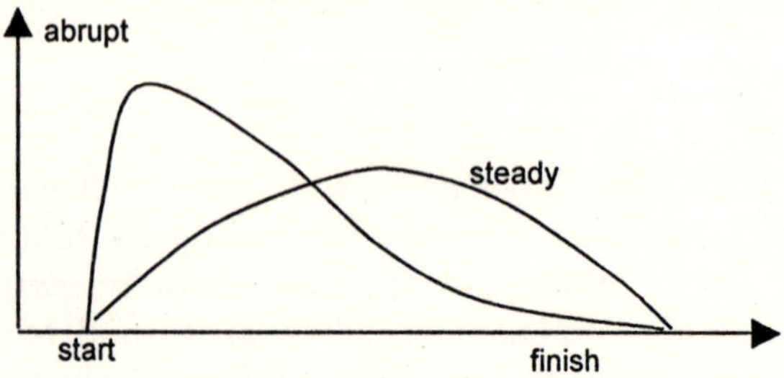

Figure 1: Temporal Structure Intensification

LVs participating in VV composites may impose fine-grained temporal constraints. Sometimes these may be derived from the heavy verb usage, as in *uThaa*, where the implicit sudden-ness of the action of standing up is intensified by moving more energy towards the start of the process. For example, the full verb *kahaa* 'speak' may have a steady energy distribution, whereas *keh uThaa* appears to have more energy at the inception. These would involve a further fine gradation depending on the host, although aspectually, all compounds with this LV appear in an inceptive aspect.

In summary, the main function of LVs participating in VV compounds appears to be the modification of event structure, including, but possibly going beyond, aspectual properties. Such LVs appear to lose all qualia features in the process of CP formation, and the qualia structure of the host prevails. Some character of its event dynamics may be derivable from the full verb counterpart, but this is a small part of its full semantic repertoire and hence the term dilution is appropriate for this class of LV. On the other hand, in other instances (e.g., jaa_{LV} above) the process involves more of a shift than dilution, as was also the case for some of the LVs participating in NV/AV compounds. In most LVs participating in VV composites, the residual meaning is very light indeed, and the temporal character of the modification it imposes is perhaps better handled through separate lexicalization.

To illustrate the structures resulting from LV-host interaction in VV compounds, we present below the semantic structures that may arise for the predicates *nikal paDaa* and *nikal gayaa*. These structures adopt the argument structures of the host, but enforce an aspectual change in the event structure by shifting the head to the moments associated with start and finish, thus encoding inceptive and completive aktionsarts.

$$(23)\quad \begin{bmatrix} \text{nikal paDaa} & \\ \text{EVSTR} = & \begin{bmatrix} \text{E1} = e1\text{:transition} \\ \text{M1} = e1.\textit{start} \\ \text{HEAD} = \text{M1} \end{bmatrix} \\ \ldots & \end{bmatrix}$$

$$(24)\quad \begin{bmatrix} \text{nikal gayaa} & \\ \text{EVSTR} = & \begin{bmatrix} \text{E1} = e1\text{:transition} \\ \text{M2} = e1.\textit{finish} \\ \text{HEAD} = \text{M2} \end{bmatrix} \\ \ldots & \end{bmatrix}$$

3.2 VV Composition Constraints: Partial Productivity in LV Usage

In VV composites, a light verb is in principle compatible with any main verb; however, semantic restrictions do apply such that many combinations are ruled out. Thus, the inceptive light verb *paD*, for

Table 1: ***Selectional Restrictions in VV CPs***

	jaa	chal	paD	Daal	uTh	De
kar	√	√	x	√	?√	√
nikal	√	√	√	x	x	√
khaa	√	?√	x	√	?√	?√
bol	√	?√	√	?√	√	√
keh	√	?√	x	√	√	√
jaa	x	x	x	x	?	x
chal	√	x	√	x	x	√
gir	√	?√	√	x	x	x
paR	√	x	x	x	x	x
so	√	?√	x	x	sv	x
de	√	?√	x	√	?x	√
baiTh	√	x	x	x	x	x
uTh	√	√	x	x	x	√
ro	√	√	√	√	√	√
has	√	x	√	√	√	√
mAr	√	x	x	√	X	√
kho	√	x	x	√	X	√

KEY: √ = accepts x = rejects sv = serial verb

example, forms verbal composites such as *nikal paDnaa, bol paDnaa, chal paDnaa, gir paDnaa,* but not **jaa paDnaa, *so paDnaa, *kar paDnaa, *khaa paDnaa, *keh paDnaa*. It seems that events with strong intentionality do not take the inceptive *paD*; it combines only with events with a low intentional content. Table 1 presents some data on selectional restrictions among VV collocations in Hindi[4].

The data presented in Table 1 is subject to variation as well as possibilities for conflation with other usage patterns. For example, regional variations may be noted – e.g. speakers from the Chhatisgarh region appear to consider *ro gayaa* as inappropriate, whereas users near Kanpur reject *baith paRaa* or *bol chalaa*. Similarly, some constructs like so *uThaa* license serial verb usage "slept, then got up", and respondents may be confused.

The semantic role of the LV in these collocations is that of imposing aspectual constraints on the event structure of the host predicate. As observed earlier, the aspectual structure associated with a particular LV may be related to its HV counterpart, or may be quite arbitrary. We have seen how the aspectual semantics of the LV *jaa* does not seem to be related to its HV semantics as the motion verb 'go', whereas the inceptive aspectual LV *uThaa* has some of the abruptness at start associated with its HV counterpart. The HV *paD* (fall) represents a lack of volition which is reflected in its aspectual semantics in the LV usage. On the other hand, the LV *Daal* has a completive aspect which does not appear related to its HV semantics (put), although it may be related to the bounded event structure in 'put'.

The aspectual semantics of the LV also appears to constrain what HVs it can select. Thus, although both *keh* and *bol* denote "talk", *keh* is less volitional, and is selected by paD, whereas *bol* is rejected. Similarly, the completive *Daal* rejects transition actions like *nikal*, which appears to prefer *jaa* for its completive form.

Looking for a generalizations underlying the semantic shifts and dilution exhibited by the LVs, we may consider the manner in which verbs such as "go" or "put" are recruited for a range of polysemous usage across a large number of languages. Some of these polysemous semantics eventually shift into increasingly grammaticalized usage. After the "be/have" class, these are possibly the most grammaticalized across languages. To consider a few examples with the English "go", his face went red in anger, as the story goes, he went on and on, Iraqi children go hungry every day, as well as idiomatic usage as in the milk went bad, go by, go dutch, go for it, etc.[5]

Based on the data above and the possible mechanisms for synchronic transfer, it would appear possible to propose a model for a degree of bleaching in LV formation. Some LVs participating in NV/AV alternations like *kar* retain almost all the HV interpretation except for some argument fusion. Others such as *ho(be)* and *ho(become)* affect both argument and event structures in their predicates, and can be thought of as a little bleached. On the other hands, LVs participating in VV alternation appear to have lost almost all of their HV semantics, and range from instances like *Daal* or *paR* which retain some aspectual or argument structures from their HV to *jaa* which appears to have become completely grammaticalized (Figure 2).

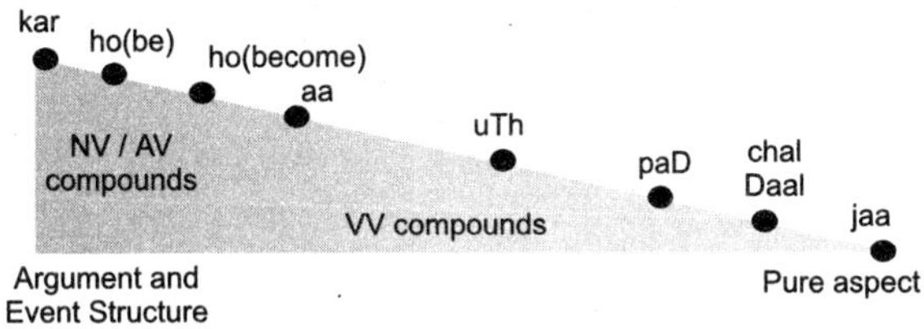

Figure 2. Cline in Light Verb Bleaching

The cline in LV semantic bleaching goes from retaining nearly complete HV meanings, to total grammticalization. LVs participating in NV/AV compounds appear to be somewhat less bleached than those participating in VV collocations.

4. Constraints on VV Composition

4.1 Non-root Verbal Hosts

In this section, we consider VV forms that involve a non-root verbal host and an LV to see whether these structures can indeed be claimed to result from event structure unification proposed in Section 3. Notable among these is the so called permissive: *jaane denaa, karne denaa, paRhne denaa,* sometimes analysed as an instance of VV compounds (Butt, 1995). Consider the following examples:

(26) a. raam ne sitaa ka kaam kar diyaa
Ram erg Sita poss work do give-past
'Ram has done Sita's work.'

b. raam ne sitaa ko kaam karne diyaa
Ram erg Sita acc work do-nom give-past
'Ram allowed sita to do the work.'

In (26a), we have a compositional structure involving the host *kar* 'do' and the LV *de* 'give', where the latter modifies the aspectual structure to completive through event structure unification mechanism outlined in Section 3.1. (26b), on the other hand, has a permissive implicature. Note that (26b) contains the nominalised host *karne* and the semantic composition may, therefore, work differently from that in (26a). In other words, since the same LV triggers different event structures depending on whether the host is in the root form or the inflected one, it would seem that the semantic composition is sensitive to the inflectional form of the root verb. However, it can be argued that the inflectional form does not really constrain the semantic composition. Rather, *de* in (26b) is a HV and the permissive implicature results from a regular polysemy of the HV *de*, which takes three arguments, *raam*, *sitaa* and *kaam karnaa*. If the latter analysis is along correct lines then the structure in (26b) does not instantiate a CP composite; rather, it is a case of the HV *de* taking a clausal complement as in (26c):

(26) c. [$_{NP}$ raam ne] [$_{VP}$ [$_{NP}$ sitaa ko [kaam karne]] [$_{V}$ diyaa] $_{VP}$]

whereas (26a) may take the phrasal structure:

(26) d. [$_{NP}$ raam ne] [$_{VP}$ [$_{NP}$ sitaa ka kaam] [$_{V}$ kar diyaa] $_{VP}$]

Consider some more constructions belonging to this class:

(27) a. raam apni baat bol paDaa
Ram self's opinión say fall-past
'Ram expressed himself'.'

b. raam ko apni baat bolni paDii
Ram-dat self's opinión say-nom fall-past
'Ram had to/was forced to express himself.'

(28) a. raam meri baat par has paDaa
Ram my opinion on laugh fall-past
'Ram laughed at my opinion.'

b. raam ko meri baat par hasna paDaa
Ram-dat my opinión on laugh-nom fall-past
'Ram had to/was forced to laugh at my opinion.'

The aspectual semantics of the LV *paDaa* in (27a) and (28a) is different from that of *paDaa* in (27b) and (28b). The (a) examples give the inceptive reading whereas the (b) examples have a compulsive meaning. Here again, it may appear as if the same LV is triggering different event structures depending on whether the host is in the root form or an inflected one. However, again it appears equally plausible to look upon the (b) instances as those involving a clausal argument of the HVs *de* and *paD*. Viewed thus, the permissive in (26b), and the compulsive in (27b) and (28b) are both instances of polysemous HVs *de* and *paD* taking clausal complements with nominalised heads.

Further investigation shows that there are a range of inflected verb forms which appear in CP-like structures. Consider *sunai paDaa* and *sunai diyaa* in (29).

(29) a. use ghar jaate hue ek awaaz sunaaii paDii

he-dat home go-part part one voice hear-part fall-past
'While going home, he heard a voice'.

b. use ghar jaate hue meri awaaz sunaayii dii
he-dat home go-part my voice hear-part give-past
'While going home, he could hear my voice.'

(29a) has a nonvolitional implicature whereas (29b) has an abilitative one. Both the structures are unproductive, appearing only with the verbs *sun* and *dekh*, and are idionsyncratic forms with a frozen meaning. Some other structures such as *sunne mei ayaa* exhibit a similar frozenness, and may not involve event structure unification proposed earlier. These structures presumably belong to a restricted non-compositional set.

Yet another class of structures sometimes conflated with those under consideration in the present work, consists of VV sequences where neither of the two verbs is semantically a LV. Examples of this class include sequences like *maar giraaya* and *soc nikaalaa*. What distinguishes this class of CPs is their co-eventual semantic structure: both the participating verbs define the event. The semantics of these predicates involves multiple levels of complexity and has been dealt with elsewhere.[6]

Similarly, a number of structures (e.g. *so uThA*, *kar aayaa*, etc.) appear to be better modelled as serial verbs and not quite as complex predicates; in these instances we find that inflection of the so-called host verb results in no change in the aspectual semantics.

Thus, while there are a range of phenomena that appear to reflect complex predicate structures on the surface, it seems that a good number of them may have alternate accounts.

4.2 Polarity Effects

Complex predicates show polarity effects which are of interest semantically. Consider the following which show that CPs of the VV type do not admit of negation (Hook, 1974; Hook, 1991):

(30) a. raam kaam par nikal paDaa
Ram work on leave fall-past
'Ram left for work.'

b. *raam kaam par nahin nikal paDaa
Ram work on not leave fall-past
'Ram did not leave for work.'

c. *raam kaam par nikal nahin paDaa
Ram work on leave not fall-past
'Ram did not leave for work.'

However, negation is possible in conditionals, where it has a positive implicature, as in (31a):

(31) a. jabtak voh kaam par nahin nikal paDtaa use chain nahin aataa
as long as he work on not leave fall-pres-hab him ease not come-pres-hab
'As long as he doesn't leave for work, he is not at ease.'

However, negation is possible in the context of inclusive and exclusive emphatics (*hii, to*) such as:

(32) a. usne kitab paDh to nahin Daali keval kharid kar rakh di hai
he-erg book read emph not throw-past only buy do keep give be-pres
'He has not read the book he has only bought and kept it.'

b. usne kitaab keval kharid hii nahin Daali, paDh bhii lii
he-erg book only buy emph not throw-past read emph give-past
'Not only did he buy the book, he read it too.'

On the other hand, a VV composite such as *paDh paanaa*, denoting abilitative event semantics, does allow negation:

(33) a. usse meraa kam ho paayaa
he-instr my work happen find-past
'He could do my work.'

b. usse meraa kaam ho nahin paayaa
he-instr my work happen not find-past
'He could not do my work.'

c. usse meraa kaam nahin ho paayaa
he-instr my work not happen find-past
'He could not do my work.'

While (33b) and (33c) are both negative, sentence (33a) has a negative implicature.

4.2.1 Polarity Sensitivity in other Indian Languages

The polarity sensitivity of CPs is a phenomenon that shows up in languages other than Hindi and Urdu as well. Thus Kashmiri, an Indic language of Dardic roots, shows polarity sensitivity in the following structures[7]:

(34) a. raaman tshun saarni vənith zi su gav phel
Ram erg wear-past all say+part that he go-past fail
'Ram told everybody that he had failed.'

b. raaman nyu saarni vənith zi su gav phel
Ram erg take-past all say-part that he go-past fail
'Ram told everybody that he had failed.'

c. *raaman tshun nI saarni vənith zi su gav phel
Ram erg wear-past neg all say-part that he go-past fail

'Ram did not tell everybody that he had failed.'

d. *raaman nyu nI saarni vənith zi su gav phel
Ram erg take-past neg all say-part that he go-past fail
'Ram did not tell everybody that he had failed.'

The data from Kashmiri (34a-d) contain VV predicates *vənith tshun* and *vənith nyi*. These examples show that CPs of the VV type in this language do not admit of negation. However, negation is possible in conditionals, where it has a positive implicature, as in (35):

(35) yotaany təmi tshun nI saarni vənith zi su gav phel, tas aav nI tasli
until he-erg wear-past neg all say-part that he go-past fail he-dat come-past neg satisfaction
'Until he told everybody that he failed, he was not satisfied.'

Similarly, negation in CP structures in Kashmiri is possible in the context of emphatics:

(36) təmi tshun nI saarni vənith-ai yot zi su gav phel, report tyi hə:vnakh
he-erg wear-past neg all say-part-emph that he go-past fail report emph show-past
'Not only did he tell everyone that he had failed, he also showed them the report card.'

From a semantic perspective, it seems clear that VV composites specify an additional aspectual constraint not present in the host by itself. Negating an aspectual form achieves nothing that is not there in the negation of the main verb alone, e.g. negation of the main verb implies that both its start and finish are negated. It is possible that the availability of this simpler mechanism then blocks the negation of the composites. However, this is at best a very partial account, and the polarity sensitivity exemplified by these structures is an offshoot of a complex interaction between negation, conditionals and emphatics on the one hand, and the inceptive, completive and abilitative aspectual semantic types on the other, needing detailed investigation.

5. Conclusion

In this paper, we have proposed a compositional account of complex predicates drawing on data from Indic languages such as Hindi, Urdu and Kashmiri. Argument and event unification have been used together with the standard co-compositional mechanisms to capture the semantic restructuring of the host predicate by the lexicalised LV. We discuss the constraints on complex predication and offer a semantic type based explanation for the various compositional constraints. Clearly, this work is merely a beginning in the direction of a fine-grained semantic approach to CP composition, and much remains to be looked at in terms of accounting for co-occurrence restrictions on CP constituents.

The issue of semantic dilution of light verbs and how a semantic typing system can account for the type alternation between a full verb and its light verb counterpart is examined. We propose a bleaching cline to account for the varying extent of semantic shift across the class of grammaticalised verbs or LVs in these languages. While we have argued for a semantic type sensitive compositional process, it is clear that certain issues such as polarity effects require further exploration. It is possible that polarity effects overrides lexical composition, and as such, interacts with the semantics of conditionals and emphatics at the discourse level.

REFERENCES

Brugman, C. 2001. Light verbs and polysemy. *Language Sciences* 23, 551-578.

Butt, M. 1995. *The structure of complex predicates in Urdu*. Stanford: CSLI Publications.

Butt, M. and W. Geuder, 2001. Light verbs in Urdu and gramaticalisation. In R. Eckardt et al (eds.) *Words in time: Diachronic semantics from different points of View*. Mouton de Gruyter, 295-350.

Butt, M. 2003. The light verb jungle, Ms., *Harvard working papers in linguistics*. Boston.

Folli, R., H. Harley and S. Karimi 2005. Determinants of event type in Persian complex predicates. *Lingua* 115, 1365–1401.

Grimshaw, J. and A. Mester 1988. Light verbs and Ë-Marking. *Linguistic Inquiry* 10, 205-232.

Hook, P.E. 1974. *The compound verb in Hindi.* Center for South and Southeast Asian Studies, The University of Michigan.

Hook, P.E. 1991. The Emergence of perfective aspect in Indo-Aryan languages. In E. Traugott and B. Heine (eds.) *Approaches to grammaticalization*. Vol. 2. John Benjamins, 59-89.

Hook, P.E. 1993. Aspectogenesis and the compound verb in Indo-Aryan. In M.K.Verma (ed.) *Complex predicates in South Asian languages*. Delhi: Manohar Publishers.

Jackendoff, R. 1990. *Semantic structures*. Cambridge, MA: MIT Press.

Jayaseelan, K. 1984. Complex predicates and the theory of theta-marking. *CIEFL Working Papers in Linguistics* 1.

Jespersen, O. 1940. *A modern English grammar on historical principles*. London: Allen and Unwin.

Matsumoto, Yo. 1996. *Complex predicates in Japanese*. CSLI Publications and Kuroshio Publishers.

Mohanan, T. 1994. *Argument structure in Hindi/Urdu*. Stanford: CSLI Publications.

Pustejovsky, J. 1995. *The generative lexicon*. Cambridge, MA: MIT Press.

Pustejovsky, J. 1998. The Semantics of Lexical Underspecification. *Folia Linguistica*, XXXII.

Raina, A.M. 2005a. Complex Predicates in the Generative Lexicon. In P. Bouillon and K. Kanzaki (eds.) *Proceedings of GL'2005, Third International Workshop on Generative Approaches to the Lexicon*. 210-221.

Raina, A.M. 2005b. Complex Predicates and Semantic Underspecification. *Indian Linguistics* 65, 89-103.

Raina, A.M. (Forthcoming). The Co-eventual Verb in Hindi, In O.N. Koul (ed.) *Indo-Aryan linguistics*. CIIL Publications.

Yokota, K. 2005. The Structure and Meaning of Japanese Light Verbs. *Language Sciences 27*, 247-280.

NOTES

1. Several commentators have used the term complex predicates to refer to a wide set including serial verb constructions, light verb constructions, particle + verb constructions, among others. According to Butt (2003), the term is used to designate "a construction that involves two or more predicational elements (such as nouns, verbs and adjectives) which predicate as a single element, i.e., their arguments map onto a monoclausal syntactic structure". In this paper, we confine ourselves to the subset of monoclausal complex predicates containing the light verbs.
2. GL posits three generative devices for generating meanings arising out of compositional contexts: (a) Type-coercion; (b) Co-composition, and (c) Selective binding. The principal motivation for these generative devices in GL is to dynamically resolve ambiguities arising out of polysemy by means of a rich lexical decomposition. All the three devices proposed in the classical GL account involve a semantic type-shifting process but the constraints on type-shifting come from different parts of the phrase
3. The term also occurs in Jackendoff (1990), where it refers to a more general process of mapping semantic arguments into subcategory structures.
4. The table reflects acceptability patterns obtained from Hindi users in and around Kanpur.
5. Cognitive Linguists assume this to reflect the ontological primacy in these motive concepts, which licenses its metaphorical transfer to other usages, and this holds across different cultures, and in some cases, leading eventually to a greater dilution in frequent usage constructs.
6. We have argued elsewhere that although this class, termed as the *co-eventual verb*, shows similarities with the regular VV composites under discussion in this paper, the similarities are purely formal in nature. In so far as the sub-event structure of the co-eventual verb is concerned, it works on principles very different from aspectual type coercion at work in the VV composites (Raina, forthcoming).
7. For a detailed account of complex predicates in Kashmiri, see Raina (2005b).

21

Limits to Compositionality of Meaning: Some Notes with Reference to English and Hindi

Rajneesh Arora

1. Introduction

The question of compositionality of meaning has attracted the attention of many linguists (Cann 1993; Cruse 2000; Saeed 2003). The strongest version of the principle of compositionality, as Alan Cruse defines it, states that 'the meaning of a grammatically complex form is a compositional function of the meanings of its grammatical constituents' (2000: 67). This definition incorporates three separate claims:

(*i*) The meaning of a complex expression is completely ***determined*** by the meanings of its constituents.

(*ii*) The meaning of a complex expression is completely ***predictable*** by general rules from the meanings of its constituents.

(*iii*) Every grammatical constituent has a meaning which contributes to the meaning of the whole. (67)

Cruse points out that 'claim (ii) incorporates claim (i) but claim (i) could be true without claim (ii) being true. Claim (iii) is presupposed by the other two' (67). The principle appears to be straightforward. For instance, in the sentence *Rakesh goes to the office and Radha stays at home* the meaning is composed of the meaning of its constituent clauses *Rakesh goes to the office* and *Radha stays at home*. Further, the meaning of the first clause can be collected from the meanings of its constituent phrases *Rakesh, goes* and *to the office*. The meaning of the second clause can be collected from *Radha, stays* and *at home*. In the first clause *to* and *the office* combine to give us the meaning of *to the office*. Similarly, *the* and *office* together give us the meaning of *the office.* In the second clause, *at home* is a combination of *at* and *home.* So the meaning of a phrase is composed of its constituent words. The words in turn are composed of their constituent lexemes and grammatical morphemes. So *goes* is a combination of the lexeme *go* and the grammatical (present tense) morpheme *es* and *stays* is made up of the lexeme *stay* and the present tense morpheme *s*. The conjunction *and* joins the two clauses. The juxtaposition of the two clauses indicates there is a relation between *Rakesh* and *Radha.* In this way every grammatical constituent contributes to the meaning of the whole sentence. We can interpret this sentence because the 'meanings are composed in rule-governed ways' out of the meanings of the constituents. However, we shall see that there are limits to the principle of compositionality of meaning.

1.1 The Scope of the paper

In this paper I will discuss the extent to which meaning is or is not compositional. In other words it will be an attempt to study the ways in which the compositionality of meaning is restricted. It will try to explore whether compositionality is a matter of degree or whether there is a cline of compositionality of meaning. Using examples from English and Hindi it will also attempt to show how the principle of compositionality works in some equivalent expressions in English and Hindi. For transcription of Hindi/Urdu words, I will use the key provided by Bhardwaj and Wells (1989: 174-7).

2. Meaning and related concepts

The words *meaning* (noun) and *mean* (verb) can be used in different contexts and in different senses. In this paper I am concerned with meaning as it is understood in linguistics, that is, linguistic meaning. A distinction is made between two types of linguistic meaning - *descriptive* and *interpersonal*. Descriptive meaning is the 'meaning that describes something' (Hofmann 1993: 2). For instance, when someone utters a sentence such as *Vinod is in Delhi,* it tells us that there is a person called Vinod and he is in Delhi. This is factual information which can be explicitly asserted and denied or can be objectively verified. This comes under descriptive meaning but this may have other purposes as well. For example, it may mean that Vinod is in Delhi to be with his brother. It may also mean that Vinod is not available or that the speaker is telling a lie. All these other meanings depend on the shared knowledge between the speaker and the listener and therefore come under the realm of interpersonal meaning. But there is more to the interpersonal meaning which we will discuss in the subsequent sections.

2.1 *Utterances, Sentences and Propositions*

Hurford and Heasley (1983) define an utterance as

> . . . any stretch of talk, by a person, before and after which there is silence on the part of that person. (It) is the USE by a particular speaker, on a particular occasion, of a piece of language, such as a sequence of sentences, or a single phrase, or even a single word. (15)

If I say *I enjoyed writing this essay* and repeat this after a brief pause, I produce two utterances. If another person says the same thing after me, it will be an instance of a third utterance. So utterances are concrete physical events. A sentence on the other hand "is neither a physical event nor a physical object. It is, conceived abstractly, a string of words put together by the grammatical rules of a language" (16). A sentence therefore is an abstract entity. The three utterances referred to earlier are three different realisations of the same sentence. Let us move on to the notion of proposition. Consider the following sentences:

1) Columbus discovered America.
2) kolambas ne amairikaa kii khoj kii (Hindi)
   Columbus America of discovery did
3) America was discovered by Columbus.
4) It was Columbus who discovered America.
5) It was America that Columbus discovered.
6) What Columbus discovered was America.
7) The one who discovered America was Columbus.

Sentence 2 is a Hindi translation of sentence 1. All the sentences have grammatical differences which are irrelevant from the point of view of logic, because if one is true all the sentences are true, and if one is false then all are false. So all the sentences have a single common proposition. 'A proposition is that part of the meaning of the utterance of a declarative sentence which describes some state of affairs' (19). Whereas utterances, sentences and propositions can be true or false, only utterances and sentences can be grammatical. Grammar is not relevant for propositional meaning and only utterances can be loud or quiet. (22)

2.2 *Context*

The notion of context is important for interpretation. For our purpose we will restrict ourselves to two meanings of 'context'. First, it can be used to refer to 'non-linguistic environment of any language activity', that is, the socio-cultural background. Second, the word 'context' is also used to refer to 'the linguistic environment of any expression'. It is also called co-text (Sinclair 1991: 171).

3. Models of Compositionality

Cruse (2000) proposes three models of compositionality of meaning depending on the position we may take vis-ë-vis compositionality. He calls them the building-block model, the scaffolding model and the holistic model respectively. In the building-block model, 'the meaning of an expression can be finitely described, and is totally accounted for by standard compositional processes acting on the equally determinate meanings of its component parts' (79). The example that we discussed in section 1 fits this model. Here we do not go beyond the descriptive meaning. The problem arises when it becomes important to include the interpersonal context which necessitates the use of the scaffolding model or the holistic model. According to the scaffolding model 'what compositionality provides is the bare bones of a semantic structure for a complex expression, which is fleshed out by less predictable pragmatic means, using encyclopaedic knowledge, context, and so on' (79). The holistic model, on the other hand, 'requires that the meaning of every item is an indefinitely large entity which consists of its relations with all other items in the language. In a sense, all the effects of combination with other items are already present in the meaning: all that is needed is to extract the relevant portions' (79-80). Let us look at the following line which I seem to recall from a billboard advertisement of a restaurant that I glanced at while walking on a road in Delhi many years ago.

> If there is juicier leg of lamb, it's still walking.

When it is presented out of context, the descriptive meaning gives us only a part of the sense. Even when the context is given, one needs to interact with one's knowledge of the world, that, *leg of lamb* is something to be eaten. The co-text also reinforces this meaning. But the interpretation becomes difficult as it forces the reader to assume that 'a leg of lamb that is walking' is the juiciest. In our situation, though the use of words like *mutton, chicken, fish, beef* and *pork* is common, *leg of lamb* is relatively uncommon. When I gave this sentence to my postgraduate students, out of fifteen only five of them could make something out of it though subsequently I gave them the context of its use. I was not surprised as almost half the students were vegetarians. For a community, imaginary perhaps, that has not experienced any non-vegetarianism, this sentence could only be a part of a story from a jungle book in which this sentence was uttered by a wolf. What I want to stress here is that the building-block model cannot explain the intended meaning in this sentence. For a fuller interpretation, we need the scaffolding model or the holistic model as we need to use the encyclopaedic knowledge or the context and /or try to extract the relevant portions from all the effects of combination of every item with all other items.

4. Additive and interactive modes

In this section I will describe some of the ways in which meanings are combined. The combinations appear to follow the principle of compositionality but meanings are understood in different ways which may pose some challenge to compositional nature of certain expressions. According to Cruse,

> A combination is said to be additive if the meanings of constituents are simply added together and, both survive without radical change in the combination [...] In interactive types of combination the meaning of at least one constituent is radically modified. (67)

Let us look at the following:

(*i*) [Raju and Meena] are good friends.
(*ii*) Rita is [smart and beautiful].
(*iii*) Rekha likes [green shirts].

(i) and (ii) are examples of simple syntactic co-ordinations, which are additive modes of combination. *Green shirts* in (iii) is an example of interactive mode. *Green shirts* are things, which are *green* and *shirts* at the same time. Such combinations are called Boolean combinations (68). It is interactive in the sense that *green* restricts the meaning of *shirts* to a class of *green shirts*. According to Cruse, there are two types of interactive modification: 'first, the endocentric type, where the resultant meaning is of the same basic type as one of the constituents, and the exocentric type, where the resultant meaning is of a different basic type to either of the constituents (68). The example given above is a type of endocentric combination. Cruse (69) illustrates another type of endocentric combination which he calls relative descriptors. He gives the example of *a large mouse*. He seems to suggest that the meaning of *large* is to be understood in relation to the *mouse,* that is *large* within the class of mice.

Exocentric combinations, on the other hand, can be illustrated by noun phrases. The initial example that I have given in the introduction contains two cases of exocentric combination *to the office* and *at home*. In *to the office, to* denotes a relation and *the office* denotes a place but together they denote a direction. These are some of the cases which indicate that the principle of compositionality does not take us far.

5. Limits to compositionality

In this section I will discuss a few areas such as ambiguity, idioms, metaphor, conversational implicature and speech act where the principle of compositionality is restricted in some ways.

5.1 Ambiguity

'A sentence is said to be ambiguous whenever it can be associated with two or more different meanings' (Cann 1993:8). Ambiguity is the result of a number of reasons. A word may have more than one sense. This kind of ambiguity is called lexical ambiguity. For example, *We'll meet at the bank* is ambiguous because of two meanings of *bank* – 'bank of a river or financial institution'. Then there is another kind of ambiguity called structural ambiguity. In a sentence such as *He slapped the boy at the counter*, the ambiguity is based on the fact that *at the counter* may modify either *the boy* or the whole clause *he slapped the boy*. The immediate constituent analysis can disambiguate the sentence giving two structural descriptions for each meaning. We have yet another example of structural ambiguity in the sentence *She found him a good worker*. This sentence is ambiguous because of the grammatical relations between the constituents of the sentence and its sense depends upon whether the noun phrase *a good worker* is understood as an object or object complement. For one meaning the sentence is ditransitive and for the other meaning complex-transitive.

Let us now look at the following example from Hindi:

use roko mat, jaane do
him stop not, go let
[Don't stop him, let him go]

use roko, mat jaane do
him stop, not go let
[Stop him, don't let him go].

This is again a case of structural ambiguity. The word *mat* (not) may modify either the first clause or the second clause thereby producing two meanings. In fact, the correct position of a comma for each meaning will resolve the ambiguity. Let us now look at the following joke which I read in a magazine sometime ago.

A: Every minute a woman gives birth to 10 children.

B: We must find out the woman.

The humour lies in the non-generic reading of A's utterance by B. This kind of ambiguity comes under logic. Such ambiguous sentences, I argue, do not restrict the principle of compositionality because for each meaning of such ambiguous expressions the principle is valid. It may be pointed out here that in such cases we either decode one of the two meanings or both meanings at the same time.

Cann (1993: 9) discusses a third kind of ambiguity which he exemplifies in *Every good politician loves a cause*. He points out that sometimes a sentence can be only assigned a single surface constituent structure so that this ambiguity cannot be directly attributed to a syntactic source and is referred to as a semantic scope ambiguity. Ambiguities such as the one above do restrict the compositionality of meaning.

5.2 *Idiom and idiomaticity*

Cruse (1986) observes that idiom has been traditionally defined as 'an expression whose meaning cannot be inferred from the meaning of its parts' (37). He goes on to state that 'the definition must be understood as stating that an idiom is an expression whose meaning can not be accounted for as a compositional function of the meanings its parts have when they are not parts of idioms' (37). He points out that it is easy to differentiate between 'idiomatic' and 'non-idiomatic expression'. According to him, an idiom must satisfy two requirements: first, it should be lexically complex (made up of more than one constituents) and second, it should be a single minimal semantic constituent. (37). For example, the meaning of the idiom *kick the bucket* cannot be derived from the words 'bucket' or 'kick' when used in isolation. Also it is an idiom because it is single minimum semantic constituent equivalent to 'die'. Idioms by definition are not compositional. So the non-compositional nature of the meaning of a group of words may be called idiomaticity. Sinclair (1991: 110) gives an example of a grammatical phrase 'of course'. Sinclair seems to suggest that the space between the two words has no meaning and predicts that it will soon disappear exactly as it happened in expression such as *maybe, anyway, everyone* etc.

Proverbs and sayings are also known to have a great deal of idiomaticity. This may suggest that idiomatic expressions have different degrees of idiomaticity and indeed it is so. For example, *might is right* is less idiomatic than *all that glitters is not gold*. In fact, *might is right* follows the compositionality to a great extent but not its Hindi equivalent:

jiskii laathii uskii bheiṅs

(one who has got a stick will take away the buffalo)

Let us now look at the compound nouns. The idiomaticity of *teRhii khiir* (a difficult task) in Hindi can be explained on the same lines as that of 'hotdog' in English. *teRhii* which means 'not straight' or 'difficult' may give some clue but *khiir* which is a sweet dish made from milk, rice and sugar has nothing to do with the meaning of the expression as a whole. Similarly, *hot* may be some help but *dog* does not provide any clue to the meaning of *hotdog*. Let us now consider the following compounds in English:

black market	black belt
black sheep	black tea
blackball	blackboard

Blackball and *black sheep* are more idiomatic than *black market* or *black belt* whereas the meaning of *blackboard* and *black tea* is more or less compositional. However, their sense is not understood the same way. We now look at the following compounds in Hindi:

ghoRaagaaRii	Horse vehicle (a vehicle pulled by a horse)
relgaaRii	Rail vehicle (a vehicle that runs on rails)
motargaaRii	Motor vehicle (a vehicle pulled by a motor)
DiizalgaaRii	Diesel vehicle (a vehicle that runs on diesel)
maalgaaRii	Goods train (a vehicle that carries goods)

The meaning as given in brackets shows that the relationship between the two 'lexemes' in each case is not the same. All these compounds have a very low idiomaticity and follow more or less the principle of compositionality of meaning but again the compositionality is understood differently in each case.

We now consider the following English proverbs:

(a) to carry coals to Newcastle

(b) to make hay while the sun shines.

The literal compositional meaning together with 'the knowledge of the world' will make them wholly compositional. It is a common knowledge that Newcastle is a place in England where coal is found in abundance and that the sun is a rarity in England. The equivalent expressions in Hindi are as follows:

(c) ulte baa̐ns barelii ko
taking back bamboos Bareilly to
[to carry bamboos to Bareilly]

(d) bahtii gangaa me haath dhonaa
Flowing Ganga in hand(s) (to) wash
[to wash hands in the flowing river *Ganga*]

Both (c) in Hindi and (a) in English are used in similar situations. Bareilly is a place which is famous for bamboo trees. The sense of (c) is same as that of (a), that is, giving something to someone when one already has it in plenty. Similarly (b) in Hindi and (d) in English have the same interpretation, that is, one should make use of the opportunity when one gets it. Such idiomatic expressions would fit the scaffolding model of the principle of compositionality.

5.3 Metaphor

Metaphors are another important area where the compositionality of meaning is restricted. Goatly (1997) defines metaphors as follows:

> Metaphors occur when a unit of discourse is used to refer unconventionally to an object, process or concept, or colligates in an unconventional way. And when this unconventional act of reference or colligation is understood on the basis of similarity, matching or analogy involving the conventional referent or colligates of the unit and the actual unconventional referent or colligates. (8)

'Colligate is one kind of collocate. Whereas the term collocation is used to refer to any kind of co-occurrence of words in a text, 'Colligation is the syntactic relation between the two words' (8).

Let us consider the following metaphorical expressions in Hindi or Urdu:

a) tum gadhe ho
you donkey are
[You are a donkey].

b) zindagii sigareT kaa dhuaẵ hai
life cigarette of smoke is
[Life is smoke of a cigarette]

c) aadmii bulbulaa hai paanii kaa
man bubble is water of
kyaa bharosaa hai zindagaanii kaa
what trust/ assurance is life of
[Man is a bubble of water. How can one trust life? (An Urdu couplet)]

d) dil ek mandir hai
heart a temple is
pyaar kii jismẽ hotii hai puujaa...(A Hindi film song)
love of which-in done is worship
[Heart is a temple where love is worshipped].

e) zindagii to bevafaa hai, ek din thukraaegii
life only unfaithfulis, one daywill kick (me)
maut mahbuubaa hai, apne saath lekar jaaegii
death beloved is, her with will take along
[Life is unfaithful as it will leave me one day, but death is (my) beloved that will take me along].

Some of the above expressions are more metaphorical than others. Goatly (1997: 38) suggests that there are clines of metaphoricity from the most active original transfer metaphors at one end to the most conventional, dead and approximative ones at the other. He uses the following diagram to show five clines of metaphoricity:

(1) Approximative Similarity .... Distant similarity/ Analogy
(2) Conventionality .... Unconventionality
(3) Marking .... No marking

(4) Non-contradictoriness ....Contradictoriness
(5) Explicitness .... Inexplicitness

Five metaphorical clines (38)

On the basis of these clines we can examine the metaphors given above. Clearly (a) is more conventional than the others and would require the least processing effort. In this case we have to move from semantic field of 'animals' to that of 'humans'. In comparison the expression 'tum paagal aadmii ho' [you are a mad man] is almost non-metaphorical and can be placed at one end of the cline (1). It is a case of approximative similarity where both 'you' and 'a mad man' are from the same semantic field, that is, 'humans'. Similarly, (c) is less metaphorical than (b). In (b) 'life' and 'smoke of a cigarette' are distant and also unconventional. The same is the case with (c) in which 'man' and 'a bubble of water' are not from the same semantic field and therefore are distant but the interpretation is made explicit by the cotext in (c). We can notice that both these metaphorical expressions suggest the transience of human life but in case of (c) it is made explicit. In (d) again which is an example of a Hindi film song the cotext makes the interpretation explicit, that is, 'heart is a temple where love is worshipped'. (e) is also an example of explicit interpretation where 'death' has been described as man's faithful beloved. So (b) again is more metaphorical than (d) and (e) in the sense that it is inexplicit. It is therefore possible to place metaphorical expressions at different points in the cline(s) of metaphoricity. Clearly the compositionality of meaning is inversely proportional to the metaphoricity of the linguistic expressions. It follows that we can talk of the cline(s) of compositionality of meaning.

5.3.1 Metaphors and Metonymy

According to Lakoff and Johnson (2003: 5), 'the essence of metaphor is understanding and experiencing one kind of thing in terms of another.' For them, it is a mapping from source domain to target domain. Source domains are from our direct experiences of everyday life which are familiar and easy to imagine. Target domains, on the other hand, are abstract concepts. Given below is a list of source domains and their corresponding target domains exemplified by Lakoff and Johnson (1980, 2003).

Source Domain	**Target Domain**
1) money	time
2) food, plants, products	ideas
3) containers	emotions, visual field, activities
4) journeys	love, life

5) buildings	theories
6) fighting	arguments
7) seeing	understanding
8) gambling	life
9) physical contact	emotional effect
10) up and down	control, health, status

[from Siewierska 2003: Lecture Notes]

The detailed discussion of different kinds of domains is beyond the scope of this paper. It is, however, significant to point out that Hindi and Urdu are also rich in such conceptual metaphors. Here are some of the Hindi examples of 'journey' as a 'source domain' and 'love/life' as a 'target domain'.

hum kaafii aage nikal aae haiˇ
[We have come a long way].
ab piichhe jaanaa mushkil hai
[Now it is difficult to turn back].
ham ek muKaam par aa gae haiˇ
[We have reached a destination].
phir maine piichhe muR kar nahiiˇdekhaa
[I never looked back again]
hum ek moR par pahučh gaye haiˇ
[We are at a cross-roads].

Metonymy on the other hand is an association between two components within a single domain. Lakoff and Johnson (2003) point out:

> In a metonymy, there is only one domain: the immediate subject matter. There is only one mapping; typically the metonymic source maps to the metonymic target (the referent) so that one item in the domain can stand for the other (265).

Given below are some examples of metonymy which exist in Hindi:

1) Place for institution
naii dillii iraaK senaa bhejne ke vishay meˇchuppii saadhe hai
[New Delhi is quiet on the issue of sending troops to Iraq].
2) Represented entity for represented
bhaarat ne Khitaab jiit liyaa
[India has won the title]
3) Part for whole
vahaǎˇpar kaii Khuubsuurat chehre maujuud the
[Many beautiful faces were present there]
4) Whole for part
kyaa meˇaapkii rasoii istemaal kar saktaa huŭˇ

[Can I use your kitchen?]

5) Container for contained
ketalii ubal rahii hai
[The kettle is boiling]

Siewierska (2003) gives a list of metaphorical expressions in which anger is conceived in terms of heat, madness, fight, animal habits, etc. Hindi and Urdu have all of them. Here are some of the examples:

1) meraa khuun khaul rahaa hai
[My blood is boiling]
2) uskaa bhejaa garam thaa
[His head/ mind was hot]
3) unmeˇgarmaagarmii ho gaii
[They had a heated argument]
4) vo gusse se paagal ho gayaa
[He became mad with anger]
5) apne gusse se laRo taaki uspar kaabuu paa sako (religious discourse)

[Fight you anger so that you can overpower/control it] 6) uskaa gussaa bahut bhayaanak hai
[He has a ferocious temper]

7) vo gusse se dahaaRne lagaa
[He was growling with rage]

One metaphorical expression which looks at 'anger' as 'object' appears to be novel.

apnaa gussa apnii jeb meˇrakhkho
[Keep your anger in your pocket]

Conceptual metaphors seem to exist in all the languages. However, certain languages may be richer than others in terms of use of metaphors. Novel metaphors become conventional after a passage of time and require less processing effort. The fact however remains that in order to see these metaphors as compositional we need to go beyond the building-block model of compositionality.

5.4 Conversational Implicature

In language it is normal to mean more than what is actually said, that is, more than what is literally expressed. Let us look at the following example from Hindi:

1. A: kyaa aapne meraa chek beĩk meˇjamaa kiyaa
(Did you deposit my cheque in the bank?)
2. B: raaste meˇradha mil gaii thii
(I met Radha on the way).

Clearly (1) is a request for information which requires a confirmation. However the information in (2) is not directly expressed. What is conveyed in (2) can be understood on the basis of the shared knowledge between A and B. If A knows that Radha works in a bank, it can be understood to mean that B might have given the cheque to Radha who would deposit it in the bank. However, it may also means that B did not deposit the cheque if both A and B understand that Radha is a talkative person and that once one starts talking to her, one loses track of time. So there is a big gap in what is said and what is meant in (2). This kind of ambiguity is based on 'sequencing structure of conversation'. Here is another example:

A: Coming to the pictures tonight? (3)

B: There's a magic show in the Tagore theatre this evening. (4)

Again B's response does not appear to be relevant to the invitation by A. But assuming that B is being relevant otherwise he would not have said so, A has to draw on the assumed knowledge that B might be more interested in the magic show and can conclude that B would not accompany A which is the implicature derived from B's utterance. The descriptive meaning of (4) does not convey this sense. So in both the examples above the compositionality of meaning is restricted. The concept of implicature is related to Grice's Cooperative Principle which states that 'make your contribution such as is required, at a stage at which it occurs, by the accepted purpose or direction of the talk exchange in which you are engaged' (Grice 1975 cited in Levinson 1983: 101). Accordingly it has been elaborated in four sub-principles called maxims—maxims of quality, quantity, relevance and manner. The examples above are cases of conversational implicature in which the maxim of relevance has been flouted. We need to apply the scaffolding model here as we need to draw upon the contextual factors in order to interpret the meaning

5.5 Speech Act:

In speech act theory developed by Austin (1993) and Searle (1969) utterances are seen as 'conventionally grounded social actions'. In other words, speech is action, and that language can actually be used to do things (Austin 1962, cited in Leech 1983, Levinson 1983, Keith 1986, Yule 1996). A speech act may be direct or indirect. For instance, *open the window* is a direct directive whereas *would you mind opening the window?* is an indirect directive. It is also possible in some cases in which the action requested may not be coded linguistically. It has to be determined by the context and other procedures such as Grice's Cooperative Principle. For example, *it's hot in here* is the most indirect directive which remains ambiguous. Such indirect speech acts may restrict the principle of compositionality of meaning. The only way to resolve this is to invoke the holistic model by considering the intended meaning as one of the effects of the combination of items in the given expression.

6. Conclusion

On the basis of our discussion we may conclude that we can certainly talk of degrees of compositionality of meaning. In case of metaphors, the compositionality of meaning of an expression is inversely proportional to the metaphoricity of that expression. The same is true of idiomaticity. We have noticed that one expression may be more idiomatic that others. We have seen some cases where some phrasal idioms were more idiomatic than the proverbs. We have also noticed that equivalent idiomatic expressions in two languages may have different degrees of idiomaticity. As far as ambiguities are concerned they do not come in the way of compositionality of meaning. Whether we decode one of the meanings or both meanings, for each meaning the principle is valid. It also follows from the above discussion that there seems to be a cline of compositionality of meaning but it is difficult to define the range of the cline in terms of certain categories. We cannot for example say that metaphors are more compositional than idioms or vice versa. Each instance has to be studied individually.

As we have seen we cannot go very far with the building-block model of compositionality. The scaffolding model perhaps would be more helpful as it would resolve the ambiguities caused by the context of language use especially indirect speech acts. If we adopt the holistic model and assume that 'all the effects of combination with other items are already present in the meaning' we should be able to see the meanings of all instances of language use including metaphors and idioms as compositional. If we go with this 'radical view' of compositionality, we can argue that when we interact with a piece of language use we bring our 'reality' to the text. If our reality does not match with what is intended and we are not able 'to extract the relevant portions', there is nothing we can do about it.

REFERENCES

Allan, K. 1986. *Linguistic meaning*. London: Routledge and Keagan Paul.

Bhardwaj, M. and G. Wells 1989. *Hindi Urdu Bol Chaal: A beginners' course in spoken Hindi and Urdu on BBC Television*. London: BBC Enterprises Ltd.

Cann, R. 1993. *Formal semantics*. Cambridge: Cambridge University Press.

Cruse, D.A. 1986. *Lexical semantics*. Cambridge: Cambridge University Press.

Cruse, D.A. 2000. *Meaning in language.* Oxford: Oxford University Press.
Hofmann, R. Th. 1993. *Realms of semantics.* London: Longman.
Hurford, J.R. and B. Heasley 1983. *Semantics: A coursebook.* Cambridge: Cambridge University Press.
Goatly, A. 1997. *The language of metaphors.* London: Routledge.
Lakoff, G. and M. Johnson 1980. *Metaphors we live by.* Chicago: The University of Chicago Press.
Lakoff, G. and M. Johnson 2003. *Metaphors we live by* Chicago: The University of Chicago Press.
Leech, G. 1983. *Principles of pragmatics.* London: Longman.
Levinson, S.C. 1983. *Pragmatics.* Cambridge: Cambridge University Press.
Saeed, J.I. 2002. *Semantics.* Second Edition. Oxford: Basil Blackwell.
Siewierska, A. 2003. 'Compositionality of Meaning' Lecture notes (unpublished).
Sinclair, J. 1991. *Corpus, concordance, collocation.* Oxford: Oxford University Press.
Yule, G. 1996. *Pragmatics.* Oxford: Oxford University Press.

22

On the Nature of Reason in the Present-day Academic Research[1]

Pramod Pandey

1. Front Matter

I am concerned here with a certain way of reasoning as a contingent historical truth about the dominant theories of today and their consequences on the growth of knowledge. This has limited philosophical significance, at best. I propose to discover here a form of rationality that can enhance our understanding about the nature of reason underlying present-day academic research, heavily influenced by western theories. I shall speak mainly from the point of view of modern language studies, and relate it at random with other disciplines and social living.

The paper is organized as follows. Section 2 presents an operational definition of the reasoning informing present-day theories. Section 3 characterizes the reasoning as Contending Dichotomous Reasoning or -AR. Section 4 deals with the characteristic features of -AR. Sections 5 and 6 discuss the roots and consequences of -AR, respectively. Section 7 clarifies the conception of -AR by showing what it is not. Section 8 discusses a way of getting out of the -AR. Finally, section 9 presents the conclusions.

2. Reasoning in modern theories

Modern theories in academic research appear in my view to employ a certain way of reasoning that may be operationally described as follows:

(1) Given an object of inquiry X, assume that it has apparent duality, consisting of the dual elements A and –A; take up one of the elements of the duality, say, A, and argue that it is of primary/ basic significance in X, while the other, -A, is of

secondary/ derived significance, and conclude that for an explanation of X the proper subject of study is A, not –A, and vice versa.

For instance, in his well-known book, *Knowledge of Language: Its Nature, Origin, and Use* (1986), Chomsky presents a general outline of the theory of Universal Grammar (UG), following a general scheme of reasoning given in (1). He divides the concept of language as a complex of two different types, one, called E-language, having to do with linguistic behaviour, and the other, called I-language, having to do with the knowledge underlying linguistic behaviour. He justifies the shift of focus from E-language to I-language for the advancement of the UG programme. The argument plan can be inferred from the titles of the chapters. There are four chapters in all. The titles and subtitles of the first two chapters are:

Chapter 1: Knowledge of Language as Focus of Inquiry.
Chapter 2: Concepts of Language;
2.1 The Commonsense Concept and Departures from It,
2.2 Externalized Language,
2.3 Internalized Language,
2.4 The Shift of Focus from E-Language to I-Language,
2.4.1 On the Reasons for the Shift of Focus,
2.4.2 The Empirical Basis for the Study of I-language,
2.4.3 Some Consequences for the Shift of Focus.

Chapter 3 is about the UG of I-Language. *Chapter 4* briefly deals with an aspect of E-language.

Several versions of this mode of argumentation can be found not only in the specific theory of language that Chomsky propounded and that is the dominant theory of language today, but also its opposites, known as the Functional theories of language, as in Foley and van Valin (1985) and in Givon (1993).

On another plane, one comes across arguments between linguists with theoretical and with descriptivist persuasions advocating their goals and relegating the goals of the other. Chomsky's criticism of American structural linguistics and of the behaviourist theory of learning (Chomsky 1959) is well-known. In recent years, descriptivist arguments have come afresh. Thus Dixon (1997) makes a plea for the documentation of languages and for developing a 'Basic Linguistic Theory' in place of formal theories, which, in his view are antagonistic to fieldwork and writing of grammars.

The line of reasoning operationally described in (1) can be termed as *Contending Dichotomous Reasoning* or *Main-and-Auxiliary* type of reasoning or –AR.

Contending Dichotomous Reasoning (–AR) needs to be

distinguished from plain Dichotomous Reasoning (see e.g. Ellis 1962, Beck 1963). If the relationship between the elements of the object is seen as complementary, the type of reasoning may be termed as Complementary Dichotomous Reasoning or +AR. If, on the other hand, the relationship between the elements of the object is seen as contending (*either-or*), the type of reasoning may be termed as Contending Dichotomous Reasoning or –AR. The main interest of this paper lies in investigating the attributes and consequences of Contending Dichotomous Reasoning (–AR) in the growth of knowledge in modern times.

3. Contending Dichotomous Reasoning (–AR)

Consider the following list as illustrations of the instantiation of –AR in different disciplines:

Philosophy: Empiricism/Rationalism, Analytical/ Synthetic.
Psychology: Behaviorism/Cognitivism.
Economics: Capitalism/Communism.
Political Science: Democracy/Dictatorship.
Sociology: Individual/Collective, Urban/Rural.
Arts: Art-for-Art's Sake/Art-for-Life's Sake, Culture/ Science.
Linguistics: Thought/Communication, (First Language) Acquisition/ (Second Language)Learning, Rules/Constraints.

The point about the dichotomies in the various fields is that the pursuit of knowledge in them requires one to choose between them. The choice having been made, one must depend on a set of concepts, categories and techniques of analysis that are unique to it and at odds with the opposite element of the dichotomy. Thus a philosopher must assume knowledge to be based entirely on either experience or innate mental dispositions. A psychologist concerned with accounting for learning in a certain domain must either devise ways and means of incorporating all the contents of learning in the domain or allow for the learning to depend on the creativity of the learner. An economic policy must not undermine either individual freedom or collective growth in any way. One can go on enumerating instances of dichotomous concepts and approaches in the various fields of human knowledge today as evidence of the force with which –AR seems to overwhelm them. There is little doubt that –AR leads to polarizing knowledge in terms of opposing concepts and methods.

However, the –AR method does not lie in simply proposing opposites and choosing between them, but rather in certain modalities that can be said to yield a complex character to it. These modalities are discussed in the following section.

Before proceeding with the discussion of the modalities of

Contending Dichotomous Reasoning, however, it is useful to briefly consider the main issue in linguistics, as it relates to other disciplines concerned with language, such as philosophy and psychology. Linguistics in the the past fifty years has been concerned with two alternative views of language, namely, as consisting in the knowledge of linguistic structure (e.g. Chomsky 1965, 1986) and the use of that knowledge (e.g. Halliday 1985). This fundamental difference in the two views of language, broadly known as the formal and functional views (see e.g. Newmeyer 1998), informs all the other aspects of theoretical inquiries in linguistics (e.g. see Pandey 2001), such as the relevant data (intuitive or from the community), valid evidence (internal or external), type of explanation (formal or functional), etc. Theoretical studies on language in related disciplines, such as psychology (e.g. Bates and MacWhinney 1982) and philosophy (e.g. McDowell 1980) are along the lines of the fundamental difference in the two views.

4. Characteristics of –AR Reasoning

Contending Dichotomous Reasoning is characterized by the following features.

Polarity. Intrinsic to –AR in the investigation of an object of study is the propensity to ascribe polarity to it. Thus, human knowledge has been assumed by philosophers (Locke and Descartes), psychologists (Watson and Piaget), political thinkers (Burke and Chomsky), aestheticians (Derrida and Mendelssohn), language philosophers (Quine and Putnam) and linguists (Bloomfield and Chomsky) to depend on two alternative properties, experience and innate abilities. Leading thinkers in these disciplines must show their allegiance to one of the elements of polarity.

It is often observed that investigations in these disciplines must be marked by a clear choice between the polar opposites in all possible aspects. For instance, in the announcement of the topic ("Experience and Experiences") of the 13th Colloquium 2007 of the International Philosophy Colloquia Evian), it is mentioned that the Colloquium "aims to provide a setting in which participants can discuss whether to understand experience as mediated or unmediated, conceptual or sensory, linguistic or prelinguistic, subjective or intersubjective, foundational or subversive, passive or active, practical or theoretical, etc." The 'etc.' here, it is easy to guess, is of other possible polar options.

Prioritization. It is not the case that only one of the elements is accepted as a true representation of reality, while the other is rejected as false. Rather, it is assumed that one of them is the main/basic/ primary, while the other is auxiliary/derivative/secondary. As an illustration, consider the following quote from Michael Dummet (1989:

192), a well-known philosopher of language, on the function of language:

> Language, it is natural to say, has two principal functions: that of an instrument of communication, and that of a vehicle of thought. *We are therefore impelled to ask which of the two is primary.* Is it because language is an instrument of communication that it can also serve as a vehicle of thought? Or is it, conversely, because it is a vehicle of thought, and can therefore express thoughts, that it can be used by one person to communicate his thoughts to others? [italics mine PP].

It is not clear to me as to why we are "... impelled to ask which of the two is primary", unless there is a ruling assumption that when presented with such dichotomies, one of them must be assumed to be primary.

Irreconcilability. There is no relationship between the opposing elements of the dichotomy. Only one of them must prevail. Thus, Chomsky, for a long time argued for the superiority of 'formal' over 'functional' explanations in linguistics, as can be seen in the following quote (Chomsky1971: 44):

> Where properties of language can be explained on such "functional" grounds, they provide no revealing insight into the nature of mind. Precisely because the explanations proposed here are "formal explanations", precisely because the proposed principles are not essential or even natural properties of any imaginable language, they provide a revealing mirror of the mind (if correct).

The development of one of the elements of the polarity must be seen as a criticism of the other. Thus a formalist explanation of a linguistic phenomenon must be seen as implying the inadequacies of a functionalist approach and *vice versa*.

The relationship of irreconcilability is one of the traits of contending theories involving a 'paradigm shift' in the words of Kuhn (1962: 103), "...the normal-scientific tradition that emerges from a scientific revolution is not only incompatible but often actually incommensurable with that which has gone before".

Reversal. Focus on one of the elements of a duality often leads to a reversal of research programmes in terms of their methods and goals. This has to do with the in-built polarity in the mode of –AR reasoning. As one of the ends of the polarity is denied any significance, the progress in the sciences takes the form of the swing of a pendulum.

Such a swing (see Kiparsky 1971) took place in linguistics at the turn of the last century, when linguists, following de Saussure (1911), turned their attention from the study of historical change to synchronic descriptions. Instances of such swings are common to a majority of disciplines.[2]

Recall the debate between Karl Popper's notion of Falsifiability and Thomas Kuhn's notion of Paradigm Shift characterizing the essential nature of the growth of science (see e.g. Lakatos et al. 1969). Kuhn's explanation of 'paradigm shift' in programmes of research, on account not of evidence or reason, as argued by Popper (1959 [1935]), but of sociological factors, seems to be a predictable phenomenon rather than 'irrational' (see e.g. Maxwell 1974)), from the present point of view. When a critical aspect of a polar reality being investigated is ignored, the search for truth is bound to lead to a reversal to it; a complete account is impossible from an investigation of half-truth.

Argumentativeness. –AR is argumentative in the following senses.

One, it supersedes evidence, that is, the evidence is used to prove the argument.

Two, it selects supporting intra-theoretic evidence. Thus, for instance, once having argued for the empirical basis for the investigation of an aspect of reality, say I-Language in linguistics, as shown above in $ 2, the evidence that will be found to have a bearing on the investigation of that aspect of reality must all come from within it.

Three, –AR reasoning ignores evidence from the opposite position as metatheoretically irrelevant. Thus, in linguistic theory of I-Language, it is unusual to find a hypothesis being justified on the basis of data from linguistic variation or language pathology, because these areas of language are assumed to belong to E-Language.

5. Roots of –AR

A strong reason for the predominance of –AR in modern theories is its instrumentality in the growth of normal science. Scientific inquiries require a problem to be broken down into smaller, distinct problems for exhaustive and in-depth analyses, so that its investigation can grow on firm, falsifiable grounds. However, the extension of –AR to all domains of inquiry, and without simultaneously seeking interrelation among the aspects of a problem can lead to an inadequate and thus distorted view of reality. The progress in natural sciences as well as in social sciences has thus come to be questioned (see e.g. Laudan 1977, Wagner and Berger 1995).

6. Consequences of –AR

The consequences of –AR reasoning on the growth of knowledge have been immense. In fact, the entire enterprize known as the Modernity Project seems to have grown in the way of –AR, as can be inferred from Habermas (1985), where he argues that the main aim of the project was to focus on the development of "objective science, universal morality and law, and autonomous art according to their inner logic. At the same time, this project intended to release the cognitive potentials of each of these domains from their esoteric forms. The Enlightenment philosophers wanted to utilize this accumulation of specialized culture for the enrichment of everyday life- that is to say, for the rational organization of everyday social life." (p. 9). Habermas's proposal, in the face of the prevailing situtation, opposed to peaceful social living, is to continue the project, not abandon it, by seeking a relinking of the three separated domains. Pandey (2001) tries to show Generative Linguistics as an exemplar case of the Project of Modernity and how it can grow in the direction suggested by Habermas. Pantham (1981, and in subsequent papers) has argued that the crises being faced in the politico-economic and socio-cultural affairs in the modern times, a topic of critical concern in the writings of Habermas, have a solution in Gandhiji's social theory and praxis. The point about the solution is that it is based not on resolving in favour of one of the opposite sides in conflict, but in striking a relationship between the opposing sides of the conflict.

7. Getting Out: Synthesis

A way out of the consequences of contending dichotomous reasoning determining the fate of academic disciplines in modern times is in seeking a synthesis between polarities. Proposals for synthesis can be found in most major disciplines today.

In linguistics, the title of Haspelmath's review article ("Why Can't We Talk to Each Other?") is a loud cry for the formalist and functionalist approaches in linguistics to come together. The growing realization of the need for a synthetic relationship between the two approaches has been felt mainly on two grounds: one, each having been found to be valid in different domains of linguistic structure (see e.g. Newmeyer 1998); two, language, their common object of study, having come to be seen as both a natural and a social kind (e.g. Pateman 1989), requiring both formal and functional approaches of investigation. In a different vein, it is such a synthesis that Agnihotri (2001) argues for: without undermining the contributions of formal linguistics, whose main concern is with the structure of language, he argues at length for the need to bring into methodological focus 'the interdependence of language and society'.

In the field of political philosophy, Gellner (1998) has argued persistently for a synthesis between two opposed visions of human society, namely individualism and communalism, with analogues in other spheres, such as rationalism and empiricism in philosophy and cognitive psychology, and capitalism and communism in economic thought. Gellner argues that neither of "these visions [individualism and communalism] will do: we are not, in fact, self-sufficient individuals, nor do we possess self-contained and self-authenticating communities. Mankind has shifted , and is continuing to shift, from relatively self-contained communities to wider community endowed with powerful knowledge, which works more or less in terms of norms conveyed by the individualist model. It is only by understanding this transition that we can come to terms with our condition. Absoluting either end of the old polarity will not do." (Gellner 1998: 188)

As another instance of the expressed need for a synthesis between contending theories in a discipline, we find Lee (1986) in the field of demography.[3] "There are two grand themes in macro-demographic theory: the Malthusian one, that population equilibrates with resources at some level mediated by technology and a conventional standard of living; and a Boserupian one, that technological change is itself spurred by increases in population. The striking association between the levels and changes in technology and population over the past million years leaves no doubt in my mind that at least one of these views is correct. But it is also possible that both are, since the two theories are not contradictory, but rather complementary." (p. 96) The writer's assumption underlying the proposal for a synthesis between the two contending demographic theories, namely, that only complementary theories can be synthesized, follows contending dichotomous reasoning. We are however concerned here with the attempt at synthesis, and skip a discussion on that assumption.

At the micro-level in a field of inquiry, it is easy to come across similar attempts at synthesis. As an illustration, phonological theory, within the broad field of linguistic theory, has experienced a recent move to reexamine the relationship between formal phonology with functional phonetics and to show their mutual influence on one another as against their strict separation as sub-components (e.g. Hayes 1999, Pierrehumbert et al. 2000, Cohn 2007).

8. What –AR is not

In trying to grasp the concept of contending dichotomous reasoning, it is necessary to distinguish it from certain cases that may appear to be its instantiations but are not. Two of the well-known cases are taken up here.

One of the cases is the 'Divide and Rule' policy that is often ascribed to the British rule in India and other places in the world. The policy has actually a long history and the expression can be traced to early Latin and Greek, as a translation equivalent of "divide et impera" and "divide ut regnes". The policy can be seen as a general negative principle of governance. Its relation to –AR, if any, is indirect. The principle, as can be easily seen, differs from –AR in its goal of application. -AR aims at proving the primacy of one over another. The objective of employing the principle of 'divide and rule' is to keep two entities divided. The two objectives are clearly non-identical.

The other case of a possible instance of –AR is the Socratic/ Elenctic method of hypothesis elimination, which depends on positing two opposites, with one of them shown to be untrue. This method too is not an instance of –AR, since it involves mutual agreement between interlocutors to engage themselves in it in order to arrive at the truth about an object of inquiry. As we saw above, -AR crucially leads to irreconcilability in the positions of its adherents.

9. Conclusions

The Contending Dichotomous way of thinking that has been a strong trait of the modern theories has had both beneficent and meretricious influence on the growth of knowledge in the modern times. As argued above, the dominant theories are based on polarity, claims about superiority of their own validity, and theoretical reversals, among others. It happens to be the case that most of the modern theories in the various fields of knowledge are Western in origin as well as growth. Considering the negligible role of developing countries from the East, such as India, where knowledge has not been based on such a mode of reasoning, it appears plausible to characterize –AR as Western, albeit purely in the socio-historical sense of having to do with the modern times. The case of that plausibility appears stronger when we notice that even in a field such as linguistics, which has had a long tradition in a developing country like India, research is guided by concerns that are seldom related to the native tradition. While there is a lot of merit in the modern Western theories, largely owing to rigorous scientific techniques of analysis and explanation, researchers in developing countries like India, not having internalized the mode of contending dichotomous reasoning that underlies them, fail to make substantial contribution to them. The foundational issues that the theories address remain obfuscated to them, especially with regard to strict allegiance to the goals and methods of one of them.

It is necessary to closely examine the nature of the –AR mode of thinking, its influence on the growth of knowledge and ways and means of arriving at beneficent modes that critically involve scientific methodology, without doubt, but that avoid partial representation of reality and avert predictable reversals.

REFERENCES

Agnihotri, R.K. 2001. *Half the battle and a quarter.* Mysore: Central Institute of Indian Languages.

Bates, E. and B. MacWhinney 1982. Functionalist approaches to grammar. In E. Wanner and L. Gleitman (eds.) *Language acquisition: The state of the art.* N.Y.: Cambridge University Press.

Beck, A.T. 1963. Thinking and Depression: Idiosyncratic content and cognitive distortions. *Archives of General Psychiatry* 9, 324-333.

Chomsky, Noam 1959. A Review of B. F. Skinner's *Verbal Behavior. Language* 35, 26-58.

Chomsky, N. 1971. *Problems of knowledge and freedom*. New York: Random House.
Cohn, Abigail 2007. Phonetics in Phonology and Phonology in Phonetics. *Working Papers of the Cornell Phonetics Laboratory* Vol. 16. Pp. 1-31.
Dixon, R.M.W. 1997. *The rise and fall of language*. Cambridge: Cambridge University Press.
Dummet, Michael 1989. Language and Communication. In George Alexander (ed.) *Reflections on Chomsky*. Oxford: Basil Blackwell. 192-212.
Ellis, A. 1962. *Reason and emotion in psychotherapy*. New York: Lyle Stuart.
Fischer, Louis 1982. *Gandhi: His life and message for the world*. Signet.
Foley, W.A. and R.D. van Valin 1985. *Functional syntax and universal grammar*. Cambridge: Cambridge University Press.
Franceschi, Paul 2007. Preprint. Complement to a theory of cognitive distortions. http://cogprints.org/5261/1/Complement_to_a_theory_of_the_cognitive_distortions_(Cogprints).pdf.
Ganeri, Jonardan 2000. *Indian philosophical theory*. Oxford: Oxford University Press.
Gellner, E. 1998. *Language and identity: Essays on Wittgenstein*. Oxford: Oxford University Press.
Givon, T. 1993. *English grammar: A function based Introduction*. Vol. 1. Philadelphia: John Benjamins Publishing Co.
Goody, Jack 1992. East and West: Rationality in Review. *Ethnos* 6-36.
Habermas, Jürgen 1985. Modernity- an incomplete project. In H. Foster (ed.) *Post-modern culture*. London: Pluto Press. 3-15.
Halliday, M.A.K. 1985. (1st ed.) *An introduction to functional grammar*. London: Edwin Arnold. [2nd ed. 1994].
Haspelmath, M. 2000. Why can't we talk to each other? *Lingua* 110, 235-255. [A review article on Newmeyer 1998].
Hayes, B. 1999. Phonetically-driven phonology: The role of Optimality Theory and grounding. In M. Darnell et al. (eds.) *Functionalism and formalism in linguistics*. Vol. 1: General Papers. Amsterdam: John Benjamin. pp. 243-285.
International Philosophy Colloquia Avian 2007 http://www.uildesheim.de/eviancolloquium/ topic.html
Kakkar, Sudhir and Katherina Kakkar 2007. *The Indians: Portrait of a people*. Penguin India.
Koller, John M. 1982. *The Indian way*. New York: Macmillan Publishing Company.
Korzybski, Alfred 2003 (1933). *Science and sanity*. Forth Worth, Texas: Institute of General Semantics.
Kuhn, Thomas 1962. *The structure of scientific revolutions*. Chicago: University of Chicago Press.
Lakatos, Imre 1970. Falsification and the methodology of scientific research programmes. In I. Lakatos and A. Musgrave (eds.) *Criticism and the growth of knowledge*. Cambridge: Cambridge University Press. 91-195.
Laudan, L. 1977. *Progress and its problems: Towards a theory of scientific growth*. Berkley, California: University of California Press.
Maxwell, N. 1974. The rationality of scientific discovery. *Philosophy of Science 41*. 123–153, 247–295.

McDowell, John 1980. Meaning, communication and knowledge. In Zak van Straaten (ed.), *Philosophical subjects: Essays presented to P. F. Strawson*. Oxford: Oxford University Press. 117-139.

Myers, Linda James 1988. *Understanding an Afrocentric world view: An introduction to a optimal psychology*. Dubuque, IA: Kendall/ Hunt Publishers.

Newmeyer, F.J. 1998. *Language form and language function*. Cambridge: MIT.

Pandey, P.K. 2001. Grammar and 'others'. In Anvita Abbi et al. (eds) *Linguistic structure and language dynamics in South Asia*. [Papers from the Proceedings of SALAXVIII Roundtable, 1997]. Delhi: Motilal Banarasidass. 277-290.

Pantham, Thomas 1983. Thinking with Mahatma Gandhi: Beyond Liberal Democracy. *Political Theory*, Vol. 11, No. 2 (May, 1983), 165-188.

Pateman, Trevor 1989. *Language in mind and language in society*. Oxford; Clarendon Press.

Pierrehumbert, Janet, Mary A. Beckman, and D.R. Ladd 2000. Conceptual foundations of phonology as a laboratory science. In Burton-Roberts et al. (eds), *Phonological knowledge: Conceptual and empirical issues*. Oxford: Oxford University Press, pp 273-304.

Popper, Karl *1959. The Logic of Scientific Discovery.* (translation of Logik der Forschung, 1935*)*. Hutchinson, London.

Prince, A. and P. Smolensky 2007. *Optimality theory: Constraint interaction in generative grammar*. Oxford: Blackwell. [Rutgers University Center for Cognitive Science].

Ramanujan, A.K. 1989. Is there an Indian way of Thinking? *Contributions to Indian Sociology* 23, 41-58.

Tully, Mark 2007. *India's unending journey: Finding balance in a time of change*. London: Rider.

Wagner, D. and J. Berger 1985. Do sociological theories grow? *American Journal of Sociology* 90, 697-728.

NOTES

1. Earlier versions of the paper were presented at the Department of Journalism and Mass Communication, The M.S. University of Baroda, Vadodara, and at the Forum for Contemporary Theory, Vadodara. I would like to thank Probal Dasgupta, P.G. Patel and Thomas Pantham for their comments on the paper and on their insightful suggestions, some of which I hope to take up in a larger study.
2. Thus, Tully (2007: 9-10), on economics: "In my own life time, the governing school of economics in the Western world has made a 180-degree swing, from the certainty that socialism is the ultimate and absolute truth to the conviction that market capitalism is the only guarantee of prosperity. Left-wing politicians, civil servants, nationalized industry employees and trade unions once espoused a socialism that came to dominate us in the West, and government became a vast vested interest. Now big business is dominating us because we have been led to believe in market economics with absolute certainty...It's not just economics but also our sexual mores that have swung 180 degrees, from one form of certainty to another."
3. I am grateful to P.M. Kulkarni for the reference.

23

Towards Branding Indian Linguistics: A Linguistic Destination Next

Shailendra Kumar Singh

1. Towards Introducing:

An enterprise of branding Indian Linguistics requires three tests to filter and examine its sprouting at new world order: 1. Recognition of new temperament and liveliness, 2. Potential of resistance and, 3. Liberation of the disciplines. First of all, Indian Linguistics must be paralleled at academic and territorial levels by scholars from a wide range of backgrounds which would help in widening the ambit of linguistic studies at all possible fronts. However, it is important to remember that Indian linguists must set their own agendas to drive attention of differences and expose the less established field. Additionally, it also requires a political act to make 'academic turn' noticeable. Recognition of new temperament and liveliness means understanding of features which will make it distinctively visible. The matter of the fact is that at-homeness has to be understood as experiencing differences and also uniqueness. The principle problem of Indian Linguistics is the order of invisible shapelessness. Hence it needs to be questioned with the sheer strength of resistance. And, if we are of opinion that the concepts underlying much of western theory are flawed then disciplines have to be liberated. In so doing, we can reach at 'academic turn'. As one of the largest hubs of non-native English speaking peoples of the world, it may not be in India's interest to be ceased in stillness. Indian linguistic brand, today, is not only aspirational but ultimate unifier.

2. In the Search of Third

With India being labeled as 'destination next' and the west heading east, it is time to trap possibilities in the field of international linguistic research and move on to become potent through fitting utilization of linguistic resources. In many cases, obviously, not all, the West's 'look east' policy is born out of demographic, linguistic, economic and political desperations. By 2025, 1.8 million immigrants would be required if we want to solve the labor market problem, especially in the faster ageing countries. It is more likely that emerging linguistic scenario will be playing major role in setting up the new world. The new world order would be welcoming linguists just as own citizens. Who knows! Linguists might play major role in strategizing and implementing major processes. Be sure of the fact that sooner or later, it's bound to happen. It will be helpful to remember that once upon a time linguists played a major role in providing the appropriate tools for carrying out the agendas of linguistic manipulation and reinforcing the status of language in the formation of nation-state. At best, we can anticipate for linguists entering into new role – specifically, this time in analyzing linguistic temptation, linguistic celebration and, in totality, a search of TRADITION THIRD. It may also turn true that linguistics as a core discipline will be helpful in enhancing cultural competencies of other fields and will also become cross culturally a more adaptable discipline. One of the crucial changes that the new world order will be witnessing in the 21st century is that language will be playing a key role in conducting the socio-cultural, political and economic affairs of the world and, not necessarily, religion. And, imagine, if India would become the host of worldwide English. Given a chance, Indian linguistics will have a global mission with global workforce. The bizarre turn of pyramid sounds like a new linguistic imperative with a new slogan 'linguistic destination next'. Here is everything for critics of globalization to chew on. The growing phenomenon would be part of deep multilingualism, in which the knowledge of language will be helpful in breaking down caste and gender inequalities while allowing the hitherto underprivileged to break into white color profession. It is the linguistic highway of social engineering. The ideal of emerging deep multilingualism, therefore, is: the best form of multilingualism is not necessarily the condition of living in permanent non-conflict conditions, but it should be simply equipped with the unique talent of translating conflict into non-conflict to nurture the meta-cognitive spirit among people. Hence, the great thing about deep multilingualism is that it tolerates changes. Are we adaptable and enjoy the changes? Indian linguists must get their act together to become globally competitive. There are some variables in which India can secure top rank, but these are few and far between. There are positive factors that India can build on. At this moment, it has not become a matter of pride. But for that to happen, competitiveness is a call and we, therefore, must make a determined trusts towards making Indian linguistics globally competitive. In so doing and so to happen, Indian linguistics needs to learn, more importantly, from Indian industry, which has been vehicle of the country emergence.

At the same time or at some point of time, Indian linguists must be challenged, tested, confronted and most importantly empowered. At the corner, there is a need for rummaging around for an enterprise to empower the linguistics of the East. We can begin with accepting the general perception that India is booming and the effects of shining could be seen everywhere. Global investment bank Goldman Sachs has suggested that the Indian economy has the potential to grow 40 times bigger by 2050. Will linguists be able to maintain, at least, some growth? Here lies the real caveat. The fact remains to be realized that linguists in India has to work much harder to achieve its potential. There is, in fact, nothing new in this appeal that we have not heard of before. Not necessarily, we have to speak in similar vein. This paper will serve as a constant reminder that India has potential to become a leading linguistic centre provided it is serious about recognizing and implementing some of suggestions. The serious problem here is that seriousness is seriously lacking.

Considering the impacts of shining India in the field of linguistics, this paper, in particular, poses a question in front of the Indian linguist - Are you [linguists] ready to get your creative hats on? The paper raises this question with serious doubt in mind because neither the mindset has changed, as people do not consider this discipline as a lucrative and competitive, nor moving into a completely different direction for getting in touch with the local flavor. The effect of boom in Indian economy must have also been credited to linguistics. Today, linguistics is being flooded by various brands, i.e. American, British, European, Canadian, etc. but it is Indian linguistics which was never branded through right channel of communication. It is in this fear, it becomes imperative for us to surface yet another harass question: Was there ever a serious linguistics in India? Or, did Indian linguistics ever exist with brand name? Do not get it wrong because Indian linguistics has done amazing job but it has been perceived or rather misunderstood as a non-serious discipline.

As an academic endeavor, it would be wise to begin with discovering the reasons of bankruptcy in Indian Linguistics and reveal the tips for branding linguistics for making it more and more convincing and overcoming the tag of bankruptcy. The inspiration springs from the realization that we should no longer wait the linguistics as pathetic victim deserving the charity of the west. We need to pose questions for ourselves: Does Indian linguistics lag behind world standards in productivity? Has there been any breakthrough in linguistics studies? Or, have we remained either stagnated or have we collapsed? Is the gap with other disciplines itself revealing?

Instead, we should provide own brand to succeed and contract with whoever and whatsoever it finds to be fit for appealing. The best and the only way to brand are to deliver right massage through the right communication channel. It is necessary to improve productivity if it has to become a sustainable academic activity and hence it calls for a massive courage. With a changing face of Indian economy, several fields are to be explored and Indian linguists can maneuver data. That is why the calls for a change in mindset are needed to recognize the potential of past and plan accordingly. It is possible as we are now in era of 'translation'- hence, we must finally break out the shackles to explore the creative Indian side.

3. Emergence of a New Linguistic Order:

Things will become seeming only when we attach importance to the imperativeness of 'cultural turn' which is shaping the new world order in which we are becoming habitual to inhabit in [...betweens]. The debate should begin with phenomenal rise of deep multilingualism which is constitutive and becoming an instrument for creating identity within [...betweens]. One may even find it extremely hard to chart out the exact definition. The best thing about deep multilingualism, more precisely in my mind, is that it is a difficult notion to define. To many, this may, more reasonably, sound third world's divisive rhetoric. Certainly, this is not an effective means of winning moral credibility. Let it be, even so it is not in its moral self. Indian multilingualism has many more things to celebrate, and even it is far more than just that. Optimistically, 21st century is transforming a world into a more comfortable place for a people who live between cultures. At the same time complexity is increasingly growing. The varying shades of political surfing, asserting the new beginning where meetings of mind are collaborative.

Placed in a given situation, India will have to be proactive and impose itself on western's linguistic radar. It is likely to be first order of linguistic business. More Likely, India should play an important role in the revitalization of global linguistic trends. Hence, it should become an enthusiastic partner and follow the ideal: it is always good to give something than receive something. In so doing, it will enter into the new domain of social-psychology facilitating the ideal of reciprocity - in fact, the deal that positive action will inspire reciprocal positive action.

The new alliance will inspire differences with reciprocity and a common sense of purpose. A new theory will encourage us to go beyond. Hopefully, we will be redrawing for a better world. Will sociolinguistics find comfortable terrain from where it can prove its own legitimacy of pasteurizing the growing alliance of [...togetherness]? Unless we come out from the compressor of old models, things may not be placed in order. Sociolinguistic enquiry is still engaged with an old strategic game. It must look at the new world order. A new mantra - deep multilingualism - is becoming universal slogan. Can sociolinguists - still settling old scores with their zero sum score - see the changes coming? If yes, what kind of change would they like to see?

4. Locating the Fitness:

There is a daunting challenge facing multilingual theory and language practice today. The key traditions of sociolinguistic thinking, all those stem from western minds, appear to be severely strained in the face of major developments in communicative behavior of the [...third] world. If the available and preconceived theories are not concerned with 'what is happening and going on' in the present world order and, thereby, with nature and prospects of deep multilingualism, then an ideal theory must be conceptualized. At issue is rethinking the nature, form and content of multilingualism in the face of the complex interlocking of local, regional, national and global relations and processes. The fitness of Western theories on multilingualism has to be rethought. The pursuit of linguistic temptation is central to this enterprise - more importantly, for discovering the actual underlying principles of linguistic behavior in the changing world order. I explore lines of argument which seek to show how the ideas of linguistic temptation and deep multilingualism can coherently be interlinked through the notion of [...betweens] - an order which is shaping and being conditioned by the laws of [....third]. In particular, the chapter argues that multilingualism can only be adequately ingrained if the law of [...third] enacts in the overall affairs of global order. The contemporary nature and scope of multilingualism can be mapped by looking at a number of disjuncture and juncture between, on the one hand, the formal domains at global level and, on the other, the actual practices and structures at local level. The explosion of interconnectedness is reinforcing facilitative relations at g (local) level with support of transnational and translational networking to induce deep multilingualism in return.

5. Experiencing and Entering into [...Newness]

Despite all programmatic failure, what makes us special? The newness has to be nursed not as formalities but as a commitment of ensuring and respecting diversity. Seeking justification in the name of diversity will be a futile exercise. It has been observed that the greatest diversity is found in the area of easy mobility but, in a country like India, multilingualism has stayed and sustained in the isolated areas also. The rules of convergence and divergence are constantly operating in own terms and conditions. India is emerging as a manufacturing hub of multilingualism which is creating new linguistic opportunities for even those who do not carry the label of [...insiders]. To an extent, the shift is already happening. Let us hope that as good as things are today, however, there could even be better tomorrow. Multilingualism has grown stronger. It is vibrant and recognized as one of the pillars of democracy. One can evenly find the multilingual pace for change is only accelerating. What else could explain the volume of growth in a country whose purchasing power has been doubled and which has among the largest networks of banks in the world and houses the research bases of 125 of the world's top companies? The good news is that grass root composition is receiving substantial support from the following recent developments:

5.1. Mobility Across:

As estimated, with almost 7, 50,000 Indians, having various linguistic backgrounds and shared habit of multilingual practices, are migrating overseas in the search of jobs. Linguistic inflows have also ballooned. The growth for white collar jobs since the mid 90s has seen millions of technology workers going abroad without detracting familial ties at home and remitting large parts of their savings to families in India. Recently, these inflows have increased dramatically to spreading all around the world and not restricted to west alone. It has also succeeded in displacing other recipients like China and Mexico. Sociolinguists, in particular, must debate on productive use of multilingualism growing rapidly with phenomenon of mobility across. Above all, one can rightly term it as process of transforming the pocket of diversity. However, we need to check whether or not this trend is in sync with global pattern.

5.2. Holy Word and Stalls

Set up over 90 years ago, the Giitaa press has published 6-34 crore copies of Gita and 6-94 crore copies of Ramcharitramanas. Rs. 1 is the price of cheapest book and 1,350 of the most expensive one. Books are now virtually engraved on the soul of spiritual India not only through reading but also through display at the common places such as railways stall ....etc. The press archives contain over 3,500 manuscripts including at least 100 interpretations of the Gita. Such press has been responsible for evolving a completely new book culture in India. One can find such stalls at remote corners of the country.

5.3. *Tongue tied and freed*

Even at the moment of high spirit and free movement, the seeds of language conflict are present. Language was a chink in the nationalist armor throughout the long anti-colonial struggle. The question of implementation of official language on union was coincided with two sharp opposite views: 1. Hindi zealots saw it as a unifying force, 2. its opponents saw it as an imposition on locals. During sixties the force of opposition was high and for many this sounded like unmanageable. The anti Hindi agitation which took final shape in 1937-39, started weakening in post 80s era. Perhaps what could not have been solved politically, the magic has been displayed by globalization and technology. The era of tongue-confusion seems to be permanently confined into corner with no hope of turning into sparks. It is now perhaps a forgotten chapter in India's history. For many, like prophet of doom, the risk of India being split into a number of totalitarian small nationalities sounded very obvious. Who goes wrong? This is a question to be answered.

5.4. *Desi-Enclaves*

Speaking in and with many languages is turning out to be both a force and a fashion. A linguistic slice of [...other] is no more visualized and understood as [...others] but stands in overwhelming [...betweens]. Multilingualism has become a holistic structure through which human communication is routed. Moreover, it is not simply a communication structure but culmination of all those structures in which socio-political, socio-cultural, religious and technological networks operate – hence, it is also a way of organizing people, a way of thinking, an ethos and a shared set of expectations. Every failure in expectation may cause serious damage to human delivery itself. Thus, multilingualism is as much a psycho-social structure as a linguistic reality. By systematically interrelating people to one another across the linguistic boundaries, multilingualism has succeeded in producing a new world, in which one can hardly rejoice with single and independent linguistic control over his or her destiny. That is to say, no person, no nation, and no culture can claim to be independently monolingual. Linguistic integration is progressive while segregation is backward. Multilingualism of the [...third] behaves and becomes big and unique in its desi- enclaves. And its architectural aesthetic is certainly distinct.

5.5. Merger Mantras:

With acquisition, emerging as an integral part of corporate strategy, Indian companies put into place ideas and initiatives in the cultural and business landscape to make the mergers deliver results. A new balance mantra has started ensuring that equals are morphed at economic levels but also at a linguistic level. Confidence building measures are an integral part of integration. Welcome to the world of mergers and cultural integration. Acquisition is not just about getting bigger but acquiring people and keeping them smiling in shared moments. For Tatas, the iconic Jaguar Rover Brands came along with 16,000 people. The rate of success depends on making bond between two parties and making people feel they are on equal foot. Such efforts are complemented by bringing in nuances of cultures into integration process. Given the diversity of languages and cultures, India has straddled the two worlds rather deftly. The new 'Linguistic Marketing Behaviorism' appears to be crispy as it is tough to bond people who cannot pronounce desi names like Aditya Birla and others know neither Spanish nor German.

5.6. Intellectual Totalitarianism

There are new things with appealing passion and attracting all those [...others] who are the proprietors of not only the linguistic codes but also [...others] mindset. New writing is becoming a site on which language has breached the borders to keep pace with contemporaries and also histories. It is needless to say that purified English has become mixed-veg. histories. Standing at this stage, we are in process of rewriting a new linguistic genealogy. A voice of expressing indebtedness is rocking with a sense of new expression of acknowledgment and signaling growth of [.....beyond] in which [.....in-betweens] are marked with new boundaries of new showcase of cultural exposition. The challenge at hand is to place the things in right direction. Accents and flavors are acceptable not with uneasiness but with taste of new voices. The direction is towards celebration and it is worthy of big prizes with whatever sense of exoticism. [...Others] are being inspired to understand the new mantras in a refreshingly new way. With polyphony and structural peculiarities, Indian English is purely Indian – a moment that led intellectual liberty define the flavor of fashion.

6. Strategic Switch

The boundary of [....within] is in capacity of breeding deep multilingualism. Deep multilingualism, as an ideal of social life, is, in its socio-cultural dynamics, much wider than political makeup, even it requires the support of political establishment. As an ideal, it expresses the need for progress beyond [.....own] linguistic boundary. Nowhere in the world are there institutions which, in fact, can deny securing full development of individuals in the absence. It is no longer utopian reality – but, in fact, it is, in a way, reconstructing and developing an interactive social process for us. Deep multilingualism supports the formation of equal social relation of [...betweens]. In comparison to rarely formal and institutional, deep multilingualism is preparing and equipping individuals to understand the value of diversity in responsive way.

Is it a signal of success mantra of emerging multilingualism? It obviously glosses indomitable spirit, ensuring user's delight with definitive satisfaction. It is the biggest victory contributing to linguistic celebration. Deep Multilingualism has come a long way. It is in this spirit that Braj Kachru's (1986) concentric circles of use of English do not move along with today's reality show, as the direction of English is no longer restricted to what is being called the inner circle, the outer circle and expanding circle. English, with centripetal and centrifugal forces, is evolving itself as a language of [...within and beyond]. Politely speaking, multilingualism in the Western world has never been the story of [...within]. It is about to experience the process of knotting with rest of [...others].

Hence, it requires theoretical rebuilding. The old model rather reminds the deep water fish that when drawn out of the elements and brought to the surface the inner system bursts. It is the time of deregulation. It so appears that the moral drama over multilingualism is played at the moral divide of [....self] and [...other] and as a result every encounter emerges with sharp demarcation. It is for this reason that [....plural] has never been found in the west without hyphenation. Above all, entering into [......deep multilingualism] means engagement with daily life, leaving the old convention aside. As a result, the moral self constituted inside the [....deep multilingualism] is unlikely to be in discomfortable position. In comparison to Kachru's formal and institutional concentric classification, English, a language of global deep democracy, has also become a way of life in its ontological and epistemological make up, not only for who owned it but also in the share of who all are willing to own. Deep multilingualism is helpful in reconstructing civil society with diverse memories, knowledge, expectations and hopes, simultaneously transforming the mechanical language laboratory into a package of life enhancement for individuals and communities. .

The present-day shining of third world countries - in terms of continuous growth of cultural, economic and political relations and structures - is, in particular, making existing theoretical models scandalous with exceptional difficulties in confrontation with live reality. No way has yet been found to solve the problems in overcoming theoretical barriers. A new approach to interpret multilingualism is, therefore, required – if, the academia has to cope up the needs of today and tomorrow. No other things than multilingualism speaks better about today's and tomorrow's social existence. It goes without saying that today's multilingualism is crucial to tomorrow's social existence. What is strange, however, is that significance of fact is still recognized by models which are constructed for someone else. However, it would be foolish to suggest that all assumptions are to be given dustbin treatment. Some kind of extra effort is ultimately necessary to encounter the theoretical imposition and to phase out our own habitual lethargy which will, in turn, highlight the distinction between external and internal knowledge. Note, however, that both of these conceptions of the reasons for theorizing multilingualism are explicitly social – that is to say, remodeling will derive justifications for new communication order not from 'pure knowledge' or 'value free science', but from the necessity of living with and in the new social order. What is indeed required is: theorizing and re-theorizing of multilingualism in the present social terms and conditions. Need for insisting upon new social order, social network, social interaction and communicative behavior has arisen to highlight the live academic show. There can no longer be a dispute that if theory is not a part of such social reality show – then, its uselessness speaks for itself. Multilingualism is a communicative action and not a static condition that can be studied in laboratory. However, it should neither be read as battles over political, academic and institutional correctness nor should it be baffled and angered over by western assumptions. Point to understand here is that nobody should tell us to understand as already prescribed. The spirit in which this debate rages is good indication of how shining is spreading in the knowledge awareness zone also. In this light, we must try to understand that suspicion over the first world order utterly felt by the third world order has to be taken as a persuasive challenge to rectify the monolith linguistic ideology for understanding the emerging order of [...betweens]. The challenge must not be read as a calculative dose for offending those who have contributed immensely in establishing and shaping the academics. While understanding the differences between two [...orders], we must not be sensitive to discriminatory issues. Such understanding must be separated from the illusion of living with two worlds and while doing so we will be pushing ourselves in cultural [...otherness] where [...betweens] does not rest. Maybe emerging signal is signaling as strategic switch.

If appearances are the indication, multilingualism is in full bloom and the mood of the multilingual is upbeat ahead of new world order and in spiraling [...betweens]. Its base is expanding in the new linguistic heartland. However, it is facing a bipolar contest: 1. experimenting and experiencing with third front and 2. struggling and dragging along with more or less collapsed theoretical models of uncontested front. Within the bipolarity, a new experiment with truth is resulting which rightly satisfies the concept of linguistic satyaagrah (urge for the truth). The urge of linguistic satyaagrah is not confined to any singular direction. As an ambition, it is an announcement of arrival of deep multilingualism in the region whose emergence has resulted not as a split from the West, but as a recognition of its very much presence. We are about to encounter and relish a new linguistic optimism.

World's greatest wealth lies in its human resources and the strength of human resources profoundly lies in linguistic diversity. Maintenance of linguistic diversity could be the single biggest move towards future prosperity. It requires substantive, not just symbolic action. The third world can act as a multiplier force and can take off some of the western theoretical burdens, if the right incentives are taken. For that to happen, the Third world must be allowed to develop indigenous theoretical modules and also be encouraged to set up own chains of branded models, which would serve both the world's human resource needs and also to disseminate theoretical knowledge to the west. Strategic shift is required in favor of craving out new theoretical models inspired from the [....within]. The Third world's switch means trying to trade with the western's declining support in the third world for the fresh support for itself. Support must stand with credibility which will generate real compulsion for the biggest. Any model that strikes the third world's target may well be vital in forming a new academic zone, even at the centre. The strategic switch is moving forward with justifications for evolving a consensus on the issues. In the situation of failing to deliver, the Third world must be accused. The strategic switch has to be underlined with urgency to forge a non-western alliance in the prospect of west joining hands with third world, in a short span of time. To draw in the better model than what we have, it is necessary to profit ourselves by legitimizing theoretical autonomy. Or else, we can also envisage the [...First world] and [...Second world] collaboration where it will throw in some combinations of mutual respects for each other in understanding the uniqueness. It is certainly needed because out- of- the-box thinking need not be dragged for an unwanted period of time.

When it comes to theorizing the multilingualism of the Third world, there are several questions that bog the mind. It requires a thorough 'rethinking' because the third world's multilingualism is not what a theory describes. Much of what makes the multilingualism new is the linguistic temptation and celebration. Linguistics temptation pluralizes the viewing of thinking on multilingualism in the capacity of the privileged and thus demanding the space for entering into newness. This project is risky because criticism will come from various corners. Every sincere effort to distance from the divides of East-West, First-Third and any such hyphenated categories will not look as a wise move. It is to be noted that the invisibility of original location is immense and sharp. Therefore, divides demand complex knowing – not alone in terms of past but also in terms of present.

7. Strategic Alliance:

We hope to build up certain strategic alliance as the changing mood of multilingual is in full boom. That also does not mean that everything is good with the Third front and everything has gone wrong with the first world. The crux of the point is to make those things visible which are trying to attain the spark of visibility in the course of takeovers. Instead, we are in no position to assert the emergence of a universal diktat of unifying the world in opposition to one which had existed for a long. In turn, we are highlighting the concrete multiplicities in which the notion of [....Mono reality] is challenged - not in terms of intended opposition, in favor of the inclusion of [....multi-realities]. These processes are at work in concrete multiplicities as real elements. Time has come to resist the totalizing view that the west had initiated and then imposed. Hence, privileges of differences over uniformity must be considered as a poly-dimensional effect.

8. Defining the border of [... betweens]

Let us assume that the Third world is neither the new world nor the fractured world of west. No need to begin with either in opposition or in subjection – better, to toss for the [...betweens] of beyond. The notion of [....betweens] needs to be promised in supporting the periphery of inclusive [...other] for sidelining the rigidity of [....others]. But, in any case, the portal of being an absolute imaginative has to be transformed as the portal of a beginner. Many are wrong in concluding that nationalist thoughts of Indians are imitative and hostile. The need of the day is to launch a constant course of reevaluating the notion of [....inclusiveness], which is to be understood in a refreshingly new way. We must review the notion of plural at the juncture of 'elsewhere' and the western world is not the only one that prepares us for a plural-based approach to social understanding. There is an urgent need to go beyond the understanding of Western universalism and nationalism. 'Diversity in unity' must be preferred 'everywhere' for expressing uniqueness and not selfishness.

9. Linguistic Temptation

The inquiry of linguistic temptation begins at this point: that, the traditional linguistic theories of language use have appropriated the experiences and tried to project the west as the originary home of diversity. The starting point here is not simply the [....exclusiveness] of the old models but, more importantly their arrogance in forgetting the [....others]. Should we feel helpless? Or, try to re-contextualize the plurals in which everyone is slowly entering into, even without acknowledging. The old fashioned meaning of multilingualism is drifting and shifting and contradictorily the new multilingualism is shaping up everywhere. Everybody in the third world has grown up totalizing himself within the theoretical paradigm of the West with utter sense of sincerity and gravity and placing himself/herself under the down slides. Some false sites have also been projected to nurture and enforce the falsity as truth. This is perfect imbalance in the name of theory building which requires serious rethinking. This will help us know where, how, why and what have gone wrong in the making of [....self] by [...others].

New beginning brings home linguistic temptation in new texture. Locals are the real experiencers and manufacturers. We need to do something seriously at least to balance the divides before we aspire to empower East to encounter West's dominance. Invisibles must be translated into visible to expose the narrowness of [....others]. Self superiority could be challenged through adopting the respectable path of balancing and avoid confrontations. The wishes of new universality must become the part of new voices under the order of inclusiveness. Consider the following ideal options:

1. [...inside] of own is also empowered as the outside of [....others].
2. Inclusiveness is morphed into coverage of [...outsider] and [....insider].
3. Presence of [...originals] complements the boundary of [...others].
4. Resistance of [...self] does not confront with [...others].
5. Temptation to use [...others] does not deviate [...self].
6. Turf of [...own] and [...others] is naturalizing.

7. Process of becoming entering into domain of [...newness].
8. Historical debris of [...others] may be used in rebuilding the hopes of entering into [...newness].
9. Textual status of past knowledge is changing to expose the dominance of [...others].
10. Breeding of [...newness] tempts [...original] to acquire new brands.

Linguistic temptation indicates the social-psychological make-up in the virtual domains of [...betweens] - comprising the borderlines of [....outsiders] and [....insiders]. One should not be warned for making early hopes that new world order has started shining with new linguistic excitement in which no one is deliberately excluded on the cost of sociopolitical dilemma of [.....inclusions]. Moreover, the linguistic temptation is enormously exciting with different brands. Hence, there is a point in getting excited about it. The question is: how much excitement this temptation is holding for the first world order? Is it as affectionate and excitable as in the Third world? The range of excitement is bound to be virtually different not only in terms of forgotten past, but more so in memorable present. Both may have just many things in common, but departure tends to concentrate upon the [...exclusion] of each other, especially while looking at the notion of multilingualism, in totality. It is yet to be adjudged whether divide is turning into a zone of [...exclusion], in which one cannot fit into the [...others] as an [.....obvious]. The invisible pretext of being excluded has turned into visible. Linguistic temptation has contracted a bond of convenience with the Third world order, not alone for the sake of preference, but for the reason of compulsion of leaving old to fancy with young for self-satisfaction of living in excitement. The [....third world] has become convenience store of multilingualism. Therefore, declaration of the end of monolingualism cannot be expressed as an early option. Needless to say, the notion of monolingualism has often been theoretically conceptualized for the linguistic defense of self and hyphenating the boundary of [....insider] and [....outsider] for self-categorization and self-identification. Hence, our entry is justified.

10. A New Journey

A common consensus is turning out to be reality show that India is on move to acquire the superpower's tag. A feature that translates its move into uniqueness is its capacity to accommodate diverse socio-cultural and linguistic groups in the vibrant democracy. Unity in diversity's formula not only corresponds to the old fashioned rhetoric of accumulative capacity but also it's enhanced velocity to maintain the pace of vibration with all encounters. Is it a quest for alternatives which is waiting for a new text yet to be written in a refreshingly new way? Or, has it entered into the process of engendering which would turn into a new genealogy? Should India involve herself into the process of redrafting, reinventing, relativizing and revising in the quest for alternates? Time is passing out for discussing the issues, which are still in private. It would be harmful to suppress and not bringing into public. Hence, such discourse has to be prioritized with uttermost sincerity. We need to consider the fact whether the move on factor is also helping India to become an attractive linguistic destination. Is India's vibrant democracy also experiencing linguistic vibration with reverberation of energy?

Before counting on the issue with uttermost care, it is indeed mandatory to find out whether or not linguistics and linguists are endangered species in India. It may not be wise to tag the issue of endangerment with discipline and species as a whole, but sensitivity must be checked out so that an answer towards justifying the course of engenderment could be established with a new sense of urgency. The fact that Indian linguists have remained insensitive to the matter of linguistic sensitivity is undeniable from many corners. Had linguists been sensitive to their linguistic sensitivities Panini would have been familiar to others much before than western European Indologists made him? India's history is certainly lost in translation. Linguists would have certainly played an affirmative role in preventing the process of endangerment of India's history. Endangerment as a process not only signifies the decay and threat but also results into the process of invisibility. Insensitivity often creates invisibility which seems to be closer to truth in the Indian case. Invisibility also reflects what is unknown to others. India's history is full of paradoxes wherein the margin of known and unknown is so thin that nothing conclusive has come out to date. Have we missed the boat? The journey of translation has always been auspicious for the western world in carrying out the mastery over another. It is the act of translation which has preserved the history. It is not to say that India has never travelled beyond, but the fact that remains to be exposed is that it has utterly failed to accelerate and systemize the process of knowing others or making herself knowledgeable to others through the act of translation.

Any issue that needs to be seriously debated in linguistic circle is the issue of sensitiveness over insensitivity that has ruled us without serious interruption. Who should take responsibility, more candidly, for such unworthiness? Should linguist alone? Or, all of us, at least in parts, before it is imposed upon the other? Did history bestow sufficient chance to bring the chronology into the order of transparency? Can linguistics be liberated? Hence, we enter into the realm of morality judgment, and questions arising within must be addressed. How wakeful we are in considering and articulating India's linguistic ecology within the realm of western's purity? On the other hand, yet another question, of similar weight, anticipates critical enquiry: To what extent western's purity has succeeded in inflicting impurity into others? Indeed, time has come, with all sincerity, to respond: Have such inflictions succeeded in creating the sharp dilemma of purity and impurity? As of now, dilemmas of purity and impurity have ignited the utter sense of wakefulness. The purity articulation derives under the inspiration of German Romanticism – that, an original Indo-European people spoke a single pure primordial language or ursprache called Indo-European. The purity version has signified that the modern languages from Europe to India developed from a single language. Rather than attempting to verify and question the logistic of imposed purity, we celebrated inclusion with proud. We paid heavily in this order of celebration – mainly on the cost of exclusion which is, otherwise, narratives of inclusion. Orientals calibrated the happiness while diagnosing the competency of others. More surprisingly, legitimacy over purity has remained unquestioned. The rise of the Third world order has certainly placed the issues for rethinking. Is it too late to clear out the cloud of confusion? To certain extent, the western world's mastery over hatching the conspiracy of confusion was politically genuine and correct. The question is: How was incorrectness transformed into the course of correctness? Truly, re-historicizing the texts reveals the one side of the coin. Does it also mean that our own insensitiveness encouraged the others to be more passionate about setting things in the order of incorrectness? Causes for allusiveness are even traceable in various empty categories. Emptiness has allocated an easy space for acceptance as desired even by others. Indian history, in its derivation, had become an open space for alternativeness. Things would have been entirely otherwise, had it been made available to others in those days through the act of translation. At this point, even the margins of insensitiveness expose our serious failure. Europeans had championed themselves in the art of knowing through the act of translation. May be we lost in the middle. Towards the beginning, some of our grammarians, writers and narrators were keen on bringing history close to linguistics. However, it has always remained in fractions. For example, Patanjali, a grammarian and commentator on Panini around 150 B.C described in the Mahabhasya, the two invasions (he uses imperfect tense – as if it was a recent event):

Arunad yavanah sa:ketam (The yavanas were besieging Saketa)

Arunad yavano madhamika (The Yavanas were besieging the middle country).

Have Indian linguists been ever sensitive to such historical misfortune?

11. Liberating Discipline

Has sociolinguistic liberated? Perhaps, it is the right time to access its descriptive or methodological principles. Notions such as "native speaker" and "native speaker intution", and "natural language", "linguistic system" "speech community" have their roots in homogeneous organs. It is no more surprising that the fundamental "vernacularism" of linguistics needs to be seen as an ideology with a complex history and real political consequences across the world. It is becoming clearer that the multiplicity of communicative behavior is compelling sociolinguistics to distance itself from the nursed biasness of theoretical constructs. As of now, sociolinguistics is modeled both as the parent and child of western mono-isms. Hence the **appeal is: at least from now onwards, the** starting point should take a lead in interpreting the trend of diversity and reclaim the role as the premier science for interpreting human diversity - elaborating distinct human "character logy' or 'typology" of ethnic groups. On many issues, sociolinguistics has struggled as a faceless discipline. Indeed, it has to be librated. Sociolinguists have taken extra care to show how monolingual behavior varies according to a number of parameters. In multilingual communities there existed a set of norms defying bilingual behavior. In particular, the firm conviction was that bilingual or multilingual communities are situated between different poles of continuum. It was also assumed that monolinguality is more commonly used in economically dominant group where as the members of minority or subordinate groups tend to be bilingual or multilingual and refer to the subordinate identity.

[....Self] at the risk of [...others] has to be recognized– or else, the liveliness in opposition will remain decorative. Hopefully, it strikes the issues of knowing in the distraction of knowing. From the domain based theory of language choice, shift and maintenance, urgent need of takeover on linguistic temptation seems to be demanding. This attempt takes over the emphasis on linguistic temptation rather than domain as the central unit of analysis. In the process of doing so, it would be possible to associate beyond the periphery of traditional narrow focus and the monistic and hyphenated modes of multilingualism. Hence, on equal footing, other ways of looking at multilingualism could be included in the mainstream. In addition, a fruitful theory of linguistic temptation may always be helpful, in a number of significant ways, to refer to the act of communicating with responsiveness. The force of temptation is an acquaintance with responsibility of attending and serving in contended multiplicity. It results in the course of social transformation which cannot be abdicated even by the west.

Begin with a naïve question: Today, should multilingualism be defined by the book or not? The straight and candid answer should be: No. However, it is a job that demands sheer strength and unusual bravery but no classroom justification. Previous experience is not required either. Is there anyone willing to challenge the Western brawl of egos? So, who will wear the badges of honor next – theory creator or theory receiver? Should we only wait and watch? No doubt, we have also made stronger statements but they are largely unnoticed today. Are we unintelligent enough to be seriously vindictive about ourselves? An imperfect model reflects the presence of imperfect examples. It needs to be addressed as to why even a large community is bound to be vindictive? Multilingualism is a question of survival as its essential entitlement is conducive to social survival, feelings of commitment, empowerment and ability. It is likely to be turning into a new set of visible formlessness of [...betweens] – where, whose who is not necessarily governed by the principles and parameters of [....Either] or [.....Or] and in which new voices of togetherness are turning out to be acceptable means of cultural, socio-economic, socio-political and social psychological realities. It is no more an accident and begins with good genes and also depends upon good habit. Multilingualism gives a new hope for our life and creates the right balance in life. The real pleasure in it remains not alone with the mouth but with ears which are capable enough of transferring [...many] into [...many others].

12. Justifying the End

Let there be no dispute over this simple fact: Monolingualism has been banished not only from unknown corner – but, even from where ever it was supposed to be rooted. Multilingualism is the mildest of the words one can use to describe the soaring effect of monolingualism. However, it still continues to be accentuated by the flag of high headless-ness. Today, there is nothing respectful, polite or modest about it. It has been declared misfit. Yet it is culminated not just by the ferocity of West but also because of the laziness of the East. Monolingualism tends to create partition: [...East] and [..West], [...self] and [others] and many more. Linguists need to redeem their pledge. It was worst in timing when multilingualism was accused. The unification of monolingualism and multilingualism remains a highly emotive issue which still reverberates in the treatment of East's hierarchical structure and western mindset. No other issue in linguistics remains as fraught and contentious as the divide. The term of this debate needs to be spelt out. Is the declaration to end monolingualism inevitable and desirable? It is likely that salutation of distinctiveness may ensure desirable victory over contested [... isms]. Let it be the part of steady integration. Obviously, both cannot be allowed to override the equal status simultaneously. The task before us, then, is to carefully balance these two competing interests as the East seeks to forge a viable and sustainable alternative to the west.

The emergence of local might sound regional, but the impact is global – only for the better and not for the worst. A small ripple from the early 80s is turning out be a rapacious revolution for diversities and aspirations have found legitimate place in the establishment of the Third world. It would be difficult to contain the revolution as it draws energy from the polyphony of the new voices which are unheard and untold so far. It appears to be capable of widening social and cultural bases while keeping regional voices in good humor. Regionalism deserves place even at apexial level. The regional surge in the form of new voices is directly proportional to the fading of monolingualism in all its expressions. New voices are asserting themselves and as a result the stature of multilingualism is widening with a new sense of popularity. Multilingualism is an embodied rainbow in which regionalism with its new voices tends to be the real voice of mainstream and always in waiting of real unfolding. The change is overwhelming everywhere. Smaller voices are in the process of multiplying. This tells the story of how the tectonic plates and flag have shifted in and around the overall linguistic ecology. With the resurgent periphery playing a defining role in shaping the linguistic destiny, the world is becoming a true linguistic federation comprising everyone at a crossroad of [...betweens], in which marginalized linguistic identities and aspirations are occupying their rightful space. Now, becoming multilingual is a lifestyle statement. It is a hot seat zone where, indeed, you pay and spend almost nothing but are rewarded exceptionally well. It is, in fact, the new world's new offer which allures us with new profitability.

Today deep multilingualism is a dynamic enterprise that continues to spread its wing and also a new linguistic behavior in the midst of makeover. That also means diversity is a correct societal form and is grounding very fast. It is likely to facilitate cross-border dialogue as never before. However, it is still a notion in progress. Within the new positioning of [...betweens], one can accept that deep multilingualism has grabbed the new fertility space, where no one is threatened and with such a rise it is poised to grow in stature in all fronts. This discussion looks at the evolution of deep multilingualism in the span of linguistic temptation. Across all sections of our life and in all professions, a new hybridism is exploding - an expression that needs new interpretation on form and aesthetics as it is trying to find its feet. There is lot more churning going on because people are getting polarized economically, socially, aesthetically faster than ever before. The language needs to keep pace. It is bit like discovering a new territory right inside your home. Everywhere we are bound to face a new linguistic toss and winners are celebrated and losers are submerged. Linguistic temptation is turning out to be a peculiar artistic enterprise. The principle of [...purity] and [...hybridity] is unlikely to pose the constraints of 'haves' and 'haves not'. What is more important today is the aesthetic of delivery which generates new charm and this is the beauty and unpredictability of art and craft of new linguistic temptation in which everybody is participating.

Deep multilingualism should no longer be viewed as synonymous with speaking many languages – in fact, in totality, it is a form of conduct which continues through honor, to the extent that we share and perceive the communicative kindness. As an expression of continuity, it suggests continuum, a dialogue of harmony in which many learn to live as an inspiration for [...US] and not necessarily between the divider of [I] and [You]. However, it was mistakably understood as a pertinent source of backwardness, conflict, dominance, etc. With vibrant energy, it is set to be the true representative of pluralism for indicating the coexistence of [....Others] and [...Self] within [... betweens]. In extreme circumstances, real pluralism tolerates annexation of boundaries or assimilation of boundaries or propagation of simplistic and mono-world view. Facilitating dialogue and thereby promoting the understanding of collective good rests with its soul. The realization of one's identity may sustain boundaries and yet at the same time, understanding of other identities may help formulate a public policy of harmony. The real pluralism approach solomonizes the fact that societies without boundaries are not possible. It is no longer only aesthetic in character but it is a blending of [....Selves] belonging to [...Own] within [....Others].

The liberalization saga of post-colonial world has had phenomenal success in making it one of biggest international markets. It has begun expanding explosively. The 'Third World Countries' urgently need to organize their linguistic sectors to fulfill the potential of a new generation genuinely. Good to hear that mundane multilingual sector has suddenly turned into an incredible techno color dreamboat as never before. It is a boundless linguistic revolution in a country where the communicative habit was even frowned upon by caste, class and clan systems. It is a complex interplay of social, economic and technological forces. Ridings on the wings of prosperities, globally connected young Indians are biting the new linguistic cake with relish. It is a revolution for a better world and it is growing in strength.

13. Towards Concluding

Candidly, neither the linguistic canon of the West has to be domesticated nor foeriegnized, but interventionist options have to be reinvented to energize the capacity of recognizing the [...betweens], which is occupying the space of [...third]. It is to be also understood that teachers are certainly not helping students to gain the cultural competency of the present by making them fixed in the western pedagogical model. At least, this is not a profitable endeavor as long as power brokers remain unexposed. Rectification of betrayal must be understood in the light of the freshness of discursive power relations with good intentions. Hence, the new breed of linguistics, in general, must call into question every aspect of fixity. In its composite outlook this is not just about discarding or avoiding the west at the outset but recognizing the emergence of a new self and attempting to locate the self [...within]. Whatever utility may be stretched in parts, however, the process of dismantling will not act as a remote control for correcting all incorrectness, in which we are also the strongest party. It is so because dismantling procedures may again be termed as irreverent experiments with [...others]. We need to bring a liberating phenomenon into picture with authentic creativity.

Whether we welcome or denounce it, it is undeniable that linguistic temptation interrogates drastically many time honored linguistic myths and, in return, may therefore also offer us alternative ways of negotiating the place of Indian Linguistics in the transitory and often distorting competency of the West. Indeed, it may help us in adjusting the place between past and present and also help in pushing us on the threshold of the future. Are we ready? .

REFERENCES

Crystal, David 1988. *The English language*. London: Penguin.

Kachru, Braj 1986. *The alchemy of English: The spread, functions, models of non-native Englishes.* Chicago: University Of Illinois Press.

Kedourie, E. 1993. *Nationalism.* Cambridge, Mass: Blackwell.

Peter, Pam 2004. *The Cambridge guide to English usage*. Cambridge: Cambridge University Press.

24

Rough Notes

Udaya Narayana Singh

Plural Voices

I was wondering if there existed an alternative way of painting the dark days and nights.

Why should it not be the case that the 63% of educated Indians would like this number to grow to 73% or even to 93%, assuming that 7% would still belong to an age where ignorance and innocence are bliss.

Perhaps not knowing how adults poison their own environment, or how they park their own garbage with open invitation to birds and insects, or how they learn the mantra that helps outsmarting the 'fellow-runners' are all bliss!

But there is no harm in still hoping that there would be some, or many, who would like 93% literacy and education.

Let me try to imagine an India of the future: What would life be like if that were to happen?

First, for that to happen in the first place, there should be 30% more facilities - more books, more teachers, more schools, more libraries, more universities etc.

Secondly, if all these happened within a foreseeable time, there would be no need to reserve or regulate admission or jobs etc, and the legal and constitutional provisions would not affect us much. (Consequently, there will be a lot of problems faced by those in politics who depend crucially on these divisions in society!)

Thirdly, there would be a tremendous expansion of markets in all spheres, with a greater amount of participation of the segments and sectors that are not dependent only on the governing forces.

Fourthly, and hopefully, the health-care and family and other kinds of planning on the front that accounts for life, living and longevity would now have the situation where it would be easier to spread the required knowledge and awareness vis-ë-vis issues of public health.

Fifthly, there would be a greater number of educated electorate that would not be possible for political parties and aspiring politicians to take for granted. It will surely reflect on the governance structure and the required balance between forces of civil society, political-economic forces, and the judicial system.

Therefore, the question is whose interest would be served by disallowing knowledge to kindle lights that make a nation's future less hazy. There will still be tsunamis, earthquakes, floods and the great depressions and recessions. But the fact is that the country will then be ready to face them, and devise strategies and action plans to pre-empt and prevent them.

To my mind, a lot of what is happening now - which is the handiwork of different political groups, is happening because we have not reached the 93%. Now we have a situation where the farmers are disallowed to talk to the investors and cartographers and economists and the strategists who could together alter their landscape and destiny. Instead, we see political egos being allowed to clash at the cost of the common man, and at the cost of public exchequer. It is easy to paint black. It is difficult to dream of rainbows, and think bigger and better. Or, for the better!

Do we need to wait for the seasons to change to imagine what a rainbow will look like, or can we invite the plural voices to air prayers of different hues? That is exactly what my friend and colleague Rama has been striving for – all his life, when he was talking about literacy education in a plural setting such as ours, or in a country like South Africa, or in the highly multilingual setting of England. For those who never worried about plurality, and its connection to the gateway of knowledge, it is worth giving a thought! And, of course, you are welcome to read Ramakant Agnihotri's work.

The Death of the Monolingual

Whom do you support when some of our mainstream politicians harp on the *sons of the soil* theory? It is not an easy decision. Protectionism somehow manages to raise its ugly head time and again in all countries, or in several states within India. The trouble is that a lot of political managers and planners think that this policy is based on sound management principles. Many even think it is inevitable, like death and income-taxes. However, we need to question as to who is a Pure Son of the Soil, and which Soil has remained pristine and pure! Since the humanities and social sciences are increasingly dedicating a portion of their scholarly agenda to the environment, it is not surprising that linguists would spend a lot of their ink on writing about the need to preserve our language ecology. But like Ramakant, I have also been questioning the notion of linguistic purity, and therefore, let me elaborate.

Let me approach it from the point of view of the *ecological humanities* which believes that for a just and equitable future of life, social and ecological justice are essential component of governance of social groups. In other words, we must make a space for or be responsive to Indigenous people's knowledge and aspirations for justice. If we did not, we would soon see the conditions of crisis, which would only be an indicator that major changes which we would like to come about through our socio-economic planning are somehow running out of control. Who throws them out of the desired path, and who or what derails these processes are important questions we need to address. Like many important ecological changes, especially during the periods of crisis, are situated across the nature/culture divide, does it say anything about the way grammarians try and bring an 'order' into the natural phenomena by bringing in the desirable homogeneity, and culture? Is acculturation (and '*Sanskritization*') an as inevitable homogenizing and pasteurizing process as several others in modern-day nation-state management? Just as shift in ecological thoughts almost goes parallel to the shifts that had been taking place from universal knowledge to situated knowledges, or in language ecology, from the concept of *monoglossia* to *heteroglossia* in all speech communities, and from the centred hierarchies to decentred networks in the art and science of political management, the time has perhaps come to declare a death warrant for 'monolinguialism', and with it – the ever-elusive search for 'the Standard', or 'the Pure'.

Let us not underestimate this shift of paradigm in Sociology of Language, of which some of us have been the spokespersons in this part of the world. Inherent in this shift is a "decentering of the scientist" (Rose and Robin 2004), including the scientist of languages. Such celebrations of the impure, the colored, the converged require a new generation of workers and thinkers who believe in this kind of shift. For the ecologists among the scientists, the shifts in thinking are revolutionary:

> ...from concepts of climax and equilibrium to concepts of pervasive disequilibrium; from concepts of objectivity to concepts of intersubjectivity; from visions of deterministic prediction to an awareness of fundamental uncertainties such that predictions must be probabilistic. (Ciancio & Nocentini 2000)

Are we being scientific when we declare that monolingualism is a myth, and pluralism is the only reality? This is a question that ghosts of many earlier generation sociolinguists will raise. But to my mind, those would hardly qualify as *science of language* today. To bring a parallel from elsewhere, let me turn to pseudo-scientism and science in another field. For centuries many believed if we allowed a substantial quantity of blood to flow out of the body of a diseased person, this bloodletting could cure-all. The Mesopotamians, the Egyptians, the Greeks, the Mayans, and the Aztecs – all subscribed to this view, and they all had in mind a model built on the process of menstruation meant for 'cleansing' women of "bad humour" (Hippocrates). But as science progressed, we know that while bloodletting could work wonders at a time when hypertension went untreated, it was far from being scientific about treating human sufferings.

And yet we are aware that many political and intellectual battles were fought on this issue of support for 'bloodletting' as a cure. The barber-surgeons continued using it in many communities. While *phlebotomy* (also known as "breathing a vein") or *therapeutic phlebotomy* does allow drawing of blood for laboratory analysis, especially to reduce the amount of red blood cells, these are not like the pre-scientific beliefs like those in favor of bloodletting. All such primitive beliefs, like the faith in *Alchemy,* have now been thrown into the dustbin of the history of science, we know.

A part of literature in Sociolinguistics will surely have the same fate, I am afraid.

Linguists' Woes: Purity too dies

I grew up with a product I came to hate during my fever quarantine. That was called the *Purity Indian Barley*. As I grew older, more than the barley, it is this 'purity' I became more and more suspicious about. In the name of 'purity of race', we ended up with a holocaust. Recall the flak 'the purity of reason' got. Although linguists and grammarians remained tied to the notion of 'ideal' and 'pristine' speech forms by an 'Ideal' speaker-listener, and believed that whatever varies from the 'Standard' and the 'Accepted' was 'vulgar' or *'praakRta'*.

Our authors in the 20th century or even earlier, however, were not married to this notion of purity. Rather, they have given up the need to preserve the purity with a vengeance. We have already had fiction writers such as Phanishwarnath Renu (in *'Mailaa Aanchal'* and *'Partii Parikathaa'*) and Nargarjun (in *'Balcanmaa'*) in Hindi, or Satinath Bhaduri (*'DhoRhaai carit Maanas'*) in Bangla, but coming to Krishna Sobti, thanks to her novels such as *'Baadalon ke ghere'*, *'Mitro Marjaanii'*, *'Ai laRkii'*, and *'Suraj Mukhii Andhere ke'*, where she uses Punjabi, Urdu, Sindhi, and Gujarati words with equal ease in her Hindi writings, we find an interesting trend that contests the so-called Standard. Once, when asked as to how the Hindi readers of her novels from other parts of India (outside the western Indian belt) would enjoy the flavor of her language, she had said that the chief concern of a good writer should be the subject matter and capacity to assimilate the external conditions and their transformation into internal ones. A reading of her *'Yaaron ke Yaar'* would reveal that she has mastered the language of tirades and abuses typically used in a colloquial code-mixed situation where Hindi was one of the codes used alongside Punjabi. The story had an office as its locale, which could be any office anywhere. But with subtle differences, she creates a whole crowd of a subordinate establishment, and to capture the atmosphere, she used actual dialogues, punctuated with usual abuses, as a part of her realistic presentation.

Obviously, for any author, it would be very difficult to satisfy - with respect to linguistic conformity - all sections of a large linguistic tract such as that of Hindi. However, she believes, and this background information helps us in appreciating her style, that it is the power of the narrative and authenticity with which an author presents the narration with respect to the locus of the story - together with the linguistic choices she makes would determine the readers' response. It is, therefore, not a question of linguistic-semantic transparency of each and every idiom or expression used in a text that is important; the simple test of a piece of prose-writing would be to assess the absorption of the content and the expression. Thus, someone like Krishna Sobti or Devaluru Mahadeva (in Kannada) would refuse to 'defend' her or his use of this 'deviance'. This is because she believes that this is the only way the history of a plural space could be captured. History is neither viewed through cyclical patterns, nor through archetypal characters in Zindaginama but through folk traditions, rituals, ceremonies and marriage ties. Feminine voices, maternal images, images of birth and nurturing and of continuity abound. Prefacing her work with a poem, Sobti states:

> History/what is not
> And history/what it is
> Not that
> which is secured in
> the royal archives with
> date and time in the
> chronicle

But that
which flows within the
consciousness of the people's mind
Flows, flourishes and spreads
and lives's in the
ordinary people
(Translated by Jasbir Jain)

When I consider these positions, as a student of historical linguistics or language history, I find that the defect in what we had been doing since the *Junggrammatiker* days is that we had always been trying to reach unique solutions. There must be one line of development that somehow branches off into so many trees, we thought. How little we realized that neat patters of sound change or other phenomena would soon break down into several course of changes that flowed on parallel, and how often we would get confusing and contrasting explanations all of which would seem to be correct. We may need to rethink about all neat explanations soon, just as the story of diffusion of traits from Dravidian to Indo-Aryan would have to be reopened to see if the traits came from other sources we never considered so far (even after S.K.Chatterji's excellent hint in his 1939 book *Kiraata-jana-kRti*). May be a lot came from the Austric or went into them, or began from the Tibeto-Burman and reached us later. Or it could be that each one was giving and taking features all the time, defying all typical historical linguistics explanations. Here too, there is a space for plurality, then.

The *Visarjaniiyas*, or the Dispensables

Talking about the *Bhasha*, or the so-called 'native' languages, there are other kinds of comparisons and contrasts that appear. In terms of '*swaramaalaa*' (or, 'alphabets'), they are neither like the '*Swara*' (=the vocalic) nor like the '*Vyanjana*' (=the consonantal). Let me quote an example from my own writing. In my youthful exuberance, back in 1966 - in my first book of poems in Maithili, yet another language on the margin in the east – I had written about the '*Anuswaara*' and the '*Visarga*' – the lowest of the lowly – neither the Vowels, nor the Consonants. I had then said – the fight is between the Vocalics – the indomitable, and the Consonantals – the noisy ones, ready to run riots on streets – but that the *Anuswaara*s and the *Visarjaniiya*s of our society are the dispensable lot. Why should anyone weep for them? Do they have the right to be read? I guess that this is what we are all trying to discover now.

"Why worry about what you can't have?" – Some may ask, while one talks about marginalization of a large number of our *bhasha* traditions? Always down in the should all be 'number game', the unanswered and unanswerable questions will be many: Who will publish books in these languages? Even if published, how will these books reach the scattered segments of people in undefined difficult terrains? Who will read them - especially in the absence of universalization of education and literacy?

In short, how will the literary traditions in smaller languages survive in the cruel market economy of publishing? Some may say – May be, they would come alive in translation into languages where books sell and are read by a large readership. If that is made possible, 'translation' would have played an important role in furthering the cause of smaller languages.

When we look at the one big cultural space that has thrown up the largest number of languages, we will have to consider the North-East. The total scenario of the North-East vis-ë-vis languages spoken is like this: North-eastern India now has seven different states, where most of them speak Tibeto-Burman languages. These states are spread over an area of over 255,088 sq. km., which is 7.7% of India's territory[1], but house the largest number of linguistic groups. Except Assam, which itself had had a chequered history, the other states were created at different period of time. In 1972, Meghalaya (with mostly Khasi and Garo speakers) was carved out of Assam through a peaceful process. Tripura, too, with Tipra or Kokborok languages (spoken by 19 Scheduled Tribes besides Bangla and Manipuri, out of which Bangla speakers account for 40% of its population)[2] had become a state in 1972. But much before that, Nagaland became a self-governing state within India (in 1960), although the state was officially inaugurated in 1963[3]. This 16,579 sq. km area has between 12 to 14 Naga languages. One of the latest to be created was Sikkim (inhabited by speakers of Lepcha, Bhutia, Nepali, Limbu), which was an independent kingdom till 1975 before it merged with India. After the memorandum of settlement between Government of India and the Mizo National Front was signed in 1986, Mizoram became an official state with Mizo and English as official languages in February 1987. At the same time, from its earlier formation as the North-Eastern Frontier Province or NEFA as it was popularly called, Arunachal Pradesh[4] was set up– on 20th February 1987. The major lingua-ethnic groups include: Adi, Nyishi (including Bangru and Puroik), Apatani, Bugun, Galo, Hrusso, Koro, Meyor, Monpa, Tagin, Mishmi (including Idu-Mishmi, Taroan and Kamman), Sajolang, Sartang, Tai Khamti, Yobin, Singpho and Tangshang (including a number of smaller groups from the Changlang district as well as Nocte, wanchoo and Tutsa from the Tirap district). In fact, ever since the British had gained the governance of Assam (in 1838), their plan was to isolate the tribal linguistic groups there. That was why we found NEFA being created in 1873 through the promulgation of the Bengal Eastern Frontier Regulation.

To give one instance of attempts to disturb the linguistic-ethnic composition of the region, take the case of migration in the North-East, because of which as against the 355,320 Muslim population of the Assam Valley (as per 1911 census), the number had grown almost three-times to 1,305,902 by 1941. It is not surprising, therefore, that violence against the speakers of 'Other tongues' erupted here repeatedly in 1979, 1987, 1989, 1990 and 1992[5], and some part of the region is disturbed linguistically even now.

The violence had its roots in the large-scale in-migration from Bangla-speaking Muslims during the last century. Among the north-eastern states, Manipur is one of the oldest as it had got full statehood. Although Manipuri speakers have the majority, about 30% are speakers of Naga and Kuki, with a number of other very small speech groups. Since 1972, the North Eastern Council Act, 1971, a North Eastern Council (NEC) has been established (with representation from all seven north-eastern states at the highest level) to act as advisory body in respect of balanced socio-economic development of the region.[6]

It is obvious now that these small languages in the North-East face the real danger of losing out in the number game. The threat is more pronounced as the model of governance we have chosen (namely, 'democracy') is crucially dependent on the factor of number or on the majority. Once they begin to lose out or are out-numbered, the three 'D's - Disappearance, Death, Danger become the real possibility. Once again, many skeptics might ask what if that happens. But we will do well to remember that this would defeat the fundamental bases of our multi-lingual and pluri-cultural ethos which the creators of our Constitution would swear to protect. In fact, in the remaining parts of the world today, disappearance of languages or linguistic bases are happening at an alarming pace, so much so that in one prediction only 10% of the current 6,000 world's heritage languages will survive by 2050.

Death of a speaker is understandable. Wiping off of an entire culture or community is painful. In many cases, the elders in the speech community are able to speak their languages in all contexts, but not the younger people who often migrate into the language(s) of Power – be it English, or Hindi or Assamese or Nepali or Manipuri or Bangla.

In one of my talks titled, 'Mother, Why don't you teach me?' (at Hyderabad status in 1972; Goethe Institute and Osmania University

Seminar) I had shown the terrible crises gripping our smaller language groups – often schooled in 'Other tongues'. In preparing the NCF (National Curriculum Framework, NCERT) document, Ramakant and other colleagues had expressed similar sentiments. A large number of Grade I students do not reach Grade V - about two-thirds of them being girls. If we have both primary and the middle schools, about 3/4th boys and 4/5th of girls drop out . How will such societies churn out readers and writers in these tongues? To reduce the Teacher-Pupil ratio from 1:42 to 1:20 level, we need an additional, 3 million primary school teachers, more than twice the number employed now.

As against this scene, consider what the latest UNESCO report says: "There are 77 million children in the world who are not enrolled in school during ... 2004 and the largest numbers ... in Nigeria, Pakistan and India together..." Here is another reason as to why we must take steps – both legal as well as political to protect the right of the smaller languages to be read as well as the oral traditions in which they are traditionally rich. Otherwise, "Education for All" will remain a distant dream for socially disadvantaged children in India even by 2015 – which is our target year for achieving it.

But by 2016, there will be 500 million with less than five years of schooling, and another 300 million not passing out of high school. The actual number of primary schools (651,381) or Upper Primary Schools (245,274) are too few to make any move towards creating a 'Knowledge Society'. Only 53.04% villages have at least primary schools somewhere near by.

The trouble in planning for these smaller linguistic groups also come from the fact that 50.66% of the total STs population is in Scheduled Areas; Which means that while a largely Scheduled Tribal space such as the North-East could attract attention and funding, the rest live as tiny minority groups in non-scheduled areas which do not make it possible for them to get the kind of attention they deserve. They lose out faster in the pressure game. Do we not sit down and plan for the protection and promotion of such cultural spaces? Indian Linguistics needs more sensitive and sensible linguists like Ramakant who could alter the face of our policy and planning documents and literature on language management.

The Beginning

When we all started as postgraduate students of linguistics in Delhi – way back in 1972, some of us were dreamy eyed freshmen, over-awed with our highly trained and knowledgeable teachers, the distinguished visitors, and the adjunct and visiting faculty. But some – like Rama,

Aditi, Kapil and Harish as well as many others – came after a few years of teaching experience in the literature programmes in the colleges in Delhi, and therefore – we had teachers on the dais as well as teachers sitting with us as fellow students. It is needless to say that some of those classes we had had with Prabodh Pandit after office hours, or with Ravindranath Srivastava in the tea-shop on Lucknow Road were the most memorable moments of our lives. A lot of what one could call unconventional ideas in linguistics came about since those days.

When I look back into how we all started, I couldn't help penning down a few lines in my language for us, our generation, which in English rendering reads like this:

Chasing the waves on the sea-shore
we return to the childhood again -
games played on the sand
hillocks that couldn't be scaled,
gasping for breath to retire early,
drinking of coconut-water together -
even now crowd the memory lane.

must turn my head
back into the past -
must take my head out of my prison
so that months and years turn into
tiny temple-bells tied to a tall flag-staff -
your gentle smile chiming and
echoing mildly into my ears.

what I like doesn't wait for time -
'cause time always drags me along
towards unknown banks.

REFERENCES

Chatterji, Suniti Kumar 1939. *Kiraata-Jana-KRti*. Kolkata: Asiatic Society.

Ciancio, O. and S. Nocentini 2000. Forest Management from Positivism to the Culture of Complexity. In M. Agnoletti and S. Anderson (eds.) *Methods and approaches in forest history*. Wallingford, UK: CABI Publishing. 47-58.

Rose, Deborah Bird and Libby Robin 2004. The Ecological Humanities in Action: An Invitation. *Australian Humanities Review*, 31-32.

NOTES

1. http://www.satp.org/satporgtp/publication/faultlines/volume12/Article3.htm; esp. Sahni, Ajai. 'Survey of Conflicts and Resolutions in India's North-East'. [*Institute for Conflict Management* (ICM)].
2. http://www.economywatch.com/stateprofiles/tripura/profile.htm
3. www.economywatch.com/stateprofiles/nagaland/profile.htm
4. http://arunachalpradesh.nic.in/
5. http://www.hvk.org/articles/1002/113.html
6. http://necouncil.nic.in/about_m.htm

25

'How Do I Know You are not a CBI Agent?': Examining the Identity of Researcher in Sociolinguistic Fieldwork

Rizwan Ahmad

Prologue

My intellectual engagement with Professor Ramakant Agnihotri started when I was studying for my Master's degree in the Department of Linguistics at the University of Delhi. As a first year student, I took a course on the principles and methods of language teaching with him. At that time, since I was more interested in the structure of language, I did not take the course very seriously in the beginning. But Rama's (nay Agni's, as we used to call him amongst us) innovative way of teaching made the course immensely interesting. Agni encouraged us to think critically and relate theoretical knowledge gained in class to real world experiences. By the end of that term, Agni had kindled a spark of enquiry in me about the social and psychological aspects of language, and my fascination with syntactic theories and the beautiful trees that they generated had started to wane. In the following semester, I decided to sit in his sociolinguistics class as an auditor. An added attraction of the course was that his class had many beautiful girls. The decision to "flirt" with the field of sociolinguistics later turned out to be a serious business. After completing my Master's degree, I wrote an M. Phil. thesis, under his supervision, examining the sociolinguistic aspects of Urdu and Hindi news bulletins of the All India Radio. By that time, sociolinguistics had become my passion, which culminated into a Ph.D. from the University of Michigan, Ann Arbor, USA in 2007.

Although it has been more than a decade since I graduated from the University of Delhi and left India in pursuit of my academic career,

I have stayed in touch with Agni through email, phone calls, and personal visits. This attests to the fact that in addition to being a fine scholar, he is an excellent human being. Our last meeting took place at the silver Jubilee celebrations of the South Asian Linguistic Analysis (SALA-25) conference at the University of Illinois, USA, in 2005. He looked as enthusiastic and dynamic as ever; he came to my presentation and asked questions and gave valuable feedback on my paper. I feel privileged to contribute to this festschrift volume in honor of Professor Ramakant Agnihotri. This paper is dedicated to his scholarship in the field of linguistics.

1. Introduction

This paper is *not* about the findings of a study; it is rather about the sociolinguistic methods that lead us to our research findings. Since our results are based on an interpretation and analysis of the *data* that we collect from our research participants, the results cannot be separated from the methods that we adopt to collect the data. Results and data are intertwined in a way that they inform each other in significant ways. Mithun, who has conducted extensive fieldwork on a number of American Indian languages notes, '...the choice of methodology can also shape the resulting product in ways researchers may not always be aware of' (2001: 35). In a way, the relationship between data and findings are quite similar to the philosophical position that holds that the means and the end are not separable. In this paper, I will discuss the factors that affect the means that lead us to the end. The paper is based on the pilot study that I conducted in Old Delhi in 2005 and full-fledged fieldwork research that I carried out in 2006 for my Ph.D. dissertation, which I completed at the University of Michigan in 2007.

2. Interconnectedness of methodology, data, and results

The interconnectedness of the methodology, data, and the results has been noted by linguists who are interested in the structure of language and those who study the social and political dimensions of language. Chelliah (2001), whose scholarly interest lies in the structure of Tibeto-Burman languages of North East India, for example, cautions that depending exclusively on direct elicitation methods could lead to incorrect generalizations about the structure of a language. She argues that it is important to combine data obtained through elicitation methods with naturally occurring texts such as conversations and narratives. For Chelliah, the very authenticity and validity of research depends on the right methodology adopted.

In sociolinguistic research, the impact of the methodology we adopt on our results was pointed out, quite early on, by Labov. Since Labov was interested in variation in speech, he wanted to make sure that the data he obtains is as close to naturally occurring language as possible. He referred to the problem of collecting natural data for sociolinguistic studies as "observer's paradox". Labov in his classic work noted, 'our goal is to observe the way people use language when they are not being observed (1972a: 61)'. The influence that the researcher can have on the quality of data goes far beyond the "naturalness" of data. In cases where the language under study is ethnically marked, the very access to research participants can crucially depend on the researcher's social and ethnic identity. Moreover, the ethnic identity of the researcher can color the responses that he/she receives from the participants, especially if the study focuses on the social and cultural perceptions about language.

Many studies have demonstrated the role of the researcher not only in the quality of the sociolinguistic data but also obtaining access to speakers and the community at large (e.g. Hazen, 2000; Schilling-Estes, 2000). Although as an outsider fieldworker, it is always difficult to get access to data without establishing a sufficient level of confidence, it becomes more difficult if the fieldworker is perceived as belonging to a community that has a hostile relation with the community being researched. In such cases, access to institutions and speakers for relevant data often depends on the social identity of the fieldworker. Sociolinguistic studies in Northern Ireland, for example, show that, due to heightened ethnic differentiations, it was often difficult for a Protestant fieldworker to conduct research in Catholic areas (McCafferty, 2000).

Although the ethnic boundaries and social divisions between Muslims and Hindus, at the time when I conducted my fieldwork in Old Delhi, were not as sharp as the Northern Ireland situation described by McCafferty, the perception of Urdu and Hindi in the twentieth century as languages of Muslims and Hindus did create a methodologically difficult situation for me as a researcher. A good example of how ethnically marked Urdu and Hindi have become can be gleaned from the protest by Hindu fanatics against the introduction of a 10-minute news bulletin in Urdu on Doordarshan in Bangalore in 1994.[1] In this paper I do not go into the history of the formation of the link between Urdu and Hindi and Muslim and Hindu identities. However, the reader can refer to King (1994), Dalmia (1997), Rai (2000), Faruqi (2001), Orsini (2002), and Ahmad (2008).[2]

3. Multiplicity of identity

In the following, I show how Muslims and Hindus of Old Delhi developed different perceptions of my social identity in different social and discourse contexts. I further show that my being Muslim did not automatically make my entry into the Muslim community of Old Delhi easier. Nor did my religious identity prevent access to the Hindu community. In many ways, I was an outsider for both Muslims and Hindus. I was able to gain access to the communities only after I had developed a high degree of trust and confidence with them. The contacts I already had with people of Old Delhi, before I started my fieldwork, helped a great deal in alleviating fears, suspicions, and misgivings among research participants and building trust and confidence. A lot of contacts with Urdu and Hindi speakers that I made on my own, without the help of the local people did not grow to a level of trust and confidence needed for conducting fieldwork research. This tells us so much about the fear that people in general have of outsiders. Once I had a referral from a known dillīwālā, a native resident of Old Delhi, people's perception of my foreignness decreased significantly, and so did their fear and inhibitions. People were willing to discuss the social and cultural aspects of Urdu and Hindi on tape, often running for over an hour.

Since Muslim and Hindu names in India are linguistically distinct, Muslims and Hindus of Old Delhi in general and my research participants in particular did not have any trouble finding out my social identity just by learning my name. In the very first meetings, whenever I introduced myself, or was introduced by others, dillīwālās, both Muslims and Hindus, right away knew that I was Muslim. They did not have to wonder about my identity or explicitly ask me for the information. Other relevant social identities are not as easily and clearly gleaned from Muslim names as the religio-ethnic identity. For example, it was not easy for anyone to find out from my name what berādrī, Muslim caste, or 'mazhab', religious sect, I belonged to.[3]

Let me start with how larger social and political contexts of Old Delhi went into the interpretation of my identity by dillīwālās. During my very first week in Old Delhi, when I was still trying to establish connections with Urdu and Hindi speakers, I went to a chemist in Chūriwālān to buy some medication. I wanted to make use of the opportunity to learn about the language situation of Old Delhi. I greeted the shop owner, Shamīm, whose Muslim identity was visible in his typical Muslim Tōpī, cap, with the traditional Muslim greeting 'as salāmu alaikum' and introduced myself to him.[4] I told him my name and my institutional affiliation. To establish my credibility and gain his confidence and trust, I further added that before going to the USA for my higher education, I was a student at Jawaharlal Nehru University and the University of Delhi. I also told him that during my college days, I would frequently come to Old Delhi. Then, I asked him a general question about Urdu and Hindi in Old Delhi. Before answering my question, Shamīm asked me for my identity card to verify my identity. I showed him my University of Michigan ID, which had my picture and my name, but Shamīm did not look convinced.

He did not believe that I was *only* interested in the issue of language. He told me that Indian secret service agents of the CID, Criminal Investigation Department and CBI, Central Bureau of Investigations, often come to Old Delhi under cover, looking for other social information. His suspicion grew further, and right in front of me, he told his colleague and friend Mr. Shafīq that I might be an agent of the American CIA, since I came from the US. Mr. Shafīq who was a little less suspicious of my identity than Shamīm, told him that some researchers indeed do study languages. Shamīm however was not convinced and did not answer my question about Urdu in Old Delhi. He then took me to a professor of Urdu, who lived in the same neighborhood, probably hoping that the professor will be able to figure out my identity better than he could and thus would know how to deal with me accordingly.

In the second phase of my fieldwork in 2006, while roaming around the Matia Mahal neighborhood in search of right research participants, I went into a small shop for a cup of tea. As usual I started to talk to the shop-owner in order to listen to his Urdu. I found his language very interesting since he did not pronounce "correctly" a couple of the Urdu phonemes, namely /k̲h/, in words such as 'k̲hayāl', 'thought' and /gh̲/, in words such as 'gh̲alat', 'wrong'. It is worth noting that these phonemes are considered to be shibboleths of the Urdu language.[5] In order to make sure that he and his family were originally from Old Delhi and not migrated recently from outside, I asked the gentleman about the original homes of his parents. He told me that they are k̲hālis dillīwālās, pure natives of Old Delhi. In fact, in order to prove his ancestry in Old Delhi, he showed me a 19th century land document of his great grandfather written in Persian. Since he could not read the document himself, he asked me if I could read it to him. With my smattering of Persian, I was able to figure out the names of the seller and the buyer and the witnesses. He was very happy to know that his great grandfather's name was mentioned in the document. Once I ascertained that he was a native of Old Delhi, I wanted to interview him. I introduced myself in more detail and told him that I am a research student and that I would like to tape an interview with him. He told me that he was not free that day, but he could do it the following day. I came to him at the time of his choosing, the following day, with my recording equipment. He talked and talked but did not agree for a taped interview. He made several promises later, and did not fulfill any. He knew I was Muslim, but I was an outsider who did not enjoy his confidence and trust. My being Muslim was not enough.

In Old Delhi, for even Muslim dillīwālās, I was an outsider in another way. I was Bihari—someone who came from the state of Bihar. The word 'Bihari' has become a term of abuse and insult in Delhi. It is not uncommon to hear people in a fight calling each other 'Bihari'. A few years ago, I noticed two people fighting over a seat in a Blueline bus. One of them, in a raised pitch called the other 'abē oē bihārī!', 'you Bihari!'. The other in response yelled, 'bihārī hōgā tū' 'you are Bihari, (not me!)'. The emergence of Bihari as a term of insult is beyond the scope of this paper. However, what I want to underscore is the stigmatized meaning that the word 'Bihari' connotes in Delhi. Among dillīwālās too, Biharis constitute an out-group that serves as the 'other' of who they are.

Since I was born and raised in North Bihar, I retain a distinct Bihari accent when I speak Urdu. Often, Old Delhi Muslims commented on my lack of control of Urdu and/or my Bihari accent. While interviewing a Muslim research participant, Mr. Nazīr Quraishī, who lives in Haveli Azam Khan, I asked him to tell me something about a neighborhood in Old Delhi known as Chitli Qabar. I was interested in hearing the pronunciation of the Urdu phoneme /q/ in 'qabar'. In order to help him locate the neighborhood, I added 'wōbāzār jahā̃ aurtẽ hī aurtẽ dikhtī haĩ', 'the market where a lot of women are seen'. I used 'dikhtī haĩ', a passive form of the verb root 'dékh', 'see', which, I realized later, is not common in Old Delhi Urdu. Mr. Quraishī commented on my "incorrect" use of the verb right away, 'āp kī bhī urdū sahī nahī haĩ' 'your Urdu is not correct either', indicating probably that my Urdu is as bad as other younger generation speakers or as bad as that spoken by other Biharis living in Old Delhi. He then provided the correct passive form of the verb 'dikhāī dētī haĩ'. This incident shows that I was not seen as an insider linguistically and socially. My Muslim identity was just not relevant for this conversational context.

Another similar incident took place at the Jāmā Masjid, where I went to offer my Friday prayer. I was not particularly dressed for the occasion. I was wearing a T-shirt and a pair of jeans. On Fridays, most Old Delhi Muslims wear a white kurtā-shalwār, 'a loose two-piece outfit', and a Tōpī, 'cap'. I was offering 'sunnat', a non-mandatory prayer, before the beginning of the sermon and the mandatory prayer. As soon I was done, somebody from the row behind me pulled me by the shoulder and, in what I considered quite a rude way, pointed at my uncovered head and elbows and unreasonably long trousers that went beyond my ankles. In a very harsh and a tone filled with anger, he told me how careless I was not to get a cap worth 10 rupees. It is widely believed by Muslims that it is forbidden in Islam for men to cover ankles and leave the elbows uncovered. It is also recommended that you cover your head. The gentleman thought that I was an outsider, and I needed to be taught a lesson. The notion of insider-outsider is complex and my being Muslim was not always interpreted as an in-group marker.

My access to the Hindu community for data was expected to be difficult. I did not have any key contacts among the Hindu community of Old Delhi, before starting my fieldwork. I made some efforts, on my own, to establish contacts with Hindus in Bāzār Sitārām and other neighborhoods, but I was not successful at all. The successful entry into the community was facilitated by the contacts I developed with people of influence and established credibility in the neighborhoods. My contacts among the Muslim community became helpful in that they introduced me to some known figures among the Hindu community, who in turn put me in touch with speakers who became my research participants. Once the key figures introduced me to possible research participants and, in a way, vouched for my authenticity and credibility, they were able to cooperate with me in my research. Without these key contacts, I would not have been able to gain the confidence and trust of the Hindu community. The struggle to find a way into the Hindu community was in no way different from the struggle to gain access into the Muslim community.

My Muslim identity, however, did play a positive role in obtaining access to Islamic institutions such as mosques. As a Muslim, my entry into mosques was not restricted. This was helpful in collecting data in an indirect way. Since a large number of homes in Old Delhi do not have enough 'public' space for outsiders like me, many people who were interested in helping me with my research were not able to meet with me in their homes. Those who had businesses would often invite me to their work place. Those who didn't often invited me to meet with them on the premises of the mosques. So, I used the mosque premises as a meeting venue, where I had several meetings with research participants. Since Turkaman Gate is a very crowded neighborhood, I used KalāN Masjid located in the vicinity as a meeting place. Secondly, I also observed the use of Urdu in mosques and recorded some 'k̲hutbās', 'sermons'. As a Muslim I exercised my right to gain entry into mosques and established contacts with the 'imāms', people who lead the prayers. It would have been difficult for me to gather data from the mosque, if I were not Muslim.

In a methodologically non-significant way, my Muslim identity was once treated as an in-group marker. While I was doing my research at Zakir Husain College with the third generation Urdu speakers, who were born in the 1980's, I contacted a young man from PhāTak Tēliyān through a friend of his, whom I had known for a long time. After I explained my research to him, I asked him if he would be willing to participate in my research. He showed his willingness to participate in my research and commented that it was good to know that I was working on Urdu. If "*I*" did not do research on Urdu, he argued, why would 'others' do. For this Muslim gentleman, Urdu was the language of Muslims and it was "natural" that I, being a Muslim, was doing research on it.

The social and contextual nature of my social identity notwithstanding, I hired a Hindu research assistant to conduct some of the interviews for me, with Hindu research participants. I did this in order to make sure that I was not influencing the quality of the data I was getting from Hindu participants. My research assistant, a female undergraduate student, was born in the city of Old Delhi. She conducted interviews with some Hindu participants including P. K. Chōprā, whom I also interviewed. I studied the two interviews with reference to the use of the Urdu phonemes and found that there were no differences in terms of frequency distributions between the two interviews. This way of triangulating my methods assured me that the data I was getting was a broader pattern and not because of my influence on the participants.

4. Conclusion

I have shown through the above discussion that the notion of insider and outsider related to the social identify of the researcher conducting sociolinguistic fieldwork research is quite complex. Different social, political, and other contextual factors go into the construction of an identity of the researcher. My Muslim identity did not automatically facilitate my entry into the Muslim community of Old Delhi, nor did it prohibit access into the Hindu community. I was an outsider for both Muslims and Hindus of Old Delhi. Since I was an outsider, it was quite natural that they treated me with fear and suspicion, especially given the subject of my study—Urdu and Hindi. I have shown that the best way to win the trust and confidence of the community you want to study is through establishing contact with key personalities in the community. Once you have established your credibility and authenticity to them, they will vouch for you and provide you with the contacts with research participants of your interest. This of course takes a lot of time. But you will be rewarded with rich and authentic data that one cannot obtain in a short period. In sociolinguistic research, there are no quick recipes, like McDonalds.

Appendix

Symbol	*IPA*	*Symbol*	*IPA*
/kh̲/	/χ/	/j/	/dʒ/
/gh̲/	/ʁ/	/sh/	/ʃ/
/C/ (capital letter)	Retroflex e.g. /T/ stands for /ʈ/	v	Short vowel
ch (consonant followed by 'h')	Indicates aspiration, e.g. /th/ stands for /t^{h}/	v̄	Long vowel
/y/	/j/	ṽ	Nasalized vowel
/ch/	/tʃ/		

REFERENCES

Ahmad, Imtiaz (ed.) 1973. *Caste and social stratification among Muslims in India.* Delhi: Manohar Book Service.

Ahmad, Rizwan 2007. Shifting dunes: changing meanings of Urdu in India. Ann Arbor: University of Michigan. Ms.

Ahmad, Rizwan 2008. Scripting a new identity: the battle for Devanagari in nineteenth century India. *Journal of Pragmatics* 40.1163-1183.

Ahmad, Rizwan 2008b. Unpacking indexicality: Urdu in India. *Proceedings of the Symposium about Language and Society (SALSA),* University of Texas at Austin. Vol. 52. 1-9.

Chelliah, Shobhana 2001. The role of text collection and elicitation in linguistic fieldwork. Linguistic Fieldwork. In, Paul Newman and Martha Ratliff (eds.) 152-165. Cambridge: Cambridge University Press.

Dalmia, Vasudha 1997. *The nationalization of Hindu traditions: Bhāratendu Hariśhchandra and nineteenth-century Banaras.* Delhi: Oxford University Press.

Engineer, Asghar Ali 1994. Bangalore violence: linguistic or communal? *Economic and Political Weekly.* 29. 2854-2855.

Faruqi, Shamsurrahman 2001. *Early Urdu literary culture and history.* New Delhi: Oxford University Press.

Goodfriend, Douglas E. 1983. Changing concepts of caste and status among Old DelhiMuslims. In Imtiaz Ahmad (ed.) *Modernization and social change among Muslims in India*. 119-52. New Delhi: Manohar Publications.

Hazen, Kirk 2000. The role of researcher identity in conducting sociolinguistic research: a reflective case study. *Southern Journal of Linguistics* 24.103-20.

King, Christopher R. 1994. *One language, two scripts: the Hindi movement in nineteenth century North India*. Bombay: Oxford University Press.

Labov, William 1972a. Some principles of linguistic methodology. *Language in Society* 1.97-120.

Mccafferty, Kevin 2000. *Ethnicity and language change: English in London, Derry, Northern Ireland.* Vol. 7: Impact: Studies in Language and Society. Amsterdam: John Benjamins.

Mithun, Marianne 2001. Who shapes the record: the speaker and the linguist. Paul Newman and Martha Ratliff (eds.) *Linguistic Fieldwork.* 34-54. Cambridge: Cambridge University Press.

Orsini, Francesca 2002. *The Hindi public sphere.* New Delhi: Oxford University Press.

Rai, Alok 2000. *Hindi nationalism.* New Delhi: Orient Longman.

Schilling-Estes, Natalie 2000. Fieldwork for the new century: papers from the SECOL 1999 panel presentation. *Southern Journal of Linguistics* 24.83-90.

NOTES

1. See Engineer (1994) for communal color that the language riot of Bangalore acquired.
2. See Ahmad (2007, 2008b) for the complexity of social meanings of Urdu in India.
3. For a discussion on caste among Muslims in India, see Ahmad (1973). For a discussion on caste and status among Old Delhi Muslims, see Goodfriend (1983).
4. In order to protect the privacy of the research participants, I use pseudonyms.
5. See a key to the transcription system in the Appendix at the end of the paper.

Section C

APPLIED PERSPECTIVE

26

Using the Mother Tongues for Learning and Teaching Other Tongues: Theory and Practice

A. L. Khanna

Introduction

It is a truth now universally acknowledged that there are no monolinguals on the surface of the earth; those who are said to know only one language actually control a highly complex and subtle range of a verbal repertoire in which different styles and varieties serve the functions that are comparable to what are called different languages in the case of a multilingual. We do need to dismantle the 'mono/multi' divide and regard multilinguality as constitutive of being human (see e.g. Agnihotri, 1995, 1997, 2000, 2007). Every human being knows (uses)/ learns more than one language/ varieties. Perhaps, we all know that the additional languages that all of us learn are learnt either non-consciously while negotiating our needs in everyday life or consciously in tutored situations. No one questions the use of the mother tongue (L1) in acquiring another language (L2) as part of one's growing up, but when it comes to learning another language in a school or college setting, there is a lot of hue and cry about whether or not to allow the use of the mother tongue (L1) in the L2 classroom. Some researchers and practitioners of second language who recommend L2 only have tended to base their claim on theoretical arguments such as the idea of learning being heavily determined by the quantity of exposure to the language. Central to forwarding this argument is Krashen who advocated maximum exposure to the target language. According to him, all teaching should be in L2 only and that there was a definite relationship between comprehensible input in L2 and proficiency (Krashen, 1985:14). It meant that time spent using L1 would detract from L2 learning .He even stressed that exposure to L2 was not always successful in increasing proficiency in the target language because learners had access to L1, either in class or out of it. Followers of this monolingual paradigm go to the extent of saying that the use of L1 should be banished completely from the foreign/second language classrooms. This sort of anger against the use of the mother tongue has also been expressed by those who do not know the native language of the students they are teaching or are those who have some vested interest in promoting only L2. For instance, emphasis on monolingual teaching of English had not only political agenda but was also tied to the economics of the global EFL field (Pennycook, 1994: 176). In Phillipson's view (1992: 193) this sort of perceived superiority and dominance of English over other languages is a case of only Linguistic Imperialism. Thus, the supporters of monolingual approach advocate that learning of L2 should model the learning of an L1 (through maximum exposure to L2).

Second Language Acquisition Research

The role of the mother tongue (L1) in teaching English as a foreign/second language has been the subject of controversy and debate in second language acquisition (SLA) research literature and professional teaching spheres, reflecting fluctuations in language learning theory that have led to advocating different pedagogies for actual classroom use. L1 was accepted by the proponents of Grammar Translation Method (GTM) which had been used in the teaching of Latin and Greek for several centuries in Europe. It had its support in long and extensive use rather than any defensible theory of language or learning. In fact, translation and rules of grammar constituted the core of this method. Gabrielatos (2001) observes that L1 was favored by the proponents of the Grammar Translation Method (the first grammar translation course was published in 1783), and Pendergast (around 1860). The grammar-translation method was universally accepted because language teaching placed an emphasis on the written word. In the 19th century, this trend slowly reversed towards monolingual approach in part due to a shift towards the spoken word. As a result of mass migration from Europe to America and spread of colonialism and bigger and mixed L1 classes (Hawks, 2001: 47) the teacher could not rely on L1 to help the students. As a result, this method was discouraged or eliminated from the recommended list by the advocates of the Direct Method who were against the use of L1 in teaching a foreign language. The Direct Method contributed to the consolidation of the idea that L1 languages should be excluded from the classroom (Harbord, 1992: 350; Pennycook 1994: 169) Gabrielatos (2001) remarks: "Moderate views were expressed by the Reform Movement (Vietor (1882/1886) and Palmer (mid 1910s to late 1920s).Therefore, it seems L1 has never been 'a skeleton in the cupboard' (Prodromous,2007: 7) rather it has been a bone of contention for more than two centuries (p 6)." It is the result this kind of negative attitudes that the use of L1 in an EFL classroom came to occupy a very low profile.

The focal emphasis of the theory and practice of second language teaching in the late nineteenth century and greater half of the twentieth century was largely behaviorist in nature. The rapid growth of structural linguistics coincided with the behaviorist principles of learning. All the language teaching methods, including audio-lingual method and grammar-translation method, developed during this period rest on the assumption that 'the major problem in learning a foreign language is to master the structure of that language and that this problem requires almost exclusive attention.'(Roberts, 1975: 96). L1 continued to be looked at negatively by the linguists working under the influence of behaviorist psychology and structural linguistics. The audio-lingual method which was in vogue from the 1950s to the first quarter of the 1970s undermined the importance of L1 in the process of L2 learning in a formal context. The researchers working in the Communicative Approach paradigm firmly believed in the use of L2 as the medium of teaching and also that L1 use actually interfered with L2 learning and brought about error interference (Pacek, 2003) and viewed all deviations from the target language as deplorable errors that needed to be eliminated. Errors, seen as interferences, became the basis of Contrastive Analysis (CA) which began to be used as a tool to predict the errors of the second language learners and preparing teaching materials. The protagonists of CA were linguists such as Nickel and Wagner (1968), Lee (1968), Nemser (1971), Duskova (1969), Dulay and Burt (1974), Ellis (1985), Larsen-Freeman and Long (1991), of course with a significant difference in the ways in which they used the tools of CA. The principles and methodology came under severe criticism (see Lee 1968; Gradman,1971; Whitman and Jackson,1972, among others). Research evidence showed (see, for instance, Buteau, 1970; Richards, 1971a, 1971b; Oller, 1972; Ghadessey, 1980; and Felix, 1981) that learner L1 interference in the learning of an L2 is just one minuscule source of error. Therefore, prediction of errors done by CA was not considered reliable. Several researchers believing in the creativity of the learner and working on the output of the learner realized that the learners' output needs to be seen in its own right rather in terms of the first or second language(s). This implicit assumption has been called, with a slightly different emphasis, 'transitional competence,' (Corder, 1967), 'approximative systems'(Nemser, 1971), 'interlanguage'(Selinker, 1972) and 'language learner's system' (Richards and Sampson, 1974). Interlanguage is the system of implicit knowledge that the learner develops and systematically amends overtime and is thought to be distinct from the learner's first language and from the target languages (Maclaughlin, 1987).

In fact, one of the crucial issues in the different views is the nature and extent of L1 influence on a learner's language (Ellis, 1994). The cognitive psychologist Ausubel (Ausubel, 1964) pointed out amongst several other things, that L1 could function as a facilitator in the process of L2 learning. Rivers (1972; 1981) observed that since L1 was ubiquitous in the process of L2 learning teachers could capitalize on the pupils'L1 mainly for giving instructions or clarifying difficult language. In her opinion, learner L1 may help accelerate the process of learning another language.

A number of researchers including Ellis (1995) view learner's L1 positively. Krashen and Terrell (1983) suggest that learners should use their L1 to bridge the gaps in communication on account of inadequacy in their interlanguage to initiate utterances. Rutherford (1987: p 7-14) as reported in Hitotuzi (2006) favours the thesis that no human being embarks on learning an L2 as a tabula rasa. He argues that, when attempting to learn an L2, the learner is equipped with two kinds of prior knowledge, which he labels knowledge this and knowledge how. The first is, in his words, 'an unconscious "foreknowledge" or innate "inkling" of what shapes the organization of the target language can assume.' This capacity is at the disposal of the learner and is activated whenever he/she needs to infer the unknown in the target language on the basis of his/her rudimentary interlanguage. Then, the second, knowledge how, mirrors the learner's L1 learning experience: 'The ability temporarily to bend the new language into forms that will, with maximal efficiency, serve the initial desire for rudimentary communication.'

Rutherford emphasizes the valuable contribution of L1 to L2 learning: 'Both of these cognitive capacities are crucial, for without them, no language learning would be possible at all (p 8).'

Deller (2003) lists seven reasons why we should use their L1 as a resource. One of the reasons cited by her is that the use of mother tongue will equip the learners with the words and expressions they really want and need in English. Brown (1987) sheds light on how useful interference errors can be for the development and strengthening of L2 learners' interlanguage. According to Rutherford (1987), this may be achieved by resorting to language universals.

Cook (2002) believes that L2 user is a person who has knowledge of his first language and L2, rather than a monolingual with an added L2. According to him, an L2 learner employs his L1 or any other language he knows for any purpose at whatever level. Cook presents multi-competence view of second language acquisition, according to which two or more languages are present in one mind which encompasses the concept of interlanguage. This conception treats the mind of the L2 learner as a whole rather than as having separate L1, and interlanguage components. Although L2 research from the 60s onwards have made use of the interlanguage concept to describe the independent language of the L2 learner, yet the research methods employed consistently measured L2 learner against the native speaker. In Cook's opinion, L 2 users should be judged by what they are, L2 users, not what they can never be by definition, native speakers. In Francois Grosjean's (1989) famous phrase, a bilingual is not two monolinguals in one.

Cook (2001) remarks: 'Acquiring a second language does not mean acquiring the self contained language system of a monolingual but an L2 that coexists with L1 in the same mind. Aiming to be a monolingual native speaker may then be impossible for all but a handful of people...The benefits of learning a second language are becoming a different person, not just adding another language.' Cook (2001) goes on to add: 'Instead of pressurizing the students to approximate the native speaker as much as possible, teaching should aim at making them independent L2 users who can function across two languages, with mental abilities that the monolingual native speaker can not emulate.' Juarez et al (2008) showed in their research that judiciously resorting toL1 in the EFL classroom is more a help than a handicap. According to them, the use of L1 and translation activities has enjoyed renewed attention (e.g. Ferrer, 2005; Deller and Rinvolucri, 2002; Atkinson, 1993, 1987; Auerbach 1993). As Rinvolucri so succinctly reminds us in a recent publication, 'the mother tongue is the womb from which the second language is born' (Deller and Rinvolucri, 2002: 4) a metaphor which clearly highlights the more favourable facilitating role currently attributed to translation and the use of mother tongue in EFL contexts. Yet it should be taken into account that such an L1- based methodological approach is principally promoted by practicing teachers than supported by empirically based studies of linguistic achievement. The two groups remain clearly distinguishable.

Practising Teachers' Views

It is equally important to know what the practising teachers feel about the role learners' L1 plays in learning the target language. Some teachers view it as a valuable tool in the developmental process of L2 learning.

Prodromou (1992) holds the view that the learner's mother tongue is an excellent instrument for the activation of his/her cultural schemata in the process of learning L2.Butzkamm (quoted in Mckenzie-Brown, 2006) remarks:

> 'Using the mother tongue, we have learned to think, learned to communicate and acquired an intuitive understanding of grammar. The mother tongue opens the door not only to its own grammar, but to all grammars, in as much as it awakens the potential *for universal grammar* that lies within all of us...for this reason, the mother tongue is the master key to foreign languages, the tool which gives us the fastest, surest, most precise, and most complete means of accessing a foreign language.' He suggests that using teaching aids in the mother tongue can 'promote more authentic, message oriented communication than might be found in the lessons where they are avoided...(Also,) mother tongue techniques allow teachers to use richer, more authentic texts sooner. This means more comprehensible input and faster acquisition.'

He further says that his theory 'restores the mother tongue to its rightful place as the most important ally a foreign language can have, one which would, at the same time, redeem some 2000 years of documented foreign language teaching, which has always held the mother tongue in high esteem.'

Buckmaster (2000) argues that the use of L1 empowers the L2 learner. He suggests that the use of the mother tongue of the students by the teacher allows students 'to compare and contrast English with the language they know best, to use translation as a means to study form and meaning, to understand jokes, to check comprehension, to understand complicated instructions, to check exercises with their partners and to learn vocabulary with direct equivalents (p2)'. Matsuda (1996) advocates the acquisition of writing skills. She in her capacity as an English composition instructor allows her pupils to avail themselves of their L1 as a technique to unleash creativity and reflection. She maintains that the various common aspects between learner L1 and L2 (if worked on a consciousness-raising basis) can evolve into precious interchangeable material to amass qualitative composition skills in both languages. Tuck (1998), however, believes that L1 should be used primarily for writing practice with lower levels and/or children. But some believe that total immersion in the target language can be very stressful for the beginning learners. One word in L1 can in many situations release tension. But a few have wondered how in a multilingual class where students from different language backgrounds come to study together (as in a class in India) use of one of the mother tongues will help the learners. In such situations the teacher would require a common language that is understood by most of the learners in the class. Some scholars have also shown how languages of children can be used for language learning and cognitive growth of children even when the teacher does not know the languages of children (Agnihotri, 1995,2007; NCF 2005).

In an email survey on the Use of English conducted by the BBC British Council on teachers teaching English as second/foreign language in different parts of the world 21% said that they used only English in their class. Others used English sometimes (58%),about half the time (6%), frequently (8%) and most of the time (7%).Those who used English only had the opinions like the following:

'I teach English as a second language to adults who are going to live in England. I never use my L1 (Gujarati) in the class. I feel it hinders from using other learning methods, listening outside classroom. (Gita Kharicha, England)

'One of the advantages of NOT speaking your students' first language is that you can't use it in class. My classes have been 100% English and always will be. My best students have all learnt English entirely through English; I really don't see how using L1 would have helped at all.'(Marcus, South Korea).

'Mother tongue should be avoided when teaching English language; the teacher should demonstrate and use pictures to pass his message across to the children.'(Muhammad Abubakar, Kaduna, Nigeria).

But there are others who feel that L1 can be very useful in L2 class. Here are some of the opinions:

'In my opinion, use of students' mother tongue in a monolingual class, is a great tool in teaching abstract vocabulary just to ensure enduced errors are avoided. It is a last resort for the teacher to spot check on the students and to further avoid frustration by slow learners. In this way, the teacher, himself, does not have to speak the mother tongue but can ask one or two of the students to say the word or expression in their L1 for the better understanding of their peers.'(Farahnaz Jafari, Dubai UAE)

'Using MT sometimes prevents wasting too much time trying to explain one single word/or phrase.'(Eleonora, Antonini, Italy)

'Sometimes I use Dutch to explain difficulties about grammar and pitfall words and idioms resembling Dutch words and expressions but with completely different meaning. All other things are done in English.'(R.G. Renes, The Netherlands)

'I use mother tongue when teaching English if it is extremely necessary for making meaning clear the meaning of collocations of word, the word order and also the prepositions. I prefer to repeat three-four times the things in English with miming and pointing to the things named.'(Annamaria D. Kalmar, Hungry)

'I feel that it depends on the level of the students' English regarding on how the teacher uses the mother tongue. It is important to be understood when explaining points.' (Robert Warren)

Ray (2007)'s survey of 72 English teachers teaching in state-funded schools revealed that nearly two thirds held the view that children's mother tongue is a great help rather than a hindrance in teaching English at the initial stages. According to her, the teachers unanimously felt that as 'the children became more confident, the teacher should slowly progress from partly L1 class to totally L2 class where the children are given a greater exposure to L2 and are provided scaffolding that uses methods not requiring L1.' (p. 5).

Khanna (2009) based on a survey of some practicing English teachers at various levels and in different teaching contexts, found that as many as 54 percent teachers engaged in teaching English at various levels admit that they make use of learners' mother tongue occasionally while teaching English. It is only a very small minority that shuns learners' mother tongue completely. Nearly 80 percent of English teachers believe that knowing the mother tongues of learners is a rich resource and many of them feel that there is nothing wrong in using it to make learning an anxiety- free experience for the learner.

As it can be seen from these surveys, the opinion is divided on whether to use L1 in L2 class. There is a very small section of teachers who believes in target - language only policy in the target language class and who sees an insignificant, or no role at all for L1 in the L2 classroom.

Learners' Perception

Since the learner is central to the issue, it is equally important to understand how learners view the use of their mother tongues in learning another language in the classroom. Schweers Jr (1999), as part of his teaching and research in Puerto Rico, Bayamon Campus, enquired of his Spanish students learning English whether Spanish had any role to play in learning English. An overwhelming number (88.7%) of his students recognized the importance of the mother tongue primarily for explaining difficult concepts. A few more studies reported in Hitotuzi (2006) favour the use of the mother tongue. But some of the studies reported here (in Matsuda, 1996) point out that the use of the mother tongue can be an obstacle. However, Burden (2000) is in agreement with the truism that the better the student, the less support needed from the mother tongue.

Implications for language Teaching: suggestions on the use of L1 in L2 classroom

A major pedagogic implication is that we put L2 user at the centre of language teaching rather than the native speaker. We need, in the opinion of Cook, a proper description of successful L2 users which can show their unique characteristics of grammar, vocabulary, pronunciation, rather than relegating them to deviation from the language of the native speaker. The students' goal is to be able to use both L2 and L1 in the appropriate situation and for the appropriate uses. Cook believes that the successful students can never become like the native speakers. These L2 speakers will not think in monolingual ways. They will think L2 user ways. They will become non-native speaker teachers who use second language efficiently for particular purposes.

After one has listened to the views of language oriented researchers, teachers and learners one can legitimize the use of L1 in the L2 classroom with certain amount of caution. If such caution is not taken about the amount of use, when and why and by whom, the recourse to L1 might be counter-productive.

Hitotuzi (2006) recommends L1 equivalents for teaching abstract items to the beginning groups whenever contextualization, mimicry and other techniques fail to gloss them convincingly. He further adds: 'Moreover, at times L1 can be used in L2 classrooms as a mnemonic strategy-e.g. association of meanings in the two languages. By and large, at this level the L1 can be used for almost every move in the classroom, both teacher initiated or student- initiated, such as organization of the class and tasks, maintenance of discipline and classification as regards testing material.'

Bowen,Tim (n.d.) lists some of the contexts in which the knowledge of the mother tongue of the learner would be very useful. The first use, according to him, is that it provides 'a quick and accurate translation of an English word that might take several minutes for the teacher to explain and even then there would be no guarantee that the explanation had been understood.' He adds that knowledge of the mother tongue is also particularly useful with younger learners and adult learners at the beginner level to check instructions, to ensure that concepts have been correctly understood and for general classroom management. He further adds that the greatest potential advantage of the knowledge of learners' mother tongue is that it enables the teacher to contrast the language with English and to know which structure are difficult and which are easy. It helps to know the potential problems with vocabulary items. Finally, he mentions that some learners need the security of the mother tongue. Such learners need to relate concepts in English to equivalents in L1.This may be the most effective way of learning vocabulary.

Hitotuzi (2006) further points out that L2 learners should be encouraged to using the target language from the very beginning lest they become complacent with the use of the mother tongue. This could be done only by engaging learners in language-building task mentioned in Nunan (1999). Hitotuzi further cites researches of Centeno-Cortes and Jimenez(2004) and DiCamilla and Anton (2004) to emphasize the pivotal role L1 plays in cognitive and meta- cognitive processes involved in L2 learning. Research and classroom practice appears to support that L1 can be used as a starting point in the production of oral/written texts in the classroom. But as learners become more proficient in the target language they must move towards using the target-language only strategy. The proficient users of the target language are not forbidden to use their L1. They could use it while reflecting and working on their own, in activities such as doing home work, writing an essay, issues in language and meta language etc. However, they must use only the target language, while interacting in the classroom, in order to gain aural/ oral fluency.

In the end one would agree with the supporters of Bilingual Approach expressed by researchers such as Deller and Rinvolcri (2002). They contend that the mother tongue that learners bring to an L2 classroom should be perceived as a rich resource in the initial stages of learning. A judicious use of the mother tongue both by the teacher and learners instead of causing an obstacle may help learners to achieve their goals faster in the target language and also make them cognitively richer and more mature. Anandan (2006) remarks that we can get maximum yield from the use of L1 by virtue of inter-sentential code switching which operates at the discourse level. This will optimize input in terms of L1 and L2 without putting language acquisition at stake.

As learners gain confidence in the use of L2, they would on their own reduce their dependence on L1. Excluding L1 may lead to higher drop out rate in ESL schools, whereas when L1 is permitted, researchers and teachers alike report much more positive results (Auerbach, 1993:18).

In the opinion of Gabrielatos (2001), in the context of learning English as a second/ foreign language by a non-native speaker, a uniform attitude to L1 use in ELT is not helpful. A more constructive range of questions is 'what for', 'when', 'to what extent'.

Any views on the utility of L1 in ELT should not be influenced by sociopolitical issues, but also take into account insights from Linguistics and Applied Linguistics.' It is very important to mention at this juncture that since there are many variations of English around the world, there is no scientific validity to support the view the notion of a native speaker being the ideal teacher (Phillipson, 1992: 1950). In addition to the quantity of exposure to the target language through the native speaker, there are several other factors (e.g. text materials, trained teachers, sound methods of teaching etc) that are necessary for achieving language proficiency in the target language. Simply increasing exposure to the target language may not yield the desired results particularly with the lower- level students. They may benefit more by explanation in L1 than immersion in the TL. Thus, inclusion of L1 (even in a multilingual class where the teacher may not know L1s of all the learners) in L2 classroom may accelerate rather than impede learning, raise learners' meta-cognitive awareness, foster guided reflection and develop both cognitive and meta-cognitive learning strategies through cross linguistic comparison. Thus, learners using L1 may stop having a sense of shame or guilt generally associated with using L1.This may in turn make learning L2 less threatening and anxiety-free and may also increase learning potential of the learners, increase positive results and may reduce the drop rate of below average learners.

REFERENCES

Agnihotri, R.K. 1995. Multilingualism as a classroom resource. In K. Heugh et al (eds.) *Multilingual education for South Africa.* Johannesborh, Germany: Heinemann, 3-7.

Agnihotri, R.K. 1997. Multilingualism, Colonialism and Translation. In S. Ramakrishna (ed.) *Translation and multilingualism: Post-colonial contexts.* Delhi: Pencraft International, 34-46.

Agnihotri, R.K. 2000. Teacher's Space in the classroom. In R. Mathew et al (eds.) *The language curriculum: Dynamics of change.*Vol 1. Hyderabad: Orient Longman. 157-161.

Agnihotri, R.K. 2007. Towards a Pedagogical Paradigm Rooted in Multilinguality *International Multilingual Research Journal* 1 (2), 1-10.

Anandan, K.N. 2006. *Tuition to Intuition: A Constructivist Perspective on Second Language Pedagogy.* Calicut: Mind Publication.

Atkinson, D. 1993. *Teaching monolingual classes.* Harlow: Longman.

Atkinson, D. 1997. The mother tongue in the classroom: a neglected resource? in *ELT Journal* 41, 4:241-247.

Ausubel, D. 1964. Adults vs. children in second language learning: psychological considerations. *Modern Language Journal* 48, 420-424.

Auerbach, E. 1993. Re-examining English only in the ESL classroom. *TESOL Quarterly* 27(1), 9-3.

Brown, H.D. 1987. *Principles of language learning and teaching* (2nd ed.).New Jersey: Prentice Hall.

Buckmaster, R. 2000. Using L1: What kind of sin? *IATEFL Pre-conference Edition* 18.Retrieved September 16, 2001 from http://www.iatefl.org.pl/nletter/nletter18/nlet18 2.html

Burden, P. 2000. The use of the students' mother tongue in monolingual English 'conversation' classes at Japanese universities. *The Language Teacher* 24 (6), 5-10.

Buteau, M.F. 1970. The students' errors and learning of French as a second language: a pilot study. *IRAL* 8 (2), 133-45.

Butzkamm, W. (n.d.). The bilingual method-an overview. Unpublished paper.

Bowen, Tim. (n.d.). Using the mother tongue in classroom. http;//www.onestopenglish.com/News/Magazine/Archives/mothertongue.htm

Canagarajah, A.S. 1999. *Resisting linguistic imperialism in English teaching.* Oxford : Oxford University Press.

Centeno-Cortes, B. and A.F.J. Jimenez 2004. Problem – solving tasks in a foreign language: The importance of the L1 in private verbal thinking. *International Journal of Applied Linguistics* 14 (1), 7-35.

Cook, V.J. 2001. Using the first language in the classroom, *Canadian Modern Language Review* 57, 3, 402-423.

Cook, V.J. 2002. Background to the L2 user. In V.J. Cook (ed.) *Portraits of the L2 User*. Clevedon: Multilingual Matters.

Cook, V.J. 2003. *Effects of the L2 on the L1*. Clevedon: Multilingual Matters.

Corder, S.P. 1967. The significance of learners' errors. *IRAL* 5 (4), 161-70.

Corder, S.P. 1971. Idiosyncratic dialects and error analysis. *IRAL* 9 (2), 147-59.

Corder, S.P. 1974. The elicitation of interlanguage. *IRAL* (special issue on the occasion of B. Malmberg's 60th birthday, edited by G. Nickel), 51-63.

Deller, S. 2003. The language of the learner. *English Teaching Professional (Jan 26):* 5-7.

Deller, S. and M. Rinvolucri 2002. *Using the mother tongue: Making the most of the learner's language.* London: Delta Publishing.

DiCamilla, F.J. and M. Anton 2004. Private speech: A study of language for thought in the collaborative interaction of language learners. *International Journal of Applied Linguistics,* 14(1), 36-69.

Dulay, H. and M. Burt 1974. Natural sequence in child language acquisition. *Language Learning* 24, 37-53.

Duskova, L. 1969. On the sources of errors in foreign language learning. *IRAL* 7, 11-36.

Ellis, R. 1985. *Understanding second language acquisition.* Oxford: Oxford University Press.

Ellis, R. 1994. *The study of second language acquisition.* Oxford: Oxford University Press.

Felix, S.W. 1981. The effects of formal instruction on second language acquisition. *Language Learning* 31 (1), 87-112.

Ferrer, V. 2005. The use of the mother tongue in the classroom: cross-linguistic comparisons, noticing and explicit knowledge. (online;http//www.teachenglish worldwide.com/Articles.htm.).

Gabrielatos, C. 2001. L1 use in ELT: not a skeleton, but a bone of contention. *Bridges* 6: 33-35.

Ghadessey, M. 1980. Implications of error Analysis for second/foreign language acquisition. *IRAL* 18.2: 93-104.

Gradman, Harry L. 1971. What methodologists ignore in contrastive teaching. *Paper presented at the Pacific conference on contrastive linguistics and language universals.* Honolulu.

Grosjean, F. 1989. Neurolinguists, beware! The bilingual is not two monolinguals in one person. *Brain and Language* 36, 3-15.

Harbord, J. 1992. The use of mother tongue in the classroom. *ELT Journal* 46 (4), 30-55.

Hawks, P. 2001. Making distinctions: A discussion of the mother tongue in the foreign language classroom. *HWA Kang Journal of TEFL,7*, 47-55.

Hitotuzi, Nilton 2006. The learner's mother tongue in the L2 learning-teaching symbiosis *Profile*, Jan/dec.2006, 160-172 ISSN 1657-0790.

Howatt, A.P.R. 1984. *A history of English language teaching.* Oxford: Oxford University Press.

Juarez, Carolina Rodriquez and Gina Oxbrow 2008. L1 in the EFL classroom : more a help than a hindrance? *Porta Linguarum* 9(1), 93-109.

Khanna, A.L. 2009. English Teachers' Views on the Place of Mother Tongue in Teaching English as a Second Language in Non-native Contexts. Research in progress.

Krashen, S.D. 1985. *The Input Hypothesis: Issues and implications.* London and New York: Longman.

Krashen, S.D. and T.D. Teller 1983. *The natural approach: language acquisition in the classroom.* Hayward: Alassany Press.

Lado, R. 1964. *Language teaching: A scientific approach.* New York: McGraw-Hill, Inc.

Larsen–Freeman, D. and M.H. Long 1991. *An introduction to second language acquisition.* New York: Longman.

Lee, W.R. 1968. Thoughts on contrastive linguistics in the context of language teaching. In J.E. Alatis (ed.) Monograph series on Language and Linguistics 21: *Contrastive linguistics and its pedagogical implications.*

Mckenzie-Brown, P. 2006. Teaching English, British Council (BBC) Nov. 28.http:www.teachingenglish.org.uk/talk/vote/vote15_mothertongue.shtml#top.

McLaughlin, B. 1987. *Theories of second language learning.* Edward Arnold.

Matsuda, A. 1996. Using the L1 in the ESL composition classroom. Paper presented at INTESOL'96 as part of the colloquium Perspectives on NES and NNS teachers in ESL writing classroom.

Medgyes, P. 1992. Native or non-native: Who's worth more? *ELT Journal* 46, 340-349.

Nemser, W. 1971. Approximative systems of foreign language learners. *IRAL* 9 (2), 115-23.

Nickel, G. and K.H. Wagner 1968. Contrastive linguistics and language teaching. *IRAL* 6, 233-55.

Nunan, D. 1999. *Go for it.* Boston: Heinle & Heile Publishers/ITP.

Oller, J. Jr. 1972. Contrastive analysis, difficulty and predictability. *Foreign Language Analysis*, 6, 95-106.

Pacek, D. 2003. Should EFL give up on translation? Talk given at the *11th annual Korea TESOL International Conference*, October 18th, 2003,Seoul.

Phillipson, R. 1992. *Linguistic imperialism*. Oxford: Oxford University Press.

Pennycook, A. 1994. *The Cultural politics of English as an international language*. London and New York: Longman.

Prodromou, L. 1992. From mother tongue to other tongue: What is the place of the student's mother tongue in the EFL classroom? *TESOL Greece*. 2007.

Ray, Shefali 2007. L1 in the English class: a survey of government primary schools of Delhi. *FORTELL Newsletter* 12 (September), 3-5.

Richards, J.C. 1971a. A non-contrastive approach to error analysis. *English language teaching*, 25, 204-19.

Richards, J.C. 1971b. Error analysis and second language strategies. *Language Sciences* 17, 12-22.

Richards, J.C. and G.P. Sampson 1974. The study of learner English. In J.C. Richards (ed.) *Error analysis: Perspectives on second language acquisition*. London: Longman.

Roberts, J.T. 1975. Recent development in ELT–part 1 and bibliography. *Language Teaching Abstracts*: 94-104.

Rivers, W.M. 1972. *Speaking in many tongues: Essays in foreign language teaching*. Chicago: Chicago University Press.

Rutherford, W.E. 1987. *Second language grammar: learning and teaching*. New York: Longman.

Selinker, L. 1972. Interlanguage. *IRAL* 10 (3), 219-31.

Teaching of Indian Languages, National Focus Group Position Paper, vol.1.3 *NCERT*, 2006.

Teaching English, British Council BBC. www.teachingenglish.org.uk

Tuck, R. 1988. Translation—still taboo? *The Journal* 9 Retrieved September 20,2001from http:www.britishcouncilpt.org/journal/j0922rt.htm.

Whitman, R.A. and K.L. Jackson 1972. The unpredictability of contrastive analysis. *Language Learning* 22, 29-41.

27

On the Teaching of Indian Language and Literatures Abroad

Omkar N. Koul

1. Language Teaching

1.1. Instructional Materials

Instructional materials are of two types: texts and supplementary materials. The texts are usually selected by the instructors of their choice or sometimes devised by them keeping in view the objectives, needs and level of the learners. There has to be wide range of available text materials the instructors can choose from. It is imperative to have the texts available in the local medium of instruction, i.e., English, French, German, Russian etc. The usual structure of the text material comprising different lessons follows a general format of text, vocabulary, grammatical and cultural notes.

The text materials are an integral part of any language teaching and learning situation. There is a long tradition of the writing of the language teaching/learning courses using different formats from structural to situational materials. Different types of instructional text materials are currently being used. The materials include certain standard manuals and the text materials prepared by the concerned teachers at different levels. As far as Hindi and Urdu languages are concerned most of the materials are available in the English medium. There are limited materials available in the medium of other major foreign languages such as French, Russian, German, etc. The traditional text materials are available in the format of narrative passages, selections from literature, conversations followed by grammatical notes, vocabulary etc. No adequate efforts have been made to select text materials from the current use of language used in the print and electronic medium.

Presently, the language samples vary a lot in content, style and variety of speech. Now there is a preference to select texts from the standard spoken variety used in electronic and print media. The newspapers present the current use of language in writing and are considered ideal for the text. Not many texts are available for teaching Hindi and Urdu languages. The principles of gradation of materials are not adhered to. The principles of simple to complex structures are adhered to. In the selections from newspapers, it is possible to grade the materials on the principles of simple news items to special reports or columns and editorials; short to long conversations, narratives or reports.

There are no standard tests. It is necessary to develop standard tests to test the development of language skills among the learners at different levels from the minimum to maximum levels of achievements using a standard five point scale.

1.2. Supplementary materials

Supplementary materials may include cultural readers, pedagogical grammars, learners' dictionaries, online courses etc. Whereas in the design of the text materials the choice is made by the concerned teachers in the design or the selection of a standard language teaching/learning course, but in the supplementary materials the teachers rely on and recommend other support materials. It is the area language experts, linguists and lexicographers of the concerned languages and institutions working for the development of the languages that have a prominent role.

1. Cultural readers are handbooks useful for explaining different cultural bound lexical terms, expressions, customs, festivals and other socio-cultural patterns of the people who speak the concerned language natively. No cultural readers are available in Hindi and Urdu for the use of language learners in these two languages. The language learners have to refer to different sources and rely mostly by the explanations provided by the teachers in class.

2. Pedagogical grammars provide grammatical descriptions of the target languages from pedagogical point of view. They are to be distinguished from linguistic grammars and must include descriptions from pedagogical point of view and exercises too. No adequate attention has been provided to this area in Hindi and Urdu. Most of the grammars written in these languages are by foreigners or non-native speakers of these languages. Though useful, they do not meet the requirements of

language learners. Pedagogical grammars must base their descriptions on the selected text and supplementary materials including the current use of spoken and written materials used in print as well as electronic media.

3. Audio-visual materials are of different types: (i) the recordings of the texts and also some supplementary materials in the pronunciation of the native speakers; (ii) free conversations related to the use of the target language in different social domains of household, market place or offices etc.; and (iii) interactive audio materials to build conversations.

4. Preparation of online language courses in target languages which would be composite courses introducing pronunciation of speech sounds, script, vocabulary, structures, grammatical and cultural notes, drills and exercises in interactive format. They can form the self-learning language learning packages. Though online courses have been prepared in some selected Indian languages like Tamil, Kannada, Bangla, the serious work is yet to begin as far as Hindi and Urdu are concerned. Materials currently being used for Hindi and Urdu are excerpts from some TV serials, stage dramas or films with no explanations. Their use in public domain is an infringement of copyright violations.

5. Websites of the target language resources are required for referring to the language resources. The materials should provide linguistic, sociolinguistic and cultural profile related to the target languages. These websites should provide (i) different kinds of text materials, (ii) supplementary materials such as conversations and narrations in socio-cultural context, excerpts from plays, TV serials with explanations and (iii) learners' dictionaries in the target languages. No serious work has been done in this area as far as Hindi and Urdu languages are concerned.

6. Learners' dictionaries form an important part of supplementary teaching/learning materials in a second/ foreign language teaching situation. Though a large number of bilingual dictionaries of different sizes are available in Hindi and Urdu languages, no useful learners' dictionaries have been prepared for the needs of second/foreign language learners in these languages. A learner's dictionary must ideally provide examples of the use of lexical items from the texts.

2. Teaching of Literatures

There is an interest in teaching the courses on Indian literature and/or the literature of a specific language in foreign universities. The universities which offer courses in Indian literature subscribe to an idea that 'Indian literature is one written in many languages.' The course contents usually revolve certain literary trends in selected languages like Sanskrit, Bangla, Hindi, Urdu, Tamil etc. The selection of texts is made from the available translations.

For offering courses on Indian literature or literature of a specific language, there is a need to have the basic material as follows:

1. Critical histories of literature in English and other prominent foreign languages like French, German, Russian, Spanish, Italian etc. The histories have to be as objective as possible so that the students are able to comprehend the literary trends and interpret them in their own way. These histories have to be pedagogically oriented.

2. Comparative literatures in Indian languages as well as selected foreign languages.

3. Authentic translation of prominent literary works from Indian languages into English and major foreign languages.

4. Publication of literary journals related to contemporary Indian languages.

5. Websites in all Indian languages providing up to date information on the concerned languages and literatures. The websites may provide the texts in translation with different interpretation.

6. Teaching of courses in literatures may not be an end in itself. Appropriate materials are to be developed for teaching Indian languages through literature.

There are no adequate materials as listed above for teaching of Indian literatures particularly Hindi and Urdu languages. Currently the selections of texts are made at random depending on the availability of literary texts in translation or interpreted in the language of medium of instruction.

2.1. Integrated courses on Languages and Literature

Assigning a definite role to literature would depend upon the objectives, levels and situations of language teaching. It is important to address the issue of selections of sample or representative literature, and also to identify the objectives of the teaching of literature. The main objectives of second or foreign language teaching are to develop linguistic, socio-linguistic, communicative, discoursal, strategic competence of the learner at different levels. It is possible to make use of appropriate selections of literature as instructional materials in fulfilling these objectives.

The role of literature can be broadly categorized at two levels: Introductory, and Advanced. At the Introductory level, selections of the literary texts can be used for imparting instructions in four basic skills: Listening, Speaking, Reading and Writing. For example, Literary text including prose and poetry can be used in developing listening comprehension.

The oral narration of pieces of prose, recitation of poems, discussions of literary topics, literary dialogues and narratives can be used in developing speaking skills. Literary texts can be used for reading comprehension too. Imitating different types of literary styles for creative writing exercise, writing of guided compositions, paraphrasing of literary texts, and preparation of summaries etc. can be used for developing writing skills.

For teaching literature at the Advance level of a language course would require the identification of clear-cut objectives. The objectives may be as follows:

1. to appreciate the literature at the target language;
2. to understand the socio-cultural patterns of people who speak the language natively;
3. to understand the literary tradition in the target language;
4. to undertake comparative and contrastive studies of the literature of the target language with that of the learner's mother tongue. etc.

In my opinion, the most difficult part of the curriculum planner and a teacher is to make selection of sample or representative literature. The process of selection involves the (a) gradation of literary texts; (b) choice of literary genres, (choice of literary styles and (d) choice of standard vs. non-standard varieties.

As far as the gradation of literary texts is concerned, it is suggested to employ the principles of 'simple to complex' or 'known to unknown'. It would mean to start with the selections from contemporary or modern literature and move to medieval and ancient texts. The simple reason being that the language used in contemporary literature is a form of living language the learner can easily encounter in the natural language environment. The transition from modern to ancient would be more smooth than from the old to modern. Similarly, it is suggested that selection of literary texts should be primarily made in the standard variety and the non standard varieties can be introduced at the advanced or higher levels.

It is possible to integrate the language and literature courses keeping in view the objectives of language teaching and learners' interest. Conscious attempts need to be made to bring the two closer.

3. Translation

Translation is becoming an important tool to enhance understanding between cultures. The source and target cultures are so different that translators face a challenge in enabling readers to understand the source culture. There is a need to present the cultural terms in a manner which represents the source culture most appropriately. A translator has three options: (a). adopting the source-language terms without any explanation, (b). adopting the source language terms with extensive explanations, and (c). rewriting the text for the target-language audience. The first choice is preferable for several reasons: (i) the text reads more fluently; (ii) the translator is closer to the source culture; and (iii) the reader of the target texts gets a more genuine image of the source culture. Globalization has made this option possible and more acceptable. Translators are facing new challenges. In the cross-cultural translation process, de-coding, re-coding and en-coding has to focus on cultural transposition. A translator has to be both bilingual and bicultural. Referring to the globalization in its expanded meaning, I will make some remarks on translation and culture, problems of translation and the development of appropriate translation tools and methodology.

Translation involves the transposition of thoughts expressed in one language by one social group into the appropriate expression of another group. It entails a process of cultural decoding, re-coding and en-coding. Cultures are increasingly brought into greater contact with one another. Multiculturalism, which is a present-day phenomenon, has an impact on almost all peoples worldwide. Moreover, as technology is developing at a hectic pace, nations and their cultures have come very close to each other. We are at the threshold of a new international paradigm. Boundaries are disappearing and distinctions are being lost.

3.1. Translation and Culture

There are three major types of translations: (i) business and social studies, (ii) science and technology and (iii) literary. As far as the translations in the areas of business, social sciences, science and technology are concerned, English has more or less emerged as a *lingua franca*. Globalization is changing the face of business, and bringing many challenges. One of the biggest challenges is how to remove the language barriers that divide people and cultures around the world. No one language will ever be universally accepted as the sole vehicle of international communication. Translation will continue to be an important tool available for obtaining information and content in different languages for multinational customers, work forces, business partners and researchers. The success of technical communication in a national and/or international context depends primarily on translation. Increasing communication between different states or regions at the national level or at the international level brings the question of the status of the transfer of meaning and the act of translation in focus with a new urgency.

In the globalized world, besides modern sciences and technologies, literatures of other cultures and languages have found a wider audience. There is so much more for translators and writers and readers to explore and share. The transfer of the culture-bound terms from the source language into the target language is more acceptable in the translation of literary texts. Translators have more access to online information, such as dictionaries of lesser-known languages. The Internet too helps the reader to understand foreign elements in the text.

3.2. *Problems in Translation*

There are practical problems of translating the terminology in different subject areas. Mostly, the misunderstandings are due to the translation or interpretation of terms. There is an urgent need for the development and standardization of the multilingual terminology.

A good source-target language dictionary is in no way sufficient in technical translation. 'Equivalence' plays a central role in translation. It expresses the correspondence of pairs of terms from the source and target language as far as their contents are concerned. There is a focus on functional equivalence of terms. An act of translation doesn't mean carrying out a word-for-word translation of terms from the source language into the target language. The contents of the terms must be transferred. There are various degrees of equivalence:

1. Complete conceptual equivalence
2. Partial equivalence or overlapping
3. Inclusion; a term merges into another
4. No conceptual equivalence

It is difficult to achieve typical equivalence or one-to-one correspondence in practice. It is not always possible to get unambiguous definitions. Meaning of a term can only be worked out completely from the context. It is a case of interpretative translation, based on interpretations. There is a danger of "interference" from one concept into another. The problem of translation is a dual one because it concerns two different systems of languages and concepts respectively. There is a problem is the lack of conceptual clarity.

3.3. *Translation Tools*

The translation tools fall into different categories: bilingual terminologies and dictionaries, encyclopedic dictionaries, cultural readers, database, linguistic corpora etc. The existing bilingual and multilingual terminologies are often incomplete and do not keep pace with the general expansion and the shift in the meaning of terms in different disciplines.

There is a need to develop a multilingual terminological database for Indian languages like "Eurodicautom' of the European Commission's Translation Service. Available at www.echo.lu/edic , it contains more than 5 million entries - technical terms, abbreviations, acronyms and phraseology - in twelve languages.

3.4. Methodology

Three types of methodologies are adopted: presenting meanings in context, emphasizing the difference, and transfer method with special explanations. The meanings of terms become clear when the terms are considered in context. The knowledge of the context is supplied by amplifications in the text in footnotes or in appendices. In order to make the meanings clear, differences in the source and target language concepts terms can be explained. In the "transfer method", further translation step is undertaken regarding the contents.

4. Agencies

Various agencies in India should have a prominent role in facilitating the teaching and learning of Indian language and literatures to non-native speakers of these languages in India and abroad. A few suggestions are made as follows:

1. The national language institutions and central universities like Central Institute of Indian Languages (CIIL), Central Institute of Hindi (CIH), Central Hindi Directorate (CHD), National Council for the Promotion of Urdu Language (NCPUL), Central Institute of English and Foreign Languages(CIEFL), National council for the Promotion of Sindhi Language (NCPSL), Rashtriya Sanskrit Sansthan (RSS), Mahatma Gandhi International Hindi Vishvavidhyalaya (MGIHV), Maulana Azad Urdu University (MANU) etc.;
2. State Academies, Textbook Boards, Language Departments and Translation Bureaus;
3. Central and State Universities;
4. Reputed publishing houses committed for the development of Indian languages and literatures;
5. Inter-governmental agencies for the development of languages, literatures and cultures in collaboration;
6. The ICCR may support the international collaborative activities in the preparation of the need based language learning materials in Indian languages;

7. The Indian Embassies and High Commissions abroad may assist the programmes related to conducting of short-term workshops, seminars, teachers training in Indian languages and literatures;
8. The language teaching programmes run by Indian Embassies and Cultural Centres may supplement the programmes conducted by the universities and other institutions abroad. Well-trained faculty has to be provided in these Centres, who can collaborate with the local scholars in running the progammes successfully.

5. Conclusion

Foreign language teaching has undergone tremendous changes lately all over the world. It is no more a routine academic job. A lot of attention is paid in framing clear-cut objectives, devising of learner-centered need-based courses, preparation and selection of instructional materials including print and audio-visual materials, developing of online courses, use of different suitable language teaching methods, administering of language tests in measuring the achievement levels. As far as the teaching of Indian languages as foreign languages abroad, especially Hindi and Urdu, we have to go a long way.

REFERENCES

Koul, Omkar N. 1983. *Language in education*. Patiala: IILS.

Koul, Omkar N. 1994. The role of literature in language teaching. In *SALR*, Vol. VI, Delhi: Creative Books.

Koul, Omkar N. 2005. *Language, education and communication*. Delhi: IILS.

Snell-Hornby, Mary 1999. *Handbuch Translation*. Tübingen: Stauffenburg.

Venuti, Lawrence 2001. *The translation studies reader*. London: Routledge.

Wiersema, Nico 2003. Globalization and Translation: A discussion of the effect of globalization on today's translation.

28

Teaching English to Young Learners: How Far Have We Come? How Far Can We Go?

Rama Mathew

> One day as I was walking across the classroom, I noticed something familiar in the rubbish bin. It was a small white paper bag. Inside the bag were the small zero-shaped Greek cookies, koulourakia, that my mother had sent to school with me the day before. I, personally, had handed it to my kindergarten teacher who graciously accepted it with a wide smile and a warm thank you. I didn't touch the bag, but I could see that it was just as I had given it to her, unopened.
>
> It was then that I must have realized that I couldn't bring anything with me to school. All that I had accumulated from birth to age 5 (language, culture, personality, talent, interests) went straight to the rubbish bin, unopened, not because it was inferior (or superior for that matter), but because it was different, therefore unintelligible, therefore useless.
>
> ......my kindergarten teacher couldn't possibly know that this gift was a symbol of honour. In my home culture, it meant that we recognized the teacher as an authority figure and accepted her position of power. She couldn't possibly know that with that small white paper bag I brought with me a wealth of experience, a rich culture, and a language that was fully developed. She thought that I brought nothing with me. But I did. So I began kindergarten ten paces behind the rest of the class and it took me six whole years to catch up....
>
> (Vasilla Kourtis Kazoullis: *Foreword in Cummins* 2001: iii-iv)

Introduction

The backdrop to this paper is the recommendation of the National Knowledge Commission on the teaching of English as a second language in all schools in India from Class 1 itself. Sam Pitroda, the Chairman of the Commission, in his letter to the Prime Minister, underscores the importance of English since '...an understanding of, and a command over the English language, is perhaps the most important determinant of access to higher education, employment possibilities and social opportunities.' Continuing his argument, he points out the irony in the situation: 'English has been part of our education system for more than a century. Yet, English is beyond the reach of most of our young people, which makes for highly unequal access'. The Commission recommends that 'the teaching of English as a language should be introduced, along with the first language (either the mother-tongue or the regional language) of the child, starting from Class I in school. This phase of language learning should focus on using both languages to create meaningful learning experiences for the child without disproportionate emphasis on grammar and rules' (National Knowledge Commission 2006).

The paper is situated within the context of Teaching English to Young Learners (TEYL) in mother tongue medium schools in India where English is taught as a subject from Class 1 onwards or from an early level such as Class 3 or 4. The decision to introduce it from primary classes in Government schools was taken to make it accessible to the underprivileged, since students in these schools are by and large from that section of the society. Although it seems that the issue of equal access has now been largely addressed in policy, the question of its implementation, i.e. to what extent students are getting opportunities to learn the language to be able to use it for different purposes, needs to be examined. Based on observation data from classrooms in different parts of the country, the paper raises questions about what is happening in the wake of the implementation of a new language policy. It also looks at what some of the principles of second language teaching and learning are at the primary level and how they may be implemented in actual classroom contexts.

Goals of Teaching English to Young Learners

Before we examine data from actual classrooms, we need to agree on the goals of TEYL. Since this is a new area of work (so far we had about 5-6 years of English during the 10-years of schooling) it is necessary to clarify what it is that we want to achieve by the end of teaching 10 (or 8-9) years of English. While a full-length discussion of the nature of English language proficiency these students can aim for is beyond the scope of this paper, the premise on which a school English programme can be based, would need to be outlined here.

Very clearly, we would like our young learners to learn English to be able to use it in a variety of situations, including those related to interpersonal communication as well as academic skills. Cummins (1981) termed these two types of competence, *Basic Interpersonal Communication Skills* (BICS) and *Cognitive Academic Language Proficiency* (CALP). This distinction is brought out by other researchers, for example, in Gibbons' (1991), description of what she terms *playground language* and *classroom language*. According to her, playground language 'enables children to make friends, join in games and take part in a variety of activities that develop and maintain social contacts' .....while the classroom language is 'associated with the higher order thinking skills, such as hypothesizing, evaluating, inferring, generalizing, predicting or classifying. Yet these are the language functions which are related to learning and the development of cognition; they occur in all the areas of the curriculum, and *without them a child's potential in academic areas cannot be realized'* (p. 3 emphasis mine).

Given this conversational/academic distinction, it is possible to argue that our learners have their mother tongue (or a regional language in some cases) as their medium of instruction, and therefore it is difficult to aim for English proficiency in academic skills since all their subjects are taught through the vernacular medium. This paper, however, makes a plea for English to be used as a medium for teaching at least one content subject such as environmental science, mathematics or some other 'academic' subject. According to the National Knowledge Commission (2006), 'Language learning cannot be separated from, and must be integrated with, content learning. Therefore, English should also be used to teach some non-language, content subjects, starting from Class III in school'. This is a very important imperative for English language teaching to be meaningful and challenging in its own right.

Thus, it seems possible and feasible to aim for (almost) equal competence in two languages i.e. in L1 and L2. In fact, the implication of the policy of introducing L2 in early primary classes is this, that we would like bilingual competence in our students. Presently, the (good) English medium school, more often than not, produces quite a good proportion of student population who are 'illiterate' in their mother tongue. Students in the not-so-good English medium schools are usually not good either in L1 or L2. In the new model with TEYL in place, we should be able to achieve equal bilingual competence, not more of one and less of the other (L1 or L2); and certainly not 'neither L1 nor L2'. While this does not seem to be a contentious issue, and the answer to the question has a sound theoretical basis as mentioned above, addressing it in practical terms requires us to confront the issue in a more unconventional manner than we have hitherto done: the import of this statement becomes clear in the remainder of this paper.

How far have we come with TEYL?

A survey of teaching-learning in different types of English classes over a period of time gives us a picture of what is happening with regard to TEYL. To begin with, we will examine the context provided by the extensive work done by Alexander (2000) in primary classes (not necessarily focused on English) across several countries. In the normal conduct of teaching, he identifies a continuum of pedagogic control in which 'anarchic' and 'autocratic' situations represent the two ends. The following Table gives us a comparative picture of the type of pedagogic control that was observed in a full range of lessons in five countries.

Pedagogic Control in Five Cultures (Alexander 2000)

	(Anarchic)	Negotiated	Directed	(Autocratic)
England		---———	———	
France		---———	———	---
India			———	———---
Russia			---———	
United States	---———	———		

It is clear from the table that the type of control ranges from *Directed* (by the teacher) to *Autocratic* in the Indian primary schools.

Soumini's study (1985) of both English class and a content class i.e. Social Studies in an English medium school, throws light on the issues that are being raised in the paper:

Class IV   ***English Class***

The class is engaged in the conversion of direct speech to indirect speech:

1 T: "Each one says the child is mine and I am his mother". (Students had to change it into indirect speech).
S1: Each one says that the child is ours and she is the mother.
T: Try, try. All of you try.
S2: Each one of them says that the child was mine.
5 T: (Shows disapproval by shaking her head)
S3: Each one says that the child is hers and I am his mother.
T: (a little impatient) Listen. When you are using 'she' how can you use 'I'?
S4: Each of them says that the child is hers and she is her mother.
T: (looks relieved) Did you understand?

This extended discourse shows that students were engaged in deleting and replacing words which would be acceptable to the teacher. Even the last one (line 8), although incorrect in terms of the meaning, probably occurred by trial and error. Students could not get the answer right because their focus here was on manipulating the sentence and not on meaning. It is debatable if this type of discourse can indeed lead to language learning.

Class IV *Social Studies*

T: Who was Akbar?
S: Akbar was the son of Humayun.
T: And?
S: ...was an emperor of Northern India.
T: You are forgetting his dynasty....
Ss: Moghul Dynasty.

Though the teacher was trying to bring the students' answer to her frame, it produced a longer discourse that resulted in better interaction. The focus was on meaning here.

Soumini's study revealed that the classroom interaction in social studies classes on the whole was better than in English classes (except when the focus in English classes was on content) as these gave more opportunities for communicative activities. When the teacher and students relied heavily on the text book /or some explicit grammar teaching as shown in the example above, although it seems that there is adequate classroom interaction it did not give rise to a language-rich environment in the classroom.

Another study by Kumar (1986) consisted of seven classes, i.e. two English classes of which one was devoted to the teaching of language structures and the other to the teaching of poetry, three content subject classes (Maths, Science, and Social Studies) and two Activity classes (Craft and Cooking). An analysis of classroom interaction data revealed that the conditions for language learning available in the Activity classes, in terms of the nature of the input to which the learners are exposed, the nature of the opportunities available for learners to participate in the interaction and the nature of the classroom atmosphere, are more conducive to language learning than those available in the English and Content subject classes.

A more recent example of a typical English class from an urban setting (see Mathew 2006) seems to confirm the above finding that English classes at best provide a pseudo-communicative situation although there appears to be a lot of interaction.

Class IV *English Class* *Hindi Medium*

T: What do you take in your breakfast?
S:*Paratha* and milk.
(Teacher looks at another student gesturing to her to answer.)

S: *Paratha* and potato *bhaji.*
T: What do you take in your dinner? (Looks at others)
S: Bread and butter.
T: Bread and butter? Do you take it in the morning or in the evening? *Bolo beta, raat ko lete ho ya subah lete ho?*
(Answer not audible: teacher abandons the 'topic'.)

The children in this school come from very poor homes and one can question the 'authenticity' of this context since they probably come to school without any breakfast not least, *paratha* and milk or bread and butter for dinner. It seems that children didn't realize the sudden switch from breakfast to dinner in line 5 and therefore the answer *bread and butter* in line 6. It is clearly not a genuine dialogue although it can be justified as just a classroom dialogue: classroom dialogues are often removed from what they are familiar with. This does not amount to the *classroom language* Gibbons (ibid.) talks about above.

Continues with the earlier question: What do you take in the morning?

S: *Chapati* and vegetarian.
T: What is vegetarian? Who is vegetarian? (No answer).
T: Are you veg or nonveg? Do you take eggs? (Children look blank)
T: Which dish do you like most?
(No answer)
S: *Poori bhaji* (makes a guess at the expected answer)
T: (gestures to go on)
S: *Rajma chaaval*
T: Don't say *chaaval,* say rice.
(When the 'dishes' are exhausted):
T: Now I'll ask you about fruit. Which fruits do you like? (Points at a student)
S: .....
T: Don't take too much time.
S: Orange
T: (Looks at the next one)
S: Madam ji banana ji.
S: Madam ji strawberry ji.
S: Madam ji grapes ji.
T: Don't say: *Madam ji banana ji* (imitates them). Say, I like...
S: I like orange...(This continues till the bell rings).

These excerpts point to several plausible interpretations: this is an example of a classroom conversation which students cannot relate to since it is not part of their everyday experience. Even when there is a chance for her to engage in a meaningful dialogue as in line 13, she doesn't choose to exploit it; instead she goes on to elicit more 'dishes' (line 16). They produced different names of fruit in quick succession not so much to reveal what fruit they like as to keep the tempo of the class going. An instance of how the 'knowledge' they bring to the classroom is not valued is apparent in line 18: *Don't say Chaaval, say rice.* In the given setting, though, Rajma chaaval is a more popular term than Rajma rice. A similar instance of discounting learners' culture is available in line 27 when the teacher asks them not to use an expression they typically use in all classes: *madam ji, ... ji*: this is not how, for example, a teacher is normally addressed in private English medium schools.

These excerpts indicate that there is no exposure to *comprehensible input*, a necessary condition for acquisition of a second language, (see Krashen 1981) which refers to the processing or negotiation of meaning in the target language. Exposure by itself is not enough, it must be exposure that learners can understand. Furthermore, they can understand input that is a little beyond what they already know: learners utilize context, extra-linguistic information and their knowledge of the world to understand the meaning. A feature that is absent in all these classroom excerpts is meaning-negotiation, which shows that they are being exposed to finished products of language and not something in which they have an investment. Another example illustrates this point:

> The teacher gets students to say sentences in direct speech and writes them on the board with appropriate punctuation marks: Amita said, "Give me my pencil" (students substitute words such as pen, book, umbrella), Shivani said, "I am a girl" (substituted by 'tall girl'). When a girl comes up to her and whispers something in her ears, the teacher says, Sanjana just now said, "May I go to the toilet?" and proceeds to write it. When Sanjana continues to stand there, says something to her again and looks a little embarrassed, the teacher ignores her; goes on to another sentence.

It was quite apparent that Sanjana had used an utterance to convey meaning in a genuine situation, but it was treated as yet another instance of the form-focus class the teacher was engaged in.

Most teachers reveal in actual practice a negative attitude about the ability of poor children to learn in general and learn English in particular. The following is an example taken from another study (Mathew and Pani 2008).

The teacher tells a story in Hindi with barely a few words in English which were wrongly pronounced, for example, 'thrusty' for thirsty, scribbles a word or two on the blackboard which are not readable, draws some pictures which again are undecipherable. When he can't proceed, turns to me (sitting at the back observing the lesson) and says, *Maine bataya na inko kuch nahin ata hai? Inke dimag me to mitti bhari hai.* (I told you they don't know anything? They have mud in their head.) The Class VI children know the story and are not excited by it.

Teachers' attitude to the disadvantaged learner is negative and vitiates the situation further. They are of the view that without home support students cannot learn a language and that their language learning ability itself is poor. Contrary to the view prevalent among primary teachers, Gee (1999) notes that almost all children. regardless of home income level have impressive language abilities and enter school with "large vocabularies, complex grammar and deep understandings of experiences and stories" (367). He further adds that what they lack is not general language abilities but specific abilities tied to school practices and school-based knowledge. A point that comes up quite clearly here is that if we continue to exclude issues of identity and power which make up the big picture, and focus on more technical objectives such as correct syntax, pronunciation, etc, our efforts to improve instruction will at best be futile and at worst result in exclusion and unequal access.

Where do we go from here?

In this section, I will try and summarize the points that have emerged in the earlier discussion and attempt to suggest a way forward.

Classroom observations carried out across regions, time periods and different grade levels reveal that classes are generally teacher directed where teachers talk most of the time. Ironically, however, teachers normally do not use English even in the English class; The class on the whole sounds and looks like a mother tongue class. This is largely due to teachers' inadequate proficiency in the language. Also their own understanding of the methodology for TEYL seems to be not very satisfactory. In an earlier case study of two States, Delhi and Orissa (Mathew and Pani 2008), it was found that teachers have very little or no exposure to ELT pedagogy let alone at the primary level. The commonly used methodology is one where the teacher makes students mechanically repeat words and sentences, reads out parts of the text from the prescribed reader and explains it in their mother tongue. All possible means are employed to get the text/story across to students: explanation in simple language, examples, easier words, comparisons, use of toys/puppets are some of the activities one gets to observe in their classes. Students seldom get any opportunity to explore meaning, if in unfinished, unsuccessful ways. In this didactic exercise which is most often teacher controlled, negotiations between the teacher and students or among students are almost totally absent. In sum, then, in English classes, English is not used as a tool or medium through which they develop cognitive/thinking skills which they could use in different situations in different ways, and simultaneously refine the language in the process of meaning-making.

We will now briefly examine what alternative approaches/perspectives, that are tried out in other contexts, may be relevant to our situation.

The seminal work by Prabhu (1987) in his Bangalore- Project, also known as the Communicational Teaching Project (CTP), pointed to the need and possibility of teaching English through problem-solving activities where the focus is on meaning and not on form. He divided meaning focused activities broadly into three types: (i) information-gap activity, (ii) reasoning-gap activity, and (iii) opinion-gap activity. His experiment demonstrated that when the attention is on the task at hand, grammar-construction by the learner becomes an unconscious process. It would be interesting to apply this experiment to teach any one subject such as mathematics, science or any other content subject through English at the primary level provided it allows of meaning-focus and learner engagement with cognitive skills.

Mercer's (2002) illustration of the practical educational value of research based on a sociocultural perspective is useful here. According to this perspective, education is a process of simultaneous enculturation and transformation, and has come to be called Cultural Historical Activity Theory or CHAT (based on the pioneering work of Vygotsky) and involves not didactic instruction but a more subtle kind of learning. The central idea underpinning this perspective is that language plays a vital role in achieving the interactive process of teaching and learning, an induction into ways with words and ways of thinking achieved through dialogue. Mercer's analysis of research into what distinguished more effective teachers from the less successful ones indicated the following:

1. They used questions and answer sequences not just to test but also to guide understanding, to discover the initial levels of pupils to adjust their teaching accordingly, they asked *why* questions to help pupils to reason and reflect on what they were doing.
2. They taught not only subject content but also procedures for solving problems and for making sense of experience.
3. They treated learning as a social, communicative process. They

> encouraged pupils to take an active, vocal role in the classroom and organized exchange of ideas.

Mercer suggests that we need to focus our attention directly on language as a means for thinking collectively - a process he calls 'interthinking' analogous to 'interaction' and find ways of applying it in the classroom.

Another perspective that we haven't brought into the second language classroom in any conscious or planned manner is that of emergent literacy. Although it is a model used for developing reading and writing in L1, its application for acquiring L2 needs to be explored fully. It reminds us to put the learner first, because children have to develop literacy skills from their own experience. It offers a variety of opportunities for children to encounter written language at their level: Children's literature which is accessible in terms of language, ideas/ stories and illustrations will have to be made available so that they can hypothesise about how language works, what words/ pictures mean, and come up with approximations to and deviations from adult language. In this approach, ways in which a child acquires the mother tongue could be examined to see what aspects of that process could in fact be brought into the classroom. Sinha (2001) provides a detailed description of this alternative model and discusses its implications for the Indian classroom. Emergent literacy ideas have a potential for the second language classroom (see Hudelson 1994 and Cameron 2001 for example), although the question of when to introduce them to the alphabets of the English language and whether this should precede meaning-based reading and other activities will need to be addressed. The important point, contrary to what most teachers believe, is that (English) language is learnt *in* the meaning-making process itself and does not *precede* it. It is because of the anxiety resulting from such a misconception that teachers 'teach' letters first, then words and their meanings, and later isolated sentences before exposing children to the 'whole language'. They explain everything so that there is 'complete understanding'. This perception would have to change if we want our young learners to learn English.

In this effort, both languages, i.e. their L1 and English can go hand in hand. The *additive bilingualism enrichment principle* and the *interdependence or common underlying proficiency principle* (Cummins 1981) suggest that when students add a second language to their intellectual toolkit while continuing to develop conceptually and academically in their first language, there is substantial linguistic, cognitive, or academic growth. Furthermore, transfer of proficiency from L1 to L2 is possible where there is adequate motivation to learn L2 and adequate exposure to L2.

The former, it seems, is a non-issue in our context, although we need to work on the latter quite concertedly.

Conclusion

In conclusion, a number of suggestions that emerge from the discussion and their implications are described below:

- Value students' languages and cultures and affirm students' identity.
- Build on what students already know: trying to find out what they bring to the classroom itself results in a meaningful dialogue in the classroom.
- Make considerable use of students' first language in the classroom.
- Devise activities that specifically ask students to use their L1 with each other, for example: a group telling a story in L1 to each other in small groups and then using as much English as possible to tell it to the others. The teacher should ensure that there is a natural transition from less to more English as children progress.

Children's literature in the class is an invaluable resource: getting them to choose the book they like to look at/read (as opposed to the teacher deciding which 'one' story they should 'teach' the whole class) is extremely crucial. The fear that they may not understand the story 'correctly' (especially the 'message' or 'moral' of the story) makes teachers narrate it, or do repeated readings until the children have lost interest in it.

These suggestions have an important implication for regular teacher orientations explicitly to serve bilingual students more effectively. Also teachers would have to be given hands-on experience of the different ways in which the prescribed text book can be used in class.

An area that needs immediate attention is teachers' own language proficiency. Do they have adequate proficiency so that they can provide comprehensible input and a language-rich environment? It seems that teachers should have a basic proficiency that they can deploy with the help of child-friendly books, without which opportunities for learning English cannot be created in the classroom. The diffidence this lack of competence in the language and pedagogy causes, it seems, is also a cause for teachers' negative attitude towards these children. Although this attitudinal problem is deep-rooted in society and would have to be dealt with in other ways, one way forward would be to ask the existing teachers to undergo a proficiency course on a voluntary basis. It stands to reason that if students want to learn English to enhance upward mobility or social prestige, so will teachers. The course should also be such that they enjoy doing the course and find it a fun activity. The English course for young children should be such that the teacher, while engaging the students in language-rich tasks in the classroom, can also learn from it. Aside from this, in-service pedagogy courses should have a built-in mechanism to improve teachers' proficiency. When teachers learn how they can get learners to read, speak, listen or write better, they would also be exposed to various effective strategies in those skill areas. Another step could be to recruit (hereafter) only those who have the required level of proficiency.

REFERENCES

Alexander, R. 2000. *Culture and pedagogy: International comparisons in primary education*. Blackwell Publishing Ltd.

Cameron, L. 2001. *Teaching languages to young learners*. Cambridge: Cambridge University Press.

Cummins, J. 1981. The Role of Primary Language Development in Promoting Educational Success for Language Minority Students. In California State Department of Education (Ed.), *Schooling and language minority students: A theoretical framework*. Los Angeles: Evaluation, Dissemination and Assessment Center California University: 3-49.

Cummins, J. 2001. *Negotiating identities: Education for empowerment in a diverse society*. (2nd ed.) Los Angeles: California Association for Bilingual Education.

Gee, J.P. 1999. Critical Issues: Reading and the New Literacy Studies: Reframing the National Academy of Sciences Report on Reading. *Journal of Literacy Research* 31, 3: 355-374.

Gibbons, P. 1991. *Learning to learn in a second language*. Newton, Australia: Primary English Teaching Association.

Hudelson, S. 1994. Literacy Development of Second Language Children. In F. Genesee (ed.) *Educating second language children*. Cambridge: Cambridge University Press.

Krashen, S. 1981. *Second language acquisition and second language learning*. London: Pergamon Press.

Kumar, K. 1986. Opportunities for Language Learning: A Comparative study of Classroom Interaction in English, Content Subject and Activity Classes. Unpublished Ph.D. Dissertation. CIEFL, Hyderabad.

http://knowledgecommission.gov.in/downloads/recommendations/LanguageLetterPM.pdf Accessed on 20 December 2007.

Mathew, R. 2006. ESL at the Primary level: Does it lead to Bilingualism? Plenary paper presented at the International Seminar on *Bilingualism in an ESL Classroom: Issues and challenges*, English Language Teaching Institute, Gauhati, Assam.

Mathew, R. and S. Pani 2008. Issues in the Implementation of TEYL: A Case Study of Two States of India. Paper presented at the International TEYL Conference on *The Way Forward: Learning from International Experience of TEYL*, Regional Institute of English, Bangalore.
Prabhu, N.S. 1987. *Second language pedagogy*. Oxford: Oxford University Press.
Sinha, S. 2001. Emergent Literacy: An Alternative Approach. *Issues in Primary Education* 3 (1), 6-12.
Soumini, P. 1985. Language Learning in English and Social Studies Classes in an English Medium Primary School in Andhra Pradesh. Unpublished M.Litt Dissertation. CIEFL, Hyderabad.

29

Restructuring General English Language Curricula at the Tertiary Level: Issues and Possibilities

S.R. Prahlad

In this paper, my aim is to identify a set of issues relevant to English language curriculum renewal at the tertiary level in the present context of globalisation. I attempt to do this by relating the rapidly changing role and status of English to the typical general English language curricula in use at the college level in our country.

1. The status of English in the world today

In 1996, Sridath Ramphal, the former Secretary-general of the commonwealth, had said in an address:

> There is no retreat from English as the world language; no retreat from an English speaking world. (cited in Crystal, 2003: 26)

Now, six years into the new millennium, Ramphal's statement is still valid, unquestioned and indisputable. Why should this be so? The following statements concerning English can offer an explanation:

a. English is now *the* language of opportunity and empowerment.
b. English is on its way to becoming the global lingua franca.
c. English is the medium of a great deal of the world's knowledge, especially in such areas as science and technology.
d. A view that is widely held in today's world is that a person is more likely to be in touch with the latest thinking and research in a subject by learning English than by learning any other language.
e. About a quarter of the world's population is already fluent or

competent in English and this figure is steadily growing – in the early 2000s that means around 1.5 billion people.

f. English is now so widely established in the world that it can no longer be thought of as 'owned' by any single nation.
g. Now English has a new, functional role, no longer associated with the political authority it once held.
h. English is essential for progress as it will provide the main means of access to high-tech communication and information over the next twenty-five years.
i. English is likely to remain the world's language for international communication for the next twenty-five years.
j. Three-quarters of the world's mail is in English.
k. About 80 per cent of the world's electronically stored information is currently in English.

(all statements drawn from Crystal, 2003)

It can be seen that most of the statements above project a picture of English emerging as a global language. Noting that a genuinely global language is one the usage of which is not restricted by countries or governing bodies, Crystal (2003) presents a functionalist account of English. He observes:

> Many factors, which include the recognition of global interdependence, the desire to have a voice in world affairs, and the value of multilingualism in attracting trade markets, all support a functionalist account of English, where the language is seen as a valuable instrument enabling people to achieve particular goals. (24)

This functionalist view and the instrumental role of English had earlier been noticed by Salman Rushdie as well:

> ...those people who were once colonized by the language are now rapidly remaking it, domesticating it, becoming more and more relaxed about the way they use it. Assisted by the English language's enormous flexibility and use, they are carving out large territories for themselves within its front. ...The children of independent India seem not to think of English as being irredeemably tainted by its colonial provenance. They use it as an Indian language, as one of the tools they have to hand.
>
> (Rushdie, quoted in Crystal, 2003: 184)

Crystal (2003) offers one major reason for English moving towards becoming a global language. He talks about the three-pronged development of users of English – first-language, second-language, and foreign-language speakers. As a result, a global language will eventually be used by more people than any other language. As it is fairly obvious now, English has already reached this stage.

What could be the significance of what has been discussed so far? I believe that the prospect of English becoming a global language has important implications for the practice of English language teaching in non-native contexts. These implications can be captured as a set of prescriptions for policy makers and language educators in L2/FL contexts:

1. Start teaching learners English as early as possible.
2. Provide learners with as much time and as many opportunities as possible for using English as a means of academic, professional, and social communication.
3. Make a serious and honest attempt to review and restructure English language curricula at all levels of formal education.

I will now turn to the topic of English language curriculum design and implementation.

2. Curricula and educational value systems

I will begin this section with a discussion of the notion 'curriculum'. Richards et al. (1985) describe a curriculum as an educational programme which states:

a. the educational purposes of the programme;
b. the content, teaching procedures and learning experiences which will be necessary to achieve these purposes;
c. some means for assessing whether or not the educational ends have been achieved.

Curriculum development in L2/FL teaching, Richards et al. observe, contains a similar range of elements:

a. the study of the purposes for which a learner needs a language;
b. the setting of objectives and the development of a syllabus, methods and materials;
c. the evaluation of the effects of the teaching procedures on the learner's language ability.

It is important to bear in mind that the notions 'curriculum' and 'curriculum development' cannot be handled fruitfully independently of a focus on the purposes of education (of which language teaching is a part.) Skilbeck (1982) was the first person to discuss the 'value systems' underlying educational traditions (Clark, 1987 and White, 1988 relate Skilbeck's ideas to language teaching).

The three major educational traditions discussed by Skilbeck are *classical humanism, reconstructionism,* and *progressivism.* I will discuss each of these in some detail because no discussion of curriculum renewal can be meaningful without our reflecting on their relevance in the present context.

a. Classical humanism

Littlewood (1992: 14) describes classical humanism as follows:

> In this tradition the main purpose of education is to *transmit valued knowledge and culture to an elite section of the next generation*, and, in so doing, to *develop their general intellectual abilities.* The curriculum is determined mainly by the *valued subject content, which exists outside the learners and should be transmitted to them.* (emphasis supplied)

In a more detailed discussion of classical humanism, Clark (1987: 5) says:

> ...classical humanism is characterized above all by the desire to promote broad intellectual capacities, such as memorization and the ability to analyse, classify, and reconstruct elements of knowledge, so that these capacities can be brought to bear on the various challenges likely to be encountered in life...The teacher is seen as someone who possesses knowledge and whose task is to pass it on to the learners...Just as knowledge is to be passed on from generation to generation, so cultural values are to be transmitted through the hidden curriculum, and through the study of works of proven moral and aesthetic value, whose inherent merits are then celebrated.

If you want to relate classical humanism to the kind of education you received, you can ask yourself why you needed to study writers like Kalidasa, Bhasa, or Shakespeare, Milton, Keats, Wordsworth and others. Did your study of these writers help you realise your goals as a learner? Did it meet all your needs and requirements in life?

b. Reconstructionism

Littlewood (1992: 14) summarizes reconstructionism as below:

> In this tradition the main purpose is to bring about desired social change. In order to achieve this, the focus shifts onto providing every individual with knowledge and skills that are useful for social life. The curriculum is carefully planned around taxonomies of objectives, which each learner should be enabled to master.

Clark (1987: 14) observes that reconstructionism is an essentially optimistic ideology which believes that man can improve himself and his environment. Reconstructionists envisage that social, economic, intellectual, and spiritual advance can all be rationally planned for. Education is seen as an important agent for bringing this about. It is seen as a means of redressing the injustices of birth and of early upbringing, and of working through consensus towards a better world in which all citizens are equally valued.

When I try to relate my understanding of reconstructionism to the kind of education I have received, I am tempted to recall my lessons in physical, organic, and inorganic chemistry; my lessons in algebra, calculus, analytical geometry, astronomy and so on; my practical lessons in how to use the spectrometer and the screw gauge. What puzzles me at this stage of my life is that I seldom need to use the knowledge or information that was transmitted to me in any of these areas. So, what am I to conclude about the value or benefits of a reconstructionist approach to education?

c. Progressivism

In progressivism, the main purpose of education is to enable each individual to develop towards self-fulfilment. Since self-fulfilment means different things for different people, the focus here is on nurturing natural growth processes rather than hoping to achieve pre-determined end-points or objectives. In progressivism, it is believed that a curriculum should be flexible enough to foster the kind of growth aspired for by every individual who wants to be educated.

Clark (1987: 51) summarises progressivism as being concerned with the following:

a. individual growth from within through interaction with a favourable learning environment;
b. learning through real experience;
c. a speculative (rather than a sure or static) view of knowledge;
d. natural (as opposed to contrived and imposed) learning processes and stages of development;
e. sensitivity to the interests, rhythms, and styles of learning of individual learners;
f. the learner as a whole, thinking person;
g. the social (and psychological) nature of the learner and the development of (healthy) relationships with others in the classroom community;
h. the promotion of learner responsibility and of learning how to learn.

Learning, as they say, is a self-driven and ongoing process. An important question that curriculum developers are faced with is: 'What kind of learning is valuable, and for whom?' However, there is no easy answer to this question. It all depends on the perceived goals, needs, and requirements of a learner. What is perplexing, however, is that a learner's needs and requirements keep changing. This leads one to the question of whether one should risk being the recipient of a loose, flexible progressive curriculum, or whether one should settle for the safety offered by an other-determined classical humanistic or reconstructionist curriculum.

This discussion of educational value systems leads me to a discussion of how these are reflected in English language curriculum design as it is commonly perceived at the present time.

3. L2/FL curricula and educational value systems

Language teaching being a part of general education, the goals of L2/FL teaching and learning must be justifiable in terms of broader educational purposes. It therefore becomes necessary for us to relate the learning of English to the three educational value systems discussed in the previous section.

As a contribution to the transmission of valued knowledge and skills (a feature of classical humanism), L2/FL learning provides knowledge of a different language system, knowledge and understanding of a new culture and civilization, and general intellectual skills. e.g., analysis and inference.

As a contribution to the individual's preparation for life as a member of society (the major aim of reconstructionism), L2/FL learning attempts to provide a useful skill for many kinds of work, extended opportunities for independent travel, wider and better opportunities for interpersonal communication, and a better understanding of other members of society.

As a contribution to the development of the individual (the major concern of progressivism), L2/FL learning provides a less restricted perspective on the world, more ways of expressing one's own self, more possibilities for future learning, and a richer interpersonal network for one's existence.

The three value systems discussed above have been reflected in three major approaches to L2/FL curriculum design. *Classical humanism* underlies the grammar/system-based curriculum; *reconstructionism* is at the heart of the function-based, or communicative, curriculum, and *progressivism* is reflected in the process-based curriculum. Let us now look at these three types of curriculum briefly.

In the *grammar-based curriculum*, the *main goal* of language teaching is help learners master the language code, i.e., to develop their linguistic competence. The *objectives* are mainly defined with reference to individual grammatical structures or vocabulary items. The *syllabus* selects and grades the structures and lexical items by appealing to criteria such as complexity, importance, teachability, learnability and so on.

The *instructional materials* expose learners to language structures and vocabulary items using specially devised or simplified texts. The *classroom activities* are meant to achieve the goal of enabling learners to internalise and use the items taught as accurately as possible.

In the *function-based curriculum*, we can see an extension of the scope of language teaching to include the goal of making learners aware of how language is used as a tool for achieving successful communication. Here, we are concerned with developing learners' communicative competence. In the function-based curriculum, the main aim is to be enable learners to realize their communicative needs in a range of situations. The *objectives* are defined mainly in behavioural terms: understanding and expressing particular notions and functions, being able to use language in a range of situations and settings, being able to handle different roles and topics, developing functional competence in the receptive as well as production skills, etc. The *syllabus* selects the various units of organisation according to criteria such as immediate need, usefulness, complexity of the language demanded, etc. The *instructional materials* provide examples of authentic (as opposed to simplified or contrived) language used for realizing a variety of communicative purposes in the real world. The *classroom activities* aim at providing learners with opportunities to practise understanding and convey meanings through an effective and efficient use of the language skills.

In the *process-based curriculum*, the assumption that educational outcomes can be rationally planned for is not entertained. Instead, it is believed that the process of education should be allowed to proceed in such a way that it can provide for learners' natural growth and development.

In this curriculum, the main *aim* is to create contexts of learning which will stimulate the potential for natural growth. The *objectives* are not set out in terms of behaviours which learners are expected to master, but in non-language terms, e.g., topics to be handled, tasks to be worked out, or problems to be solved. The *syllabus* is flexible, and provides a rough specification of contexts intended to promote learning (by no means prescriptive, however), which can be graded and used via consultations between teachers and learners, according to the demands these make on learners' communicative ability (at a given point of time) rather than by strict structural or semantic criteria. The *learning materials* act as a stimulus for using language in order to exchange meanings about the topics, activities, or tasks to be handled at a particular point of time during learning. The *learning activities* consist mainly of the transaction of meanings through the use of language for a variety of communicative demands and purposes.

Having discussed the three main types of language curricula that are currently under discussion and debate, I would like to move on to a discussion of 'curriculum renewal', which is particularly relevant in the context of the globalisation of English.

4. Curriculum renewal in L2/FL teaching and learning

However well-planned and rigorously implemented it is, no curriculum can ever be perfect or theoretically pure. This is because: a curriculum is always negotiated differently by its different consumers; it has to serve the needs and requirements of a large, and usually ill-understood, learner population; a curriculum that is viable in one context may not necessarily be so in another; what is considered adequate or satisfactory in a curriculum now might be viewed as being of little use, or even irrelevant, a few years hence. Consequently, curriculum renewal needs to be seen as an essential part of curriculum development, which involves continuing negotiation, accommodation, and change of the various parts of the curriculum. As Clark (1987) puts it, curriculum renewal implies an ongoing process of refinement and re-creation.

Clark (1987: xiii) defines curriculum renewal as making attempts to effect change in the various interrelated parts that go to make up the L2/FL curriculum. In his view, curriculum renewal is like the creation of a never-ending jigsaw puzzle, in which the various parts are cut and re-cut to fit together into a whole that is itself evolving to respond to changing insights and values. A change made to the shape of one part of the jigsaw will inevitably affect other parts.

According to Clark (1987: xii-xiii), curriculum renewal entails the following:

a. the review of principles to guide the language teaching/learning process in the light of applied linguistic theory and classroom experience;
b. the reworking of syllabuses embodying aims, objectives, content, and a broad methodology;
c. the review of classroom teaching/learning strategies;
d. the choice, adaptation and creation of resources embodying appropriate learning experiences;
e. the review of assessment designed to monitor, record, report, and provide feedback on learner progress;
f. the review of classroom schemes of work relating all of the above together;
g. the review and creation of strategies designed to assist teachers to evaluate classroom practices and to improve on them;

h. the identification of areas for research to determine possible ways forward in any of the above areas;
i. the review or devising of in-service education designed to assist teachers to widen their conceptual and pragmatic base in particular areas, and to find solutions to their own classroom problems.

It is important to note here that Clark (1987: xiii) also observes that there is not only a need for an evolutionary approach to curriculum design, but also a need for coherence in the bringing about of change.

What has been said above brings me to a discussion of curriculum renewal in the context of the growing importance of English as an emerging global lingua franca.

5. English language curriculum renewal at the tertiary level: issues and possibilities

By now, it should be reasonably clear that we need to pay serious attention to the way we handle English language teaching, given the growing importance of English at the present time. In this final section of this paper, I will try to voice my views on how ELT curricula organised at the tertiary level can be renewed so as to make the learning of English fruitful and emancipatory for non-native users of English.

We will first look at the aims and objectives of ELT at the college level. The demands made on the users of English in the world today are so diverse and also different from what used to be the case in the first half of the previous century that a detailed and rigorous review of the aims and objectives of ELT is urgently called for at this point of time.

Realistically speaking, the typical non-native learner's motivation for learning English in the present context is 'instrumental' rather than 'integrative'. People now view English as a means of ensuring their survival in a ruthlessly competitive world and also as an instrument which can fetch them better rewards in the form of good financial returns and social visibility.

English for general purposes (EGP) courses typically have a rather general and loosely-specified set of aims and objectives. But if educational planners have to retain their credibility in today's world, they have to ensure that even EGP courses are as beneficial and rewarding to learners as possible. This is now a greater social responsibility than before.

However, arriving at a precise and accurate specification of the aims and objectives of an EGP course at the college level is by no means an easy task. Some of the main reasons for this are the following:

1. English language educators at the college level seldom have a clear idea of what the terminal behaviour (in terms of knowledge, skill, abilities) of a typical school-leaver in the country truly is. Regardless of which school-level curriculum a student might have gone through (CBSE or ICSE or state-administered), there are no detailed performance indices which curriculum planners at the college level can rely on.
2. A typical group of college entrants in any part of the country almost invariably represents a heterogeneous population, marked by wide variation in terms of the quantum and quality of exposure or instruction received, attitude, motivation, aptitude for learning English, empathy for the language, perceived present and future goals and needs, economic viability of studying English, and so on. Consequently, designing or renewing a common language curriculum for such a diverse learner population can become an exceedingly difficult task.
3. Then, there is this curious bifurcation in many parts of our country, between education at the intermediate level and that at the degree level. I have not been able to understand the academic reasons behind this, but I believe that if these two levels can be seen as a continuum, rather than as two independent phases of education, then planners of the English language curriculum at the tertiary level will be able to design a more comprehensive and user-friendly curriculum.

At the present time, there can be no dispute about the fact that communicative competence should be the major aim of ELT. Let us now look briefly at what communicative competence is.

Canale and Swain (1980) describe communicative competence as the underlying systems of knowledge and skill required for communication (for example, knowledge of vocabulary, and skill in using the sociolinguistic conventions for a given language). Canale and Swain emphasize that communicative competence refers to both knowledge and skill in using this knowledge when engaging in actual communication. Knowledge refers to what one knows (consciously and unconsciously) about the language and other aspects of communicative language use. Skill refers to how well a person can perform this knowledge in actual communication.

As presently understood, communicative competence minimally includes four areas of knowledge. These are grammatical competence, sociolinguistic competence, discourse competence, and strategic competence (Canale, 1981).

Grammatical competence is concerned with mastery of the language code itself. It includes features and rules of the language such as vocabulary, word and sentence formation, pronunciation, and linguistic semantics.

Sociolinguistic competence addresses the extent to which utterances are produced and understood appropriately in different sociolinguistic contexts depending on contextual factors such as the status of participants, purposes of the interaction, and norms or conventions of interaction.

Discourse competence concerns mastery of how to combine grammatical forms and meanings to achieve a unified spoken or written text in different genres. Genre is the type of text which one needs to comprehend or compose. Unity of a text is achieved through cohesion in form and coherence in meaning. Cohesion deals with how utterances are linked structurally and facilitates interpretation of a text. Coherence refers to the relationships among the different meanings in a text, where these meanings may be literal meanings, communicative functions, and attitudes.

Strategic competence is composed of mastery of verbal and non-verbal communication strategies that may be employed for two main reasons:

(*i*) to compensate for breakdowns in communication due to limiting conditions in actual communication or due to insufficient competence in one or more of the other areas of communicative competence, and

(*ii*) to enhance the effectiveness of communication.

It can be seen from the discussion above that in curriculum renewal, we need to constantly keep in mind our increasing awareness of the complexity involved in mastering an L2 or FL and keep reworking our conceptualisations of what needs to be taught to learners. In brief, we can say that communicative competence in all its richness and complexity needs to be accommodated within the ELT curriculum by framing a comprehensive set of well-formulated, realistic, and meaningful objectives. Further, the objectives should also take into consideration the importance of helping learners to learn how to learn, so that they can become self-directed individuals and take responsibility for their own learning in instructional as well as real-world contexts.

I will now try to relate our discussion of curriculum renewal to the second major component of 'curriculum', viz. *content*. In any discussion of the content of a curriculum, we need to consider two types of content – *syllabus content*, and *instructional content*. A syllabus is basically a plan for teaching and facilitating learning. Designing a syllabus involves the selection, gradation, and staging of the items to be handled by the teacher during the transaction of a curriculum. Instructional content is the realization of syllabus content in the form of projected learning activities and experiences which are expected to realize the aims and objectives set out in a particular curriculum.

If we can recall our earlier discussion of the vagueness regarding the entry-level proficiency in English of a typical college entrant, and of the several components that make up the construct of 'communicative competence', we can see that none of the three types of language curriculum we discussed earlier – the grammar-based curriculum, the function-based curriculum, and the process-based curriculum – can independently nurture a learner into becoming an efficient and successful user of an alien language like English. So, how can we handle this problem through curriculum renewal?

One possible solution, I think, is to opt for a 'variable focus curriculum' (Allen, 1984), or an 'integrated language curriculum' (Stern, 1992). Let us look at these two related ideas in some detail.

Yalden (1987) notes that there are three principles which can inform the design of language syllabuses. These are:

(*i*) a view of how language is *learned*, which would result in a grammatical or system-based syllabus;
(*ii*) a view of how language is *acquired*, which would result in a process-based syllabus, and
(*iii*) a view of how language is *used*, which would result in a function-based syllabus.

Allen's (1984) formulation of the 'variable focus syllabus' is very similar to Yalden's conceptualisation of the types of language syllabus because it is made up of the following related components: *structural, functional*, and *experiential*. Allen feels that the language syllabus should include all these levels or components all the time, but the emphasis should change during the different stages of learning.

Stern (1992) also highlights the need for a curriculum which can address several complementary and interrelated goals of language learning. He proposes an integrated curriculum, which comprises several syllabuses, each of which is aimed at achieving particular goals. The different syllabuses which make up Stern's conceptualisation of an 'integrated language curriculum' are the following:

a. The language syllabus. This type of syllabus has *proficiency* as its major goal. It attempts to plan learners' systematic study of the language in terms of its formal and functional characteristics.

b. The culture syllabus. This type of syllabus addresses the goal of helping learners to acquire knowledge by studying people who use the language in terms of their society, history, beliefs, values, etc.

c. The communicative activities syllabus. This syllabus type is also proficiency-based. Its goal is to enable learners to use language in its socio-cultural context, both inside and outside formal instructional settings.

d. The general language education syllabus. This syllabus has as its major goal, the transfer and application of one's knowledge and experience. It aims at making learners reflect on language(s), cultures, and learning (of other languages or the varieties of a language, cross-cultural awareness of various kinds, processes and strategies in language learning and use, etc.).

From this discussion it should be clear that an integrated language curriculum is best suited for learners at the tertiary level in non-native contexts, where levels of language attainment can seldom be predicted in accurate terms. I will now proceed to a discussion of how a syllabus of syllabuses such as Stern's can be translated into instructional content that can serve the needs of a heterogeneous group of learners.

Instructional materials constitute an important part of the language curriculum as they involve the translation of syllabus content into a set of activities and tasks that are aimed at promoting learners' language development and growth.

Tomlinson (1998) identifies a set of principles of second language acquisition relevant to the development of instructional materials, which is basic to our discussion here. These are:

1. Materials should achieve impact on learners.
2. Materials should help learners to feel at ease.
3. Materials should help learners to develop confidence.
4. What is being taught should be perceived by learners as relevant and useful.
5. Materials should require and facilitate learner self-investment.
6. Learners must be ready to acquire the points or items being taught.
7. Materials should expose the learners to language in authentic use.
8. Materials should provide learners with opportunities to use the target language to achieve communicative purposes.
9. Materials should take into account that the positive effects of instruction are usually delayed.
10. Materials should take into account that learners differ in learning styles.

11. Materials should take into account that learners differ in affective attitudes.
12. Materials should maximize learning potential by encouraging learners' intellectual, aesthetic and emotional involvement.
13. Materials should not rely too much on controlled practice.
14. Materials should provide opportunities for feedback on learning outcomes achieved by learners.

Thus, materials designed for a particular language curriculum should be sensitive to the different phases that mark the process of learning, such as noticing, assimilating, restructuring, and proceduralizing the items being taught. It should also be clear from the principles cited above that all the consumers of a curriculum cannot benefit equally from a common and fixed set of instructional materials.

We must also realize that if an integrated language curriculum is opted for at the tertiary level, then the quantum and range of materials to be designed would be much greater than what is common practice today. That is, in place of the currently common anthologies or coursebooks, there will be tasks, exercises and activities of various kinds, focusing on the different components of communicative competence. In short, the materials would be very different and much larger in scope.

But this leads us to another problem: how can the time constraints operating during the implementation of the English language curriculum accommodate such a radically different view of instructional materials? A partial answer to this question is that we need to draw a distinction between instructional materials which are teacher-directed, and those that are used of the learner's own volition while receiving guidance and assistance from the teacher as and when necessary.

In an important paper titled *Materials as support; materials as constraint*, Prabhu (1988) draws a distinction between 'course' materials and 'source' materials. According to Prabhu, 'course' materials provide all and only the inputs that need to be presented to learners; they constitute both the teaching content and the teaching agenda, and they incorporate a number of decisions made by the materials producer on behalf of the teacher on the desirable forms, difficulty levels, quantities and sequence of teaching inputs. 'Source' materials, on the other hand, provide a wide range of possible inputs, without assuming that all of them would be used in any classroom; they are not organized into lesson-units, and they may provide learning inputs at different levels of difficulty and in different quantities, leaving it to the teacher (learners too, in my view), to select from a range of inputs on offer. Prabhu goes on to observe:

> Course materials represent a good deal of support, but also a large degree of constraint in teaching; source materials represent those forms of support which are likely to act minimally as constraint. (p.13)

Personally, I would like to view the transaction of the English language curriculum at the tertiary level of education as involving contributions from both the teacher and the learners, in order to help learners achieve their individual and personal goals. This would result in a rather complex mix of other-determined and self-determined assessment of the learners' personal goals and proficiency levels, and their judgements regarding what kind of instructional inputs can contribute to the kind of language growth or achievement being worked towards.

In sum, I am arguing for a pedagogic framework in which instructional materials are to be used in a flexible fashion, partly teacher-directed, and partly determined by the learners themselves. So, we can have a centrally-developed coursebook to be used by the teacher in the classroom in a rather prescriptive way, and a set of sourcebooks designed for the whole stretch of tertiary-level education, which can be used by the typical college-level learners as dictated by their wants and preferences at a particular point of time in their educational development.

I will now attempt a brief discussion of how 'methodology' can be handled in college-level settings in the context of curriculum renewal.

One of the major problems related to English language education in colleges in our country is that the size of a class is surprisingly large. From a class-size of sixty to seventy, which was the typical scenario in my student days, it has risen to even greater numbers now. As a result, many teachers opt for a set of fixed teacher-centred methods, rather than accommodating learner-centred or learning-centred methodology in their work. This choice generally has a rather pernicious effect, which is that learners are often deprived of appropriate and useful training which can help them become responsible and efficient learners and users of English.

A second problem concerning the practice of English language education in our country is that language learning or teaching is generally not considered to be a complex or specialized process or activity that requires continuing support to teachers also. Few teachers enjoy the benefit of continual professional training or development through teacher orientation or refresher programmes during their careers. The outcome generally is a fossilization of teacher competence and expertise: teachers are expected to deliver the goods, but the system is seldom sensitive to their needs as developing and growing professionals.

It is important for policy makers and educational planners to address problems of this kind, especially in the context of the rapidly changing status of English as a global language. But now, leaving these harsh and nagging realities behind, we have to return to the topic of methodology.

In discussions of language teaching these days, we are often told that we are now in a 'postmethod era'.Kumaravadivelu (2006) notes that towards the end of the twentieth century, the L2 profession witnessed a heightened awareness of language teaching. This awareness centred round the following realizations:

1. there is no best teaching method ready or waiting to be discovered;
2. the artificially created dichotomy between theory and practice in language teaching has been more harmful than helpful for teachers;
3. teacher education models that merely transmit a body of interested knowledge do not produce effective teachers, and
4. teacher beliefs, teacher reasoning and teacher cognition play a crucial role in shaping and reshaping the content and character of the practice of everyday teaching.

In order to shape the practice of everyday teaching, Kumaravadivelu says, teachers need to have a holistic understanding of what happens in instructional settings. They need to systematically observe their teaching, interpret their classroom events, evaluate their outcomes, identify problems, find solutions, and try them out again to see what works and what doesn't. That is to say, they need to become strategic practitioners.

In contemporary discussions of language teaching we often come across the statement that there is no best method of teaching language. We are also told that we now exist in a 'postmethod condition' (Kumaravadivelu, 1994). As discussed by Kumaravadivelu (2006), the postmethod condition signifies three interrelated attributes, which are summarized below.

Firstly, the postmethod condition signifies a search for an alternative to the 'method' concept rather than an alternative method. Alternative methods are seen primarily as products of top-down processes in curriculum design and implementation, whereas alternatives to method are mainly products of bottom-up processes, i.e., those that are initiated by people who are actually involved in the actual process of teaching and learning, in order to ensure that the curriculum is negotiated and implemented efficiently.

Secondly, the postmethod condition signifies teacher autonomy. Unlike the conventional concept of 'method', which ignores teachers' experience and their tacit knowledge about teaching, the postmethod condition recognizes teachers' potential to know not only how to teach but also how to act autonomously within the academic and administrative constraints they need to work under. It further promotes their ability to know how to develop a reflective and critical approach to teaching.

Thirdly, a crucial attribute of the postmethod condition is 'principled pragmatism'. This is based on the pragmatics of pedagogy, where the harmony or tensions between theory and practice, ideas and their actualisation, can be realized and acted upon only through actual teaching. Thus, principled pragmatism involves self-observation, self-analysis, and self-evaluation on the part of teachers.

What could be the relevance of this discussion of the postmethod condition to curriculum renewal? ELT practitioners like ourselves need to keep in mind that there are bound to be differences between curricula as they are perceived and designed by educational policy makers, syllabus designers, and materials producers on the one hand, and curricula as they are interpreted and negotiated by teachers and learners in real classrooms, on the other. That is to say, curricula as intended plans will be different from curricula as they may be realized in different instructional settings handled by different teachers. However, teachers need to take responsibility for ensuring that any teaching/learning event undertaken is based on informed decisions and that it leads to learning outcomes which are deemed as being productive and significant in some way by learners.

I would now like to get back briefly to our earlier discussion of the postmethod condition. An important way in which teachers can practise principled pragmatism (a crucial attribute of the postmethod condition) has been discussed by Prabhu (1990). Prabhu observes that teachers need to develop 'a sense of plausibility', which is their subjective understanding of the teaching they do. Prabhu says that teachers need to operate with some personal conceptualisation of how their teaching leads to desired forms of learning, and that their sense of plausibility may arise from several sources, such as a teacher's personal experience as a learner, a teacher's earlier experience of teaching, exposure to various teaching methods, what a teacher knows or thinks of other teachers' beliefs, opinions or actions, and so on.

Prabhu (1990: 172) goes on to observe that it is when a teacher's sense of plausibility is engaged in the actual context of teaching that the teacher can be said to be involved and the teaching can be productive instead of being mechanical. When a teacher is satisfied or dissatisfied about a particular act of teaching that has been handled, that feeling itself is a further influence on the sense of plausibility, confirming or rejecting or revising it, usually in small measures, and generally contributing to its growth or change.

We can conclude from Prabhu's discussion of the teacher's sense of plausibility that he is addressing the question of how involved teachers constantly accommodate and enrich their schemata for 'teacher' and 'teaching', thus paving the way for their development, growth and enrichment as professionals.

I would like to conclude this discussion of methodology in the context of curriculum renewal by discussing a concept which I believe is important in discussions of English language education at the tertiary level. This is the concept of 'experiential learning', which was first articulated by Kolb (1984).

In experiential learning, the learner's immediate personal experience is seen as the point of departure for every incoming learning experience. Learning is said to occur when learners engage in, and reflect on, a particular learning activity. The active involvement of the learner is crucial in experiential learning, and the focus is on 'learning by doing'. Experiential learning stands in contrast to the 'transmission' approach to education in which the learner is seen as acquiring knowledge passively from the teacher.

Kohonen (1992) relates the concept of experiential learning to language teaching by deriving a set of instructions for the teacher, which are as below:

1. Encourage the *transformation* of knowledge within the learner rather than the *transmission* of knowledge from the teacher to the learner.
2. Encourage collaborative learning among learners.
3. Embrace a holistic attitude towards the subject matter rather than a static, atomistic attitude.
4. Pay attention to the process of learning rather than the products of learning. Emphasize learning how to learn, self-inquiry, and social and communication skills.
5. Encourage learner-directed rather than teacher-directed learning.
6. Promote and exploit intrinsic rather than extrinsic motivation.

Kohonen (1992: 37) observes that experiential learning can be viewed as part of learners' individual growth. It encourages learners to become increasingly self-directed and to become responsible for their own learning.

From the preceding discussion, it can be seen that at the present point of time, teachers need to make informed decisions regarding their choice of teacher-centred, learner-centred, and learning-centred activities in the context of English language education. These decisions depend on a number of factors, such as the teacher's received knowledge, and wisdom, an understanding of and reflection on teacher and learner beliefs, attitudes, and actions in the context of teaching and learning, ideas related to the realization of projected learning outcomes, acceptance or rejection by fellow-professionals of innovatory practices initiated by individual teachers, and so on.

I will now discuss the fourth component of the language curriculum, viz. evaluation and assessment in relation to curriculum renewal.

In the preceding discussion of curriculum renewal of English language courses at the tertiary level, I have suggested the need for opting for an integrated language curriculum and also for the use of a structured coursebook and a set of flexibly-designed sourcebooks, the use of which is to be determined primarily by the learners themselves. In addition, I have also suggested the integration of English language curricula at the intermediate and degree levels into one common, comprehensive curriculum. These suggestions obviously have important implications for issues related to assessment and evaluation, which form an integral part of any curriculum. Here, I will first attempt a brief discussion of 'assessment' and then move on to a discussion of the notion of 'evaluation'.

The term 'assessment' refers to a variety of ways of collecting information related to a learner's language ability or achievement. It is important to note that although the terms 'testing' and 'assessment' are often used interchangeably, 'assessment' is a more general term that subsumes measurement instruments such as tests and also a range of methods used for monitoring and recording students' learning. Assessment should also be distinguished from 'evaluation', which is concerned with the overall language curriculum and not merely with what individual learners have been able to learn or achieve during a particular course of study.

Brindley (2001: 138) observes that assessment is carried out to collect information about learners' language proficiency and/or achievement which can be used by the stakeholders in language learning programmes for a variety of purposes, which include:

> *selection:* e.g., to determine whether learners have sufficient language proficiency to pursue studies at the tertiary level,
>
> *certification:* e.g., to provide people with a statement of their language ability for employment purposes,

accountability: e.g., to provide educational funding authorities with evidence that desired learning outcomes have been achieved and to justify expenditure,

diagnosis: e.g., to identify learners' strengths and weaknesses,

instructional decision-making: e.g., to decide what material to present next or what to revise, and

motivation: e.g., to encourage learners to study harder.

The emphasis given to each of these purposes is influenced to a considerable extent by the social and political context in which assessment takes place. However, in non-native contexts, especially in the present context of the globalization of English, the purposes of *certification* and *accountability* merit particular attention and thought on the part of English language educators and policy makers. This is particularly due to changing and increasing demands made on learners, as when they try to seek admission to specialized or professional courses, or when they seek employment in sectors where specific kinds of proficiency in English are deemed important. In short, we now need to view 'assessment' beyond narrow pedagogic contexts and relate it to a wider context that is sensitive to individual, societal and national needs and goals.

Language teachers are usually concerned with two forms of assessment: *formative assessment* and *summative assessment*. Formative assessment is assessment carried out by teachers *during* the learning process with a view to using the results to improve instruction. On the other hand, summative assessment occurs at the end of a course, term or college year, for purposes such as accrediting students, or for providing aggregated information on curriculum outcomes to educational authorities.

Language teachers should, at this point of time, seriously concern themselves with yet another distinction, that between *proficiency assessment* and *assessment of achievement*. Proficiency assessment refers to the assessment of general language abilities acquired by a learner at least partly independently of a course of study. As opposed to this, assessment of achievement aims to establish what a student has learned in relation to a particular course or curriculum. Assessment of achievement is frequently carried out by teachers who are in charge of a course of instruction.

Assessment of achievement has its own goals, such as determining the quality and quantity of inputs, learners' intake and uptake of what has been presented to them, and the nature of output that results as a consequence of instructional inputs. However, we have to accept the fact that assessment of achievement, however important it may be in pedagogic contexts, is of limited value when an individual's language ability is sought to be measured or evaluated in the real world. In real-world settings, what matters is proficiency, not achievement. The question therefore arises as to how we can accommodate proficiency assessment within the perspective of a renewable English language curriculum, which we have been discussing so far. I now turn to this topic.

I believe that proficiency assessment should be based on observable or inferred facts concerning the progress made by a typical ESL learner in his attempt to learn the target language, given variables such as the quality and quantity of exposure to language, learner effort and degree of involvement in the learning process, attitude, motivation, and empathy for the language being learnt, and so on. Thus, proficiency assessment is not concerned with a simple causal relationship between teaching and learning, but with an estimation of what learners have been able to achieve in terms of language ability, both as a result of the learning experiences they have encountered in the classroom and also the *incidental* catalysts to language learning they might have encountered during their lives outside the English classroom.

When we focus on proficiency assessment, we need to move away *from* testing learners' knowledge and understanding of specific instructional inputs they might have received *to* testing their ability to handle the various elements and skills of language for realizing a variety of communicative purposes in academic as well as social settings. Consequently, our assessment instruments need to emphasize *skill* rather than *content*. It is the learner's ability to demonstrate how well he can handle the skills of language that can throw light on his proficiency in the target language.

Now, how can we get an idea of what kind of test items we need to include in proficiency tests for continuous as well as end-of-the course assessment? Allen (1984: 65) says that target language proficiency can be represented as consisting of at least three competence factors (grammatical, sociolinguistic, and discourse), interrelated with four skill factors (listening, speaking, reading and writing), which in turn interacts with two awareness factors (unconscious/conscious or implicit/explicit). This gives one a combination of twenty-four factors which have to be taken into account in the development of teaching materials as also tests.

Thus, proficiency assessment tasks for formative as well as summative assessment need to be designed keeping in mind the type of competence being sought to be tested, the language skill or skills through the use of which this type of competence is to be demonstrated, and the kind of awareness factor that is implicated in the performance of a particular test stem.

Further, in the design of items in proficiency tests, it is also important to strike a judicious balance between declarative knowledge and procedural knowledge. Declarative knowledge is knowledge that can be stated (as opposed to demonstrated). Procedural knowledge, on the other hand, is knowledge of how to use language to get things done. Thus, this type of knowledge manifests itself as skills, being a matter of 'knowing how' rather than 'knowing that'.

Having discussed what should constitute the content of a proficiency test, we now need to turn our attention to a few other aspects of proficiency tests. These are the setting in which the test has to be taken, the educational level of learners who are to take the test, the projected level of performance that is expected of learners (in terms of a set of behaviours), descriptors of the degree of skill that is to be demonstrated, the aspects or parameters specific to the language skill to be used, pattern of scoring and so on. Detailed attention to these aspects contributes not only to comprehensiveness in test design but also to transparency, objectivity, and fairness in assessment.

I wish to make one final point related to proficiency assessment. The current forms of accreditation of students used at the college level involve either giving them aggregate scores and/or slotting them into one of several divisions. However, in proficiency assessment, our concern is to let people know what skills they can handle, and how well they can do so. Also, since language proficiency of most individuals is variable across skill areas, merely awarding aggregate scores or divisions is of little value.

A possible alternative to the current practice of accreditation of students in our country is to work towards an assessment system that can be modelled along the lines of the International English Language Testing System (IELTS) or the American Council for the Teaching of Foreign Languages (ACTFL). For example, in IELTS, a person taking a proficiency test in English is rated on a nine-point scale in which the candidate is judged as being, for example, an intermittent user or a modest user or a competent user or an expert user. This system also makes use of band descriptors or interpretations which detail the level of performance the candidate is capable of in each of the four language skills. Similarly, the ACTFL system uses a holistic scale comprising ten levels, with the descriptors for each level mentioning, in detail, the situations that individuals can cope with and the language activities they can perform, as also the strong and weak points of their language.

Moving towards proficiency assessment schemes such those cited above is a complex, rigorous, and time-consuming process. However, in the present context, we have no choice except to make the transition. I will now attempt a very brief discussion of how curriculum renewal can be related to the notion of 'evaluation'.

The life of a curriculum can be divided into three broad phases – planning, implementation, and evaluation. Here we are concerned with the third phase, which is evaluation.

Richards (2001) observes that curriculum evaluation focuses on collecting information about different aspects of a language programme in order to understand how the programme works, and how successfully it works, enabling different kinds of decisions to be made about the programme, such as whether the programme is responsive to learner needs, whether students are learning sufficiently from it, or whether further teacher training is required for teachers who are handling the programme.

There are many aspects of a language curriculum which can be focussed on in curriculum evaluation. These include:

(*a*) *curriculum design*: this involves generating insights about the quality of programme planning and organisation.

(*b*) *the syllabus and programme content*: here questions are raised about the relevance, engagement or sustainability of a syllabus, its level of challenge for the target learners, the degree of success met by the assessment procedures used in the programme, and so on.

(*c*) *classroom processes*: here, the focus is on collecting detailed information about the extent to which the curriculum is being implemented by teachers as well as learners.

(*d*) *instructional materials*: here, the concern is to find out whether the materials used in the instructional settings are aiding learning and development.

(*e*) *the teachers*: here, evaluation involves finding out what teachers actually taught, how they went about the business of teaching, what their attitudes to the curriculum were, what their perceptions about the different parts of the curriculum were, etc.

(*f*) *the students*: here, we are concerned with what learners were able to get out of the curriculum, how well they participated during its implementation, and how relevant and useful the programme was in their view, etc.

(*g*) *monitoring of learners' progress*: this involves formative evaluations of student learning while a language programme is in progress.

(*h*) *learner motivation*: here, the individuals who are evaluating a curriculum are interested in finding out how well teachers are encouraging learners to understand and appreciate the aims and goals being addressed in a curriculum, and how well they are succeeding in ensuring learners' continued involvement with an externally-imposed plan of study.

(*i*) *the institution or the system prescribing the curriculum*: here, the aim is to find out what kind of administrative support was provided, and to what extent; what resources were made available and to what extent they were utilized, and how responsive and accommodating the institution or the larger system was, when faced with instances of incompatibility between the planned curriculum and its users, viz. learners and teachers.

(*j*) *the learning environment*: here, curriculum evaluators are concerned with finding out to what extent learners are provided with a responsive and supportive environment in terms of their educational needs, goals, and aspirations, and actually occurring learning experiences.

(*k*) *staff development*: here, the concern is to find out to what extent the system provides the staff opportunities to increase their expertise and effectiveness as handlers of the curriculum.

(*l*) *teacher training*: here, our aim is to find out whether teachers handling the curriculum are well-equipped to do so, and if they are not, what further training is needed in order to equip them suitably.

(*m*) *decision making*: here, the aim is to determine how well the persons involved in the implementation of a curriculum, such as administrators, teachers, and others, make decisions that result in an optional use and utilisation of a curriculum.

(adapted from Sanders, 1992 and Weir and Roberts, 1994)

I think that it can be seen from this discussion that in the context of curriculum renewal, evaluation of a curriculum should receive as much attention as curriculum planning and implementation. At the risk of sounding philosophical, I wish to say that a curriculum never dies in the true sense, because it is subject to the processes of continuing birth and rebirth. It is important for English language educators to keep this in mind during the process of curriculum design and transaction.

Conclusion

In this paper, I have tried to demonstrate how curriculum renewal is necessary, and also important, in the present context of the changing status of English as a language which can hold the world together in many important ways. I have read somewhere that the renowned educational thinker P.W.Jackson, in his book titled *Life in classrooms,* said: 'The path of educational progress more resembles the flight of a butterfly than that of a bullet.' Few people who have experienced education in one form or another would disagree with this statement. Still, I would like to say that, for involved and responsible educators, the path of the butterfly is something to be tracked, however challenging and elusive the process of doing so might turn out to be.

REFERENCES

Allen, J.P.B. 1984. General purpose language teaching: a variable focus approach. In C.J. Brumfit (ed.) *General English syllabus design.* Oxford: Pergamon/British Council.

Brindley, G. 2001. Assessment. In R. Carter and D. Nunan (eds.) *The Cambridge guide to teaching English to speakers of other languages.* Cambridge: Cambridge University Press.

Canale, M. 1981. From communicative competence to communicative language pedagogy. In J.C. Richards and R. Schmidt (eds.) *Language and communication.* London: Longman.

Canale, M. and M. Swain 1980. Theoretical bases of communicative approaches to second language teaching and testing. *Applied Linguistics* 1(1) 1-47.

Clark, J.L. 1987. *Curriculum renewal in foreign language learning.* Oxford: Oxford University Press.

Crystal, D. 2003. *English as a global language.* Cambridge: Cambridge University Press.

Jackson, P.W. 1968. *Life in classrooms.* New York: Holt, Rinehart and Winston.

Kohonen, V. 1992. Experiential language learning: Second language learning as cooperative learner education. In D. Nunan (ed.) *Collaborative language learning and teaching.* Cambridge: Cambridge University Press.

Kolb, D. 1984. *Experiential learning: Experience as the source of learning and development.* NJ: Prentice-Hall.

Kumaravadivelu, B. 1994. The post method condition: (E)merging strategies for second/foreign language teaching'. *TESOL Quarterly* 28 (1), 27-48.

Kumaravadivelu, B. 2006. *Beyond methods: Macrostrategies for language teaching.* New Delhi: Orient Longman.

Littlewood, W. 1992. Curriculum Design. *Review of English language teaching* 2(1), 11-23.

Prabhu, N.S. 1988. Materials as support; materials as constraint. Paper presented at the *RELC Seminar,* Singapore, April 1988.

Prabhu, N.S. 1990. There is no best method – why? *TESOL Quarterly,* 24 (2), 161-176.

Richards, J.C. 2001. *Curriculum development in language teaching.* Cambridge: Cambridge University Press.

Richards, J.C., J. Platt and H. Weber 1985. *Longman dictionary of applied linguistics.* Harlow: Longman.

Sanders, J.R. 1992. *Evaluating school programmes: An educator's guide.* Newbury Park, CA: Corwin Press.

Skilbeck, M. 1982. Three educational ideologies. In T. Horton and P. Raggatt (eds.) *Challenges and change in the curriculum.* London: Hodder and Stoughton/Open University Press.

Stern, H.H. 1992. *Issues and options in language teaching.* Oxford: Oxford University Press.

Tomlinson, B. 1998. Introduction. In B. Tomlinson (ed.) *Materials development in language teaching.* Cambridge: Cambridge University Press.

Weir, C. and J. Roberts 1994. *Evaluation in ELT.* Oxford: Blackwell.

White, R.V. 1988. *The ELT curriculum.* Oxford: Blackwell.

Yalden, J. 1987. *Principles of course design for language teaching.* Cambridge: Cambridge University Press.

30

English at the Primary Level: A Study of Teaching Vocabulary

Panchanan Mohanty

1. Introduction

Learning of a language at the most basic level involves two things: grammar and vocabulary. In other words, it is the mastery of some grammatical rules and vocabulary items. It is needless to mention that grammar being a closed system can easily be subjected to abstractions and generalizations whereas the same is not true of vocabulary which is an open set. Unlike grammar, the limits of vocabulary is hard to specify because of its open-ended nature. Due to this reason coupled with the emphasis on formal rules of grammar, teaching of vocabulary was relegated to a secondary position after the rise of structural linguistics between 1940s and 1970s. Another reason is that there was too much emphasis on vocabulary during the preceding period which was dominated by the Grammar-Translation Method. As structural linguistics was against such a teaching method, it was natural for vocabulary to be neglected during its heydays.

But a lot of attention has been given to English vocabulary teaching in the recent years because of the dismal performance of learners even after years of learning English as a second/foreign language. In fact, vocabulary has now occupied the central place in all language teaching/learning activities and grammar has been pushed to a secondary place. Vermeer (1992: 147) states: "The bulk of learning a new language consists of learning new words. Grammatical knowledge does not make for great proficiency in a language." Gass and Selinker (1994: 270) reinforce this view: "The lexicon may be the most important component for learners." Cook (1993: 125) opines that "... communication strategies seem linked to lexis rather than to other levels of language" and "... communication strategy' is reiterated to lexical 'compensatory strategy'".

Keeping all these in view, I want to look into the issue in learning English vocabulary in India and discuss the problems involved therein in this paper.

2. The Data

Though some Indian states like Manipur, Tamil Nadu, Tripura, West Bengal, Goa, Lakshadweep, and Pondicherry, etc. are reported to be introducing English from Class III, all other states do it in Class IV. So I have chosen the English textbook *English Reader,* published by the Government of Andhra Pradesh and prescribed for Class IV in the schools of this state for a close scrutiny. I hope the generalizations which will be drawn on the basis of this book will also hold for the text books prescribed in other states. The prelude to this book bearing the caption "To the teacher" states: 'The main objectives of teaching English at this level are to develop in the pupils:

- (*a*) the ability to listen to English spoken by their teachers and classmates, and understand it;
- (*b*) the ability to speak English with their teachers and classmates in asking and answering questions as well as discussing simple topics of interest to them;
- (*c*) the ability to read prescribed textbooks, stories and other reading materials and understand them;
- (*d*) the ability to write simple English in answering questions and generally expressing themselves, and
- (*e*) the ability to read, understand and enjoy simple poems in English. (p.iii)

The point to be noted is that though the second/foreign language teaching materials meant for the first stage must consist of those vocabulary items which are easily learnable and basic, there is no mention of these criteria here. It implies that this textbook is not seriously concerned about these criteria.

3. Methodology

All total fourteen prose lessons and seven poems included in the above mentioned Class IV English textbook which runs into the hundred and forty six pages were fed into a computer. The total number of word tokens used in this book is 13205 whereas the word types are 2160. It should be mentioned here that the machine treats the same word written in small letters (e.g. the), with a capital letter in the beginning (e.g. The), and in capital letters (e.g. THE) as three different words. It also counts different inflected forms of nouns and verbs as different words.

4. The Learnability Criteria

Scholars have argued that a language is acquired through incidental exposure, and vocabulary acquisition is no exception to it (Coady 1997, Elley 1989, Hulstijn 1992, Simcock 1990). Though it is very true of L1 vocabulary acquisition where the learner is exposed to a very large amount of data, the L2 learner is certainly not so very fortunate. So Meara (1997: 113) states: "The basic assumption - sometimes described as a hypothesis - is that learners can acquire words from incidental exposure to written or spoken test, and the research is designed to find experimental evidence in support of this common-sense hypothesis'. This strikes me as a fairly unproductive approach: at the end of the day, if the research is successful in that unequivocal evidence of incidental learning occurs, then we are not really any better off than we were when we started. After all, we knew that learners could acquire words from exposure to text anyway, and a formal confirmation of this doesn't really help very much. In some ways, research of this sort is a bit like a gardener planting seeds in a plot in order to confirm that they will grow into flowers. A good crop of daisies would indeed confirm the hypothesis', but it's not exactly thrilling science, and it doesn't do much to help us understand the process of germination, or how this process is affected by various relevant environmental factors." So of late, both the incidental and systematic or direct learning strategies have been emphasised. In this connection, Nation and Newton (1997: 241) state: "In any language course it is worth looking at the opportunities for direct and indirect vocabulary learning to see that there is a systematic programme of vocabulary development."

Though in his review of Cook (1993), Gregg (1995: 90) has argued that contrastive analysis and error analysis are "unrelated to linguistic theory in particular" and "dead meat in general", there is plenty of evidence that the first language influences learning of a second/foreign language in a considerable manner (Odlin 1989, Perdue 1993, Ringbom 1987). The following pronouncement of Perdue (1993, Vol. 2: 245) should drive home the point: "I have claimed that each native language has trained its speakers to pay different kinds of attention to events and experiences when talking about them. This kind of training is carried out in childhood and is exceptionally resistant to restructuring in ALA (adult language acquisition)." For this reason, the Keyword Method as well as certain other mnemonic devices have been proposed by scholars (Kasper 1993, Hulstijn 1997).

Therefore, learners cannot be left to themselves in order to learn mainly from their exposure to the second/foreign language; rather certain strategies have to followed so that they can learn it quickly and properly. These strategies, in fact, demand a discussion on different criteria of learnability.

4.1. Language and Cultural Distance

There are a number of recent studies which show that language and cultural distance can facilitate or hinder learning of second/foreign language vocabulary. Odlin (1989: 77-80) has reported that Swedish and Spanish speakers learn English vocabulary more easily and successfully than their Finnish and Arabic counterparts. In other words, learning of English vocabulary by Swedish and Spanish speakers is facilitated as they share a lot of common vocabulary whereas it is less successful in the case of Finnish and Arabic speakers who perceive their languages and cultures as distant from the English language and culture. Kasper (1992) has also shown that Danish speakers transfer their first language usages frequently while using German whereas it does not happen when they speak in English.

All these force us to think that a similar thing must be happening to Indian language speakers learning English. In fact, it does happen. For example, many Indian languages do not make distinctions among a tree, a plant, and a shrub, and they use only one word for all the three English words. That is why chilli tree, banana tree and banyan tree are often heard in Indian English. Again, I have come across a lot of instances where people confuse one of the following words with another belonging its group:

(*a*) arm, hand, palm
(*b*) foot, leg, thigh
(*c*) desk, table, teapoy
(*d*) tomorrow, yesterday
(*e*) honour, respect
(*f*) to catch, to hold
(*g*) to laugh, to smile

All these distinctions are expected to be made clearly in the initial stage except probably honour and respect because of their abstract nature. But a frequency count of these words in the said textbook reveals that their use is neither properly planned nor equally frequent. The following figures will substantiate it:

(*h*)	plant - 1 tree - 31 shrub - 0	(*j*)	arm - 3 hand - 20 palm - 0	(*l*)	foot - 2 leg - 3 thigh - 0
(*i*)	yesterday - 1 tomorrow - 2	(*k*)	to catch -6 to hold - 7	(*m*)	to laugh - 0 to smile - 2

It is clear from the above that it is a lacuna which has to be overcome to achieve the goal the book has set for itself.

4.2. *Pronounceability*

Quite some time ago, on the basis of their experiments on the learning of nonsense words, some of which were pronounceable while others were not, e.g. *sland*, and *ndasl*, Gibson and Levin (1975) showed that the pronounceable words were perceived quite accurately compared with the unpronounceable ones. Celce-Murcia (1978) has also reported that her daughter Caroline, who was simultaneously acquiring English and French, used those equivalents which were easy to pronounce irrespective of the language. For example, she preferred English *boy* to French *garcon* on the one hand and French *couteau* to English *knife* on the other hand most probably due to the presence of /r/ and /f/ in the latter words.

The Arabic example has become a classic one to prove that phonological differences between Arabic and English cause serious problems in learning the latter by the speakers of the former. Let us take some examples cited in Ryan (1997: 186):

(*n*) We get water from deep *wheels*. (wells)
(*o*) You get upstairs in a *left*. (lift)
(*p*) I met my friend in the *model* of the square. (middle)
(*q*) Goods are carried on a *fright* train. (freight)
(*r*) He went to *present* for the crime. (prison)

According to Ryan (1997: 188), the cause of this confusion is the difference in root-structures between Indo-European languages and Arabic. When stable roots are a norm in Indo-European languages, Arabic words normally possess three consonants which in combination with different suffixes consisting of vowels create words that belong to one semantic domain. For instance, from the root *k-t-b* words like *kita:b* 'book', *kataba* 'he wrote', *maktaba* 'library', etc. can be formed. It means that vowels perform different functions in Arabic and English. The hypothesis is that Arabic speakers ignore the vowels while storing words in their mental lexicon and they also demonstrate" ... an almost indiscriminate choice as to which vowel to use when one is needed". (Ryan 1997: 189). This may be the cause of Arabic speakers" problem which Haynes (1984) calls 'vowel blindness'.

Before subjecting the textbook under consideration to scrutiny from the above points of view it is necessary to point out that there is a basic difference between the scripts of Indian languages in general and that of English. Indian languages have syllabic scripts whereas the English script is alphabetical. Though it is a very important problem it is surprising that there is hardly any detailed study on this aspect.

There is a report by Wydell (1996) of a Japanese-English bilingual who was found to be dyslexic in the foreign language English without showing any real problem in the first language Japanese. The point to be noted here that English script is significantly different from that of Japanese. So this is an indication that difference in script may cause a serious learning difficulty. There cannot be a better place than India for such a study.

However, coming back to the main problem we were discussing, it can be stated that Indian languages have more or less a stable relationship between letters and sound whereas spelling and pronunciation of English words do not match with each other due to their orthographic idiosyncrasies. That is why Indian language readers find it very difficult to properly learn a lot of English words. In an experiment that was conducted a few months ago I found that even postgraduate students pronounced who as /ho/ like 'go', good as /gu:d/ like 'food', and spelt quote as 'coat'. The textbook under discussion contains many such words which will confuse the learners. The following examples are illustrative:

> arrows book child country daughter deal hear our
> arose blood could country laughter dear heard hour

Besides, there are lots of words whose inflected or derived forms have been used in this text without giving their bases. For instance, annoyed, arose, blurred, boasted, calmed, dashed, dug, spoilt, bruises, butterflies, charmingly, dustbins, floating, flowing, personal, teeth, etc. Even the very first lesson, i.e. 'The False School Master' contains the following words: anxiety, anxiously, brought, continued, could, dying, furniture, guessed, head, hearing, house, knit, know, minutes, neighbours, received, their, there, trouble, wallet, etc. These are certainly going to create problems for the young learners who know neither their meanings nor their structures which are sometimes idiosyncratic.

4.3. Use of Basic Vocabulary

More than half a century ago, Fries (1945: 3) had remarked: "A person has learnt a foreign language when he has thus, first, within a limited vocabulary mastered the sound system and has, second, made the structural devices matters of automatic habit." We may not agree with every bit of his statement, but his idea of 'a limited vocabulary' is quite important even today. It is better known as 'core' or 'basic' vocabulary in the literature on language teaching/learning. Scholars have used criteria like frequency, range, availability, coverage, etc. to determine the basic vocabulary of the man language.

In this paper I have taken the 207 basic vocabulary items listed in from Sridhar (1990: 323-327) to find out if and how these are used in the textbook under consideration. A careful scrutiny reveals that out of these 207 words, 37 have not even found a place though a few of them have been used in their inflected or derived forms. That means almost 20% of the basic vocabulary has been ignored here. Interestingly, this 20% includes very frequently used words, like belly, bone, dig, dust, flower, laugh, leaf, person, salt, snake, tooth, and yellow.

Again, the frequencies of the occurring words are neither regular nor proportionate. The following data will make this point clear:

big - 23	hand - 20	hear - 11	live - 29	head - 20
small - 16	leg - 3	say - 19	die - 8	tail - 2
long - 45	good - 39	old - 45	play - 6	one - 11
short - 6	bad - 7	new - 5	sleep - 32	two - 47
	three - 27			
	four - 10			
	five - 9			

A close look at the distribution and age-appropriateness of the lexical items used in the textbook should be quite useful and revealing; but it has to be a separate and full-fledged study.

5. Conclusion

To conclude, this paper intended to discuss why learning of English in this country is so disappointing inspite of a strong motivation of the part of learners to learn it, and the concentration was for learning of vocabulary. For this purpose, *English Reader*, published by the Government of Andhra Pradesh and prescribed for Class IV all over the state, was selected for a close study. Three major criteria of learnability, such as language and cultural distance, pronounceability, and use of basic vocabulary were used to test the lexical items employed in this book. It was found that none of these have been adhered to seriously especially when learners are exposed to the language for the first time at the primary level. Therefore, non-adherence to these criteria can be claimed to be the major factor for poor learning of English. It follows from this that all such textbooks have to be revised and rewritten if we are sincere about improving the standard of teaching and learning English in India.

REFERENCES

Allen, V.F. 1983. *Techniques in teaching vocabulary*. Oxford: Oxford University Press.

Carter, R.A. 1987. *Vocabulary: Applied linguistic perspectives*. London: Allen and Unwin.

Celce-Murcia, M. 1978. The simultaneous acquisition of English and French in a two-year old child. In E.M. Hatch (ed.) *Second language acquisition*. MA: Newbury House.

Coady, J. 1997. L2 vocabulary acquisition through extensive reading. In Coady and Huckin (eds.).

Coady, J. and T. Huckin (eds.) 1997. *Second language vocabulary acquisition*. Cambridge: Cambridge University Press.

Cook, V. 1993. *Linguistics and second language acquisition*. London: Macmillan.

Ellis, R. 1994. *The study of second language acquisition*. Oxford: Oxford University Press.

Elley, W. 1989. Vocabulary acquisition from listening to stories. *Reading Research Quarterly* 20 (2), 305-325.

Fries, C.C. 1945. *Teaching and learning English as a foreign language*. Ann Arbor, Michigan: University of Michigan Press.

Gass, S.M. and L. Selniker 1994. *Second language acquisition: An introductory course*. Amsterdam: John Benjamins.

Gibson, E.J. and H. Levin 1975. On the perception of words: an application of some basic concepts. In E.J. Gibson and H. Levin (eds.) *The psychology of reading*. Cambridge, MA: MIT Press.

Gregg, K.R. 1995. Review of V. Cook 1993: Linguistics and Second Language Acquisition), *Second Language Research* 2 (1), 90-94.

Haynes, M. 1984. Patterns and perils of guessing in second language reading. *On TESOL 1983*. Washington D.C.:TESOL.

Hulstijn, J.H. 1992. Retention of inferred and given word meanings: experiments in incidental learning. In P.J.L. Arnaud and H. Bejoint (eds.) *Vocabulary and applied linguistics*. Basingstoke: Macmillan.

Hulstijn, J.H. 1997. Mnemonic methods in foreign language vocabulary learning. In Coady and Huckin (eds.).

Kasper, G. 1992. Pragmatic Transfer. *Second Language Research* 8(3), 203-231.

Kasper, L.F. 1993. The keyword method and foreign language vocabulary learning: rationale for its use. *Foreign Language Annals* 26, 244-251.

McCarthy, M. 1990. *Vocabulary*. Oxford: Oxford University Press.

Meara, P. 1997. Towards a new approach to modelling vocabulary acquisition. In Schmitt and McCarthy (eds.).

Nation, I.S.P. 1990. *Teaching and learning vocabulary*. New York: Newbury House.

Nation, I.S.P. and J. Newton 1997. Teaching Vocabulary. In Coady and Huckin (eds.).

Odlin, T. 1989. *Language Transfer*. Cambridge: Cambridge University Press.

Perdue, C. (ed.). 1993. *Adult language acquisition: Cross-linguistic perspectives*. Cambridge: Cambridge University Press.

Ringbom, H. 1987. *The role of the first language in foreign language learning.* Philadelphia: Multilingual Matters.

Ryan, A. 1997. Learning the orthographical form of L 2 vocabulary - a receptive and a productive process. In Schmitt and McCarthy (eds.).

Schmitt, N. 1997. Vocabulary learning strategies. In Schmitt and McCarthy (eds.).

Schmitt, N. and M. McCarthy (eds.) 1997. *Vocabulary: Description, acquisition and pedagogy*. Cambridge: Cambridge University Press.

Simcock, M. 1993. Developing production vocabulary using the "ask and answer" technique. *Guidelines* 15 (2), 1-7.

Sridhar, S.N. 1990. *Kannada*. London: Routledge.

Swan, M. 1997. The influence of mother tongue on second language vocabulary acquisition and use. In Schmitt and McCarthy (eds.).

Vermeer, A. 1992. Exploring the second language learner lexicon. In L. Verhoeven and J.H.A.L. de Jong (eds.) *The construct of language proficiency*. Amsterdam: John Benjamins.

Wydell, T. 1996. Why English is hard on the brain. *New Scientist*, January 20, 1996.

31

Communicative Language Teaching and Large Classes: Conflicts and Convergence

Mohammad Aslam

Introduction

Communicative Language Teaching (CLT) emerged as an alternative approach in language teaching and learning in the 1960s and 1970s of the twentieth century when teachers and students felt dissatisfied with grammatical approaches, especially Audiolingualism which had established itself as an 'effective method' in teaching foreign languages after World War II. In the UK and the Council of Europe at Strasbourg, a need was felt to teach each others' languages within the European Council so that they could communicate both orally and in writing with the native speakers and, thus, satisfy their linguistic needs (Ellis 1996).

CLT is based on the linguistic theory of communicative competence, an expression coined by Dell Hymes (in Pride & Holmes (eds)1972 and Brumfit & Johnson (eds) 1979) as a reaction to Noam Chomsky's (1957) narrow-band 'competence' which he believed all native speakers possessed innately and which enabled them to create and understand innumerable sentences of their mother tongue. While Chomsky's *competence* restricted itself to the grammatical well-formedness or correctness of the native languages, *communicative competence* moves beyond grammar and defines the use of language as a vehicle for negotiating meaning and meaningful communication. It includes the following competencies: *grammatical, lexical, discourse, strategic, sociolinguistic* and *pragmatic* (See, Richards & Rodgers 2001; Aslam 2007). Obviously, the language learning and teaching becomes a much more complex process than understood in GT Method and/or Audiolingualism. Grammar is just one aspect of the language which, anyway, gets a back-seat as the major focus here is on how language is used to create social and personal relationships in the society. For this purpose, CLT focuses on students' needs and individual affective factors which play a vital role in developing communicative ability, or communicative competence, in learners. It believes in active participation of learners in whatever happens in the classroom and creates a learning environment that encourages learners to take risks so that they play their roles in a collaborative and interactive way. The primary concern of CLT is to develop fluency in the target language through a variety of strategies that address different learning styles and language skills (Rowe, *online*).

CLT recognized that learners learn better by using the language in real communication rather than by concentrating on its grammar or structure. Stephen Krashen (1982) spoke against explicit teaching of grammar. He went to the extent of saying that 'the learned system' (ie, consciously learned grammar of the language) did not add anything to the learner's competence. In fact, it acted only as a monitor or editor to check form or accuracy in one's speech. "Conscious learning can function as a monitor or editor that checks and repairs the output of the acquired system" (Richards & Rodgers 2001: 181). Language is therefore viewed as a vehicle for communication and its acquisition "can take place only when people understand messages in the target language" (Krashen & Terrell 1983: 191).

By nature, CLT is eclectic as it does not have a well articulated learning theory. It therefore draws on several language teaching methods so that the *best bit* of each method is employed to enable learners to use language in real communication. That is why CLT has been looked at more as an approach than a method. Learning is not the end; it is only means to a communicative end. The teacher therefore used authentic materials (*authentic* here refers to those materials which are not basically meant for language teaching/learning. For instance, a newspaper report, a magazine etc could be used as a help for the learner). Classroom activities have to be related to the real world which is possible only when learners are encouraged to use language effectively by focusing on the messages and meanings and not on grammar.

CLT and the Learner

The kind of activities that CLT envisages is varied and demands an active participation and role of the learner. Since the primary concern of the approach is to facilitate uninterrupted and un-interfered USE of the language, it uses games, role plays, simulations, cue cards, activity cards, jigsaw, communication-gap tasks and many other procedures in order to help learners interact in the target language. Naturally, the teacher's role is more of a facilitator of these activities so that the learners are really engaged in real communication in the classroom. This has given the learner a lot of importance in the class and made him/her the pivot of all activities. "The emphasis in Communicative Language Teaching on the process of communication, rather than mastery of language forms, leads to different roles for learners from those found in more traditional second language classrooms" (Richards & Rodgers 2001: 166). Learners have to shoulder the responsibility of learning on their own, through interaction within the group and by contributing his/her bit to the activity that the class takes in hand (Breen & Candlin 1980). Active collaboration and cooperation are *sine quo non* in CLT. Often there is no specific text used and no grammatical rules are explained. Learners are led through a task through pair-and-group work and it is only through plenary sessions that the entire class is involved in one go. CLT teachers therefore tolerate learner errors also for they know that in order to develop communicative competence it is important that learners are allowed to USE the language freely so that they comprehend on their own how language works: "CLT teachers look for patterns of errors in a learner, rather than all the mistakes, and the CLT teachers correct the patterns. CLT teachers do not focus on accuracy at the expense of fluency or communicativeness. CLT teachers aim first for fluency, then for accuracy" (Rowe, *online*).

Since CLT is learner-centered, it has put a lot of responsibilities both on teachers and learners. While the former are supposed to act more as facilitators and managers and very less as teachers, the latter have to shoulder the responsibility of participating and engaging themselves in all the classroom activities and tasks. Expected classroom behaviour among teachers and students is definitely different from what it was in say the GT-Method. As the stakes are high for both, the approach has brought to the front an important issue with regard to the number of students that a CLT class can have which would be easily managed by the teacher and which would really become meaningful for students.

CLT and Class Size: the Conflict

In order to enable teachers to manage and monitor learning in the class, many scholars (See, for instance, Nasco and Arthur 1988; Hywel 1989; Yuan and Wan 2006; Ke 2008, to name a few) have discussed the issue of a number of students that can ideally be taught through CLT procedures. It is commonly believed that 20-30 students would be an ideal number and 50-60 in a single class is considered a crowd. Some teachers feel that even class with 25 students should be considered large (Renaud et al 2007). And, if the number touches something between

100 and 150, one can imagine how difficult it would be for the teacher to manage the class and undertake tasks which are meant to involve learners while the teacher spends time in monitoring whether or not the task in hand is being carried out the way s/he wanted. Renaud et al (2007) report their Haiti experience of having a 80-student limit "in which student-centered methods can be used without creating chaos...and where communicative activities were successfully used." However, they also report a teacher saying that "a class with more than 80 students becomes a congregation rather than a class, and the teacher must become a preacher: lecturing, writing notes on the board for students to copy, and hoping that at least some of the students will learn something".

Large classes "present teachers with a number of challenges. First, the teacher should be able to easily identify the students and this is especially difficult if one is to teach several large classes at the same time. Second, the teacher needs to have a way of monitoring an individual student's progress. Third, the teachers must be able to have easy access to data about the students' language strengths and weaknesses. Fourth, the teachers should be able to respond to the students as individuals, with interest outside the classroom" (Duppenthaler 2006). These challenges are so difficult, if not impossible, to overcome that one is forced to believe that CLT is not meant for large classes at all.

In 1989, the Lancaster-Leeds Large Classes Research Group carried out a series of pioneer projects in South Africa, Nigeria and Japan which threw enough light on different approaches that teachers adopted to manage large classes (Coleman 1989). The report identified three broad categories of approaches to large-size classes: (1) Plenary approach: This is teacher centered and teacher controlled. "The lesson is primarily a lecture ('There is no alternative!'), or . . .there may be some audience involvement in the form of choral work ('let the people sing!'). . .This type of plenary approach argues basically that a lecture is the only way of handling large classes" (Coleman 1989). (2) Interactive approach: This is not a single approach. "It is, rather, a continuum—and a very 'extended' continuum at that. At one end of the continuum we find teaching which is still largely teacher-centered and teacher-dominated but which nevertheless deliberately grants occasional opportunities to learners to interact, either with each other or with the teacher. . .At the other end of the continuum, we find highly interactive teaching in which the central and public role of the teacher has almost disappeared" (Coleman 1989). (3) Compromise approach: "The distinctive feature of this approach is that a lot of learning is expected to take place outside the context where learners meet the teacher. The classroom is seen not as the place where learning takes place, but instead, as a place where administration is dealt with, where learners are advised and given feedback, and where learners are inspired to go out to do their own learning" (Ke 2008).

Large classes make it difficult to maintain discipline, interest level of students, effectiveness in teaching and so on. "The frequent teacher-student interaction will decrease significantly owing to the limitation of time and the super size of the classes. Teachers feel harder to respond to the students as individuals. To manage a large class successfully, the essential points are: (1) how to involve students in active learning and how to carry on in-class activities and communicative tasks; (2) how to engage students in language communication to enhance meaning negotiation; (3) how to personalize the classroom environment" (Yuan and Wan 2006). Gluscevic (1999) also feels that teaching a class of 100 to 150 students poses a real challenge to the teacher in developing communicative ability in students in one, two or all the four language skills. Facing such a situation, any teacher would want to give only lectures and forget about practical work and interactive tasks. But, a teacher favouring CLT cannot do that. As we will see below, lecturing continues to be the most favourable mode of teaching in large classes, in CLT this can't be heavily relied on for many disadvantages as will be discussed soon.

Large-sized classes is a global phenomenon, except in situations where English is taught/learnt for specific purposes (ESP), for instance, in medicine, engineering and so on. But, in situations like ours where English is taught for general purposes (EGP) and the number of students taking English courses is larger than what would, perhaps, be found in other parts of the world, adopting CLT becomes a challenging task. Although the premier academic bodies like Boards of School Education and the Central Board of Secondary Education (CBSE) have adopted communicative materials, it is yet to be ascertained whether the classroom teaching/learning actually has become communicative in nature. It won't be out of place to mention that traditional methods, especially using the learners' mother tongue (MT) or the regional language, continue to be a part of teachers' handy tools in teaching English in most of the Indian schools, if not at the Undergraduate level(though some use is made there also). This fact has been recognized the world over that the classical method of teaching, the GT Method, continues to be used in one form or the other in many countries especially in multilingual communities (Richards & Rodgers 2001; Aslam 2007).

The problem gets compounded more because of the demands that CLT makes on both teachers and students. CLT requires high proficiency in English from teachers and a lot of time in preparing effective activities. Since the approach doesn't have any fixed materials to be used, a teacher has to utilize whatever resources s/he could lay hands on in order to make classes interesting and motivating. Therefore, s/he needs lot of time even in implementing the activities, and in our situation, time is a great constraint in teaching English at any level of education—time given to English teaching/learning is 40-45 minutes a day in a 6-day week programme.

Physical condition of the classrooms also poses a challenge to the teacher favouring CLT. Normally, we have tiered classrooms with fixed furniture. Such a classroom is suitable only for lecturing (or, at the most pair-work), but arranging group work in such a situation is virtually impossible. And, group work activities are the most favourable tool with the teacher in engaging students in real communication and for monitoring the success or otherwise of the activity in hand. In fact, management problems creep up every now and then because the teacher cannot attend to individual problems which often creates chaos (at times, frustration also) in the class. Although some scholars feel that large classes could be advantageous also as they provide a rich variety of human resources and there are a lot of students or interaction. They also believe that since the teacher cannot attend to individual problems, "the students must develop strategies for helping themselves and their classmates through peer-teaching and collaboration, thus fostering an atmosphere of cooperation" (Ur 1996, quoted in Renaud et al 2007). However, the fact of the matter is that large classes pose very grave challenges to the teacher in managing the class, maintaining discipline, sustaining the interest level and carrying out communicative activities with ease. Wilhelm (2006) reports his experience at Sam Ratulangi University, Indonesia, in which even "basic" teaching resources were not available. He says, "In one class in particular, I was troubled to learn that the enrolled students consisted of over 150 first-year undergraduates from a variety of majors with English proficiency levels ranging from low-beginner through intermediate. The class was to be taught in an auditorium area covered by a metal roof and open at the walls. There were not enough chairs for the students, and since there were no fans, the doors at the back had to be left open for air flow. When it rained, I could hardly hear myself talk because of the noise on the metal roof. The open walls and doors meant that I had to compete for the students' attention with noises from outside the class, including shuttle buses, crowing roosters, and singing groups practicing next door in the student canteen". This is not an unusual situation in India where classes are conducted at many places under tents which become virtually no classes during rainy days. Dr Ives has written in *A Survival Handbook for Teaching Large Classes* (google, online) about the many challenges that teachers and students in large classes can face. For the teacher, the following are a matter of concern:

- Management of the paperwork: handing out, collecting and recording tests and other assignments, make-up work;
- Management of distractions: talking, late arrivals, early departures;
- Perceived anonymity of the students: difficulty of learning names, of taking attendance, of getting students to come to class, of getting students to participate in class, of getting students to do assignments in a timely manner;
- Lack of flexibility in class activities: difficulty in varying activities, in doing group work, in enhancing critical thinking and writing skill.
- Diverse background and preparation of the students.

Students also experience difficulties in large classes chief among them, according to Dr Ives (op cit) are:

- Not knowing what is relevant or important information
- Hesitation in asking questions or in other ways indicating a lack of knowledge
- Hesitation in appearing "smart" to their peers (the nerd curse).
- Lack of experience with time management, studying, or other skills necessary for success in college.
- Perceived anonymity which allows them to challenge authority and to push boundaries.

These are very formidable challenges and cannot be easily resolved. There is a tremendous risk of losing control and authority of the teacher if necessary steps are not taken to overcome the difficulties that large classes pose both to the teacher and students.

Resolving Conflict

However daunting the large-sized classes might be, today teachers can hardly afford to ignore tremendous responsibilities that current trends in English language teaching (ELT) have put on their shoulders. We cannot ignore that English has globally become the most favoured language of international communication, even in those countries where it used to be castigated as the coloniser's language (for instance, India,

Nigeria and many other African countries). Almost everybody would want to be 'communicative' in English as it has opened up new exciting vistas of global interaction—especially through the Internet—and job opportunities in multinational companies (MNCs). This is evident from the fact that numerous English teaching centres/institutes have been established across India which fetch a large number of students and non-students. Some very popular and expensive English coaching centres notwithstanding, there are innumerable not-well-to-do centres in every state of India that offer English language courses, and they are doing pretty good selling by using the buzz word, 'communication' to attract their clientele. The focus therefore remains on developing spoken skills so that people can use the language in day-to-day communication events.

It is the formal mode of education that poses a serious threat to CLT which we have discussed a great deal above. Some basic issues which need out attention in order to resolve the conflict between large-sized classes and CLT are:

1. How can we make our classes interesting and motivating?
2. Given the constraints, is it possible to undertake learner-centered activities like pair work and group work?
3. Is there any *one* way of teaching a large class?
4. What could be the best survival kit for handling a large class and how could students be more responsive while teaching English?

Dr Ives (op cit) suggests many ways of making classes interesting and motivating. He states that by adding "variety/entertainment to lectures (animations, slide shows, demos, video clips, music, guest speaker, etc)", it should be possible to make large classes more informative, interesting and relevant to the lives of students.

My personal experience says that in tiered classes with fixed furniture, it is very difficult to undertake group work activities because it is not possible to sit face-to-face and in a circular mode there. However, pair-work is possible and even if some adjustments have to be made (like shifting a student or two from one place to another), they can be easily done. However, where chairs can be moved easily group work can be undertaken, though difficulties of management remain. MacDonald et (*online*) suggest "Team English" which "is the ability to identify teams and individual members quickly and easily. Each team has a designated color. Each student wears the team color and a team number...In teams of six students, numbers 1-6 are used; if there are nine team members, students are numbered 1-9 and so forth...For each activity, you form pairs or groups appropriate for that activity...In effect, each team represents a small class, which allows students to develop team loyalty while still interacting with a variety of classmates." The teacher can then engage the groups in different activities ranging from Total Physical Repose (TPR) commands to learner-centered communicative activities.

Gluscevic (1999) suggests using student assistants or demonstrators (ie, students who have completed two-year course of Medicine and have passed final exam with the highest mark) in teaching large classes. She points out, "One of the main advantages of this technique is in being able to teach in small groups. Since the course is based on the communicative approach, we have succeeded [in the School of Medicine at the University of Belgrade] in engaging almost all students actively in the activities. A three-way communication among assistants, students, and the teacher results in a more natural environment". She further states that using teaching assistants proves helpful in encouraging students speak more freely with their seniors and that learners get individual attention. However, since the assistants are not language teachers, they might commit mistakes or may not be able to correct student errors. " This problem needs to be faced and resolved", Gluscevic (op cit) opines.

Wilhelm (2006) suggests "in-seat activities" and "out-of-seat activities" to help large classes develop communicative skills in English. The former are those activities where in students mostly remain seated and the latter "are useful and important but not always feasible with extremely large groups because [they] are time-consuming to get the activities underway." In-seat activities include question-answer drill involving different groups: "Group 1 reads a question from the homework, and Group 2 gives a choral response. The trick is to ask each group to respond in unison so that you can hear whether answers are correct or incorrect" (op cit). "Chaining" is another activity that Wilhelm suggests. It is used to practice a particular grammatical category which are incorporated into a dialogue of at least four line. "Four to ten students sit in a row, and the first student on one end is told to begin the first line of dialogue. The next student listens and repeats the line, then turns and gives the third student the second line of dialogue. This process continues with each student until the end of row is reached...".

Touba (1999) reports her experience of handling groups in large classes in Egypt. She suggests group work and Content Based Instruction (CBI) as effective models in teaching classes with 60 students or more. "CBI is the most appropriate model of instruction because it is based on the assumption that for successful language learning to occur, the course content must take into account the eventual use the learner will make of the target language" (op cit). She feels that group work in CBI promotes "cooperative learning and peer tutoring".

Ke (2008) experimented with 80 first year Chinese students who had already learned English in their secondary school for 6 years. He suggests an eclectic mode of teaching which involves procedures—teacher's instruction, students' participation and consolidation work—based on three approaches—*teacher-controlled, student-oriented* and *learning centered,* respectively. It is only in "student-oriented" teaching where basic skills are developed through group discussion, pair-work, role play, debate etc. A teacher controlled class is very traditional in nature as the focus here in on knowing about the language whereas in the "learning centered" class, focus is on accuracy. Ke warns that the three procedures are not "rigid". He says, "They should be used in accordance with the objectives of each lesson" (op cit).

Yuan and Wang (2006) suggest a "collaborative learning" which they define as "a classroom interaction method with which students a various performance levels work together toward a common goal. Within the group students discuss the material to be learnt with each other, help and assist each other to understand it and encourage each other to work hard. Students are responsible for one another's learning as well as their own...During the cooperation, it is vital that each student hold individual accountability and positive interdependence toward the others, which are considered to be the two most crucial basic elements in CL".

What has been said so far, should give us a clear idea that there is no single way of teaching large classes. "We have to take into account our teaching style, the characteristics of our students, and the goals and objectives of our course" (Dr Ives, *online*). Even when one is using the lecture mode, it can be made interesting by adopting different strategies to maintain the tempo of the lecture and also bring attentiveness in students. For instance, as "a lecture interruption or in the closing minutes of a class session, ask students to take out a sheet of paper and for one minute, summarize main points of a lecture or note any muddy points of the lecture. Collect these and use feedback to target problem areas" (Dr Ives, op cit). If possible, one can use OHPs or Powerpoint presentations to enhance the interest level of students.

Conclusion

Large classes pose very tough challenges and most of them are related to management, whether it is attendance, attention or activities. In such a situation, lecture mode seems to be the only feasible and 'effective' way of handling the class. But, Communicative Language Teaching (CLT) being a learner-centered approach believes in the active participation of the learners in the learning process so that they shoulder the responsibilities of developing skills on their own with minimum teacher interference. The various proposals mentioned above cannot and should not be taken as sacrosanct or absolute. In fact, a lot would depend on individual teachers who must gauge his/her students in terms of proficiency, interest, attitude and aptitude. Any decision regarding how to use different activities—communicative or otherwise—should therefore rest with the classroom teacher. A teacher's right judgement would play a very vital role in planning the lessons in such a way that the learner harvest maximum benefits from classroom teaching. Whether it is the lecture mode, group and pair works, role play, simulation or any other techniques, the teacher must not lose sight of the ultimate goal of teaching and learning of English—developing *communicative competence*. The teacher who is knowledgeable about the various methodologies will not unnecessarily enslave himself/herself to any one methodology, but will adopt a balanced or eclectic approach in which s/he choose the best part in all or some and make language classroom interesting and motivating. Perhaps, that could resolve some of the problems that we confront in teaching large classes!

REFERENCES

Aslam, Mohammad 2008. *Teaching of English for B. Ed.* New Delhi: Cambridge University Press.

Coleman, Hywel 1989. *Approaches to the management of large classes.* Project Report No 11. Britain: Lancanster-Leeds Language Learning in Large Classes Research Project.

Duppenthaler, Peter 2006. Managing and Monitoring Large Classes. *English Teaching Forum* 38, 3 (July-September). Available online.

Gluscevic, Mirjana 1999. Is it Possible to Successfully Teach Oversized Classes? *English Teaching Forum* 37, 1 (January). Available online.

Hymes, D. 1972. On communicative competence. In J.B. Pride and J. Holmes (eds.). *Sociolinguistics.* Harmondsworth: Penguin. Also, in Brumfit, C.J. and K. Johnson (eds). 1979. *The communicative approach to language.* Oxford: Oxford University Press.

Ives, Sallie M. 2000. *A survival handbook for teaching large classes.* Online: www.Google.com.

Ke, LI. 2008. Teaching College English to a large class: Problems and remedies. *Sino-US English Teaching* 5 (2). Available online.

Macdonald, Marguerie et al. nd. Classroom management: Team English for large classes. Online: www.onestopenglish.com.

Touba, Nahida Ahmad 1999. Large Classes: Using Groups and Content. *English Teaching Forum* 37, 3 (July-September). Available online.

Renaud, Susan et al. 2007. Student-Centered Teaching in Large Classes with Limited Resources. *English Teaching Forum* 45, 3 (July-September). Available online.

Richards, Jack C. and S. Rodgers Theodore 2001. *Approaches and methods in language teaching* (2nd ed). Cambridge: Cambridge University Press.

Rowe, Alexander. nd. An Overview of Communicative Language Teaching. Online: http,//fc.sc.ed.

Wilhelm, Kim Hughes 2006. No Books and 150 Students. *English Teaching Forum* 44, 3 (July-September). Available online.

Yuan, Ximing and Wang, Jian 2006. A Collaborative Learning Perspective on EFL Large Class Meaning Negotiation. Sino-US English Teaching 3 (2). Available online.

32

Process of Learning ESL vs. EFL: A Study of Errors in Acquisition vs. Learning

Vaishna Narang
Mi Yang Cha

This study is an attempt to explore if there could be some empirical support for the hypothesis that the SL, a language which is used as a second language in a given sociocultural context is acquired by a process different from the process of learning the same language in another context where it functions as an FL, a Foreign Language. In other words, the hypothesis that we would like to explore is that *(i)* the process of acquisition of an SL is different from the process by which an FL is learnt or acquired? (ii) the process of acquisition of an SL is similar to the process of acquisition of the native language/ first language/ mother tongue, hence 'acquisition' and the process of learning a FL is different from the process by which L1 is acquired, hence' learning' rather than 'acquisition'. Continuing the argument we wish to go a step further and ask if it is possible to define a second language in terms of some features of the process by which it is acquired, such that another language may be defined as a 'foreign language' which is learnt differently. Through this empirical study of the errors of learners of ESL and EFL we wish to re-examine the 'acquisition' and 'learning' distinction (Krashen, 1982) in terms of 'natural order' in case of acquisition and 'conscious focusing on linguistic forms' in learning, (Krashen, 1982) , 'creative construction' in one and 'error correction' and 'rule isolation' in the other, (Krashen, 1982). The SL situation, we assume provides 'input' which is different from 'input' that the learner receives in the FL situation.

Before we continue with the issue /s pertaining to the SL- FL debate, let's briefly examine the MT and L1 and the process of acquisition since the Second Language is being defined in relation to the socio-cultural contexts and functions it shares with MT/ L1. A layperson's definition of Mother Tongue may include all or most of the following features: language acquired from the cradle; first in the order of acquisition; language of the process of socialization and acculturation which makes a biological being a social being; language of maximum proficiency; language of home and family and therefore the language of one's emotional life; language of one's ethnic identity; language of thinking, and language of dreams. A cognitive scientist and a linguist would say MT is the language of cognition; means of the process of conceptualization and symbolization, language through which learning metalanguage is made possible. This metalanguage serves as a filter and influences every subsequent attempt at learning a language MT and the process by which it is acquired serve as the means to acquire and to enhance the individual creative abilities.

All these features together define our notion of 'Mother Tongue' only as long as we visualize a speech community as a monolingual speech community and the child acquiring the same as the only language at least initially in the first four to five years of his/ her life. As we look around today, the reality is quite different. Bi-/ multilingualism seems to be the norm and monolingualism, an exception to the rule. Most often the modern child is brought up in a bi- or a multilingual environment in which s/he acquires two or sometimes more than two languages simultaneously and only one of those is identified as the MT of the individual. We examine the criteria, all the ten parameters we used to describe the concept of MT and find that it is perhaps only the criteria of 'ethnic identity' which defines a language as MT in this new linguistic context. All the other parameters point to what we call 'the first language' (L1) rather than the MT.

The Other Tongue, (OT) is different from both the MT and the L1, and it is this other tongue, which may be situated differently in the context in which it is being acquired/ learnt. As language teachers, today we do not want to define a second language as the second language of an individual, and a foreign language as foreign to the learner. It is the SL situation and the FL situation that we wish to distinguish between. It is the sociopolitical conditions and contexts of situations which define language as a SL of the region, the state, the city, the village...in which the learner happens to be located. So the SL and the FL situation actually helps us examine the nature of input when it comes to a learner being situated in that specific context and learning/ acquiring the FL/SL of that sociopolitical context. Let's briefly review what has been said earlier about the SL and FL (Wilkins, 1972; Lewis,

1974; Srivastava, 1979; Narang, 1989, 1996;...)

A foreign language is a means to understanding/interpreting the culture of another speech community different from the user's own speech community, while a second language is used as an alternate means to express one's own culture. So, there may be no social pressure for learning a foreign language while the social pressure for learning the second language translates into economic pressures in terms of better job opportunities for those fluent in the language and greater involvement in the social and cultural life of the region. All of these factors lead to a greater motivation for learning the language. Therefore, the second language, in contrast with the foreign language, is more likely to influence the psychological development of the learner. In terms of E. Glyn Lewis, the second language is "acquired under the stress of close social or environmental requirements" and ... "is more deeply embedded than a foreign language in the fundamental psychological development of the child" (Lewis, 1974: 33).

Wilkins discusses these two points in terms of social functions saying that the second language 'does have some internal, social function', while the foreign language 'has no internal communication function', and that 'whereas the second language learner needs the language for use within his own community, the foreign language learner needs it so that he can form contacts with a community other than his own' (Wilkins, 1972: 150-5).

Being a part of the verbal repertoire, the second language is parallel to the user's own language, while the foreign language is not a part of the user's total verbal repertoire and therefore cannot be placed parallel to his 'own' language. It is, however possible that a language initially used as a foreign language may gradually become a social necessity and thus acquire the status of a second language in the same society.

The user of second language is active and creative in this language while the user of a foreign language does not have this language available to him for creative use to that extent. Learning a foreign language is a process of 'cognitive enrichment rather than fulfillment' (Lewis. 1974: 34).

A language accepted as a second language in society has a tendency to evolve a new 'standard' which is invariably different from the 'norm' or the 'standard' of the language as accepted in its native society For instance Indian English and its varieties spoken in the region are different from the native standard as spoken, say for instance in different parts of UK. Similarly the status of Hindi in countries like Fiji, Guyana, Mauritius, Surinam is that of a second language with an acceptable standard variety in each one of the regions different from what is accepted as standard in any of the Hindi speaking regions of India.

Thus, it is important, first of all, to examine the sociolinguistic status of a language in the society and find out whether it is that of a second language or a foreign language, because the language teaching materials and teaching strategies for the two are bound to differ accordingly. For example, the second language learner needs the language for use within his own community and the context of his learning should be his own culture. The foreign language learner, on the other hand, needs the language mainly for the interpretation or expression of an alien culture and therefore, the context of learning should not be his own culture but that of the group whose culture has provided justification and motivation for his learning the language.

This study limits itself to the analysis of the learner language samples of written compositions produced by the Korean EFL students in Korea and by the Korean ESL students in Delhi, India. It does not deal with aspects of phonology or spoken language. The analysis focuses mainly on errors in syntax, lexicon and morphology. The analysis of the students' writings does not concern itself with the rhetorical organization, writing style and discourse. It is a cross sectional study and therefore none of the learners have been studied over a period of time as it happens in longitudinal case studies. Some of the findings of the present study serve as hypotheses for a detailed longitudinal Learner Language study.

The subjects in this study were two groups of Korean students; an EFL group in Korea and an ESL group in Delhi, India. The EFL group consisted of 50 second-year university students majoring in English Literature at Taejon national University of Technology in Korea who had received about 8-9 years of English instruction. The ESL group was composed of 50 high school students enrolled in international schools in Delhi. These ESL students were further subgrouped according to the length of learning period in ESL settings: ESL A was a group of 23 students learning English for less than 3 years and ESL B was a group of 27, learning for 3-10 years in the ESL situation.

Written compositions of these 100 students served as the primary source of data for errors while a questionnaire was prepared to elicit relevant information about subjects, curriculum, teaching methods and materials, use of English in daily activities, etc. Some informal interviews with teachers and students in Korea and in Delhi were also carried out to obtain extra information.

Some of the results are presented in this study to show how the rates and routes of learning can be very different in ESL situations as compared to EFL situation. The number and nature of errors in the two groups of learners can serve as an important indicator of different kinds of cognitive processing involved in SL / FL processing.

Results and Discussion

A comparison of overall performances between the EFL, ESL A and ESL B groups is presented in Table No.1 below.

	EFL Group (50 Subjects)	*ESL Group (50 Subjects)*	
		ESL A Group (23 Subjects)	*ESL B Group (27 Subjects)*
Average length of composition	175 words	263 words	407 words
Total No. of words	8734	6056	10990
Total No. of Sentences	985	476	687
Mean of Words in a Sentence	8.9	12.7	16.0
No. of Error-free sentences	149 (15.1%)	180 (37.8%)	465 (67.7%)
Total No. of Errors	**1837**	**524**	**364**
Percentage of Errors	21.0%	8.7%	3.3%

As is evident, there is a sharp contrast in the overall performance and in the error percentage in the performance of EFL and ESL students. The EFL students produced greater number of errors in a wider range of types than the ESL students: 1837 errors of 71 types occurred with the EFL students and 888 of 55 types with the ESL students. Further, of these 888, 524 (59%) of 55 types were found in the ESL A students and 364 (41 %) of 45 types in the ESL B students. The error rate of the EFL group (21%) was about four times that of the ESL groups (5.2%). The number of errors of individual students ranged between 19-62 in the EFL group and 2-53 in the ESL group.

There were also qualitative differences observed in the learner languages of the learners in the two learning situations. While the ESL students' well-expressed ideas were constructed in long and complex constructions using many embedded, coordinate and subordinate clauses, the EFL subjects produced very short, choppy, simple and basic-structured sentences in their writings. Moreover, most of such constructions in the EFL students' compositions were erroneous containing very low number of error-free sentences.

Table 2 below shows the number and percentage of errors at the level of syntax, morphology and lexicon in the EFL, ESL A and ESL B groups.

Error Types	*Number of Errors (%)*		
	EFL Group	*ESL A Group*	*ESL B Group*
Syntactic Errors	1024 (55.7%)	310 (59.2%)	216 (59.3%)
Lexical Errors	550 (30.0%)	115 (21.9%)	69 (19.0%)
Morphological Errors	263 (14.3%)	99 (18.9%)	79 (21.7%)
Total	1837 (100%)	524 (100%)	364 (100%)

Syntactic deviations comprised the largest number and frequency of occurrences among the three main linguistic categories, indicating that syntax is the most troublesome area for both the Korean EFL and ESL students. Syntactic errors are spread across a wide range of error types.

Different error types were counted for each one of the following types of morphosyntactic structures and tabulated separately for the three groups of learners EFL, ESLA and ESLB, (see Table 3 below).

Error Types	*Number of Errors (%)*		
	EFL Group	*ESL A Group*	*ESL B Group*
Article	279 (27.2%)	94 (30.3%)	87 (40.3%)
Preposition	227 (22.2%)	80 (25.8%)	45 (20.8%)
Pronoun	109 (10.6%)	41 (13.2%)	20 (9.3%)
Tense Sequence	103 (10.1 %)	35 (11.3%)	25 (11.6%)
Conjunction	91 (8.9%)	19(6.1%)	17 (7.9%)
Word Order	68 (6.6%)	11 (3.6%)	4 (1.8%)
Quantifier	29 (2.8%)	7 (2.3%)	3 (1.4%)
Relative Clause	11 (1.1%)	8 (2.6%)	4 (1.8%)
Miscellaneous	107 (10.5%)	15 (4.8%)	11 (5.1%)
Total	1024 (100%)	310 (100%)	216 (100%)

The results of this study show significant differences in the nature of LLs of the Korean learners in the EFL and ESL situations. The main findings of this study are summarized in the following sections.

1. The overall language performances of Korean students differed in the EFL and ESL situation. The ESL students far outperformed the EFL students. The EFL students wrote on an average 175 words per composition (ranging 64-242 words) and the ESL students, 341 words (ranging 129-619 words) in their writings; The EFL students produced greater frequency and a wider variety of deviations from the target language than did the ESL students. Total 1837 errors of 71 types

occurred in the writings of the EFL subjects and 888 of 55 types in their ESL counterparts; The error rate of the EFL students (21.0%) was approximately four times that of the ESL students (5.2%); The number of errors of individual students ranged between 19-62 in the EFL group and 2-53 in the ESL group.

2. There also existed some notable differences among the ESL students according to the length of the learning period in the ESL situation. Those exposed to the ESL setting for a longer period (ESL B group) performed better than those exposed for a shorter period (ESL A group); of 888 errors, 524 (59%) of 55 types were made by the ESL, A group and 364 (41%) of 45 types by the ESL B group. These ESL A students appeared to operate in a similar but less primitive way as the EFL students did, showing their background of EFL training before learning in the ESL situation. Lexical errors show a significant decline in ESL situation.

3. As compared to the ESL students who had overall better linguistic abilities and a wider control of English usage, the EFL students were found less competent in English use. Their writing reflected cognitive and linguistic insufficiency or regression in use of the target language that was inconsistent with their intellectual maturity. While the ESL students generated well-expressed ideas and concepts in long, complex and target language-like constructions, the EFL students produced inconsistent usage in very simple, short, choppy and basic-structured sentences. Moreover, in most cases, they repeated the same words and phrases and yet produced a higher percentage of incorrect usages.

4. While most of the errors produced by the ESL subjects occurred at the word level EFL students' errors occurred at the phrase or sentence levels, which resulted in greater amount of distortion. In addition, the majority of errors produced by the EFL subjects were systematic in nature mainly due to systematic Ll transfer in contrast to the non-systematic nature of ESL students' errors occurring once or twice on arbitrary basis.

5. While the ESL students showed syntactic maturity, many EFL students appeared not to have internalized a large number of grammatical rules nor understood how to apply them to construct sentences appropriately to get their meanings across. Thus, due to a lack of syntactical knowledge and limited vocabulary, the EFL students generated a number of deviant constructions that were not intelligible. The Grammar-Translation method used in the EFL situation in Korea did not necessarily lead to the students' better competence in language use or even in grammar *per se*.

6. As compared to the ESL students', the EFL students' LLs were far more deviant and unstable and revealed greater gaps at the syntactic, morphological, lexical and semantic levels:

(a) the EFL students produced more number and types of syntactic deviations that comprised the largest frequency of occurrences among the main linguistic categories: 1024 (EFL), 310 (ESL A) and 216 (ESL B) representing 55.7%,59.2% and 59.3% of the total errors of each group respectively. Syntactic errors were spread across a wide range of error types: Article, Preposition, Pronoun, Tense Sequence, Word order, Quantifier, Relative Clause and Miscellaneous Syntactic errors;

(b) lexical errors accounted for 30.0% (550 of 1837 EFL), 21.9% (115 of 524-ESL A) and 19.0% (69 of 364 - ESL B) of the total number of errors of each group, but resulted in the most serious interruption in communication. Lexical errors were found in the use of Noun, Adjective, Adverb, Verb and Modal/ Auxiliary Verb. The most frequent occurrence of lexical errors occurred in the inappropriate choice of verb;

(c) Morphological errors appeared in the EFL and ESL students with varying frequencies: 263 (EFL), 99 ESL A) and 79 (ESL B) representing 14.3%, 18.9% and 21.7% of the sum of errors of each group respectively. Morphological errors involved misuse of Plural/ Singular markers, Subject-Verb Agreement, Participle Ending, Tense markers, Comparative/Superlative Forms, Negative Markers and Possessive Markers (See Table 4).

	Lexical Errors	*Morphological errors*
EFL	30%	14.3%
ESL-A	21.9%	18.9%
ESL-B	19%	21. 7%

7. The EFL students' LLs, in most cases, consisted of rules of their NL. In particular, they exhibited an additive mixture of structural patterns of NL and TL: with the TL pre-posing verb placement remained, TL elements were restructured, reclassified and expanded to follow the NL structure, which reflected their current LL grammar systems. (see Table 5)

Error Type	*EFL Group*	*ESL A Group*	*ESL B Group*
Transfer	1093 (59.5%)	131 (25.0%)	29 (8.0%)
Overgeneralization	656 (35.7%)	310 (59.2%)	236 (64.8%)

8. Hierarchy of Errors : The morphosyntactic errors were divided in to three types:

Articles as one category where there is a significant difference in percentage of errors with ESL B group showing 40.3% errors despite a lot of exposure and learning as compared to EFL group relying only on formal teaching- learning of English. Article in English seems to be one aspect of language which has to be learnt by all Korean learners no matter what the context of learning is. Tenses and Relative Clause form the second group where ESL shows a slightly greater percentage of errors indicating that ESL exposure does not help much in the acquisition of the same, and the learner has to make conscious effort to learn the two in English as distinct and different from their native language. Prepositions, Pronouns, Conjunctions, Word Order and Quantifiers form the third group where EFL learners show more errors than the ESL group suggesting an easier access to the same in ESL situation facilitating the process of learning/ acquisition. (see Table 3)

While use of articles was the most frequent and common problem in learning English for both the EFL and ESL students, there were notable differences in the hierarchy of errors, which indicated the differences in routes and rate of the LL development between the EFL and ESL situation.

The ESL students as a whole showed a better pace and rate of the language learning development because of a variety in their conditions of exposure to the target language. The EFL and ESL students were also found to operate differently in specific aspects of language use. The sources of deviations included L1 transfer and overgeneralization, and they varied in their extent according to the ESL or EFL learning situations.

In this respect, preposition usage was chosen as one of the areas for close inspection in this study. The comparisons were made through the random sampling of ten subjects selected from each group. The total number of preposition usage and obligatory contexts in which prepositions were omitted was counted for each subject.

The number of correct and incorrect usage was also counted separately. A comparison of the preposition usage between the EFL, ESL A and ESL B groups is presented in Table 6 below.

	EFL Group	*ESL A Group*	*ESL B Group*
No. of Usage	138	191	257
Obligatory Contexts	9	5	2
Correct Uses	92 (62.6%)	163 (83.2%)	244 (94.2)
Incorrect Uses	55 (37.4%)	33 (16.8%)	15 (5.8%)

As shown in the above table, there were significant differences in overall preposition usage between the EFL and ESL groups. The ESL students outperformed their EFL counterparts in terms of total number of usage and error rates. Apart from those quantitative differences, there were also major qualitative differences in the use of English prepositions between the two learning situations. There was a great variability between the EFL and ESL students. While no specific patterns or consistencies were discerned in the ESL subjects', some systematic patterns were found in the EFL-LLs. That is, the EFL subjects tended to use only certain prepositional phrases correctly in limited contexts that were basic, frequent and familiar as seen below:

(a) In summer, our family go to the sea.

(b) The air was different from here one.

(c) I'll plan to go *on* a picnic *with* my college fellow.

In most other cases it appeared a direct transfer of L1 structure, not only in the choice of the preposition but also sometimes using it after the noun or at the end of the phrase like a postposition (as in Korean). The sources of errors of prepositions also differed in the EFL and ESL situation. In most cases, the EFL students' incorrect preposition usage was closely related to inter lingual influence while that of ESL students was associated with the confusion or misunderstanding of collocational prepositional phrases.

To sum up, generally speaking, while the interlingual process is prominent in the EFL students' LL development, intralingual process is dominant in the ESL student' LLs. The difference in cognitive process in EFL and ESL learning situations can account for this contrast. As the students' proficiency levels increase, reliance on transfer decreases and reliance on overgeneralization increases, that is, as proficiency increases, the LL becomes more independent of the NL and becomes more dependent on the TL.

The Korean students, with considerable differences in the EFL and ESL situations, showed a common tendency to employ some learning strategies and communication strategies in trying to overcome their difficulties in using English. They also produced deviant constructions that reflected a number of differences in the learning strategies they employed in EFL and ESL situations. While the authors are exploring the learning strategies of Korean learners of ESL and EFL, the present study shows both the Korean EFL ands ESL learners' active involvement in the process of learning the target language. To sum up, the present study provides strong evidence for significant differences in the whole learning process between the EFL and ESL situation. The EFL situation triggers more transfer-based LLs, and the occurrence of L1 transfer is systematic. On the other hand, the ESL situation shows a different route and also the rate of the LL development due to a greater variety in their conditions of exposure to the target language. The cognitive and psychological factors also operate differently in the EFL and ESL learning situation. In addition, the interlingual process is prominent in the EFL whereas intralingual process is dominant in the process of LL development in ESL. We wish to suggest at the end of this paper that further studies on the development of LL are needed to show the subtle differences between the process of acquisition which seems to operate in a Second Language situation, and process of learning which seems to be at work in a Foreign Language situation.

REFERENCES

Agnihotri, R.K. and A.L. Khanna 1995. *English language teaching in India.* New Delhi: Sage publications.

Cha, Kyung Whan 1990. An error analysis of English writing through Korean college students' English compositions. *English Teaching* 40, 39-156.

Cha, Mi Yang 2000. *Learning of English by Koreans: Cross-sectional study of learner language in EFL/ESL Situations.* Unpublished Ph.D. Dissertation. JNU, New Delhi.

Choe, Yongjae Paul 1996. English education in Korea: Past, present, and future. *Theses Collection (Soong Sit University)* 26, 331- 157.

Corder, S.P. 1981. *Error analysis and interlanguage.* Oxford: Oxford University Press.

Dulay, H., M. Burt, and S. Krashen 1982. *Language two.* Oxford: Oxford University Press.

Ellis, Rod 1985. *Understanding second language.* Oxford: Oxford University Press.

Gass, S. and L. Selinker (ed.) 1983. *Language transfer in language learning.* Rowley, Mass.: Newbury House Publishers.

Han, Sang Ho 1997. Transfer and overgeneralization in Korean children's English utterances. *The Journal of English Language Teaching* 773-98.

Krashen, S. 1981. *Second language acquisition and second language learning.* Oxford: Pergamon Press.

Lewis, E. Glyn 1974. *Linguistics and second language pedagogy: A theoretical study.* The Hague: Mouton.

Narang, Vaishna 1996. *Communicative Language Teaching.* New Delhi: Creative Books.

Narang, Vaishna (ed.) 2006. *Contemporary Themes and Issues in Language Pedagogy.* New Delhi: Books Plus.

Nickel. G. 1989. Some controversies in present-day error analysis: 'Contrastive' vs Ňon-contrastive' errors. *IRAL* 27 (4), 293-305.

Odlin, T. 1989. *Language transfer.* Cambridge: Cambridge University Press.

Park, Heung Gi 1983. A critical review of teaching English as a Foreign Language at university level in Korea. *The Journal of Education (Pusan Teacher's College),* 9, 109-116.

Richards, J. 1985. *The context of language teaching.* Cambridge: Cambridge University Press.

Selinker, L. 1972. Interlanguage. *IRAL* 10, 209- 231.

Selinker, L. 1992. *Rediscovering interlanguage.* Harlow: Longman.

33

Kashmiri-English Contact: Some Phonological Issues

Aadil A. Kak

Background Survey

A contact situation is one where two or more languages come in close proximity to each other. According to Weinreich (1968: 1), "...two or more languages will be said to be in contact if they are used alternately by the same persons. The language-using individuals are thus the locus of the contact".

Appel and Muysken (1987: 5) distinguish five basic types of linguistic contact:

(*i*) The linguistic archipelago, in which many unrelated languages coexist in a relatively small area leading to bilingualism and widespread diffusion of words and elements of grammar.

(*ii*) Situations of language contact involving more or less stable borders between language families.

(*iii*) Language contact in which some languages have a high social status. This leads to evolution of several non-native varieties including Pidgins and Creoles.

(*iv*) Speakers of a minority language surrounded by a dominant national language.

(*v*) Language contact due to migratory movements.

Contact has resulted in varying degrees of transfer of features of one language into another. In the course of its history, English for instance, has borrowed vocabulary from French, Latin, Greek, and many other languages with which it has come in contact. In most of the cases languages in contact have been situations of speakers - in - contact i.e. languages have come in contact when their speakers have come in contact. Language contact in terms of speaker contact usually involves multilingualism with diffusion of both vocabulary and grammar across the languages. Examples include areas of Papua New Guinea, the Amazon basin, and the Australian desert. Other situations of language contact may involve geographic proximity between different language communities with only a slow spread of features across languages, creating a so-called 'sprachbund' or linguistic areas e.g. speakers of Greek, Albanian, Romanian, Bulgarian, etc have adopted features from each other over time. Yet another kind of a contact situation may involve the use of distinct languages within the same community by speakers who are bilingual or multilingual. This can lead to a high degree of convergence between very different languages, as is observed in the case of languages like Urdu, Marathi, and Kannada in the village of Kupwar in India (Gumperz and Wilson 1971). It has also been observed that the ability to manipulate two codes can lead to very intricate patterns of code alternation and code mixture. Some communities have highly regular patterns of code alternation which depends on the setting or context of speech resulting in 'diglossia'. It is important to point here that language contact does not always require speakers to have 'actual contact', as is the case in the present study.

Contact between languages can have a wide variety of outcomes ranging from borrowing, code mixing/switching, interference, language change and at times leading to the creation of whole new languages. According to Thomason and Kaufman (1988: 37-38) the two basic mechanisms in contact - induced language change are borrowing and interference through shift. Borrowing is defined as the incorporation of foreign features into a group's native language; the native language is maintained but is changed by the addition of the incorporated features. Shift-induced change, on the other hand, results from imperfect group learning during a process of language shift. Though these concepts were developed to explain contact - induced language change in a wide range of historical data, they are also used to explain recent (or ongoing) contact - induced change.

The results emerging from a contact situation depend on various factors like the length and intensity of contact between the languages; the types of social, economic, and political dimensions; the functions which communication must serve; and the degree of similarity between the languages.

Galindo Sole (2003) has outlined some ways of classifying the results of language contact.

Table 1: Some criteria and classificatory systems of language contact phenomena (Galindo Sole, 2003)

Criteria	*Classification systems*
1. Linguistic level language	phonic, lexical and morphosyntactic language contact phenomena
2. Process	substitution and importation
3. (Lack of) Integration into the recipient language	
3.1. Frequency of appearance	borrowing and code-switching
3.2. Morphosyntactic integration	
4. Integration process stages	interference in speech and in language, interference as process and as result, etc.
5. Relation between interfered and interfering structures	underdifferentiation, overdifferentiation, reinterpretation, substitution, import and loss
6. Etc.	

Galindo Sole (2003) further mentions that Ludi (1987) has used the term 'transcodic marker' in the context of language contact to cover a broad range of typologically organised phenomena. Though these typologies are many, they have been distinguished into two broad groups: Code switching and Interferences. Code switching indicates alternate activation of more than one language and is only available to bilingual speakers. Interferences are phonetic, lexical, morphosyntactic or semantic material transferred from one language to another; becoming integrated inside the recipient language and are available to monolingual speakers as well, not only to bilinguals.

Other classificatory techniques include the one which adopts the level of social integration as its starting-point. Using this criterion Weinreich (1953: 49) distinguished between interferences in speech and interferences in language. The same distinction is carried on by Payrató (1985) to differentiate between interferences used only by bilinguals, used by the whole of population explicitly accepted as normative and those which have entered the language many years before.

Other classification systems take into account the relation between the interfered and interfering structure. Weinreich (1953) analyses this relation at the phonic level, and Payrató (1985) extends it to other linguistic levels. Still other classifications distinguish between positive and negative transfers, segmental and suprasegmental interferences, proactive and retroactive interferences, etc.

Kashmir and its Language Scene

Kashmir is the most populous province of the state of Jammu and

Kashmir, the northernmost state of India. Regarding the linguistic scene in Kashmir, it is observed that Kashmiri is the native language and English and Urdu are the non-native or 'outsider' languages. Contact between Urdu and English with Kashmiri is not through any migrant population but chiefly through political patronage, education and mass media. This contact situation has led to bilingualism in active, as well as, passive forms and has also resulted in a relatively high degree of code mixing (Kak 1995, Kak and Agnihotri 1996). According to the 1981 census report (no census was held in 1991 and the complete results of the latest census report are not yet available) 89.5% of the population numbering 2,806,000 people of the Kashmir province speak Kashmiri, and even in the absence of any significant (if not negligible) native speaker population of English and Urdu, the impact of these two languages in different domains of life is obvious (Kak 2001), with both these languages even encroaching on those domains which were previously restricted to Kashmiri only.

The official language of the state of Jammu and Kashmir is Urdu. It is used for many official purposes like for writing the revenue records, for land assessment, land deeds, in the lower courts and so on. Furthermore, Urdu is also a language in the curriculum. English, again a language in the curriculum, is the only language used in higher studies (other than in specific language courses). English is also used for certain official purposes like in most of the High court documents, in revenue and land records by the younger generation (who find themselves more proficient in English than in Urdu) etc. Kashmiri, the native language, is not a language in the curriculum, has no role in the official domain, has almost no 'practical' value attached to it and its knowledge or proficiency gives no special benefit or status to the individual, thereby, placing it at the lowest rung of the language hierarchy. Among the three languages mentioned above, maximum status is attached to English because of its extensive application and its global significance, and because for every 'good' job, knowledge of English is a prerequisite.

In the absence of any effective number of English and Urdu speakers, language contact is by means of the curriculum and mass media which include newspapers (Urdu newspapers have the highest circulation, followed by English newspapers). There are no Kashmiri newspapers in Kashmir (though attempts were made to start some but they were all short-lived). Local Radio and TV station telecast and broadcast news and programmes in Urdu and Kashmiri. Cable TV which features more than 50 private channels telecasts most of the programmes in Hindi followed by English. No private channel caters exclusively to Kashmiri.

Aim of the Study

Languages in contact may influence each other in many ways: lexically, morphologically, phonologically, phonetically, prosodically, syntactically, semantically, pragmatically etc. Normally, these differences are apparent when the language/languages other than the mother tongue is/are used by speakers. Broselow & Park (1995) working on Korean (which does not have long vowels) and English (which has long vowels) observed that the Korean speakers perceived the contrast between long and short vowels, but in production, they essentially used Korean phonology. Han (1992) observed that Japanese distinguishes geminate from non-geminate stops (consonant length; k vs. kk, e.g., black owl vs. black cat) which English doesn't (*kkæt vs. kæt). English speakers of Japanese (even highly proficient ones) either missed this contrast altogether or produced long consonants that were not native-like (too short). However, at times L2 speakers are observed to adjust their speech to eliminate the mother tongue influence and gain closer proximity with the 'standard'. The reasons for this behaviour appear to be sociolinguistic and the ambivalence towards or the striving for the 'standard' has more to do with the status and prestige of the language/languages in question in comparison with the status and prestige of the mother tongue. Thomason & Kaufman (1988) argue that social factors alone determine the linguistic outcomes of language contact; linguistic factors are said to play no role. In other words, reacting to someone's speech with a positive or negative attitude indicates reacting to the whole complex of social, economic and political connotations associated with that code.

The present study takes into account the influence in terms of phonology in Kashmiri-English contact situation in Srinagar, the summer capital of the state of Jammu and Kashmir and the centre of the Kashmir province. The focus of the study is on phonological elements which are absent in one of the languages in contact and present in the other.

Kashmiri, Urdu and English are observed to be in contact in Srinagar. However, this study involves only the phonology of Kashmiri and English. Urdu is not considered because of the lack of any statistical significance.

Phonological Issues

It is observed that Kashmiri native speakers speak Urdu and English with certain phonological variations, which are typically characteristic of them. These 'characteristic features' observed in their use of Urdu and English, the non-native languages, are because of the influence of the native language, Kashmiri.

In the case of English spoken by Kashmiri native speakers, statistically significant variables were observed. For this study three frequently occurring phonological features were identified. They were selected because they were easily identifiable, frequent in occurrence and were statistically significant. Responses regarding phonological features were elicited from the informants who were native speakers of Kashmiri with varying levels of English proficiency. The phonological features, which were taken into consideration, were:

a) The variable (f) of English,
b) Consonant clusters of Kashmiri and English, and
c) The variable (p^h) of Kashmiri.

Variable (f) of English

The labiodental fricative /f/, which is present in English in words like 'fail', 'five', 'fin' and 'life', does not occur in Kashmiri. Typically, the influence of the mother tongue should cause the Kashmiri native speaker to substitute this /f/ with the voiceless, aspirated, bilabial stop /p^h/. Consequently, /f/ of 'fin', /f in/, 'five' /faiv/, and 'life' /laif/ should be and mostly is normally pronounced by the Kashmiri native speaker as /p^hin/, /p^haiv/ and /laip^h/. However, the /f/ → /p^h/ replacement is not absolute and the incidence of variable (f) in the English spoken by Kashmiri native speakers would provide us with an insight into the extent of influence of English on the phonological repertoire of the Kashmiri native speaker.

Other sounds like /θ/ and /ð/ (produced with friction), which are present in English but absent in Kashmiri, were not taken into consideration because of the lack of any significant statistical significance as almost all Kashmiris use /d/ (frictionless) for /ð/ and /t^h/ (frictionless) for /θ/. The difference lies in friction only. Similarly, other features which showed an almost 100% similarity of pattern were also not taken into consideration.

Consonant clusters of Kashmiri

Consonant clusters are sequences (combinations) of two or more consonant phonemes. In Kashmiri such consonant clusters are seen to occur in the initial, medial as well as the final position. Initial and final clusters are syllable based while medial clusters are word based and are found to occur across morpheme boundaries.

Though only the initial clusters can be called pure Kashmiri clusters, final clusters are mostly found in the borrowed words, but by now such words have become part of the whole system of Kashmiri and are widely used.

Kashmiri has only double consonant clusters, which occur at all the three positions. In the initial and the final position, the occurrence of these consonant clusters is restricted i.e. only certain consonants can combine with certain other consonants to form a cluster, as is discussed below. Clusters consisting of more than two consonants is not possible. To elicit data in terms of the phonological variables only word initial (and syllable initial) and word final (and syllable final) consonant clusters were taken into consideration. Care was taken to include only those consonant clusters in the study which are absent in Kashmiri.

Word initial consonant clusters of Kashmiri

Kashmiri has a regular pattern for word initial consonant clusters. The second consonant of the initial consonant cluster is always /r/. The first consonant may be a voiceless unaspirated stop /p/ or /t/, a voiceless aspirated stop /p^h/ or /k^h/, voiced unaspirated stop /b/ or /d/, voiced retroflex /ḍ/ or velar /g/, voiceless aspirated affricate /ts^h/, voiceless fricatives /s/ or /š/ or voiced fricative /z/.

Table 2: Patterns of Kashmiri initial consonant clusters

	p	p^h	b	t	d	ḍ	k	k^h	g	ts^h	s	š	z
r	*	*	*	*	*	*	*	*	*	*	*	*	*

The examples of Kashmiri consonant clusters are as follows /prasun/ 'to give birth', /p^{h}ru:ts/ 'auspicious', /bram/ 'illusion', /tra:v/ 'leave', /drog/ 'expensive', /ḍram/ 'drum', /kra:l/ 'potter', /k^{h}ra:v/ 'wooden slippers', /grekh/ 'boil', /ts^{h}raṭh/ 'mischief', /srog/ 'cheap' and /zror/ 'piece of land'.

Word final consonant clusters of Kashmiri

The frequency of the word final consonant clusters is lesser than that of the initial clusters even though their choice is comparatively more varied (Bhat 1987). Nasal /n/ or /m/ or a fricative /s/ or /š/ is always the first member of the cluster. The second member of the cluster is always a stop. E.g. 'mp', 'mb', 'nt', 'nd', 'nḍ' 'nk', 'nkh', 'ng', 'st', 'št' and 'šṭ'. E.g. /ka:mp/ *'fear'*, /amb/ *'mango'*, /and/ *'end'*, /khanḍ/ *'sugar'*, /mast/ *'care free'*, /gašt/ 'a round', /lang/ 'branch/thigh', /šankh/ 'conch shell' and so on.

Use of English consonant clusters by native speakers of Kashmiri

In case of the consonant clusters of English, which do not conform to the phonology of Kashmiri, Kashmiri native speakers are observed to resort to breaking the consonant cluster by inserting a vowel between the consonants e.g. 'school' /sku:l/ would be pronounced as /sәku:l/, 'strike' /sṭraik/ as /siṭraik/, 'plate' /pleiṭ/ as /paleiṭ/ or /pileiṭ/ etc. This is because of the reason that no triple clusters are found in Kashmiri and the combination of double consonant clusters of English is different from that of Kashmiri. In the preliminary investigation again, it was observed that the breaking up of the consonant clusters is not invariable but varies. So, consonant clusters were taken as variables for checking the informant's assimilation to English.

Feature (p^h) of Kashmiri

The main aim of taking this feature into consideration was to see if the influence of variant [f] of a more prestigious language (in this case, English) was strong enough to encroach upon the phonology of Kashmiri. As indicated earlier, the general practice of the Kashmiri native speaker is his tendency to substitute the Kashmiri /p^h/ for the English /f/ while speaking and reading English. What would be interesting to observe is if the influence of English is so strong that it would prompt Kashmiri native speakers to use /f/ in place of Kashmiri /p^h/ (this was to some extent observed in some cases in the preliminary investigation). This, in a way, could be indicative of a much strong assimilation to the prestige code and the interference would, instead of being unidirectional, be bidirectional.

Method

As already indicated, the study is based on Kashmiri native speakers of Srinagar. Kashmir, and along with it Srinagar is a sensitive area and social and political dimensions make it extremely difficult to undertake an empirical sociolinguistic study in the area. It was impossible for me therefore to draw out a random sample from a given list of the population. I therefore, depended largely on personal contacts. I started with a family known to me and from that point on I used the contacts provided by each family I visited. The sample thus represents a network of families spanning Srinagar.

The features mentioned above i.e. incidence of [f] in English, handling of double and triple consonant clusters in English and incidence of [f] in Kashmiri along with certain social-psychological features were taken as variables and the responses elicited in terms of these variables were codified. After codification, these variables were tabulated and subjected to correlation analysis.

Sample

Data was collected from 30 informants for this study. Care was taken to have a representative sample which included male and female informants from different parts of Srinagar, including the old area, broadly termed Downtown, the so-called Posh areas called the Civil lines like Rajbagh and Sanatnagar and the outskirts of Srinagar such as Ganderbal. All the informants were native speakers of Kashmiri with varying levels of English and Urdu proficiency. The informants belonged to different socio-economic backgrounds, with different educational levels. The break-up of informants as per age and gender is given below.

Table 3: Break-up of informants (a)

OM	OF	MM	MF	YM	YF
5	5	5	5	5	5

where arbitrarily, OM stands for Old Males, OF stands for Old Females, MM stands for Middle-aged Males, MF stands for Middle-aged Females, YM stands for Young Males and YF stands for Young Females.

The age range of the different categories of informants is

Table 4: Break-up of informants (b)

Group	*Age Range*
Old (O)	Above 40 years
Middle-aged (M)	26 to 39 years
Young (Y)	Upto 25 years

Tools

A questionnaire was designed to elicit the socio-psychological features of the sample. For determining the incidence of the use of the variable /f/ in English and to test the handling of English consonant clusters, the informants were asked to read from a prepared passage in English. This passage had words which contained the sound /f/ and the consonant clusters (initial and final). The reading was recorded for each informant and the percentage of 'standard use' of /f/ and that of the consonant clusters of English was calculated.

However, for the second part of the exercise, which included testing the sound /f/ in Kashmiri, a Kashmiri passage was not used because almost all the informants showed at least some degree of inability to read Kashmiri. So, to measure this variable, individual interviews were conducted with each informant and the percentage of incidence of /f/

instead of /pʰ/, if any, was noted in the case of each informant.

The data was tabulated and subjected to analysis. For the correlation analysis Window's based SPSS package was used.

Analysis

Variable (f)

Fig 1 presents the graphic representation of the incidence of use of variant [f] in English among the informants.

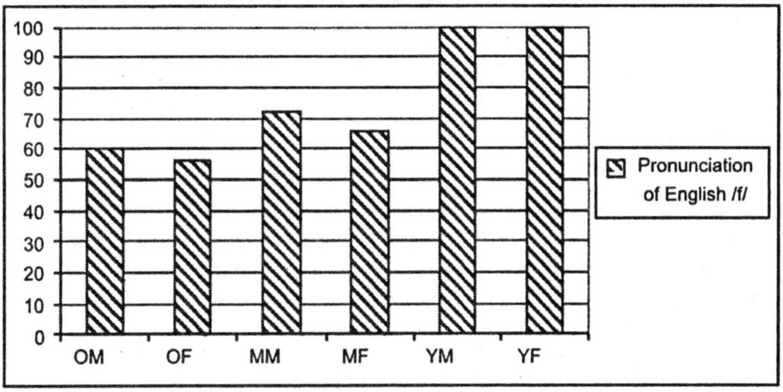

Fig. 1: Incidence of [f] of English among informants.

It is observed that the use of variable /f/ increases with decrease in age, with its lowest incidence among the 'Old' group and the highest incidence among the age group representing the 'Youth'. It is also interesting to observe that the variation in terms of gender in the use of this variable is very low indicated by little differences between males and females within age-groups.

The variable (use of /f/ in English) shows positive significant correlations with the Variable 'Educational Institutions' ($r=.64$, $p\leq.001$) and negative significant correlations with Variables 'Age' ($r= -.64$, $p\leq.001$), 'Occupation' ($r= -.67$, $p\leq .001$), 'Level of Education' ($r= -.36$, $p\leq .01$) and 'Claimed Proficiency in Kashmiri' ($r= -.45$, $p\leq .001$).

Table 5: Correlations of Variable 'Use of /f/ in English' /with other Variables

	Educational Institutions	*Age*	*Occupation*	*Level of Education*	*Claimed proficiency in Kashmiri*
Use of /f/ in English	0.64	– 0.64	– 0.67	– 0.36	– 0.45

These correlations indicate that informants who are able to pronounce the /f/ of English 'properly' have been educated in missionary schools. Furthermore, the incidence of this sound is high among the informants who belong to the lower age bracket. The negative correlation with 'Occupation' and 'Level of Education' indicates that these informants are not holding substantial posts and their level of education is not high. This may be because most of the better performers of this variable are the youth who, as compared to the older generation, are either students or hold positions low in the job hierarchy because in most of the jobs in Kashmir, seniority is important for being at the upper end in the hierarchy. Another correlation, with 'Claimed proficiency in Kashmiri' is also to some extent related to the 'youth' factor. Claimed proficiency was measured in terms of 4 skills namely, Reading, Writing, Speaking and Comprehension. It is a common observation that almost all Kashmiri youth (except those who have academic qualifications in Kashmiri) are unable to Read and Write Kashmiri, though their Comprehension and Speaking skills may range from average to good. The inability to read and write Kashmiri is because of the absence of Kashmiri in the curriculum and lack of Kashmiri reading and writing opportunities.

Consonant clusters of English

Two occurrences of consonant clusters (both double and triple) were taken into consideration: in words which had a consonant cluster at word initial position only i.e. they consist of only one cluster, and in words which had consonant clusters at the word initial position and the final position as well i.e. they consist of two clusters.

Single consonant clusters (one cluster within a word/syllable): Here, informants were tested for words which had only one consonant cluster (either double or triple) in them. The testing was done at two positions,

Word/syllable initial position e.g. *scream* /skri:m /, *split* /split/ *strange* /streindʒ/, *spring* /spriɳ/, *plate* /pleIt/, etc and

Word/syllable final position e.g. *called* /kɔ:ld/, *alarm* /əlarm/, *ghosts* /gousts/, *lift* /lift/, etc.

The overall percentages of the 'standard' articulation of the initial and the final consonant clusters were 79% and 70.2% respectively, indicating that the informants had 'handled' the consonant clusters reasonably 'well' with comparatively lesser frequency of nativization. Furthermore, the articulation of the initial consonant clusters, with respect to the standard, was relatively better than the final consonant clusters. A graphic representation is given below.

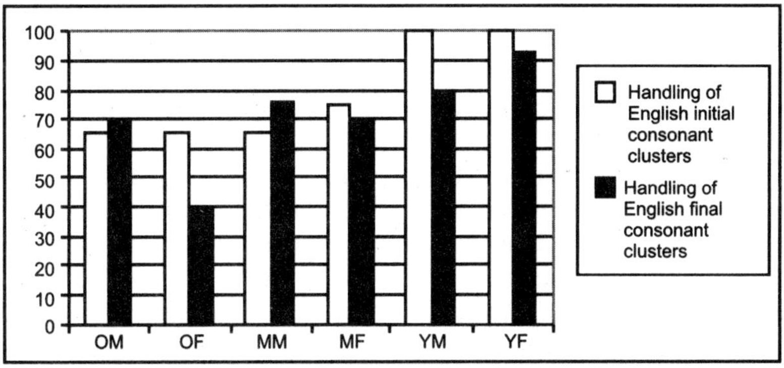

Fig. 2: Standard handling of initial and final consonant clusters of English

From the figure, it is clear that the young males and females seem to handle both the initial and the final consonant clusters better than the other groups, especially in the case of the initial consonant clusters which show a 100% score for both the 'Young' males and females. What is interesting to observe is that even the 'Old' age group shows 60-70% standard pronunciation of the consonant clusters.

It was observed that the variables 'English single consonant cluster (at word/syllable initial position)' and 'English single consonant cluster (at word/syllable final position)' both correlate positively with Variable 'Family's English proficiency' ($r=.62$, $p \leq .001$) and ($r=.39$, $p \leq .001$) respectively and correlate negatively with Variable 'Age' ($r= -.61$, $p \leq .001$) and ($r= -.57$, $p \leq .001$) respectively.

Table 6: Correlations of Variables 'English single consonant clusters (word initial and word final)'

	Family's English Proficiency	*Age*
English single consonant cluster (word initial)	0.62	– 0.61
English single consonant cluster (word final)	0.39	– 0.57

These correlations indicate that the informants who handle the consonant clusters well rate their family's English proficiency highly. This may be an indication that the improvement in the standard articulation of consonant clusters depends on the exposure to English within the family. The correlation with 'age' is a recurring one and indicates that the youth are better at handling consonant clusters as compared to the middle-aged and the old informants. The reasons are greater peer pressure, greater exposure as already indicted, and consequently greater fine-tuning to nuances of English among the youth as compared to the older generation.

Double consonant clusters (two clusters within a syllable/word): These included words like *dreams* /ḍri:mz/, *clocks* /klɔks/, *schools* / sku:lz/, *sticks* /stIks/, *plots* /plɔṭs/, *scarf* /ska:rf/, etc with consonant clusters (syllable initial and final) both at the beginning and at the end of the same word/syllable.

In the case of words with consonant clusters at initial and final positions, the overall percentage of standard articulation of the initial consonant cluster and the final consonant cluster is 68.6% and 62% respectively. This indicates that final clusters are comparatively difficult for Kashmiri native speakers to articulate as compared to the initial clusters, indicated by the comparatively lower scores of the former as compared to the latter .

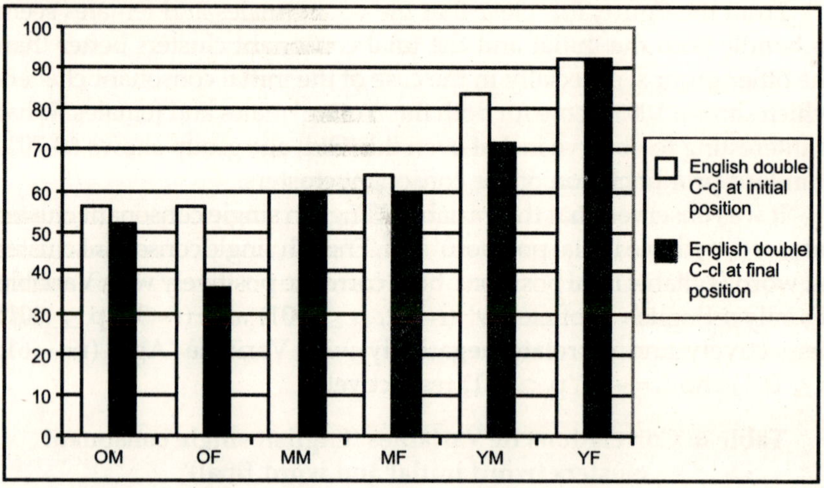

Fig. 3: Standard articulation of double consonant clusters of English

Fig. 3 graphically shows the Standard articulation of the consonant clusters by the 6 groups. It is evident here that overall in all the groups, initial consonant clusters (in words with double consonant clusters at initial and final position) are comparatively easier to handle than the final ones. As in the case of the words consisting of one cluster, 'Old Females' again appear to have difficulty in handling the word final consonant clusters. The highest score for handling both the initial and the final consonant clusters is observed in the case of the 'Young Females.'

In the case of words with two clusters, it was again observed that Variable 'English consonant clusters (at word initial position)' and Variable 'English consonant clusters (at word final position) correlate positively with Variable 'Family's English proficiency' ($r=.58, p \leq .001$) and ($r = .40, p \leq .001$) and with Variable 'Duration of use of English'

($r = .40, p \leq .001$) ($r = .44, p \leq .001$)and negatively with Variable 'Age' ($r = -.50, p \leq .001$) ($r = -.39, p \leq .001$).

Table 7: Correlations of Variables 'English consonant clusters (word initial)' and 'English consonant clusters (word final)'

	Family's English proficiency	*Duration of use of English*	*Age*
English consonant clusters (word initial)	0.58	0.40	– 0.50
English consonant clusters (word final)	0.40	0.44	– 0.39

These correlations indicate that informants who handled the double consonant clusters at word initial and final position well, again rated their family's English proficiency highly. The exposure is augmented by the positive significant correlation with 'Duration of use of English'. Again, we see the negative correlation with Age which is indicative of better performance in this sphere among the Youth.

In Srinagar, it is commonly observed that the usual 'mistakes' while speaking English are generally committed by the older generation. The 'Youth' usually attempt to 'improve' their English as compared to the older generation who generally appear to be satisfied with the way they speak English and don't seem to care about their accent and pronunciation. The youth on the other hand try their best to speak English as close to 'the standard' as possible and are more conscious of it. This to a great extent is influenced by the educational institutions to which the youth belong and the exposure they have, including the exposure, from other family members who have good English proficiency. On a number of occasions students persistently ask the teachers about how a particular word is pronounced indicating their inquisitiveness in this matter. Good pronunciation is admired and bad pronunciation is frowned upon and becomes the butt of ridicule. Sometimes the youth carry the practice a bit farther when they try to inculcate this habit in their elders, if they find the elders 'deficient' in this matter. The reason is that among their peers they would like to present their parents as having a good command over English (including English phonology). In one instance, I observed a young girl correcting her mother who used to pronounce /blu:/ 'blue' as /bIlu:/ (which is the Kashmiri way of pronouncing it and quite common). She pestered her mother so much that now her mother uses /blu:/ instead of /bIlu:.

Variable (p^h) of Kashmiri

In the case of this variable, the incidence of replacing Kashmiri variant [pʰ] with the non-Kashmiri variant [f] is observed as a whole and along different socio-psychological variables.

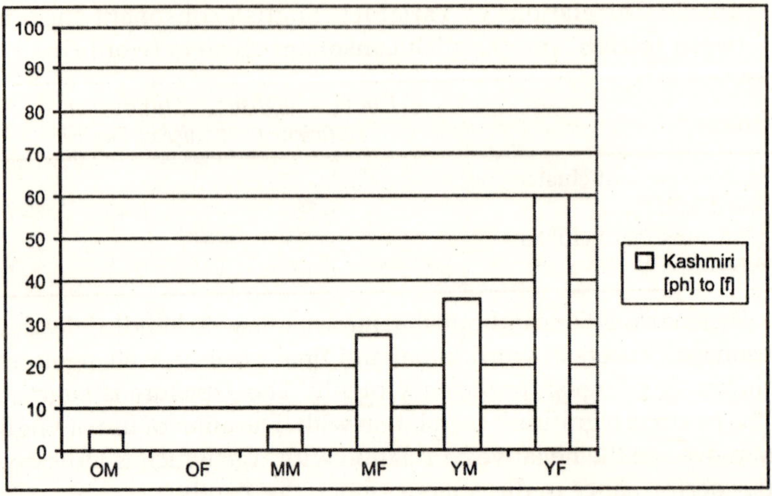

Fig. 4 Incidence of [pʰ] to [f] phenomenon in Kashmiri.

Fig. 4 graphically shows the incidence of re-placing Kashmiri [ph] with [f]. It is observed that among the informants an increase in the use of /f/ instead of /pʰ/ is inversely proportional to age i.e. the younger informants show greater use of /f/ in place of /pʰ/ in Kashmiri as compared to the older informants. The interesting point is the use of /f/ in Kashmiri even by some 'old' informants. Some of the instances include /pʰə:tir/ 'fool' pronounced as /fə:tir/, /ṭɔpʰ/ 'sting' as /ṭɔf/, /pʰot/ 'basket'as /fot/, etc.

Among the informants the group representing 'Old Females' show no use of /f/ in Kashmiri (though >55% showed the use of /f/ in English). The 'Youth' show the highest use of /f/, and among them the 'young females' with a score of 60% show its maximum use while using Kashmiri. Overall, the graph shows a steep increase for this trait with a wide margin between the young and the old informants.

The Variable 'Incidence of [f] in Kashmiri' is seen to correlate positively with the Variables 'Educational Institutions' ($p=.42$, $r \leq .001$) and Family's Education ($p=.72$, $r \leq .001$) and negatively with Variable 'Age' ($p = -.62$, $r \leq .001$).

Table 8: Correlations of Variable 'Incidence of /f/ in Kashmiri'

	Educational Institutions	*Family's Education*	*Age*
Incidence of /f/ in Kashmiri	0.42	0.72	– 0.62

These correlations indicate that being educated in prestigious institutions (in this case, the missionary schools) and belonging to families who are educated seems to play an important part in this phenomenon. The negative correlation with 'Age' is an indication that this phenomenon is more prevalent among the 'Youth'.

Overall, it is observed that 'Age' is a common factor in all the above mentioned instances. This may be because the younger generation is more susceptible to prestige and status as compared to the older ones. This may also be an indication that the younger generation are subject to greater pressures for achieving the prestige forms, and better English proficiency means a better profile and thereby, a better job. Another factor can be peer group pressures which may also be a reason for the greater attempt at reaching the standard.

As already indicated, exposure also plays the role of an important factor. Exposure to English comes from different areas like curriculum, TV and Radio programmes, reading habits, friends and relatives, etc. This exposure is more prominent among informants belonging to prestigious educational institutions (where proficiency in English is stressed upon, with some prestigious institutions even going to the extent of fining those students who don't use English), or/and belonging to educated families with high levels of English proficiency (which provides a boost to English proficiency in the domain of home itself) and duration of use (where more a native speaker of Kashmiri practices the more closer to the standard does he get).

Another point which is relevant here is that /f/, which may be seen becoming a part of Kashmiri phonology appears to be the /f/ of English rather than of Urdu. This assumption is made because Kashmiri native speakers are not generally conscious about and do not show much of a tendency to acquire aspects of the Urdu phonology as is indicated by the lack of any significant correlation, as mentioned earlier. We do observe the presence of strong Kashmiri phonological features in the Urdu of most Kashmiri native speakers. Though it cannot be denied that the presence of the Kashmiri phonological features are present in English as well but as per my observation the intensity and passion with which proximity to the 'standard' in English is desired is higher, as compared to Urdu. English learners frequently make use of English pronunciation dictionaries (and computer mediated pronunciation aids, in these days) to improve their pronunciation. Pronunciation dictionaries of Urdu, if present, are hardly ever used. Another point which is also relevant here is that among Kashmiris the number of Urdu proficient people is much higher than the number of English proficient people, because of the longer duration of Urdu in

Kashmir as compared to English (which showed its presence in Kashmir in the late nineteenth century and was taken up seriously in the curriculum etc only in the past 40 years or so). Furthermore the official status of Urdu in the state leading to greater use and greater exposure to it has granted it, if it may be so called, the status of 'the second native language'. This has resulted in a form of a 'native standard' of Urdu in Kashmir which is very much 'Kashmiricized'. The target of a Kashmiri native speaker is attainment of this 'local standard'. However, in the case of English, no such 'native standard' has been attained which leaves the field open to 'greater chances of improvement' thereby leading to attempts at proximity to the 'standard' (as opposed to the 'native standard').

In the case of the use of /f/ in place of /p^h/ in Kashmiri, as also indicted by the correlation matrix, the older generation don't show much of a difference between them. I have also observed a difference between the [p^h] of the older generation and the younger generation. The older generation uses more aspiration as compared to the younger generation while pronouncing [p^h]. It appears that educated Kashmiri native speakers subconsciously associate aspiration of [p^h] with non-eliteness. Hence, greater the aspiration less elite the speaker. The younger generation is more prone to this 'elite' pressure and it is observed more so in the young females, where in the case of certain young females, who were educated in missionary schools, an almost 100% incidence of '[f] in the place of [p^h]' is observed whenever they speak Kashmiri.

Conclusions

Overall, it is observed there is a progressive phonological assimilation towards English, the top-most language in the hierarchy. This assimilation is bidirectional and is evident not only in the phonological features of English like the /f/ sound and English consonant clusters which are progressively in the process of being de-nativized but evidence also indicates that the 'English influence' has spread to Kashmiri as well, as is evident by observing the presence of the non-native /f/ sound in Kashmiri phonology. Among the sociopsychological factors, 'Age' appears to be playing an important role in this assimilation. Younger generation is observed to be more amenable to English influence as compared to the old and the middle-aged generation. The emphasis on 'proper' English, greater peer pressure and greater acquiescence to social status symbols among the youth appear to be the primary motivators for this phenomenon. Other factors like exposure to English in the form of 'English prowess' of the family and prestigious educational institutions also play an important role.

This issue is further assisted by the prevalence of English, the language with status and global utility, and to its easy access in Srinagar through curriculum and mass media. The increase in status of English, its global value and greater dependence on it in many spheres indicates that the influence of English on Kashmiri and the level of assimilation is going to increase, rather than decrease, with the passage of time.

REFERENCES

Appel, R. and P. Muysken 1987. *Language contact and bilingualism*. London: Arnold.

Bhat, R.K. 1987. *A descriptive study of Kashmiri*. Delhi: Amar Prakashan.

Broselow, E. and H. Park 1995. Mora conservation in second language acquisition. In J. Archibald (ed.) *Phonological acquisition and phonological theory*. Hillsdale, NJ: Lawrence Erlbaum Associates.

Census of India 1981. New Delhi: Government of India.

Galindo Sole, Mireia 2003. Language Contact Phenomena in Catalonia: The Influence of Catalan in Spoken Castilian. In Lotfi Sayahi (ed.) *Selected Proceedings of the First Workshop on Spanish Sociolinguistics*. 18-29.

Gumperz, J.J. 1982. *Discourse strategies*. Cambridge: Cambridge University Press.

Gumperz, J.J. and R. Wilson 1971. Convergence and Creolization: A Case from the Indo-Aryan/Dravidian Border. In D. Hymes (ed.) *Pidginization and creolization of languages*. Cambridge: Cambridge University Press.

Han, M. 1992. The Timing Control of Geminate and Single Stop Consonants in Japanese: A Challenge for Non Native Speaker. *Phonetica* 49, 102-127.

Kak, A.A. 1995. Acceptability of Kashmiri-English Mixed Code Sentences: A Sociolinguistic Study. Unpublished M.Phil. Dissertation. Delhi: University of Delhi.

Kak, A.A. 2001. Language Maintenance and Shift in Srinagar. Unpublished Ph.D. Dissertation. Delhi: University of Delhi.

Kak, A.A. and R.K. Agnihotri 1996. Acceptability of Mixed Code Sentences and its Social Psychological Correlates. *CIEFL Bulletin* 8, 5-28.

Payrató, L. 1985. *La interferËncia lingìistica. Comentaris i exemples catalë-castellë*. Barcelona: Curial; Publicacions de l'Abadia de Montserrat. Somerville, MA: Cascadilla Proceedings Project.

Thomason, S.G. and T. Kaufman 1988. *Language contact, creolization, and genetic linguistics*. Berkeley: University of California Press.

Thomason, S.G. 2001. *Language contact: An introduction*. Edinburgh: Edinburgh University Press.

Weinreich, U. 1953. *Languages in contact: Findings and problems*. The Hauge-Paris: Mouton.

Weinreich, U. 1958. Yiddish and Colonial German in Eastern Europe: The differential impact of Slavic (*American contributions to the Fourth International Congress of Slavicists*, Moscow, September 1958). The Hague: Mouton and Co.

34

Lexico-Semantic Features of Indian Pidgin English

Priya Hosali

1. Pidgin languages are simplified link languages. They are concomitants of situations where we have had languages in contact: either a contact between the ruler's language and the language of the ruled, or between the languages of two groups of people coming together for trade and commerce. When a pidgin becomes the mother tongue of a speech community we call it a creole.

1.1 During the epoch of colonization, as Europeans came into contact with aboriginal populations, many pidgin forms of Portuguese, Spanish, French and English became common. So arose Pidgin Portuguese, Pidgin Spanish, Pidgin French, and Pidgin English. Pidginization occurred not only with European but also with non-European languages. So arose Swahili in Central Africa, Fanaga- Lò or Kitchen Kaffir in South Africa, Tupi–Guarani in Brazil, Pidgin Motu in Papua, and Bazaar Malay in Indonesia.

1.2 From the beginning of colonization in India, a Pidgin English was spoken between the first colonists and the natives. Hugo Schuchardt, the German armchair linguist divided this pidgin language into five types: Butler English of Madras, Pidgin English of Bombay, Boxwallah English of Upper India, Cheechee English and Baboo English. (1891:38)

Yule and Burnell define Butler English thus: it is "the broken English spoken by native servants in the Madras Presidency, which is not very much better than the Pigeon English of China.... The oddest characteristic about the jargon is (or was) that masters used it in speaking to their servants as well as servants to their masters." (1968: 133-134)

Reinecke says: "Certain dialects which may be classed with the trade jargons arise, it must be admitted from master and servant relationships; but...these dialects remain supplementary and tend to disappear without attaining a stable structure." (1964: 538) These dialects are the Tamil–English of Madras known as Butler English; Tây Bôi of Saigon, and the Tagalog-Spanish of Manila.

2. This paper concentrates on Butler English: the Pidgin English spoken in India by native servants to their English–speaking masters. The head of the domestic staff of a European household in India used to be called the butler: hence the English spoken by the butler was labelled Butler English. In my study the range of the term has been widened and applies to the English spoken by domestic staff in general. The term 'butler' is synonymous with 'any domestic.' Guides, vendors, and taxi-drivers (among others) also speak Indian Pidgin English, but they are outside the scope of this study.

2.1 In his article **'Indo–English'** (1891: 47) Schuchardt gives a sample of Butler English quoted in **The Times**, April 11, 1882: 8c.

> (1) Butler's yevery day taking one ollock for own-self, and giving servants all half half ollock; when I am telling that shame for him, he is telling, Master's strictly order all servants for the little milk give it – what can I say, mam, I poor ayah woman?

Schuchardt (1891:48) further quotes a handful of sentences in Madras English, which are sprinkled throughout the text of **Gup** (Indo–English gossip) **Sketches of Anglo–Indian life and character.** (1868)

> (2) I all right now, ma'am. Missus want amah for the baby? (34) Master not believe she give "garley!" Master not believe she throw knives! Master now see what that missus doing. (45) Yes ma'am, I speaking English – same as missus. (55) How I telling? English people very clever; can do everything. (169)

2.2 Here are some samples of **Butler English from Hosali** (2000)

Drinks / Foods

Thomas and Khaddar are adept at mixing drinks.

> 1. Bloody Mary's is eh tomato's juice, pepper, salt, pepper, salt, eh rum, Worcester sauce, all mixing and what is the quantity.... Put it eh one slice lime also. Bloody Mary is red colour. That's tomato colour no. Tomato juice.
>
> 2. Tom Collins. I will say whisky with sour – some fresh lime, whisky, soda.

Most chefs employed in hotels and clubs have mastered the culinary arts.

> 3. First to boiling **dα|l**; after some time putting chilly; all this, this all mixing.... No **haldi** I put first. After that **dα|l** is tch boiling...that mixing

all. After I put pepper and some oil. Put it the oil, something chillies, **jIrα|** all this thing is **baghα|rα|**.

4. Yes. Caramel custard. Beat the eggs, egg and milk and sugar – and beat it and bake it. Essence also, sugar.... Only for the English **khα|nα|** I cooked very well. Because that **desi** I don't know.

Tradition of Domestic Service

Raji is in charge of the swimming-pool in the Secunderabad club.

5. Swimming-pool because is the **sahibs** coming, want some clothes, and sh shorts, and clothes and towels. Then give it: give some money and purse. And keep in my **almirah**. Then I bring: when they will finish their swim then give back again. Ha?

Anthony worked in the house of one of the Nawabs of Hyderabad.

6. Hm, **mα|harα|jα|** of **nε|zEm** Hyderabad.... Eh eh eh cook and dressing–boy. Travelling–cook. Eh that master's eh **mα|harα|jα|** going anywhere and travelling – I'll go with him and cook and dressing–boy – everything.

Lourde Marie looks after the garden.

7. The master room **ma**. Master – any guest coming – who so keeping here. Yes **ma**. That the garden. I only looking garden – **mα|lι|** coming – the children helping for pouring water and all.

Helen is a baby–**ayah**.

8. Baby–**ayah's**. Just eh I'll look after baby and eh washing baby's clothes – washing, ironing. Just I'll taking walking – that's all.

And Mary, the most endearing of my butleresses talks of the many facets of her life.

9. My mother is working British – cook-**ayah.** His name is Teresa.... I been working Mrs. Pattison.... He's take me four month – London. When I'm hyoung. Oh London is here only little little house upstairs and after he.... I been working baby–**ayah.** Then after he's take me there he's giving all the inside work. Then he's giving me warm clothes – then every evening he giving me drinks. Brandy. Hm. My **memsahib**. Whisky, brandy, anyone.... I had lot of gold things and rich. I'm eh working British times – monthly eighty eighty I taking.... Yes I going five–o' clock in the morning time for the milk – then I put the bottle all there – I going to the church – Richmond Road.

2.3 About Butler English, Schuchardt wrote: "In vain, I have tried to obtain from Madras more substantial samples of this English, written down with reasonable care. In recent years it has appeared to be on the wane." (1891: 48)

Butler English has developed its present form as a result of a particularly intense contact situation, which disappeared subsequently when India gained independence in 1947. However, the samples quoted from the newspapers of 1882 and 1868 when compared with samples from my data collected from 1980–2000 show that the variety is very much alive, and that though the samples are separated by a century, they have many features in common. The implication is that there still is a contact situation, which is influencing Butler English today. Butler English has been stable enough to allow it to be described linguistically.

2.4 It should be remembered, however, that Butler English is never spoken among butlers: it has its roots only in the master - slave relation of the dominant and the dominated. The label "pidgin" for it has been questioned on this ground. Whinnom has pointed out that the languages we today recognize as pidgins are spoken not by foreigners nor even primarily by dominant speakers of a standard language but **by natives in subordinate positions who do not share a common language among themselves.** (1968: 102-104) Verma (Personal communication, 1981) labels Butler English a semi-pidgin. Mühlhäusler (1978: 15) terms Butler English a minimal pidgin. Aitchison (Personal communication, 1987) suggests that the easiest way to solve this controversy over labels is to distinguish between stable pidgins and unstable pidgins. Butler English is a pidgin but an **unstable** pidgin.

3. As the analysis of the lexico-semantic features of Butler English is data based, a word about data collection is necessary. Data collection for this study took place in Hyderabad, Bangalore and Madras, in hotels and in clubs – those hangovers of colonial rule in India. Some army establishments were also included. Many domestic staff were from homes of friends known to the family for the last three decades. A rough–and–ready questionnaire was prepared to elicit information on the domestic's general family background, tradition of domestic service and special interests, if any. This was used when recording the speech of seventy–five domestics – some of them indeed very important like the Nizam of Hyderabad's butler, the Dewan of Mysore: Sir Mirza Ismail's dresssing–boy, and the Maharajah of Mysore's cook. They include both sexes, embrace different religions and range from the ages of twenty to seventy. Some of them are totally uneducated; others semi-educated. All of them are bilinguals, while many have a nodding acquaintance with three or more languages.

The tapes were first orthographically transcribed. The corpus comprises 275 foolscap typed pages of text containing 4,205 utterances. Next each sentence of Butler English was matched with its corresponding equivalent in standard Indian English. Inspiration in this area has been derived from Gumperz who suggests as quoted in Bailey

(1971: 342) that the translatability measure be applied in order to determine how a given text differs from its educated equivalent.

4. I now proceed to describe some of the lexico–semantic features of Butler English. All examples are taken from Hosali. (2000) Comparisons between Butler English and other pidgins and creoles are made wherever appropriate.

4.1 Considered from the point of view of their vocabularies all Pidgin and Creole Englishes are closely related to each other and, through English, to the Indo–European family of languages. (Todd, 1974: 12) An example is: English **arm/hand**; Krio **an**; Cameroon Pidgin **han**; Jamaican Creole **han**; Sranan **ana**; Melanesian Pidgin **han**; Butler English **hand**. An examination of the syntactic evidence, however, suggests the need for caution in their classification.

4.2 Apart from lexical similarities due to their core vocabularies deriving from English, all pidgins and creoles have lexical items from local languages which reflect the local culture. Pidgin languages are characterized by a simplification of the "superstrate" language and an admixture from native tongues.

4.2.1 In Butler English a number of Indian words occur in an otherwise English sentence. Some examples are:

> (servants) (1)...Yes first I be the cook's **meti** (= assistant domestic servant) then afterwards the **chokrα|** (=boy)... (2) I only looking garden – **mα|lι|** (=gardener) coming – (masters) (3)...I working in English **sahib** (=European gentleman). (4)...I work only for eh cook eh cook and bearer and **memsahib** (=the wife of a **sahib**) houses. (foods) (5) Only for the English **khα|nα|** (=food) I cooked very well. Because that **desi** (=indigenous) I don't know. (6)...Then he's eating nice meat – nice **biryα|nι|** (=dish of rice, cooked with meat and vegetables) – then all the roast – (7)...After I am put **kari** (=dish (of meat)) boiling...(8)...And he is come saying **α|lu|** (=potato) **matar** (=edible pea), **capα|tι|** (=small round of unleavened bread, baked on a griddle) in North India. (words related to daily chores) (9) In the Regimental **bazα|r** (=shopping area). He is working...(10) I give for Christmas **baksι|s** (=tip) for one HMT watch – one bottle whisky.

It will be seen that the Indian words designate servants and masters and relate to domestic duties like cooking. This is not surprising as servants (who spoke Indian languages) were naturally familiar with the Indian elements which were in turn tolerated by the colonial master who had himself picked up a smattering of the Indian vocabulary. In an article in **Blackwood's Edinburgh Magazine** "The Anglo-Indian Tongue" (1877: 541) we have: "The mixture of English and native words...constitutes an idiom in the speech of the governing class, and really forms a bond of union between them and the governed."

But one can ask the question: "How did this mixture of English and native words originate?" This aspect is described in The **Anglo-Indian Tongue.** (1877: 543) "Strange to say, it must be held to have been initiated rather by natives than Englishmen. The Anglo-Indians, early in the last century, did not trouble themselves much about the oriental tongues. They might acquire a knowledge of Persian because it was the diplomatic language of the country, and intelligible to all educated Muhammadans; **but the vernaculars spoken by the people among whom they lived and traded were altogether neglected.**

To obviate the consequent inconvenience, **dubashes** or 'two-tongued men'" (=interpreters) arose – ... "who had picked up as much English as enabled them to become the medium of communication between the strangers and their countrymen. The stamp which these men left upon official writing and communication is by no means wholly effaced at the present day. It was by their agency that the bulk of the untranslated native expressions which give a character to the speech of Anglo-Indians was introduced into the English language. Although succeeding generations of Anglo-Indians became better orientalists, and the profession of interpreter fell into desuetude, men still adhered to the old phraseology of the **dubashes,** and went on adding to their vocabulary whenever they fell in with a word of more than ordinary aptness. Each branch of the public service has contributed its quota to the development of the Anglo-Indian tongue: the law and the courts are especially well represented; the army has introduced a large stock of phrases, which, however, are not so generally used outside military circles; but, above all, **intercourse with native servants has produced the most expressive and remarkable terms in the glossary.**"

4.2.2 Some examples from Atlantic and Pacific Pidgin and Creole Englishes (Todd, 1974) are:

> (Atlantic) (1) akara (=beancake) (2) mboma (=boa constrictor) (3) mukala (=whiteman) (4) ngOmbi (=spirit).
>
> (Pacific) (1) balus (=bird/pigeon) (2) kapul (=tree kangaroo) (3) mbambu (=mother's brother's son) (4) ngambwa (=spirit).

These lexical items, from local languages not unexpectedly, relate to local culture and conditions.

4.2.3 In Tây Bôi, the Pidgin French of Vietnam, (Reinecke, 1971) most of the Vietnamese words are names of foods and plants, or of distinctive features of Vietnamese life. A few are onomatopoeic names of animals, such as **mèo** (=cat).

4.3 All English pidgins and creoles make use of some Portuguese words. (Todd, 1974: 15) They vary from a few per cent in most cases to approximately thirty per cent in Saramaccan a Surinam Creole. All

Pidgin and Creole Englishes, for example, possess a form of **saber** (=know) and of **pequeno** (=little / offspring).

4.3.1 Some examples from Butler English are:

(1) Yes **bearer** (=waiter/domestic servant)...afterwards the **bearer**.

The term perhaps originated in the habit of the early Europeans of employing their palanquin bearers as personal servants: English "palanquin" from Portuguese **palanquim** from Hindustani **pα|lki|**. (Schuchardt, 1891: 41-42) Although "bearer" has come into Indo-English via English it is classified with words of Portuguese origin as in meaning it is closely connected with "boy."

(2) ...I come for ball–**boy** (=male domestic servant)...

Yule and Burnell also define "boy" as "servant." I quote: "In Southern India and in China a native personal servant is so termed, and is habitually summoned with the vocative 'Boy.' The same was formerly common in Jamaica and other West Indian Islands... The word, however, came to be especially used for 'Slave-boy' and applied to slaves of any age. **The Portuguese used moco in the same way. In 'Pigeon English' also 'servant' is 'Boy,'** whilst 'boy' in our ordinary sense is discriminated as 'smallo-boy'!" (1968: 109-110)

Boy "A palankin–bearer" relates to the name of the caste, Telugu and Malayalam **boyi**; Tamil **bovi**. Wilson gives **bhoi** as Hindustani and Marathi also (as quoted in Yule and Burnell, 1966: 50)

An excerpt illustrating the use of the word is:

"Yes, Sahib, I Christian **Boy**. Plenty **poojah** do. Sunday time never no work do." (Yule and Burnell, 1968: 110)

Schuchardt gives supporting evidence, when he notes that the Indo-English word "boy" is modelled on Portuguese **moco** "boy/servant" and has come to mean in India any kind of servant. "There is also Hindustani **bhoi** or **bhu|ι|**... **'palanquin bearer.'** (This is the origin of **boi** 'parasol bearer' of the Indo-Portuguese, who as early as the sixteenth century, used not merely **bo|y do sombreiro**, but also **bo|y d'agua**). In the latter sense, one can say either 'boy' or 'palanquin boy'." (1891: 43)

(3) ...They are keeping one butler, cook, car driver and **ayah** (=nanny/ female servant)...

Yule and Burnell give a more detailed gloss: "A native lady's–maid or nurse-maid. The word has been adopted into most of the Indian vernaculars in the forms **α|ya** or **α|yα|**, but it is really Portuguese. (f. **aia** 'a nurse, or governess;' m. **aio** 'the governor of a young noble')." (1966: 22)

(4) Small boy. **ammα|** (=madam) know also.

It is very probable that **ammaǀ** is a semantic extension of the Portuguese **amah** – "wet–nurse." (Oxford Dictionary (OD), 1979: 689) In India its range of meaning extends from "mother" (=term denoting kinship) → general term of respect → "madam" (=term of address).

Yule and Burnell define **amah** as "a wet nurse; used in Madras, Bombay, China and Japan." It is Portuguese **ama.** (1966: 9)

Whitworth relates **amah** to the Marathi **αǀma** "the breast." "A term used in Anglo-Indian nurseries for wet-nurse." (1976: 11)

Two more words of Portuguese origin which were used very often throughout the text were **brinjal** and **almirah**.

(5) Cut all the **brinjal** (=edible fruit of the egg-plant) small small...

The word in Portuguese is **beringela, bringiela, bringella.**

(6) ...And keep in my **almirah** (=ward-robe/cupboard)...

Yule and Burnell note that the word is in general use, by masters and servants in Anglo-Indian households, in both North and South India. It has come to us from the Portuguese **almario,** and in Hindustani has become **almari** – "a wardrobe, chest of drawers, or like piece of (closed) furniture." (1966: 9)

4.3.2 Schuchardt maintains that Portuguese is the fifth most frequent source of loans after Aryan, Dravidian, Persian, and Malay into the English spoken by the Indians. This is not surprising since the Portuguese were "the first European rulers in India." (1891: 41)

In our examples (see 4.2.1) the languages which have served as sources are chiefly the indigenous languages of India, both Aryan and Dravidian – especially Hindustani. Also making a contribution are Asian languages (Arabic) followed by Portuguese, as mentioned by Schuchardt. As for parts of speech, nouns make up the majority – followed by adjectives.

4.4 Compounding is a device by which the vocabulary of pidgins is increased. Butler English too combines a number of lexical items with other lexical items to form compounds. The compound may have more than two parts. The parts are usually words and can be taken both from English (English Compounds), both from Indian languages (Indian Compounds) or one from English and the other from Indian language(s) (Hybrid Compounds). If the compound is Indian it is marked by the letter (1); if Hybrid, by the letter (H).

4.4.1 Some examples from Butler English are:

(English Compounds) wine-waiter, room-waiter, glass-cleaner, plate-washer, special-cook, soup-cook, travelling-cook, squash-marker, billiard-marker, tennis-picker.

(Indian Compounds) **Monda** (=the name of a market in Hyderabad) **ku|li|** (Hybrid Compounds) **varEndα|** (=open roofed portico) – boy, **paŋkhα|** (=fan) – boy, house-boy, telephone-boy, ball-boy, lady-**ayah** (=female servant), cook–**ayah**.

The above is by no means a comprehensive list: it excludes a host of servants who are named after the multifarious duties they are expected to perform.

The following passages are cited as they are singularly striking examples of the use of compounds in context.

(1) Yes ma'am. Small the boy is coming here – that tennis-boy. Start is the tennis-boy. Tennis-boy to the bar-boy – bar-boy to that coffee-room-boy – coffee-room–boy to plate-**meti** (=assistant domestic servant) – plate-**meti** to silver-**meti** – that working.

(2) Butler and in starting small work. Running-boy; tennis-boy; **paŋkhα|**-boy. After I start butler second-boy; dressing-boy.

A number of compounds are formed by using **sahib** (=master/lord) as a general title and suffixing it to names; **Bakshi sahib** (I), **Dr. Mahadevan sahib** (I), titles of men of rank; **rα|jα|** (=Indian prince) **sahib** (I), or to official titles; **colonel–sahib** (H), **court–master sahib** (H).

sahibah (=mistress/lady) performs a similar function.

The same is true of other lexical items used as terms of address.

Pattison master (E); **Bharatpur mα|harα|jα|** (I), **Safir begam** (I) (=lady of high rank); **Hosali master** (H).

I mention the lexical item **kari** (=a dish cooked with bruised spices and turmeric and usually served with rice), because in combination with other lexical items it has produced many compounds.

dα| (=soup made from split peas) **kari** (I), **masα|lα|** (=spices) **kari** (I), **meat kari** (H), **mutton kari** (H), **chicken kari** (H).

4.4.2 Compounds have been catalogued on the basis of syntactic similarity. The alternative approach of cataloguing compounds on the basis of the semantic relations which obtain among their components would suggest a slight re-arrangement in classification.

I illustrate the point with some examples. (a) **head-bearer** (b) **second-bearer** (c) **dining-bearer** (d) **glass-bearer** and (e) **service-bearer** while displaying surface similarity are semantically dissimilar. In (a) and (b) the first element denotes the rank of the bearer: one is "head" or "chief" (he does not serve that part of our anatomy termed "a head") while the other is "second in command." In (c), (d) and (e) no rank is indicated: a **dining-bearer** is one who "serves in a dining-room;" a **glass-bearer** one who "cleans/serves glasses" and a **service-bearer** one who generally "serves."

4.4.3 A number of compounds are the direct result of nouns being juxtaposed without the possessive suffix:

> butler work, butler job, bearer work, bearer job, waiter job, cook work, **chokrα|** (=boy) job, **ayah** job.

Although the ordinary pidgin language has 700/1500 words compared to other languages' stock of 20,000/25,000, pidgin vocabularies are not poor. Scarcity of individual words is counterbalanced by a wealth of combinations into which they may enter.

4.4.4 Some examples of compound words from Atlantic and Pacific Pidgin and Creole Englishes (Todd, 1974) are:

> (Atlantic) (1) bushbif (=bush+beef) wild animal/game (2) daiman (=die+man) corpse (3) bigai (=big+eye) greed/greedy (4) taifes (=tie+face) frown.
>
> (Pacific) (1)bigsonde (=big+Sunday) feast day (2) bushnaif (=bush+knife) strong knife (3) draibon (=dry+bone) tough (4) klaudibrok (=cloud+broke) thunder/cloudburst.

Different items are combined from the pidgin either on the analogy of English patterns or in direct translations from the mother tongues.

4.5 Although pidgin languages have an inadequate lexicon when compared with other languages, pidgin speakers are conversant with certain registers (or occupational varieties) – here **the register of the kitchen** – for those who live under what Tennyson calls the sooty yoke of kitchen vassalage, and whose job it is to serve dinners of six, eight or even ten courses must be familiar with the **names** of the endless succession of items they are called upon to prepare and serve.

4.5.1 Some of the names used by butlers are given below:

> (drinks) brandy, whisky, gin and lime cordial, vodka, Bloody Mary, Tom Collins, Rumbullion, brandypawnee, punch.

Bloody Mary was the nickname of Mary 1, queen of England (1558), notorious for her persecution of Protestants. (The drink has a red colour because of the addition of tomato juice). (Websters International Dictionary (WID), 1961: 238)

Rumbullion (obsolete Rum) and an alternative form of Rum-bowling is also known as Grog. Old Grog was the nickname of Edward Vernon (1757), an English admiral who ordered the sailor's rum to be diluted. Grog, short for grogram, referred to his habit of wearing a grogram cloak in bad weather. (WID, 1961: 1001)

Brandypawnee is brandy + **pα|ni|** (=water) (OD, 1979: 711) and punch, a drink of five ingredients from **pα|nc** (=five). (Punch, of course, has long since lost its Indian association).

It was Ude (as quoted in Turner, 1963: 156) who voiced the noble thought that "man will raise cookery to the class of the sciences and its professors will be **Artists**, not servants." Our "artists" name some of the dishes they make to perfection.

(soups) chicken sweet corn, minestrone, Scotch broth, American soup, consomme.

(chicken) chicken paprika, chicken cacciatore, chicken a la king, chicken au gratin, chicken mayonnaise.

(mutton) chops, mutton cutlet, mutton roast, vindaloo.

(fish) fried fish, fish mayonnaise, fish au gratin, fish macaroni.

(roasted meats) turkey roast, duck roast, beef roast.

(steak) hamburger steak, billiard steak, Salisbury steak.

(stew) Irish stew, brown stew.

(sauce) white sauce, tomato sauce, tartar sauce, soya-bean sauce, minus sauce (=mayonnaise sauce).

(dessert) lemon souffle, coffee souffle, chocolate souffle, caramel custard, chocolate pastry, cake.

(teas) Indian tea, English tea, lemon tea, mixed tea.

4.5.2 Apart from "English khα|nα|" made in the "British style" butlers are equally familiar with "Mughlai dishes" made in the "Mughlai style;" and the ingredients that go into the making of both types of foods.

(vegetables) carrot, beans, turnips, radish, onions, tomatoes, capsicum, green peas, celery, parsley.

(powders) chilly powder, **haldi** (= turmeric) powder, mustard powder, yellow powder, jelly powder.

4.5.3 Terminology to express the various processes that are involved in cooking is not lacking.

make, boil, pour, cut, mix, set, mould, cover, grind, fry, mince, bake, garnish, mash, add, beat, clean, pound, soak, brown.

We can conclude that Butler English has a large repertoire of words restricted to certain registers for pidgin languages like Cinderella are relegated to the scullery and the kitchen.

4.6 One word denoting a wide range of meanings is a feature characteristic of pidgins.

4.6.1 Some examples from Butler English are:

do: (=make) ...I doing only toast... Omelette eh I do very nice. ...I can do...caramel custard.

put: ...putting (=casting) vote ma that vote I'm putting there. How can you put (=lay) table – fruits – put (=cut) it to pieces... – put (=make) all the beds... Is putting (=giving) money.

long: I long (=tall) that's why they calling **lambu** | Tirupal. ...Very far long (=high) up...

many: (=much) ...then asking madam how many tea – how many milk, how many sugar... That's all.

4.6.2 Some examples from Melanesian Pidgin (Hall, 1955) are: **papa** (=father/mother's brother). If one needs to distinguish, however, the physical progenitor can be referred to as **papa tru** (=real father) and the mother's brother as **smolpapa.**

Wairles (=wireless) connotes the fact that speech is being received without any visible means of transmission and so the word was applied to other similar situations which involve secret or underhanded talk. So **tok wairles** (=gossip). **Em i-tok wairles long mi** (=he is conducting a whispering campaign against me).

4.6.3 Some examples from Tây Bôi (Reinecke, 1971) are:

peau (=skin/bark); manger (=eat/bite).

4.6.4 Some examples from Korean Bamboo English (source unknown) are:

skoshi (=few/ little); ketchee (= get/ take /have); taksan (=much / many/ large).

4.7. As pidgin languages have a smaller vocabulary when compared with other languages, particular lexical items are overused.

Studies of languages have revealed that the one preposition (=structural word) to be retained when all others are omitted is **of.** In pidgin languages, however, the overworked preposition is **for.** (Personal communication, Corder, 1982)

4.7.1 Some examples from Butler English are:

(1) I'm teaching here **for** service **for** between seventeen years **for** service **for** Madras. British High Commissioner **for** twelve years. That I'll come **for** Mangalorkar two years. Now. (2) Make **for** first one make custard. After **for** mix it up in gelatine, keep some five minute, ten minute on the fridge – after white eggs **for** beating –

Want is another overused lexical item.

... **want** to the carry the club...and **want** to go ....we **want** to carry...we **want** to give... we **want** to take... – and **want** to arrange – we **want** to do...**want** to watch the ball... – **want** to show... – then you **want** to watch... – again he **want** to go ... you **want** to work with him...

In this example **want** (=has/ have).

4.7.2 In Melanesian Pidgin (Hall, 1955) English **screw**: referring not only to the metal object that holds two pieces of wood together, but to anything which acts as a joint.

So **skru** bilong arm (=elbow) and **skru** bilong leg (=knee).

English **grass** appears as **gras,** referring not only to the green plant which grows up out of the ground, but to anything which grows outward in blade–like shape.

So **gras** bilong hed (=hair) and **gras** bilong maus (=beard).

Again **bilong** is an overused lexical item in phrases such as:

haus **bilong** mi (=house of me / my house); singsing **bilong** lotu (=song for worship / hymn).

4.7.3 In Beach La Mar (source unknown) **belonga** is used in phrases such as:

diss **belonga** master (=master's dishes); hands **belonga** you (=your hands); clothes **belonga** essepoon (=napkin).

4.7.4 Korean Bamboo English (source unknown) uses numbers in a special sense:

number one (=the best); number five (=mediocre); number ten (=the worst).

4.8 Neologisms occur in pidgin languages as they do in other languages.

4.8.1 "Butlerian" users of English have been very productive in coining new English words: they are particularly fond of neologistic creations using the suffix **time**.

Some examples are:

English time, British time, morning time, evening time, night time, Easter time, marriage time, election time, dressing-boy time.

4.8.2 This capacity to coin new words is especially evident in word compounding (see 4.4.1 – 4.4.3) **many** of which are striking examples of the propensity of speakers to condense into compound noun phrases (presumably for reasons of brevity) what speakers of standard Indian English would communicate by a clause or a phrase of greater length.

4.8.3 Creativity is revealed in the following passage.

...I am going some hotels also. Any **beach time** Tank bund. Very **enjoysome** there. From here I'm working is eh **one-self boss**. There is not boss. For me only boss.

Beach time is a neologistic creation with **time** probably on the analogy of "playtime;" and **enjoysome** (=enjoyable) a neologistic creation on the analogy of "troublesome." **One-self boss** (=my own boss).

Other analogical creations formed by the suffixation of **-ly** are:

straightly (=straight), **goodly** (=well), **troubly** (=trouble):

formed on the analogy of words like "nicely, rightly, wrongly."

Also used were **simmerer** (=to simmer) on the analogy of "to bake → baker" and "to cook → cooker."

> ...keep it **simmerer**;

and **eggsy** on the analogy of "mixie."

> ...eggs will be done in the **eggsy**...

These neologisms are instances of the expansion of rules, whereby a suffix is added to a word (often on the analogy of another word) to which it would not normally be suffixed in standard Indian English.

4.8.4 For examples of Melanesian Pidgin, Beach la Mar and Korean Bamboo English (see 4.6.2 – 4.6.4; 4.7.2 – 4.7.4).

4.8.5 Butlers also took recourse to onomatopoeia (=the formation of words in imitation of the sounds associated with the thing concerned) as **ha| ha|** for "asthma."

> This **ha| ha|** taking no this very young age;

and **dhum dhum** for "rain."

> Rain coming sir, rekulu (=tin roof) **dhum dhum** sir.

4.9 Many idiomatic expressions (exemplifying the butler's innovative powers) characterize Butler English. Wherever they can be attributed to Indo-Aryan/ Dravidian languages the expressions in these languages are given.

> (1) I am **give temper** (=season it with) from onions...

(Hindi) **ta|rka| / bagha|r do / choyk** (=season give). One meaning of **temper**(v) is to "bring (e.g.) clay to the required condition by moistening, mixing, kneading, etc." (Advanced Learner's Dictionary (ALD), 1974:906) Perhaps butler John has this in mind when he uses **temper** here.

> (2) **Real** brother.

In all Dravidian languages **svanta** (=own) is used in expressions such as the one given above.

> (3) See I cannot do to say **my my my mouth...**

(Tamil) **va|yile cola mudiya|du**

(Kannada) **ba|yali helalikke barodila|/a|godila|** (=mouth say cannot).

Ingenuity in coining new words/idioms (which may have their roots in Indian languages) is a pidgin speaker's forte by means of which he extends the pidgin's limited vocabulary.

4.9.1 Tây Bôi, the Pidgin French of Vietnam (Reinecke, 1971) is a literal translation of Vietnamese.

Tôi di chō (=moi aller marché) (=I go to the market).

But the French words, which translate Vietnamese particles of time and place often do **not** follow the same order.

Tôi sɛ~di (=I subsequent-time go) (=moi aller ce soir) (=I go this evening).

4.10 One of the striking characteristics of pidgins is iteration or reduplication. Standard European languages also can and do duplicate forms, but not as extensively or as systematically as any of the pidgins and creoles. In English iteratives of the rhyming type are found in phrases such as "razzle-dazzle, hoity-toity," and of the ablaut type in "ding-dong." Such iteratives, which are forms of semi-duplication are quite rare in pidgin, though instances of their use have been recorded. The common pidgin type is total iteration or duplication which is represented in standard English by only a few combinations like the "choo–choo train" and the "go–go girl." Duplication occurs in baby–talk too: "naughty-naughty."

The high frequency of reduplication of items is usually a South Asian English marker. The reason for this reduplication is attributed to the underlying structure of these languages. Passé gives the following examples from Sri Lankan English showing the transfer from Sinhalese: **punci punci keeli** (=to cut into small, small pieces); **unu unu** (=to eat something hot, hot); **hemin hemin** (=to proceed slowly, slowly); **andaa andaa yanavaa** (=to go crying, crying); **monava monava** (=what and what did he say?); **kavuda kavuda** (=who and who came to the party?). (quoted in Kachru, 1969: 653)

In Indian languages (such as Hindi) reduplicated adjectives either have an intensive or a distributive meaning. (Kachru, 1980: 76) Some examples are **lα|l lα|l sa|rϕi|** (=very red saree); **hare hare pepϕ** (=green trees); **bapϕe bapϕe maka|n** (=big houses). The affix **sa|** **or si|** added to colour adjectives signals diminished quality: **la| l-si| sα|rϕi** (=reddish saree). Added to other adjectives it signals intensive meaning: **barϕa|-sa| maka|n** (=very big house); **caurϕi|-si| sarϕak** (=very wide road).

Semi–duplication (which is nonsensical) such as **kha|na| va|na|; da|l va|l; biskit viskit** also occurs.

Some examples of reduplication of items from Indian languages (in my data) are:

Hindi **konsa konsa** (=which which); Kannada **salpa salpa** (=little little); Tamil **volupa volupa** (=loudly loudly).

As all languages make use of this mechanism we see that in the past reduplication was given undue prominence as a feature of pidgins and creoles. In their use of reduplication pidgins and creoles differ from

English only in **degree** rather than in having introduced an entirely new method of qualifying meanings.

4.10.1 The following exemplify the widespread use of reduplication in Butler English.

> **Big big** hotel that... **Different, different**... – only **little little** house upstairs... English is **little little**... **Small small** childrens... Cut all the brinjal **small small**... **Little little** piece...**little little** slowly fry it – ...just now I make **soon soon**...

Although any part of speech can be reduplicated, the adjectives little and small occurred most frequently in reduplicated form. In the examples given, the standard language would prefer to strengthen adjectives and adverbs by means of intensifying adverbs such as **very**.

Other examples of reduplication with the meaning of "a lot" were:

> ...take the white and **beat it. Beat it, beat it** ...then both getting **fight, fight, fight, fight**... –the woman worried, **worry, worry** –

Still other reduplicated forms meaning "every" were:

> ...**Saturday Saturday** I go...**Tuesday Tuesday** I'll go there.

Reduplication is used for plurals:

> –keep it piece – small **piece piece piece** (=small pieces) and diamond cut –

4.10.2 Semi–duplications of the rhyming type were:

> linen ginen, bed ged, tip gip, Desai gesai, breakage greakage, book gook, party varty, feed geed, meeting geeting.

4.10.3 A hybrid semi–duplication with one element from English and another from Hindi was:

> ...Half loan giving, half taking **half ma|f** (=forgiven).

4.10.4 Some duplication appeared to be hesitation phenomena.

> ...that top top tea–pot eh tea–pot...Last last last last not not sir last year last June.

4.10.5 Some examples from Atlantic and Pacific Pidgin and Creole Englishes (Todd, 1974) are:

> (Atlantic) (1) san (=sun) sansan (=sand) (2) wan (=one) wanwan (=one by one) (3) fain (=lovely) fainfain (=very lovely).
>
> (Pacific) (1) sip (=ship) sipsip (=sheep) (2) sing (=sing) singsing (=ritual singing) (3) bik (=big) bikbik (= very big).

Reduplications reduce the number of homophonous forms as in (1); extend the meaning of the simple form as in (2); and intensify: this type being confined to the adjective/verb class as in (3).

4.10.6 Worth recording is an example from Cameroon, where an old man, lamenting the fact that his wife was perpetually scolding, exclaimed:

> **ene dei ene dei soso miamia** (=any day any day so so nagging).

4.10.7 Examples of reduplication from Jamaican Creole (source unknown) are:

> (nouns) fufu (=mashed starch - vegetables: Yam etc.); nyam nyam (=food / flesh / meat). (adjectives) fool fool (=foolish); wee wee (=very small).
>
> (verbs) talky talky (=to talk a lot); shi shi (=to drive away).

4.10.8 Examples of reduplication from the story of Cinderella-san narrated in Korean Bamboo English (source unknown) are:

> Poor little Cinderella-san ketchee (=have) no fun, hava-no social life. Always **washee-washee** (=washing), **scrubee-scrubee** (=scrubbing), make **chop-chop** (=food)... **shine-shine** (=polish) boots.

4.11 Butler English has stylistic limitations and a reduction of options, which is a feature of pidgins. Consequently syntactic duplication occurs.

(1) I told ma – **separate tea, separate milk, separate sugar.** If he asking cup of tea, I put first tea then asking madam **how many tea – milk, how many sugar?** That's all.
(2) Ah **my life is very bad.** My life is eh **I playing too much card** – I eh **I'm going too much picture – I'm going too much race – horse race. My life is very bad...**
(3) Father does **house shoe making. House seeing.**
(4) Ah she already done so many problems for the **unemploy's problem** and **poor family's problem...agriculture problem – employee's problem.**

4.11.1 The style then in general is quite simple and straightforward. In earlier times, the normal European regarded the native as mentally less advanced than himself and incapable of following involved or complicated reasoning. Consequently there grew up, along with pidgin itself, the habit of making short, simple utterances, stopping and recapitulating often to make sure the hearer has understood, and then resuming the discourse with **achal** (=all right) in Butler English and with **orait** (=all right / very well) in Melanesian Pidgin – a style suited to both sides. As pidgin languages are mainly oral, words are spelt according to the way in which they are pronounced.

5. I conclude by saying that pidgins/creoles as repositories of man's innate "communicative competence," have proved themselves indispensable in socio–historical contexts. The study of these linguistically poor relations of the great language families, bred in harsh

and limiting conditions, may yet have much to tell us about the nature of human interaction – from the first halting attempts at communication to the ultimate recognition of a shared identity.

REFERENCES

Anglo-Indian tongue, The. May 1877. *Blackwood's Edinburgh Magazine*. 121:739. 541-551.

Bailey, B.L. 1971. Jamaican Creole. (Can dialect boundaries be defined?) In D. Hymes (ed.) *Pidginization and creolization of languages*. Cambridge: Cambridge University Press. 341-348.

Hall, R.A. Jr. 1955. *Hands off Pidgin English!* Sydney: Pacific Publications Pty. Ltd.

Hosali, P. 2000. *Butler English: Form and function*. Delhi: B.R. Publishing Corporation.

Hosali, P. 2000. *Communication and grammar: From pigeons to pidgins*. Hyderabad: Central Institute of English and Foreign Languages.

Kachru, B.B. 1969. English in South Asia. In T.A. Sebeok (ed.) *Current trends in linguistics*. 5. The Hague: Mouton. 627-678.

Kachru, Y. 1980. *Aspects of Hindi grammar*. Delhi: Manohar.

Mühlhäusler, P. 1978. *Pidginization and simplification of language*. Canberra: The Australian National University.

Reinecke, J.E. 1964. Trade jargons and creole dialects as marginal languages. In D. Hymes (ed.) *Language in culture and society*. New York, Evanston and London: Harper and Row. 534-546.

Reinecke, J.E. 1971. Tây Bồi: notes on the Pidgin French of Vietnam. *Pidginization and creolization of languages*, D. Hymes (ed.) Cambridge: Cambridge University Press. 47-56.

Schuchardt, H. 1891. Indo-English. *Pidgin and creole languages (selected essays by H. Schuchardt)*. G.G. Gilbert. (ed.) 1980. New York: Cambridge University Press. 38-64.

Todd, L. 1974. *Pidgins and creoles*. London and Boston: Routledge and Kegan Paul.

Turner, E.S. 1963. *What the butler saw. (Two hundred and fifty years of the servant problem)*. Great Britain: Unwin Brothers Ltd.

Whitworth, G.C. 1885 (reprint) 1976. *An Anglo-Indian dictionary: a glossary of Indian terms used in English, and of such English or other non-Indian terms as have obtained special meanings in India*. Delhi: Indian Documentation Service. Yule, H. and A.C. Burnell. 1886. Yule, H. and A.C. Burnell (second edition) 1903. (new edition ed. W. Crooke) 1968. *Hobson-Jobson: a glossary of colloquial Anglo-Indian words and phrases, and of kindred terms, etymological, historical, geographical and discursive*. Delhi: Munshiram Manoharlal.

Yule, H. and A.C.Burnell. 1966. *Dictionary of Indian English*, ed. G.B.T. Kurian. Madras: Indian Universities Press.

35

Globalization and English Language in India: An Overview

Raj Nath Bhat

Prologue

The word 'global' is over 400 years old but it became a common usage in such words as 'globalization', 'globalizing', 'globalize' only in the 1960s.

Giddens (1990: 64) defines globalization as "the intensification of worldwide social relations which link distant localities in such a way that local happenings are shaped by events occurring many miles away and vice-versa." Robertson (1992: 8) defines globalization "as a concept that refers both to the compression of the world and the intensification of consciousness of the world as a whole...both concrete global interdependence and consciousness of the global whole."

The world of scholarship is divided into there 'camps' with regard to the phenomenon called globalization : i) *hyperglobalists*- who believe that globalization indicates progress and that it is essentially 'done' or at best 'in progress' (at a rapid pace); ii) *skeptics*- who hold that it is the new form of (American) imperialism that crushes local creativity and cultural identities through market forces, goods, foods, icons, and above all, language (for instance, Phillipson, 1992); iii) *faithful-optimists*- who propose that globalization is a complicated phenomenon that cannot be considered either benign or evil (Pennycook, 1994; Canagarajah,1999).

Similarly there are differing views regarding the origins of globalization. According to some it began in the fifteenth century with the expansion of European countries across the globe. Some others consider it a post-Second World war phenomenon that weakened Europe and hastened the process of decolonization on the one hand, and allowed the USA to assume the status of a world power, on the other. Amartya Sen (2005), however, argues that globalization has been there in varying measures in all periods of known history. Says he: "I would argue that globalization, in its basic form, is neither particularly new, nor, in general, a folly. It is through global movements of ideas, people, goods, and technology that different regions of the world have tended, in general, to benefit from progress and development occurring in other regions...Around 1000 CE, globalization of science, technology and mathematics was changing the nature of the old world, even though, as it happens, the principal currents of dissemination then were typically in the opposite direction to what we see today...Europe would have been much poorer had it resisted the globalization of mathematics, science and technology at that time, and to a great extent the same - working in the converse direction - is true today...Through persistent movements of goods, people, techniques and ideas, it (globalization) has shaped the history of the world. India has been an integral part of the world in the most interactive sense" (345-7).

Significantly though, the phenomenon of the expansion of English as the sole global language is unprecedented. The shocked but optimistic thinking minds of Europe put forward the proposals for building an international language towards the end of the 'Great War'. Ogden (1944: 171) remarked: 'What makes a nation is a common language. What will make men international, will be a common language.' In his Basic English project, Ogden (1944: 9) believed that "it would be possible 'to say almost everything we normally desire to say' with just 850 English words if these were 'scientifically selected'. The intention was that this 'scientifically' reduced form of English should become an international auxiliary language. This proposal was supported politically by the British wartime premier, Winston Churchill". (Harris, 2003: 207-08).

Harris further observes: "Ogden, one of Saussure's trenchant critics, seems to have seized on two of Saussure's ideas and made them the theoretical point of departure for Basic English project. The first idea was that a language (*langue*) both provides and interconnects all the concepts its users need for analytic thought, and the second was that, because of the structure of the system, if one word were removed from the vocabulary, the effect would be to 'redistribute' its meaning over neighbouring words... Although as a socialist Orwell (1944: 108) welcomed in principle the idea of an international language, he also found the notion of promoting one's own national language for the purpose imperialistic...Four years after the end of the 2nd World War, George Orwell published his (celebrated) novel *Nineteen Eighty Four*, with its chilling vision of a future in which systematic mind-control would be exercised through systematic (*Newspeak*) language-control".

Today one can only assess the impact that English expansion has made on the world of scholarship. The upwardly mobile social classes across the globe consider a person educated if s/he has the capacity to use English. Consequently, scholars like Kachru (1988) divide the world into three *'circles'*- the *'inner'*-where English is the first language of the majorities like the USA, England, Australia, Canada etc.; the *'outer'*- the former British colonies like India, Singapore, South Africa, etc.; and the *'expanding'* - Eastern Europe, China, Japan etc. where English is expanding at a fast pace.

English in India: The Initial Phase

The first English word was probably heard/uttered in India way back in the sixteenth century much before the merchants of London formed the East India Company. Mesthrie and Bhatt (2008: 13-15) call it "the third crossing of English.[1] Kachru (1983: 19-21) identifies three stages in which English was introduced in the sub-continent: i) a missionary phase that began around 1614; ii) a phase of 'local demand' from leaders; and iii) the educational phase that began in 1765 with formal colonization. English became the language of the Supreme Court at Calcutta (now Kolkata) in 1776 but its official teaching began in the first quarter of the nineteenth century[2]. Although missionaries and several Europeans including non-natives, had begun to teach the language to 'interested' Indians much earlier yet, during the first quarter of the nineteenth century, British administrators in India were divided in their opinion regarding introduction of English on a large scale.

In 1853, arguing in favor of establishing universities in India, Charles Hay Cameron (the then, President Law Commission, & President Council of Education for Bengal) in his address to the British Parliament on 'The Duties of Great Britain to India in respect of the Education of the Natives', said : "India with an indigenous literature, which is thought to have received its highest polish from the hand of Kālidāsa, about the time when Virgil was performing in the Georgics the same process with the language of Rome... No scholar, no man who reverences antiquity, no man who rejoices to recognise in his own mind an inheritance of thought and feeling derived to him through many centuries, and which the stream of time has gradually augmented by successive alluvions would willingly give his assent to the doctrine that patriotism requires us to prevent the descendants of those who in the first century of our era illustrated in the literary court of Vikramaditya, from acquiring all the knowledge that we possess, and from developing under that potent stimulus all the talent or genius which may exist in themselves."

"What I am asking is the establishment of Universities in India, (not only to educate the natives, and give them European knowledge to which must attach power, and give them European ideas, but at the same time to raise them in the Civil Service), with a declaration that the natives honoured with their degrees will be admitted to offices from which natives are now practically excluded."[3]

Eventually, the M.A. Course in English literature began in India in 1858 barely a year after it was introduced in Great Britain. But the syllabi largely laid emphasis on Elizabethan and Romantic texts that had to be analyzed through "received critical opinion" (Agnihotri & Khanna, 1995: 14). The high-stationed and a few mid-stationed found themselves empowered with a degree in the new language but the low-stationed continued to be unlettered. (However, women of all strata were deprived of English education during a larger part of the Nineteenth century).

The Outcome

A couple of decades later, the first generation of university educated Indians with a creative talent began to write English fiction demonstrating the birth of a class of individuals English in thought and '*un*-white' in color. The '*language-powered*' elite began to seek recognition, status and comforts; he considered himself nearly equal to the English but far too superior to the powerless native. Around this period a District Commissioner observed: (Earlier) "we had to take account of local nationalities and particular races. The resentment of the Marathas did not involve that of the Bengalese. (The situation is different now). We ...are beginning to find ourselves face to face, not with the population of individual provinces, but with 200 millions people united by sympathies and intercourse which we have ourselves created and fostered." (cf. Seal, 140). In 1830s, a member in the council of Governor Elphinston of the Bombay Presidency had opposed teaching of English in India on these very grounds.

During the freedom struggle the Indian leaders, like Gandhi, Bose, Gokhale, Azad, Nehru, Raja Gopalacharya and so on, from various linguistic backgrounds could get together and communicate among themselves through English. They could argue with the colonial masters as well in his language.

Decolonization and English

The pre-independence political leaders in India considered English as the language of *Satan* that deserved to be dwarfed to whatever extent possible. But the language riots in different parts of the country and also the realization that it was impossible to equip the youth with scientific and technological knowledge without English encouraged them to have a second look at the issue and English eventually came to occupy a place of pride in education, administration, and judiciary. The elite across the country had already extended power and prestige to English. The political endorsement for continuation of English further strengthened their position resulting in causing a social divide between the English-educated and English-less people in the country (Agnihotri & Khanna, p. 15).[4]

A similar situation obtained on the African continent where the indigenous languages were ill-prepared to replace English/French in the erstwhile colonies. According to Said (1993: 167-174), Fanon believed that "unless national consciousness at its moment of success was somehow changed into a social consciousness, the future would hold not liberation but an extension of imperialism. Throughout *The Wretched of the earth*, Fanon wants somehow to bind the European as well as the native together in a new non-adversarial community of awareness and anti-imperialism". Language certainly has the power to bind peoples of differing cultural hues and traditions together; it builds bridges of understanding and friendship; provided there is a desire to appreciate 'other's' point of view.[5]

Evidently, the new rulers in multilingual, multi-religious, multi-ethnic nation-states were ill-prepared to face the linguistic-challenge. A shift to an indigenous language would have uprooted a vast majority of the elite who had their own agendas and 'programmes'. Multilinguality turned out to be a serious barrier to a switch over to native languages, benefiting English whose expansion was ensured. Shreesh Chaudhary (2001) aptly remarks: "In 1857, the mutinous sepoys had captured the telegraph system, but could not use it. They had no language to link Kamptee with Kanpur, the two main centres of mutiny. Today English links Kohima, on the North-East border of India, with Kochin, on its South-West Coast, though their languages and cultures are more different than are those of Manchester, Madrid, Munich and Moscow. English holds whatever remains of India together. Today English is India's obsession number one (number two is secularism). For many here, education is synonymous with English (*Englis for many).* English is their best bet for a good career... Forty years ago there were only three English medium schools in Bihar, the second most populous state in India. Now there is one even in my village, in Bihar, which is yet to have electricity, telephone, hospital, or an all-weather road".

Contemporary Scenario

Legislation, riots, lockouts, etc. notwithstanding, English is the main official language of the union government and of many states. It is the medium of education at national institutions for arts, law, polity, science, technology, medicine, business and commerce. Over 400 million Indians use English in their daily lives. India is the third largest publisher and one of the largest buyers of English books. Even the so called English Hatao agitators have fallen silent on the issue; on the contrary those who removed English from the curriculum or delayed its introduction to the post-primary stage have, on a second thought, enforced it from the primary stage!

The advancements in and expansion of computer technology (*almost coinciding with the disintegration of the former Soviet union*) has given additional strength to English language to make inroads into domains where it was earlier less 'intrusive'. Internet, e-mail, software technology, e-conferencing, e-governance, mobile (cell) phone, and other technologies associated with communication and computer engineering have given an edge to English over other languages and it is expanding at a rapid pace. Eighty percent of 'digital information' is now stored in English and the job is accomplished by professionals from various linguistic backgrounds including those from India. It is estimated that nearly 1.3 billion people will speak English as a first or second language by 2050; more than 40% of them may be Indians.

In India, the generation that is comfortable with English is strongly in favor of Indianization of English curriculum. It proposes that 'Bhasha' literatures (*'authentic creations'*) in translation and Indian-English writings (*'adjunct creations'*) as well as Indian literary theories be taught from school to the university. They argue that 'Bhasha' literatures in particular (and some Indian-English writers too) represent our socio-cultural moorings and values that are easily comprehensible and analyzable, India has a rich and long tradition both in aesthetics and linguistics which has enriched the western thought a great deal (like Sir William Jones, Max Muller, Saussure, Bloomfield, Eliot, Chomsky, to name but a few); but we on our own continue to ignore or denigrate our ancestral scholarly heritage. Dasgupta (1993) forcefully argues that English is a 'loan language' and that 'we need to relativize our English studies to our Indian studies'. The world outside deserves to know about our traditions, culture and creative abilities which can be achieved only through translation. Hence, there is a need to shift to a curriculum that represents India and Indians.[6] Also there are voices that argue that English is a forceful agent of decolonization that enables the marginalized and peripheral sections of (urban) India to access the global economy. They argue that this is a progressive shift where the disenfranchised and the 'subalternaized' groups have been able to gain access to linguistic capital (Vaish, 2005).

Today India has several thousand trained professionals in English, some of who teach in the universities of Africa, Near East and elsewhere. Of late, French and German universities have begun to offer special graduate programmes through English to attract students from across the globe. India has a longer tradition in English teaching. She has been the pioneer in the arena of experimentation with ELT methods. Her capacity to attract students from Asia-Pacific, Africa, East Europe, Latin America, etc., if harnessed in right earnest, can make Indian universities richer and their educational programmes shall consequently become qualitative and competitive.

As of date, the future of English in India and the world stands unchallenged and the Indian higher education has the potential to make best from it. Indians in the years to come may man the celebrated institutions of learning across the globe. The contributions of the twentieth century *non-whites* have rarely been acknowledged in the English world of scholarship but the present century may prove to be another phase of 'Enlightenment'.

REFERENCES

Agnihotri, R.K. and A.L. Khanna (eds.) 1995. *English language teaching in India: Issues and innovations.* New Delhi: Sage.

Bradley, John H. 2003. *The power of scale: A global history approach.* M.E. Sharpe Publications.

Cameron, Charles Hay 1853. *The address to the British Parliament.* London: Longman, Brown, Green and Longmans.

Canagarajah, A.S. 1999. *Resisting linguistic imperialism in English teaching.* Oxford: Oxford University Press.

Chaudhary, Shreesh 2001. English takes India from Raj to riches. In the *Times Higher Education Supplement,* London, 23 March 2001, 20-21

Dasgupta, Probal 1993. *The otherness of English: India's aunty tongue syndrome.* New Delhi: Sage.

Giddens, A. 1990. *The consequences of modernity.* Cambridge: Polity Press.

Harris, Roy 2003. *Saussure and his interpreters.*Edinburgh: Edinburgh University Press.

Kachru, Braj B. (ed.) 1983. *The other tongue: English across cultures.* Oxford: Pergamon.

Kachru, Braj B. 1988. The sacred cows of English. *English Today* 16: 3-8.

Krishnamurthy, N. and L. Krishnamurthy 2006. *The story of English in India.* New Delhi: Foundation.

Mesthrie, R. and R.M. Bhatt 2008. *The world Englishes: The study of new linguistic varieties.* Cambridge: Cambridge University Press.

Patnaik, B.N. and S. Imtiaz Hasnain (eds.) 2006. *Globalization: Language, culture and media,* Simla: IIAS.

Pennycook, Alastair 1994. *The cultural politics of English as an international language.* London: Longman.
Phillipson, Robert 1992. *Linguistic imperialism.* Oxford: Oxford University Press.
Said, Edward W. 1994. *Culture and imperialism.* US: Vintage Books.
Seal, Anil 1971. *The emergence of Indian nationalism: Competition and collaboration in the later nineteenth century.* Cambridge: Cambridge University Press.
Sen, Amartya 2005. *The argumentative Indian.* Penguin.
Shankar, S. 'Bikne wala Sahitya' in *Bharatiya wangmay.* Dec. 2008.
Vaish, Vinita 2005. A Peripherist view of English as a language of decolonization in Post-colonial India. *Language Policy 4 (2),* 187-206.

NOTES

1. *According to Mesthrie and Bhat* the first (450 to 1100) and the second (1164-1500) crossing of English coincide with the 'migration/invasion of Anglo-Saxon from north-western Europe', and 'the conquest of Ireland by Henry II' respectively. The demand for English has grown immensely over the last three-four decades in erstwhile [French/Spanish/Portuguese/etc.] colonies as well as in Eastern Europe, China, Japan etc.; Mesthrie and Bhatt (2008) call it the "fourth crossing of English".
2. Krishnamurthy & Krishnamurthy (2006) term the phase between 1830 and 1892 as "The Grand Design", and the following one- 1893 to 1947- as "The Dissemination Phase".
3. Charles Hay Cameron in his historic address also remarked that "the natives of India are generally sunk in profound ignorance and superstition; secondly, that they are evidently capable of very high intellectual attainments." Marx echoed the first part of Cameron's remark with a high degree of scorn. Marx wrote: " we must not forget that these idyllic village communities, inoffensive though they may appear, had always been the solid foundation of oriental despotism, that they restrained the human mind within the smallest possible compass, making it the unresisting tool of superstition, enslaving it beneath traditional rules, depriving it of all grandeur and historical energies. Indian history has never been anything but the chronicle of foreign invasions and foreign domination. India has never really been ruled by her own sons". (*New York Daily Tribune,* 1853). Elsewhere Marx continued: "We must not forget that this undignified, stagnatory, and vegetative life ... evoked... unbounded forces of destruction and rendered murder itself a religious rite in Hindostan... this brought about a brutalizing worship of nature, fell down on his knees in adoration of *Kanuman,* the monkey, and *sabbala,* the cow." *Selected Works,* 1. 350-51.

   Said (168) has rightly observed that "Marx and Nietzsche interpreted the reified data of bourgeois society by translating them back into primitive but productive impulses toward dominance and accumulation".
4. Bradley (2003) opines that "individuals not social classes have been the agents of social change and in the process a small elite gain

disproportionate power that makes democratic control more difficult to achieve and maintain".

5. Prof. Yash Pal, the eminent scientist, in one of his lectures makes the point rather more succinctly: "Global consciousness", as a different entity from globalization, "comes from scientific exploration." The same scientific laws govern everything in this cosmos: the sun, moon, houses etc. Global consciousness would prepare us to consider each space as the center - so long it gives the same right to everybody else. One should be able to recognize that there will be tremendous diversity on earth. Global consciousness should create a new type of world in which decentralization is considered productive and valuable, where different ways of living are preserved.
6. The dominant position that English occupies gives the Indian English writers freedom to paint India in their own mould. In a Hindi periodical S. Shankar laments Adiga's derogatory reference to the Indian tradition of '*Deva-stuti'(offering prayers to god)* in his 2008 booker prize winner novel '*The White Tiger*'. He believes that 'no author writing in an Indian language would resort to such cheap tactics to earn awards.' Do such portrayals pose a threat to Indian culture? It seems difficult to spell out an unambiguous answer to this question.

36

The Study of Lexical Phrases Among Proficient Users of English

Anju Sahgal Gupta & Madhu Gurtu

BACKGROUND

The lexical approach is based on the idea that an important part of language acquisition is the ability to comprehend and produce lexical phrases, as unanalyzed wholes or chunks, postulating the hypothesis that these lexical chunks become the raw data by which learners perceive patterns of language traditionally thought of as grammar (Lewis, 1993, p. 95).

It was initially Becker (1975) and then Pawley and Syder (1983) who noted the phenomena of lexical phrase which gradually caught the attention of applied linguists leading to a lexical approach in language pedagogy and to considerable research in first language acquisition, some in second language acquisition (SLA), with not much evidence of research done in the Indian context.

The lexical approach advocates argue that language consists of meaningful chunks that, when combined, produce continuous coherent text, and only a minority of spoken sentences are entirely novel creations. As Wray (2002) argues, as mature native speakers of a language, we apparently produce and interpret ready made surface structures (p. 13) for nearly all our communicative functions, retrieving sometimes quite lengthy strings from memory as single lexical units, while using our live grammar and lexicon (p. 33) sparingly, mainly for stitching the precasts together. This approach makes a distinction between vocabulary (which concerns itself with individual words) and lexical phrase which includes not only single words but also word combinations that we store in our mental lexicon. Language production thus, is not a syntactic rule governed process but is instead the retrieval of larger units from memory (Moudraia, 2001).

Justification for this theory comes from statistical analysis of language which shows that we do indeed speak in chunks and collocations. We thereby reserve our main energies for idea generation and interpretation and of course for an occasional novel construction, should the need arise. The concept has implications which, if taken seriously, could revolutionize our views of language use, acquisition, and pedagogy, and possibly even human cognitive architecture (Cobb 2002). Theoreticians and practitioners of SLA have stressed their importance. While the collocations are frequently used by native speakers, their acquisition is considered a problem by second language learners.

While the interest in the use of lexical phrases in language use was apparent, until recently there were no means of proving that it was more than a marginal phenomena. It was only with the computer analysis of large corpora (including the COBUILD Bank of English Corpus, the Cambridge International Corpus, and the British National Corpus), that the extent of our reliance on pre-cast formulaic language became clear. With the phenomenon thus noted (by Pawley and Syder) and also validated by Corpus Study there has been a burgeoning of research in this area.

Michael Lewis (1983) who initially used the term 'lexical approach" made the following suggestions:

- Lexis is the basis of language (not mastery of grammatical system; lexis being distinguished from vocabulary which refers to a stock of individual words with fixed meaning).
- Language consists of grammaticalized lexis, not lexicalized grammar which suggests that lexical phrases offer far more language generative power than grammatical structures.
- The central organizing principles of any meaning centered syllabus should be lexis.

Problems of terminology

The role of formulaic, multi-word units has been stressed in both first and second language acquisition research. Researchers and linguists have coined their own idiosyncratic terminology. Corder (1973) refers to "subroutines or ready-made sub-plans", Hakuta (1974) talks of "routines and pre-fabricated patterns", Peters (1983) uses terms such as "formulaic frames", Keller(1979) uses "gambits", Pawley and Syder

(1983) and Nattinger & DeCarrico (1992) use the term "lexical phrase". The terms which are now more widely acceptable are "lexical phrase" and "lexical approach" and we use these in our study.

Methodology

Research questions

Our paper addresses these research questions:

- What kinds of lexical phrases do educated second language users make use of in their writing?
- How correctly and appropriately are these lexical phrases used?

Sample: With the aim of investigating these issues we selected a sample consisting of 20 students of second year English honours of a women's college, affiliated to Delhi University.

Tools: The lexical phrases were analysed on the basis of the written scripts of the sample. The students were asked to write an assignment in class from their course material which was an extract from the Mahabharata. The assignment was:

Draupadi's protest in the assembly hall is a protest against the patriarchial system that reduces her to a non-entity, her question aims to assert a women's sense of self, her right to her independence. Discuss.

Since they were familiar with the content and held strong views on the topic, we felt that they could better concentrate on the language – which would give us a clearer understanding of their linguistic ability and use of lexical phrases.

The basis of our analysis of lexical phrases was the framework suggested by Nattingar (1992) and Lewis (1993) with minor modifications. A detailed description of the lexical phrases we have considered for the study is given below with examples:

1. **Idioms**: Frozen phrases where the meaning is not derivable from its parts or the sum of its parts, i.e. kick the bucket
2. **Polywords:** Short phrases that function as a single lexical item. These are non-variable in nature – continuous (can't break them up), can be both canonical and non-canonical.

   Canonical Phrases: which follow the structure of an English phrase or sentence and these could be *phrasal words, compound words* and *prepositional phrases.*

   Example:

   Phrasal word *put up with*

Compound word *blackboard*
Prepositional phrase
as a discourse marker *in this way*

Non-canonical Phrases: These do not follow the structure of an English sentence or phrase. Example:

Waste not, want not
Down with the King
The more the merrier

3. **Collocations**: These are essentially word partnerships - 'Strings of specific lexical items that co-occur with a mutual expectancy greater than chance' (Nattinger and DeCarrico, 1992) i.e. they co-occur in natural texts with greater than random frequency (Lewis, 1997). Native speakers intuitively 'know' which words frequently combine and which do not. Knowing the frequent collocations is essential for accurate natural English. In Lewis's approach collocations are thought to be the most important types of lexical phrases.
4. **Sentence Frames**: which tend to extend the discourse, moving the ideas forward.

   Examples

   As far as I think...
   What I want to explain...
   It doesn't mean that..

Analysis

Since our focus in this study was to investigate into the kinds of lexical phrases that were used, we did not take into account isolated words nor did we look into the appropriate/inappropriate use of such words. For this reason, we did not make note of discourse markers such as *therefore, thus, now, then,* etc. Further, we did not make note of the incorrect grammar of words used, for example, *but still her question quaked the elders in the clan.* We did not isolate the word *quaked* as a deviant word used here as a transitive word, instead of an intransitive one. We only noted it as a deviant collocation *quaked the elders,* for even if the phrase was *made the elders quake* it would still be a deviant collocation. Incorrect use of affixes with words such as *unjustice* in the place of *injustice* was also not taken into consideration.

We will now give a detailed analysis of the lexical phrases found in the written samples taking each of the items outlined in the methodology section one by one:

Idioms

What was interesting about the scripts was the fact that though in Indian classrooms, idioms are taught as part of vocabulary, very few of them occur in the scripts of the students. Of those that were used, most were well formed although there were some that were deviant.

Well Formed

The well formed ones were

danced to the tune of
made up her mind
fair play
cross their limits
shook the basic foundation of

Some of them were slightly informal for academic discourse, for example:

play tricks on

The deviant idioms used were

adds fuel to the enmity, on the analogy of *add fuel to fire*

the foundation of dharma <u>gets a serious blow</u> when the elders of the house are mute spectators.
brings to a narrow past
went in vain instead of *was in vain*

Phrasal Verbs

Phrasal verbs are taught all through the school years; however, phrasal verbs did not occur in the scripts of the students. In fact when they did, they were used inappropriately/incorrectly and by students who were not very proficient users of the language. This is not surprising as phrasal verbs belong to the spoken genre rather than a written one. In the scripts of more competent writers, the phrasal verbs were either missing or when used, they were used appropriately, for example:

lashed out at, gave in

Deviant/inappropriate phrasal verbs were

if he was <u>taken over</u> in the game, he was not more a free man
she did not <u>call for</u> any man's power
she raised her voice against injustice done to her and it <u>paid off</u> for her.
Draupadi <u>looked up</u> to the elders for support.

Compounds

Again very few compounds were used in the scripts of the students. Some of the well formed ones were:

> *self respect, assembly hall, set-up, life partner, dumbstruck, evil-doers, noble men, frame work, daughter-in-law, gambling match, etc.*

The deviant ones were *freeman* (which was used several times),

> *women-hater, earthy-woman, dicing game.*

Prepositional Phrases as Discourse Markers

Not many prepositional phrases occur in the scripts of the students, those that were attempted were correctly used and were primarily used as discourse makers. Some of them are listed below:

> *at first, at last, in this way, at that point of time, in a way, after that, on the other hand*

Sentence Frames and Linkers

Sentence frames were very few in number and mostly used by proficient users, for example, *that's why*. The sentence linkers were mostly isolated words and many times used incorrectly by less proficient users.

Collocations

The most productive use was that of collocations and there were several well formed collocations used primarily by proficient users. The well formed collocations had the following patterns:

1. adjective + noun	*moral law*
	ideal character
	fine picture
	extreme pain
	collective appeal
	central figure
2. verb + noun	*gained status*
	raised this question
	met her fate
	followed the right path
	protect her honour
	suffer humiliation
3. verb +preposition phrase	*protect against patriarchal system*

	appealed to the divine forces
	came to her rescue
4. verb + adjective	*remained unresolved*
	sit mute
	remained unanswered
	felt sorry
5. adverb + verb	*meekly agrees*
	persistently questions
6. adverb + adjective	*extremely humiliating*
	highly learned
	ritually impure
	truly pitiable
	hugely embarrassed
7. adjective + preposition phrase	*shaken at the sudden attack*
	subjected to such humiliation
	treated as commodity
	deprived of their rights

Some of the well formed collocations were not used appropriately in the sense that they were too informal for academic writing of this kind. Examples:

could not say no, had no say in, she kept asking about

Deviant Collocations

Place the question instead of *'put the question'*.

Place and *put* are semantically similar. Because *place* is more formal, the students seemed to use the word *place* instead of *put*.

Put her at the stake
Put their heads down in shame
Puts a light on the position of women
Put the assembly in a state of dilemma

Put seems to occur in most of the deviant collocations.

face disrespect (instead of *face humiliation or show disrespect*).
suffer insult (instead of *suffer humiliation*)
freedom was limited by the system (instead of *'restricted'*)

Restricted and *limited* are synonymous terms. Students are not aware of the appropriate collocations and use the more commonly used word *'limited'*.

joint wife (generalization from the Indianism*'joint family'*) *legal husband* (instead of '*lawful husband*')

As we can see, these collocations are due to over generalization which has resulted from imperfect understanding of the nature of collocation.

Now look at the following examples,

drugged with misfortune
declared as mere servant
expert cheat

The deviance in the above cases can be traced to the lack of awareness on part of the users of positive/negative connotations of lexical phrases. In English 'drugged with' will occur with success – a positive thing; 'declare' will occur in a positive sense,for example, 'be declared a winner, a hero,' etc. Similarly, 'expert' is used in a positive sense as well. Here these words are used in a negative sense. The distinction is blurred between positive and negative sense of word for the second language learners.

Some other deviant collocations were

suppressed argument, strict follower, materialistic possessions, lived a veiled identity.

Another interesting aspect seems to be that many students make use of innovative collocations which are culturally appropriate and follow the rules of English syntax, for example

women were kept as birds in the four walls of the house
burn with a lot of shame

Among the deviant ones many of them were influenced by the L1 transfer, for example:

put their head down in shame
placed the question in front of the elders in the assembly (instead of 'in the presence of')
women were not allowed to raise their voice before the elders (in Hindi *before/in front of* has a metaphorical meaning as well, besides the locative meaning, whereas in English these words are primarily used as locatives).

Generalization

The analysis throws up interesting insights.

1. There is a near absence of idioms, phrasal verbs, compound words, sentence frames and prepositional phrases as discourse

markers. This is surprising because these students would have spent a considerable part of school time practicing idioms, phrasal verbs and compound words. The absence of phrasal verbs is perhaps expected since they are much more informal in nature and belong to the spoken realm. Perhaps idioms and compounds are not so productive in discourses of this kind.

2. Sentence frames and prepositional phrases as discourse markers were used by the proficient users of the language leading to greater cohesion and coherence in their discourse. There was a certain flow to their language which was enhanced by the use of these devices.
3. There were an overwhelming large number of collocations. The occurrence of collocations in the sample seems to validate the findings of the lexical phrase proponents that collocation is the main organizing principle of language. Though it is a well known fact that students have not received any conscious practice in the use of collocation in their school or college studies, they display a good awareness of how collocations help create language. As the students are English honours students with a lot of exposure to good writing it seems that these collocations have been imbibed by them with varying measures of accuracy. It is also interesting to note that certain innovative collocations were attempted (sometimes incorrectly) in consonance with the cultural context of India. In fact, the areas which are taught such as idioms, phrasal verbs, prepositional phrases and compounds were not productively used; collocations which are generally not part of formal instructions occurred in large numbers. The only difference was that the less proficient students made more mistakes in their use.

Conclusion

Finally the question that can be asked is, do lexical phrases function for second language learners as they do for the native speakers? There are no clear answers as yet. This theory is still in its nascent stage and not enough research has been conducted, especially in SLA. Cook (1996) cautions us not to go overboard for a single all embracing theory on how second language acquisition works, in particular on account of the sheer complexity of SLA itself. However, the works of Nattinger, DeCarrico and Lewis represent a significant theoretical and pedagogical shift from the past. They challenge the traditional view of language which is primarily a syntactic rule-governed process and suggest that learners need to perceive, use, and retrieve patterns of lexis and collocations from memory.

REFERENCES

Cobb, T. 2002. Review of Alison Wray (2002) Formulaic language and the lexicon. Cambridge UK: Cambridge University Press.

Cook, V. 1996. *Strategies and UG theories. Conference at Seville* (paper taken from internet)

Keller, E. 1979. Gambits: Conversational strategy signals. *Journal of Pragmatics*, 3, 219-237.

Lewis, M. 1993. The lexical approach: *The state of ELT and the way forward*. Hove, England: Language Teaching Publications.

Lewis, M. 1997a. *Implementing the lexical approach: Putting theory into practice.* Hove, England: Language Teaching Publications.

Lewis, M. 1997b. Pedagogical Implications of the Lexical Approach, in J. Coady and T. Huckin (eds.) *Second language vocabulary acquisition: A rationale for pedagogy*, Cambridge: Cambridge University Press, 255-270.

Nattinger, J. 1980. A lexical phrase grammar for ESL. *TESOL Quarterly*, 14, 337-344.

Nattinger, J. and J. DeCarrico 1992. *Lexical phrases and language teaching*. Oxford: Oxford University Press.

Olga Moudraia 2001. *Lexical approach to second language teaching*, http://www.cal.org/resources/digest/0102lexical.html.

Pawley, A. and F. Syder 1983. Two Puzzles for Linguistic theory: Native-like selection and native-like fluency. In J.C. Richards and R.W. Schmidt (eds.), *Language and communication*. New York: Longman. 191-226.

Peters, A. 1983. *The units of language acquisition*. Cambridge: Cambridge University Press.

Sinclair, J.M. (ed.) 1987. *Looking up: An account of the COBUILD project in lexical computing*. London: Collins COBUILD.

Wills, J. and D. Willis 1989. *Collins COBUILD English course*. London: Collins COBUILD.

Wray 2002. *Formulaic language and the lexicon*. Cambridge UK: Cambridge University Press.

Rama Kant Agnihotri:

Publications, Awards, Current Projects and Activism

LIST OF PUBLICATIONS

Books

Crisis of Identity: A Sociolinguistic Study of Sikh Children in Leeds. Delhi: Bahri Publications, 1987.

Tense in Indian English: A Sociolinguistic Study. Delhi: ICSSR and Bahri Publications (with A.L. Khanna and A. Mukherjee), 1988.

Prashika: Eklavya's Innovative Experiment in Primary education. Delhi: Ratna Sagar (with Subir Shukla and A.L. Khanna), 1994.

English Grammar in Context. Delhi: Ratna Sagar (with A.L. Khanna), 1996.

Hindi Morphology: A Word-based Description. Delhi: Motilal Banarsidass (with Rajendra Singh), 1997.

Problematizing English in India. New Delhi: Sage Publications (with A.L. Khanna), 1997.

Adult ESOL Learners in Great Britain. U.K.: Multilingual Matters (with A.L. Khanna, M.K. Verma and S.K. Sinha), 1998.

Half the Battle and a Quarter. CIIL Foundation Day Lectures. Mysore: Central Institute of Indian Languages, 2002.

Hindi: An Essential Grammar. London: Routledge, 2007.

Indradhanush Elementary Textbook Series: From Creation to Reception. Delhi: State Council of Educational Research and Training (with Janaki Rajan and A.L. Khanna), 2008.

Language, Learning and Knowledge. Delhi: Macmillan (with H.K. Dewan), 2010.

Edited Volumes:

Second Language Acquisition: Socio-cultural and Linguistic Aspects of English in India. New Delhi: Sage Publications (with A.L. Khanna), 1994.

English Language Teaching in India: Issues and Innovations. New Delhi: Sage Publications (with A.L. Khanna), 1995.

Social Psychological Perspectives on Second Language Learning. New Delhi: Sage Publications (with A.L. Khanna and I. Sachdev), 1998.

Bha:sha: Bahubha:shita: aur Hindi. New Delhi: Shilalekh (with P.K. Vandyopadhyaya), 2000.

Bhasha, Boli aur Samaj: Ik Antah Samvad. Delhi: Deshkal (with Sanjay Kumar), 2001.

Noam Chomsky: The Architecture of Language. New Delhi: Oxford University Press (with N. Mukherjee and B.N. Patnaik), 2001.

Construction of Knowledge. Udaipur: Vidya Bhawan Society (with Tista Bagchi, a book based on Proceedings of the seminar held in Udaipur in 2002), 2004.

(Forthcoming) *The Non-Native Phenomenon: English in India* (with Rajendra Singh), USA Palgrave, 2009.

(Forthcoming) *Construction of Knowledge* (with Tista Bagchi and H.K. Dewan, a book based on the Proceedings of the seminar held in 2004), 2009.

Translations

I shall face you. New Delhi: Ankur Publishing House. (Translation of the Hindi Poem of Pranav Kumar Vandyopadhyaya), 1978.

Naxalbari. Delhi: Sunday Press (Translation of the Hindi Poem of Pranav Kumar Vandyopadhyaya), 1980.

One day in Biharipur. Penguin India. (Translation of Pranav Kumar Vandyopadhyaya's Hindi novel *Khabar*), 1991.

Several poems and stories translated into Hindi published in *Anyatha*, Chandigarh and Minneapolis, 2004.

Papers/ Chapters Published in books:

1977 Choice of Styles in Hindi: A Pilot Study. In *Papers in Linguistic Analysis*. Delhi: Dept. of Linguistics, University of Delhi. 43-52.

1977 Research Associate and co-author in Srivastava R.N. et. al. *Evaluating Communicability in Village Settings*. UNICEF.

1982 A Cross-cultural Study of Spatial Ability in Children. *Educational Psychology*. 2.1: 37-46. (with M.V. Cox and D.C. Bryant).

1982 Kannadigas' Assimilation of Hindi in Delhi: A Sociolinguistic Study: Paper presented at the Third *International Conference on South Asian Languages and Linguistics*. (Jan. 13-16) Mysore: CIIL. (with T.S. Satyanath).

1982 Predicators of Achievement in English Tenses—a Socio-psychological Study. *IJOAL* 8.2: 89-105. (with A.L. Khanna and A. Mukherjee).

1984 The Use of Articles: Errors and Pedagogical Implications. *International Review of Applied Linguistics* 22.2:115-28 (with A.L. Khanna and A Mukherjee).

1985 Syntax-The Common Bond: Acceptability of Syntactic Deviances in Indian English. *English World-wide* 6.1:117-129 (with Anju Sahgal).

1985 I Deny that I'm Incapable of Not Working all Night: Divergence of Negative Structures in British and Indian English. *Current Issues in Linguistic theory* 4.1: 3-14 (with Jean Aitchison).

1987 Readability Levels of a Hindi text: A Study Using Cloze Procedures. In *Indian Journal of Applied Linguistics* Vol. 13, No. 1. (with Anju Sahgal).

1988 Indian English Phonology: A Sociolinguistic Perspective. *English World-Wide* 9.1: 51-64 (with Anju Sahgal).

1989 *The Structure of Modern English: Sentence Structure I, Block 5* (Units 21-25), Course E E G 02, pp 1-52. New Delhi: Indira Gandhi National Open University. (IGNOU Teaching Materials).

1990 Gricean Maxims and Conversational Goals. *International Journal of Dravidian Linguistics*. 19.2: 111-125 (with Neeti Ahluwalia and K.V. Subbarao).

1990 Conflicting pressures: The Case of Sikh Children in Leeds (U.K.). *South Asia Newsletter* 6: 18-22.

1990 Attitudes and Motivation of Adult ESOL Learners in Great Britain: A Cross-Cultural Pilot Study'. *Language Issues* 4.1: 4-8 (with A.L. Khanna, M.K. Verma and S.K. Sinha).

1990 *The Structure of Modern English: Sentence structure II, Block 6 (Unit 26-30)*, pp. 1-51. New Delhi: IGNOU. (IGNOU Teaching Materials)

1991 Acquisition of Articles in Learning English as a Second Language: A Cross-cultural Study. *South Asian Language Review* 1.2: 67-80.

1991 Evaluating the Readability of School Textbooks: An Indian Study. *Journal of Reading*. 35.4: 282-288. (with A.L. Khanna).

1991 Syntactic Strategies and Politeness Phenomena. *International Journal of the Sociology of Language* 92: 35-53. (with K.V. Subbarao and Aditi Mukherjee)

1991 Sound Patterns of Indian English – A Sociolinguistic Perspective: In Gupta, R.S. and Kapoor, K. (ed.) *English in India: Issues and Problems*. Delhi. Academic Foundation. 175-188.

1991 Linguistic Situation in India and Computer Applications. In Sarma, V.S., Viswanadham, N., Yegnanarayana, B. and Deekshtulu, B.L. (ed.) *Artificial Intelligence and Expert System Technologies in the Indian Context*. Vol. 2. New Delhi: Tata McGraw Hill. 53-57.

1991 Application Oriented Course in Translation. Block 6. Unit 1 and 2. Delhi: IGNOU. (IGNOU Teaching Materials)

1992 India: Multilingual Perspectives. In Crawhall, Nigel T. (ed.) *Democratically Speaking: International Perspectives on Language Planning*. Salt River, South Africa: National Language Project. 46-55.

1993 English Tense and the Indian learners. In Lakshmi Bai, and Mukherjee, A. (ed.) *Tense and Aspect in Indian Languages*. Hyderabad: Osmania University and Booklinks Corporation 143-154. (with Aditi Mukherjee and A.L. Khanna).

1994 Campaign-Based Literacy Programmes: The Case of the Ambedakar Nagar experiment in Delhi. In Barton, D. (ed.) *Language and Education* 8.1 & 2: 47-56 (special issue on 'Sustaining Local Literacies).

1995 Evaluating Classroom Performance. Paper presented at the CBSE-ELT *International Seminar on Curriculum Development: Dynamics of Change*. (August 22-25). Hyderabad: CIEFL.

1995 Language, Limited Identities and Canada. In Mohan, C. (ed.) *Regionalism in Canada*. Delhi: Allied Publishers, 113-130.

1995 Comments on Sadhna Saxena and Kamal Mahendroo's paper 'Politics of language'. In Gupta, R.S., Abbi, A. and Aggarwal, K.S. (ed.) *Language and the State: Perspectives on the Eighth Schedule*. New Delhi: Creative Books, 152-54.

1995 Multilingualism as a classroom resource. In Kathleen Heugh, Amanda Sieruhn and Peter Pluddemann (eds.). *Multilingual Education for South Africa*. Johannesburg: Heinemann, 3-7.

1995 Bahubhashita, Saksharta, Bhasha-Shikshan Evam Baudhik Vikas. *Pashyanti* July-Sept., 17-20.

1996 Shared Socio-Cultural Norms: The Case of Second Person

Pronouns in Indo-Aryan (Hindi) and Dravidian (Telugu and Tamil). In Verma, S.K. and Singh, D. (ed.) *Perspectives on Language in Society*. Delhi: Kalinga. 253-267.

1996 Is Coming Together Growing Apart: Review of Fred E. Jandt's book International Communication *The Book Review* 20.4: 31-32.

1997 Hindi and Urdu: A Case of Lexical Divide. Paper presented at the XVIII SALA Roundtable Delhi: JNU. Jan. 6-8. (with Rizwan Ahmad)

1997 The Social Psychological Perspective on Second Language Learning: A Critique. In Singh, R. (ed.) *Grammar, Language, and Society: Contemporary Indian Contributions.* New Delhi: Sage. 325-342 (with A.L. Khanna).

1997 Contributions to Tabouret-Keller, A., Le Page, R.B., Gardner-Chloros, P. and Varro, G. 1997. (ed.) *Vernacular Literacy: A Re-evaluation*. Oxford: Clarendon Press. (in particular Vol. 43-45).

1997 Multilingualism, Colonialism and Translation. In Ramakrishna, S. (ed.) *Translation and Multilingualism: Post-colonial Contexts*. Delhi: Pencraft International. 34-46.

1997 'Sustaining Local Literacies' and 'Literacy Teaching in India'. Both in Edwards, V. and Corson, D. (ed.). Literacy: Encyclopedia of Language and Education. Vol. 2 Dordrecht: Klewer Academeic publishers. 172-180; 199-207.

1998 Retention and Use of Mother Tongue Among Adult ESOL Learners in Great Britain. In Verma, M.K. *Sociolinguistics, Language and Society*. New Delhi: Sage Publications. 167-83. (with M.K. Verma, A.L. Khanna and S.K. Sinha)

1998 Mixed Codes and Their Acceptability. In Agnihotri, R.K., Khanna, A.L. and Sachdev, I. (ed.) *Social Psychological Perspectives on Second Language Learning*. New Delhi: Sage Publications. 191-215.

1999 Regional Report on India: English in India (A Report). In Singh R. (ed.) *The Yearbook of South Asian Language and Linguistics*. New Delhi: Sage Publications. 161-183.

1999 Is *Ghursvaar* a Compound? *Linguistics Today*, Jan-June, 43-56.

1999 Bacchon ki Bhasha Sikhne ki Kshmta: Dhavni Sanracna, Varnmala aur Vartni (Part 1). *Sandarbh* 28: 9-14.

1999 Bacchon ki Bhasha Sikhne ki Kshamta: Vartni ka Manakikaran. *Sandarbh* 29: 39-45.

2000 Writing and Written Language. In Gupta, R.S. (ed.) *Directions in Indian Sociolinguistics*. Shimla: IIAS. 94-102.

2000 Teacher's Space in the Classroom. In Mathew, R., Eapen, R.L. and Tharu, J. (ed.) *The Language Curriculum: Dynamics of Change*. (Vol I).Hyderabad: Orient Longman, 157-161.

2000 What can you do with 'The kind-hearted Carter and the Crafty Crocodile'. *Issues in Primary Education* 2.1: 7-10.

2000 Bhasha ka Bazarikaran. *Hans*, Oct., 121-23.

2001 Srivastava, Ravindra Nath (1936-92). In Mesthrie, R. (ed.) *Concise Encyclopedia of Sociolinguistics*. Amsterdam: Elsevier (Pergamon), 914.

2002 English in Indian Education. In Daswani, C.J. (ed.) *Language Education in Multilingual India*. New Delhi: UNESCO. 186-209.

2002 A farce called literacy. In *Practice and Research in Literacy*. Edited by A. Mukherjee and D. Vasantha. New Delhi: Sage Publication, pp. 29-48.

2002 Khubchandani, Lachman M. (1932-) In Mesthrie, R. (ed.) *Concise Encyclopedia of Sociolinguistics*. Amsterdam: Elsevier (Pergamon), 884.

2002 A Pre-Partition Partition: The Case of Hindi and Urdu. In Settar, S. and Gupta, I.B. ed. *Pangs of Partition*, Vol. II. New Delhi: ICHR and Manohar, 29-46.

2003 Sociolinguistic Theory and Practice: The Indian Counterpoint. In Singh, R. ed. *The Yearbook of South Asian Languages and Linguistics*. New Delhi: Sage, 11-26.

2003 Shikshkon ke liye Bhasha Vigyan. *Shiksha Vimarsh* 4.2: 7-13.

2004 Relative clause attachment in Hindi: Effects of RC length and RC placement. (with Shravan Vasishth, Eva M. Fernandez and Rajesh Bhatt) In *Proceedings of the AMLaP Conference*, Aix en Provence, France.

2005 Noun Modification Preferences in Hindi. (with Shravan Vasishth, Eva M. Fernandez and Rajesh Bhatt). In Bagchi, T. and Agnihotri, R.K. ed. *Proceedings of the International Seminar on Construction of Knowledge*, Vidya Bhavan Society, Udaipur, pp. 160-171.

2005 Translations of the poems of Alfonso Reyes and Cesar Vallejo. *Anyatha* 6: 57 -65.

2006 Identity and Multilinguality: The Case of India. In Tsui, Amy B.M. and Tollefson, James, W. ed. *Language Policy, Culture, and Identity in Asian Contexts*. New Jersey: Lawrence Erlbaum Associates, 185-204.

2007 Towards a Pedagogical Paradigm Rooted in Multilinguality. *International Journal Multilingual Research*1.2: 1-10.

2008 Orality and Literacy. In Kachru, Braj, B., Kachru, Y. and Sridhar, S.N. ed. *Language in South Asia*. Cambridge: Cambridge University Press, 271-284.

2008 Continuing Debates over the Native Speaker: A Report on a Symposium on English in India and Indian English. *English Today* 24.4: 51-58. (Cambridge: Cambridge University Press)

2009 Multilinguality and a New World Order. In Mohanty, A.K., Panda, M. Phillipson, R. and Skutnabb-Kangas, T. eds. *Multilingual Education for Social Justice: Globalizing the Local*. New Delhi: Orient BlackSwan, pp. 268-77.

2009 Language and Dialect. *Learning Curve* 13: 21-24.

2010 Language in the Material World: Multilinguality in Signage. *International Multilingual Research Journal* 4.1: 55-81 (with Kay McCormick).

2010 Noun Modification Preferences in Hindi. In Agnihotri, R.K. and Dewan, H.K. eds. *Language, Learning and Knowledge*. Delhi: Macmillan, pp. 165-171 (with Shravan Vasishth, Eva M. Fernandez and Rajesh Bhatt).

2010 Multilinguality and the Teaching of English in India. *The EFL Journal* 1.1: 1-14.

AWARDS

1980 Project Director: Variation in the Use of Some English Grammatical Forms: A Sociolinguistic Perspective. ICSSR.

1980 Area Director, University of York Project on Spatial Skills among British and Indian Children.

1981-84 Developing Suitable Materials for Primary School Children in a Sociolinguistic Perspective, Eklavya, Bhopal.

1982 Language Pedagogue in Evaluating a Manual for Training Health Workers, WHO.

1990 Canadian Government 'Faculty Enrichment' Fellowship to work at the Univ. of Concordia, Montreal.

1991 Univ. of Montreal Fellowship.

1991 British Council Grant-in Aid to participate in the Sociolinguistics Symposium, IX.

1992 National Language Project (Cape Town, South Africa) Award to participate in a Conference.

1994 Director, ICSSR Project on Norms of Indian English.

2000 University of California Education Abroad Programme Fellowship.

2001 UGC Major Research Project on Developing an Intelligent Hindi-Urdu Lexicon and Machine Translation (with K.V. Subbarao and Gautam Sengupta).

2002 Director, Sir Ratan Tata Trust Assessment Report on the Vidya Bhawan Basic Education Rediscovery (BER) Project.

2003 Director, MHRD Project on Understanding Pedagogical Innovations under DPEP in Tamil Nadu.

2004 Guest Professor at the Interdisciplinary Centre for Cognitive Studies, Potsdam, Germany.

CURRENT PROJECTS

Faculty and Resource Person for the Tata Institute of Social Science MA in Education Programme.

Feedback Study of Indradhanush Elementary School Textbooks published by SCERT, Delhi (in collaboration with Janaki Rajan and A.L. Khanna with inputs from a large number of teams and investigators.

Textbooks in English for Rural Children, Vidya Bhawan Society, Udaipur.

Selection of Materials for Elementary School Children, Eklavya, Hoshanganbad.

Textbook Project on Applied Linguistics (with A.L. Khanna).

UGC Major Research Project on Acquisition of Reading and Writing Abilities in Literacy Programmes (With A.L. Khanna, A. Mukherjee and Sadhna Saxena).

Editing a collection of papers (with M.K. Verma) by Prof. R.B. Le Page, University of York, UK (likely to be published by Sage).

Editing a book (with Rajendra Singh) on English in India.

Coordinator for the Language, Mind and Society paper in the TISS, Mumbai project in developing the MA Education programme in Hindi.

Consultant, UNICEF, Bhopal Project on the Status of Girls' Education in MP.

ACTIVISM

Association with School Programmes

1982- Academic Advisor and Teacher Educator, Innovative School

Programmes of NGOs: Eklavya, Digantar and Vidya Bhawan Society.

1983-90 Prashika (Primary Education Programme), Eklavya, Bhopal.

1999-04 Conducted Orientation and Content Workshops in several states including Rajasthan, West Bengal, Kerala, Karnataka, Andhra Pradesh, Haryana and Bihar as part of District Primary Education Programme (DPEP).

2003-05 Chairperson, SCERT, Delhi English Textbooks.

Consultant to several States including Madhya Pradesh, Rajasthan, Chattisgarh, West Bengal, Kerala, Karnataka, Andhra Pradesh, Haryana and Bihar governments on Language Education, Teacher Training and Textbooks.

2004- Chairperson, NCERT National Focus Group on the Teaching of Indian Languages.

2006- Chairperson, NCERT Source Book for Teachers for Teaching Languages.